THIS IS OUR WORLD

THIS IS
OUR WORLD
Louis Fischer

GREENWOOD PRESS, PUBLISHERS
WESTPORT, CONNECTICUT

Library of Congress Cataloging in Publication Data

Fischer, Louis, 1896-1970.
  This is our world.

    Reprint of the ed. published by Harper, New York.
    1. World politics--1945-   I. Title.
[D843.F53 1974]   327'.09'045   74-1514
ISBN 0-8371-7389-2

Copyright © 1956, by Louis Fischer

All rights in this book are reserved. No part of the book may be used or reproduced in any manner whatsoever without written permission except in the case of brief quotations embodied in critical articles or reviews.

Originally published in 1956 by Harper & Brothers, New York

Reprinted with the permission of Harper & Row, Publishers, Inc.

Reprinted in 1974 by Greenwood Press,
a division of Williamhouse-Regency Inc.

Library of Congress Catalog Card Number 74-1514

ISBN 0-8371-7389-2

Printed in the United States of America

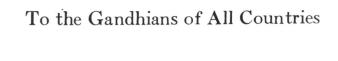
To the Gandhians of All Countries

CONTENTS

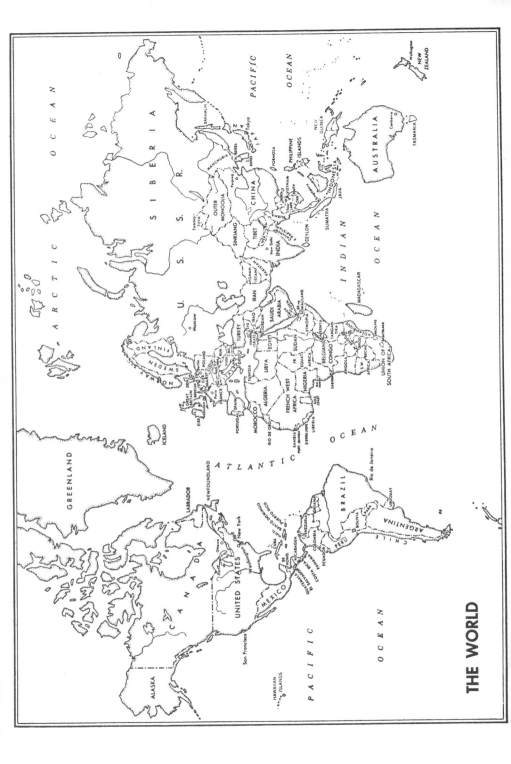

THE WORLD

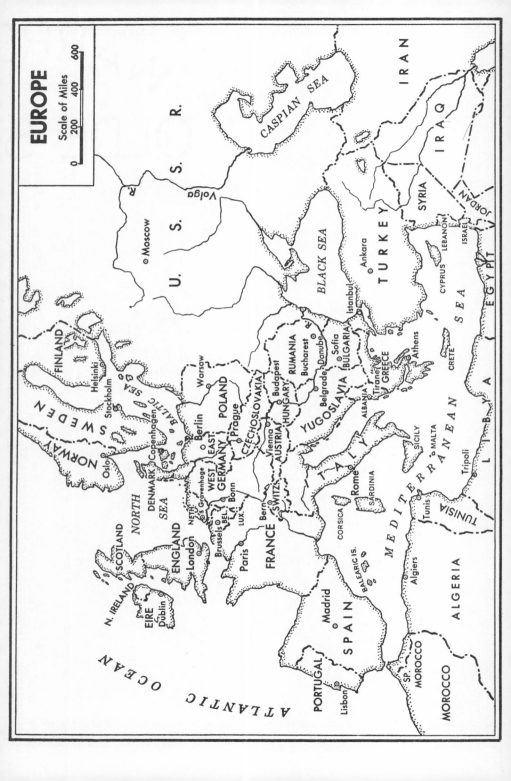

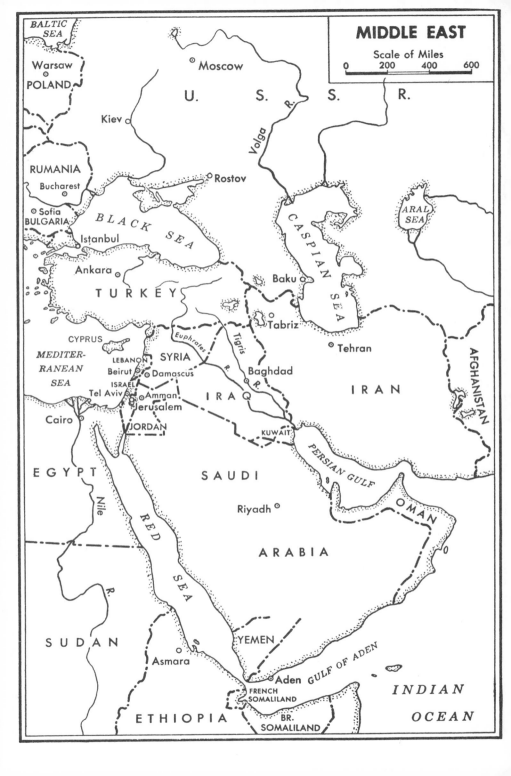

MIDDLE EAST

Scale of Miles

0 — 200 — 400 — 600

BALTIC SEA

Warsaw
POLAND

Moscow

U.   S.   S.   R.

Kiev

Volga R.

RUMANIA
Bucharest

Rostov

Sofia
BULGARIA

ARAL SEA

B L A C K   S E A

Istanbul

CASPIAN SEA

Ankara

Baku

T U R K E Y

Tabriz

CYPRUS

Euphrates

Tigris

Tehran

MEDITER-
RANEAN
SEA

LEBANON   SYRIA
Beirut   Damascus
ISRAEL   R.
Tel Aviv
Amman   Baghdad
Jerusalem   I R A Q

R.

I R A N

AFGHANISTAN

Cairo

JORDAN

KUWAIT

E G Y P T

SAUDI

PERSIAN GULF

Nile

Riyadh

OMAN

RED SEA

A R A B I A

R.

S U D A N

YEMEN

Asmara

Aden   GULF OF ADEN

FRENCH
SOMALILAND

INDIAN
OCEAN

E T H I O P I A

BR.
SOMALILAND

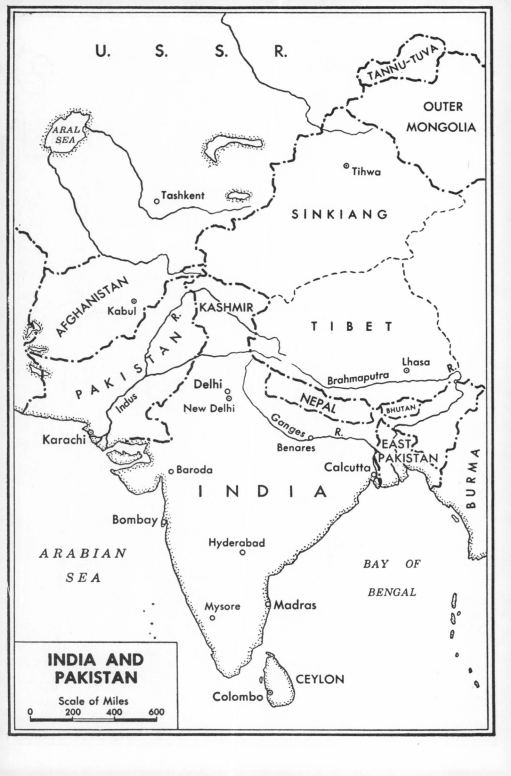

U. S. S. R.

TANNU-TUVA

OUTER
MONGOLIA

ARAL
SEA

°Tihwa

○Tashkent

S I N K I A N G

AFGHANISTAN

KASHMIR

Kabul ○

T I B E T

Lhasa
○

Brahmaputra

R.

NEPAL

Delhi ○○

New Delhi

BHUTAN

Indus

Ganges ○

R.

Benares

EAST
PAKISTAN

Karachi ○

Calcutta ○

B U R M A

○ Baroda

I N D I A

Bombay ○

A R A B I A N

Hyderabad
○

S E A

B A Y   O F

B E N G A L

Mysore
○

○ Madras

CEYLON

Colombo

**INDIA AND
PAKISTAN**

Scale of Miles

| 0 | 200 | 400 | 600 |

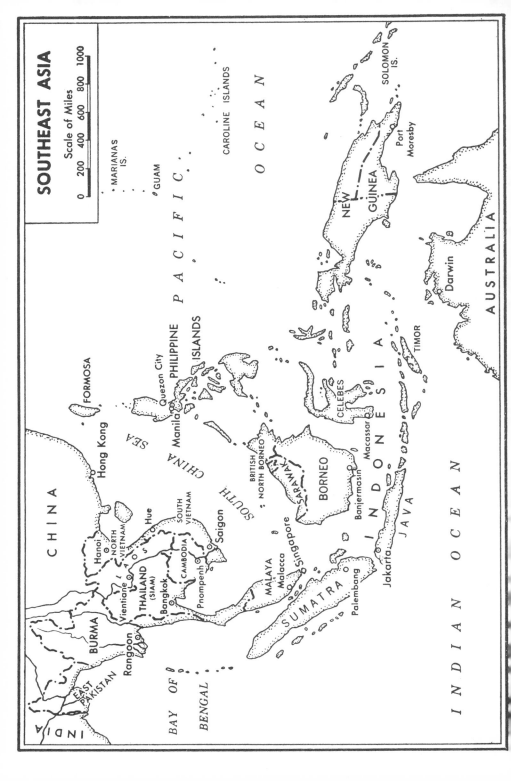

SOUTHEAST ASIA

Scale of Miles

0 200 400 600 800 1000

MARIANAS IS.

GUAM

CAROLINE ISLANDS

P A C I F I C   O C E A N

SOLOMON IS.

NEW GUINEA

Port Moresby

Darwin

A U S T R A L I A

TIMOR

CELEBES

Macassar

Banjermasin

I N D O N E S I A

J A V A

Jakarta

Palembang

S U M A T R A

Singapore

Malacca

MALAYA

B O R N E O

SARAWAK

BRITISH NORTH BORNEO

FORMOSA

Hong Kong

Quezon City

Manila

PHILIPPINE ISLANDS

SEA

C H I N A   S E A

S O U T H

C H I N A

Hue

Hanoi

NORTH VIETNAM

SOUTH VIETNAM

Saigon

CAMBODIA

Pnompenh

Vientiane

Bangkok

THAILAND (SIAM)

BURMA

Rangoon

EAST PAKISTAN

I N D I A

BAY OF BENGAL

I N D I A N   O C E A N

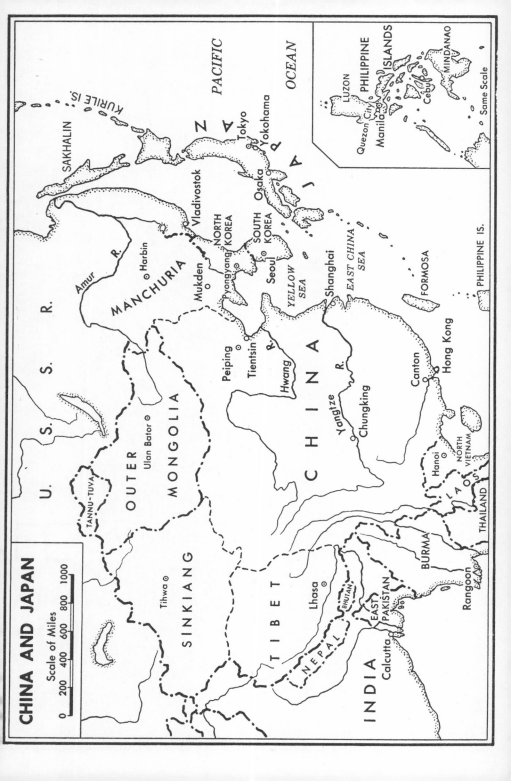

Part One
THE CURTAIN RISES

CHAPTER ONE

The Beginning of a Diary

I N ROME or Washington, Tokyo or Jerusalem, New Delhi or
New York or Bonn or Saigon or London or anywhere, whenever I
have an interesting interview or conversation I write it down, sometimes verbatim, and file it. Occasionally I write it in the form of a
letter to my family or a friend and keep a carbon copy. These diary
entries are supplemented by notes of my impressions, observations,
and reflections as I travel abroad and in the United States. I also
keep bulging files of clippings from newspapers and magazines of
several countries. To these, from time to time, I add letters that come
from persons throughout the world about their living conditions,
work, and thoughts.

In 1940, when I finished writing *Men and Politics*, an autobiography, I began a new file and marked it "The Next 20." *Men and
Politics* dealt with my first seventeen years as an American journalist
abroad. I vaguely assumed that this new collection of papers would
cover a slightly longer period.

I started work on *Men and Politics* when the Second World War
broke out. That was the end of an era; the world I knew in Europe,
Soviet Russia, and Spain had collapsed, with all its hope, and the fire
kindled by Hitler was spreading over the globe. Today, another era,
the postwar era, is coming to a close. It has been a dark era, with
bright spots, but the outlook is one of some hope—and no war. So I
am not waiting for the "20" to terminate. I am recording my experi-

ences with world affairs from 1945 to date, and where I had no personal contact with such major events as General George C. Marshall's mission to China to bring the Nationalists and Communists together or the Blair House conferences at which President Truman decided that America would fight in Korea—a turning point in history—I have interviewed some of the principal participants.

I am the victim—or beneficiary—of a boundless curiosity. I am the eternal questioner. I like to know about people and things and to delve for facts and causes. If there is anything I enjoy as much as asking questions it is research work, which is another form of diving for information and explanations. On a visit to a country, or before or after, I study its history, background, customs, and so forth. In Hong Kong I read a mountain of English translations from the Chinese Communist press and talked with businessmen and diplomats who had seen China after Chiang Kai-shek left. Later I made a survey of Moscow-Peking relations since Mao. When the East German revolt occurred in June, 1953, I flew to Berlin and spent a month in intensive conversation with the rebels. Yet one never knows enough, and it is often depressing to come suddenly upon a situation several years old which all one's reading had not disclosed. Hence my incessant travels.

There was a time, years ago, when I concentrated on high politics: the statements of governments, the acts of leaders, official documents, conferences, and statistics. These still absorb me. Governments invade the lives of all of us—too much, probably, but there it is, and what they do is enormously important. But nowadays I find enlightenment in a chat with a London policeman as he patrols his beat or in examining a class of children in a village school in Yugoslavia or in bull-session discussions with university students in Munich and Calcutta or visiting a Japanese novelist and sitting on the floor and eating raw fish or going to a Buddhist temple in Japan to have tea with a priest or talking with peasants in the rice fields of Indo-China. I ask Prime Minister U Nu about his development plans for Burma, but with a little prod he tells me, too, about swimming excursions with his family. Chancellor Adenauer tells about his desire to make Germany a part of Western civilization, as it was before unification in Goethe's time, but I get a better insight into his thinking from some comments on a book he has been reading. I used to look down my nose, in a kind of intellectual snobbery, at the idea of describing what a statesman wore. But I have discovered that the eye-piercing shirts and energetic gestures of President Magsaysay of the Philippines and Tito's clothes—and the drinks he serves—are not only interesting, they are part of the man.

The interaction between populations, politicians, and politics is almost the most fascinating aspect of world affairs. What makes England a democracy—laws or the automobile driver's road manners and the public's attitude toward sports? I would say that laws are a result rather than a cause. Family life is as good a key as any to post-war Japan. What a Hindu will not eat is one of Prime Minister Nehru's big economic problems. The Indian attitude toward the cow, monkeys, and a fast is reflected in election figures. These subjects belong in a living record of our times. A country is a complicated tapestry or rather a symphony of politics and poetry, economics and religion, law and language, tradition and imported isms, and of prejudice, pride, hope, hate, fear, faith, geography, natural resources, natural catastrophes, and many other things. One must not listen only to the brass and big drums, and although the conductor—the Prime Minister or President—occupies the center of the stage he would be nothing more than an acrobat without the orchestra and the composer. Moreover, the people always pay for the performance and consequently should always remain in focus.

Whenever possible, I return to the same country trip after trip. One goes to a place the first time in order to go there the second and third time. Moving from country to country also helps one to compare and see better. In 1952, traveling eastward around the globe, I understood more about India after I arrived in contrasting Burma, and my next stop in Siam (Thailand) gave me a clearer view of Burma. In 1954, I was in Texas seven weeks after leaving India and it occurred to me (I made a note on the Pullman-diner menu) that, "In the face of an impassable mountain range like the Himalayas which bars the way with beauty, or of a desert which acts as a frustrating frontier, man may be inclined to stand still and meditate on the inscrutable nature of God and the futility of life. But on the vast fields of Texas, laden with wealth in the form of oil, cotton, cattle, chemicals, and cereals, the tendency is to gallop ahead and not look fate or fortune in the mouth. The emphasis would be on work rather than contemplation, on enjoying the surface rather than plumbing the depths of existence. In Texas the only fear is that somebody might destroy a system capable of bearing such rich fruit; in India that circumstances might prolong its life. Texas wants more

of the same; India, when awakened, wants much that is different."
Or compare France, whose loss of glory and power has given her a sick
heart, with Italy which, in similar conditions, wears a smile over
rags and riches. Why the difference? The answer might be more
revealing than all the Cabinet crises and election results since
1945. . . . My Soviet experience from 1922 to 1938 pried open some
of the secrets of Communist Yugoslavia and, in turn, Titoland was
a searchlight on Stalinist and post-Stalin Russia.

Time also leads to comparisons: India struggling to be free under
Gandhi's leadership in 1942 and 1946, and working and progressing
under Nehru's leadership in 1948, 1952, and 1954; Pakistan under
the British and under the Pakistanis; Turkey in 1934 and 1952; Israel
in 1919, 1934, 1942, 1946, and 1952—a small country chipping away
at a big dream; neighboring Lebanon in 1920 and 1954—big things
are impossible, little things come easy, the result, Levantine laziness
and cleverness; Italy under Mussolini, De Gasperi, and Scelba, at war
and in peace; London appeasing, bombed, rebuilding; Germany—
sipping tea in a Berlin café, amid ruins, in 1946 with Germans I
had met in the same café in 1927 when German literature, painting,
and the theater were excitingly creative, and German democracy was
sprouting wings. Why had it spawned Hitler? . . . and so on.

I have not been able to return to the Soviet Union. But since I
left there in 1938, I have tried to keep in touch by reading Soviet
publications and through contacts with former Soviet citizens now
living abroad and with foreign diplomats and journalists stationed
in Moscow. Nevertheless, after so long an absence I cannot rate as
an expert on Soviet affairs. Yet every statement about the Soviet
Union in these pages is checked and double-checked and usually
derives from a Soviet source with an exact quotation and reference.
Moscow's activities have bulked large in the postwar and consequently
have their place in this journalist's-eye view of the period. What I
write about Russia is not born of hate. Even before I sat at Mahatma
Gandhi's feet I did not hate, and now certainly I could not hate
a country or a people or a race or religious group or individual. I
know of no pure government, and the Soviet government, because
it can ignore the popular will—though not entirely—is very impure.
But that is a matter for analysis, description, and proof, not for emotion, venom, and invective.

Criticism is the medicine of politics and I indulge in it. I would not
gloss over world dangers or ignore dark spots in Russia, America,

India, Germany, or anywhere. Yet after all the knocks my hopes have received I remain an optimist and do not think that progress is a Victorian illusion. When we stop regarding atomic fission as a nightmare it may become mankind's blessing. The atomic and hydrogen bombs have given us a glimpse of the final abyss and should enable humanity to move in the opposite direction. On the other hand, I am not writing to prove this or any other thesis. The book is just the story of the postwar world as I have seen it, how it arrived where it is and why, and what its prospects are.

Naturally, however, my observations and researches are bound together by ethical and intellectual cements. One of them is faith in individuals despite the many mighty forces arrayed against them. I find good people everywhere, even in governments; people want to be helped to be good. A second cement is a horror of injustice and poverty. The more I know about tortures and judicial lies in totalitarian countries and about material suffering in large parts of the world, the more I feel that we all, and civilization with us, are being dragged down by a dwindling capacity for indignation; with that goes a reluctance to act against injustices at our elbows, to "turn the searchlight inward," as Gandhi advised.

On another level, the thread that connects my facts and reflections about the world since 1945 might be called revolution, which simply means accelerated evolution without bloodshed, barricades, or destruction: in America, the permanent revolution sparked by the Ford Motor Company; Alcoa; General Motors; Walter Reuther; Atom, Electronics, and Brothers; Science, Inc.; the Supreme Court; some college professors and presidents; and all Americans with a trust in the future; in Russia, the counterrevolution engineered by Stalin because he was afraid of man; in England, the unfinished revolution inaugurated by Attlee and preserved by Churchill and Eden; in France and Italy, the revolution which the Communists cannot make and the capitalists refuse to make; in Turkey, a successful old revolution now somewhat imperiled; in Israel, another permanent revolution—within siege walls; in India, the delayed beginnings of a revolution; and so on. This angle of vision gives postwar history three dimensions. It is linked with another thread: an aversion to such terms as "Communist" Russia, "capitalist" America, "feudal" Latin America, "Socialist" Burma, et cetera. I use them myself out of habit, but no single adjective is big enough to wrap around any country, even a little one. Every country combines several social systems. This plural approach is a great teacher; it has solved a number of problems for me as I visit and revisit the continents.

The first of these journeys into the postwar world took place in 1946. I had seen parts of Europe and of the Middle East during the First World War and lived in Europe for many years in the 1920's and 30's. I saw England, Africa, Palestine, and India during the Second World War and wrote about that in a separate book. Now, returning to familiar countries after this second conflict, I was aware that the trip had some kind of special significance for me; the Old World would be different after five years of bombs, and fires, and killing, and I had to be able to look at it with different eyes. So, flying the Atlantic at eight thousand feet with only sky above and the boiling, billowing, constantly erupting white-cotton sea of clouds below, I made notes on a pad, I scribbled my "marching orders" —how to see, whom to see:

"I am looking into a ditch. It used to be wider but time has been filling it in. I will cross it in eight and a half hours; soon we will be crossing it in jets between lunch and dinner. Yet what a difference the ditch makes. I have just left a country of plenty and relaxation. Temporarily, to be sure, because of the late war, nylons, steaks, butter, and houses are somewhat scarcer than usual. But we enjoy great luxuries, the luxury of uninterrupted electric current, of the crowded ice cream parlor, the fully stocked drugstore, the swollen clothing emporium, the luxury of fat newspapers and thick magazines, the luscious luxury of liberty. I am crossing the ditch to see people in Europe, Africa, and Asia again. Bombs have shredded their nerves and shattered their homes. Their stomachs are never quite full, their minds never altogether quiet.

"I must remember all this when I meet them. These people died. Now life makes them live again amid the rubble. I will spend evenings with old friends. What will they think of me? I am sated. My worst suit will make me look well dressed. I will leave them in a few months and go back to the other side of the ditch. Will they hate me? Will they say, 'He is not one of us, he is an American, he cannot understand us, he has never been dead'?

"Must America help all the world? Can one country undertake such a big job? Can it refuse the job if that is the only way of saving itself? The uncertainties of the Old World are moving across the Atlantic and injecting the United States with a sense of insecurity. Is the ditch growing narrower for fears as well as planes and wider, too wide, for affection and understanding? . . .

"What happens to persons who have had twelve years of Hitler rule? Can France survive? Will England revive? Will India go free? Will Palestine drown in blood?"

I see the dark green coast of Ireland.

CHAPTER TWO

Egypt, India, and Palestine: 1946

MY FIRST goal was India. En route, I stopped for several days in Cairo. The chief topic of political conversation was the exodus of the British from the land of Egypt. The first evening I dined at the home of Sir Walter Smart, the Political Adviser of the British Embassy, whose Egyptian wife, daughter of a Cairo newspaper magnate, I had met years earlier in Moscow. Sir Walter assured me the British were getting out. They had already evacuated Cairo and Alexandria. But before they relinquished military control of the Suez Canal they wanted an assurance, written into an Anglo-Egyptian treaty, that they could come back in case of an emergency which threatened the safety of the Canal.

But what is an emergency? Would an attack on Greece constitute an emergency? (I had just flown from Athens to Cairo in three hours.) No, King Farouk replied. An attack on Turkey? No, said the twenty-six-year-old monarch. Only if an Arab country was attacked —Iraq, for instance, or Syria—would the British be entitled to return to Egypt with their military forces.

The British reminded the monarch and Prime Minister Sidky

Pasha, who doubled as president of the National Association of Manufacturers, that a war which began in far-off Poland reached one of its great climaxes at El Alamein, near Suez. If that battle had been lost, Hitler's Marshal Rommel might have conquered Egypt, swept on to India (the dream Napoleon dreamed more than a century earlier), joined forces with the advancing Japanese, and won the war.

The Egyptians resisted such logic. Egypt is surrounded by deserts and seas. Large oceans of sand sometimes give the same false sense of security that comes to nations from large bodies of water. Isolationism apart, the Egyptians just wanted the British out. The King could not forget the biggest political day of his life, that day in February, 1942, when British tanks and soldiers surrounded his palace and the British Ambassador, Sir Miles Lampson, a mild, plump, jovial man, entered the palace and politely intimated that His Majesty could be very comfortable in exile, for a very long time —unless he promised to help fight the Nazis. He promised—and bore a grudge.

The Egyptian army officers disliked the limitations on their power and duties resulting from the presence of foreign military forces on national soil. The new small middle class, just beginning to push into politics, resented outside occupation.

The rising tide of Egyptian nationalism disturbed not only the British. The Copts, who are Christians and constitute 10 per cent of the population of the country, were worried. I also talked to an Italian waiter, a French owner of a gift shop, and the Yugoslav maid in my hotel who had fled from Belgrade after the Germans bombed and took the city. They all expressed a fear of being forced to emigrate. So did Jews, Greeks, and Poles. Many tens of thousands of foreigners had settled in Egypt to do the work and conduct the trade which the natives had felt was beyond their capacity or beneath their dignity. Now middle-class Egyptians coveted their positions.

Xenophobia and anti-imperialism were rife. An odor of social ferment filled the air. I had lived in Egypt, in cities and in the desert, for several months in 1918. Disease and filth were somewhat less rampant now. But wealth was more concentrated and the peasantry poorer. The glaring contrast between the ostentatious luxury of the thin upper class and the near-starvation of villagers and slum-dwellers irked the intellectuals, who threatened to submit to

Russian embraces. They were disgruntled, politically impotent, and anti-British. Moscow was anti-British. They therefore thought of Moscow as a new Mecca. But they did nothing. They were loquacious and indolent and apparently infected with the pervading social decadence.

Unemployment riots in Alexandria had recently moved the government, for the first time in history, to dole out a pound, then about four dollars, to 250 workless. An additional £750 were available for distribution among the unemployed. There were 400,000 unemployed.

Did the Prime Minister believe that labor unrest was due to Communist activity, a member of Parliament asked him at question time. "Possibly," he answered, "and if so it is regrettable." These words would not butter the underdog's unleavened bread. Azzam Pasha, the General Secretary of the Arab League, advised the Prime Minister "to combat Communism in Egypt by encouraging the growth of a Labor party. The Prophet Mohammed," he added, "was the first Socialist and it is the duty of his present-day followers to do all in their power to encourage the growth of Socialism."

Labor leader Clement R. Attlee was then Prime Minister of the United Kingdom. He and Ernest Bevin, his Foreign Secretary, were adamantly anti-Communist and anti-Soviet. The strength of Socialism in England kept British Communism weak. Hence probably Azzam Pasha's assumption that a middle-of-the-road Labor party could likewise serve Egypt as a preventive and an antidote to Communism. But Egyptian employers even refused to tolerate free trade unions. Though most trade unions were company unions, they were not allowed to form a nation-wide federation. A Socialist party would have been labeled Communist and suppressed as subversive of the upper-class interests which paid a farm laborer five to eight piasters, or twenty to thirty-two cents, for a twelve-hour day. Factory hands received not much more.

I was born and raised in the family of an impecunious Philadelphia fish-and-fruit peddler; my mother sometimes supplemented his meager income by taking in the neighbors' laundry. Poverty has always aroused my elemental resentment. But actually it is not poverty which breeds revolt so much as poverty in intimate proximity with conspicuous wealth.

In 1942, I had flown up from Khartoum, capital of the Sudan, to Cairo. Somewhere over southern Egypt, Captain Raymond Wise,

Jr., also a native Pennsylvanian, invited me into the seat just vacated by the copilot, and showed me how to take over the controls of the DC-3. I felt this was too great a responsibility for one who could not even drive an automobile, and so I merely took advantage of a perch in the cabin to observe the countryside ten thousand feet below. In the center of the scene flowed the Nile, a straight silver ribbon glittering in the blinding sunlight; on each bank was a narrow strip of life-giving brown mud and silt deposited seasonally after the swollen river retreats into its channel; beyond these, to the eye's infinity, stretched the dead desert. This was Egypt. And this was Egyptian society too: rich life for the few who owned the precious land, arid misery for all the rest.

In such a situation the famished millions dream of equality and the Communists have a field day telling lies about the equality which does not exist in Soviet Russia.

After digging a long deep trough and raising a high spray, the British seaplane took off before noon from the surface of the Nile, circled so the passengers could see the Giza pyramids and Sphinx, flew over the Suez Canal and the Sinai Desert, and in less than three hours "landed" on the saline waters of Palestine's Dead Sea at Kaliya. The next evening I reached New Delhi, the capital city. I remained in the country exactly a month.

I learned to like India. Four years earlier, on my first visit, I met many fine Indians and grew attached to some, but I failed to establish an emotional bond with the Indian people as a whole. India, to me, was a problem. I was eager to see the problem solved by the granting of independence—for the sake of India and of humanity. But I did not feel drawn to Indians in general as I did to the Russians, say, or the British or Spaniards.

This time, however, I played with a brown baby girl of two and as I held her soft little hand in mine I found myself hoping that she and her generation would grow up in a well-fed, happy country. I walked in poor city districts and saw boys and girls going to school, their clothes threadbare but white and clean, their sandals old, their black hair well kempt, their brown faces bright. And such big eyes, big white-and-brown eyes reflecting a desire to live! In Bombay I got a sense of dynamic energy in the mass, vitality despite suffering. At mammoth meetings in small towns and village centers I watched congregated thousands listening patiently to long speeches, waiting for guidance and a word of hope. These folk, I felt, would follow either selfless or sinister leadership. I was optimistic yet apprehensive. I was participating, not merely observing.

Indians, to risk a generalization, are cynically suspicious yet touchingly, naïvely trusting. Not having experienced much generosity from the rich or much justice from the powerful, the people tend to see a selfish motive behind every friendly act. But once convinced of a leader's idealistic renunciation for the common good, their adulation recognizes no bounds. They are hero worshipers and autograph collectors. They rewarded Mahatma Gandhi, Jawaharlal Nehru, Mrs. Sarojini Naidu, Sardar Vallabhbhai Patel and other nationlist leaders with tender devotion.

I stayed with Gandhi at Dr. Dinshah Mehta's Nature Cure Clinic and submitted to its ministrations—but not its diet—and then traveled with the Mahatma, third class, to Bombay. On bidding him farewell there he suggested that I visit him eleven days later at Panchgani, a health resort in the Maharashtran hills. Jayaprakash Narayan, the Socialist leader of India, and his wife, Prabhavati, were also going there to see Gandhi, so we traveled together by the Deccan Queen express from Bombay to Poona, and continued the journey in a car loaned to Jayaprakash.

Before long the car broke down and we changed to a cross-country bus. The Socialist party had arranged little welcoming receptions for Jayaprakash at villages en route. The bus halted at each of these request stations. Jayaprakash, his wife, and I would alight and listen to greetings addressed to him in Maharashtran, which he does not speak. He replied briefly in Hindi which was translated, and then each of us was garlanded with leis of most fragrant flowers threaded together on a wire—very heavy—and touched at the juncture of the thumb and forefinger with a metal hand that had been dipped in solid incense. Thus perfumed, and bearing armfuls of fruits and flowers as gifts, we returned to the bus whose driver and passengers, crowded like herring in a barrel, had waited while the ceremony lasted. Six times we got out in two hours. Nobody murmured a complaint. I suppose our temporary fellow travelers' complacent acceptance of these delays was due to a mixture of apathy, the low cost of time, and respect for Jayaprakash. They had perhaps never heard of him, but if he deserved such receptions he was worthy of their deference.

I myself received much attention in India because it had become known that I had spent a week with Gandhi in 1942. Once, on leaving a Nehru press conference in Bombay, I was encircled by autograph seekers. The scene struck me as comic, for on my right was Lillian Smith, popular American author of *Strange Fruit*, and on my left Dorothy Dunbar Bromley, a well-known staff member of the New York *Herald Tribune*. But they had not been touched by the Mahatma.

"One day," Mrs. Bromley wrote in her paper on August 11, 1946, "I heard two hundred Indian newspaper men . . . put questions on India and international affairs to the American writer Louis Fischer, who is known and loved throughout India. . . . Their questions ranged from 'What are Russia's intentions?' to 'Why do you in America discriminate against Negroes?' "

On that occasion and during my subsequent visits to India when the latter query was invariably posed, I gave more or less the same reply. "Yes," I said, "the discrimination against Negroes is a blot on America; I condemn and combat it. But in my own lifetime I have seen a tremendous change for the better. There is less mistreatment, less segregation, less discrimination in employment. The situation in some parts of the North and South is still a disgrace, yet the outlook for Negroes is brighter and many of them are rising in their professions and occupying honored places in society. I will be happy," I concluded, "when the sixty million untouchables of India are as well treated and as well situated as our Negroes." This statement was always met with embarrassed silence, and I did not mind.

Indians have their own strong color prejudices. Even shades of brown may make a difference in social status. Light skin is preferred. Nevertheless they indignantly, ferociously attack all manifestations of racial discrimination outside of India, especially in the United States and South Africa.

The dropping of atomic bombs on Hiroshima and Nagasaki left a deep scar on many Indians and on other "colored," that is, non-"white" peoples. The subject came up the day after my arrival in New Delhi at lunch in Birla House (where Gandhi was later assassinated). Mr. G. D. Birla's other luncheon guests were Sardar Vallabhbhai Patel, the "strong man" of the Indian Congress (Independence) party, and Chakravarti Rajagopalachari, an in-law of Gandhi, future Governor-General and Minister of Home Affairs in free India, who, next to Gandhi, has the astutest political mind in the country. During the table talk, Rajagopalachari said America subjected the Japanese to atomic bombing because they were colored; the Germans were not atom-bombed. I argued that the first report of the first successful atomic explosion in New Mexico reached President Truman when he was in conference with Stalin at Potsdam *after* Germany's defeat. The United States, therefore, did not have the A-bomb during the war with the Nazis. But Rajagopalachari could not be convinced by the facts. Even his great brain surrendered to emotions.

Most of the discussion at the luncheon, however, centered on the British offer to grant India independence. An impressive British Cabinet Mission, consisting of Lord Pethick-Lawrence, Secretary of State for India, Sir Stafford Cripps, President of the Board of Trade, and Albert V. Alexander, First Lord of the Admiralty, had arrived in New Delhi on March 24, 1946, to consult Indians and decide with them how power could best be transferred to Indian hands. But few Indians trusted British intentions. Jawaharlal Nehru and his adviser on foreign affairs, a long-time resident of England, V. K. Krishna Menon, told me they did not believe England would leave India. Even Gandhi wavered. He welcomed the Cabinet Mission with the emphatic statement that "it betrays want of foresight to disbelieve British declarations." Later, however, he too entertained doubts. The negotiations and debates were long and painful, and determined the future of India.

On reaching New Delhi, the Cabinet Mission had asked Gandhi's Congress party and Mr. Mohammed Ali Jinnah's Moslem League to submit a plan for the liberation of India. The two organizations failed to agree, and Gandhi, accordingly, advised Pethick-Lawrence, Cripps, and Alexander to formulate their own proposal.

They did, and it unequivocally rejected the idea of partitioning India. The three Ministers argued that if Britain gave Mr. Jinnah everything he asked—an independent Pakistan embracing all of the Punjab province in northwest India and all of Bengal and Assam in the northeast—his Moslem state of seventy million Moslems would include fifty million Hindus and Sikhs, while twenty million Moslems would remain in predominantly Hindu India. How did that solve the problem of religious minorities? The Cabinet Ministers accordingly considered an alternative: the partitioning of the Punjab, Bengal, and Assam, and assigning the Moslem sections to Pakistan.

But this, the Cabinet Mission reported, "would be contrary to the wishes of a very large percentage of the inhabitants of these provinces." Moreover, the two lobes of Pakistan would then be separated by a thousand miles of India. "Such a Pakistan," the three Ministers declared, "is regarded by the Moslem League as quite impracticable." (Yet that is the Pakistan of today.)

The Cabinet Mission, consequently, recommended against "two entirely separate sovereign States." In view, however, of the "very genuine and acute anxiety of the Moslems lest they be subjected to a perpetual Hindu-majority rule," the Mission wanted to grant considerable autonomy to the provinces with Moslem majorities. To do this, Article 19 of the Cabinet Ministers' report provided for three federations: one in the center which was overwhelmingly Hindu, and two on the sides with small Moslem majorities and massive Hindu and Sikh minorities. Although the three regions would belong to a united India, each would draft its own constitution. But if a province like Assam, which had more Hindus than Moslems, did not like the constitution of the northeastern federation it could join the Hindu federation in the center.

This British plan for Indian independence, first published on May 16, 1946, represented a complicated compromise. The Moslem League did not get Pakistan. Neither did the Congress party of Gandhi, Nehru, Patel, and Azad achieve its aim of freedom in unity. The three-federations scheme seemed to them to contain the germ of partition, Pakistan by two side doors, with tens of millions of non-Moslems subjected against their will to Moslem rule. Congress party spokesmen protested against the coercion. Gandhi feared that the Moslems in the two peripheral federations would make laws preventing the non-Moslems from exercising the option of secession.

Vocal India engaged in endless, agitated, inconclusive discussion on the British plan. To accept or not to accept? The answer might determine the fate of India with her 350 million inhabitants and perhaps, too, the fate of Asia for a century or more. Week after week, Congress party and Moslem League leaders sat in separate conclave weighing and maneuvering. Meanwhile Lord Pethick-Lawrence, Cripps, and Alexander consulted both Indian camps. Often the British Cabinet Ministers came to negotiate with Gandhi in the slum for untouchables where he chose to live. It was there that I saw Gandhi for a moment early on the evening of my arrival in New Delhi on June 25. He said he could not give me any time because Lady Cripps had brought a message from her husband. Nehru was there too and I drove with him to Maulana Azad's home where he was staying. I talked with Nehru in his room for a while and then we went downstairs to dine with President Azad and several other members of the Congress party's Working, or Executive, Committee. At five-thirty the next morning I walked with Gandhi for half an hour, lunched with Patel, Rajagopalachari, and Birla, and spent the evening with Sardar Patel. The outlines of the situation were growing clear to me. I felt as though I was looking down into the crater of history.

On June 27, I accompanied Gandhi again on his walking-talking constitutional which began at 5:30 A.M. and lasted half an hour. I was seeing Nehru at 2:30 P.M. Now I had to get the British and Moslem viewpoints. I made an appointment with Mr. Jinnah for 10:30 A.M. the same day.

Of the three British Cabinet Ministers I knew Cripps best. I telephoned his office and learned that he was leaving for London in the afternoon but would receive me at 9:30 A.M. I realized immediately that, given the intervening distance, the Cripps date would probably make me late for my Jinnah appointment, and I am punctual. Perhaps that is due to my fourteen years as a foreign correspondent in Russia, where "*seichas*" or "right away" may mean never or next week, and to my extended experience in Spain, where "*mañana*" or "tomorrow" is an expression of a way of life. But knowing Jinnah's pride, I would not dare try to change a rendezvous with him, and as Cripps was going to London that day, he would find it impossible to fit me in at another hour.

I arrived at the Cripps quarters at Number 2 Willingdon Crescent, a little ahead of time, kept my taxi, and went inside. Isobel, Lady Cripps, was in the reception room and received me cordially. In a minute she escorted me to the entrance of Stafford's study. He looked more gaunt than ever and no wonder, for May and June, with their oppressively torrid heat and all-invading dust storms, are the worst months of the year in New Delhi, and Stafford had spent them in endless, weighty, and sometimes heartbreaking conferences. His long, hollow cheeks were longer and hollower still. Yet the usual gentle smile played around his mouth. He was immensely affable and said he felt optimistic. The Cabinet Mission's proposals of May 16, 1946, would go through, he declared, and India would get independence. The accomplishment seemed to buoy him. He also gave me his view of British domestic politics.

After thirty-five minutes, Sir Stafford took me to the door and handed me over to Isobel with whom I sat in the antechamber for ten relaxed minutes while she knitted and chatted charmingly about her beloved theme: Stafford.

The taxi started, made good progress, then coughed, sputtered, and stopped. The turbaned Sikh driver puttered, tinkered under the hood, and finally made a motion of despair. No other taxi was in sight. Near by some government cars were standing under a shed for shade. I offered one of the chauffeurs some extra money but he refused; it was not regular. So I accosted a tonga. A tonga is a one-horse, two-wheeled cart in which the passenger sits with his back to the cabbie in order, perhaps, to keep his mind off the inadequacies of the conveyance. We moved at Delhi-horse's pace; neither whip nor oath affected the emaciated animal's speed. I arrived at Jinnah's house thirty-five minutes late.

Mohammed Ali Jinnah, the genius of Moslem politics, stood over six feet tall and weighed only 120 pounds. His elongated face was a series of bony ridges and hollows which gave the impression of a forbidding earnestness, and he rarely laughed or smiled. Frigid and formal, his presence generally reduced the temperature to freezing. He dressed either in fashionable European clothes or in a knee-length straw-colored tunic, tight, white Indian trousers that clung to his bony legs, and black patent leather pumps. A monocle dangled from a black cord. Somebody called him "one of the best-dressed men in the British Empire." He drank liquor, ate pork, seldom went to mosque, knew no Arabic and little Urdu. In these respects, as well as in surname, origin, and temperament, he was as un-Islamic as anyone could be, and he adopted the program of a separate Moslem state very late in life. Yet chiefly by dint of his unrelenting, embittered, fanatical advocacy of that program, he made himself the political leader of India's Moslems and, ultimately, the father of Moslem Pakistan.

As I entered Jinnah's room I apologized for being late and explained the circumstances: a broken-down taxi and only a tonga as an alternative. "I trust you are not hurt," he said stiffly. I told him there had been no accident, only an engine that refused to function. He kept the conversation on the incident.

When I finally extricated myself from the talk about taxi and tonga I said, "It seems India is about to become independent." This remark echoed Cripps's optimism and tested Jinnah's sentiments. He pulled in his chin, looked at me sternly, stood up, extended his hard hand, and declared, "I will have to go now."

The interview broke all records for brevity; it had lasted about ninety seconds. As Mr. Jinnah bade me good-by at the door, he made it clear that he would not see me again.

I do not know even now whether he was offended by my lateness or by my suggestion that India's freedom was imminent. Probably the latter. For Jinnah did not want a free India, he wanted two free Indias, one of them Pakistan. The British Cabinet Mission had vetoed Pakistan. Gandhi called the vivisection of India "blasphemy." But that merely stirred Jinnah's cold ruthlessness; he hated Gandhi.

The Congress party leaders made the historic blunder in 1946 of wavering and weighing nice distinctions about the constituent assembly, provisional government, and constitutions. They should have accepted the Cabinet Mission's May 16 proposal forthwith and without amendment for it was far better than what they got and it preserved the framework of a united India in which, in calmer times, they might have tried to achieve better relations between Hindus and Moslems. The difficult May 16 plan would have been far better than the deficiencies and horrors of the ultimate settlement.

Congress acceptance of the Cabinet Mission's plan would have obliged the British government to put it into effect. But when Congress delayed and indulged in detailed analysis of its own doubts and of the proffered democratic devices, Jinnah saw his chance to torpedo the scheme entirely.

The Congress leaders were operating on the legal plane and apparently underestimated Jinnah's choice of weapons. He had no use for subtly balanced constitutional skyscrapers. His monistic eye saw that he would never attain Pakistan through law or order. The Koran could not help him, so he unsheathed the sword. Deliberately, he proclaimed August 16, 1946, "Direct Action Day." The day lasted months. Thugs, arsonists, and death dominated city and countryside. Hindus, Sikhs, and Moslems reveled in competitive killing. Rivers of blood washed away reason. Religious passions tore India in twain. On August 14, 1947, Jinnah crowned himself ruler of Pakistan.

I had argued with Mr. Jinnah in 1942 against multiplying discords in the world. "I am a realist," he replied. "I must deal with the divisive characteristics which exist." Gandhi, Nehru, and Azad hoped to bridge the gulf between Hindus and Moslems. Jinnah aimed to make the chasm unbridgeable.

Jinnah's Moslem League consisted overwhelmingly of large land-lords who feared that independent India's first act would be a land reform designed to divide their estates among the land-hungry and always hungry peasants. Hence the Moslem landlords' coldness toward Indian independence.

The Moslem peasants, therefore, felt little sympthy for the upper-class Moslem League, and in the Northwest Frontier Province, in the Punjab, Bengal, and Sind, it was usually defeated by other parties.

Jinnah needed a device to link Moslem landlords and Moslem peasants. He found it in Pakistan, the Moslem Zionism, and pro-claimed it in 1940.

Pakistan promised to be a poor, reactionary, landlord-ridden state, another Iran. Moslem feudals would naturally desire it. The new Moslem middle class might be lured to it by the prospect of more government jobs than they could get in a united India in competition with Hindus. But the peasantry seemed to have nothing to gain, and industrialists and tradesmen could not prosper in a feudal country.

The unreligious Jinnah, however, whipped them all into a frenzy of religious nationalism. In 1946, he unleashed the whirlwind. In 1947, he reaped the power. He made history and misery. The two travel together far too often.

The bisection of India represented a triumph of Jinnah's mad realism compounded by maniacal religion.

Just as Jinnah was planning "direct action" in India, violence flared in another country held by the British: Palestine. Indian Congress party spokesmen and editorialists were generally pro-Arab and anti-Zionist. In 1946, I asked Nehru why. "That is the least we can do for our Moslems," he answered with disarming candor. Gandhi was watching the Arab-Jewish conflict, and asked me to write him from Palestine. I promised.

I left Karachi, on the west coast of India, at one minute past midnight and landed in Palestine nine and a half hours later, after a 2,079-mile nonstop flight in a converted Lancaster bomber. The land of the Bible flowed with military and hate. Cities were dotted with pillboxes, barbed-wire barricades, and roadblocks. Concrete bastions with slit windows for guns dotted the countryside. British soldiers went about in pairs, carrying light but deadly Tommy guns.

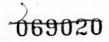

The vital statistics of Palestine were: 1,200,000 Arabs; 600,000 Jews; 100,000 British soldiers. Each of the camps was descended from one of the three religions born in the Holy Land, and now they were defiling the cradle with murder, terror, and intolerance.

A four-way boycott gripped the little country: the British boycotted the Jews; the Arabs boycotted the Jews; the Jews boycotted the British and Arabs.

A Jewish journalist friend took me to a Jewish restaurant. Pointing to a couple at another table, he said, "She's a traitor, she married an Englishman."

I said, "This is racism. You're as bad as a Nazi."

"A month ago," he confessed, "I felt differently. Now the British are out to ruin us."

Near the city of Jaffa, I interviewed Major General Cassels at his divisional headquarters. I asked him where he had served in the war. He and his division had fought their way into Germany in 1945 and remained there until a few months ago. I wondered about fraternization in Germany and Palestine. "Oh," he answered, "a great deal of fraternization went on between our soldiers and Germans. There's none here between us and Jews." An ironic reversal a year after the war! The King David outrage made matters worse.

Jerusalem's King David is the finest hotel in the Middle East. A few minutes after noon, on Monday, July 22, 1946, a delivery truck drove up to the kitchen entrance of the hotel and men dressed like Arabs began unloading large metal milk cans. When all the containers had been placed inside the kitchen, a thunderous explosion occurred, sheets of flame enveloped the building from basement to roof, glass, masonry, and timber flew through the air, and shots were heard as a truck and a small automobile escaped from the scene. The entire front corner of the hotel's south wing, all seven floors, had been shorn off as though a thousand-ton bomb had dropped on it. The south wing was used at the time by the Secretariat of the government of Palestine and as British military headquarters. Ninety-one officers and officials, many of them highly placed, were killed, including Julius Jacobs, Finance Under Secretary, and Captain M. Levy, two pro-Zionist British Jews. Hundreds were seriously hurt.

I arrived in Jerusalem three days after this crime had been committed. Most Palestine Jews were incensed by the act of brutality and had no doubt about its authors. The next day indeed, Irgun Tsvai Leumi, a Jewish terrorist organization, admitted the deed but contended that it had telephoned the hotel switchboard twenty-two minutes before the explosion and given instructions that the building be evacuated. This attempt at extenuation was apparently addressed not to the public in general but to the larger Jewish paramilitary defense body, the Hagana, which had agreed to the Irgun's attack on the British headquarters in the King David Hotel provided it took place before working hours so that no personnel was harmed. The terrorists argued, however, that the only way of bringing the explosives into the premises was via the milk cans and these were always delivered during the lunch hour.

One effect of the King David midday madness was a schism between the Irgun gunmen, who had already staged kidnapings of British Tommies and other Wild-West coups, and the Hagana, the underground but "regular" Jewish army subject to the responsible Jewish leadership. The Hagana too was at war with the British in Palestine, but limited itself to such acts as the sabotage of bridges and railways without attacking persons or engaging in fierce vendettas and tit-for-tat terror. The Hagana now took steps to curb the Irgun. But while the sober segments of Palestinian Jewry might be shocked by the Irgun's senseless barbarity, no Jew could very well turn an Irgun man over to his British pursuers or refuse shelter to a hunted terrorist. For it was generally felt that however misguided its methods, the Irgun was devoted to the ideal of a Jewish state.

Inevitably, the British authorities imposed a curfew on Jerusalem and spread a net over all Palestine for the apprehension of the King David culprits. The curfew required every resident to remain indoors, and neither stand on roofs nor lean out of windows, from 6 P.M. to 6 A.M. As the curfew hour approached, say at 5 P.M., one could notice people on the streets looking at their watches. Fifteen minutes later the pace of pedestrians quickened. By a quarter to six everybody was running. At six the city was empty and silent, except for the rumble of military vehicles.

Though the sight of Jerusalem's populace, Englishmen, Arabs, and Jews, hastily disappearing into their stone houses by foreign fiat was not without a certain fascination, it scarcely added to the sum total of human dignity. A violent few had brought it on the innocent many.

Journalists were given special passes exempting them from curfew restrictions. Every evening I would leave the Hotel Eden (not named for the British statesman) to watch the strange phenomenon of a city's public life ebbing away without signal or siren. Two or three minutes after the lethal hour of six, a British patrol would appear either on foot or in a truck or small armored car. I kept the official permit in my front handkerchief pocket, for a rapid motion of the hand into any other pocket might suggest the intention of whipping out a weapon. The military were very nervous, and not without reason, for a terrorist threatened with arrest is like a lion at bay, and British personnel had been ambushed before.

One evening, climbing up a deserted street, I overtook a tall British officer, and as I glanced sideways I saw a sensitive, troubled face. My "Good evening" seemed a godsend and was eagerly reciprocated with the obvious added comment that it could not be very good in the midst of "this mess." I identified myself and so did the Englishman. He was from London and we talked nostalgically about it. He wanted to be home, to leave all of this behind and have some peace. "We are hated here," he said, "and we hate the whole dirty business. But we had to have the curfew for our own protection. Besides, the Jews and Arabs will massacre one another if we get out."

The gulf between the British and the Jews was growing wider. After the murder at the King David, Lieutenant General Evelyn Barker, British Commander-in-Chief in Palestine, issued a secret circular, which was soon published by the Jewish press and acknowledged as correct, stating that "all Jewish places of entertainment, cafés, restaurants, shops and private dwellings" were put "out of bounds." Then for emphasis, "No British soldier is to have any intercourse with any Jew. . . . These measures will inflict some hardship on the troops," it was admitted, but "they will be punishing the Jews in a way the race dislikes more than any: by striking at their pockets and showing our contempt for them."

It was a Nazi-ish ukase, and Herbert S. Morrison declared in the House of Commons that the British government "disassociates itself" from General Barker's order. But British officials in Jerusalem defended Barker. "Can you blame him after the King David?" they argued.

The Arab-Jewish rift was even worse than the British-Jewish quarrel. Lieutenant General Sir Alan G. Cunningham, the British High Commissioner, told me that he could get Arabs and Jews to attend his cocktail parties because they stood around in separate groups. But they would not accept an invitation to a dinner in his house where they had to sit down together.

An Arab maid asked her Jewish mistress to buy her a frock in a Jewish shop. "If I went in myself," she explained, "my relatives would slit my throat."

An Arab merchant changed to European clothes, so as to be inconspicuous, when he visited his Jewish attorney's office.

This was not a new situation. The isolation had increased with the years. The Jewish young men and women I knew in Palestine in 1919 and 1920 spoke Arabic. Their children knew only a few words of the language. In 1919 and 1920, Arab peasants sold vegetables and fruits to Jewish housewives in the cities. In 1934, Arabs in Jewish Tel Aviv were either tourists or window-shoppers; Jews occasionally went slumming in Arab Jaffa. Arab farm labor had been ousted from the Jewish agricultural colonies. This was a deliberate policy, known as "The Conquest of Labor," designed to open jobs for newcomers from Eastern Europe and regenerate ghetto Jews through creative physical work. A laudable purpose but politically divisive and disastrous!

The 1947 partition of India was surgery, a painful severing of limbs and tissues intimately interlinked, for Moslems, Hindus, and Sikhs were one body though they worshiped differently and had different outlooks. But Palestine was partitioned long before the politicians cut the map in two. Jews and Arabs were different not only in religion, but in culture, living standards, social patterns, political goals, and economic interests. Hates and fears built a high wall between them. The bisection of Palestine into an Israeli state and an Arab state merely clothed a condition with a constitution.

The British were caught in the middle. The Zionists charged that anti-Zionism was dominant among the permanent British officials who implemented their policy through Foreign Secretary Ernest Bevin, the allegedly "anti-Semitic" Labor leader. The Arabs believed that under American pressure England, loyal to Biblical tradition and the Balfour Declaration of 1917, would favor the Jews.

I went to dinner in the magnificent villa of the Grand Mufti, situated on the road up to Mount Scopus and occupied by Kathy Antonius, whose late husband George, author of *The Arab Awakening*, I had known in America. Kathy, sister of Lady Smart of Cairo, was a spirited lady, interested in people and ideas, who kept an Arab-British salon in the best European manner. Her Arab guests were tense, upper-class young men uncertain of what role to play in the drama they knew impended. "If the British adopt a pro-Jewish policy, we will turn to Russia for help," Hadar Hussein Effendi, nephew of the Grand Mufti, exclaimed.

"That," replied an Arab friend, "would be like catching hold of a shark to save yourself from drowning." He too, however, took an intransigent attitude on Zionism.

I spent a morning with a group of young Arab leaders in the Arab political office in Jerusalem. Over cups of Turkish coffee, and in an atmosphere of European urbanity, they passionately pleaded their national cause. "They are not anti-Jewish, they say," I reported to Mahatma Gandhi by letter. "They merely think that the Jews should go elsewhere. The Palestine Arabs object to Palestine being converted into a Jewish state and they object, too, to the establishment of a Jewish state or any Jewish government in only a part of Palestine. They therefore reject the British plan recently adumbrated by Herbert Morrison in Parliament which provides for a Jewish province and an Arab province and the retention of some territory by the British."

The young Arab leaders maintained that if Britain tried to impose a pro-Jewish solution they would rise in revolt. I said they could not cope with the British military; an insurrection would cost the lives of a few Englishmen and many Arabs. The Arabs shrugged their shoulders.

The soil of the Holy Land was thickly sown with the seeds of violence.

Thus far, my trip had taken me to three countries. All three wanted the British to withdraw. Before long, England did leave India, which was a colony, and Palestine, a mandated territory, which was in effect a colony. She stayed in Egypt, an independent country, for the sake of Suez.

At most, Suez was an imperial key. India was the imperial crown. Palestine too was valuable property. Yet the British gave them up and held on to the Canal. The reasons why this was possible are illuminating:

Egypt's pashas, beys, and royal courtiers were torn between a controllable nationalistic hostility to foreign occupation and a dominant social or class hostility to change. They could have unleashed a popular movement to force the British out. But they feared the people; they knew that a mass upsurge against foreign rule might teach the miserable millions how to oppose their native overlords. These revolutionary possibilities persuaded the political and economic rulers of Egypt to let sleeping dogs lie and let the British stay. With more faith in itself and closer ties with the people, the upper class might have experimented, as their peers have elsewhere, in using nationalism to expel the foreign power and thereby enhance their own power. But at that moment the masters of Egypt took no chances; an occasional inexpensive, ineffective riot served quite adequately as a patriotic vent for university students and as a patriotic fig leaf for themselves.

Neither was England under any foreign pressure to abandon Egypt. On the contrary, the retention of the Canal by a Western nation seemed an insurance against Soviet expansion.

The United States, however, did maintain a constant barrage of criticism against British rule in India and Palestine. Never having had an empire and having prospered without one, America saw no wisdom in imperialism. The first colony to wring independence from a foreign regime, America easily generated a vague yet vehement sympathy for any colony bent on the same purpose.

American influence apart, the British Labor government which came to power in 1945, and its supporters in and out of Parliament, would have felt acutely uncomfortable if called upon to suppress a revolt provoked by their obstruction of Indian independence after having championed it for many years out of office. The physical cost and financial expense of such a military-police operation right after the exhausting Second World War would have been back-breaking and, as a matter of fact, was never contemplated. Organized and guided by the genius of Mahatma Gandhi and enriched by his moral quality, the Indian freedom movement had attained nationwide, mass proportions with millions of followers in all classes and castes. As early as Gandhi's famous Salt March in March, 1930, it had become clear that the Indians were invincible. After that it was only a matter of time before the immovable object called British raj would have to remove itself or the irresistible force would eddy around it, dig under it, and finally wash it out to sea.

In an interview I had with Prime Minister Clement R. Attlee at Number Ten Downing Street on October 14, 1946, he said, apropos of Palestine, "If we are attacked by both Arabs and Jews and if no one wants us, we will get out." Further in the discussion he returned to this theme: "We cannot stay if no one wants us," he asserted. The same principle applied to India. "No one" would have been an exaggeration. But so many Indians and Palestinians wanted Britain to leave that Britain did.

The British people, amply endowed with that complicated virtue which carries the simple label of political maturity, knew that they could not accomplish the numerous pressing, postwar creative tasks at home while seated on the lid of a pot containing several hundred million seething Indians. It was for this reason, among others, that they voted the Labor party into power only two months after they had won a difficult war under the able leadership of their beloved Winston. He would not have freed India. The Labor government had to. The liberation of India was among its chief historic functions. A country either copes courageously with the surgical operations history demands of it or it deteriorates, and victorious Britain did not intend to deteriorate. Other nations that had flinched in the war failed in peace. But England faced her domestic problems, as she had met the Nazi threat, with stamina and stubbornness and the self-sacrifice born of self-confidence.

CHAPTER THREE

New England?

THE DAY I arrived in London from India in 1946 I thought back to an experience in wartime Britain five years earlier. During a visit to a military airfield near Bath, Captain Ian Gleed, age twenty-five, leader of a night-fighter squadron in the Royal Air Force, took me up over the English Channel in an open training plane, and then two Hurricane pursuit ships came up and maneuvered in mock combat around us. When we landed, Ian, hero of the Battle of Britain, walked me over to his own Hurricane fighter and pointed to the fifteen little yellow swastikas painted on its flank. Those were "for the fifteen Jerries I've shot down so far," he said. He patted the Hurricane as one would a favorite horse. Suddenly he grew meditative and said, "Do you think we shall be unemployed when it's all over?"

Ian never knew the answer. He was killed in combat in 1944. But he knew that right after the First World War, when he was a baby, British officers begged in British streets and British soldiers peddled pencils or sang for alms. Hence Ian's query. He was wondering, he must have wondered often, whether he would be penniless though England owed him so much.

Ian, a middle-class boy, would have voted Labor. Military like Ian and civilians by the millions wanted to try out new faces and new ideas. England would not tolerate conditions similar to those that existed in the 1920's and 1930's when the unemployment of two million adults—out of a total national population of forty-eight million men, women, and children—was considered normal and ineradicable. If anything it was this unemployment in the prewar period, reflected in Captain Ian Gleed's worry, that explains Labor's smashing electoral victory in the summer of 1945. The nation's mood prompted it to turn away from the old.

There was, to be sure, no zeal to set the world on fire; the bombs had done too much of that. The people were too tired and too patriotic to discard the ancient foundations which had withstood the onslaught so sturdily. The superstructure, however, seemed to need renovating. There would always be an England, but not the same kind.

Despite bombs, blood, and crashing buildings, the war was exhilarating, the future a remote and gnawing uncertainty. When the future arrived with the peace, the British, proud that they had single-handedly stemmed the tide which engulfed a continent, looked back somewhat nostalgically to the wartime equality of sacrifice and brotherhood-under-the-bombs. Some of this, they hoped, would be salvaged for the years ahead.

I asked a London tailor in 1946 whether he could make me a suit. He said yes, but the best British woolens were being exported. With the proceeds England bought food abroad so her people could eat. He explained, he did not complain. Further in our conversation he said he missed the war. "Not the air raids," I commented.

"No, but their spirit," he replied. He had "fire-watched" many a night with a lord and a bank director.

The social leveling did not survive the war and was incomplete during it. Money quickly drove a wedge between different income groups. But a strong tendency persisted after the war (1) to level incomes through taxation, (2) to level living standards through food rationing, (3) to level available medical aid through a national health service, and (4) to level down the political power of the business community by withdrawing a number of industries from its control and placing them under government operation.

Nations must make rearrangements day by day and month by month in their politics, economics, and social structure. But if the *status quo*, the existing order, acquires too much resistance to change, a backlog of unmade adjustments accumulates and hampers growth and hurts health. Reform blocked too long breeds revolution.

England possessed the flexibility and wisdom to reform. The war had a lot to do with it. All the people, rich and poor, men, women, and children, military and civilians, had stood firm like a high rock in a storm. National cohesion reduced class consciousness. The ubiquitous evidence that dignity and nobility in danger inhered in individuals irrespective of class strengthened the trust of one class in another.

"This country survived the Battle of Britain," a titled English-woman said to me with more than a touch of emotion. "No harm can come to us from within. We"—she meant the upper class—"we should have been frightened by Labor's innovations had they taken place before the war. Fancy nationalizing the Bank of England! And coal! And the railways! But let them experiment. It's only fair that Labor should have its innings."

The Communists' blind loyalty to Moscow and their irritating, un-British methods, made British Labor far more anti-Communist than anticapitalist. Its original fund of idealism was heavily weighted with pacifism, but it had backed wars and military budgets in the national interest. Labor's nationalism, however, is tempered, except in the demagogues, by internationalism, Christian brotherhood, and anti-imperialism.

The British Labor party is first of all British, not merely loyally

British, as demonstrated by its participation in the Churchill government during the war and by its actions before and since, but characteristically British. It lacks a rigid dogma. Its discipline permits differences. Jesus Christ inspires more of its members than does Karl Marx. It depends on and caters to workers' support but does not make a religion of the class war. It recognizes the clash of classes without aggravating it in Parliament or industry. Neither is class equated with country or placed above country.

The Labor government's reforms after the Second World War were not designed to establish a working-class or proletarian state. Twenty per cent of British industry was nationalized; some thought it insufficient, a number were disappointed with the results.

Most of the nationalized industries had been inefficient; the coal industry was derelict for decades. The community and the owners profited too little. British capitalism had run down. Productivity was low. The rate of reinvestment in industry fell below modern requirements. Whenever private business lacks the capital or withholds the capital for the renewal and expansion of its equipment it grows technologically inefficient and socially delinquent and opens the door to action by the state. In 1945, British working-class and middle-class votes accordingly raised into power a party committed to the use of common funds for national economic uplift.

British Labor, however, never intended to nationalize farming or retail trade or the larger part of industry. Even its radical wing would have been content with a few additional firms in the state's grip. British Labor, like Britain, was wedded to liberal democracy. Nobody and nothing was expropriated. The state paid compensation for all the enterprises it nationalized.

Labor also undertook a redistribution of income, goods, and benefits so that the poor would be leveled up and the rich down. Building materials were government-controlled. Aneurin Bevan, risen from pony boy in a Welsh mine to striped-trousered Minister of Health and Housing in Whitehall, consciously pursued a policy of houses for workers only, denying the wherewithal for repairs to anyone else. England had always been slum-ridden and now, due to the Nazis, there were not even enough slums.

Food was rationed. The country consumed more food than before the war. Workers were eating better than ever, and their children fared extremely well. Other classes consumed less for more money.

The government also rationed clothing. Under the new national health service, millions of poor who had never been able to have their teeth fixed—one could see the ugly results in any street crowd—or visit a doctor received adequate medical care. The privileged upper-income strata complained, talked about the numerous abuses, but accepted the innovations as inevitable. No Conservative government would dare tamper with the health service or with housing priorities.

Money ceased to be the only medium of distribution. Red tape competed with pound notes as a means of getting goods and facilities. But there was no black market. Though they might resent official policy, Englishmen played fair out of a sense of national dignity—which is more than patriotism. Having fought the war so nobly they could not ignobly let their country down in peacetime by allowing material scarcity to lead them into immorality.

Probably the scarcest commodity was labor. Signs in office and shop windows pleaded for stenographers, saleswomen, waitresses, maids, and so forth. Men were quitting the mines in droves and seeking better-paid jobs. Prime Minister Attlee told a deputation of high-minded citizens that if all German prisoners of war were sent home England could not gather in the harvest. Nor were enough hands available to clear the debris from blitzed sites. Working men enjoyed this condition and frowned on government proposals to encourage immigration.

It was the labor shortage and the demand for high or full employment that constituted the revolutionary leaven in postwar Britain. Scarce labor, favored by state rationing, costs more; to pay the added expense private enterprise had to increase productivity. It became wise and desirable to spare the man and introduce more machines. The government paid for much of the new mechanization. In London I obtained a list of more than a hundred factories which the government was financing and building but which were to be operated by private enterprise for a small rental. Laborites called this "Mixed Economy": state capitalism in partnership with private capitalism in the national interest. All the new plants were located in the former derelict industrial areas, centers of chronic unemployment for decades.

The British state was spending more and needed money. Several items of national bookkeeping stood out in bright red ink: less coal would be exported; fewer cotton goods would be sold to India; more food would be imported. The sizable deficits could only be covered by tapping America's good will and purse.

It was ironic that billions from the American capitalist government to the British Labor government should have facilitated the nationalization of British capitalist industry. But foreign policy is often shot through with social contradictions. A Socialist Britain was sure to be on America's side in the battle with Soviet imperialism; therefore London got loans from Washington. "It is not really important to us," said George F. Kennan, chief of the U.S. State Department's Policy Planning Staff, "how much of the economy of England is controlled by the British government as long as the rights of individual Englishmen are still protected by a system of justice second to none that the world has known. . . . As long as these conditions prevail we need have no fear that the national strength of England will ever be used for purposes basically hostile to this country."

Britain is America's door and corridor to Europe. There are always differences and clashes of interests between nations, but without or against Britain the United States could have no effective policy in Europe, and perhaps none in Asia either. This practical consideration was emotion-coated with the admiration which Americans felt for England during her wartime struggle to survive. Nor was the admiration diminished by her austere peacetime struggle for revival with state aid.

For America the only alternative to supporting Labor Britain would have been the impossible one of watching British economy collapse. The Labor government also had no choice; it felt compelled, under its electoral mandate, to feed, clothe, and shelter the people adequately. The process involved a legal, peaceful transition from old-time capitalism to a new kind of capitalist-socialist welfare state which might become typical on all continents in the second half of the twentieth century. Historically, this was exciting.

But the millions of men and women, chiefly women, who stood in queues from morning till evening did not see their humdrum lives in epic perspective. Gradualism had no thrills. My hotel displayed an "Old England" sign which read, "The management would be grateful if visitors dining in the restaurant would kindly wear evening dress." Man does not live by bread alone. He yearns for something tasty, elegant, and colorful. He needs circuses and pageantry. Soldiers and officers, back in the treadmill after great wartime adventures, were irked by the monotony and tedium. The yawn is as politically destructive as the laugh.

Friends asked whether America would launch a war against Russia. Richard Crossman, Labor M.P., said England would be neutral in the next war. "There will be no neutrals," commented Kingsley

Martin, editor of the weekly *New Statesman and Nation.*

Herbert Morrison, economic co-ordinator in the British government, told me of a dinner "which some of our Labor chaps gave to Soviet Ambassador Gusev to get better acquainted and make him feel at home. I asked him why they acted with so much suspicion toward the West. He made a long speech about the bravery of the Red army. I said to him, 'No, no, my good man, you misunderstood my question,' and repeated it. The ambassador delivered another long speech about the Red army. Then I understood that he didn't dare talk freely.

"But surely the Kremlin doesn't want a war," Morrison reflected. "Isn't it much better to let Molotov and Vishinsky fire away on every occasion and answer them without bitterness? We just state our case. That way they will be put in the wrong with world public opinion."

I suggested that Western statesmen ought to keep asserting their belief in the foreign policy of former Soviet Foreign Commissar Maxim Litvinov, the policy of collective security against aggressors.

Regarding Palestine, Morrison urged the adoption of his plan for partition into an Arab and a Jewish province. "But the Zionists want a state," I interposed.

"They could get it, after a period, out of the autonomous provinces," he explained. "They could have control over immigration."

"Not completely?"

"They could," he insisted, "unless they went wild, which I don't think they would."

I asked him how he got on with Ernest Bevin, the Foreign Secretary; there were always stories about friction between them. "Ernie and I have been getting on very well," Morrison replied. "I like Ernie. In the last government we had some scraps, but not in this one. I leave him alone and he leaves me alone. The government is functioning well as a team."

The "team" functioned well because it had a good captain in Prime Minister Clement R. Attlee. Immediately after my talk with Morrison I had an interview with Attlee at Ten Downing Street.

Mr. Attlee received me in a large room with a large table surrounded by chairs. At each place was a pad of Ten Downing Street stationery and four or five pencils. Apparently, the Cabinet would soon meet. In front of Attlee stood two black telephones, one marked "Secret," the other "Normal." The Prime Minister looked much grayer than when I last saw him in 1941. He also looked disheveled, and later I realized why: he kept curling the hair that fringes his bald pate.

Attlee asked me about the German leaders I had met. He asked whether India had a second generation of able young leaders. He asked about Russian policy and said, "It's remarkable how the Soviet government has dissipated the great amount of good will they had in this country." He said Britain had urgently requested the United States to persuade the UN to take over the Palestine problem. He made few other statements. Mostly he put questions, and the only indication I had of his views was when he occasionally took his pipe out of his mouth to say, "Quite, quite." This was far from satisfactory, but I had no choice; he obviously intended to remain uncommunicative.

If Attlee did not seem a dynamic figure he was a fighter, and in the House of Commons he was a tenacious, incisive debater. A middle-class intellectual who had identified himself with Labor, he served as the fulcrum moderator between factions, always positive, never obstrusive or abrasive. He had a faculty of withdrawing without yielding ground, and therefore made a fine chairman. A Churchill Cabinet meeting often became a forum for Winston's brilliant if business-impeding disquisitions, whereas Attlee, a consummate listener, drew the maximum from his colleagues and helped the government function as an efficient, unthwarted unit. A lesser man than Churchill, it is a question whether Attlee was not a far better peacetime Prime Minister.

The British, one felt, were creative; they had decided to build a better Britain and the government was resolved to implement the decision. This required another type of popular heroism, less spectacular than war heroism but more impressive because so dull. Morale was sustained by the work on new hospitals, factories, and homes, by full employment, the government's moderation, Ernest Bevin's firm foreign policy, peace in industry (few strikes), the occasional appearance of peaches and grapes on side-street pushcarts, and the occasional appearance of the sun. Many Englishmen were taking their first summer holiday since 1939 and reveling in it. September saw less rain. Good weather meant clear sailing for the government.

Captain Ian Gleed would not have been unemployed. His surviving colleagues found jobs. No bemedaled heroes in faded raincoats were hawking lead pencils in 1946. Ian, so vital, would have rejoiced in his country's virility despite the wartime drain on blood and energy and in its creativeness despite economic hardships. But if, some black night, flying high over England on the prowl for Nazi raiders, the mysterious stars and his loneliness had moved him to dream a dream of a bright new world when the fighting was over, he would have been disappointed. The postwar is hardly a time for dream fulfillment. People were living close to the earth, worried about rations, a roof, and the next war. The old England was not dead, and a new England had not yet been born. The in-between phase tried Britain's patience.

Nevertheless, the postwar years confirmed the British people's wartime faith in themselves. Under stress they were firm. In weakness they were great. There was a promise in all this that England would be strong again.

CHAPTER FOUR

Little Belgium

THE STORY is told of a headline in a big London newspaper which read: "STORM OVER CHANNEL. CONTINENT ISOLATED." The entire European Continent was seen as a satellite somewhere off the coast of the center of the universe. The truth is that even after the wartime decline in Britain's power, the British, and foreigners like myself, had this same sense of her position as the sun of the political solar system. After my stay in Egypt, India, and Palestine, I felt cut off from world currents. The East holds one concentrated on itself. I had to re-establish contact with the switchboard of international politics, and that was England. From London I hopped over to Belgium, then back to London, then on to France and Germany, and again to England.

In Belgium, the entire population of eight and a half million seemed to live by the black market. I talked to poor, middle class, and rich. They all depended on the black market. Prime Minister Camille Huysmans said to me, "Our people learned during the war to live legally and illegally." Blackmarketing, which was an anti-Nazi adventure in wartime, remained a habit in peacetime. Though coupons were required for the purchase of certain commodities, merchants announced quite openly, in the hearing of other customers, that by paying extra you could buy without coupons. Shops were well stocked, and the restaurants, especially after Asia and London, were dizzily luscious. I bought some food for London. After austere, law-abiding England, the easygoing cynicism of Belgium was impressive and depressing.

But the farms with their shaggy horses, the men in patched corduroys, the women bent over vegetable rows, the country roads lined with neatly pruned trees, the low houses, the canals, the street cars, the factories, everything seemed fastened to the earth with the steel bands of history. No invader could carry them away.

A controversy was shaking Belgium and because it concerned the future of a king it really interested the people and not only politicians, intellectuals, and journalists. On the day the newspapers reported that Greece had voted to return King George to his throne in Athens, Prime Minister Huysmans told me in Brussels that Leopold III would never be king of Belgium again. "The King," the seventy-five-year-old Premier declared, "was and is a Fascist. During the Ethiopian War he sent a friendly message to Italian Marshal Graziani. He sympathized with General Franco."

I wondered whether Leopold had any choice but to surrender the Belgian army to the Nazis on May 28, 1940. "Of course he did," M. Huysmans exclaimed and slapped the side of his thigh for emphasis. "Perhaps he had to surrender the troops under his immediate command in one battle area. He did not have to order the entire Belgian army, part of which was in France, to lay down its arms. He could have left the country, as the Belgian government did, and continue the resistance from abroad. Leopold was never a prisoner of the Nazis." By implication he was their voluntary guest.

Was it not a fact, I argued, that the Belgian army helped cover the retreat of the British and French to Dunkirk where they slipped into the water and out of the Nazi noose to live to fight another day? Some isolated units acting independently had, the Prime Minister agreed, but Leopold deserved no credit for it.

I inquired whether the powerful Catholic party might not bring the King back. "Impossible," M. Huysmans affirmed, "there will be blood in the streets. The workers will fight. In private many Catholics are antiroyalists. The Catholics are too intelligent to try restoring Leopold."

The Prime Minister's vehement opposition to the return of the King from Switzerland did not spring from any intention to end the monarchy. "I am a republican," he asserted, "but I am also a practical man, not a dogmatic theoretician. In view of the division of Belgium between Walloons and Flemings and between Catholics and Socialists, in view, moreover, of the divisions between the nations of the world, a king is an element of strength and unity." I had no difficulty assimilating this view. An American used to become an antimonarchist as soon as he learned about George III in primary school. As he grew older the Sultan, the Czar, and the Kaiser made royalty synonymous with tyranny. But after the First World War and during and after the Second, uncrowned heads—Hitler, Mussolini, and Stalin, for instance—incubated much mischief, whereas in Scandinavia, Britain, and so forth kings and queens, by preserving tradition without obstructing change, came to symbolize stability, democracy, and middle-class normality.

Postwar Belgium experienced trouble finding the right king and spent considerable care and emotion on the matter because Belgian freedom depended on it. M. Huysmans hoped Leopold would renounce the throne and thus clear the way to the ascension of the liberal Regent, Prince Charles, Leopold's brother. Charles, however, was a bachelor and therefore a problem, for a king should have an offspring, and Charles refused to marry.

Belgium is mainly Catholic, and the Catholic party, heavily pro-Leopold, was the largest. The issue of the royal succession, however, was so acute that in 1946 an anti-Leopold coalition, a strange pudding consisting of Socialists and the Big Business liberals with a bitter sauce of Communists, had taken office under Camille Huysmans.

"I am a Socialist and a democrat," M. Huysmans said. "That distinguishes me from the Communists who are Socialists but not democratic. When I was in London during the war I published the names of two hundred Polish Socialists whom the Russians liquidated in Poland. The Soviet authorities never denied my charges. Russia has established her bloc in Central and Eastern Europe," the Prime Minister continued, "but when there is talk of a Western bloc Moscow screams that it is threatened." He had the old-style Socialist's venomous hatred of Communists. They reciprocated.

On taking leave, I asked M. Huysmans to arrange an interview for me with his Foreign Minister, Paul Henri Spaak. He telephoned and an appointment was fixed for five the next afternoon.

Monsieur Spaak, a vigorous man with round face and black, horn-rimmed glasses, received me in his cluttered office. It was soon obvious that he was granting me a perfunctory interview because his Prime Minister had requested it. When I asked him what happened to a country like Belgium after its second invasion in a generation, what sort of safety it expected from its foreign policy, he replied that Belgium believed in the United Nations and would be loyal to its obligations. "Those are mere words," I commented with intended bluntness, and I added, "You won't mind my saying so, will you? I have never learned to be diplomatic with diplomats." He appeared shocked, but my remark elicited the statement that he was opposed to the veto in the UN Charter and had opposed it at San Francisco and subsequently.

I inquired about the Paris Peace Conference which he had just left for a brief stay at home. He thought it would result in peace treaties with Italy, Bulgaria, and other ex-enemy states.

"Treaties," I said, "but no solutions."

"There can be no basis for peace," he declared, somewhat testily, "so long as one of the three big powers, which is in fact the second, behaves in a mysterious fashion."

"The fact that Russia is mysterious," I suggested, "really solves some of the mystery. America is not mysterious, nor England, nor Belgium. Russia is mysterious because it is a walled dictatorship and that is the source of her foreign policy."

Suddenly he said, "What is your name?"

I told him. "Ah," he exclaimed. "Now I know who you are. I have read your *Men and Politics*." Thereafter the tone of the interview changed. "We must find safety," he said, "in a united Europe united with the United States." Meanwhile, Belgium hoped to consolidate a federation (Benelux) with Holland and Luxembourg.

I asked how he could report on the Paris Peace Conference to a Cabinet that included Communist ministers. "I can't," he declared frankly. "They would be sending my words to Moscow the same day. So I reported to Prince Charles"—and, presumably, to the Prime Minister and individual ministers.

"Charles," he stated, "is very intelligent. 'Van Zeeland [veteran Belgian Prime Minister and Foreign Minister],' he said to me once, 'is like a brilliant light in front of my eyes which blinds me. You stand behind me and shed light on what is in front.' We are trying to find the Prince a wife. That is not easy."

Spaak explained that to get the Communists out of the Cabinet the Socialists would have to form a coalition with the Catholics, and he, as a Socialist, favored such a combination. But he could not countenance Leopold's restoration.

(In 1950, Leopold, tired of waiting in Switzerland, and hoping, by a dramatic act, to precipitate a decision in his favor, returned to Belgium. His presence, however, provoked street rioting which forced him to abdicate. Later, his young son took the crown as Baudoin I.)

M. Degrelle, the wartime Belgian Rexist or Fascist, had been in the news. He had fled to Spain and Franco refused to return him. "What can be done about Spain?" I inquired of Spaak.

"I would get rid of Franco," he replied, "but, first, we must avoid a civil war, and, two, I would make sure the Communists don't get in. I think," he added, "that immediately after the war the great powers, and that means chiefly England, could have removed Franco. London actually considered restoring the Spanish throne."

At the end of our talk he invited me to lunch at his house the next day. Madame Spaak, a gracious political hostess, the Spaaks' two grown-up daughters, Marie and Antoinette, and Ferdnand, age twenty-three, a lieutenant in the British navy during the war, as well as Victor Larock, editor of the Brussels Socialist daily, *Le Peuple*, were present in the simple family dining room. At table, the Foreign Minister and everybody else interrogated me about Russia. Spaak could scarcely disguise his indignation at Moscow's imperialism outside and cruelties inside. He was an internationalist, and favored a united Europe, in fact world government if possible. Meanwhile, he was nursing Benelux (Belgium-Netherlands-Luxembourg) a three-in-one union which some day would have a single currency, maybe a single government. "Belgium," he affirmed, "cannot stand alone."

"When the Nazi scum withdrew," he said, "some Hitlerite weeds remained. Among them is anti-Semitism, a phenomenon Belgium had never known. This is one of the results of our using totalitarian methods to win the war."

Presently, Ferdnand opened a sideboard drawer and drew from it a copy of my *Men and Politics*. "Autograph it only to me," M. Spaak suggested teasingly. The children protested, and I wrote, "To M. Spaak and his extremely pleasant family."

"Now," the father said, "Marie and Antoinette will quarrel as to who should read it this evening." We promised to meet in New York when he would be presiding at the United Nations Assembly.

Politics has exciting drama for me. But I like it best mixed with warm personal contact. The Spaak lunch combined people and politics.

The next day, I mixed art with politics in near-by Antwerp, spending most of the day in the old house of Peter Paul Rubens, who died in 1640, and the rest of the day discussing the seamen's strike in the port. *Le Peuple* asserted that the strike had no economic justification and was merely a rehearsal for emergency events which favor a foreign power. The editor of an Antwerp Catholic newspaper told me that Russia intended to seize the city and hold it as a loaded revolver pointed at Britain's temple. I remarked that Antwerp was safe as long as England and America occupied Germany. But the editor's apprehension reflected the nervousness of that first postwar year when it was not yet certain whether the West could contain Russia. Many Europeans had measured the distance between themselves and the nearest Soviet soldier.

CHAPTER FIVE

"Peace" at Paris

APPARENTLY neither war nor peace can dim the exquisite, eternal beauty of Paris. It is a place where one wants to have much time just to sit and sip, and eat. It is a wonderful place to do nothing. That made it a wonderful place for the peace conference.

An international peace conference had been convened in Paris early in 1946 to write the peace born of the Second World War. I attended a session of the conference in the ornate Senate chamber of the Palais du Luxembourg. With the delegates from many countries seated around a huge oval table, the after-lunch meeting was called to order at 3:50 P.M. instead of 3:30, and thereafter, until five, the diplomats discussed how to save time. The Englishman limited himself to a few brief sentences. The American talked less than a minute. The Soviet spokesmen made long speeches. It was not difficult to make war on time at this peace conference. If you talked twenty minutes you killed an hour, for a speech in English had to be translated into French and Russian, and a Russian speech into English and French, and a French speech into Russian and English.

The delegates looked and were bored. Inside the sessions they discussed shipping on the Danube, Hungarian deportees, Rumanian reparations, Italian frontiers. Outside, there was one topic: Russia.

Paris was down-at-the-heel but I enjoyed walking the streets. France still suffered from an automobile and bus shortage and gasoline scarcity; many people walked, and many women rode bicycles as they had during the war. They developed powerful calf muscles.

In the hotel barbershop, I had my hair cut by an old French barber. When he had finished I asked whether I could have an olive oil shampoo. "Olive oil?" he exclaimed. "On your head? We haven't even got it for our stomachs." This led straight into a discussion of politics. "I'm voting Communist in the next election," he said. He was not a Communist, but "everybody else has failed and the Communists are making promises, so I'm going to let them have a chance." There must have been hundreds of thousands of French voters like him.

I visited several famous art galleries which I had not seen since I was last in Paris in October, 1939, and viewed one fine collection that owed its existence, so to speak, to Goering and his brother Nazis who had "liberated" the paintings during the war and carried them off to Germany. Detectives and experts had searched out the canvases and now they were on special exhibit as returned loot.

One day I passed the hotel where Jan Masaryk, the Foreign Minister of Czechoslovakia, was staying. I went into the lobby to phone him and make an appointment. He asked me up. "Isn't it awful!" he said after the usual greetings.

"What?" I asked.

"Everything," he replied.

"Czechoslovakia?"

"The Russkies still leave us alone in domestic matters," he responded. "I have told them the minute they limit our freedom of the press I quit. I can always go to America and earn my living by making four broadcasts a month.

"But my dear fellow," he exclaimed, changing the subject somewhat, "those Russkies have a wonderful delegation here, much better than yours. Molotov and Vishinsky are a powerful team though they hate one another. They work hard and have five hundred people helping them."

Jan Masaryk liked to pepper political talk with profanity and to salt serious conversation with a sexy anecdote. He always seemed gay and full of fun, a pessimist in his thinking but an optimist in his conduct. He often scoffed. One might have called him a cynic were it not for an intuitive devotion to freedom and decency. Once he had to fill out a questionnaire. After the item, Race, he wrote, "Human."

This was his sixtieth birthday. "Look at this room," he pointed, "look at all the flowers. Looks like a fancy brothel." He invited me to lunch the next day. "What would you like, steak?" he suggested. He said we would eat in his room—"We can talk more freely up here."

Food in Paris was a problem—even in his excellent hotel—and therefore a special pleasure. Jan Masaryk ordered a martini for himself and steak for two if they had it, otherwise veal, and soup. We got veal. "You take all the butter," he urged when the lunch was brought in. We had white bread, a rarity in Europe those days. "I saved this peach for you from yesterday," he said.

"Young Masaryk," as friends called the Foreign Minister to distinguish him from his father, Professor Thomas G. Masaryk, the scholar and founder of the post-World War I Czechoslovak republic, was an enemy within the Soviet gates, a Westerner imprisoned by circumstances inside the Russian empire. His years were therefore numbered. He sensed it. "Louis," he declared, "you know I'm no Bolshie. I can never be a commissar. If they suppress our press I'm through. That will be my cue. But what can I do in the meantime? I can't just desert the people of my country and go to my mother's land." (His mother was American.)

I let him eat. "I'm considering going to the UN session in New York," he resumed. "But I'm overflown. Not that I'm afraid, but I've flown too many thousands of miles."

"Sail on the *Queen Elizabeth*," I urged. "I've booked on her for October 16. You must come to America. Czechoslovakia needs a balance. U.S. help would be a counterpoise to Russian power."

"Of course, but you people aren't present," he argued. "How can I have an independent policy when America gives me no real support? Without America, our entire future will be decided in Moscow."

I told Masaryk of a conversation I had had at a New York dinner party with a Polish diplomat who said he was not a Bolshevik, he was a Menshevik, but he had entered the service of the puppet Polish government on the assumption that the Big Three would settle their differences. "If you are relying on that," I had told the Pole, "you better quit right away."

"If the Big Three remain at odds," Masaryk said quickly, "Czechoslovakia is finished."

Masaryk said he was in Moscow two days before the peace conference opened in Paris. Marshal Zhukov (the conqueror of Berlin in 1945) had had "a tiff" with Beria (the head of the secret police) and was demoted to a minor post in Odessa.

"You don't think Beria concocted 'the tiff' to please the boss?" I suggested. "Stalin would want to get rid of a popular military hero. He wants to be thought of as the only person who won the war."

"Maybe," he replied. "Zhukov had been saying that when his soldiers are demobilized after six months in Czechoslovakia they demand a better life at home."

Masaryk switched the conversation to Germany. He was afraid a pro-German policy in the West would alienate many Czechs. "Our people suffered throughout the entire war from the Nazis," he emphasized.

Masaryk glanced at his watch and offered to let his driver take me to the Palais du Luxembourg. "I'm not going today," he announced. I felt sure he preferred his siesta.

How could a man with Masaryk's experience take the peace conference seriously? It was a farce conference. The Big Three Foreign Ministers (Molotov, Byrnes, and Bevin) had agreed at a meeting in Moscow in December, 1945, to draft the peace treaties in advance, not treaties to define relations among themselves, but treaties which they would impose on former enemy countries. Having drafted the documents, all nations concerned would assemble to discuss them. They could talk, make objections, suggest changes. But the conference itself would have no power to alter the drafts. When the conference adjourned, the Big Three would adopt the final texts. If they wished they might consider the views expressed by the small nations at the Paris sessions. But only if they wished.

So the Big Three planned the conference and so it actually functioned. Moreover, it was already clear that Stalin would not allow Poland, Rumania, Bulgaria, and Hungary to conduct the "free and unfettered" elections which he and Roosevelt and Churchill promised them at Yalta in 1945. An agreement was being honored in the breach. Time to make more agreements.

The Paris Peace Conference debated the inescapable manifestations of East-West rivalry, not its causes. It accordingly got nowhere.

The only material issue before the conference was Trieste, the Adriatic city garrisoned by British and United States troops. The Russians wanted them out. Had the West yielded, Moscow would have won a concrete advantage. One hot Sunday afternoon, September 15, 1946, I kept an appointment with a member of the American delegation. To probe his thinking I suggested that there be no treaties, and no agreement over Trieste.

He was horrified. "And keep our troops in Trieste?" he exclaimed.

The troops stayed in Trieste until 1954—desite the agreement.

For some diplomats a conference is like punching a time clock, it means they have been on the job; for some diplomats who are lawyers a treaty is proof that they have accomplished something. There is, to be sure, a virtue in getting together with the other side as long as that is possible, and the drafting of treaties clarifies issues. But these formalities must never be mistaken for reality.

The skeptical Masaryk had no illusions about the Paris Peace Conference. Neither had General Walter Bedell Smith. General Smith, Eisenhower's Chief of Staff during the war and at the time of Germany's surrender, now Ambassador in Moscow, was in Paris to assist the American delegation. I telephoned him the morning after I reached Paris. We had never met, but he knew my book on Soviet foreign affairs and asked me over to his hotel. An orderly told me the General was in his bath; would I wait? A few minutes later General Smith appeared dressed in a purple silk robe. He said, "What can I do for you?" I replied that I wanted nothing except to chat with him about Russia. He said, "What do you think is the Soviet government's foreign policy?"

"To keep what they have and try to get as much more as possible."

"What is their long-term goal?" he asked.

"Stalin is not thinking in long terms."

"I agree with you," the Ambassador fresh from Moscow declared. Then he talked. "I knew Moscow would be a difficult post," he began. "I did not seek it. Eisenhower urged me to take it. A businessman wouldn't take the post because there is no fun in it. Moscow didn't want a career diplomat. The idea back of sending me was that Stalin fancies himself a military man and likes to talk with military people. I took it on for six months. [He stayed three years.] The first three months were a honeymoon. I brought Stalin a letter from Truman which said that any statement I made was as if it had come from the President. You know, when you are talking to Stalin, especially when you are telling him something unpleasant, he looks at you from the corner of his eye, never full-face; then when he talks to you he eyes you squarely and tries to bore into you. I went to see him alone. Molotov was there and Pavlov, Stalin's interpreter. Molotov never said a word."

"Literally?" I wondered.

"Literally," General Smith confirmed. "I told Stalin," he continued, "that our relations needed clarification. We had to know whether the Soviet government intended to increase its armaments. We also had to know whether the Soviet Union proposed to advance beyond its present line, whether they wanted more territory."

"We don't want much more," Stalin asserted.

" 'Much' is a vague word," General Smith commented. "Does it mean you want Turkey?"

"Stalin's reply," the General told me, "was evasive." But the Ambassador made it clear to the dictator that America would not sit by idly if Turkey were menaced. "Now Stalin knows we are serious about that," General Smith declared. I felt there had been a decision at the highest American level to go to war, if need be, in defense of Turkey.

Turkey had come under Soviet pressure. Immediately after the war, Stalin officially asked the Turks to cede their northern provinces of Kars and Ardahan to Russia. At the Potsdam Conference in July, 1945, he tried to obtain President Truman's assent to a Soviet fortress in the Dardanelles, a transparent device for converting Turkey into a Russian vassal. Truman said no.

Ernest Bevin, the British Labor government's blunt, sometimes ungrammatical Foreign Secretary, charged that the Kremlin was conducting "a war of nerves" à la Hitler against Turkey. A few months later, when Molotov put in a bid for Tripolitania in North Africa, Bevin exclaimed that Russia "is reaching across our throat."

The Dardanelles are a waterway into the Mediterranean. Tripolitania is part of its coast. The French and Italian Communist parties wanted power. It seemed as if Stalin wished to transform the Mediterranean into a Red sea. The Russian bear was stretching a paw into the British orbit.

Britain's alarm was shared by America. Hence General Smith's frank question to Stalin about Turkey. Hence Stalin's unsatisfactory rely.

"The Soviet Union," General Smith said, "is the most nationalistic country in the world. A few weeks ago I talked with Maxim Litvinov in Moscow. Litvinov declared, 'The important decisions have been made in the Kremlin. There will be no friendship with the West.'"

As Foreign Commissar for ten years, Litvinov had courted England, France, and America. He was dismissed in May, 1939, to make way for the Soviet-Nazi Pact. After Hitler's invasion of Russia in June, 1941, Stalin reverted to Litvinov's policy, took Litvinov out of the mothballs, and sent him to the Washington Embassy. Now Hitler was gone and, Ambassador Smith said, "Litvinov is on the way out," a tragic figure, the last of the Bolshevik Mohicans. All other high-ranking survivors of the purges and trials of the 1930's—the Malenkovs, Berias, and Gromykos—were political technocrats, bureaucrats without faith in revolution. Their internationalism, an essential component of Communism, had died. "An internationalist," Stalin once stated, "is one who unconditionally, unwaveringly, without conditions is ready to defend the Soviet Union." Thus Communist internationalism equals Russian nationalism. General Smith noted the phenomenon for a practical reason: this nationalism was the mother of Soviet imperialism, America's foremost problem.

Soviet imperialism, as I saw it, resulted from inside pressures and outside opportunities. To frighten England and France into another Munich appeasement over Poland and to avoid a two-front war if they fought, Hitler wooed, won, and neutralized Russia in August, 1939. Stalin exacted a price: the freedom to annex Esthonia, Latvia, and Lithuania, the eastern half of Poland, and parts of Finland and Rumania. They were Soviet imperialism's first meal.

During the Second World War, the Red army seized German and Czechoslovak lands which had never belonged to Czarist or Soviet Russia, and overran and subjected Poland, Rumania, Czechoslovakia, Hungary, Bulgaria, Yugoslavia, and Albania. Therewith, the Soviet empire reached its furthest European limits. In Asia, Russia annexed Southern Sakhalin and the Kurile Islands and returned to the Czarist bases and railroads in Manchuria.

This foreign expansion reflected Stalin's domestic failures. There had been much new construction in Russia and impressive industrial development, but the cost of the economic system in terms of money and lives was enormous and the return to the individual disappointing. Grain production was down, livestock had been seriously depleted, and supplies of consumer commodities failed to gratify elementary needs. In the circumstances, citizens could not be expected to put the necessary effort into their work or remain loyal to the regime in a crisis. The situation induced a search for new mass incentives, some nonmaterial stimulus that would compensate for physical privations. Stalin chose nationalism. He would substitute love of country for the lost faith in the practical benefits of Communism. He would give the nation glory instead of goods.

Having killed the spirit of the revolution by murdering so many revolutionists Stalin resurrected the dead heroes of the Czarist past and revived the once-reviled attributes of the buried monarchy: Cossack military units, guard regiments, gaudy uniforms, epaulets, army titles, and so forth. This was an attempt to weave Communism like an invisible patch into Russia's national fabric.

Further to rekindle the Russian patriotism of the Great Russians who constituted half the country's population and had little love for their Georgian despot, Stalin in 1939 and 1940 regained the Baltic states, Poland, and other Czarist-Russian areas, and restored the Czar's stranglehold on Manchuria. He expected the Russians to be grateful to him and to forgive him his sins and their misery.

To reconcile the forty million Soviet Ukrainians to Muscovite domination, their heavy cross for three centuries, Stalin annexed all European regions with Ukrainian populations: Eastern Poland, Czechoslovakia's Carpatho-Rus, and Bessarabia and Moldavia in Rumania. He expected the Ukrainians to thank him for having created one big Ukraine.

In all Soviet citizens, the Kremlin's expanded world power would presumably evoke helpless submission, or pride, or the hope of consumer-goods imports from the newly acquired territories.

A central purpose of Soviet aggression abroad was thus to reinforce the Soviet system at home.

But appetite, the French say, comes with eating. The more territory Moscow swallowed the more it craved.

The Kremlin was yielding to the suction of the power vacuum created by the defeat of Germany, Italy, and Japan, the weakness of Britain and France, and America's demobilization after the war. Opportunities to get rich quickly are difficult to resist especially when their realization seems essential to life. I was one of fifteen Americans to whom Stalin accorded a six-and-a-quarter-hour interview in Moscow on September 9, 1927. In the course of this long confrontation, Stalin asserted that as the world situation developed "two world centers will be formed: a Socialist center attracting to itself the countries gravitating toward Socialism, and a capitalist center attracting to itself the countries gravitating toward capitalism." These two camps would compete, Stalin predicted, and the side that won would achieve world domination.

Stalin's concept of Russo-American rivalry dominated his thinking until he died. Uncertain of the outcome of the contest between the two colossi, he aimed to attach pieces of the capitalist world to Russia and thus improve the Kremlin's competitive position. The Second World War was his first chance of doing this. He thought he could make further gains after the war.

This was the background of the Paris Peace Conference.

The overture to the conference was conducted by two maestros: Joseph Stalin and Winston Churchill. Stalin made a speech. Date: February 9, 1946—the turning point in postwar history. It contained no new notes. Stalin simply declared that the development of Soviet heavy industry from 1928 to 1941 had saved Russia from defeat in the Second World War and that the Communist party accordingly intended to "organize another powerful upswing of our national economy" till it attained, by 1960, approximately three times the 1941 level: fifty million tons of pig iron, sixty million tons of steel, sixty million tons of oil, and five hundred million tons of coal. "Only when we succeed in doing that," Stalin said, "can we be sure that our motherland will be ensured against all contingencies."

The same week Lazar Kaganovich and Georgi M. Malenkov, members of the top Politburo, spoke on the same theme. "Our country continues to be within a capitalist encirclement," Kaganovich declared. "We must not lose our conquests," Malenkov warned. "We must consolidate our victory."

If, despite annexations and new colonies, Russia still felt imperiled by "capitalist encirclement," she might seek more annexations to safeguard those already made. Was that what Malenkov meant by the consolidation of victory? Stalin's emphasis on heavy industry, which produces armaments, and on "contingencies," which means war, frightened the West.

America and England knew they would not attack Russia. Would Russia attack?

Asia was helpless, Europe exhausted, America relaxed. But the Kremlin master called for intensified military preparations. This drop of incongruity precipitated understanding in the West. Nationally prominent American and European journalists and commentators who had closed their minds to suspicions of Russia grew more critical. U.S. Supreme Court Justice William O. Douglas, after reading Stalin's speech, said it was "The Declaration of World War Three."[1]

It remained for the outstanding word artist of world politics, Winston Churchill, speaking on American soil, to answer Stalin and therewith usher in the new, cold-war phase of postwar history. Indeed, his address, delivered at Westminister College, in Fulton, Missouri, on March 5, 1946, made history. He rode through the small town to the college in an official car with President Truman who had flown a thousand miles from Washington for the occasion, and Mr. Truman introduced him to the assembly.

"Time is short," Churchill advised. "Prevention is better than cure." For "nobody knows what Soviet Russia and its Communist international organization intends to do in the immediate future, or what are the limits, if any, to their expansive and proselytizing tendencies."

Here he introduced a new term into the languages of the world: "From Stettin in the Baltic to Trieste in the Adriatic, an Iron Curtain has descended across the Continent." Behind it stood a chain of police governments subservient to the Kremlin. Turkey and Persia "were profoundly alarmed and disturbed." Russia had designs on all of Germany. "The future of Italy hangs in the balance." She and France felt the full force of a Communist fifth column which constitued "a growing challenge and peril to Christian civilization."

"From what I have seen of our Russian friends and allies during the war," Churchill continued, "I am convinced that there is nothing they admire so much as strength, and there is nothing for which they have less respect than for weakness, especially military weakness."

He did not believe Russia wanted war, only "the fruits of war and the indefinite expansion of their power and doctrines." Therefore the resources of America and Britain should be joined to create "an overwhelming assurance of security."

[1] *The Forrestal Diaries*, edited by Walter Millis, with the collaboration of E. S. Duffield, New York: Viking Press, 1951, p. 134.

Years later, at a press conference in Washington, D.C., on June 28, 1954, Churchill, once more Prime Minister, recalled that his Fulton speech "didn't get a very warm welcome in the United States because it was so anti-Russian and anti-Communist." Some harbored too many illusions to believe him. Some rejected his cure—a military alliance—though they accepted his facts and their interpretation. Many made the wish father to the thought and were therefore reluctant to abandon the assumption of Big Three unity, for the alternative was confusion, struggle, perhaps even war. The consequences of an open Russia-versus-West antagonism were so horrible to contemplate that good people just refused to contemplate them. Their love of peace led to see-no-evil appeasement. Nevertheless, Churchill's Fulton performance did induce a more realistic appraisal of the three ingredients of Stalin's postwar design: nationalistic megalomania, isolationism, and imperialism. They usually walk together.

The delegates to the 1946 Paris Peace Conference sensed the new attitude toward Soviet Russia. They saw that the conference was merely another arena where the big powers sparred for advantage, a battlefield, not a peace conference. Most conferees recognized that after the treaties were signed Moscow would continue to dominate Hungary, Rumania, and Bulgaria, while Italy would remain under Western influence.

Actually, nothing changed. The sessions devoted no time to Asia or Africa. Austria and the biggest European headache—Germany— were not even on the agenda. Sixteen months after the defeat of Hitler, thirteen months after the collapse of Japan, the differences between the two victorious camps were already so sharp that they saw no use in discussing them. The conference accordingly limited itself to confirming what could not be altered without war.

The explanation of the postwar no-peace situation begins with the simple circumstance that Moscow wanted the territories it annexed during the war, and that any attempt to prevent their seizure might have required the Western powers to stop fighting Hitler and start fighting Stalin. This they would not do. At Teheran in December, 1943, and at Yalta in February, 1945, Roosevelt and Churchill were the victims of this stern military fact.

But it is also true that they underestimated the perils of Soviet expansion and were overoptimistic, especially the President, about the prospects of collaboration with Soviet Russia. Moreover, the capture of Vienna, Berlin, and Prague by the Russian army, when they could have been taken earlier by an Anglo-American force which was kept waiting, displayed a tragic lack of statesmanship. Worse still, the zoning of Germany and the isolation of Berlin from the Western zones would seem to reflect political myopia, ignorance of elementary geography, and lack of plain common sense.

I think there is also a moral explanation for the failure to block Soviet expansion. The Western leaders could not deny to Stalin what nations in their own orbit refused to forgo. England, France, Portugal, and Holland had not yet relinquished their empires. Churchill said in November, 1942, "I have not become the King's First Minister in order to preside at the liquidation of the British Empire." Russia consequently felt justified in establishing hers. The members of the anti-Fascist coalition destroyed the German, Japanese, and Italian empires, but they were incapable of renouncing their own. How could they oppose Soviet imperialism?

This diagnosis contains the cure. During my stay with Mahatma Gandhi in India in 1942, I mentioned President Roosevelt's Four Freedoms. "Does that include the freedom to be free?" Gandhi asked. The question was on the minds of the spokesmen and leaders of several hundred million Asians and Africans.

On a trip around the world in 1952, I interviewed Ismet Inonu in Ankara. Ismet, the successor of Kemal Pasha Ataturk, was the head of Turkey's Republican party, Ataturk's party, which wielded dictatorial power from 1923 to 1945. In the latter part of 1945 Inonu, then President, allowed a second party to come into existence. Subsequently, the new party won the national election and ousted Inonu. I asked Mr. Inonu in 1952 why he had permitted the formation of a second party.

"Because the democracies had won the war," he replied.

That suggests the possibilities which the 1945 military victory opened for political reform, social change, colonial liberation, European unity, and economic advancement. The United States could have made itself the beloved leader of democratic mankind by becoming the champion of a new world throughout the world.

CHAPTER SIX

Germany in Rubble

IN PARIS I asked General Walter Bedell Smith for a letter of introduction to somebody in Germany who could help me understand conditions. He took a sheet of paper and wrote, "Dear Lucius. You can talk freely to Louis Fischer, the bearer of this note." General Lucius D. Clay was the U.S. assistant military commander and later became top military commander in Germany with headquarters in Berlin.

To enter Germany, an American journalist had to be accredited to the American army in Germany and have its visa as well as that of the French, British, and Soviet military authorities. One could fly to Berlin only in an American army plane on payment of U.S. dollars. Since, according to regulations, everybody transported in an American military plane had to be furnished with a parachute which he knew how to operate, all passengers were summoned into a room at Orly Field and given a parachute plus six minutes' instructions, with practice, on harnessing oneself with it. As I dragged my luggage and parachute across the field I could only hope that the old DC-3 would hold out as far as Berlin. I did not think I would have made a very graceful jump.

I had looked forward to getting an air view of post-Nazi Germany, but the cloud blanket was unbroken from Paris to Frankfurt to Berlin. The shock of Berlin was all the greater. At the giant Tempelhof Airport there were no taxis in sight and so I boarded an OMGUS bus. OMGUS stood for Office of the Military Government of the United States. Five Americans rode on the lower deck of the bus.

Occasionally the spacious vehicle stopped at street corners for Germans who held up cards. They were employees of OMGUS and rode upstairs, a sort of Jim Crow arrangement. The pedestrians one saw through the bus window did not seem badly dressed and wore fairly good shoes, but looked pale and miserable. Here and there, men and women passed bricks on hills of rubble.

I first went to Berlin in December, 1921, lived in it for long periods between then and Hitler's accession in January, 1933, and had seen it under his rule in 1936 and 1937. I knew many parts of Berlin as well as I knew London, New York, and my native city of Philadelphia. But now the city was unrecognizable. Whole streets had disappeared. The British and American "blockbusters" were literally that; they crushed entire blocks of homes and office buildings into heaps of broken brick amid jungles of twisted iron. I wondered how many stinking corpses still lay under the ruins.

At the press camp—everything was in military terms—a German shouldering a rifle and wearing a steel helmet with "GUARD" painted on it let me pass into the American information office. There I was assigned a "billet" in a house across the street, given a list of official telephone numbers and a PX card, and warned not to go into the Soviet sector of Berlin at night.

I shopped in the PX army store, bought an armful of German newspapers at a corner kiosk, and went to dinner in the club situated in a building behind the billet. The meal, consisting of American food, cooked or canned, cost twenty-five cents. At the table were Kathleen McLaughlin of the *New York Times*, Sam Lubell of the *Saturday Evening Post* and his wife, and May Craig of Maine newspapers. They were talking Russia. When I remarked on it, they said yes, two or three months ago they would have been arguing whether or not they should like Germans, but that question had been overshadowed by the Russian problem.

The next day, Saturday, I walked to the shining marble OMGUS building, inherited unscathed by bombs from the Nazis, where I had an hour with General Clay. He impressed me as having a precision brain. The Russian problem preoccupied him too. His aim was an arrangement for Germany like that in Austria where the four zones, Russian, American, British, and French, were ruled by one Austrian government. This, Clay hoped, would supersede the existing division of Germany into East Germany under a Communist regime and the three Western zones. If Moscow wanted ten billion dollars in return for its consent to this unification of Germany, General Clay felt the money would be well spent. I thought eighteen million East Germans were worth more to Stalin than American billions.

The next day I jeeped to the Soviet sector for lunch. The further east one went in Berlin, the more gruesome the ruination grew. Through the once-beautiful Grunewald section, in the Koenigsallee, Bismarck Strasse, and Alt-Moabit, the destruction was wholesale and frightening. How did people survive bombs that pulverized such massive buildings? The Schiller Theater where my wife and I had seen many plays in the Weimar Republic period was an ugly, burned-out shell. The Siegessaeulle victory column was erect and its surmounting angel's gold glowed brightly. Several churches had been completely gutted. The lion protecting its cubs against snake attack in Alt-Moabit Square was untouched though everything around the monument was in ruins. Lehrter Railway Station had no superstructure at all but the subway trains continued to run through it.

I was lunching in Pankow, in East Berlin, in the apartment of Friedrich Wolf, a popular German Communist writer and playwright—author of *Professor Mamlock* among other plays—whom my family and I had known for years in Moscow. I brought them sweets, coffee, and cigarettes from the U.S. army PX, and Friedrich and his wife Else took them with undisguised joy. After inquiries about relatives and friends, I asked about several Soviet writers, and the pained expressions on my hosts' faces indicated that they would rather not talk about the departed, for since I last saw the Wolfs in Moscow in 1937 a purge had swept all Soviet strata and professions. Friedrich limited himself to stating that the purge was like a lottery; if you happened to be home when the Black Maria of the NKVD passed they took you along. He said, "We will do things differently here. We need an opposition in the party. We will avoid the mistakes of Russia." (German Communists often assumed a superior attitude toward Russians.) Presently he checked himself; he was talking too freely, and, to change the subject and try to make me take my turn at being embarrassed, he asked whether the American economic depression would not force the U.S. to wage war on Russia. There was only one answer and I gave it: a long laugh. He then inquired how strong was Henry Wallace, would he be the next President? "His chances," I replied, "are about as good as yours to replace Stalin." They both laughed.

Wolf, who subsequently became East Germany's Ambassador in Sovietized Poland, said, "Well anyway, I was never really interested in politics. I'm a writer and I intend to write more children's books." (Escape into the nursery.) He autographed one for me. The conversation tapered off to personalities and generalities.

The street signs in the Russian sector of Berlin were in German and Russian. On the drive back to the press camp I stopped to pick up two Red army soldiers in poor-quality, ill-fitting uniforms, looking forlorn, like peasants in a big town. They had been window-shopping at a miserable lean-to hut which displayed cheap knicknacks and tinsel. At first they seemed surprised and pleased that anybody should address them, and in their own language, but soon I noticed a look of dismay. A foreigner talking to them! They were from a village near Vinnitsa in the Ukraine; I had visited the town in 1922. East Berlin, they said, was so bright and gay, but strange. To me it was a rubbled slum.

When the German driver of the jeep delivered me at my billet I gave him the usual tip: two American cigarettes. He clicked his heels, saluted sharply, and bowed low over my extended hand. He would either smoke them with delight or, more likely, sell them. American cigarettes were the best currency in Germany.

Sunday at noon I walked over to OMGUS for an interview with Ambassador Robert D. Murphy. Our chief topic was Russia and we stayed on it more than an hour. What might happen if Stalin died, he wondered, and would the Russian military take over in that event? How strong was Russia in her new satellite colonies? The truth, we both realized, was clouded, shrouded in rumor, hopes, and deliberate falsifications. But it was clear to me, I said, that Stalin would go to any length to reinforce his grip on Russia's recently acquired puppet states. In this connection I told Ambassador Murphy of Stalin's letter to Pope Pius in the autumn of 1944 in which the dictator proposed a pact of friendship to the Vatican. His purpose, obviously, was to lessen Catholic opposition to Soviet rule over Poland. The Holy Father, however, was not co-operative.

"That's interesting," Murphy, himself a Catholic, commented, "I hadn't heard of it. But about the same time, the end of August or in September, 1944, I talked with Soviet Ambassador Alexander Bogomolov in Rome—we were both members of the Allied Control Commission—and Bogomolov suddenly said, 'Why is the Vatican so hostile to the Soviet Union?' "

"Well," Murphy had replied, "you believe that religion is the opiate of the people."

"Oh," Bogomolov explained, "that plaque has been taken down in Moscow. It was the slogan of some Frenchman and we Russians don't approve of it anymore."

"Well," Murphy persisted, "you have closed many Roman Catholic churches and arrested priests."

"That," Bogomolov asserted, "belongs to bygone days. We can change all that. Why is the Pope so antagonistic to us? I should like to discuss the matter with him."

Ambassador Murphy had an appointment with the Pope for the next day and told him about this conversation with Bogomolov. The Pope said the Vatican would wait until the Communists translated their words into deeds; then he could judge. "We have time," the Pope said.

That evening, at seven-forty, I had dinner with General and Mrs. Clay at their home. The framed photograph of a young Clay in military uniform touched off an exchange of data on our respective sons' wartime services, and then, till eleven, we talked politics and persons. Clay, a man of piercing dark eyes and penetrating intelligence, talked about his father, A. S. Clay, United States Senator from Georgia from 1896 to 1910 when he died. The General called his father a "liberal" who advocated personal income tax legislation and had sponsored the bill for the introduction of the Rural Free Delivery, or free rural postal service. Lucius D. was an engineer by training. He gave evidence of having a filing-cabinet mind; when he talked about his work he first described all the multifarious aspects of administering the American zone in Germany and then fitted them together neatly. A strong person given to clear-cut views and quick decisions, Clay naturally disliked divided power. He therefore favored a civilian rather than a military chief for the American government in Germany. He might have preferred a military chief with unquestioned authority, but in peacetime the State Department would of course assume an important role in so decisive a foreign situation as the occupation of Germany, and since this meant that the army alone could not dominate, Clay saw the wisdom of a political head instead of a military one. That was out of the question, however, until Russian intentions had been clarified.

Opposed in theory and practice to state ownership, Clay prohibited the government of the Land, or state, of Hesse, from writing nationalization into its constitution. What if some future regularly elected government, he argued, rejected nationalization? It would have to amend the constitution. He also would not allow a Land to statify an important industry. That right, he felt, should be reserved to the federal government. If the federal government favored state ownership he would have been in a quandary, but there was no federal German government.

General Clay, representing the Defense Department, and Ambassador Murphy, representing the State Department, did not, according to a view widely held in the American colony, see eye to eye on several key issues. Such clashes, due to differences of personality or policy, do occur between departments of government and between officials in democracies and even in dictatorships. It was said, for instance, that Murphy favored U.S. aid to the German Social Democratic party and to the Christian Democratic Union party, which was chiefly Catholic in leadership, whereas Clay felt that a party compromised itself by taking help from a foreign government. Actually, Murphy told me he shared Clay's opinion. But several State Department men were anti-Clay and pro-Socialist, and the Socialists complained that the Christian Democrats got a great deal from OMGUS, above all newsprint for their daily newspapers, while their party received next to nothing. Both parties were in fact recipients of American benefits but the relative extent was an official secret. When I talked in Berlin with Jakob Kaiser, a Catholic party man and later minister at Bonn, he did not appear dissatisfied, whereas Dr. Kurt Schumacher, leader of the Social Democrats, deeply resented the discriminations against his organization, and he made a statement to me which carried tremendous significance for the future of German politics and, it would seem, for the future of Socialism throughout the world. "If the Western powers," Dr. Schumacher exclaimed with bitterness, "do not allow us to be Socialists we will become nationalists."

Irrespective of party sympathies, the American military and the American journalists in Berlin were increasingly sympathetic to Germans. At lunch with several colleagues in the home of one American newspaperman we argued whether this new friendliness could be ascribed solely to rising anti-Russianism; you cannot hate two enemies. No, they all thought a defeat, literally so smashing as that administered to Nazi Germany, coming after the loss of World War I, could not but affect more than politics, it had to affect individual psychology and create personal doubts about militarism and nationalism.

One morning I was standing outside the billet waiting for a jeep when two German women asked me where Goethe Strasse was. I said I didn't know, I was a foreigner. I told them I was a foreigner in order to start a conversation. "Ja," one woman commented, "a foreigner. That's why the gentleman looks so healthy." She said she was fifty; I would have guessed seventy. Her companion, age sixty-eight, informed me she weighed seventy-four pounds, "with my clothes and keys," she added. They lived in the Russian sector. Yesterday, they reported, each of them had received two hundredweight of coal. Every person in the sector did. "That is very good," they declared. Bad weather was coming. But the reason the Russians had distributed the coal was that elections were coming.

I visited two young Germans, a man and his adopted sister, friends of my family. The girl, seventeen, attended school in the Communist sector because there was no adequate school for her in the Western sectors. Each day for the past week, she and the other pupils had been receiving a tasty, less gray bread roll. She had also been given a copybook in which was a printed message from the SED or Socialist-Unity (Communist) party. "This is a gift from the SED," the message read. "Instead of using the paper for propaganda purposes we are presenting it to you." (The entire city, West as well as East, was plastered with many huge SED propaganda posters bearing on the impending poll.) My young friends said that residents of the Russian sector had indeed received two hundredweight of coal in the form of lignite, or brown-coal, briquettes. I brought one of their briquettes to America and showed it at lectures. It was probably the strangest piece of election propaganda ever seen. On both sides of the coal brick were pressed the words: "WAEHLT SED." ("Vote for the SED.")

The seventeen-year-old pupil described a meeting of her class addressed by a Soviet army major in resplendent uniform. He discoursed on the social system in the Soviet Union and the government's bounty to citizens. When the class dispersed the German students winked at one another. "Practically the same as Hitler's 'From the Cradle to the Grave' arrangement," several of them whispered.

Germans in Berlin were confused and apprehensive. The past was a nightmare, the present nerve-racking, the future darkly uncertain. They wondered what would be the fate of Berlin, a city of three

million, an island completely surrounded by the Red sea of the
Russian zone, a metropolis divided into four parts. They feared that
their island would be inundated by the Communist tide. The Soviet
NKVD was already pushing fingers into the three Western sectors
and into Western Germany too.

In August, 1946, the Berlin daily *Telegraf* had reported that the
Soviet secret police was kidnaping boys between the ages of fourteen
and seventeen from the Western areas. East German boys were also
being abducted to Russia. The Soviet authorities issued a denial: the
whole thing was "an anti-Soviet invention." However, a Socialist
functionary in Berlin gave me the photostat of a letter confirming
the charges. The communication, dated May 7, 1946, was from Otto
Buchwitz, secretary of the Saxony (Soviet zone) provincial section
of the Russian-dominated SED party, to Otto Grotewohl, the national
head of the same party in Berlin.

DEAR OTTO,

I have talked to you once or twice about the following matter. Circumstances compel me to take it up again. I have in my portfolio approximately forty cases of persons who have been arrested by the
N.K.V.D., most of them quite young persons fifteen to eighteen years old
who were arrested last year. They were members of the Hitler Youth
organization, some perhaps had leading positions in it. Practically all the
parents are members of our party [the Communist party] and have been
in our party since 1933. Here and there adults too have been arrested,
presumably the victims of personal denunciation. The reasons usually are
unknown. I am besieged by relatives for help. The same thing has happened in other districts. . . .

I decided to ask for an interview with Otto Grotewohl. He granted
it. To enter his office in the SED building in East Berlin, I had to
fill out a form and leave my passport at the guard box just inside
the entrance. In return I received a slip with my name and the name
of the person I wanted to see. I could not get back my passport or
leave the building without that person's signature on the slip. This
was the exact procedure followed in Soviet Russia.

After discussing various matters with Herr Grotewohl I said I had
a photostat of the letter sent him by Otto Buchwitz about the
arrests. He did not seem surprised. Without hesitating a moment, he
said, "Armed with that letter I was able to persuade the police to free
fifty of the young men."

"But I understand," I pressed, "that several thousand young men have been arrested."

Grotewohl sat silent.

"Since almost all German teen-agers, millions of them, had been compelled to become members of Hitler Youth units, the arrest of young men and women as former Hitler Youth members was only a formal excuse for the kidnapings," I ventured.

Grotewohl gave an almost imperceptible nod of assent.

Grotewohl had been a Social Democrat and gone over to the Communists; now the Communists were using him as their chief administrator. At the end of our talk I therefore said to him, "Your mistake was to think the issue was Socialism versus capitalism. But the issue is freedom versus tyranny."

Perhaps I imagined I saw a sad look in his eyes. "You don't want my confession right now, do you?" he replied.

Two worlds, Communist and non-Communist, met in one ruined, rubbled, troubled city inhabited by sophisticated Germans and many thousands of foreign officials. Here Soviet Russian bureaucrats were having their first prolonged contacts with the Western world. Here the Western world would discover whether it could co-operate with Communists. Berlin was a proving ground for East-West relations, a traffic sign to the future.

The only government the city of Berlin had was a four-power "Kommandatura." Representatives of the four occupying powers were responsible for feeding, housing, and supplying the big town, operating its transportation facilities, waterworks, electric stations, and so forth. You could not, one assumed, allow sector boundaries to cut water mains in two, or sever electric cables, or block the subway. Berlin had to live as a united city, and it was the Kommandatura's business to keep it living.

At a regular session of the Kommandatura, Soviet General Kotikov brought up the subject of baseball. It had come to his attention, he stated gravely, that every Friday afternoon American GIs taught German boys and girls in the United States sector to play baseball. That was a "paramilitary activity" which led to "regimentation."

The American and British representatives lifted their eyebrows and exchanged shoulder shrugs. U.S. General Ryan spoke up. "Will my Soviet colleague," he said, "honor us with his presence at the baseball field next Friday?"

General Kotikov announced he would take the matter under advisement; probably phone the Kremlin. Weeks later when I left

Berlin the Russians had not yet disclosed whether they thought base-ball was anti-Communist.

On another occasion, after the Russians had entered the American sector and arrested some German judges, General Lucius D. Clay informed the Kommandatura that if there was one more illegal, armed invasion he would post tanks and machine guns at the sector frontier. Such arrests stopped.

The only government of Germany was the four-power Allied Council which sat in Berlin. It functioned through 125 four-power commissions, usually consisting of from 8 to 16 members, which dealt with every conceivable business of government: finance, im-ports, taxes, health, reparations, police, railways, and so forth and so on.

I put the same question to a score of American officials in Berlin, all of them participants in one or more four-power commissions. "Give me a specific instance," I demanded, "in which the United States or England took one position and Russia another and where the Russians eventually yielded." Nobody could mention a single case.

Here one saw the small beginnings of big differences, a brook be-came a river and then a gulf. The Russians sat with the Westerners in the same commissions, the same rooms, and personally they could have communicated without difficulty, for Russians tend to be warmly companionable. But they were under Moscow's instructions to build a barrier.

Among the four-power commissions was one dealing with the resti-tution of property stolen by the Nazis. The American member of this commission was Nicolas Nabokov, born in Russia into a well-known political family of acute anti-Bolshevik leanings. Nabokov, age forty-three, a man of vast culture and great musical erudition, had become an American citizen and was working for the U.S. State Department in Berlin where I met him. One day he informed me that his Russian opposite number on the commission had invited him to dinner at Karlshorst, a suburb of East Berlin, and assuming, quite correctly, that I would like to go along, Nabokov had asked the Russian whether he could bring an American friend. The Russian agreed and sent his car for us. It was to be a Russian-speaking evening and I felt quite elated at the prospect of discussing Soviet affairs.

The drive took us past the Tiergarten, once the delightful central park of Berlin, now a vast, treeless, burnt-out field, and through the Brandenburg Gate into Unter den Linden, formerly Berlin's most elegant thoroughfare, today a shambles; thence to the Lustgarten Square littered with bronze anatomy—here a headless horse, shot full of big holes, lying on its flank; there the hollow, metal torso of an armored warrior and swept-together piles of assorted arms, legs, and feet, and of hands holding conch shells and trumpets; near by, parts of a fountain, sections of a frieze, and twisted scrap. In this neighborhood, the last, desperate German soldiers, still ready to die for a mad Fuehrer who, with his consort, was soon to commit suicide on a burning pyre, had fought the advancing Russians for worthless square yards of urban asphalt, and every home and building was a blackened, jagged skeleton.

In Karlshorst, however, many one-family German middle-class villas had been preserved unharmed, and Russian military and civilians were now in occupation. Colonel Gulayev, our host for the evening, came quickly out of the door of his little house and met us affably at the curb as the car stopped. With Nabokov and me in the car was another Russian-born State Department official and his Russian-born wife.

Gulayev wore his Red army uniform. He was thirty-two. His wife gave her age as twenty-four, and her maiden name as Serafima Holtzman—from which I concluded she was Jewish. She wore the khaki jacket and black shirt of the Russian army and two small five-pointed stars on her flat-board epaulettes indicating the rank of full lieutenant. Another young woman, a junior lieutenant with one star, whom they called Zinaida, was dressed in the same outfit and leather boots halfway up her shins. She worked as a typist in a military office and was studying German four hours a day. A Soviet civilian, employed by the army, and a Russian couple whose identity I never quite established completed the company.

Vodka-drinking commenced immediately we entered the parlor. I said I never drank vodka, but accepted a glass of wine which I touched to my lips at each of the many toasts of the evening. A light atmosphere of gaiety filled the room. The desultory conversation centered on the comparative virtues of national alcoholic beverages.

A German maid announced dinner. We moved into an adjoining room where the table was completely covered with an endless variety of fish and meat cold cuts, pickled cucumbers, pickled tomatoes, pickled watermelon, black olives, and several kinds of bread, from black to almost-white, which the guests were constantly prodded to consume and wash down with refilled glasses of alcohol. The talk dealt with every possible aspect of eating and drinking. I tried to start a discussion of wine-drinking in the Caucasus in the hope that we might at least arrive at the fringe of a Soviet topic. But I failed. We now discovered that the enormous meal so far served was merely a preliminary. There followed red beet borscht with sour cream and floating boiled potato, a meat entree plus several vegetables, and a compote of fruit succeeded by fresh fruit. As the maid presented the large serving platter to each American guest, host and hostess and the Russian visitors watched, and if the American failed to scoop up an ample portion loud protests rose from the Soviets. "Ha, ha, ha," they would laugh, "so America is weakening!" "Hey, American, surrendering already?" By the time the meat came around, I had no stomach to defend America's reputation against this great Soviet challenge.

Nicolas Nabokov had been graduated from the Annen-Schule, a select private German-language high school in Petrograd. Apparently, Colonel Gulayev attended classes in the same building after the November, 1917, Bolshevik Revolution. I heard Nabokov and Gulayev exchanging schoolday reminiscences. Skillfully, Nabokov inched over into a forbidden realm and mentioned the recent purge of Soviet writers. Gulayev said they were old and had nothing to say. Nabokov suggested that the poet Pasternak had been writing some very stimulating verse. "They must write what can be published," Gulayev proclaimed.

When we finally managed to lift ourselves from the table and return to the living room for coffee I noticed the latest issue of the Moscow daily *Pravda* lying on a sofa. The first page featured an interview with Stalin by Alexander Werth, a British journalist. "An interview rich in content," I ventured, addressing Gulayev.

"I hope it will relax the international atmosphere," Gulayev declared in a tone which clearly indicated that this was the last thing he would say on the subject.

Most of the Russians present hailed from Leningrad. I said I had once spent a week living on the premises of the big Putilov metal works in that city. Nobody uttered a word. The Soviet civilian told me, in reply to a question, that he used to be employed in the Council of Ministers in Moscow. I said in my time in Russia, until 1938, the ministers were called commissars and I had known a number of them: "Mikoyan," I enumerated ("*Da*," he commented,

"Yes") "Chicherin, Litvinov, Rosengoltz." Rosengoltz had been sentenced to death in a Moscow trial. I kept his name for last. No comment.

Seated near Gulayev sipping coffee, I informed him that in India recently I had gathered that the British intended to leave soon. "The British won't get out of India for fifty years," he announced with finality.

The party was jolly, even warm and friendly, but, just as in Moscow, after 1936, there was no conversation, only talk, only chitchat. Before many months, even this kind of association between Russians and foreigners came to an end.

We left for home at one o'clock. Driving through dark canyons of ruins made one feel endlessly sad. Occasionally a black figure groped his way over the rubble-covered streets. When he got to his room it would be very cold, and there might be no light and maybe no food. Colonel Frank Howley, America's man in Berlin's Kommandatura, told me that 32,000 cases of galloping consumption were walking the streets of the city. Every morning dozens of dead bodies, suicides, were found floating on the canals.

We averaged fifty miles an hour on Hitler's *autobahn* to Düsseldorf in a fast, smooth, small, four-seater Volkswagen, the car the Fuehrer said he intended for the masses. Now only the Allies used it. My driver was a German from Stettin, hard-working and silent except when I asked questions. For sustenance he had a thick hunk of soggy, brown bread. He had fought in the Wehrmacht in Holland, France, Greece, in Germany on the West front, and for two years in Russia; he got as far as Mozdok, near the oil fields. He liked the Dutch best. "They are clean," was his comment. "The Russians will need fifty years to catch up with Europe." Foreigners usually acquire their Soviet impressions in Moscow, Leningrad, and a few other cities. The German army never took the big cities; its troops froze and floundered in backwoods and backward villages.

I asked the chauffeur what happened when the Russians entered Stettin. "They tried to rape my eighteen-year-old sister," he replied. "She committed suicide. Then my mother killed herself." He said this in the same matter-of-fact tone I heard from a Jewish refugee woman in London. "My parents?" she said in answer to a question. "They were put into the furnace at Auschwitz." Europe had no more emotions left; it had seen too much.

Düsseldorf in the British zone was near the heart of the Ruhr, Europe's greatest industrial region, Hitler's central arsenal. Now, as we traveled through the area, most of its smokestacks were smoke-free, most of the road bridges down and replaced with temporary construction spans installed by the foreign military.

Entering Düsseldorf I told the driver to go slow; I wished to confirm my first impression. Every building and home was at least half-demolished, most of them were total wrecks. In Berlin ruined structures were abandoned. But in Düsseldorf so much had been bashed in by the bombs that blitzed places had to be used. You looked at a house. It seemed a complete ruin. But you looked closer and noticed that above the two lower stories, which were burned out with only the upright girders remaining, a fresh brick wall had been built and crude windows put in, and behind them was a light. Next to this solitary eyrie the family wash hung in a space open to the elements.

Mayor Arnold told me that Düsseldorf had almost the same population as before the war: five hundred thousand. They now lived in cellars, in windowless air-raid shelters, in built-in nests and eyries in ruins, and in wooden huts. But the people were well dressed, wearing the booty Hitler collected in Europe.

Walking down a street one Sunday I passed a group of young Germans. "English?" I heard one of them say. He wanted to buy British cigarettes. I stopped. He would buy American cigarettes. Another young man displayed an imported can of sardines in oil. Did I want to buy it? Or some tea? I interrogated one fellow. He was twenty, an electrician, earned forty marks a week. A foreign cigarette brings seven marks, sometimes ten marks. The young German was working for the equivalent of four or five or six cigarettes a week.

A woman has a chicken. The chicken lays one egg a week. Any British soldier in Germany would pay seven cigarettes for an egg. The seven cigarettes fetch fifty marks on the black market. That is a week's salary. Why work? Prostitution flourished. A bar of chocolate, a packet of cigarettes was a temptation. Men and women were demoralized. The German usually loves to work but now the incentives were gone along with the normal rewards. An article in the *British Zone Review* of September 14, 1946, a fortnightly published by the British Military Government in Germany, stated that more consumers' goods had to be supplied to Germans firstly to establish at least the elementary conditions of modern life, secondly to stimulate a desire to work, and thirdly to give some hope for the future to the German people that will lead them away from the feelings of despair which a conquered people normally develop, and which ultimately leads to bitterness, hatred. . . . An abnormal Germany will remain a blot on the map of Europe and a threat to the rehabilitation of Europe and the world. . . . The world is one economically. And if one part of this economic unit is sick then the whole body must suffer.

The American authorities, and obviously the British, saw no wisdom in the so-called, short-lived Morgenthau Plan to lower Germany's standard of living through deindustrialization and "pastoralization." But the Communists enthusiastically welcomed this scheme because they hoped to gain from the poverty and resentment which it would generate. A weak, unhappy Germany might even overcome its repugnance and welcome Russia to spite the West. With the whole world in need of more food, clothing, shelter, and other commodities the forceful curtailment of civilian production in Germany would have entitled the West to the name of "peace criminals." With humanity suffering from a shortage of shipping right after the war the deliberate blowing up of the gigantic shipbuilding wharves of Blohm and Voss in Hamburg was not only political and economic madness, it reflected an intellectual bankruptcy that boded ill for the solution of postwar problems. World statesmanship would have to find some other way of preventing a resurgence of the German peril. It could not be done by creating an economic vacuum in the center of Europe which the Soviets would gladly fill first with their agents and propaganda and then with their power and officials.

My Volkswagen driver dropped me at the central railroad station in Düsseldorf. A wooden ceiling had been built in under the bombed, crumpled, permanent ceiling of the main waiting room. At the left end of the waiting room was a beer *keller* where, according to the newspaper, a Communist election meeting would be held that morning. A man in topcoat and felt hat stopped me as I approached; I must buy a ticket. Tickets are a mark apiece. I have only a fifty-mark bill and he has no change. I offer an American cigarette. He says, "Fine. There I make a profit of six marks."

The beer *keller*, about sixty yards long and twenty wide, was half above and half below the pavement level. Four electric bulbs cast some rays of light on the dimness. The audience consisted of ten women and about two hundred men, all middle-aged, seated at round tables. One frail, bald waiter in white jacket tiptoed from table to table dispensing tall tumblers of beer from a tin platter.

A well-dressed man was addressing the meeting. I hastily scribbled down what he said: "The intelligentsia needs the prosperity of the workers in order to be prosperous. This is not a matter of sentiment but of science. Many argue about Marx and Marxism. But how many have read *The Communist Manifesto* or *Das Kapital?*"

The speaker, a physician, adverted to the Nazi regime: "Twenty-five per cent of all German physicians joined the Nazi party." I looked at the reverse side of the paper on which I was writing. It announced today's meeting as that of the "Düsseldorf Middle Class." At the entrance I had also been handed a thin Communist election leaflet entitled, "Little Nazi, What Now?" It read: "There were twelve million members of the Nazi party in Germany. Men, women, and youths, hundreds of thousands of them, were forced into the Nazi party either by moral pressure or fear of losing their jobs. . . . Shall all these twelve million be thrown into the same pot?" The Communists were courting them. Colonel Howley had told me in Berlin that 130 Nazis whom he dismissed in the American sector found employment in the Soviet sector.

The doctor droned on. "We can clearly predict," he asserted, "that catastrophe is inevitable unless we follow the teachings of Marxism. It is significant that the American statesman Byrnes said in a recent speech that the catastrophe which overtook Germany after 1918 could have been avoided if the Germans had taken the advice of Karl Liebknecht.

"Communists want planned science," he affirmed a moment later. "That is Socialism. The Nazis had a plan and an organization, for instance in aviation and medicine. Then what is the difference between Socialism and Nazism? The Nazi goal was destruction and collapse. Socialism in Russia, on the other hand, is making fascinating researches in history, medicine, and all other sciences. I recently read an American book on the atom. The authors declare that atomic energy must never be used for civilian purposes. America wants to confine atomic energy to the field of militarism and diplomatic pressure. In the U.S.A., atomic energy means retrogression, death, and constraint. In the U.S.S.R., it means scientific advance and benefits for humanity." He finished with a flourish: "We must either move toward progress or disappear under atomic bombs." Hand-clapping rewarded the speaker as he rushed to the door. I ran after

him and caught up with him in the station waiting room. I gave
my name, said I was an American journalist, and asked his name.
"Dr. Karl Hagedorn," he replied. (The name was on the printed
announcements of the meeting.)

"You mentioned the American Secretary of State Byrnes," I
began. "He is a conservative. If he ever heard of Karl Liebknecht, and
I'm not sure he did, he would never have praised him, he would
never praise a Communist leader."

"Yes," Dr. Hagedorn said, "then who could it have been? I read
it in the newspaper."

"You spoke of the civilian uses of atomic energy in Russia," I continued. "How do you know these things? There has been nothing in
the press about them. Even less important matters are kept secret in
Russia and certainly everything about atomic energy. You just thought
this up yourself."

He seemed embarrassed and spoke not a word. "Here Germany has
just come out of twelve years of false propaganda by Goebbels and
now you and the Communists are starting the same business over
again," I exclaimed.

He looked around as if seeking an avenue of escape in the immense waiting room. "Excuse me, thank you," he said, and rushed
away.

This was a day of meetings for me; the evening of the same day
I attended a gathering convened by the Zentrum, or Center party.
In pre-Hitler days the powerful organization of Chancellor Bruening,
Chancellor von Papen, and others, it had now dwindled and lost most
of its strength to the Christian Democratic Union (CDU) of Jakob
Kaiser and Konrad Adenauer. Nevertheless, I wanted to hear what
the chief speaker, Dr. Karl Spiecker, a prominent Catholic leader,
thought of the present situation.

The meeting, admission free, took place in a public school, and the
main address was preceded by an overture by Franz Schubert and the
Larghetto from the second symphony of Ludwig von Beethoven and
followed by Edvard Grieg's "Solvejg's Song" from *Peer Gynt* and an
aria from Halévy's *Jewess*, all rendered by an eighteen-piece orchestra
conducted by a man in cutaway and white tie. The audience numbered about five hundred, divided more or less evenly between men
and women, most of them over fifty with a considerable sprinkling
of persons in their thirties and twenties.

As in the case of the morning's Communist meeting, I made an instantaneous translation from German into English and made notes which lie before me now. Dr. Spiecker began with a reference to the verdict in the Nuremberg trial of German war criminals. The generals, he asserted, deserved the sentences they got because "they looked on while their colleagues who had tried to kill Hitler on July 20, 1944, were hung."

"*Sehr gut!*" "*Sehr wahr,*" and similar expressions of approval resounded throughout the hall.

Coming to the domestic political situation, Dr. Spiecker said, "Today the CDU fights Marx. But the Nazis came from the right, not from the left. Nazism was materialism wrapped in nationalism and all men of religion should therefore have fought Hitler. The real guilty ones were those who put the Nazis in power."

The audience cried, "*Sehr gut,*" in approval.

"Now we punish the little fellows and let the big ones go free. The danger is not Nazism, it is nationalism. We must prevent an alliance between big business and nationalism." ("*Sehr gut.*")

Dr. Spiecker then discussed next Sunday's elections. He wanted them to keep the Center party alive even though it would be tiny. "Religion cannot unite Germany," he stated. "There is idealism on the left, too, among the Socialists. It would be a misuse of Christianity to use it as a screen for reactionary materialism. The Center party is the party of the Sermon on the Mount, of the rich and the poor, of high and low.

"Only the SPD [Socialist Party of Germany] can stop the KPD [Communist Party of Germany.] That is why it is wrong for the CDU to fight the SPD. The CDU is a Christian bourgeois bloc. It must not provoke the formation of an anti-Christian, anti-bourgeois bloc."

On Germany's role abroad he said, "It will be decades before we can walk with raised heads. We carry a heavy responsibility for the damage in Europe. Europe has sunk, and we must recognize the need of European unity and prepare for it. We have lost our role as a national state. We must aspire to serve Europe, not rule it. We will never again be a dominant nation.

"Now we must work. And the victors must allow us to work. They must let us pay with goods for the food they are giving us. [Loud applause.]

"Power in Germany must never again reside in a small group.

Leave the middle class alone. The state must not be a night watchman. ["*Sehr gut*," "*Sehr gut*."] As a result of a century of Junkers
education we are a nation of subalterns. We in Germany don't know
what freedom is. We must learn it."

Dr. Spiecker sat down and wiped his face as he listened to the
vigorous handclapping. I rejoined my jeep driver without waiting for
the final musical numbers.

Actually, Germany was under a foreign authoritarian government,
or rather governments, and the elections, therefore, were a kind of
dry run, or flight in a wind tunnel, for the Germans elected would
have no power. Election politics is usually promises, but promises
without executive authority are fatuous. Accordingly, the parties,
with the exception of the Communists, merely engaged in identify-
ing themselves to the public. The Christian Democratic Union
(CDU) covered innumerable walls and fences with a poster reading,
"*Der Christ Waehlt* CDU." ("The Christian votes CDU.") Assiduous Socialists gave almost every poster a neighbor reading, "*Der
wahre Christ ist Sozialist. Waehlt* SPD." ("The true Christian is a
Socialist. Vote SPD.") Superimposed on a photograph of ruins, the
CDU blazoned its slogan, "Never again dictatorship." An SPD
streamer, directed at the Communists and Russia, proclaimed,
"Where there is fear there is no freedom; without freedom no Socialism."

Only the Communists made promises. "Do you want coal for the
winter?" their Düsseldorf placard asked. "Vote Communist." Every
German knew that coal was being mined and distributed by the
foreign occupation. "Do you want prices reduced?" another Communist circular demanded. "Vote Communist." But prices, and
wages, had been fixed at the Nazi-time level by the Soviet, British,
and American governments as soon as they occupied Germany, and
no German party could change them.

The election returns in the British Zone on October 13, 1946, gave
the Socialists 173 seats in the provincial legislature, the Christian
Democrats 144 seats, the Communists 36, the Center party 26.

In Berlin on October 20, the Socialists received 48.7 per cent of the
votes, the Christian Democrats 22.1 per cent, the Communists 19.8
per cent, the Liberal Democrats 9.4 per cent. The polling took place
throughout all of Berlin, including the Eastern (Russian) sector,
where the Communists enjoyed many advantages.

The Communists in West Germany were weaker in 1946 than they had been under the pre-Hitler Weimar Republic. The Nazis did not figure in the elections. The extremes, for the moment at least, were insignificant.

Foreigners in Germany always argued whether Germans had undergone "a change of heart" or "a change of mind" since the war. This involved the question of guilt for the war and for the atrocities. I asked a German physician. He said, "We could no more alter Hitler's policy than we can the policies of the present occupying powers. You remember, of course, that Hitler was a dictator. Those who were not converted by one-sided propaganda were frightened into acquiescence. Others, far too many, believed we could win the war. So they went along with the Nazis. I did it too. The alternative was to lose my skin."

I asked an old man. "What could we little folk do?" he exclaimed.

My own view was: Germany and Germans had committed innumerable, horrible crimes. Some were inherent in the conduct of war, some antedated the war, some were deliberate, unnecessary cruelties. Obviously, not all eighty million Germans personally engaged in those cruelties, and most of the inactive ones were innocent both individually, in jurisprudence, and politically, in a dictatorship. Even democratic electorates do not always govern their governments. Millions of Americans would refuse individual responsibility for the acts of recent Administrations, and the same is true in France, England, and other free countries.

But is there not something perverse in the German character? Or are the atrocities attributable to Nazi teachings? With all the rigors of German occupation in Western Europe during the Second World War, and by the Kaiser's troops in the First World War, whole populations, in millions, were not exterminated as were the Poles, Jews, and Russians of Eastern Europe from 1939 to 1945. This difference between the treatment of West and East Europeans must be due chiefly to the indecent, heathen Hitlerian "philosophy" that the victims of Nazi genocide belonged to "inferior races" inhabiting land the Germans could use to greater advantage.

This Nazi ideology was born and bore its poison fruit on German soil, in German souls. The subject continued to torment me on every successive trip to Germany. But I always had the feeling that collective guilt and collective evil were wrong whether attributed by Nazis to Jews or by anti-Nazis to Germans. Hate of an entire people is Nazism, and anti-Nazis must avoid it or court the charge of being subconscious Nazis themselves. Better kill hate and misery, and thereby perhaps induce a change of heart.

Punishment to fit her crimes would have meant starving Germany and sowing the country with salt. This was impossible without inviting epidemics and revolution. In fact, toward the end of 1946, the United States was shipping 300,000 tons of food to Germany per month; that was Germany's monthly deficit. Commenting on the announcement, General Clay asserted, "Democracy can win Germany only if food is made available to keep the German people alive and able to work."

CHAPTER SEVEN

Roosevelt and Truman. A Diagnosis of Appeasement

WHEN the Second World War began, President Roosevelt encouraged those who wanted America to aid the Western Allies, and later he seconded Prime Minister Churchill's offer of help to Russia, broadcast the very day Hitler attacked her.

Mr. Roosevelt's wartime Russian policy was partly, perhaps largely, shaped by a stubborn fear that Stalin would flip-flop again, as he had in August, 1939, and sign a separate peace with the Nazis. Considering the disastrous effects such a defection would have had on Allied fortunes, the dread was understandable. But I always felt that, having gone to war, Stalin and Hitler would not enter into a pact, and on several occasions I set forth my reasons to Under Secretary of State Sumner Welles. Finally he said, "You begin to convince me. But suppose you were President Roosevelt, and suppose you knew that if they did sign a separate peace it might mean the death of a million or two million American boys, would you be so sure?" I had to confess that I would not. The unattached observer and the critic without executive responsibility always finds it easier to believe in the flawless logic of his conclusions than the leader whose decisions involve the fate of millions.

This discrepancy between correct analysis and correct policy lies near the root of much Western appeasement of Russia. Given the unknown and uncertain in international affairs, appeasement often seems the safer course especially since it means doing nothing—which generally suits governments better than taking a decision for drastic, costly action.

During the Second World War, moreover, President Roosevelt assumed that the future of humanity would depend on amicable relations between America and the Soviet government. This assumption flowed unavoidably from the policy of "unconditional surrender" and the total destruction of Germany's and Japan's political power. With these two nations crushed, and with France and England weakened by war, no balance of power against Russia in Europe or Asia was possible except by the presence of massive American strength on both those continents, a development then neither desired nor contemplated. Therefore there had to be friendly agreement with Russia —in other words, unanimity among the great powers and, in the United Nations, a veto for each of the great powers to guarantee that unanimity.

Mr. Roosevelt realized that friendship with the Kremlin required the successful courtship of Joseph Stalin. The President felt well equipped for the assignment. U.S. Supreme Court Justice Robert Jackson once told me how, as Attorney General, he would come to President Roosevelt and propose the prosecution of certain firms for violation of antitrust laws. But Roosevelt would say, "Ah, Bob, bring them in to see me, I'll take care of it." F.D.R. had a towering faith in the conquering power of his charm, will, eloquence, intelligence, dexterity, and destiny. And it was quite justified, for had he not surmounted a cruel physical handicap and become President four times?

In Stalin, however, Roosevelt encountered a figure whose few human traits had been extinguished by the impersonal code of a brutal despotism and whose domestic-political needs were better served by an insulating Iron Curtain than by evidence of friendly coexistence with the West. When Roosevelt, therefore, indulged at

Teheran in planned and rather low-grade ridicule of Churchill in the Prime Minister's presence with a view to making Stalin laugh and thus breaking the ice of aloofness and moving on from there to personal intimacy and good fellowship, he elicited the brief show of mirth but otherwise fell lamentably short of his target.

At the Yalta Conference, in February, 1945, there was no longer the least likelihood that Stalin would withdraw from the war. On the contrary, he looked like its chief beneficiary. Roosevelt was again the chief suitor. Not only did he and Churchill want Russia's continued action against Hitler; they were bent on winning Soviet participation in the war with Japan. From the Chief of Staff, General George C. Marshall, down, the military urged the politicians to make certain of a Russian effort in the Pacific theater, and their promptings, plus the fact that Russian troops had swept through Poland into Germany while the Anglo-American forces were not across the Rhine, explain some of the errors and giveaways at Yalta.

At the end, Mr. Roosevelt knew that his attempts at Russian-American friendship had failed and the last three weeks of his life he quarreled with Stalin by cable over Communist usurpation of total power in Poland in contravention of the Yalta agreement.

By the time the Potsdam Conference met in July, 1945, appeasement of Russia was no longer necessary as a war measure, for Germany was out of the war, and Japan, facing defeat, had, Truman knew, sued for peace. Nor was appeasement likely to yield the sweet fruit of friendship. But every new top-level policy-maker apparently needed a private course of instruction in the folly of appeasement, the fee to be paid by the nation. Secretary of State James F. Byrnes took longest to learn, and he was therefore of little help at Potsdam to an inexperienced President recently inducted into an awesomely high office.

Before the Potsdam Conference, W. Averell Harriman, U. S. Ambassador to Moscow, advised his government against drawing the Soviet Union into the war with Japan. At the conference, General Dwight D. Eisenhower and General Lucius D. Clay called on Mr. Truman to put the same point of view. But Truman said he was President and he wanted to save the lives of as many American boys as possible. Generals assume men will die in war, a Chief Executive considers the sentiments of mothers, wives, and fathers. But how Truman and Byrnes failed to see Russia's poorly disguised, frantic efforts to get into the Pacific war before it ended (she entered four days before the end) is history's puzzle. And why should Secretary Byrnes have sat up till late in the night, as he states in his book, *Speaking Frankly*,[1] to devise means not of blocking but of facilitating the step which enabled Moscow to alter the entire course of Asian politics to Communism's advantage? Secretary of the Navy James Forrestal reports in his diaries that in this matter President Truman acted "under the pressure of Secretary Byrnes."[2]

For months after Potsdam, Secretary of State Byrnes continued to condone Soviet imperialism. As late as October 31, 1945, he said, "Far from opposing, we have sympathized with, for example, the effort of the Soviet Union to draw into closer and more friendly association with her Central and Eastern European neighbors. We are fully aware of her special security interests in those countries."

But against whom was Russia seeking security? England, France, and Germany could not fight the Soviets without American assistance. So the U.S. Secretary of State was supporting Russia's security measures against the U.S.? This made no sense. Moreover, if a small nation must be friendly to a great power like Russia how can it be free? The Kremlin could always veto the neighborly government on the ground of unfriendliness. Mr. Byrnes, the worst American appeaser, was blessing Russia's subjugation of her border countries.

The wish to appease, whether in the United States, France, or England, was a natural desire springing from a normal impulse to get along with one's fellowmen and avoid war. Americans, a traditionally isolationist people, were particularly eager not to become involved in quarrels with Russia which would require the United States to keep the Soviets under permanent guard.

Specifically, the appeasement of Russia after the Second World War drank at many fountains: the Soviet Union fought gallantly, effectively, and at great cost against the common enemy; Communism was different from and preferable to Fascism; a stop-Russia policy would lead to war with Russia; Moscow was seeking satellites for security; the East European countries undergoing sovietization were never democracies anyway; the Soviet appetite would soon be sated, after which, given patience and good will, a workable relationship would emerge.

All these propositions except the first were wholly or largely false

[1] James F. Byrnes, *Speaking Frankly*, New York: Harper & Brothers, 1947.
[2] *The Forrestal Diaries*, p. 70.

and dangerously misleading. Even the first ignored the fact that Russia fought only after she had been attacked; before she was attacked Soviet Communists collaborated with Nazi Germany while Communists elsewhere sabotaged the anti-Nazi cause. Official Communists and official Fascists were brain brothers. There was more of Hitler in Stalin than of Marx. The elements which originally distinguished Communism from Fascism—internationalism, absence of racial discrimination, and anti-imperialism, for instance—lived shorter lives than the oppression of the individual and other totalitarian characteristics which the two movements shared. Ignoring this development, Henry A. Wallace, who quit the Truman Cabinet on the appeasement-of-Russia issue, said on November 4, 1946, after his resignation, "As between Fascism and Communism I prefer Communism." But nobody in a free country has to make that choice and nobody in a Communist country can. Not all Communists, to be sure, are Fascists. But Communism is political cannibalism: it destroys the good intentions of its idealistic adherents and the effectiveness of its liberal fellow travelers. Mr. Wallace himself was a tragic example of the latter.

The further thesis that resistance to Russia might precipitate an armed conflict stood refuted at its first test: In Iran, in 1946, the Shah, encouraged by Americans, marched his troops into Persian Azerbaijan to retrieve that province from Soviet agents who had converted it into a puppet state. Faced with the alternative of defending it or withdrawing, Stalin withdrew. This retreat set a precedent for the future.

Soviet Russia took when she could and desisted when resisted. This is the best argument against postwar appeasement. Stalin subjugated only the weak and unprotected. No potential satellite voted itself into Communist slavery. If prosperity and democracy had been considered, Czechoslovakia would have remained free. Even Hungary and Poland would have been spared, for Hungary under Admiral Horthy's personal regime and Poland under Rydz-Smigly enjoyed more liberty than the Soviet people. But Stalin was not worrying about the wishes of his newly acquired colonial subjects. He was building an empire.

Nevertheless, illusions deeply anchored at the time of Soviet revolution in 1917, when Lenin was anti-imperialist in deed, resisted the erosion of subsequent facts. As a result, Henry A. Wallace from the left joined Mr. Byrnes from the right in approving Russia's sphere of influence in Eastern and Central Europe. Persons who waxed indignant over India's lighter yoke and hailed her deliverance easily reconciled themselves to the forced submersion of a hundred million Europeans in the Red sea.

However, light kept coming from the East; each new postwar Kremlin insult and injury destroyed another fraction of Western appeasement. The climate of opinion was clearing quickly; liberals and intellectuals who could never quite see the moral degradation of the Bolshevik regime were being convinced by Moscow's behavior. As Mrs. Roosevelt, then a member of the U.S. delegation to the UN, told Henry Wallace in a polemic, "I have worked rather more steadily and more closely with the representatives of the U.S.S.R. than Mr. Wallace" and they taught her much. "They understand strength, not weakness," she explained to Wallace, "and they say many things they know are not true because they think they can make others believe they are true." On October 23, 1947, in a column about a UN session, Mrs. Roosevelt wrote, "This speech of Mr. Vishinsky destroyed the belief of our people that conciliation is either wise or possible in dealing with the representatives of the government of the U.S.S.R. . . . Our gesture of good will was misunderstood," she continued. "And we learned a lesson which perhaps Mr. Vishinsky did not mean to teach us: namely, that no modification would ever be made in a position once taken; that no conciliation should ever be attempted." With characteristic charity and broad vision she then added, "We have learned our lesson well, but from my point of view it is unfortunate, because it will mean more votes [in the UN] against the U.S.S.R. and a greater antagonistic feeling."

In government circles, appeasement of Russia neared the vanishing point in the second half of 1946. In May, 1946, Stalin had rejected President Truman's telegraphic invitation to visit him in the White House, and this, following the rejection of a similar invitation made in person at Potsdam, convinced official skeptics that Moscow desired no settlement, no compromise, and no friendship. Appeasement, therefore, could yield no dividends. Give-and-take, in Moscow's language, meant that others give and it takes.

Nevertheless, no positive American policy had been evolved. The atmosphere that once conduced to one-sided concessions to Russia was gone, but Mr. Truman had not yet lost patience with the

Soviets. There were still several irons in the fire of negotiation, and a counteroffensive accordingly waited upon events. Ideas, to be sure, were at the blueprint stage on State Department planning boards, but they needed the hammer blow of a sudden emergency to shape them into a program of action. The emergency came early in 1947.

Part Two
THE AWAKENING

CHAPTER EIGHT

Truman Doctrine and Marshall Plan

I HAD MY first talk with Mr. Dean Acheson on January 3, 1947, when he was Under Secretary of State. Replying to an initial question about recent dealings with Russia, he said, "All that has happened is that Molotov, having decided he couldn't get anywhere by kicking people in the teeth, has changed his tactics. But it would be self-hypnosis to think everything is all right. We must not allow ourselves to be set back by their offensive strategy. They keep us busy. They throw bricks through the window and we push a newspaper into the hole, then we try quickly to plug another hole, and so on. I had my people in here this morning and told them to be on their toes instead." Mr. Acheson was planning a propaganda offensive. In a conversation lasting an hour and twenty-five minutes, I noted not a single trace of appeasement; rather the contrary.

Unusual tension was noticeable in the Department of State on February 24, 1947. Early that morning, Lord Inverchapel, the British Ambassador, called on Acheson to tell him that Great Britain could no longer afford the $250 million which financial-military support of Turkey and Greece would require in the current year.

Acheson immediately telephoned George F. Kennan at the National War College and he came over to the State Department where, with Loy Henderson, head of the Department's Division of Near and Middle Eastern Affairs, he jointly chaired a meeting of officials which examined the problem posed by the British Ambassador. It decided that the Administration had no choice but to accept the new responsibility.

From the meeting, Loy Henderson, whom I had known when he was in the U.S. Embassy in Moscow, returned to his office where I was waiting for him by previous appointment. I sensed that a sudden disaster had descended. Loy is a sincere and tense person and his hands shook with excitement.

After my talk with Loy, I walked over to Acheson's antechamber to keep a lunch date. There, two high-ranking State Department economists were exchanging animated whispers. One said, "We must do something about their tobacco."

A moment later, Acheson came out and we walked down the corridor. "Isn't this a hell of a world," he exclaimed.

"That's a mild way of putting it," I responded, "and you never know what place is going to fall on you next."

"That's the sort of situation we're faced with today," he stated.

"What is it now?" I asked.

"Greece," he said.

In the limousine he cranked up the window behind the driver. "The British are getting out of Turkey and Greece," he told me, "and if we don't go in the Russians will."

That was the Truman Doctrine.

In the Metropolitan Club, everybody greeted Acheson by his Christian name with a "Hi" and wave of the hand, and he responded in the same informal manner. At a desk downstairs he wrote an order for the dishes I wanted and ordered the same for himself. I had the feeling he did not much care what he ate.

I had said in the car that General Marshall, who succeeded Byrnes as Secretary of State in January, 1947, ought to have a show-down talk with Stalin at the forthcoming foreign ministers' conference in Moscow. When we settled at the lunch table, Acheson said, "Now go on, talk to me about this showdown talk. I discussed the same thing with the Secretary this morning. 'Well, what would you say?' Marshall asked. I replied that I would talk about their expansion and recall that the Communist parties everywhere were working for Russia. We are going into as many countries as possible and try to stop them. Stalin would then argue that he had nothing to do with foreign Communist parties. He knew they were friendly to the U.S.S.R., but he had nothing to do with them. 'And so,' Marshall queried, 'what would you have accomplished?' "

"The point is not to accomplish anything," I interjected. "What we need is an unsuccessful conference." I explained: the road from the First World War to the Second was paved with "successful" conferences which yielded satisfaction but no solution. A conference now might produce treaties, resolutions, or another conference, but it would delay the basic transformation of the non-Soviet world on which effective resistance to Soviet expansion depended. A conference with Russia that failed would direct the democratic world's attention to its own disunity and economic weakness which were, perhaps, the real causes of the failure.

Acheson and I agreed that Stalin was having trouble with demobilized soldiers who had seen and liked Europe, with the national minorities, and with the satellite countries. One way of coping with the situation was rudeness toward America; it gave the people of Russia and her new colonies an impression of Kremlin strength. Diplomatic difficulties would therefore continue, Acheson said.

Acheson was most worried about England—and money. "It's queer," he mused, "how poor the government of a rich country can be." Congress controlled the funds and had already appropriated a great deal for foreign aid. Now the President would have to ask for more millions. He looked grim. He was afraid that the Near East and France would go Communist and disastrously affect the world situation.

In the first instance, however, Soviet pressure was on Britain. (Stalin had not yet flung his challenge at America.) The Kremlin's primary purpose, like the Czar's in the nineteenth century, was the break-up of the British Empire. Weaker things first. Walter Lippmann might argue in his columns that since England was a "whale" or sea power and Russia an "elephant" or land power they could agree on spheres of influence and not collide. Unto each his element. But Britain was also a land power. She faced the Soviets in Germany, Austria, Greece, and the Near East. Russia, moreover, stood astride the Baltic Sea, coveted a foothold in the Mediterranean Sea, and was constructing a strong navy.

The question, therefore, was not whether the Red elephant would saunter out of his jungle and swim into the ocean to grapple with the whale. The question was whether the lion and the bear could lie down together. The lion was obviously willing. But the bear was brimful of vim and going places. He displayed no desire to lie down at all and certainly not with old Leo whose mane was growing thin and whose roar sounded to Kremlin ears like a bleat.

The men in the Kremlin were expecting Britain's collapse. Always viewing themselves through rose-colored glasses but observing others with the darkest lenses procurable, the Soviet leaders can make themselves see what they want to see and it is usually the same imminent triumph of Communism which Marx and Engels predicted so dogmatically and prematurely in 1848. England, it is recorded, did not collapse. Yet the situation after 1945 was critical indeed. Her prewar economic derelictions and the cost of the war were catching up with her. In 1947, the Scientific Research Board appointed by President Truman reported that, "Since the turn of the [twentieth] Century the British have been paying, in terms of technological obsolescence, the penalty of their early industrial leadership.

"Today," the Board found, "one of the most serious long-term problems still facing the British government is the modernization of industrial facilities."

In the circumstances, Britain had neither the resources nor the heart to continue holding up Greece and Turkey, and it remained for America, therefore, to block the bear while resuscitating the lion. The United States, in effect, interposed itself between Russia and England, and became, consequently, the primary target of Communist vituperation.

Congress granted $100 million to Turkey and $300 million to Greece.

Innocents and Communistic fellow travelers let out a shriek: the United States was supporting a reactionary government in Athens and a near-dictatorship in Ankara. Both governments were indeed far from democratic, and this, with persons devoted to principles in politics, was painful. But the descent of Greece and Turkey into the Soviet orbit would have extinguished what freedom they had and the chance of developing it. There is general agreement that the Second World War should have been, could have been, stopped in Manchuria in 1931, in Abyssinia in 1935; there was general support in Britain for her belated 1939 offer of support to Poland. What was Manchuria in 1931? A dictatorship under the Chinese war lord, Chang Hsueh-liang. What was Abyssinia in 1935? A backward, slave-holding state. Yet liberals did not want it subjected to Mussolini's mustard-gas culture. Poland in 1939 was ruled by a rightist junta. Yet the British people went to its defense.

Each case of this kind involves more than the nature of the regime to be saved. It raises the entire issue of aggression, for the sad prelude to the Second World War demonstrated that aggression led to further aggression and then to war. If Turkey or Greece or both had succumbed to direct or indirect Communist expansion, Russia would have outflanked Southern Europe and looked into the Mediterranean, and humanity would have teetered on the edge of a third world war. Not the nature of the victim but the nature of the assailant, and his intention, is the criterion.

The Truman Doctrine, enunciated March 12, 1947, sounded the death knell of American isolationism. After the Second World War the United States might have relapsed into seclusion as it did after the first. But there was a big job to be done, as big as the two wars themselves, and Americans love to do big jobs, especially when the implement is the one they know best: money. The job was in fact a new war with cold weapons, the American counteroffensive against Soviet imperialism.

The Truman Doctrine implied that for a long time to come the United States would try to stop any breach in the Western wall against Russian expansion. Since the actual and potential breaches were numerous and enormous, the Truman Administration, widely supported by the public and the Republican party, now stood committed to a global economic and military program of resistance to Russian designs. The Truman Doctrine was actually the new American doctrine: it did not belong to one man or one party. It contained the seed of the Marshall Plan and of NATO (North Atlantic Treaty Organization).

Would not the Truman Doctrine and its further elaborations constitute a new American imperialism? It might. The future would show. Help to a foreign country is, of itself, neither an evil nor a menace. Everything depends on whether the help is accompanied by acts of suppression and enslavement.

Aid to Greece and Turkey was followed, within four months, by the statement which led to the Marshall Plan.

President Truman modestly considered General George C. Marshall the greatest living American. Marshall was deeply respected in the army and by the public, and by many foreign countries. His personality and prestige no doubt did much to make possible the Plan which carries his name, and his political evolution from the time he left the office of Chief of Staff to the moment he uttered the words which launched that extraordinary, unprecedented scheme, is, therefore, very interesting.

During the Second World War, General Marshall's relations with Soviet officers in the Soviet purchasing mission in Washington and at various conferences abroad had been fruitful and friendly. Nothing in his personal experiences would have given him cause for pessimism in judging the prospects of negotiations with Communists.

A few months after Japan's defeat, Mr. Truman appointed him Ambassador to China with the special assignment "to bring about the unification of China and, concurrently, to effect a cessation of hostilities"[1] between the Communists under Mao Tse-tung and the Nationalists under Generalissimo Chiang Kai-shek. The task presented mammoth difficulties. The goal was a Chiang-Communist coalition interim government and the merging of the Communist army with the Nationalist army by peaceful means and persuasion. Marshall believed it could be done. This was the moment of postwar innocence now so remote and incomprehensible; but though past events should be analyzed in the perspective of history, they must be judged in the context of their time.

The proposed coalition, moreover, was not conceived as a free gift to the Communists or as a voluntary opening of the Chiang government's door to Red members. It did not resemble the temporary coalitions between non-Communists and Communists shortly after the war in France, Belgium, and Italy. "In China," Secretary of State Dean Acheson explained in 1951,[2] "the Communists were not scattered through the population as an element of the population. They were people who had a defined area, with a large population subject to their control, 116 million. They had a government of their own; they had an army of their own; and, in effect, they had a separate country within China, and the task was to put these two things together so that there would be one country and one government."

Marshall's efforts to bring about a coalition were preceded by similar action on the part of U.S. Ambassador Patrick J. Hurley, later a fierce critic of the Marshall mission. Hurley, encouraged by

---

[1] *Military Situation in the Far East, Hearings Before the Committee on Armed Services and the Committee on Foreign Relations, United States Senate, Eighty-Second Congress, First Session, To Conduct an Inquiry into the Military Situation in the Far East and the Facts Surrounding the Relief of General of the Army Douglas MacArthur from His Assignment in That Area,* August 17, 1951, Washington: United States Government Printing Office, 1951, Part 5, Appendix and Index, p. 3184.

[2] *Ibid.,* Part 3, p. 1844.

Chiang Kai-shek, flew to Yenan and on August 28, 1945, returned to Chungking with Mao Tse-tung. After a month of talks between Mao and Chiang, Hurley wired Washington that "the spirit shown by the negotiators is good, the rapprochment between the two leading parties of China seems to be progressing, and the discussion and rumors of civil war recede as the conference continues."[3] No solution had been reached. But President Truman, Secretary Byrnes, and General Marshall felt it was worth further effort.

The Marshall scheme envisaged a reorganized army consisting of fifty Nationalist and ten Communist divisions, and a provisional state council or cabinet consisting of forty members, all of whom the Generalissimo would appoint, twenty from his own party and twenty from the Communist and minor parties. In the council he would exercise a veto which could only be overridden by a three-fifths vote.[4]

Not only Marshall expected this coalition fantasy to come to life. So did Chiang; it was the only practicable alternative to his subsequent defeat. So did Stalin.

Whatever one thinks of Marshall's political qualifications, Chiang and Stalin were far from naïve; they were shrewd, intriguing opportunists. Stalin had read Machiavelli and must have regarded him a kindergarten babe, or a rural tyro; Chiang, whom Moscow had once financed and whom, in the midst of the civil war, Moscow and Chinese Communists had helped to escape from a dangerous kidnaping by a war lord, would certainly not exclude any possibility because it seemed improbable. In Europe, nations had changed sides often throughout history, abandoning partners to embrace opponents, and in China provincial war lords had flip-flopped with smiling blandness and the mental reservation that tomorrow some other combination might prove more desirable.

Chiang could easily see himself in a coalition with Communists. He probably hoped, and even expected, that Moscow would force the Chinese Communists into such a coalition, and that he could some day buy off Moscow to prefer him to Mao Tse-tung. This seemed like madness. But Chiang had his reasons:

[3] Herbert Feis, *The China Tangle; the American effort in China from Pearl Harbor to the Marshall Mission*, Princeton: Princeton University Press, 1953, p. 360 *et seq.*

[4] *Ibid.*, p. 1850.

One assumes that the Soviet Communist Stalin would naturally prefer the Chinese Communists. But in 1927, Stalin had preferred Chiang to Chinese Soviets. Stalin had no unalterable predilection for Communists. He had destroyed many Communists. He hounded Leon Trotsky till his death in Mexico City. He executed foreign Communists who were refugees or visitors in Russia. He liquidated them because they were in his way, they were his opponents. The basic reason is that Stalin was antirevolutionary. A Communist would normally be a rebel, a dissident, a troublemaker for a dictator. Stalin drained the rebellion out of Communism. He conceived of the world Communist movement as a pale carbon copy of the Kremlin. Karl Radek, famous Soviet publicist, later lost in the purge, used to say, "Revolutions are not an article of export." Moscow never expected to export a revolution, because a revolutionary Germany, for instance, might be anti-Russian, and Stalin never gambled. Instead, when he got his chance during the war, he exported the Red army and the NKVD to Rumania, Poland, Hungary, and the other new colonies, not, obviously, to foment revolution but to impose a Russian regime from above.

In China, too, Stalin sought power. The Yalta Agreement on the Far East and Russia's four-day performance in the Pacific war enabled her to occupy North Korea, Manchuria, Southern Sakhalin, and the Kurile Islands off Japan. Under regrettable pressure from the United States, Chiang Kai-shek granted the Soviet government rights over Manchuria's railway system and the ports of Port Arthur and Dairen. These were a bird in the Russian hand. Mao Tse-tung was two, or maybe only one, in the wild Asian bush.

In return for favors, the Soviet government promised, by treaty, to support "exclusively" the Chinese Nationalists under Chiang Kai-shek. Such promises, of course, are as easily broken as given. For Moscow, morality that does not pay dividends is immoral; materialism triumphs over ethics on the Red Square—and in high places in other countries.

Whether Moscow could get more from Mao than from Chiang was a question not easily answered. Stalin, in the first place, did not think Mao could overthrow Chiang. Since he lacked faith in foreign Communists acting without Soviet military aid, he took a dim view of Chinese Communist prospects. He is on record as having said so at a meeting in Moscow on February 10, 1948, of front-rank Russian, Bulgarian, and Yugoslav Communist leaders. This conference was strictly confidential and Stalin could not have anticipated that his words would ever see the light of day. But for Yugoslavia's defection from the Soviet orbit they would never have been published. Stalin declared that "after the [Second World] war we invited the Chinese comrades to come to Moscow and we discussed the situation in China. We told them bluntly that we considered the development of the uprising in China has no prospect, and that the Chinese comrades should seek a *modus vivendi* with Chiang Kai-shek, that they should join the Chiang Kai-shek government and dissolve their army."[5] This was General Marshall's goal in China and it is not inconceivable to imagine circumstances in which he could have reached it. So long as there were "comrades" in Chiang Kai-shek's government it could not have pursued an anti-Russian policy or a completely pro-American policy, and that, much more than revolution, was the task Moscow assigned to foreign Communist parties. For this reason the French and Italian Communists had participated in conservative-led coalition cabinets of their countries. They were adjuncts of the Soviet foreign office, not agents of revolution.

Stalin did not want a strong China which would limit Russia's expansion and weaken Russia's position in the Far East. In Manchuria, immediately after the end of the war, the Soviets looted tremendous quantities of movable machinery and carried it off to Russia. This might be explained on the ground of need. But the Russians also blew up Chinese powerhouses and other permanent industrial installations. They wished to destroy the base of China's future industrial development. Russia, Czarist or Stalinist, did not want a strong China. A China ruled by a Chiang-Mao coalition, with Communist subversion a constant threat or even an actuality, would not be a strong China.

The alternative to a Chiang-Mao coalition was Soviet military and monetary support on titanic scale to the Chinese Communists. But Moscow had shrunk from this sort of adventure even in Iran, a much smaller theater much nearer home and much further from American power. The Soviet leaders, never very intelligent about America, did not realize how little the United States would do to save Chiang, and they probably feared that intensified civil strife

[5] Vladimir Dedijer, *Tito*, New York: Simon and Schuster, 1953, p. 322. This is Marshal Tito's autobiography as told to Mr. Dedijer.

in China looking to a Communist victory might touch off a war with the West for which Russia was ill prepared. Stalin, accordingly, advised Mao to make peace with Chiang.

Strangely enough, the United States faced a similar dilemma: America likewise did not relish the costly alternative to a Chiang-Mao coalition. The American people had no yearning to send a million GIs to China. Moreover, General Wedemeyer later came to the conclusion, which he communicated to the Nationalist government, that "the Chinese Communist movement cannot be defeated by the employment of force."[6] In this context the Marshall mission made sense. It was neither a fool's errand nor treason.

When Marshall reached China in December, 1945, famines involving millions were already raging, and every morning hundreds of corpses were shoveled up in city streets. Inflation had made money worthless. More of this and Communism would triumph no matter who won the military battles.

As a first step toward the contemplated coalition, five Nationalist divisions were to combine with one Communist division. Areas were actually designated where the Nationalist and Communist troops would meet and merge, but the Communists never arrived. Marshall was apparently induced to believe that they failed to appear because their ragged uniforms and poor arms would have caused them to lose face! So they were clothed and armed, and still they did not appear.

The reason is that Mao, craving power, rejected a coalition with Chiang, and insisted on fighting. At the secret Moscow conference of Soviet, Yugoslavia, and Bulgarian chiefs on February 10, 1948,[7] Stalin, continuing, said, "The Chinese comrades agreed here with the views of the Soviet comrades, but went back to China and acted quite otherwise. They mustered their forces, organized their armies and now, as we see, they are beating the Chiang Kai-shek army." It was Mao who defeated Marshall.

After almost a year in China, General Marshall returned to the United States and, on January 7, 1947, issued a statement in which he attributed his failure to "irreconcilable Communists" as well as to the "dominant reactionary group" in the Chiang government. The right-wing Nationalists, he suggested, felt they need not accept American advice because they were sure they would get American

[6] *Military Situation in the Far East*, Part 5, p. 3238.

[7] See p. 88.

support whatever they did. The disappointed Ambassador declared, further, that the only solution lay in the assumption of power by middle-of-the-road liberals in the government and small parties outside it. Marshall had attempted to persuade Chiang to join these center elements and thereby give China stability and reform. But Chiang, though a dictator, was actually in the grip of powerful reactionaries who opposed a land reform, fiscal reform, and all other changes that might have saved China from Communism.

The Nationalists, General Wedemeyer reported to President Truman after his 1947 mission to China, "must effect immediately far-reaching political and economic reforms." "Promises," he wrote, "will no longer suffice, and performance is absolutely necessary." The Chinese Communists were not "agrarian reformers," but without agrarian reform Chiang could not win. It was up to the Chinese Nationalists. Nobody from the outside could save them from the Reds if they remained black reactionaries. Only Chinese could "lose" China.

It followed that Marshall would not blame himself for his failure. Nor did he blame the Communists only. To be sure, he no longer harbored the naïve thought that the Communists would compromise on a coalition; they aspired to undivided power. But he felt that both sides were bad.

In this still trusting yet somewhat chastened and suspicious mood Marshall, now Secretary of State, went to the Moscow foreign ministers' conference (March 10–April 24, 1947). There, as one of the General's colleagues in the U.S. delegation said to me years later, "Marshall learned the facts of life." The proceedings were frustrating. "Marshall was new," a second member of the U.S. delegation said shortly after the event. "He had been catapulted into the situation straight from China. He scarcely spoke at the conference the first fortnight. After that he handled himself so well he had Molotov stammering. You know, when Molotov's in trouble his old stammering trouble returns." Nevertheless, some in the U.S. delegation, and perhaps the Secretary himself, believed, or hoped, that the Soviet government's economic difficulties would make it eager for foreign economic aid and therefore more conciliatory.

Marshall's worst experience in Moscow was his interview with Stalin. It lasted only forty minutes (including translation). The Secretary of State did almost all the talking. He listed the American grievances: pledges forgotten, agreements broken, complaints unanswered, letters unanswered. At one point, Stalin interrupted to exclaim, almost derisively, "Don't take these matters so seriously." In his most revealing remark, the dictator said, "Well, after diplomats exhaust themselves in dispute they are ready to compromise." The non-Soviet negotiators would presumably succumb to exhaustion first.

The Stalin-Marshall meeting and the Moscow conference resulted in nothing constructive. Meanwhile, the European economic situation continued to deteriorate. Assistant Secretary of State William L. Clayton, having studied conditions in Europe, reported that the villages were not feeding the cities adequately. Hunger was in prospect. European recovery, General Marshall told the nation on April 28, after his return from Moscow, could not await "compromise through exhaustion." America would have to take the initiative despite Stalin's unco-operative attitude. This was all the more necessary because, what with the growing impression of an intransigent Russia preparing for war, even highly intelligent and highly placed Americans were beginning to weigh the wisdom of preventive war with atomic bombs. But a war to prevent a third world war would be the Third World War, and Marshall had reached the conclusion that, "The only way human beings can win a war is to prevent it."

Out of this thinking and out of Marshall's Moscow experience the Marshall Plan was born. Its basic idea had been under discussion in the Administration. Under Secretary of State Acheson outlined it in a speech in Cleveland, Mississippi, on May 8, 1947. He was substituting for President Truman who could not attend, and had gone over what he would say with the President. His address called attention to Europe's dollar deficit, the need of achieving "a coordinated European economy," and, finally, the urgency of Congressional decisions to extend certain executive powers (to export commodities) which were due to expire on June 30.

The Marshall Plan actually came to life in General Marshall's pronouncement at Harvard University on June 5, 1947. "Our policy," he asserted—the sentence was drafted by Charles E. Bohlen—"is not directed against any country or doctrine but against hunger, desperation and chaos." America proposed to help the nations of Europe in their economic rehabilitation. But, General Marshall added—and the following was written by George F. Kennan—"it would be neither fitting nor efficacious for this government to draw up unilaterally a program designed to place Europe on its feet economically. This is the business of Europeans. The initiative must come from Europe. . . . The program should be a joint one, agreed to by a number, if not all, European nations."

These simple phrases inaugurated one of the greatest acts of statesmanship in American history. Indeed, seldom in history has a nation, vaguely sensing its own remote interests and the world's urgent needs, behaved with such maturity and generosity.

CHAPTER NINE

The Death of Jan Masaryk

THROUGH the Marshall Plan, America undertook, for selfish and for larger reasons, to prevent world bankruptcy and world war. The Plan was not directed against Communism. A week after he sketched the Plan at Harvard University on June 5, 1947, Secretary Marshall stated explicitly that Russia would be included in it. During the Senate committee hearings on the dismissal of General MacArthur in May, 1951, Marshall again declared that America had intended to include Russia and her satellites in the Marshall Plan.[1]

It has been contended that if the Communist governments had joined the Marshall Plan, the U.S. Congress would have refused to appropriate the money. Then Moscow might have wrecked before birth the Plan which it fought so bitterly in subsequent years. The probability, however, is that Congress would have provided the funds. Between November, 1943, and March, 1948, the United Nations Relief and Rehabilitation Administration (UNRRA) spent

[1] *Military Situation in the Far East*, Part 1, p. 664.

$2,903,412,000, of which the United States contributed $2,648,989,
000. With direct U.S. approval, $1,434,000,000 of this sum was
disbursed in the Soviet Union and its satellites.[2] Under Truman and
Marshall leadership, America would very likely have taken the same
broad view, for the European gulf was then not yet so wide as to
deter the political engineers from trying to build an economic bridge
over it.

The Soviet Union and all the satellites were actually invited to
the preliminary Marshall Plan meeting convened in Paris by England
and France. Czechoslovakia accepted. But Stalin personally ordered
Czechoslovak Foreign Minister Jan Masaryk not to go. Only Molotov
went to Paris. He went with a gigantic delegation and said No.

Observers wondered why the Soviet Foreign Minister should have
required the support of ninety-one assistants to utter a monosyllabic
negative. The key to the puzzle was to be found in the authoritative
Moscow *Pravda* of June 12, 1947, which, commenting on Marshall's
speech at Harvard just a week earlier, wrote,

There is no doubt that for the rapid and successful fulfillment of the
plans for the development of industry and agriculture in Poland, Yugoslavia, Czechoslovakia, Rumania, Bulgaria, Hungary, and other countries,
foreign credits are required. . . . However, when it is a matter of receiving American credits, it is quite natural that the East European
governments prefer to deal directly with the creditors and not with
intermediaries, such as the British and French governments strive to be.

To make this doubly clear, Molotov stated at Paris that the
European governments should limit themselves to making available
to the United States "applications for the American aid required."
In other words, the Communists would take American money, but
they did not want Europe organized, they did not want a Marshall
Plan organization.

Molotov's many aides came to Paris carrying brief cases bulging
with bids for American dollars. But they flew home without opening
them because the Kremlin was averse to the kind of European
economic co-operation which the preliminary Marshall Plan conference was studying.

Moscow had adequate reasons. Under the Marshall Plan, Moscow

[2] UNRRA, *The History of the United Nations Relief and Rehabilitation Administration,* Prepared by a Special Staff under the Direction of George Wood-
bridge, Chief Historian of UNRRA, in Three Volumes, New York: Columbia
University Press, 1950, Vol. 3, p. 428.

would have had to publish statistics on Soviet economic life, which it had not done since 1935. Marshall Plan offices would have been set up in Russia and in the satellites. Information would have been exchanged. Satellite representatives would have traveled to Western Europe and America for conferences. Friendship might have developed.

But Russia was worried about her satellites. The process of integration and subjugation had gone far but was not yet complete. Before the Second World War, the economy of all of Eastern Europe depended on trade with the West, not with the Soviet Union. After 1945, Russia sought to correct this in her favor. But the ties were still thin and might easily have been rent by Marshall Plan arrangements. Thus the Plan, had it embraced the Soviet Union and its satellites as originally intended, would indeed have constituted a threat to the new Soviet empire, and it speaks for the clear-sightedness of Stalin that he immediately saw the danger and took steps to ward it off. The first known move was a conference near Warsaw in September, 1947, to launch the Cominform.

The meeting was directed by no less a figure than Andrei A. Zhdanov, then a member of the Russian Politburo and often mentioned as Stalin's heir. Georgi Malenkov also attended. Present were delegates from the Communist parties of the Soviet Union, of the six satellites (Poland, Czechoslovakia, Hungary, Bulgaria, Yugoslavia, and Rumania), and of France and Italy. The last two were presumably added because their countries were then regarded as candidates for the satellite honor. Little Albania seems to have been overlooked or omitted as unimportant.

At the meeting Zhdanov delivered an address which filled two whole pages of the Moscow *Pravda* of October 22, 1947. "The U.S.S.R.," he promised, "will exert every effort to prevent the Marshall Plan from being realized." America, he declared, aimed to "restore the power of imperialism in the countries of the new democracies and compel them to repudiate close economic and political collaboration with the Soviet Union." Whether or not Zhdanov understood America's purpose, he certainly knew Moscow's fear: that by bringing the "new democracies" of Eastern Europe into an international economic unit which might help them solve their problems instead of exploiting them for the greater good of Russia their Soviet fetters would be loosened. The Cominform tightened them.

In rejecting the Marshall Plan and interposing the Cominform,

Moscow was fighting for its empire. Stalin was pursuing his policy of isolationism.

There had never been any doubt that Moscow regarded all the satellites as permanent Russian colonies. But Stalin was the genius of installment-plan politics. In the Soviet Union and in the empire he crushed opponents and independents slowly, in stages, over a period, in some cases, of years.

In each of the seven satellites and in Russian-occupied Eastern Germany and Austria, the Soviet secret NKVD arrived with the advancing Red army and, working through native Communists, established a network of espionage, terror, and administration. All governments were, in the beginning, coalitions of Communists with non-Communists, but everywhere the Kremlin insisted at least on a Communist as Minister of Interior; he controlled the political police, the instrument of compulsion.

After that, the fulfillment of the Stalinist installment plan of complete subjugation was determined by the degree of resistance to Communism and the dangers from the West. Almost always it followed the same pattern. In Rumania, for instance, Stalin sensed danger in March, 1945, when the Allied armies began moving east through Germany toward the Balkans; his suspicious mind, always judging others by himself, feared they might penetrate into areas he had reserved for himself. The Rumanian government seemed undependable. Soviet Deputy Foreign Minister Vishinsky accordingly flew down from Moscow, called on King Michael, and, eyes on his wrist watch, told the young monarch to sanction the formation of a new Cabinet or abdicate. The King yielded, and the more amenable Petrua Groza succeeded General Radescu as Prime Minister. For his pain, Michael, who not so long before had been fighting on the side of Hitler, received the Order of Victory from Moscow.

The Communists took additional places in the new government. Still, the large anti-Communist National Peasant party continued to function and Juliu Maniu, its leader, remained the most influential Rumanian politician. During 1946, the Communists worked at two tasks: undermining the prestige of the King and terrorizing the population. In June, 1947, Maniu was arrested and the Peasant party banned. Rumania thereupon became a "People's Democracy." At the end of 1947, Michael, under Moscow pressure, gave up his throne. Satellization was now a fact; in effect, Rumania had become a province of the Soviet Union.

In Hungary everything was different—except the results. Despite
numerous arrests and shootings of village and urban anti-Communists,
the national elections of 1945 gave the party of Small Holders, or
peasants, 57 per cent of the votes, while the Communists, who had
already swallowed the Social Democrats, received only 17 per cent.
Arpad Ssakatis, a pro-Communist politician, however, warned the
Small Holders party "to abandon arithmetic illusions."[3] It was an
arithmetic illusion to assume that fifty-seven is more than seventeen.
In totalitarian mathematics, one is more than a hundred million,
and seventeen, therefore, is obviously more than fifty-seven if the
dictator so decrees. In fact, according to the same "science," seventeen
would soon become one and fifty-seven would become zero. The
seventeen party, accordingly, ordered a purge of the fifty-seven party.
A fraction of the latter, led by Parliamentary Deputy Sulyok, was expelled together with twenty-one other members of Parliament who
formed a new party. But when Sulyok made a speech in July, 1946,
in favor of a United States of Europe, the new party was suppressed.[4]

The Hungarian Communists, abetted by the Russian authorities
in Budapest, continued to split the Small Holders party, force the
resignation of that party's ministers in the government, and foment
unrest. The Communist organization, which had become the refuge
of many Fascists, engaged in anti-Semitic outrages but blamed them
on the Small Holders party. All the while, Minister of Interior Rajk,
a Communist (later executed by the Communists), actually dictated
to the non-Communist Prime Minister.

The climax came when Soviet policemen seized Bela Kovacs, the
general secretary of the Small Holders party, on February 26, 1947,
and accused him of espionage.[5] He disappeared. Small Holders ready
to co-operate with the Communists became Cabinet ministers.
Cabinet ministers who were anti-Communists were arrested or fled
abroad. The Prime Minister himself, a Small Holders member, was
forced to resign while on vacation in Switzerland. To eliminate anyone from office, the Minister of Interior simply implicated him in a
"conspiracy."

Not unnaturally, the Communist showing in subsequent elections

[3] *New York Times*, January 18, 1947.
[4] Hugh Seton-Watson, *The East European Revolution*, New York: F. A.
Praeger, 1951, p. 195.
[5] *Ibid.*, p. 198.

improved, especially since the franchise was denied to relatives of arrested persons while arrests multiplied. In this heat, the opposition melted away or fused with the Communists into a "people's bloc." Ultimately, an election took place without opposition candidates. Ever since this triumph of freedom, Hungary too has been a "People's Democracy" closely linked with the other chained members of the Soviet system in which all cast their ballots for the one who, at the moment, controls the bullets. A more appropriate name, therefore, would be "Pistol Democracy."

By such spaced hammer blows, the Communists of Hungary, Rumania, Yugoslavia, Albania, Poland, and Bulgaria had seized all commanding positions when Secretary Marshall broached his historic Plan at Harvard University on June 5, 1947.

Alone Czechoslovakia retained a semblance of independence. Unlike the other satellites, Czechoslovakia in the 1930's had been friendly to Moscow; Prime Minister Dr. Eduard Beneš sought Russian protection against Germany. After the Second World War, Beneš became President of the Republic. He and Foreign Minister Jan Masaryk enjoyed tremendous reputations in Western countries. Czechoslovakia's trade flowed to the West. Her traditions were democratic. Industrially she was advanced, economically she was strong. All these factors saved Czechoslovakia from abrupt satellization. Stalin did not wish to upset a well-balanced apple cart. Too little would be gained.

Next to Marshal Tito's Communists in Yugoslavia, the Czechoslovak Communist party was the best organized and the most firmly grounded. A Communist, Klement Gottwald, was Prime Minister; Communists also headed the Ministry of Agriculture which distributed former German lands to peasants, the Ministry of Information, the Ministry of Finance, and, of course, the Ministry of Interior. The Communists likewise exercised considerable influence in the army's General Staff. Czechoslovakia would have been easy to satellize. Therefore Stalin did not do it. Some civil liberties survived, and the Communists in power acted less ruthlessly than in the other Russian colonies.

Nationalism was strong, even among the Communists, and Beneš and Masaryk were its popular symbols. Not wishing to lose them or antagonize them prematurely, Moscow acted with patience. Stalin's forbearance must have been due not only to the pro-Russian sentiments of many Czechoslovaks but also, perhaps chiefly, to his certainty that, as Masaryk said to me in Paris, Czechoslovakia could not escape; she had no alternative to a Russian orientation. America was not present.

Suddenly, America loomed on the horizon; the Marshall Plan appeared. Stalin's brutal order which forced the Czechoslovak government to revoke its own decision and abstain from participation in the Plan was an offense to national pride and a proof of national slavery. Of course, Stalin had no choice; he could not permit a satellite to shed its chains. But Czechoslovaks were shocked. Many of them had voted Communist under the illusion that they could remain free though linked with the Soviet Union. Now, anti-Communist opposition stiffened.

Moscow, accordingly, resorted to the bulldozer tactics employed in the other puppet countries. The Communists decided to achieve a parliamentary majority.

Such is the power of real democracy without quotes, that even dictators pay respect to it in the abstract while flattening it under their steam rollers. Though they obtain their majorities by arm-twisting politics, chicanery, and misrepresentation, they nevertheless want them, and the bigger the better; a 99.7 per cent majority, as in the Soviet Union, is best. Such a vote is obviously faked and forced; all the people never agree on anything anywhere. Moreover, if 99.7 per cent of the voters support the government why have a dictatorship? Nevertheless, totalitarians seek a formal popular majority which is as near as possible to unanimity. Partly this is a means of fooling some innocents at home and more innocents abroad. Partly it indicates that opposition is vain. Partly it satisfies the strange desire of dictatorships for legitimacy. Hitler too craved legitimacy for his regime in Germany and his aggressions outside.

In Czechoslovakia, in addition, the Communists wanted a formal parliamentary majority because then President Beneš would have to approve the government based on it, and his approval would create a link with Czechoslovakia's past. The Reds could then cloak themselves in the useful garment of nationalism. Beneš, long ill, had been living far from the capital in a small town. His strongest wish was to avoid civil strife and preserve the unity of the country. The Communists played on this and tried to demonstrate that the only alternative to a Communist government was national disaster.

Elections were scheduled for the summer of 1948. In preparation the Communist Minister of Interior began purging the police of non-Communists and filling it with Reds. The Cabinet ordered him to stop. He refused. Thereupon the opposition members of the Cabinet, including representatives of Beneš' own party, the National Socialists, and of the Social Democrats, resigned.

The next day, February 22, 1948, Communist gangs marched through the streets of Prague and of provincial towns, took control of government offices, beat up citizens who refused to join them in demonstrating, and formed local committees which were, in effect, soviets ready to supplant the government.

Beneš was isolated and powerless. Under the threat of a violent Communist coup, he sanctioned the formation of a Communist-dominated Cabinet. That day, February 25, 1948, Czechoslovakia's freedom and independence died.

The new government included Communists and Communist stooges in all important posts. But because of his name and prestige, Jan Masaryk was retained as Foreign Minister. There is no precise information on what terms. The only known fact is that exactly two weeks after the formation of the new government, the press and radio, now tools of the Reds, announced that Jan Masaryk's dead body had been found on the pavement of the Foreign Ministry courtyard. He had jumped from his window, the bulletin said, and killed himself.

As long as men recall the shame of Czechoslovakia's seizure by the Communists, they will continue to wonder whether Masaryk's end on March 10, 1948, was suicide or murder. If the Communists pushed him out the window they obviously would not admit it. But it is possible that he did indeed jump. If the Communists had appointed him Foreign Minister against his wish and then prevented him from protesting as well as from carrying out his duties, or if they had held him prisoner in his rooms so that he could not leave the country, as he said he would when civil liberties were destroyed, a jump to the courtyard below his window was the only free act left to him. In that case, they murdered him. Hand a person a pistol and tell him that unless he shoots himself he will be shot, and it is murder though he pulls the trigger. Masaryk was trapped, and without freedom he was dead or, what was worse, a slave serving the Communists he hated. In such circumstances the Communists pushed him out of the window even though his own muscles and brain may have made the jump.

President Beneš, broken, resigned on June 6, and died on September 6, 1948. Czechoslovakia had been solidly soldered to the Russian empire.

CHAPTER TEN

Tito Passes

I N JUNE, 1948, when Moscow had tucked all the seven little satellites under the coarse blanket of Soviet rule, one—Yugoslavia—slipped out, and then there were six. Though the Communists of Yugoslavia were better entrenched than their comrades in any other Muscovite colony they suddenly found themselves outside the fold. Thereafter, Tito moved by stages toward collaboration with the anti-Soviet West. Nothing since November, 1917, has shed a brighter light on the nature of the world Communist movement. Nothing since 1945 is more revealing of the character of the present international struggle.

In 1952 I spent five weeks in Yugoslavia and talked with Tito and four members of his Politburo. I revisited the country in December, 1953. Both times I asked many questions about the 1948 rupture between Communist Russia and Communist Yugoslavia. The answers I received can be summarized in a sentence: Yugoslavia did not wish to be a Russian colony. During long centuries, the peoples of the present Yugoslavia resisted Turkish, Austro-Hungarian, and German imperialism. In fact, they had fought foreign domination ever since, as Illyria, they came under the Roman heel. They had no desire, now, to be incorporated into the Russian empire.

When Yugoslavia nationalism and Soviet imperialism met they

clashed, split, and stayed apart. The Communism that presumably united Russia and Yugoslavia was far weaker than the colonialism which separated them.

Proponents and naïve opponents have often described world Communism as the wave of the future, the new conquering idea. Yugoslavia was Communist; the idea had conquered. But the Moscow masters, who are dialectical materialists, put no trust in ideas. They never feel they have conquered until arms and terror give them power over life, death, property, and profits.

Communism has ceased to be a faith; it is the idolatry of organization. Lenin and Stalin made the party a fetish. Later Stalin's purges ruined the party; he then deified the government, or state. Always the goal was centralized power, ruthless, abusive.

The seven satellites, accordingly, were expected to obey and honor Moscow, Tito, the Communist, dissented.

"It is not true," Marshal Tito said to me in June, 1952, "that the June, 1948, rupture was due to differences of theory." It was due, he said, to "economic exploitation, attempts to take over everything, to control everything, in a word, directly to subordinate Yugoslavia so that we appeared to be independent but actually became a completely dependent colony."

"Nevertheless," I said to Marshal Tito, "you did not break with the Cominform. You waited till it expelled you."

"We had no intentions of breaking off relations," Tito retorted.

It follows that Yugoslavia would have stayed in the fold had Stalin not pushed it out. This altered the world balance of forces to Moscow's disadvantage. Russia lost a valuable satellite occupying a strategic position; the West won a friend.

Yugoslav leaders told me they thought the June, 1948, expulsion was intended as an act of intimidation to be followed quickly by Marshal Tito's appearance on his knees at a Red Canossa begging forgiveness for having talked back when Moscow began slipping the chains of imperial enslavement on Yugoslavia. Mosha Piyade, a member of the Yugoslav Politburo and old comrade of Tito's, said to me in Belgrade, "Stalin trusted in his authority and refused to believe that we could unite the country while defying him." Milovan Djilas, another member of the Politburo, said, "Stalin imagined his spies and supporters here would make us fall apart."

But this plausible hypothesis of Piyade and Djilas raised a second question, which I posed to Tito: Why, having seen after several months that the Tito regime remained standing and defiant, did not Stalin send the Red army into Yugoslavia to subdue the recalcitrants?

"Why Stalin did not invade Yugoslavia?" Tito repeated slowly. "It would have been another Finland with who knows what results for Russia. Stalin does not enter upon adventures lightly. He is a cautious person. The Soviet workers would not have understood."

Stalin did not strike at Yugoslavia in 1948 because he probably remembered that what commenced in September, 1939, as a limited operation to destroy Poland subsequently engulfed the planet and destroyed the destroyers. Stalin knew that the first Balkan War of 1912 inseminated the second Balkan War of 1913 which contained the germ of the First World War. Just so, a Soviet war on Yugoslavia, immediately successful though it would be—for America and England would have found it difficult to rush to the side of a Communist country fresh from Stalin's embrace—might produce a disastrous though delayed chain reaction. The other satellites were restive because of Titoist nationalism; inside Russia necessary postwar reconstruction and urgent problems of postwar morale curbed Stalin's punitive appetites. The Soviets, moreover, did not yet have the atomic bomb and were planning a major industrial effort to get it. These considerations, not Communism, saved Communist Yugoslavia from Communist Russia's vindictiveness. Communism had become little more than a name, a liturgy, and a religion canned for export to the dark continents of capitalism and therefore could not unite that which nationalism and the problems of power and organization sundered.

Nor did Communism divide ideologically divergent nations whose self-interest required co-operation. Witness the aid which America and England gave Russia between 1941 and 1945. The Soviet Union was then as Communistic and dictatorial as ever, but the Western democracies overlooked this giant fact and supported the totalitarian despotism which ruled from the Kremlin because another, led by Hitler, menaced their national existence.

This suggests that nationalism shapes policy while ideology and isms cloak it.

The Marshall Plan was another lend-lease, hands-across-the-ideologies concept. Moscow accepted wartime lend-lease for the sake of Russia's national salvation, and rejected the Marshall Plan for equally nationalistic reasons, reasons of empire. It feared that the colonies, especially Czechoslovakia and Yugoslavia, would be weaned from Mother Russia.

Moscow had been having trouble with Tito long before 1947. The friction dated almost from the moment Tito began to exercise even limited sovereignty on the territory of his country. In November, 1943, for instance, while the Yugoslav Communists were still fighting in the mountains against domestic anti-Communists and the Germans, they convened a meeting at Jajce, in Bosnia, where they proclaimed themselves the government and declared that Peter, the young exiled King of Yugoslavia, would not be allowed to return. On hearing of this development, Stalin sent a message to Tito saying he was "extremely angry" and considered the move "a stab in the back of the Soviet Union."[1] The Yugoslavs were baffled and horrified and did not accept Moscow's excuse that Stalin's anger was due to his fear of losing Anglo-American military support if Tito liquidated the monarchy.

During the Second World War, Tito received more assistance from the Western capitalist nations than from the Soviet Union. The Kremlin, however, gave so much advice that Tito, enraged, once dispatched a telegram to the Soviets which began, "If you cannot send us assistance, then at least do not hamper us."[2]

In September, 1944, Tito left the battlefield to confer with Stalin in Russia. Of this confrontation, Tito wrote,[3] "We were more or less at cross purposes on all the matters we discussed. I noticed then that Stalin could not bear being contradicted." Stalin urged Tito to let King Peter return. Tito objected. "You need not restore him forever," Stalin counseled. "Take him back temporarily, and then you can slip a knife into his back at a suitable moment."

With peace came Russian economic penetration of Yugoslavia. The Soviet government asked for and received a monopoly hold on Yugoslav civilian air transport and river shipping. Moscow promised Tito goods on credit to the value of $135 million. It sent $800 thousands' worth. Belgrade paid at an exhorbitant rate for Soviet technical aid. The Soviet Union made use of this aid "to develop its intelligence and similar services . . . the Soviet Union intended to subjugate Yugoslavia economically, to turn it into a raw-material appendage

[1] Dedijer, *Tito*, p. 209.
[2] *Ibid.*, p. 232.
[3] *Ibid.*

of Soviet economy, to prevent Yugoslavia's industrialization and to delay the further socialist development of our country."[4] How quickly Soviet imperialism slipped into the classic pattern of all imperialisms! "It came as a surprise to many Communists in Yugoslavia and in other East European countries when after the war they saw that the relations between their countries and the Soviet Union were based on purely capitalist principles."[5] The surprise, which political sobriety might have spared them, quickly turned to chagrin and, in Yugoslavia, to insubordination.

A poor country without alternative sources of credit, Yugoslavia would have submitted if the trouble had been restricted to economic relations. The rupture followed difficulties in the area of international politics. "One thing especially was a thorn in the flesh of Soviet leaders," Tito wrote subsequently,[6] "and that was our attempt to establish good-neighbor relations with the surrounding peoples in the Balkans, the Bulgarians, Albanians, Hungarians, Rumanians."

Russia opposed not only collaboration with non-Communist Europe through the Marshall Plan, and not only the unification of non-Soviet Europe for economic and military purposes, it opposed, and opposes, any intimacy among the satellites not channeled and controlled by Moscow. The only form of internationalism acceptable to the Soviet Union is that which binds the maximum number of nations to Russia.

In January, 1948, Georgi Dimitrov, top Communist of Bulgaria and former head of the Comintern, advocated a federation or confederation to include "Rumania, Bulgaria, Yugoslavia, Albania, Czechoslovakia, Poland, Hungary, and Greece; mind you, and Greece!" His emphasis on Greece was loud but the omission of Russia was even louder. The Moscow *Pravda* of January 29, 1948, reported Dimitrov's statement and appended a ferocious attack on the venerable Communist leader. "The editors of the *Pravda*," it read, "consider that these countries require no questionable and fabricated federation or confederation, or a customs union."

The Kremlin then sent a telegraphic summons to the leaders of the Yugoslav and Bulgarian governments to appear in Moscow forthwith. Tito preferred to stay home. Yugoslavia was represented by Edvard Kardelj, Number Two leader, and by Milovan Djilas and

[4] *Ibid.*, p. 289.
[5] *Ibid.*, p. 300.
[6] *Ibid.*, pp. 299-300.

Stjepan Bakarich: Bulgaria by Dimitrov, Vassil Kolarov, Number Two Bulgarian Communist, and Traicho Kostov, Number Three. These six met with Stalin, Molotov, Zhdanov, Malenkov, Souslov, and Zorin on the morning of February 10, 1948, twelve days before the Communist coup in Czechoslovakia.

Molotov opened the discussion by saying that the serious differences which had arisen between Russia on the one hand and Yugoslavia and Bulgaria on the other were "inadmissible." Throughout Molotov's remarks "Stalin was glowering and ceaselessly doodling in his notebook."[7]

Dimitrov replied and apologized for his advocacy of a Balkan federation. "You wanted to shine with new words," Stalin interrupted. "That's all wrong, because such a federation is an impossibility."

Dimitrov tried to conciliate humbly. "There is no essential difference between the foreign policy of Bulgaria and that of the Soviet Union," he said.

"There are huge differences," Stalin disagreed.

Repeatedly Stalin rudely insulted Dimitrov ("You've plunged like a Komsomol youth"; "You bandy words about like women in the streets"), and treated the other foreigners with natural discourtesy. At one point, Kardelj contended that customs unions sometimes yield good results. Stalin demanded an example. Kardelj named Benelux.

"Benelux, that's nothing," Stalin asserted angrily.

"There is Belgium, there is Luxembourg," Kardelj began.

"And nobody else," Stalin interrupted.

"There's the Netherlands," Kardelj finished.

"No," shouted Stalin.

"Yes," Kardelj insisted, "the Netherlands are in. Look at the name Benelux. It means *Bel*gium, *Ne*therlands, and *Lux*embourg."

"When I say 'No' it means no," Stalin decreed.

Kardelj held his tongue.

At midnight of the next day, Kardelj was ordered to appear in Molotov's office at the Foreign Ministry. The moment he entered Molotov handed him two sheets of paper, one a copy of the other, and said, "Sign this." The document provided for Yugoslav consultation with Moscow before making any move in foreign affairs. "I was boiling with rage," Kardelj writes. "I was thinking what to do,

---

[7] *Ibid.*, p. 315 *et seq.* The author of Tito's authorized biography reports this meeting on the basis of the notes and oral descriptions of the Yugoslav participants.

whether to sign or not. At last, I decided to affix my signature. I did this so that I would not complicate the situation which was already very tense."

After these demonstrations of the fraternal affection among world Communist leaders and of Russia's love for her chained children, Moscow exerted pressure to break Yugoslav's back. The Soviet government refused to negotiate a new trade agreement, thus cutting off Yugoslavia's supply of cotton for her textile industry and oil for her transport and factories. On March 18, Moscow informed Belgrade that it was withdrawing its military advisers and instructors from Yugoslavia; the next day it ordered all Russian industrial experts to leave.

In the latter half of June, 1948, a special Cominform session was convened in Bucharest. The Yugoslavs were invited. Stalin apparently expected Tito to appear, apologize, prostrate himself, and submit. But the Yugoslav Communist party refused to attend. The session accordingly expelled the Yugoslavs, after which Russia and the six remaining satellites put Yugoslavia under a diplomatic and economic blockade. The world Communist movement stood exposed as an instrument of Soviet imperialism.

Tito's defiance was Stalin's biggest defeat. And it has been a disaster to Moscow's pretensions as a champion of aspiring nationalism. The Soviets champion nationalism when that inconveniences an enemy. For their own aggrandizement they suppress nationalism. They suppress Communism. What Moscow cannot control it seeks to destroy.

Thus, Yugoslavia's defection in 1948 showed that the menace was Soviet imperialism which had to be checked in the interest of peace, national independence, and freedom.

CHAPTER ELEVEN

The Air Bridge

FOLLOWING Yugoslavia's defection from the Soviet orbit in June, 1948, Moscow had to make sure it would not lose another colony. Many East European Communists were accordingly accused of "Titoism," a strange disease, first diagnosed by Moscow medicos, which impels individuals to prefer their own country to a foreign conquerer. Such "nationalists" were replaced by Moscow-trained stooges whose careers, in turn, also came to an end with a bullet in the back of the neck or a one-way ticket to Siberia. The object of this repeated process of unnatural selection was the breeding of a species of political animals who crawl on their bellies in Moscow and try to look like men at home. Meanwhile, the Kremlin cattle-raisers, aided, no doubt, by the anti-Mendelian geneticist Lysenko, concentrated on the quick evolution of a four-legged, long-necked, small-brained beast which grazed in the satellite colony but was milked in Moscow.

Stalin, however, could not have been satisfied with this alone. In politics, he followed military rules, and he apparently felt the need of covering the defeat in Yugoslavia with an offensive elsewhere. Within a week of Tito's expulsion from the Cominform, the Moscow mastermind from whom all actions flowed imposed a complete blockade on Berlin. Somehow the prestige lost in Belgrade had to be retrieved.

On July 3, eight days after the Soviet military authorities ordered the city of Berlin sealed off from all contact with the West, I flew nonstop across the Atlantic to Frankfurt on the Main. There and in near-by Munich it was immediately obvious that the stakes at Berlin were high. Nobody quite knew how high, and nobody knew what were the Soviet government's ultimate intentions. Was the blockade the prelude to World War III?

Years later, when he could judge past events in perspective, I asked General Lucius D. Clay, who was U.S. military governor in Germany at the time of the Berlin blockade, what, in his opinion, was Moscow's aim. He discerned three alternative objectives, rising from minimum to maximum: to get the Western powers out of Berlin; to win all of Germany; to get the United States out of Europe.

The Berlin blockade was a major Moscow bid—the last—to take over Europe. The blockade, and the Anglo-American airlift which frustrated it, thus constitute the most decisive chapter in the postwar struggle for Europe. After that, the center of the cold-hot war for world supremacy shifted to Asia.

A crisis had been building up in Europe for exactly a year. Moscow's rejection of the Marshall Plan was a necessary measure of imperial protection, but it meant that Europe would be divided, and if Europe was divided Germany would be divided between East and West and Russia would thereby lose the rare historic opportunity afforded by the war and its aftermath of dominating all Germany.

To Moscow control of Germany was synonymous with hegemony over Europe. Many leading Bolsheviks of the Lenin period spoke German, had lived in Germany as exiles, had fed on German Socialist classics written by Marx, Engels, Kautsky, Bebel, and others, and had learned to respect German industry, military prowess, and power. The geopolitical Russian mind thinks of Germany as the European heartland, the hub, motor, body, and brain of the Continent. The Kremlin's highest postwar hope was to dominate Germany, in whole preferably or in part.

As long as Germany was industrially derelict and kept so by Western policy decisions which, in some cases, were Communist-inspired, Moscovite aspirations to win Germany were not completely fantastic. Hunger, joblessness, and hopelessness are mighty agents of subversion. But after Russia had excluded herself and her satellites from the Marshall Plan, the United States conferred with Great Britain, in July, 1947, on measures to raise German coal output, and in the same month, the U.S. State, War, and Navy Departments drew up a new directive to General Clay to stimulate German industrial output generally. On neither matter was Moscow consulted. London and Washington were also merging their German zones into Bizonia, the beginning of a federal German state.

Stalin saw Western Germany moving out of reach. He counterattacked energetically. Strikes broke out in the Ruhr. The Communist-controlled trade unions became more aggressive. Terror increased. A friend who was an official of the U.S. military government in Germany wrote me on December 30, 1947, "The pressure from the East is getting vicious, especially in Berlin—people disappearing by the dozens." Christian Democratic and Socialist opponents of Russia and of the German Communists were being kidnaped and transported to Siberia.

The February, 1948, Communist coup in Czechoslovakia raised the specter of a similar adventure in neighboring Germany. General Clay, a cold calculator, was apprehensive. "Within the last few weeks," he cabled Washington on March 5, 1948,[1] "I have felt a subtle change in Soviet attitude which I cannot define but which now gives me a feeling that it [war] may come with dramatic suddenness." There is, he added, "a feeling of new tenseness in every Soviet individual with whom we have official relations. I am unable to submit any official report in the absence of supporting data but my feeling is real."

The same sense of peril and uncertainty had invaded a number of West European capitals, and in March, 1948, Great Britain, France, Belgium, Holland, and Luxembourg signed the Brussels Treaty pledging the participants to join in fighting an external attack.

Meanwhile, since the beginning of 1948, democratic elements everywhere had been striving to prevent Italy from voting Communist on April 18 of that year. The effort succeeded. But nobody knew— and everybody wondered—how Moscow would respond to this new setback. Would it reconcile itself to the loss of Europe? Or would it feel that in the still disorganized state of the Continent now was the time, and soon it would be too late, to strike for control?

Observers agreed that, with Italy and Yugoslavia gone and Germany going, Stalin could not remain passive. Western military weakness dictated the guess that Russia's armies would move. My friend in the U.S. military government, on the other hand, said in a letter from Berlin dated April 28, "The situation here doesn't look good, and I cannot see what we can do about it. I think they can get us out of here without getting into a fight." Perhaps Moscow planned a bloodless victory. The Kremlin had already imposed a partial blockade on Western military personnel movements into and out of Berlin.

General Clay declares in his book[2] that the Soviets wanted above

[1] *The Forrestal Diaries*, p. 387.

[2] Lucius D. Clay, *Decision in Germany*, New York: Doubleday & Company, 1950.

all to prevent the rise of a three-zone federal state closed to Russian influence. Already, Bizonia functioned well and the French zone co-operated with it. The West was consolidating its position in Germany. For a year, industrial production had been on the increase.

One factor was missing: solid money. As long as German economy remained based on the cigarette, Germans would not work with their usual zest, and chaos and Communism were not precluded. The Soviet government therefore refused to sanction a currency reform which would end inflation. England, France, and America accordingly overrode the Russian veto and introduced a new stable mark in their zones.

The results of the reform were immediately discernible. The American cigarette became a crumpled figure, spurned for a starchier rival, the new crisp mark note (which has been stable from that day to this). Germans, taking courage, found a new faith in work and a new assurance that the Western powers would not abandon them to the Russians.

The June, 1948, German currency reform marks the beginning of the German mid-century economic miracle and its corollary, the integration of West Germany with the West. The June, 1948, defection of Tito subtracted a second vital European area from Russia's grasp. These historic events raised the curtain—the stage had been set by earlier developments—on one of the most dramatic episodes of our dramatic age: The Berlin Airlift.

Berlin, completely surrounded by turbulent Red waters which flooded the great city's high politics and lapped against its homes, washing individuals out to their death in the sea, must have seemed to Stalin like a sitting duck. Clay's premonitions notwithstanding, Russia had no intention of risking all in war. Berlin could be easy prey without war. It was cut off from the American, British, and French zones by Soviet-held German territory. All the Kremlin needed to do was to bar the West from crossing this territory to and from Berlin, and the three Western sectors with their 2,500,000 inhabitants, deprived of food, coal for house heating and industry, raw materials, and markets, would collapse into Moscow's arms. This might introduce bigger events: driven ignominiously from Berlin without firing a shot, the Western powers might decide that all of Germany was now untenable. And who knows what would happen in the train of such a tremendous retreat? Thus Russia might regain everything lost in Yugoslavia, Italy, and Germany.

In these calculations, Stalin forgot one big thing. There is a Russian saying, "He went to the circus but didn't see the elephant." Stalin too, failed to notice the biggest reality of the situation: that this is the air age. He knew much about aviation, he had thousands of airplanes. But knowledge is never enough. Stalin was psychologically earth-bound, because Russia's culture was. Under Soviet leadership the country had made enormous industrial and technological progress. But it was still the land of the peasant's cart, and this major fact affected the cultural bloodstream, shaping thought and influencing political decisions. "If I block all trucks, trains, buses, wagons, cars, and canal barges from entering the Soviet territory which surrounds Berlin," Stalin must have mused, "what is left for them to do but go home?" Even if the possibility of an airlift had occurred to him he would have dismissed it as too fantastic to consider seriously. "How can the food, coal, and raw materials for a city of 2,500,000 be moved by air? And for how long?"

Stalin was guilty of another psychological blunder. At the Yalta Conference in February, 1945, he had asked President Roosevelt how long the United States would keep its army of occupation in Germany after the war. "Two years would be the limit," the President replied. Now it was June, 1948, three years after the end of the war, the two-year limit had expired and the Americans, and the British and French, were still occupying Germany. "Perhaps," Stalin might have thought, "if I give them a prod, they will leave." Nothing was better calculated to keep the Americans in Germany.

At 6 A.M. on June 24, 1948, Russia threw a tight blockade around the three Western sectors of Berlin and cut off their electric current supply which originated in the Russian zone. That same morning, General Clay telephoned from the beleaguered city to Lieutenant General Curtis E. LeMay, air commander at Frankfurt in the American zone, and instructed him to start an airlift. Twenty-four hours later the first C-47 cargo planes arrived with food for the inhabitants of Berlin.

The United States had no more than one hundred of these old planes, each with a capacity of only two and one-half tons, available in Germany. They could never have transported the 4,500 tons of goods which was Berlin's minimum daily requirement. But Clay felt that if he proved an airlift was practical he would get the necessary equipment. He therefore started it, he told me in 1954, without authorization. For twelve days he got no authorization from his superiors in Washington. The U.S. government feared war with Russia. Clay, however, reassured the Army Department. "We do not expect armed conflict," he asserted.

At the end of twelve days the American public was so enthusiastic about the airlift that Clay got his authorization and more planes. In July, he went to Washington, talked with President Truman and Secretary of State Marshall, and was given 160 C-54 planes, each capable of carrying ten tons.

Within a few days these new C-54's began arriving with markings which showed that they had just come from service in Alaska, Hawaii, Panama, and other distant parts. In October, Clay flew to Washington again and received sixty-four more C-54's. The British also increased their contribution. The R.A.F. used C-47's, C-54's, Yorks, Handley Page Hastings, and numerous civilian planes of old and new vintage. The story was told of a Texan pilot in his giant C-54 (Skymaster) approaching Berlin in the general stream of air traffic when he saw a British plane which was unfamiliar. So he called the British control tower on his crackling radio and asked: "What's this coming in now, fella?"

He was told it was a Wayfarer, a British civilian plane.

"Did you say the Mayflower?" the Texan called back. "You guys sure are throwing in everything." They were.

In January and February, 1949, the airlift averaged 5,500 tons a day, or 1,000 tons above Berlin's minimum needs. In the spring, total deliveries rose to a daily average of 8,000 tons, which was equal to the volume carried into the city by land and water before the blockade. On the record-breaking day, nearly 13,000 tons were delivered.

America was gleeful, Europe impressed, Russia stunned. Foreign diplomats in Moscow reported that high Soviet officials raised their eyebrows and heavy-epauletted shoulders when asked about the airlift; they still found difficulty believing it. The same diplomats wondered how they would get out of the Soviet capital when, or if, war broke out.

I once asked General Clay what he would have done if the Russians had shot down one or more airlift planes flying over their German zone. "I had an agreed signal with General LeMay," he replied, "which I was to give him if the Soviets shot down an American plane. Without further orders LeMay would then have bombed every Soviet airfield in Germany."

"You would not have consulted the War Department?" I said.

"It was my duty," he explained, "to act in self-defense."

From time to time, the Soviet authorities announced that they would be engaging in aerial gunnery practice in the corridor which the airlift used. But no incident ever occurred. Occasionally, Soviet fighters buzzed an airlift transport but never fired.

During the blockade-airlift period rumor had it that General Clay wanted to push an armored column from the American zone in West Germany, across the Soviet zone, to Berlin. In 1950, I mentioned the matter to Sir Ivone Kirkpatrick, British High Commissioner in Germany. Yes, he remarked, there had been such a proposal, but Britain was opposed to it on the ground that the Russians would blow up all the bridges in the path of the armored column and it would look ridiculous and never get through. When I later repeated this to General Clay, he said, "My division could build bridges as fast as the Russians could destroy them." But, he added, there was a possibility, though minor, that Soviet troops would bar the way and then the Americans would have to shoot, and since this might mean war he could not do it on his own authority but had to ask Washington for permission—which was refused. He still thinks the division could have marched to Berlin undeterred and broken the blockade.

Clay was equally certain that the airlift would not provoke a war. "I had no fear of physical aggression by Soviet forces," he declared. So, month after month, the planes droned on. Radar was installed, runways lengthened, new runways built, new airfields constructed. The planes flew day and night, through rain and storm and sleet in all kinds of autumn and winter weather when visibility was nil and landings had to be made by instrument. At the peak of the airlift activity a plane was arriving or departing every thirty seconds. Bumper to bumper, or nose to tail, they flew. The stream of airlift machines was so steady that Germans called it *Die Luftbruecke*, "the air bridge." Berlin slept soundly under the thunder of the four-motor mammoths. The citizens would have suffered from insomnia only if the noise of the planes had stopped.

For the crews aloft and on the ground, and for the entire airlift personnel it was a grueling, unceasing, tense job. The distances were: Frankfurt to Berlin, 268 miles; Hamburg to Berlin, 164 miles; Düsseldorf to Berlin, 300 miles; and so forth. Planes often made more than one trip a day. The men gave up week ends and holidays whenever necessary. Everybody realized that they were not just carrying sacks of flour and bags of coal; they were writing history, they were deciding the fate of a country, perhaps of a continent. Berlin named a square after the airlift and erected a plaque to the Americans and Englishmen who lost their lives serving in it.

The bravery, devotion, and perseverance of the men of the airlift notwithstanding, the real heroes of the 1948-49 Battle of Berlin were the Berliners themselves. Early in the airlift, the food ration fell far below normal and citizens experienced serious want. Gradually, the daily ration doled out to individuals rose to slightly above preairlift times, but it always remained meager, and unrationed foods, previously brought in from the Soviet zone, were now unobtainable. Nobody starved but everybody was always hungry. Since raw materials could hardly be carried to Berlin in ample volume by air, industrial unemployment mounted sharply. The worst hardship was the raw weather of autumn and the cold of winter. Most of the coal delivered by the airlift was consumed by power plants and factories. Some coal went to hospitals, schools, and local "warming centers" where freezing men, women, and children came to thaw out their bodies. Private homes depended on wood for heating, and the supply was limited. The city fathers permitted the cutting down of every other tree along the streets and in suburban parks and woods. Electricity was available for two hours, or even less, per day. Those two hours shaped the twenty-four. If the current came on during the afternoon, children did their homework by good light. When it came on in the evening, moving picture houses might show a film. If it came on at 2 A.M., that is when the women flocked to the hairdressers.

The success of the airlift depended in the first instance on the skill, endurance, and organizing talent of the Americans and British, but in the final analysis on the stamina and wish of the Berliners. They always had a veto on the airlift. No foreign generals could have compelled millions of democratic people to suffer; no American, British, and French soldiers could have shot down a populace in revolt against prolonged, gnawing privations. As in besieged Madrid during the Spanish Civil War, so in Berlin it was the civilians who stood in the front line of defense; the military were the auxiliaries. The key to Berlin lay in the hands of its wan, weary, undernourished citizenry and they kept it there. Berliners are quite a special breed of German. In adversity, they are firm, stoic, nonchalant. They see the comic in the tragic, the gold in the gray, and can laugh at themselves. Having known Hitler barbarism and Russian terror, they were ready to pay in flesh, nerves, and pain for their honor and liberty. Tossed on an ice floe in the Red sea, they did not complain, they would not surrender. It was a triumph of spirit over matter, of spirit over force, of the will of man over the man-crushing machine of dictatorship. Berlin was—is—a crown on the brow of democracy and a thorn in the side of the Communists. When a committee of all the democratic parties of West Berlin called an antiblockade protest rally in a square in the British sector a stone's throw from the Soviet boundary line, three hundred adults and youths assembled despite bad weather and inadequate transport, and shouted their defiance of the totalitarians across the road. One of the demonstrators climbed to the top of the near-by Brandenburg Gate in the Soviet sector and pulled down the Red flag. In the municipal elections of December 5, 1948, 86.3 per cent of the eligible electors actually cast their ballots, and Ernst Reuter, an ex-Communist who was now a passionate and wise anti-Communist Social Democrat, became mayor of the surrounded, suffering metropolis. Berlin voted with calm dignity, unruffled by the provocative acts of Red toughs. Berlin was voting for its own freedom and for the freedom of free humanity.

Berliners had a joke about it. One of the staples of their flat diet was powdered potato, in lieu of potatoes, which they called *Pom.* So the people said, *"Lieber Pom als Frau, komm."* ("Rather *Pom* than woman, come.") *"Frau, komm,"* was the command the Russian soldiers gave German women whom they desired. Berlin preferred its privation to Russian domination.

But how long could the airlift go on? Judging by the spirit of Berlin and the mounting traffic efficiency of the bridge of planes, it could go on for years. Moscow saw this. The longer the airlift lasted the more clearly it demonstrated to the world the West's highly developed technique and Russia's helplessness. It displayed Russian weakness and Western strength on an island, the island of Berlin, deep in the Soviet empire. Moscow accordingly lifted the blockade at midnight, May 11, 1949. There were no intermediaries. Direct negotiations between Soviet and Western leaders had taken place from time to time during the blockade but without result. Moscow simply called off the blockade and thus made a frank and undisguised admission of its total failure.

During the 312 days of the blockade, 1,402,644 metric tons (more than three billion pounds) of goods had crossed the air bridge into Berlin.[3] Of this, the British carried almost a third—as well as 67,373 German passengers leaving the city.[4] Altogether, American planes flew 69,257,475 miles; British planes 23,071,377 miles.[4] The whole was a modern miracle.

Berlin, Germany, and Europe remained divided after the airlift. But the lines which divided them were also barriers to the forward march of Bolshevism. In 732, Charles Martel defeated the Moslems at Poitiers and thus kept Islam south of the Pyrenees and out of Western Europe. In 1683, the Turks stood before Vienna and besieged it, but their attempts to capture the city were unsuccessful. That set a limit to the Turkish tide in Europe. Historians may assign similar significance to the ten-and-one-half-month Anglo-American-German resistance at Berlin in 1948-49 and point out that it had the additional virtue of being not an exercise in killing but a manifestation of man's love of liberty and of his fellow man. It gave free Europe another opportunity of discovering the means and faith for survival.

[3] *Ibid.*, p. 391.

[4] *Berlin Air Lift; an Account of the British Contribution,* Prepared by the Air Ministry and The Central Office of Information, Text by Dudley Barker, London: His Majesty's Stationery Office, 1949.

Part Three
THE PROBLEM OF ASIA

CHAPTER TWELVE

Gandhi and the Western World

FTER four weeks in Germany, I took the train from Munich to Rome. In Kufstein, in the French zone of Austria, the train stopped for an hour and I walked into town across an iron bridge built over the rushing river in 1896. The people appeared gay; some said if they had to be occupied they preferred the French whose chief purpose seemed the good worldly life. There was another long stop at Bolzano in Italy. From the station platform I could see the sun set pink on the Dolomites. Since the train carried no diner, I bought a ready-packed bag of delicious food: sausage, fried chicken, fried potatoes, two rolls, fruit, and a small bottle of Italian wine.

The night in the soft *wagon-lits* was comfortable; but only black coffee and sugar for breakfast. Still the austerity of war.

The center of Rome looked prosperous and the people beautiful. Automobiles were scarce because gasoline was scarce, but the shops seemed well stocked and the prices extremely high. Who are these Italians who can live so well in 1948?

I spent hours wandering through my favorite part of Rome, the ruins: the Trajan Forum, the Roman Forum, the Arch of Titus, the Colosseum. Here one can daydream history.

Later I kept an appointment in the ornate Senate with Count Carlo Sforza, Italy's stately Foreign Minister, whom I had known when he lived as an anti-Mussolini exile in New York. He said Italy could prosper only in a united Europe. Would I urge Prime Minister Nehru, Sforza suggested, to initiate a movement for international co-operation among the lesser powers of the world?

118

I was on my way to India to see that fascinating and decisive country again and to gather material for a biography of Mahatma Gandhi. It might seem that the sudden leap from Italy to India would bring a rude shock—the people, geography, history, and problems of the two countries are so different. But having friends in both made the transition easy. And though the problems appeared different, the necessary solution was the same: a social revolution by legislation to erase the cruel contrasts between poor and rich and between lower and upper classes.

Nor is Gandhi so remote from Italy, Europe, the Americas, and Africa. The more I have thought of his life the clearer becomes his relevance to the worries of the Western world today. The postwar period would have been very different everywhere with an infusion of some Gandhian principles and techniques.

I had lived in Gandhi's village as his house guest, or hut guest, for a week in 1942, and found him wise, relaxed, moderate, articulate, and communicative. He did not expect visitors or associates to be awe-struck or reverent. In fact, he encouraged intimacy, banter, and laughter. He lived on the same level as everybody else—on the bare earth. When I jumped from the horse-drawn conveyance which first brought me to the edge of his village, he was there, waiting to welcome me, a man of seventy-three in white loincloth and leather sandals, and he was all the greater because he did not need distance to enhance his importance. He was what he was.

One afternoon, during an hour's interview, I alluded to the only decoration in his mud-walled hut: a black-and-white print of Jesus Christ with the inscription, "He Is Our Peace."

"How is this?" I asked. "You are not a Christian."

"I am a Christian and a Hindu and a Moslem and a Jew," he replied. He went beyond tolerance and attained the identification with others which is the synonym of love. Gandhi, therefore, was more Christian than most Christians; he was Christlike. Had Gandhi been born in India three thousand years ago, his birth would have been wrapped in myths and his youth in miracles, and he would have been worshiped as a god. By being pure in politics he became a states-man-saint.

Just four years had passed since my visit in 1942. Without bathing or shaving after the long, hot flight from Cairo, or even occupying my hotel room, I drove off to the untouchables slum in New Delhi where, I was told, Gandhi would be conducting his daily public prayer meeting. Posting myself at the foot of the three wooden steps that led down from the prayer platform, I waited for the services to close. When he saw me, he said, "Ah, there you are, Fischer. Well, I have not grown better-looking in these four years."

"I would not dare to differ with you," I replied. He laughed loudly.

I followed him around to various parts of India. I traveled with him by third-class railway car from Poona to Bombay. Wherever the train stopped, immense crowds gathered despite a very heavy monsoon rain. At one station, two boys, aged about fourteen, wet to their brown skins, their black hair dripping, jumped up and down outside Gandhi's window, moved their bent arms up and down rhythmically and yelled, "Gandhiji, Gandhiji, Gandhiji." (The "ji" is a suffix of respect.) Gandhi was amused.

"What are you to them?" I asked.

He put his fists with thumbs pointed upward to his temples. "A man with horns, a spectacle," he replied. He always regretted that people gave him adulation when what he wanted was acceptance of his way of life.

That year I spent eight days in his company. I hesitate to use too big a word to describe my relation to Gandhi; I probably grew to love him.

Two years later, at eight o'clock on the morning of Saturday, January 31, 1948, I turned on the radio in my New York apartment and heard that Gandhi had been killed at his prayer meeting in New Delhi the day before.

When the news of Mahatma's death reached him, Leon Blum, the former Premier of France, said, "I never saw Gandhi. I do not know his language. I never set foot in his country, and yet I feel the same sorrow as if I had lost someone near and dear. The whole world has been plunged into mourning by the death of this extraordinary man."

I had seen Gandhi, eaten with him, walked with him, talked with him, joked with him. I counted as golden the hours he gave me. Now, reading the accounts of how the three bullets pierced his body and how he lay helpless before death, I wept though I had not wept for many years, and felt numb. Later, when I could think again, it seemed that maybe this was the best way to die. He was a fighter all his life, and it would have been strange if he had died of a cold. His violent death was one more service. Pearl Buck called it "another crucifixion." It turned the world's attention upon his life. On hearing of the assassination, U.S. Secretary of State George C. Marshall said,

"Mahatma Gandhi was the spokesman for the conscience of mankind." U.S. Senator Arthur H. Vandenberg declared that Gandhi "made humility and simple truth more powerful than empires."

Everywhere, men in big buildings and plain folks in homes and huts mourned his passing. Humanity felt bereft, impoverished; for Gandhi owned nothing but was rich in real values. The tributes showered on him in death celebrated not so much his political achievements, great though they were, as his spiritual qualities and ethical practices; the world praised what it needed most and lacked.

Gandhi is India's gift to the Western world; his life contains a prescription for some of our worst ills. Viewing man's estate with the prophet's global eye whose X-ray vision penetrates iron curtains and national boundaries, Gandhi saw that the size of the individual has been dwindling in the democracies and dictatorships alike.

Dictatorship, whether Bolshevik or Fascist, is, by definition, a powerful state in which man is powerless. Elements of such power and powerlessness exist in varying degree in the democracies as a result of the expansion and growing complication of government functions, and the increasing concentration of economic strength in a decreasing number of enterprises. The individual, as a result, becomes dependent on institutions and on forces at least partly and often largely beyond his control, even beyond his comprehension.

To these vast, objective factors in twentieth-century civilization, the postwar international tensions have added the requirements of military defense, which enhance the state's power, and suspicion and distrust of the individual, which curtail his.

Many are aware of the differences between the Communist and non-Communist worlds. They fail to realize that the greater danger lies in similarities between them. Pressures toward conformity and obedience, the subordination of personal ethics to national interests, and the search for security at the expense, if need be, of individual independence are corroding democracy too.

The chief objection to the Soviet type of totalitarianism has been that when the state takes over all private property the individual also becomes the private property of the state and his liberties are extinguished. But now it is becoming clear that the individual can be repressed in a capitalist country where private property is presumed sacred. The tyranny of a democratic majority intolerant of the nonconformist may ultimately be nearly as damaging to the spirit of individualism as the tyranny of a police dictatorship. When a democracy, as some have urged, "fights fire with fire," and begins to use the methods of totalitarianism to combat totalitarianism it grows more totalitarian itself, and what has the individual gained? Security regulations, endless investigations, vigilantism, and character assassination by legislators and volunteer thought-policeman are methods of control not so different in their intention, though different in their intensity, from those practiced to our apparent horror in Russia and China. The fear of losing a job or of not getting one because of independent thinking or controversial reading or ideological experimentation or an interest in unpopular ideas sears the individual's soul and clips his wings and reduces his stature just as surely as the constant fear of arrest in the Soviet Union. Here Mahatma Gandhi with his emphasis on means and his love of the individual stands as a warning beacon. The individual was Gandhi's major concern, and it is this concern, in particular, which makes him so intimately relevant to the problems of the second half of the twentieth century, the century not of the common man or uncommon man, but of the assault upon the independence, integrity, and mental health of both.

For mental health, Gandhi prescribed truth. He sought for himself a unity of what he believed, what he did, and what he said. Creed, deed, and word were one. This is the integration which is integrity or truth. When utterances conflict with actions and actions with beliefs the individual is split, and sick. Gandhi preached what he practiced, and practiced what he believed. I found him healthy, happy, and lighthearted despite his many sorrows and burdens. He enjoyed inner harmony.

Most of Gandhi's ideas can be ascribed to some quality of his mental eyesight which kept him from seeing people as a mass. He never saw or judged Indians or Frenchmen or Christians or Moslems in millions. He considered each human being too holy, too important to be the mere instrument of a remote impersonal terrestrial power called the state.

Communist governments say their end is a perfect society in the future. This is their excuse for sacrificing people now. In the process they lose their humanity and their love of humanity. Gandhi hallowed means, not ends, and the means is always man. Actually there are no ends; each apparent end is a means to another means. Life consists only of means, and if the means are corrupt or ugly, all of life becomes corrupt and ugly and so does man himself.

To solve problems, Communist regimes resort to government action and violence. They trust in dehumanized institution and power instruments because they have no faith in human beings.

This system is bound to have an enormous lure for the hundreds of millions in Asia, Africa, Latin America, and even Europe. The problems of these millions are so urgent that they may not care by what methods they are solved, just so someone tries to solve them; they are already so weakened and humiliated by poverty and other degradations that they feel Communism could not make things any worse. Each person conscious of his own insignificance compared to the colossal task of wiping out the widespread misery yearns for the intervention of a mighty government, ruthless though it might be, and is ready to submit to it because it promises to save him.

As an Asian whose ear and heart were open to the cries of the simple peasant, Mahatma Gandhi faced this situation and evolved a cure. Basic to all else was his love. He loved people individually and in multitudes. Everybody who came in contact with him felt it and paid him back with love. This was the source of his authority and effectiveness. He had no power, he could not punish or reward materially; his only weapons were warmth and truth; with these he liberated India.

In the midst of his historic 1946 negotiations with British Cabinet Ministers on India's impending independence, I watched Gandhi try to patch up a marital dispute between two untouchables. This was his idea of democracy. He took the misdeeds and faults of others as a reproof to himself; he had not done enough to improve them. He regarded the good in a person as all of that person, and did not look for the bad. The person tried to be worthy of Gandhi's faith; the person grew. Gandhi endeavored to degrade, debase, humiliate, and hurt none, to elevate all. That is democracy too.

Gandhi was not born great. He was a blundering boy, a mediocre student, a poor lawyer, an ordinary individual until he remade himself. He was a self-remade man. He had faith in himself. But above all he had a deep, touching faith in the peasants, peddlers, miners, laborers, and young unformed men and women whom he drew into his work. He fed them all an elixir of growth which often transformed nameless, uneducated people into leonine heroes. The elixir was fearlessness.

A fervent, lifelong champion of nonviolence, Gandhi stated that "where there is a choice between cowardice and violence I would choose violence," for cowardice, or fear, makes a small man who will yield to pressures and not defend his freedom, his principles, or himself.

The individual's fear is thus the dictator's permit. Gandhi, on the other hand, took the proverbial docility of the Indian and, adding courage, forged it into the weapon of freedom: men and women, defying authority, would lie down in the tracks of automobiles and trains, in the path of galloping police horses, would allow themselves to be beaten without raising a protective elbow or a cry. "Gandhi has straightened our backs and stiffened our spines," Nehru asserted. Dictators and bullies cannot ride on an upright back.

Civil disobedience, or large-scale deliberate flaunting of the law in obedience to the higher law of conscience, was Gandhi's unique political weapon. He borrowed the term from Henry Thoreau's essay by that name which was published in 1849. "It left a deep impression on me," Gandhi wrote of Thoreau's paper. Gandhi, like Thoreau, insisted on the individual's right to oppose governments, even governments at war, and to resist their enactments. For democracy is hollow without the right to dissent. And dissent withers where fear enters.

Gandhi's philosophy of individualism made him an adversary of Communism or, as he preferred to call it, Bolshevism. His opposition, however, was based not on the fear which leads to suppression but on his attachment to a higher morality. Experience taught Gandhi that men fear most what is within them. It may well be that the fear of Communism varies in different countries not with the proximity or imminence of the threat as with the hidden presence of Communist elements in the democratic mentality. "Turn the searchlight inward," Gandhi advised repeatedly. The evil you fight may be inside.

The central evil of the modern world, Gandhi felt, was materialism. Communism grew from it and so did the weaknesses of democracy. "Bolshevism," he said, "is the necessary result of modern materialistic civilization. Its insenate worship of matter has given rise to a school which has been brought up to look upon materialistic advancement as the goal of life and which has lost touch with the final things in life. . . . I prophesy that if we disobey the law of the final supremacy of spirit over matter, of liberty and love over brute force, in a few years' time we shall have Bolshevism rampant in this land which was once so holy." He spoke of India; he might have been referring to any country. Matter or materialism, in Gandhi's sense, was not only wealth but power, the accumulation of "brute force" to crush the spirit of freedom, the building of a machine whose motor fuel is hate.

Gandhi never urged anyone to renounce wealth or power. He taught a set of values that might make happiness less dependent on material possessions. "As long as you desire inner help and comfort from anything, you should keep it," he suggested tolerantly. Otherwise, he said, you might renounce a worldly asset "in a mood of self-sacrifice or out of a stern sense of duty" but want it back and suffer. "Only give up a thing," he wrote, "when you want some other condition so much that the thing no longer has any attraction for you, or when it seems to interfere with that which is more greatly desired." In such a spirit, a family might give up living in a city and reside in communion with nature, or a man might relinquish government office or a business to be his own master, do his own work, and grow.

"I wholeheartedly detest," Gandhi declared, "this mad desire to destroy distance and time, to increase animal appetites, and to go to the ends of the earth in search of their satisfaction." None of this "is taking the world a step nearer its goal."

When I told him in 1946 that he ought to go to the West and teach his doctrine, he replied, "Why does the West need me to teach them that two times two are four?" His preoccupation was that the Western world knew the truth but, being enslaved to things, would not rise to the defense of principles if this involved a risk to a job, public approval, personal safety, economic security, or life. He himself paid for his principles—by going to jail, by inviting death, by courting poverty—and it made him rich in the coin of the spirit which was the only currency he valued.

Gandhi is known for his successful efforts to liberate India. Actually, for him the development of the Indian into a free man was more important than the freeing of India. Most of Gandhi's followers in India were not Gandhians and did not share his ideals; they merely accepted his leadership because it smoothed the way to their objective which was an Indian nation without the British but with all the usual attributes of nationhood. For them, national independence was an end, a good in itself; for him it was a means to a better man and a better life, and because his heart was heavy with doubts whether these purposes would be furthered by the manner in which independence was achieved—two bleeding children torn violently from the body of Mother India—he did not celebrate on August 15, 1947, the day the Indian nation came into his own world— he was sad and refused congratulations.

Gandhi was a nationalist, he loved India, but he was no Indomaniac, he said he would not hurt England to help India. All the years he fought British-Boer racial discrimination in South Africa and British imperialism in India he never despised or reviled "the enemy." He wanted to understand him. The British in India were victims of their past and their caste system; in liberating India Gandhi thought he was also freeing England for a new future.

The nature of any conflict is shaped by the attitude of the antagonists to one another. Gandhi tried to evoke the best in an antagonist rather than the worst in himself. That was indeed the way he won most of his victories. His great victory in South Africa in 1914 came not when General Smuts had no more strength to fight but when he had no more heart to fight. Likewise in India. Because Gandhi fought without arms he disarmed his antagonist. By translating the Sermon on the Mount into modern politics he became a mighty adversary. He did not always succeed, but on balance it was a practical as well as a noble form of combat and, given the will, it could be employed more often than it has been—especially in the prolonged era of cold war.

When at "war," Gandhi remembered he would have to live with the enemy after the fighting was done. He fought accordingly. He managed to lead his people against England without allowing them to hate, without fostering anti-West or antiwhite sentiments. Having resisted "white supremacy," he condemned brown arrogance.

Perhaps the best symbol of Gandhi's philosophy is the two parallel bars of the equal sign. All nations, races, religions, and persons were equal though not similar. Gandhi did not exclude preferences. He preferred Hinduism, he loved India more than other countries, he wrapped some of his immediate associates in tender affection. But nobody was second-class. He abhorred status and worked all his life against its ugly manifestations in India: the caste system, the torture of the untouchables, pride, and provincial and religious separation.

On all these and many other subjects Gandhi wrote voluminously and precisely for many decades. He spoke on innumerable occasions. But his big contribution to modern civilization is his life. Gandhi demonstrated that it is possible to be a Christ in the twentieth century. He showed that it is possible to be both good and effective. "Perhaps," the Indian poet Rabindranath Tagore wrote of Gandhi, "he will not succeed. Perhaps he will fail as the Buddha failed and as Christ failed to wean men from their iniquities, but he will always be remembered as one who made his life a lesson for all ages to come."

Gandhi grows as one watches small men coping with mounting problems. The life of Gandhi, the Hindu-Christian-Buddhist-Jewish Moslem, reveals a purity of purpose, a humility, a devotion to truth, and a greatness of mind, spirit, and character which easily make him the outstanding individual of the twentieth century and maybe, too, of the preceding nineteen. He was an Indian. He belongs to the world.

CHAPTER THIRTEEN

Indian Diary

August 1st, 1948. The first impression I got at the Bombay Airport was of sun-white, broiling, tropical, August sun. The next impression, which erased the first, was of human warmth. The airlines people and the reporters knew me and showed their friendliness. I had been an advocate of Indian independence, but more particularly, I had lived with Gandhi and that gave me a place in the hearts of many Indians and a prominence which I did not enjoy in my native land or in foreign countries I had known for decades.

August 2nd. Early this evening I received a visit from a young woman whom I had known as a Junior Miss in the United States when her father was stationed there as an Indian diplomat. She had been married recently. I asked whether the marriage was an "arranged" one.

"Oh, of course," she replied, "Granddaddy in Allahabad wrote to Daddy when we were still in the States and they settled things with my husband's family."

"When did you first see your husband?"

"The evening I married him," she said. "Our families," she added, "have been intermarrying for centuries."

"And you lived so long in America!" I chided. "Don't you believe in love and courtship?"

"Love comes after marriage," she assured me. "The Indian way is better."

I told this story at lunch the next day to an Indian who was a graduate of an English university and his Indian wife who had lived long in Europe. "My dear darling behaved no better," she confessed. "We met three times before our wedding but he kissed me only once —on the forehead." Their marriage was also "arranged." India has the largest motion picture industry in the world next to that of the United States, but no kissing is permitted in Indian films. They usually portray romantic love, adventure, and heroism.

One of the reasons why most Indian marriages are parentally planned is the desire to maintain caste purity; after all, if girls and boys were allowed to fall in love and marry their heart's choice, emotions might lead them astray into another caste, and, though intercaste marriages multiply, the objection to them, especially among the older folks, remains strong. Another factor conducing to arranged marriages is the joint family in which parents and their married children and their children, sometimes forty or more persons, live under one roof and accept the guidance of the eldest who says who shall marry whom. The joint family is breaking down for financial and housing reasons, but even when it does the tradition of parental authority persists.

August 5th. Jayaprakash Narayan, tall and handsome, age forty-six, came for a forenoon chat. "Jayaprakash," Nehru had said to me in 1946, "is the future Prime Minister of India."

J.P., as he is usually called, is a fascinating figure, the kind only India breeds. He arrived in the United States from India in 1922 to study, picked fruit in California, and later enrolled in the University of Iowa and the University of Wisconsin. In America he became a Communist. But when he returned to India in 1929, he noted the unethical ideas and unscrupulous methods of the Communists, abandoned Communism, and became an anti-Communist, Democratic Socialist. During his country's fight for independence, the Socialist party, led by J.P., was part of the Gandhi-Nehru-Patel-led Congress party. Subsequently, however, the Socialists left the Congress organization; they found it looked back too much to the national revolution that brought liberation from Britain and forward too little to the social revolution which would relieve some of the people's misery.

In 1946, I sat on the floor at Gandhi's feet while he and J.P. argued the pros and cons of violence in politics. J.P. was for it, the Mahatma, naturally, against. J.P. had supported the anti-British revolt in 1942-43 which resulted in attacks on persons and destruction of property. Gandhi criticized him for it.

Yet though J.P. differed with Gandhi on this vital principle and although he had dissociated himself from Gandhi's Congress party, he is the Gandhian, whereas Prime Minister Nehru, the Congress leader and Gandhi's political heir, is not a Gandhian.

In an Indian group consisting largely of Nehru admirers, I started a game of naming the Gandhian Indians.

"Nehru?" I queried.

Most of them laughed at the very idea.

"Jayaprakash?"

Most of them said yes.

The test of Gandhism, or Christianity, or of any noble creed lies in personal conduct and character. Nehru is tempestuous, impatient, belligerent, irritable, vain, scornful, storm-ridden. In a letter dated July 15, 1936, Gandhi told Nehru that Indian political leaders "have chafed under your rebukes and magisterial manner and above all your arrogation of what to them appeared your infallibility and superior knowledge. They feel you have treated them with scant courtesy."

Nobody would say that about J.P. He is soft-spoken and gentle, modest, polite, temperate, considerate, conciliatory, kindly, deferential. He smiles as often as Nehru scowls. His personality has doeskin softness, Nehru's bristles. J.P. possesses inner peace and firmness, Nehru lacks them. J.P.'s calm speaks of strength, Nehru's temper attests to weakness and insecurity. J.P. searches for a deep truth, Nehru enjoys playing with ideas in public. Despite his Western education and his devotion to the West, Jayaprakash Narayan is very Indian; despite his flirtation with the East, Jawaharlal Nehru is very Western. "Nehru is an Englishman," Gandhi once said to me. One can see J.P. living in a village, Nehru the aristocrat belongs in a palace. I can imagine J.P. fasting, not Nehru. J.P. likes to get close to people, Nehru shows best on a stage. Nehru is a Hamlet playing Hamlet but enjoying the role of king.

August 6th. Yesterday evening I dined on Malabar Hill at the home of Raja Hutheesing, a businessman by birth, and his wife Krishna, a Nehru by birth, the younger sister of Jawaharlal and of Mrs. Pandit. Raja prefers politics to textiles and abandons his merchandise whenever he can to run for Parliament or do a book or edit a newspaper. Being the Prime Minister's brother-in-law has its advantages, he knows some things from the inside, but his nonconformism usually leaves him in the cold outside. "In India," he said, "politics are personalities." Krishna, the author of several books, can write but usually doesn't. Unlike her brother and sister, who are built for the platform, Krishna's femininity, frankness, and pointed personality shine best in the small salon or at the dinner table.

The Hutheesings and all my Indian friends know that my fondness for India does not extend to Indian food; I find it overspiced. Instead of their "hot" exotic dishes I ask for prosaic chicken or some such dish. When the dessert was served at the Hutheesings', I looked into it with mock disappointment and exclaimed, "What! No gold?"

"What do you mean," Krishna wondered.

"Well," I said, "when I lunched with Jawaharlal at R. K. Nehru's in New Delhi in 1942, the *pièce de résistance*, for me anyway, was a sweet covered with silver leaf to be eaten. I pronounced it delicious. 'Wait,' Jawaharlal commented, 'someday we will serve you a dessert of gold.'"

Krishna clapped her hands and called Nathuram. He entered noiselessly on bare feet. Krishna spoke to him in Hindustani and he disappeared. Several minutes later he returned with a gold-roofed sweet: a bowl of rice (*pulao*) covered with gold beaten to the thinnest paper fineness by experts in Benares, Lucknow, and Delhi and said to have health-giving qualities. "There," Krishna said, "no Nehru promise shall go unfulfilled."

It was exquisite.

Except that the women wear colorful saris, bangles halfway up their bare arms, flowers or jewels in their hair, and bright sandals on their stockingless feet, and that some of the men may be in Indian costume, an evening party like the one at the Hutheesings is rather similar to an evening party in Bloomsbury or Mayfair or on Park Avenue, the Boulevard St.-Germain, or the Via dei Monte Parioli, and produces much the same kind of gossip and discussion.

Perhaps many of the Indian political arguments tend to be more emotional than factual but this is not an exclusively Eastern failing.

August 7th. Today is the Moslem feast of Id which marks the end of the month-long Ramadan fast. Below my hotel windows on the pavement of the sea wall, and near by at the massive Gateway to India arch where the British Viceroys used to land on their arrival to assume office, the scene is a blaze of color. Moslems abound; one knows them by their headgear and costumes, especially the men and boys in fur caps and red fezes. I see a boy of about six in black fur cap, and tomato-red blouse over his white pants. Moslems, Hindus, and Parsis, all easily recognizable by some or all articles of dress, mix freely and amicably. The only policeman in sight pays no attention to the crowd. He smartly directs vehicular traffic. Inter-religious hate undoubtedly lives, but its passion burned itself out in mid-1947 in the arson, the murder, and the march of the weary fifteen million human beings who had to flee their homes when India and Pakistan were born.

Friday, August 13th. Smooth morning flight of about four hours from Bombay to New Delhi. On arrival, an officer asked me the purpose of my trip. I said, "To be in New Delhi." This apparently sufficed and was duly recorded. I suppose the question was put to passengers because the assassin of Gandhi came from Bombay to Delhi just a few days before he killed the Mahatma earlier in the year. What would he have given as his reason for the visit?

Most of New Delhi is an official city with broad, tree-shaded, paved streets in which autos and bicycles greatly outnumber horse carriages and oxcarts. In the residential districts, each home prominently displays a name plate of its occupant. The houses, set far back from the street, are usually surrounded by half an acre or an acre of park and garden; there live the rich and powerful. In this year of the assassination, the homes of ministers are watched day and night by detatchments of military guards who camp in tents and cook on the premises.

The most prominent feature of New Delhi is the Viceroy's palace located in the midst of vast formal Mogul gardens with beautiful flower beds, grass plots, ponds, pools, walks, trees, and tennis courts but no benches or chairs. The building is all that the words "oriental splendor" call to mind: spacious, marble-floored corridors, a tremendous throne room, tremendous windows, mammoth oil paintings of all of Britain's Viceroys, and halls and halls and rooms and rooms and offices abounding in gold decorations, wood paneling, sculpture, richly inlaid furniture, enormous rugs, priceless tapestries, tiger skins, and so forth. Here now, in place of the Viceroy, reigns the Indian Governor-General, Chakravarti Rajagopalachari, or C.R., Gandhi's friend, an old champion of independence, perhaps the wisest man in India, emaciated, minus many teeth, head shaven, his weak eyes always hidden behind dark spectacles, and dressed in a white homespun blouse that falls halfway down his thighs, a homespun loincloth which leaves his shins bare, and old leather sandals on bare feet. Little bald Lenin in crumpled shirt and wrinkled suit as master of the Czar's Moscow Kremlin presented the same kind of sharp contrast with the past. C.R.'s simplicity was not only a calculated rejection of the formalities of the late foreign raj; it represented a hope that independence would mean spiritual purification as well as national liberation. He had differed with Gandhi in private and public, but he was a Gandhian at heart and in purpose; like Gandhi he quarreled with mere nationalism. Merely to replace the British Viceroy with an Indian Viceroy did not suffice.

The morning after my arrival in New Delhi, Mr. Rajagopalachari received me in the palace. As I took a long look around his immense reception room a mischievous smile played on his pale lips and he chuckled but said nothing, and neither did I. He was the head of state and as such outside politics, like the King of England; therefore he could not talk politics except off the record. He also talked about Gandhi. He cautioned me especially not to assume, in writing about Gandhi, that the Mahatma calm and self-control had always been there. Gandhi, he stressed, was a man of passion, all kinds of passion, and of temperament; the detached saint the world knew was the product of many a wrestling match between soul and body.

The same morning I went to see Sardar Vallabhbhai Patel, Congress party "strong man," Home Minister and second to the Prime Minister Nehru in the government. Wrapped in white homespun, his big round bald head slightly raised, he reclined on a sofa looking very much like a Roman senator after a meal. But the Sardar was sparing his sick heart. With him, as with everybody else I met, I was torn between the wish to discuss Gandhi and the desire to talk about today's politics. I usually compromised by doing both. I listened long to Patel. He had a clear and brilliant mind and could lay out all of the factors of a situation so that one saw them individually and in their relationship.

When we came to India's foreign policy, I suggested that it was more pro-Soviet than neutral in spite of the fact that Nehru had declared, "We propose, as far as possible, to keep away from the power politics of groups aligned against one another." Apparently that had proved impossible, for at the United Nations 1946 session, where India's new interim government was represented, the conduct of the Indian delegation had created the general belief that India was in the Soviet-Slav camp. This impression was strengthened by the personal attitude of Mr. Krishna Menon who, though only an alternate delegate, was Nehru's "personal representative," and dominated the Indian delegation headed by Mrs. Pandit. "Surely," I said to Patel, "it is neither neutral nor moral for India, just released from imperial bondage, to vote so often with the aggressive, expansionist, clamant Soviet empire against the West whose imperialism, to be sure, you know better, but which is obviously recessive."

"I agree with you," the Sardar said, "but have you talked with Jawaharlal?"

This remark signified that though Patel was in some respects the most powerful man in the country, the differences between him and Nehru had resulted in a delicately poised "spheres of influence" agreement which allotted foreign affairs to the Prime Minister. A few minutes before the bullets struck, Gandhi was still trying to iron out those differences, but he succeeded only in arranging a tense truce. If Patel had been Prime Minister or Foreign Minister India's foreign policy would not have resembled Nehru's.

August 15th. This is the first anniversary of India's national freedom. Imperial rule had made India, or at least the vocal part of India, seriously ill. Emotional diseases tormented the politically conscious section of the population so much that independence had to come, and it is lucky the British saw this in time. It was also good for the world's morals that one nation had ceased to insist on the right to rule another in the name of "the white man's burden" or "might makes right." Despite all the consequent problems and perils, the independence of India, and of Pakistan, Ceylon, and Burma did rid the white man's conscience of a big, black blot. This act was purifying and inspiring, but only for those who performed it—the British—and not for the direct beneficiaries and witnesses. Or maybe national independence is not a fundamental cure but merely a necessary and inevitable surrender to the normal modern craving to expel the uninvited stranger who nests in your home and is its master. Conceivably, too, Indian independence was robbed of its moral lift by the shedding of blood, including Gandhi's blood, which accompanied it.

Such thoughts ran through my mind during the day, but they were often interrupted by the anniversary celebrations. These began at 7 A.M. with songs and short speeches at Gandhi's tomb near the river. Immediately thereafter, but the sun was already sizzling hot, Prime Minister Nehru reviewed an army honor guard in front of the Red Fort and then mounted its high battlements to broadcast to the nation in Hindi. Massed squares of teen-age girls in white dresses, their big dark eyes aglow with excitement, black plaits hanging down their backs, sat on their haunches for almost two hours eagerly listening and watching the celebrities who passed. Multitudes lined the approaches to the Fort. I saw several stark-naked sadhus, or Hindu holy men, their bodies streaked with colored ash, begging. One lay on the roadway writhing; suffering opens purses. In the afternoon, the Governor-General entertained over a thousand guests with soft drinks and light refreshments in the Viceregal gardens.

As soon as I arrived at the party, the editor of a Bombay news weekly accosted me with a strange question. "What is America's attitude toward Goa?" he asked.

I smiled and said, "Most Americans have probably never heard of it. And as to the United States government, I do not know that it has an attitude."

"I understand," he exclaimed ferociously, "that America will not permit Portugal to liberate Goa because it wants a naval base on the West coast of India."

"You have a rich imagination," I commented. "When your brain lacks an explanation your emotions invent one." This is a widespread failing—and not only in India.

The next two days I interviewed several of Gandhi's close co-workers, both Indians and Quakers, lunched with the Maulana Abul Kalam Azad, a Moslem now Minister of Education, and dined on rice and fermented milk with the Governor-General and his family, he in white homespun, the waiters in elaborate red costumes with breastplates of gold embroidery.

The following day I canceled all appointments, and the next morning young Sudhir Ghosh, whom Gandhi had used as an intermediary in negotiations with the British, and his wife, Shaanti, a physician, came to my hotel room and with an insistence too firm and friendly to be denied, carried me off to the Lady Willingdon Hospital. I had foolishly infected myself with a calcium injection, and was running a high temperature.

October 19th-25th. The Willingdon Nursing Home is a municipal institution, clean and efficient. Almost all the nurses are young Roman Catholic Anglo-Indians, daughters of mixed British-Indian marriages; they look like Indians, but wear European clothes at work and outside, and are emotionally torn between a deep attachment to India, their native land, and a pride in being somewhat better than its inhabitants. They tell me that Moslem women shun nursing because it would bring them in contact with strange men; this and other taboos kept Hindu women from entering the profession until very recently.

The nurses administer the medicines, register the patient's temperature, and accompany the doctor, but do not touch the night table. That is the untouchable's department. Old man Narayan brings the food tray and my newspapers, and makes the bed. One afternoon I noticed him carefully stepping over a piece of gauze on the floor. I suggested he pick it up. He left abruptly; a moment later the untouchable came in and removed it. The floor and the bathroom and all similar "dirty" menial tasks are the province of the silent untouchable in faded blue blouse, trousers, and cap who salutes me meekly every time he enters and leaves my room. This is the caste system in practice.

After undergoing a twenty-four-hour intensive attack with penicillin and sulfa drugs, my temperature sank to normal and thereafter I needed only local treatments.

As soon as I felt well I began receiving visitors from the outside. At my request, the nurses also sent me every day a number of fellow patients who spoke English. Uppermost in the mind of nearly everyone of the latter, I found, were the horrible events of exactly a year ago when India went mad and at least a million Hindus, Moslems and Sikhs died in a flash civil war slaughter. A young woman from Calcutta, speaking with great emotion, said, "My daughter, Lakshmi, was born just as the big massacre in our city got under way. I had gone to the clinic with my mother who could not return home because of the rioting. The hospital, situated in the heart of the Hindu area, was twice attacked by Hindus bent on killing the Moslem servants. The second time they succeeded in stabbing the night watchman to death. The Hindus suffered as badly in the Moslem districts. Hindus and Moslems who had lived together as brothers and good neighbors for years suddenly slashed one another's throats. Our newspaper delivery boy, a Hindu, who had served his route for more than a year, was stabbed in the back. Fortunately, a patrolling police car picked him up within a few minutes of the incident and rushed him to the hospital. The daily *Statesman* paid all the expenses of his treatment and now he is again delivering our papers. Others, less fortunate, lived after their bellies had been slit open. One such victim crawled several yards in this condition but nobody helped him for fear of reprisals. Stray killings continued for months. A Sikh taximan cruising in a deserted street would spy a Moslem, move up from behind, stab him with his knife, and speed away. In private, Moslems boasted that twelve- and fourteen-year-olds of their community chalked up a record number of stabs-in-the-back. Christians wore crosses prominently, and Moslems took to doing the same for protection."

Tales other patients told varied in circumstances but followed the same pattern of cruelty, vengeance, and bloodshed. Millions in Pakistan and India could relate similar stories. They circulate in the national bloodstream.

On visitor's day, whole Indian families arrive to camp on the cement apron of the courtyard. I notice in particular how tender they are to their young ones who are fondled and cuddled, never scolded or beaten. It passes understanding how people as humane and gentle as these could have been so murderous a year ago. I suppose the fabric of decency burns quickly when religious and nationalistic passions mingle in one flame. Normally, Indians would not hurt a fly, much less tear babies limb from limb as happened in the Punjab, or stuff wounded into water wells.

I sense that the folks in the hospital have a feeling of inferiority to whites. A demagogue's tricks could easily convert this into hatred.

August 29th. I went to lunch with Jawaharlal Nehru. His daughter and Miss Naidu were present. After the meal he and I withdrew to a reception room for an interview. Since he was reluctant to discuss foreign policy with a critic we discussed Gandhi. Nehru also talked about himself. As he grew older, he said, he judged individuals more by their integrity and character than by the isms they embraced. Of all the spiritual leaders, Buddha and Christ appealed to him most. Throughout the hour Nehru yawned several times and looked very tired. The black rings below his eyes were bigger and blacker than ever.

August 31st. I left the hospital today for good after paying my bill. Lunch with a Moslem woman leader from the United Provinces who said Moslems were afraid to be themselves and were, in fact, second-class citizens. I reminded her of the Moslems high in the Cabinet and government service. She said, "Yes, that is Nehru's influence. But the masses do not follow him in this matter."

September 2nd. I drove to the village of Okla, about fourteen miles from New Delhi, where Dr. Zakir Hussain, a great Islamic scholar with noble, bearded visage, presides over a primary-school-to-university Moslem academy housed in a number of small, neat buildings. Zakir Hussain had his tale of horror about the events of August, 1947. In retaliation for the wanton killing of Hindus by Moslems elsewhere, the Hindus and Sikhs of the area around Okla were out for the blood of Moslems. At night, in a complete blackout, the teachers and older students stood guard, expecting an assault. In a circle around them they could see Moslem villages going up in flames. Night after night they heard Moslem peasants jumping into the near-by Jumna River to escape their pursuers, but the pursuers jumped in after them, and then there was a scuffle and struggle, and the victim would be held down by several pairs of arms till he drowned or gave one last ghastly shriek as a knife cut his throat. The ring of murder and arson began to close on the academy.

One evening, a taxi drew up at the gate of the academy and out of it jumped Jawaharlal Nehru. Oblivious, as usual, to danger, he had driven, accompanied only by the chauffeur, through that wide belt of maddened men to stay with Dr. Zakir Hussain, prepared no doubt to harangue and if necessary grapple with any attackers. The defenders were encouraged. No assault eventuated.

Indians call the antagonism between Hindus and Moslems communalism. With approximately forty million Moslems left in India after the partition, and about eleven million Hindus left in Pakistan, any flareup of violence between the two religious communities spells widespread pillage and death and threatens the peace between the two new nations carved out of the Indian subcontinent in 1947. Nehru is adamantly opposed to communalism; he stands above it. In this important matter, he is Gandhi's true heir.

September 3. Early in the morning I had a talk with Dr. B. C. Roy, who practices medicine while serving as Prime Minister of the populous West Bengal state. Later we drove over to Patel's house. Dr. Roy carried several rolled-up military maps. The two men conferred on measures of internal security to be taken simultaneously with the incursion of the Indian army into Hyderabad. For Prime Minister Nehru, a Hindu himself, insisted that before the army marched, Patel, charged with maintaining domestic law and order, take precautions to protect the forty million Moslems of India against Hindu ire in case the Nizam resisted the Indian army. The Nizam submitted. There was no trouble.

On September 7, I flew to Ahmedabad for a visit to neighboring Sabarmati where Gandhi had lived for years in an *ashram* by the river. I found the place still softly suffused with his spirit; he had given it to a community of untouchables.

Raja Hutheesing and his wife Krishna had come over from Bombay to Ahmedabad and I stayed with them in Raja's ancestral home where we talked sitting on the floor or with bare feet pulled up on a couch (a very restful position) and ate sitting on the floor at low individual tables placed around the walls of the dining room. In deference to my lack of skill, I was provided with silver; the Indians ate with their fingers. The food was vegetarian. Many Hindus never eat meat, and some even abstain from eggs because they regard them as having life. The influence of the Jain religious sect is strong in and around Ahmedabad. I saw several Jains with gauze masks over their noses and mouths—lest they breathe in and kill small insects.

On two evenings the Hutheesings took me to dine at the home of Ambalal Sarabhai, a textile millionaire. Gandhi knew the family very well. The senior Sarabhais and the married Sarabhai children with their offspring, as well as the unmarried children when they are in Ahmedabad, live together in the big house and in annexes.

The big house has a telephone operator and private switchboard with twenty lines.

I remarked to Krishna that the sari hides the female figure. "It can be worn to serve a different purpose," she replied. The next evening my eye was happier.

Ahmedabad is a very crowded city of over a million inhabitants most of whom live in slums hedged in by ugly factories. At almost any hour of the day pedestrians who find no room on the narrow pavements overflow into the streets and obstruct traffic. A few minutes' walk from town are beautiful empty meadows but the million live packed like herring in a barrel because they cannot afford to move. The city has an unhealthy intensity.

I addressed an indoor crowd, chiefly students, of at least a thousand on world affairs. The questions, in the main, reflected hostility to my views. At one point, Krishna sent me a note saying, "Don't answer idiotic questions." I answered them all. When the meeting adjourned half the audience milled around me asking for an autograph. The majority had little autograph books.

Three days later I left Bombay on the forty-eight-hour flight to New York. I left with a feeling that I wanted to come back soon and delve some more into the dark underground rivers of emotion which rumble through Indian life. The West has long assumed that the Oriental or Asian is lethargic, passive, stolid, indifferent, dreamy, philosophic, and unworldly. Many are, especially in the villages. But among those who shape the politics and culture of India and of other new republics in ancient Eastern countries, many are volatile, excitable, emotional, passionate, proud, irrational, color-conscious, Asia-conscious, power-conscious, ambitious, suspicious, fear-ridden, and insecure. Yet these same persons can be kindly, co-operative, responsive to goodness, and endlessly tender. Love lifts them to unusual spiritual heights, hate converts them into animals.

CHAPTER FOURTEEN

Asia Fights the West

I WAS ASTOUNDED when I first went to India in 1942, how often the Russo-Japanese War of 1904-5 came up in conversation. It was the first time a colored people defeated a white country, and Indians said it had stimulated their nationalism. On subsequent study trips to the Orient I noted deliberate efforts to weld the consciousness of color with the protest against poverty and the dislike of Western imperialism into an Asian mood, a sense of Asianhood. It is coupled with an attempt to make Africa a sentimental peninsula of Asia. This Pan-Asia, if achieved on an emotional or political or any level, would by its very nature constitute a bloc of brown, black, and yellow races antagonistic to the white West. The prospect presents the world with a subtle problem transcending in importance most of the tasks that now occupy overburdened foreign offices and state departments.

"Asia is one by its culture and art," said C. Rajagopalachari, then India's Minister of Education, at a conference on Asiatic Art and Culture in Calcutta, in January, 1947. Mr. Rajagopalachari's thesis is a doubtful one, but he linked it with a statement that goes to the heart of the crisis of the West. "Europe's culture," he affirmed, "is very beautiful and its civilization very attractive. But I do not know whether there is more wisdom in Asiatic culture or in European culture. I think there are men in Europe who are doubting the beauty of their culture."

In his last sentence, Mr. Rajagopalachari was being polite and moderate. He knew very well the elements of decadence in Western

140

culture and the intellectual insecurity they engender. The East thinks this is the chink in the West's armor.

"I am fascinated by the American people," said Dr. Rammanohar Lohia, a leading Indian Socialist, during a visit to the United States, "but have doubts about modern civilization, of which America is the climax." He was reflecting a widespread Asian skepticism not merely toward capitalism and democracy but toward the Western way of life.

"I come," Lohia added, "from the oldest but not the wisest country, to the youngest and most vital." Like many Asians, Lohia is preoccupied with age and vitality. India is an ancient land; it boasts a long, perhaps the longest, continuous known cultural existence. Actually, age is not a matter of calendar years or even of the unconscious markings of the past on the present; in India and a number of other Asian countries it is more a matter of the conscious retention of bygone centuries and millennia as factors in today's living. India, Jawaharlal Nehru once declared, is like a palimpsest. A palimpsest is an old parchment or canvas which has been written on or painted on and then varnished over at a subsequent period and written on or painted on again and so on for a third, fourth, and fifth time. Experts have now learned how to scratch off the newer coats and varnishes to reveal the precious originals. In the case of India, however, the varnishes have, so to speak, dissolved, and all the words or figures of past ages are visible simultaneously in one contradictory jumble of old and new. This explains the complexity of Indian culture and of the individuals formed by it. The tendency is to discard nothing. Certain Western peoples have moved from idolatry to polytheism to monotheism and, in some individuals, to atheism. But in Asia, monotheists may prostrate themselves before idols and tolerate Buddhist atheism.

The turbulent meeting place of two rivers or seas is regarded by Indians as holy, and the confluence of three rivers is very holy. The Eastern mind would rather make a synthesis than a choice. Asia could very well try to merge capitalism with Communism, or democracy with dictatorship, or neutrality with partisanship, or pacifism with militarism. The objective is not purity or consistency, it is more likely to be vitality and national regeneration with a view to achieving equality with the West. Sometimes, in fact, vitality is an end in itself or at least the major goal. Thus the anti-Communist Mr. Lohia, writing in September, 1948, stated that "Russia is today probably the most vital state in Europe and Communism has done this."[1] Vitality for what? Brute force is not vitality. Soviet culture is moribund, its popular will dormant, its individual a puppet. Dictatorship represents the impotence of a people lashed into antlike activity by the vigor of its oligarchs. Yet Lohia is not the only Asian anti-Communist who bows to the Red monolith. Power is god. Action has fascination. Men of crude power and forceful action attract even when their methods repel. This is not surprising in a society inclined to passivity and long deprived of power.

Lohia assumed that whereas Communism has vitalized Russia it has weakened Asia by civil wars. He accordingly concluded that Communism in Russia's hands "is verily the latest weapon of western civilization against Asia, Africa, and similar regions." However fallacious the reasoning, it feeds the notion of a Western plot to emasculate the East. It feeds the new Asian separatism which is as pernicious as the "Asia for the Asians" doctrine of Japan's militarists. Translated into foreign policy, this isolationism subordinates everything to the pursuit of vitality and material progress and leads to the immoral position of equating imperfect Western democracy with despotic Communism or even of preferring Communism when the democratic process seems slow.

Somewhere in this soil are the roots of many Indian thoughts on world affairs. Thus the Bombay *Free Press Journal*, a capitalist daily, wrote on August 6, 1948:

The average Indian does not care, at the moment, what label is given to the form of governance under which he lives. All he knows and cares about are the twenty-four hours of the day which are entirely taken up by the battle for survival. To the man, or to the system, which offers and gives him some respite from the battle, he will give his unswerving allegiance.

The same newspaper's comment on my lecture before the Indian Council on World Affairs in New Delhi therefore came as no surprise. "Mr. Fischer," it wrote, "would like India to align itself with the democracies but he does not tell us where these democracies are to be found." England, the United States? "Neither is a true democracy. Both are Imperialist. To align ourselves with this bloc which totters on the verge of a holocaust, appears to be an act of

[1] Dr. Rammanohar Lohia, *Fragments of a World Mind*, Calcutta: A. K. Gupta.

folly." Moreover, "what concrete benefits would India enjoy," the materialistic editor asks, "if it declared itself openly in favor of the Anglo-American bloc?" America, he argues, is "heavily engaged" fighting Communism in Europe and the Far East by economic means, and since India has "nipped Communism in the bud for the moment . . . we can get nothing out of the U.S.A. which will materially assist our rehabilitation." Nor could Britain help.

Audiences and editors in India reveal fascinating contradictions. The same lecture auditorium applauded a questioner who asked, "Why does America not extend the Marshall Plan to Asia?" and another who inquired, "Does the United States intend to take over India by means of loans and trade?" Editorial criticism reflected a power urge, a fear of foreign power, hurt pride, and nationalistic megalomania. *Janata* weekly of September 5, 1948, commenting on one of my speeches, wrote,

He cannot understand . . . that Indian state of mind which would regard American lust for leadership quite as bad as Russian lust for world direction. Neutrality, he says, is impossible. The American approach to India has never been different from the American approach to Luxembourg or Denmark. It irritates. . . . The Indian state, even in the present phase of precarious transition, is conscious of the fact that it is the crux of an economic and social order that will eventually embrace over a thousand million people [that is, all of Asia]. New India . . . will be a bloc-leader if blocs are inevitable.

Blocs were inevitable.

An Indian publisher, attempting to explain the unpopularity of anti-Soviet publications in India, said in a letter, "Following the trend of Nehru's mind, people, somehow, do not like to be dragged into Power Politics." This confirmed my own observations. Nehru "neutralism" tended to close minds to criticism of Russia while stimulating a less-than-friendly attitude toward the Western democracies. Some of the sympathy for Communism in India obviously grew from the fact that the movement is anti-West in its politics. Eager to avenge historic transgressions, Asia enjoys the efforts of Red China and Soviet Russia to hurt and humiliate the West. Their power to do so is regarded as benign and benevolent, their motives progressive and revolutionary.

I argued against these psychological phenomena because I was convinced they were wrong and harmful to India, Asia, and the world. But I did not think I would do any good. I recognized that, in a way—and this is perhaps basic—the antagonism of some Indians to the West was a struggle for independence, a hopeless struggle, for they needed Western technology and intended to use it in order to eliminate the economic lag of centuries. The West, moreover, was in them; most of India's leaders are, like Nehru, Western Easterners, or European Asians, and in combatting the West they are reacting against a split in their own psyche which makes them unhappy but is too deep to be eradicated. East and West are not "twain"; they have met in Asia. The West is there to stay, but the conflict with it goes on, for the West is their rejected past as well as the future.

The least the Western powers could do in these circumstances was to reckon with Asia's psychological difficulties and not aggravate them, not rub salt into Asia's wounds by retaining their colonial power for a few more useless years in Indonesia, Indo-China, and elsewhere. "The worst charge that can be levelled against the Dutch is that they do not know what time it is," I wrote in the Madison, Wisconsin, *Progressive* of August 25, 1947. The time was ten days after India's hour of freedom, time to quit Indonesia. But at the end of 1948, the Dutch were still engaging in "police actions" in Java, the Celebes, and Sumatra. On December 15, 1948, therefore, I sent a letter to Sir Benegal Rama Rau, the Indian Ambassador in Washington, suggesting an international conference on Indonesia. I urged that Holland be invited, and that British and American delegates also attend because their governments had the power to oust the Dutch. The next day the Ambassador cabled the contents of my letter to New Delhi. On January 1, 1949, Prime Minister Nehru, after branding the Dutch action as "naked and unabashed aggression," announced that he was summoning thirteen countries—Turkey, Egypt, Syria, Lebanon, Saudi Arabia, Iran, Iraq, Afghanistan, Pakistan, Ceylon, Siam, Burma, and Kuomintang China—to deliberations on the Indonesian problem. Holland, Britain, and America were not invited.

Nehru's conference fed Asian anger but did not stop Dutch military measures against the fighting Indonesians. Holland did not grant freedom to Indonesia until a year later. It was in that year, according to American officials who dealt directly with the Indonesian problem, that United States policy underwent a change. The "police action" of December, 1948, gradually inflamed American public opinion against the Dutch regime in Indonesia, and State Department diplomats told the Dutch that they were no longer in a position to defend them before Congressional committees or in speeches. The U.S. delegation to the UN, under instructions before December, 1948, not to castigate Dutch behavior in Indonesia, did so liberally in 1949, and the result was a Security Council resolution ordering a cease-fire in Indonesia. Dutch defiance of this order incensed the U.S. Congress; the withdrawal of Marshall Plan aid to Holland loomed as a concrete prospect. Holland was receiving about $400 million under the Plan and expending approximately the same amount in Indonesia, and the embarrassing conclusion could not be escaped, therefore, that in effect the United States was financing the Dutch war against Indonesia. American pressure on the Dutch in Washington, at the United Nations, at The Hague, and in Jakarta mounted perpendicularly, and in August, 1949, the truce signed several months earlier became a fact. Negotiations were then opened in the Netherlands which finally lead to Indonesian independence.

In private, Indonesian leaders acknowledged their indebtedness to the United States, and in private other Asian leaders paid tribute to America's and England's contribution toward Indonesian freedom. But it was not politic to say so openly.

With Indonesia free, Asian attention shifted to Indo-China where continued bloodshed fed continental antagonisms toward Europe and America. Good deeds went unrewarded, bad deeds were excoriated. Any opportunity to be anti-West was avidly welcomed. But a situation calling for an anti-East response—the Chinese Communists' militarization of Tibet, for instance—was glossed over.

All this, however, does not imply the unity of Asia. That, like the political unity of Islamic states, is a myth, and those who speak in its name are spinning fantasies. The desire to unify Asia politically is the pursuit of an abstraction, a type of endeavor in which, alas, quite a few Indians gladly indulge. Continents are classroom conveniences, not political facts. Politics works havoc with geography. It moves Turkey and Greece to the Atlantic Ocean, links Thailand with the United States, and lumps Egypt with Asia. India and Saudi Arabia are both in Asia, but what has the progressive, democratic Indian republic in common with the absolute oil monarchy of Arabia? The aspiring, finely chiseled, cultivated mind of a Nehru is a million cultural miles from Jordan, and Delhi is on the same continent with Damascus but much closer to the Thames. Half of Asia has more to fear from the other half than from the West. Was it not the Atlantic nations that rescued Asia from Japan's imperialistic embrace?

Asians, nevertheless, are right in resenting Western lack of friendship and comprehension. The West must understand that Asians will not allow themselves to be treated like dead weight in the world balance of power. They want a larger share of world leadership and of the world's wealth. Less than this reminds them of their colonial past.

The inhabitants of Asia and Africa sense what Dr. Charles F. Kettering, president of the Association for the Advancement of Science, said in 1946: that "the antiquated social systems, ignorance, stupidity and fear prevent a large percentage of the peoples of the world from enjoying even the most fundamental of the benefits of science." Three-fourths of the world's population, he added, lack sufficient food. This breeds rebellion. Since the existing system does not satisfy, Asians and Africans listen to voices describing a remote rival system. Backwardness and poverty have grown a crop of bitterness, unhappiness and hate which the Communists try to harvest. The real revolutionists are Western science and progress. As long however, as the miserable billion of Asia and Africa are denied their deserved share in science and progress the false revolutionists or Communists will flourish.

The Western summons to fight Communism therefore leaves the East cold. The East would rather fight the conditions which enable Communism to rally the unhappy to its banner.

On the other hand, the East tends to overlook its own faults. Much of its misery is homemade, and pointing an accusatory finger at the foreigner does not help. The foreigner's rule created evils, but he could not have become ruler except for evils that existed when he arrived and persist after his departure.

The East must heal itself. Fear of Western arms, machines, and money stems either from masochistic pride or feeble self-confidence which turns some Asians inward to isolationism and others backward to the obscurantism of obsolete centuries. The closed door shuts out a friend, but is sometimes opened for the enemy.

Leaving India in 1948, I felt that out of the East would come trouble. "The United States," I said to a friend, "ought to have a Secretary of State for Asia." (Britain too.)

"What would be his qualifications?" he asked.

"Greatness and an understanding heart," I replied. Treaties, trade, technical aid, and financial assistance are very important. But without warm sympathy machines and money are barren. For at bottom Asia's relation to the West is a problem of the mind, the nerves. The pain of the past gets in the way of the needs of the present. A great and understanding physican-statesman, therefore, would not only apply balm to old wounds, he would tell the patient the cold facts about his illness and some of the hard facts of modern life. In 1949, he would have made him see, feel, and understand the recession of Western imperialism and the menacing advance of Soviet imperialism in Asia. For a major shift was taking place in Soviet foreign policy; Russia was turning toward Asia.

After the Second World War, America and Europe disappointed Soviet hopes. Moscow had predicted a severe postwar economic depression in the West, followed by America's withdrawal from Europe and the inability of European capitalism to withstand the Communist tide. Just the opposite happened. America was in Europe with both feet and billions of dollars, witness the Truman Doctrine, Marshall Plan, Berlin airlift, and the beginning of European rearmament. All of this demonstrated that the Soviet Union and the European Communists did not possess the economic, political, or ideological weapons to expand into non-Soviet Europe.

Quickly drawing the logical conclusion from this situation, Moscow shifted the center of its interest from Europe to Asia. Frustrated in the West, Stalin probed for weak spots in the East. He was walking in the footsteps of the Czars. For almost a century before its death, the absolute monarchy restlessly sought to expand along the many thousand miles of its Eurasian land frontier. When it failed on one segment it tried to advance on another. Blocked in Central Asia by Britain, it eyed the Far East. Defeated in the Far East by Japan, it craved conquests in the Balkans and Turkey. Incapable of solving problems at home, Czarism remained extrovert, expansionist, unsated, and unsuccessful till it died.

Soviet policy likewise shuttled between Asia and Europe. The years from the close of the Soviet civil war in 1921 to 1929 were the Asian period in Bolshevik history when Soviet Foreign Commissar Georgi Chicherin courted Turkey, Persia, Afghanistan, and China. Maxim Litvinov, Chicherin's successor, on the other hand, culti-vated good relations with England, France, and America, and refused to antagonize these for the sake of questionable Eastern victories. Asia receded into the background.

Litvinov's dismissal in May, 1939, the Soviet-Nazi Pact of August, 1939, and the Second World War inaugurated an era of Soviet imperialism; since the war against Hitler was fought in Europe that is where Russia made her biggest territorial and political gains.

After the war, Stalin endeavored to expand in Europe by nonmilitary means. But when America returned to Europe in 1947, and more particularly in 1948, and showed that it meant to halt any new Soviet encroachment, Moscow realized that the European balance of power, smashed by the war, was being re-established with American help and could only be challenged in a major war.

In the Russian tradition, Stalin accordingly concentrated on Asia.

Asia became Moscow's primary target after important personnel changes in the Kremlin. Joseph Stalin, Czar without a crown, exercised supreme authority, but he frequently allowed the lesser men of the Politburo to engage in personal quarrels and to advocate divergent policies. Watching this play, the dictator was able to test alternative programs, and compare rival candidates for the succession.

In the Politburo after the Second World War, Andrei Zhdanov was the "European" who believed that Moscow should attempt to expand into the capitalist half of Europe with the help of the French, Italian, and other Communist parties. Stalin shared this view and supported Zhdanov. It was Zhdanov, then generally regarded as Stalin's heir, who played the leading role at the conference near Warsaw in September, 1947, which knitted the Communist parties of the East European colonies and France and Italy into the Cominform.

But observers noted at the time that Malenkov, another member of the Moscow Politburo, also attended the conference. Malenkov was Zhdanov's rival. Thanks to Malenkov's maneuvers, in fact, Zhdanov's star descended so low during the war that he remained conspicuously absent from the January, 1945, ceremonies commemorating Leningrad's liberation from Nazi siege though he had conducted the city's defense. Several months later, however, he climbed back to the top and Malenkov slipped. Malenkov, therefore, obviously did not go to the first Cominform conference to be helpful to Zhdanov, unless it was to help Zhdanov fail.

Zhdanov's foremost protégé among the satellite leaders was Marshal Tito, and the Cominform accordingly, established its headquarters in the Yugoslav capital. Tito's defection in June, 1948, seriously weakened Zhdanov's position already shaken by the failure of the Communist-led political strikes in France and Italy in the autumn of 1947, and by the victory of the democratic elements in the April, 1948, Italian elections. Zhdanov suffered a further and final setback because the Berlin blockade did not produce the desired result of ousting America from Germany, and perhaps from Europe.

Zhdanov's time had come. He died on August 31, 1948, of "paralysis of the heart," the official bulletin announced. To be sure, people in Russia, and even Soviet leaders, do sometimes die of natural causes, but the suspicion exists that, as the Russian saying goes, "he was helped to die." Indeed, the Soviet physicians, most of them Jews, who were arrested in January, 1953, on the charge, since officially repudiated, of plotting against their government, were specifically accused of administering the wrong medicines to Zhdanov. And, notoriously, crimes thus attributed to individual Soviet citizens have been the work of the Soviet government.

The death of Zhdanov brought Georgi Malenkov into the ascent. He was Stalin's political child and not a revolutionist.

Stalin frequently manifested his distrust of revolution. At a Central Committee session on January 24, 1918, for instance, he said, "There is no revolutionary movement in the West . . . and we cannot reckon with a potential." Lenin flayed him for this view and stated that if it prevailed "we would be traitors to international socialism."[2] Stalin nevertheless remained skeptical about popular revolutions till he died. His totalitarianism, based as it was on fear of the people, precluded any spontaneous initiative which might give them power. The sole contribution expected of citizens was passive obedience. Stalin's creation of the Soviet empire during the Second World War was a military operation without benefit of a single uprising. In fact, Stalin delayed the Russian capture of Warsaw until the one revolt which did occur had been crushed by the Nazis, for if they had not done it the task would have fallen to him; the Warsaw revolt was non-Communist.

Malenkov, born January 7, 1902, was too young to have had a revolutionary past or to be stirred by the revolutionary myth. If the dream of a better world or a higher type of human being ever in-

[2] V. I. Lenin, *Sochinenya* (*Collected Works*), Second Edition, edited by N. I. Bukharin, V. M. Molotov, and M. A. Savelyov, Moscow-Leningrad: State Publishing House, 1929, Vol. 22.

spired him he kept it a secret. He is a hard-boiled power man. When he succeeded Zhdanov as Number Two to Stalin, he took Asia for his arena and resorted to arms, the instruments of power. In 1949, Zhdanov's associates having been purged, Moscow greatly increased its military assistance to the Chinese Communists. Several Soviet army marshals visited China to plan campaigns and supervise field operations against the Kuomintang forces. "On October 1, 1949, the Central People's Government of the People's Republic of China was formally inaugurated"[3] in Peking. In June, 1950, Malenkov showed his hand again when the North Koreans invaded South Korea.

American resistance to Soviet imperialism in Europe had turned Moscow Asiaward, but Washington's top policy-makers were not aware of the shift and did not become aware of it until several years later. This cannot be attributed merely to lack of wisdom or information. Europe normally impedes U.S. vision of Asia and even of Latin America. For Europe is the mother of America and enjoys a natural priority in U.S. foreign affairs. In 1947, Europe seemed on the brink of collapse and Communism. Hence the Truman Doctrine and Marshall Plan. But the Marshall Plan made sense only on the assumption that war could be prevented. It was no use fattening up Europe for Russian conquest. The Marshall Plan therefore led to the rearming of Europe under NATO (North Atlantic Treaty Organization). And that raised the issue of German rearmament which, beginning 1949, absorbed an enormous amount of State Department energy.

In 1947 and 1948, moreover, when the United States was assuming heavy commitments to the economy and defense of Europe, few persons foresaw how quickly Red China would emerge as a formidable and disturbing factor in world affairs. Russia seemed the sole menace and Europe seemed to be her target. The Truman Administration therefore rushed to the rescue with dollars and guns.

Nevertheless, nothing fully excuses the failure of the Truman Administration to meet the Communist challenge in Asia before 1950. The basic cause, I feel, was the deficiency of Asia-mindedness in the American people and officialdom. The Pacific Ocean is very wide, especially for those states not bathed by its stormy waters. To most Americans, Asia meant Japan, then resting snugly under Douglas MacArthur's military occupation, and China, where the defeat of the Communists would have required the employment of a much larger

[3] A *Guide to New China*, Peking: Foreign Language Press, 1953, p. 6.

American armed force than the generals or citizenry, in the postwar mood of demobilization, were ready to assign to that task. To be sure, President Truman and Secretary of State Acheson did take the country into the expensive Korean struggle in 1950. But Korea was a case of outside aggression recognized as such by the United Nations—and that made a big difference—whereas to fight in China would have been intervention in a foreign civil war that had been going on indecisively for many years. In 1947 and 1948, when America was diving deep into Europe, an additional major commitment of U.S. power in China might have seemed excessive and, too, an adventure in mistaken emphasis, for all hearts were set on containing Russia in Europe. And by 1949, it was probably too late to enter the Chinese struggle. The Communists were winning it. At all stages, the widespread impression that Generalissimo Chiang's regime hesitated to introduce the social reforms on which alone a military victory could be built dampened American ardor for his cause.

As to large-scale economic aid: anything like a Marshall Plan for Asia was hobbled by the technological backwardness of all countries except Japan. In Europe, plant equipment, experienced management, and skilled working men, as well as markets, merely lay dormant awaiting America's golden touch before springing back into life. In industrially retarded Asia, big American loans or grants and mammoth shipments of raw materials could not have been put to creative use.

Yet when all this has been said, America's neglect of Asia remains a surprising and dismal fact. Europe, the crumpled, wrinkled old peninsula dangling from the bloated body of the Eurasian Continent, had a first and almost exclusive claim not only on U.S. attention but on the U.S. exchequer even when it was a matter of small sums. Point Four of President Truman's Inaugural Address of January 20, 1949—"We must embark on a bold new program for making the benefits of our scientific and industrial progress available for the development and growth of underdeveloped areas"—was an inspiring sentiment, but it remained a row of dead letters for many months, and when it came to life its meager blood supply of dollars prevented it from acting vigorously. Asia felt left out.

To an increasing extent, moreover, American thinking on world affairs was being shaped by military needs, or current concepts of military needs, and the military were determined to rearm Germany. For that, the assent of France was necessary. America, accordingly, did not wish to antagonize the French by insisting that they withdraw from Indo-China as it had successfully insisted on Dutch withdrawal from Indonesia. The United States was also late in demanding military and political independence for Vietnam, Laos, and Cambodia. French governments were sensitive and Washington hesitated to irritate them. Paris politicians held that a retreat in Indo-China would undermine France's position in North Africa where America wanted air bases. In fact, the abandonment of a French colony in far-off Asia might have done the reverse of reinforcing anti-imperialism in Tunisia, Algeria, and Morocco; it might have blunted it by proving French good intentions toward rising nationalisms with which a liberal Paris Cabinet could have reached a compromise solution. England had converted Indians, Pakistanis, Burmese, and Ceylonese from subjects into friends, but the narrow French concept of private property prevented them from giving up the disappearing substance to keep the essence, and U.S. statesmanship followed the alluring mirage of early German rearmament with French consent and lost sight of the Indo-Chinese problem and its inevitably embittering effect on all of Asia.

Presently, an event occurred which might have brought Asia and America close together: in October, 1949, Prime Minister Jawaharlal Nehru arrived in the United States for an official visit. No foreigner, except the British King and Queen and Churchill, ever received a more ecstatic welcome from the American people. "India" has always spelled glamour. Nehru himself had glamour, charm, and beauty. He wore Gandhi's mantle and it was synonymous with a noble idealism and high moral purpose which inspire reverence:

Nehru had written that this was "The Century of Asia." But others proclaimed it the American Century. Europe too reached toward rebirth, and the dark African giant was rattling his chains. All continents crackled with creative energy and craved a new self-expression in freedom. None wanted a leader, all needed partners. None would dominate, each had to co-operate. The Mahatma, Nehru's acknowledged master, had lived as a Christan-Jewish-Moslem-Confucian Hindu. His gifted pupil could be an American-Australian-European-African Asian, a unifier in a world too poor to pay the mounting cost of disunity. He might have been the channel through which America could save Southeast Asia from bloodshed, misery, and imperialism. But on arriving in New York, almost his first words were, "I think I don't want any ties, and I think the best ties are no ties."[4] Many

---

[4] *New York Times*, October 16, 1949.

hearts sank. Several days later, on receiving a Doctor of Laws degree at Columbia University, Nehru said, "We do not wish to forfeit the advantage that our present detachment gives us. . . . That detachment," he contended, "is neither isolationism nor indifference, nor neutrality when peace or freedom is threatened. When man's liberty or peace is in danger we cannot and shall not be neutral; neutrality, then, will be a betrayal of what we have fought for and stand for."[5] Yet a moment later, when he expressed the hope that Indonesia, Indo-China, and Africa achieve liberty, his "detachment" did not impel him to express the same hope for the East Europeans enslaved by Russia.

Not that Nehru was pro-Communist. Speaking at a reception in the home of Mrs. Dorothy Norman in New York he called the Communists of India "a party with a foreign allegiance," and answering a question from Nicolas Nabokov as to whether the Soviet government could be trusted, the Prime Minister said, "Normally not."

Yet Indian anti-imperialists frequently overlooked Soviet imperialism. In a conversation at a public luncheon, I asked Nehru's chief foreign adviser why the Prime Minister had referred to the liberation of only Indonesia, Indo-China, and Africa but not of Poland, Rumania, Hungary, and so forth. "On Hungary," he replied, "we do not know the facts."

"That," I remarked, "is your pro-Soviet prejudice." I was probably unfair in this comment. Nehru's Asian eye simply had better vision than his European eye.

The Nehru problem was not one of the mind. "I can only guess what is the purpose of Nehru's visit," I wrote to the *New York Times* of October 16, 1949. "Our purpose should be to win his heart." In Washington, President Truman and Secretary of State Acheson tried to reach Nehru's heart, but it remained inaccessible. Some time after the Prime Minister's stay in Washington, newspapermen reported that Truman had been saying to Congressmen, "Nehru practices color prejudice in reverse, he hates white people." Subsequently, Norman Thomas, the Socialist leader, told me of a talk he had had with Truman. The President said, "Mr. Thomas, not very long ago, Prime Minister Nehru was sitting in the very chair where you are now sitting, and I got the impression that he doesn't like white folks." Actually, Nehru has liked many white folks. But what Harry Truman may have sensed was the attitude of superiority assumed by the Kashmiri Brahman when facing a Missouri ex-haberdasher. That the

[5] *Ibid.*, October 18, 1949.

Midwestern plebeian occupied the U.S. White House made it even more satisfying to look down on him.

Acheson was present at most of the talks between Truman and Nehru. He also had several private conversations with the Indian visitor. At none of these meetings was any request made or promise given by either side. Truman and Acheson regarded Nehru's stay in Washington as an opportunity to create a fruitful personal understanding. But there is no evidence that they succeeded even partially.

On October 12, 1949, Secretary Acheson tendered Mr. Nehru a state dinner attended by some sixty persons, among them General George C. Marshall, Justice Felix Frankfurter, Secretary of the Treasury Snyder, Secretary of Defense Johnson, Secretary of Labor Tobin, Senator Tom Connally, Admiral Chester W. Nimitz, David E. Lilienthal, and James B. Reston. Acheson's speech was warm and imaginative. He regretted, he said, that Thomas Jefferson was not present to greet the Indian guest, the two democrats would have found much in common; he was sorry President Andrew Jackson and Nehru could not have met, both were outstanding social reformers and practical statesmen; how delighted Abraham Lincoln would have been to welcome India's freedom leader, their spiritual qualities would have woven a strong bond between them.

Nehru, in reply, disclaimed, with appropriate modesty, the virtues thus lavishly attributed to him, but in so doing he left the impression of eluding the web of friendship which Acheson had spun. As the evening wore on, the Secretary of State felt he wanted to make one last attempt at intimate mental companionship with Mr. Nehru and, having passed his duties as host to his wife Alice and to General Marshall, he took Nehru to his house. The butler served Nehru a ginger ale and Acheson Scotch and soda, and went up to bed, and the statesmen sat together from eleven to two in the morning. Since neither man is given to small talk, nor was this the purpose of the occasion, conversation was very slow in getting started. Nehru did not respond to several of Acheson's opening gambits. Finally, the Secretary of State said that something was obviously lacking in America's grasp of Indian and Asian affairs and he would welcome enlightenment. Nehru replied that everything was wrong. Would the Prime Minister specify? At first he felt reluctant to do so, but on being prodded, he said, yes, he would mention one difficulty: the problem of Kashmir. Thereafter, until he left, Mr. Nehru talked about Kashmir, talked passionately and well, and gave his avid listener the impression of having a quick, agile, perceptive mind. But the gulf had been widened. Mr. Acheson was not aware at the time that this was Nehru's purpose, and Nehru may not have been conscious of it, yet the Kashmir issue could only be a barrier, Acheson had no way of settling it, and to devote to it the final opportunity for contact was an indication that no contact was wanted.

Acheson has a keen, far-ranging, distinguished mind; the evening might have yielded pleasure and profit. It was barren. Nehru was resisting capture. He always resisted capture. His haughtiness in early manhood caused frequent clashes with his mighty father Motilal, a brilliant lawyer and public figure. Jawaharlal Nehru also resisted Gandhi: examples can be found in his autobiography[6] and other books. While most Indian champions of independence bowed to the Mahatma's intuition when his wisdom failed to convince them, Nehru was apparently too rational, Western, and proud to do so.

After Nehru had seen President Truman and Secretary Acheson in Washington he went to New York and, at the first public function, declared, "I have asked for nothing." This was proof of pride and isolation. Why not ask when there is so much need? But Nehru, new to sovereignty, did not realize the strength that inheres in it; he suspected an American assault on India's independence. Perhaps this is a natural and justifiable response to the past of India, a country which has been invaded and looted by many foreign armies. The Moslem conquest produced a sense of fear, and the British conquest a sense of inferiority. The Hindu reacted to the former by shutting himself in a big house with a tiny gate; he built cities with very narrow lanes for streets so that marauders could not attack in great numbers, and he sought safety in his own province, caste, and joint family. Isolation gave him security, and consorting with his own kind gave him confidence. Thus the complicated Indian wants a wall against those who are big, bad, and different and a bridge to those who are considered equal and similar. Here may lie the roots of Indian foreign policy and of the failure of Nehru's stay in America. He would not forge a link because he feared it might grow into a chain. A great opportunity to advance international understanding was thereby lost.

Nehru's stay in the United States in October, 1949, antedated the troubles that developed between his country and America on the

[6] *Toward Freedom; the Autobiography of Jawaharlal Nehru*, New York: The John Day Co., 1941.

Korean issue, on China, and a number of other complicated matters. The slate of Indo-American relations was relatively clean. No black clouds had yet appeared. In the United States there was great good will; in India the memory of America's friendly attitude toward her national struggle for independence was still fresh. Yet Mr. Nehru proved unco-operative.

CHAPTER FIFTEEN

No Third World War. The Korea Story

PRIME MINISTER NEHRU'S coldness toward America was due to psychological factors. Events in China were destined to deepen it. On October 18, 1949, seventeen days after the establishment of the Mao Tse-tung regime in Peking, Mr. Nehru, answering a question by John Gunther, advocated its diplomatic recognition at a luncheon of the Overseas Press Club in New York. India's Prime Minister could not ignore the Red China government even if the United States chose to do so. Mao's march to power would affect India deeply. In fact, the Chinese Communist victory was sure to affect all of Southeast Asia. Many capitals marked the event.

Moscow was particularly concerned. Malenkov had helped the Chinese Communists in the last phase when victory was inevitable. The help was born more of fear than of friendship, fear that Mao might ultimately challenge Russia's position in the Far East and Moscow's control of Asian Communist parties. The Soviets were certainly not overcome with joy by Mao's triumph and apparently felt the need of meeting it by some forward move of their own. The forward move was the invasion of South Korea by the Soviet-sponsored North Koreans.

The June, 1950, attack on South Korea has usually been regarded as directed against American interests. It was. But it actually represented an attempt to "kill" two birds, and the second was Communist China.

South Korea under a pro-American government was a Western beachhead on the Asian Continent, a wedge into the Communist world, and Moscow probably felt as uncomfortable about it as the United States might with a pro-Soviet military force in Mexico or as Europe might if Greece or Portugal went Communist. The South Korean beachhead was all the more unpleasant to the Soviet bloc in view of U.S. armed strength in Japan. North Korean conquest of the beachhead would have been a shattering blow to American power in the Far East and given Russia an invaluable advance position from which to threaten Japan politically and militarily. This alone would have justified the adventure. But in addition, a victory of Moscow's North Korean puppet would, by relieving Russia of the presence of America on her border, reinforce Soviet power in general and on Red China's flank in particular and thereby enhance Soviet influence over China and Manchuria. The North Korean attack on June 24, 1950, was thus a Kremlin attempt to push America back and hold China in check.

The double jeopardization of America and China by Soviet control of South Korea was emphasized by Lieutenant General A. C. Wedemeyer, in his report to President Truman about his mission to China and Korea. The report, submitted on September 9, 1947, declared that "A Soviet-dominated Korea would constitute a serious political and psychological threat to Manchuria, North China, the Ryukus, and Japan, and hence to United States strategic interests in the Far East. It is therefore in the best interest of the United States to ensure the permanent military neutralization of Korea. Neutralization can only be assured by its occupation until its future independence as a buffer state is assured."[1]

With General Wedemeyer's report in front of them, and seventeen days after its official submission, the United States Joint Chiefs of Staff nevertheless decided unanimously to do just what Wedemeyer

[1] *Report to the President Submitted by Lt. Gen. A. C. Wedemeyer, September, 1947: Korea,* Washington: United States Government Printing Office, 1951, p. 24.

had advised against, they decided to withdraw the American forces from South Korea because, they wrote, "from the standpoint of military security, the United States has little strategic interest in maintaining the present troops and bases in Korea."

This startling evidence of military myopia and lack of Asia-mindedness was contained in a document which remained secret for five years, and it might have remained secret to this day had it not been that General Eisenhower, campaigning for the Presidency at Detroit on October 24, 1952, attacked the Truman Administration for abandoning South Korea. When President Truman heard of this attack he picked up the telephone, spoke to Senator Wayne L. Morse of Oregon, and told him of the existence of the top-secret decision of the Joint Chiefs of Staff of September 26, 1947, to withdraw the U.S. troops from South Korea. Mr. Truman pointed out, and Senator Morse revealed in a speech at Minneapolis on October 27, 1952, that the decision of the Joint Chiefs of Staff had been unanimous; Eisenhower himself, as Chief of Staff of the Army, had voted to abandon South Korea. A few days later, on November 3, 1952, President Truman allowed the full text of the document to be published in the newspapers.

At the time the Joint Chiefs decided on withdrawal there were 45,000 American military personnel in South Korea, and, lest American prestige be damaged, they cautioned against "precipitate withdrawal." The withdrawal, accordingly, took place in stages and was completed on June 29, 1949.[2] Having determined on the evacuation of South Korea, the United States was instrumental in persuading the United Nations to adopt a resolution in favor of the departure of all foreign troops from the Korean peninsula; Soviet troops then left North Korea, but not before a large, well-equipped, well-trained North Korean army capable, as events proved, of mounting a smashing offensive, had been created. The American generals knew this was going on, but they did not expect North Korea to attack. The military crystal ball was murky.

Seven months after American combat forces were out of Korea, Secretary of State Dean Acheson told the National Press Club on January 12, 1950, that the United States "defensive perimeter" in the Far East "runs along the Aleutians to Japan and then goes to the Ryukus [Okinawa]. . . . The defensive perimeter runs from the

[2] *Military Situation in the Far East*, Part 3, p. 1811.

Ryukus to the Philippine Islands." Since American troops were stationed in all these places, the United States would defend them against aggression. But, Acheson continued, "as far as the military security of other areas in the Pacific is concerned, it must be clear that no person can guarantee these areas against military attack. . . . Should such an attack occur . . . the initial reliance must be on the people attacked to resist it and then upon the commitment of the entire civilized world under the United Nations."[3]

Acheson spoke from notes instead of from a prepared text as befits such a delicate subject. In fact, he need not have mentioned the matter at all. The statement created no furor when he made it. Subsequently, however, his words were related to the North Korean attack; it was charged that by saying South Korea lay outside the United States defense perimeter and would, in case of aggression, have to rely on its own resources, which Moscow knew to be weak, and on the United Nations, whose military potential Stalin held in contempt, Acheson encouraged the Communists to assail South Korea. In his defense, he would say that the crucial factor was not his words but the actual withdrawal of the U.S. armed forces from the lower half of the peninsula.

The objective situation, in any case, was clear: but for the abandonment of South Korea by the U.S. military the North Korean attack would have been impossible.

The United States decision to intervene against Communist aggression in Korea has a dramatic history. The State Department in Washington first learned of the North Korean attack from a press flash. It immediately telegraphed an inquiry to U.S. Ambassador John Muccio at Seoul. Before he received it he cabled a report which reached the State Department's code room at nine-twenty Saturday night, June 24, 1950. "Within a matter of minutes, the message was decoded and the Department was alerted for action."[4] Ambassador Muccio's message made it clear that a major military action had commenced. Dean Rusk, Assistant Secretary of State for Far Eastern Affairs, John D. Hickerson, Assistant Secretary for United Nations affairs, and Ambassador-at-Large Philip Jessup were immediately summoned to the State Department. They conferred among themselves

[3] *Ibid.*, p. 1812.

[4] Address by Secretary Acheson before the Convention of the American Newspaper Guild, Washington, D.C., June 29, 1950.

and with Secretary of the Army Frank Pace; meanwhile one of them telephoned Secretary Acheson at his farm in Maryland and told him the bad news. Acheson gave instructions that Mr. Trygve Lie, the Secretary-General of the United Nations, be asked to convene a special Sunday session of the UN Security Council. Then he telephoned President Truman who had arrived at his home in Independence, Missouri, only a few hours earlier after a long flight from Washington. Truman approved of the calling the UN Security Council and said he would return to his plane and fly to the national capital. But Acheson felt there was no need for night flying and promised to phone again the next morning when there was sure to be more information from Korea.

I asked Acheson whether he was excited and what he did next.

"No," he replied. "I was conscious of the seriousness of the situation but ᵀ wasn't excited. I talked to Alice for a while and went to bed."

The next morning, Sunday, Acheson drove to the State Department. The news from Korea and from General MacArthur's headquarters in Japan was grave. Acheson asked several of his aides—Rusk, Hickerson, and others—to his office. They talked for three-quarters of an hour. "By that time," says Acheson, "my mind was made up." He knew immediate U.S. action in Korea had become inevitable.

Acheson then telephoned Truman, gave him the contents of a report from MacArthur's office in Tokyo that the South Korean situation was deteriorating. Truman then said that he would fly to Washington immediately, and asked Acheson to convene the top Presidential military and diplomatic advisers for a dinner meeting that same day. He left it to Acheson to draw up the list of names.

Sunday afternoon, while the Presidential plane was winging over the Mississippi Valley, the Security Council at Lake Success, by nine votes to zero—the Soviet delegate having taken a walk weeks before and not returned, and the Yugoslav delegate abstaining—adopted a U.S. resolution which declared North Korea guilty of breaking the peace and demanded that it withdraw its troops from South Korea.

The President's plane landed at Washington airport at 7:15 P.M. He was met by Secretary of Defense Louis Johnson, Secretary Acheson, and Under Secretary of State James Webb. A photograph of Truman, Johnson, and Acheson taken at the plane shows the President not his usual jovial, jaunty self, but hollow with worry, mournful as though someone close had died and he were going to see the body. He looks like a person weighed down by the tragedy of a fateful decision yet to be made.

With Louis Johnson and Acheson, President Truman drove to Blair House, his residence while the White House was being remodeled and repaired. The President went upstairs to wash and change his shirt and telephone Mrs. Truman in Independence that he had arrived safely. Meantime his advisers were assembling and drinking cocktails. They had gathered together to make one of the most important decisions in twentieth-century American history, and it was a pure decision in the sense that the decision to enter the Second World War, for instance, was not, because that decision was really arrived at by the handful of Japanese militarists who planned the attack on Pearl Harbor and then the United States had to go to war.

Present at the dinner, in addition to Mr. Truman, were Secretary of Defense Louis Johnson, Chairman of the Joint Chiefs of Staff General Omar N. Bradley, Secretary of the Army Frank Pace, Secretary of the Air Force Thomas K. Finletter, Secretary of the Navy Francis P. Matthews, Chief of Staff of the Army General J. Lawton Collins, Chief of Staff of the Air Force General Hoyt S. Vandenberg, Chief of Staff of the Navy Admiral Forrest P. Sherman, and, from the State Department: Acheson, Webb, Jessup, Rusk, and Hickerson.

During the three-course, fried chicken dinner the President permitted no talk about the impending decision. When coffee had been served he waved the waiters out of the room and then the fourteen men got down to the business before them. They conferred till eleven, and since the dinner had started a few minutes after eight, and assuming it lasted about forty-five minutes, the time devoted to Korea was a little over two hours. Acheson spoke first. He urged the immediate dispatch of military supplies to South Korea and the evacuation of American dependents under the protection of the U.S. air force and fleet which were to be authorized to shoot at North Koreans attempting to interfere with their operations. He also recommended sending the Seventh Fleet from the Philippines to Formosa.

Mr. Truman then went around the table asking those present to state their views freely. General Hoyt Vandenberg said the air force could deal adequately with the North Koreans and no U.S. ground troops would be necessary. A number of his military colleagues were not so sure, but neither were they sure that armed action by the United States would be required. Despite the rapid Communist advance, the generals tended, that evening, to underestimate North Korean power and exaggerate the strength of the South Korean constabulary.

Somebody mentioned and others discussed the chances of Russian and Chinese intervention. Views were vague, and the President asked for information on what could be done if it did occur in Korea or elsewhere.

Under Secretary of State Webb suggested that some thought be given to possible political opposition at home by the Administration's critics. The President quickly brushed this aside and said he would be ruled only by considerations of national interest and national defense.

All the President's thirteen advisers concurred in Mr. Acheson's three propositions: send arms to Korea; evacuate Americans under armed guard; and move the fleet. The President thereupon gave them his approval and ordered the necessary instructions sent to the Far East. Mr. Truman's guests then left by the back door to avoid reporters.

This first Blair House conference on Korea was inconclusive because of the inevitable paucity of information and the regrettable optimism of the military.

The next evening, while the President was having dinner alone at the Blair House, he "was interrupted at 7:29 by a phone call from Acheson, who said the Korean news was now so bad that another meeting was advisable. 'Have them here at nine P.M.,' the President said. At that hour the same group as the night before—minus Under Secretary of State Webb—gathered around the mahogany table."[5] Mr. Acheson again drew up the list of participants and issued the invitations.

The second Blair House conference, which lasted forty minutes, dispelled any doubts—and hopes—that remained after the previous evening. America would fight in Korea. The President, acting on Acheson's advice and with the agreement of all present, declared that the fullest air and naval combat support was to go to the rapidly-disintegrating South Korean forces. As the President's advisers dispersed, he said, "Everything I have done in the last five years has been to try to avoid making such a decision as I made tonight."[5] The die was cast.

[5] Beverly Smith, "White House Story: Why We Went to War in Korea," *Saturday Evening Post,* November 10, 1951.

The second Blair House conference, in additional to sanctioning U.S. military action in Korea, decided to expand military aid to the Philippines and Indo-China. Mr. Thomas K. Finletter believes that this might have been an excellent opportunity for negotiations to "internationalize" the Indo-Chinese War and link it, like Korea, with the United Nations, for both were aspects of the struggle for collective security, and the Indo-China conflict, therefore, should not have been allowed to remain an attempt to prolong Western imperialism in Asia.

Mr. Finletter, watching Mr. Truman at the Blair House meetings and at subsequent sessions, noted, and shared, the President's devotion to the United Nations. So did some others. When I asked Ambassador-at-Large Philip Jessup, who attended the Sunday and Monday night Blair House talks, what, in his opinion, had motivated the conferees, he said, "Well, the military here probably reacted to the military challenge, while those of us from the State Department who were handling United Nations affairs were reacting to the challenge to the UN and to the whole system of collective security. All had in mind the ultimately dangerous consequences to the United States if this aggression was not resisted. The case of Korea was nothing like the sinking of the *Lusitania* before World War I. We could not just send a note. The North Korean invasion left us no choice. We had to act. We could not wait and see. I felt proud of President Truman. The Blair House conferences were democratic government at its best. The President made the decision. But he acted on advice."

Motivations in men—and even in the highest officials—are manifold and complicated. Perhaps the U.S. military wished to atone for the mistake of withdrawing the U.S. armed forces from South Korea in 1949. Probably, however, the chief reason for the Blair House decision was the realization that American acquiescence in South Korea's quick death would encourage Communist depredations elsewhere. And this raised the specter of a third world war. If the Korean aggression succeeded it might, like Manchuria in 1931, be the first step down into the abyss of another global struggle, this time with atomic bombs.

The men in the Blair House agreed that the chances were against Russia's armed intervention in the Korean fight. But there was a risk that she would intervene and the risk had to be taken because America's failure to protect South Korea would have wrecked all efforts to organize Europe or Asia for defense against Communist imperialism.

If the United States did not aid South Korea other exposed nations would expect to be similarly abandoned in case of attack or trouble. Then why join any U.S.-sponsored security bloc? American abstention in Korea would have ruined NATO in Europe, crippled the UN, and caused Asian countries to quail and crumple in the face of internal or outside Communist threats. It seems no exaggeration to say that if Truman and his advisers had resolved against action in Korea they would have been forced to scrap America's foreign policy, revert to isolationism, and surrender the Eastern Hemisphere to Russia and China. From this point of view, the Blair House decision was an easy one. It involved heavy responsibilities, but there was no escape from it. The almost universal acceptance of the Blair House decision by the American people, despite grumbling, would suggest that isolationism was dead as a policy.

In the Korean crisis, as in the case of the Truman Doctrine and Marshall Plan, the President and the executive branch made wise decisions with speed and the Congress and country followed. These three decisions alone would distinguish Mr. Truman as a great President and a great little man. Franklin D. Roosevelt made a bigger impact on the American social system but both before and during the war, he often fumbled foreign policy, and at least in the field of international relations, therefore, it is likely that the historians will mark Truman up and Roosevelt down. Considering that Harry Truman was a provincial from Missouri and Mr. Roosevelt the man of the world from New York this is a rather remarkable personal feat, a tribute to Truman's civil courage and readiness to lead, but also a reflection of the more mature understanding of world affairs which the American public acquired in the Roosevelt era.

This does not mean, however, that the U.S. objective in Korea was clearly understood. The purpose of American intervention in Korea was not to unify Korea or to destroy Red China or Red Russia. Its purpose was to repel an aggressor and thereby reinforce the structure of peace in Asia and Europe. Both these objectives were attained. When hostilities ceased the invader had been driven out of South Korea and a third world war was at least delayed and perhaps prevented entirely. Western resistance to Russian-sponsored aggression in Korea did what the democracies had failed to do before the Second World War: it served notice that in the event of aggression they would act on the side of the victim. This is a mammoth deterrent. It is altogether conceivable that largely as a result of the UN and U.S. fight in Korea there will never be a third world war. That is victory enough.

The idea of No-Third-World-War, to be sure, conflicts with the widespread notion of an inevitable armed clash arising out of un-bridgeable differences between the Communist and non-Communist social systems. Yet though the democratic nations are adamantly anti-Communist they are not likely to start a war against Communist nations. Will Russia fight the democratic world? I have always taken a special interest in Bolshevik foreign policy and have written a two-volume book on the Soviets in world affairs. Yet I have never been convinced that the Soviet government had a plan for world conquest. Aside from quotations from Bolshevik scriptures—which can usually be canceled out by other quotations; and both sets are subject to interpretation—I have not seen any proof of the existence of such a plan or a timetable. No doubt, Communists hope that Communist power will be extended at the expense of the democracies just as democrats would applaud the opposite, and each side might, given favorable conditions, contribute to the fruition of its desires. But I feel that the government of the Soviet Union is unlikely to risk its own involvement in even a minor war or risk a major embarrassment in its international relations in order to advance the cause of world Communism.

Moscow has always looked upon the Third International or Comin-tern, on its rump successor the Cominform, and on foreign Com-munist parties as instruments of Soviet foreign policy and, in propi-tious circumstances, as agencies of the Russian secret police. The spread of Communist power outside the confines of the Soviet Union has always been subordinated to Russian national aims. I find no evidence in the record to suggest the contrary. I see no case in which the Soviet government was ready to sacrifice anything more than sums of money which hardly count in its enormous budget, or some persons, always expendable in a dictatorship, or a slice of its reputation with foreign powers, also always expendable, in order to promote world revolution. Even Lenin, who had a Communist faith which has ebbed to the vanishing point in his present Russian suc-cessors, refused, during the crisis over the Brest Litovsk peace nego-tiations with Kaiser Germany in 1917-18, to offer up Russia on the altar of foreign revolt. To those who pleaded for military resistance to Germany in order to stimulate revolution in that country, Lenin replied, "Germany, you see, is only pregnant with revolution, but here in Russia a perfectly healthy child—the socialist republic—has already been born, and we may kill it if we start a war." Of course, that was at a time when the Soviet regime was too weak to try to expand for either revolutionary or imperialistic reasons. In 1939, and thereafter until 1945, it had the power, will, and opportunity to expand and did, but first it obtained Hitler's initial approval and later it sought the consent of Russia's Western wartime allies. Whether the purpose was the extension of the Soviet empire or the spread of Communism—and at this point there is no need of jousting in that bog—the governing consideration was always caution. To date, Lenin's no-war-for-revolution approach and no-war-for-anything has guided the lesser men who inherited the master's pinnacle.

Nevertheless, fears of a third world war launched by Russia commenced to multiply shortly after the end of the second. These were induced by Moscow's apparently insatiable imperialist appetite. It had annexed a vast territory during the war yet seemed intent on taking more.

Soon, however, evidence began to accumulate that though the Soviet authorities wanted to enlarge their dominions they would not do so at the cost of war. They were in no sense pacifist or humanitarian, and they had no compunctions about shedding Russian blood, they had shed plenty of it; but they did not intend to gamble with the future of their regime. Their postwar policy was No War and No Peace. They would raise international tension to the maximum. This would provide a propaganda argument at home in justification of the rigors of the dictatorship; abroad, the Western powers might mistake the tension for warlike intention and grant more concessions to assuage Moscow's apparent fury. The atmosphere of tension was a congenial climate for Stalin; he flourished in it. And it never worried him because he knew that no matter how irregular, irritating, and menacing his conduct, the West would not attack. He could therefore set the tone of world politics. If the danger became too great he could always retreat.

One by one, situations arose in the postwar period in which Russia actually did retreat. As these episodes occurred I began to move toward the comforting conclusion that there would be no war. Some tentative thoughts of this kind germinated in 1946 and grew in 1947 and 1948, but not till much later did I dare formulate the No-Third-World-War thesis either to myself or others. However, Russia's passivity in the face of the buildup of UN, chiefly American, military strength in Korea confirmed my optimism about the world outlook, and one day, when challenged, I put it in words.

It happened on September 9, 1950, while I was a week-end guest of Mr. and Mrs. Eustace Seligman at their place near Greenwich, Connecticut. Eustace, a senior law partner in the firm of Sullivan and Cromwell, takes special delight in presiding over after-dinner discussions at his home in town or country. While he cleans, knocks, blows into, fills, empties, and occasionally even puffs on his silver-stemmed pipe, he keeps the conversational ball in play until departure hour. This time the company, which included Charles W. Cole, President of Amherst College and his wife; Ordway Tead, President of the Board of Higher Education in New York and his wife, the President of Briarcliff Junior College; François Puaux, the French Consul in New York and his wife Anne; and about twenty others, had just settled in an ellipse of chairs in the big sitting room when Eustace—both hands fully occupied with his smoking paraphernalia—tossed the ball to me. "Louis," he said, "now tell us, is Russia going to fight in Korea?"

Obviously, I did not know.

"Well, make a prediction," Eustace urged. I tried to pass the ball to a neighbor but it came right back, and, realizing that there was no escape and sensing serious interest in the problem, I enumerated the postwar situations in which the Soviet government refrained from war although it might have found sufficient provocation or reason to fight. These were: (1) 1946, when Moscow accepted the Shah's reconquest of the puppet Soviet state of Azerbaijan inside Iran, a powerful position from which the whole country might have been drawn into the Soviet empire, instead of going to war to preserve it; (2) 1946, when Moscow failed to press its territorial and other claims against Turkey because, since the Turks refused to yield, Russia would have had to fight; (3) Russian abstention from the Greek civil war where a Communist victory seemed so near in 1947; (4) Stalin's failure in 1948 to use military force to bring recalcitrant Yugoslavia back into the empire; (5) Russia's passivity and retreat at Berlin in 1949 in face of the Anglo-American determination to hold the city by means of the airlift; and (6) Soviet abstention, so far, from active participation in the Korean War.

The French lady asked whether this "seeming peacefulness" was not due to the Communist belief in the ultimate triumph of their cause throughout the world. It was a factor, I replied, "but the

Bolsheviks are not fatalists, they believe in the final push that brings victory, and if they thought they would get away with it, they would try. They did not hesitate to gobble up one country after the other during the war; they knew nobody would attempt to stop them. But now they are afraid to act, afraid chiefly of the U.S.A."

I also enumerated some internal difficulties: the Soviets were short of meat and dairy products and had never solved even their grain problem. In 1946, Turkestan suffered from famine. The satellites were a swamp of discontent and not a solid base, therefore, from which to launch an attack on Western Europe. Even in the war to save Russia from the Nazis, many Soviet citizens and whole areas had been disloyal to the Soviet regime. The disaffection would be greater in an offensive war. The Soviet peoples would long remember and feel the tremendous cost of the Second World War—an estimated fifteen million civilian and military dead, and many more million wounded and incapacitated—and could have no desire for another war. A dictator must reckon with such deep sentiments in his subjects.

"How can we be sure," Eustace wondered, "that the Soviets are not simply waiting for an opportunity to make more conquests?"

"We cannot be sure," I said. "There are no guarantees in politics. The only way, in this phase, of preventing a third world war is to continue building up deterrent military power in the West. Our readiness to use that power in Korea is as much of a guarantee as there can be."

And so the friendly discussion rolled on and on. I had a feeling that some persons were shielding their pessimism against assault; it was too good to be true that we could avoid a third world war. But some were convinced. As events unfolded in subsequent months and years, I myself became more confirmed in the view that humanity would probably be spared the ultimate tragedy of total destruction in an atomic-hydrogen war. In such a war the losses would always be infinitely greater than any conceivable gain. And since gain of some kind is the purpose of war, major wars are unlikely.

Moreover, postwar experience has demonstrated through many concrete events that accidents and incidents need not cause wars. The Soviets and the Chinese Communists have shot down American and British planes and Western planes have shot down Communist planes, but since neither side was seeking an excuse to go to war they looked the other way and there was no war. If the cold war can be kept cold a few more years, therefore, it seems highly probable that the hydrogen-atomic bomb stockpiles of both blocs will become so towering as to make world war the quick equivalent of world suicide and hence unthinkable. Already, the power of each side suffices to deter the other. To keep the antagonist at peace it is not necessary to be stronger than he; it is only necessary to have enough hydrogen and atomic bombs to inflict major wounds on his cities and industries, and this point seems to have been reached by the Soviet Union as well as the West.

I understand well the sentiments of those who argue that co-existence with Communism is impossible. But neither is an atomic-hydrogen war possible. President Eisenhower put it positively on October 19, 1954: "Since the advent of nuclear weapons, it seems clear that there is no longer any alternative to peace."

Part Four
AMERICA AND EUROPE

CHAPTER SIXTEEN

The Sick Man of Europe

"FRANCE is asleep," Georges Bidault, former Premier and former Foreign Minister, said when I visited him at his home in St. Cloud, near Paris, in February, 1951. But the French men and women whom I saw in Paris and in the provinces were very much awake and vibrant; they ran to catch street cars, jumped on and off buses, talked animatedly in cafés, kissed in streets, argued and conversed with wit and verve in homes, and debated endlessly in Parliament and the press. And the children in the parks and gardens were charming. But apparently men, women, and children are not enough to make a nation; a nation must also have a soul, and the French soul was asleep, gone to sleep, perhaps, in a desire to forget.

All those months I looked for France but could not find it. There was no France, there were only forty-three million Frenchmen, individuals with great and just concern for themselves, and much less, if any, for the community. They were not even searching for their soul or a goal. At most they were searching for a Man. Many thought he was General Charles de Gaulle.

France had no focus, no magnet at the center to hold everything together, so the units flew off into space and described their own wild orbits. The country was atomized into its human components. This could be a very civilized way of living, a sort of liberty in anarchy. But nobody felt happy about it.

At the home of M. and Madame Rodolphe d'Adler, who had translated one of my books into French, I spent an evening with twelve

French men and women in their early twenties invited, at my suggestion, by young Josie d'Adler. They were handsome, well informed, articulate, friendly, and despondent. They said they did not plan long careers, did not save or intend to save money, and hesitated to get married and have children. In the midst of a gay party they might subside into a serious discussion about their dark prospects. Frenchmen would fight if war came, they said, but without much hope. One idea moved them; European Union, a United States of Europe.

Paris in 1951 was suffused with the perfume of pessimism. The French defended their gloom against all silver-lining interpreters. A former lieutenant colonel of the French army said, "The Russians will thrust to Gibraltar and Suez and then close the pincer and squeeze us in between. For me the war with Russia is a *'fait accompli,'* and I think we will have it this autumn, or next year."

Frenchmen drew the same conclusion from Korea. By diabolical cleverness, they declared, Stalin had forced America to concentrate most of its fighting power in Korea. Europe, consequently, lay unprotected and would succumb to the Soviet army. France, of course, would die again. Some people already showed that predeath pallor. "Monsieur," the elevator man in my hotel whispered, "we survived the Germans, we will survive the Russians too." Businessmen were advertising in Communist publications as insurance. Georges Garreau, a Paris columnist and friend of Premier René Pleven, told me the chief bookkeeper of a newspaper was warned that if he refused to sign the Stockholm Communist "peace pledge" a cross would be marked on his door when the Russians arrived. The same informant said he knew that high permanent officials of the French Foreign Office had signed the pledge "just in case." The Communist party was putting pressure on corner grocers to sign the Stockholm pledge. A "peace" pledge had thus become a plebiscite on war: will you submit to the Russians, the French Reds were asking.

The panic had not yet started, but preparations for it were in full swing. A perceptive Frenchwoman who represents American publishers in Paris said to me, "Many rich Parisians have bought boats which they keep on the Mediterranean for a quick escape to North Africa. Several industrialists I know, including a member of my family, have set up branch factories in Kenya, Latin America, South Africa, and in other distant lands so as to have capital abroad when they quit France before the Russians take over." Marshall Plan money was thus being shoveled out of France. "The mass of the people, however," the Frenchwomen added, "are thinking in terms of adaptation to the occupying force."

The political adaptation to Russian military occupation was also in the making; I discerned its outlines during a dinner debate with Jean Paul Sartre, the Existentialist philosopher and playwright. On December 10, he and I were the speakers at the inaugural meeting of the Franco-American Fellowship launched by Richard Wright, the American Negro writer, and Ligon Buford, a Negro formerly associated with UNRRA. Several hundred Africans, Americans, and Frenchmen attended, and their interest in M. Sartre, or in his ideas, was obvious from the way they surrounded him when the proceedings ended.

At nine M. Sartre, his friend Simone de Beauvoir, Richard Wright and his white wife, and I adjourned to a restaurant where we ate and talked till midnight. Sartre had said at the meeting that of course there was no freedom in Russia, but neither was there freedom in France, for the world was in a state of war, and war does not conduce to freedom. Therefore the only thing left to save was peace. With this as my text, I suggested at the dinner table that, maybe, since the French enjoyed no freedom they had nothing to fight for, and so, if the Russians came the only choice would be to save the peace by submission. "The Russians are not here yet," Madame de Beauvoir interjected angrily, "but the Americans are."

It would have been easy to be deflected by this sally into an evening-long wrangle about America. I preferred to explore Sartre's ideas on France. He, moreover, wanted to develop his thesis rather than follow the lady's lead. The French worker's condition, he began, is worse than the Soviet worker's. I questioned his rosy view of the Soviet economic situation and recalled a seminar of experts on Russia convened by the *New Republic* magazine in New York in April, 1949, where it was submitted that real wages in the Soviet Union were higher in 1928 than in 1938, and higher in 1938 than in 1948. The French workers, Sartre insisted, were earning less now than before the war. I could not dispute that, but it did not prove that they had sunk lower in the economic scale than Russian working men. "In any case," Sartre affirmed, "if the Russians came the French proletariat would not be inclined to worry. You cannot reach the French worker with anti-Communism."

"Then how can French workers be weaned from Communism?" I asked.

"By a positive program of Socialism," he replied. Here he attacked the U.S. for not helping France go Socialist.

"How can you expect capitalist America to make France Socialist?" I argued. "But if France had gone Socialist, America would have supported her just as it supports Labor Britain and Communist Yugoslavia."

"Yes," he retorted, "but Yugoslavia has become less Communistic since receiving American aid, and Tito is now less interesting to the French Left."

I said that was the impression the French Communist party tried to create. I didn't know, I wanted to see Yugoslavia and judge for myself. "But," I hastened to add before he could reply, "I would rather talk about France. Why do you say France is not free?"

He said *France Soir* had refused to print an article of his, and the same Paris daily rejected an article by Joseph Kessel on the Warsaw "peace" conference.

"And the same is true of America," Madame de Beauvoir interposed. Her voice was as hard and unfeminine as her face and personality. "The Taft-Hartley Law," she continued, "has paralyzed the trade unions. Fear and hysteria rule your country. Senator McCarthy is making America Fascist."

For as long as I could I was sticking to France and Russia. "So," I said, "a newspaper would not print two articles. Now may I give you a list of editors shot in the Soviet Union?" I did so. "May I mention some of the writers who have disappeared forever into Siberian banishment?" I did so. "May I mention a few of the talented novelists and poets who have been silenced in Russia?" I did so. Their vehemence subsided somewhat, and Sartre remarked that he appreciated my arguing with him, people were so far apart nowadays they refused to discuss controversial issues.

Madame soon renewed the fray with a thrust at American diplomacy which pushed other countries around. I did not deny this. I told them my opposition to McCarthy's method and effect was no less than theirs. Finally we talked of America. I noticed how readily they had given credence to any misstatement and distortion.

Through the three hours, during which my jaws grew tired from speaking French, Richard Wright usually sided with M. Sartre and Madame de Beauvoir. When I said that Soviet citizens had to lie to live he recalled how he had had to lie to the white man in Mississippi and say, "Yes, sir," with a smile. Like Sartre, Wright is an absolutist; both lack a dialectic sense; quantity and quality are slighted; things

are usually black and white, all bad or all good. Wright had with-
drawn from Communism and written eloquently to explain its fraud.
But his judgments remained extreme; they were formulated by the
brain but born in the heart or wherever emotions originate. His bitter
youth held him in its grip. The white man's supremacy ruled him and
riled him.

Some time later I repeated to Albert Camus, the author of *The
Plague* and other novels, what Sartre had said about the lack of
freedom in France. "A French intellectual," he commented, "would
rather you said his mother worked in a brothel than that he was a
moderate." Camus had had his flirtation with Communism; now, at
thirty-seven, he was writing an essay, which slowly assumed the dimensions of a book, on revolt. The theme, he explained, was that revolution stifled revolt. Russia had become conformist. I asked whether
he had considered Mahatma Gandhi as the supreme rebel of our age,
the individual in revolt against power and therefore opposed to those
revolutionists who think of solutions only in terms of a strong state
against which no revolt is possible. He said, yes, but the only books
he knew on Gandhi were eulogies, not analyses.

At the start of our conversation, M. Camus, looking pale—he had
just recovered from a tuberculosis flare-up—insisted that I first give
him my impressions. France, I said, apparently hates to think of the
recent past, of wartime defeat and postwar weakness, and is afraid
of the future, so she lives in the present, and when a nation, or
person, lives in the present it overeats, overspends, and rejects austerity, which is accumulation for tomorrow out of today's savings.

"You are quite right," Camus exclaimed. "France is living beyond
her means. We have lost what the British call civic spirit. Each of
us lives for himself. A wide gulf separates people from government,
and people from parties. The people inhabit one circle, the government, the parties, the political newspapers another, and they meet
only occasionally, on election day, or when taxes are collected, or men
conscripted. The people do not care about Indo-China and would
give it up anytime. The bureaucrats and militarists want to keep it.
The people are not deeply interested in German rearmament. But the
government doesn't dare agree to it."

He took a deep breath; his delicate friendly face showed fatigue and
I offered to leave. He shook his head in the negative, and continued,
"We have no politicians of vision or caliber, no Churchill or Eden
on the right, no Attlee, Morrison, or Bevan on the left. Life for the

poor is harder than before the war and if it were not for the social security legislation and family allowances introduced by Leon Blum's government in the late 1930's there would be serious distress.

"Nation," he concluded, "does not mean much to the Frenchman. We lost too much blood between 1914 and 1918 and from 1939 to 1945. Our best youth died. Now we lack the vitality for revolution and the loyalty indispensable to drastic reform."

"What about your literature and art?" I queried. "They seem vital."

"Yes," he said, "in the trash there is much of value. But our art and literature were never bourgeois. They are the individual in protest and in freedom."

André Malraux, on the other hand, declared that the renewed interest in painting did not signify that there was good painting; good French painters and writers were few.

I first met Malraux in Moscow in 1934. He did not speak Russian and did not know the country, but he quickly found the key to the new Soviet evolution: "Russia is becoming a class society," he announced, whereupon we enumerated three classes: the privileged bourgeoisie (the praetorian guard of the dictatorship consisting of top rank officials, officers of the army and secret police, leading industrial experts, the chained, high-pay writers, artists, etc.); the bureaucratic ant class; and the wage slaves.

Along with his great intelligence, Malraux also revealed his major obsession: death. When I next met him, he was, in a manner of speaking, a "merchant of death." I called on him in Paris in his rue du Bac apartment, an incredibly disorderly place, and found him buying tanks and planes for the Spanish Loyalists and devising schemes, which only his fertile novelist's brain could concoct, of getting them—illegally in most cases—out of their country of origin and to the anti-Franco fighting front. At intervals, Malraux would rush down to Spain to do some fighting himself. This was in the latter half of 1936.

I saw Malraux often in those days, usually at Barajas, Madrid's airport where, apart from other tasks, he was sometimes called on to persuade his temperamental Mexican, French, British, and other pilots that they ought to take to the air instead of keeping a date in town.

Later, we met in Paris, and in 1937 in New York, and again in Barcelona where he was shooting a film based on *Man's Hope*, his novel laid in Spain. When the Spanish Republic had gone down and the Second World War had commenced we sat in Paris cafés for hours discussing life and politics. He did most of the talking. Malraux's talk is like Niagara, a dynamic tumble of energy. His chief characteristic is generosity; he gives endlessly of himself in action and in writing because his wealth fills him to overflowing, chokes him, and roars out of him like a torrent. As he talks his protruding eyes assume a far-off yet piercing look; he expels air through his nose with the noise of a dry cough; his neck makes short, quick jerks which bring his silken, chestnut-colored hair falling down over his forehead, and his fingers, brandishing the ever-present cigarette, keep punctuating the discourse. "*Mais, attention,*" he cautions; in other words, here comes a new thought amplifying something already said. Lithe in body and mind, restlessly throbbing, he is like a mighty motor, and when he shuts himself off from the world and gives the motor only one narrow outlet, his pen, the result is overwhelmingly powerful.

Malraux has lived richly in Indo-China, China, Afghanistan, Arabia, and Spain, but he is deeply French in his earnestness about ideas and his love of exact verbal formulations. His temperament is constantly bursting inside in a series of unending explosions governed, however, by the mind. He is a Niagara harnessed to a purpose. Having faced death in fact and in imagination he is free to live a full life without fear. Over age when the Second World War broke out and ineligible therefore for the air force, he enlisted in the tanks though he knew, as he told me when we talked in Paris in October, 1939, that France was lost. Wounded and captured by the Germans, he escaped, and led the anti-Nazi underground in a large region of France. At the end of the war, he was again in the army fighting under General de Gaulle.

When Malraux joined De Gaulle politically after the war and entered the General's "Brain Trust," I was surprised and inquired from New York whether it was true, and why. Between July and December, 1947, he wrote me four long letters on the subject; we were conducting a transatlantic political argument by airmail. His letters, like his conversations, are streams of machine gun bullets, one, two, three. "It is true that I am working with General de Gaulle," his first letter began. He had broken with the Stalinists because they were "dishonest and immoral, anti-democratic," and servants of Russian imperialism. The crisis for him was the Soviet-Nazi Pact of August, 1939. France (like the rest of continental Europe) was being polarized between the Stalinists and Gaullists. The Socialists would split; their left would join the Communists, the right would go to De Gaulle. "I do not believe that General de Gaulle's desire for personal power is greater than President Roosevelt's, for example." The Gaullists were the last hope; "After us, Thorez [the French Communist leader] or Fascism, the real Fascism." "It is wrong to affirm that General de Gaulle is a man of the Right." Only Stalinist propaganda made him a Fascist. Malraux hoped that he and other Leftists could dominate the Gaullist movement. "The chief of the Rally [*Rassemblement du peuple Français*, RPF, De Gaulle's organization] in Paris is a Socialist; the director of the Socialist Press Service is a Gaullist." Historic parallels are always inexact but "the least erroneous" comparison would be between De Gaulle and Pilsudski or Mustapha Kemal Pasha Ataturk. "Now," Malraux warned me, "be careful about your statement, 'He is supported by reactionaries.' If your point is that the old, mustachioed military men of the provinces vote for General de Gaulle, that is naturally correct. That, however, is of no great importance. But if you want to assert that the real reactionary forces are with him, you are wrong. The truth is that those forces detest us." France is certainly not dreaming of a Mussolini. Rather of a Clemenceau." "We do not glorify force, we glorify energy; the whole tradition of the first Republic was to glorify both liberty and energy. Moreover, what the devil do you want us to do, glorify weakness?"

My position, to put it in a sentence, was: Double rejection—reject the two extremes of Communism and Gaullism and work for a moderate, stable middle.

When I arrived in Paris in December, 1950, I wrote Malraux—his telephone never answered—and he picked me up at my hotel and drove me out to his home in Boulogne sur Seine, not far from the city. He had just left the General and was flushed. De Gaulle was the talk of France.

The Gaullists did not call themselves a party, they were a "rally"; they assumed the country was sick of parties and would not follow another. Even more interesting was De Gaulle's attempt to present his movement as moderate, as something in the middle between the extreme of Communism and the extreme of decadence. Actually, what he called decadence was the Third Force, a jumble of feuding parties which had ruled France since 1946, and which was itself the buffer between Communists and Gaullists. Everybody in France tried to create the impression of being mildly center; even the Communists paraded as reasonable, gentle lovers of peace, the Catholics, the middle class, and France. They did this in order the better to appeal to the popular French mind which, to risk a generalization, soberly shuns black-or-white alternatives. The French national genius, except at time of sharp crisis, prefers the tentative and temperate. The extremes, consequently, were in a quandary: the situation, they felt, required drastic change but they had to appear moderate and safe. Communists as well as Gaullists therefore pretended to represent the sanity of the middle position. France, as someone said, had to choose between the two horns of a dilemma but was trying to invent a third. It seemed quixotic yet it proved realistic. France actually did avoid both piercing horns and stayed in the center—proof of maturity, civilized skepticism, and balance.

At times during the postwar instability and desperation, however, many Frenchmen turned to Communism as an easy, total panacea and others sought a positive pole, a Man who would bring quick solutions. Malraux, too much of a brain to be the Man, had nevertheless thrown in his lot with the Man, General de Gaulle.

When we settled in his apartment, one of the most beautiful I have seen anywhere in the world, Malraux said, "De Gaulle is national, not nationalist. In other words, he wishes to unite the nation, not expand it. He left the government in January, 1946, because every minister was lying to every other minister and to the Cabinet as a whole. . . . The recent Communist anti-Eisenhower demonstration was a failure and showed that the Communist shock troops are weaker. We have our shock troops, and we mean to use them to block Communist violence. De Gaulle will put the top French Communist leaders on a boat and ship them to the Black Sea," to the warm Soviet south. "The General will never make a coup d'état. He is a fervent democrat. He will not try to achieve power by force. He is neither a Napoleon nor a Boulanger." "Go to a De Gaulle meeting," Malraux urged when I took my leave. "It is the Metro" (the subway, the masses, the people).

I went to the May First rally of the Rally in the Bois de Boulogne, a mammoth meeting which was indeed a cross-section of France. Malraux's impassioned oratory stirred more enthusiasm than the talk of the tall, stiff, cold General. De Gaulle's closest collaborators admitted that he was arrogant and inflexible. "He believes in his destiny," one said, "and that makes any man difficult to live with."

"But he is honest and a patriot," another Gaullist observed.

Georges Bidault, who had formed and sat in several Cabinets of the Third Force, told me he would not join a De Gaulle government. The General, he declared, would make an impossible Premier. He had no sense of parliamentary affairs. He thought in 1945 that his mere presence would solve problems; then he discovered that he had to deal with complicated questions like taxes, budgets, relations between ministries, and a thousand other vexing matters which interested him too little. "France needs national unity," Bidault asserted, "but De Gaulle thinks *he* is national unity." De Gaulle gave no incentive to the politicians to support him. He would be haughty, they humble. He would have all the power, they none.

The problem of De Gaulle was obviously one aspect of a larger situation. Former Premier Paul Reynaud called France "the sick man of Europe." France had suffered and was suffering. The fear of war when no war impended would have to be registered as a pathological phenomenon were it not for the fact that the French people had paid so heavily for wars in the living past. A monument to the dead of 1914-18 occupies a central place in every French town and hamlet. The nation had scarcely dried its eyes after that conflict when France began bracing itself for another German attack and building the expensive Maginot Line. For twenty years, fear of a second world war divided France and shredded her nerves. I was in Paris on September 3, 1939, the day France, and England, declared war on Nazi Germany. Women stood around in groups biting their fingernails and gazing morosely into nowhere, into black memories perhaps, and into an empty future. There were many little traffic accidents in the streets and many petty quarrels over the accidents; men were nervous. The railway stations were crowded with families leaving for the provinces. Before the fighting started, France had a premonition of defeat. Contrary to the general impression, the war did not end for her with the 1940 collapse; her best sons fought and fell till the end in 1945. In 1946, 1950, and 1951, I rarely visited a French home but that a mother, or wife, or sister, would indicate the photograph of a young man who had died on active service. And now Korea. "Will France become another Korea?" Frenchmen asked. The national temper rose and fell with the tide of battle in the remote peninsula. When it looked as though the Communists would win, the French feared a Russian invasion. When it looked as though Douglas MacArthur's policy of extending the war to China might be implemented, they asked whether America intended to drag them into another world war. "Is it possible for America to arm and arm and arm," Bidault wondered in my second talk with him, "without a day arriving when she will precipitate herself—and us—into a war?" The apprehension was understandable. Even the most pro-American, pro-collective-security, anti-Soviet Frenchmen shared it. "Scratch a Frenchman," I wrote at the time, "and you find a neutralist." They hoped to abstain from the next war. "We would rather be occupied by Russia without fighting than after fighting," a mother of two reserve officers said to me.

Nevertheless, and with all this awareness of weakness and fear of the future, France yearned to be a great power and reacted emotionally to De Gaulle's appeals to her "glory" and "grandeur." France had not yet learned to live as a second-class power. Her glory had died too recently to be a painless memory. The French had no taste for being an enlarged Switzerland, prosperous, contented, bourgeois, and unheroic. They found no substitute for power. The beauty of France, the intelligence of her people, the high quality of their art and culture were no balm to an aching heart. Demotion among the nations humiliated and hurt, especially when transatlantic salt, in the form of crude American statements and, yes, hundreds of millions of dollars were sprinkled on the open wound. They documented France's decline. Anti-Americanism was a reverse nationalism. An official of the swollen U.S. Embassy in Paris asked several Americans how best to bring to the attention of all Frenchmen the generous assistance America was giving them. "Let them forget it," I urged, "don't rub it in." Not so long ago France was the first world power.

Many Frenchmen who supported General De Gaulle saw him as a miracle restorer of the glory of France without any appreciable effort on their part. He possessed that intangible something, they thought, which could evoke a sense of national community and induce national optimism. But several enthusiastic Gaullists admitted to me that "of course we defraud the Treasury" by not paying taxes. They craved a national transformation yet refused to make the necessary sacrifices, complaining about conditions which only a government with powers they declined to give it could eradicate. They wanted to be cured but would not pay the doctor or take his medicines. Nor would they cure themselves. That is really being sick. Five million Communist votes, and Communist control of a sixth of the seats in the National Assembly were the patient's high-temperature readings.

France needed so many drastic economic reforms that together they would constitute a social revolution. But Communists and conservatives tacitly conspired to prevent it, and the multiplicity of parties zealous of their power barred the rise of a government strong enough to make it. A government could get enough votes to be born and to live precariously, but the moment it made a move toward the rebirth of France it was killed. French politics had reached a nothingness, a nihilism. Its goal was a point of perfect balance where there is no movement except the motions required for keeping the balance.

All nations are divided by class lines, economic interests, regional loyalities, and so forth. But they unite in an emergency. France had been unable to unite in the emergency of the war and in the crisis of the postwar. The knowledge of these failures depressed the people and created a desire, in wide circles, to find a remedy, but none had been found, and that caused further depression.

Because the nation was not yielding enough fruit in the form of peace, security, and prosperity, the individual abandoned it and proposed to look after himself alone. This is individualism turned against itself, destructive and undisciplined, an individualism which weakens the nation still more. At the same time, the Frenchman's heart ached for his country and mourned its declining strength.

But he also ached for a community which could command his respect and inspire his faith. He suspected that France could find health, power, and inner unity only in a larger unity outside herself.

Intellectually, and philosophically, France has outlived nationalism and advanced beyond it, some to individualistic selfishness, some to internationalism. But emotionally, internationalism is hobbled by fear of Germany, by lingering dreams of national glory, and by the natural hesitation to plunge into cold, unknown waters.

Beached on the sand bar or stuck in the mud between nationalism and internationalism, France cannot navigate. It is this historic difficulty that explains the peculiarities of her domestic politics.

CHAPTER SEVENTEEN

One Dilemma and a Paradox

PART of the pavement of the antique Appian Way near Rome is still in use. At a ruined theater near Minturno village in central Italy in 1951, I saw the ruts made by the iron wheels of chariots which carried their owners to the show. Italy is an old country—inhabited by a young nation. History is everywhere. Age is measured not in years or decades but by centuries. The Borgias are recent compared to the Caesars. Michelangelo and Raphael, who worked in the sixteenth century, are considered "moderns."

On a wall along the Via dei Fori Imperiali, not far from the massive Colosseum and other millennial ruins, Benito Mussolini erected four maps in varicolored marble showing the expansion of Rome from a city to an empire which embraced England, Egypt, Rumania, and the Caucasus—all in a thousand years. There is no chart tracing the contraction of that empire. But Italians know it no longer exists. They also remember the disappearance of Mussolini's punier realm overseas.

The flow and ebb of power has given Italians a cynical attitude toward it. Italy perpetuated her glory in stone and bronze many centuries ago, and now it is no longer painful to be without it. Power means trouble, its fruits are sour.

The Italian people's memory has recorded the conquering and retreating tramp of many armies up and down their narrow peninsula. Today Italians are more mild than martial. The private secretary of Prime Minister De Gasperi asked me whether America would start another war. But if war came the Italians hoped it would pass them by. They believe they are off the beaten path of world power politics. They do not aspire collectively. They do not think they can change Italy, much less the universe. Too much history obstructs history-making. Too much past obstructs the future.

Mussolini aimed to inject the Italian nation with ambition. The inoculation did not take. France is tortured by her descent from the top rank. Italy is relieved. India needs to feel important. Italy bids for a minor role.

Italy is the land of the grape and the sun. The Italians love to smile and relax. They shun hate and tension, the two pillars of dictatorship. They are neither crusading nor rhetorical. Mussolini, who pretended to be both, represents a brief aberration.

Many Germans vociferously deny ever having been Nazis. Italians who were Fascists gracefully avow it. Clearly, Hitler was a deep disease, Mussolini a passing rash.

Like Bolshevism, Fascism is irrational. It attempts to substitute faith for reason. Mussolini tried to create a Fascist mystique but failed because the Italians incline to doubt and rationalism. Masses followed the Duce; they enjoyed the pageantry, the uniforms, the drama; it was sport. But few believed him.

Disappointment with the territorial spoils of World War I and unsolved economic problems raised Mussolini into power in 1922. He claimed to be the answer to Bolshevism. But his solutions defeated themselves and then they defeated him. Italy is like the old lady, she lived in a shoe, she had so many children, she didn't know what to do. There are forty-eight million in the boot, and the old-lady government doesn't know what to do; neither do the people. Outlets to the Continent and to the United States are blocked by inhospitable immigration practices. In his time, Mussolini dreamt of draining off some of the unemployables to a place in the African sun. More died fighting for it than living in it—at least in Abyssinia. Meanwhile he paid premiums to old ladies and young ladies to have more babies to make the boot more unlivable and thus create additional pressure for imperialism. In the end his imperial appetite killed him.

After the Second World War, Italy's population expanded at about four hundred thousand per annum. Yet the country could not expand imperialistically and her economic expansion was sadly inadequate. So she longed for another form of internationalism: a united Europe or a united world with wide-open doors. But that high ideal remains a remote goal. American financial aid was substitute internationalism. It was also substitute immigration. Instead of admitting excess Italians into America, America boarded them in Italy.

Economic difficulties were again at work, and this time, instead of breeding Fascism, they bred Communism. Hence the ease with which ex-Fascists have enrolled in the Communist party and risen high in its hierarchy.

The best way to understand Italian Communism—and French Communism—is to discover what is wrong with the non-Communists.

Unemployment in Italy rose from about 1,700,000 in 1949—which was approximately 10 per cent of the working force and double the prewar level—to 2,000,000 in 1951. Add an estimated two million underemployed in the cities. Add millions of idle and semi-idle in the villages. Multiply each of these by three dependents. The result, according to Mr. M. Leon Dayton, American chief of the ECA (Economic Co-operation Administration) or Marshall Plan in Italy, was that two-thirds of the Italian population were underconsumers.

In Rome, in April, 1951, I talked for hours with Mr. Dayton about Italy's pressing problems. Dayton is a Portland, Oregon, businessman, a convinced American capitalist, a devotee of free enterprise. But he found that Italian capitalism was not sufficiently capitalistic, and he tried to teach his fellow capitalists how to be better capitalists. A basic tenet of American capitalism was one stated by Paul G. Hoffman, the first director of ECA and board chairman of the Studebaker automobile corporation: "We must make better and better goods and sell them at lower and lower prices." But Italian industrialists aim to sell at higher and higher prices. Dayton gave me the text of a speech he had delivered to a meeting in Genoa on October 19, 1950, in which he castigated them for it. "I should like to ask," he exclaimed to the consternation of his audience, "how it is that a meter of woolen or cotton material costing one to two thousand lire to produce is sold to consumers at five times that amount; or why it is that a pair of shoes, which costs (including taxes) only one or two thousand lire to make, finds its way to the feet of the wearer only after 200 to 500 per cent has been added."

"To increase production and profits," Dayton urged, "the earning power of the people must be increased proportionately." The Italian capitalists rejected this doctrine as revolutionary. They were interested only in increasing profits; what else is there? They therefore raised prices. That narrowed the market and that, in turn, limited production, and that, in turn, created unemployment, and that, in turn, narrowed the market. This unmerry merry-go-round so disturbed Mr. Dayton that he tried to sting the industrialists into action. "We cannot afford to tarry, to sit on a rock and bask in the sun," he told those Genoa businessmen. Imagine telling Italians not to bask in the sun! But he warned them that "through inaction" they might lose their leadership and let it "slip by default into the willing hands of Joseph Stalin."

Italian industrialists, Dayton asserted, paid "lip service" to the principles of high production and low costs, "but of all the firms in Italy, you can count those who practice these precepts on the fingers of your two hands."

The ECA under Dayton preached "a better distribution of income" in order to increase the number of consumers and thereby raise production and create new jobs. But the upper class found the idea revolting. In addition to producing too little and charging too much, it spent lavishly and lived in luxury while the poor looked on. Instead of using available capital to expand factories and employment, money was being exported, sometimes to the United States. This was another dismal merry-go-round. The United States put money into Italy ($1,225,700,000 between April 3, 1948, and February 26, 1951, through the ECA alone) and rich Italians deposited part of it in their personal accounts in the United States. "Better distribution of income" was further sabotaged by tax evasion. Taxation is a universally abhorred yet tolerated means of partially redistributing national income. It helps governments care for the underpriviledged. In Italy, persons with small fixed incomes—clerks, minor officials, and so forth—pay taxes in full because their salaries are a matter of record, but the upper brackets notoriously tend to practice tax fraud and evasion. Businesses have been known to keep two sets of books, one for themselves, another for the revenue collector who, moreover, is not incorruptible, for a bribe which is picayune to the company may exceed his woefully inadequate annual salary.

The Italian capitalist class has an underdeveloped social conscience.

It neglects national interests. It practices an obsolete form of selfishness which consists in being selfishly selfish instead of unselfishly selfish. American business is wiser. It grows rich by enriching the consumer.

This conflict between America's philosophy and Italy's psychology ultimately cost Leon Dayton his job as head of the ECA in Rome. I asked Mr. Dayton why he did not bring his troubles to the attention of Italian leaders like Prime Minister Alcide De Gasperi. "I have," he replied.

"What do they say?" I inquired.

They told him he was in too great a hurry; they advised him to learn patience. Dayton, nevertheless, continued to press for tax reforms and a new and more capitalistic policy toward mass production and unemployment. He met with a little success in the field of tax legislation, but the antisocial mentality continued to dominate the business world, and when he tilted against it with unabated zeal the United States embassy in Rome intervened, and Mr. Dayton was transferred to Turkey. Politics triumphed over economics. Unwilling to irritate the Italian government which was shielding archaic social forms, the United States relaxed its pressure for reform. It was a victory for the conservative Italian outlook and, therefore, for the Italian Communists.

I consulted an Italian industrialist about the psychology of his friends. He said most charmingly, "You see, I have enough for myself and my family, and my two sons will take care of the enterprise when I am gone. Why should I work myself to death prematurely by accepting additional burdens? Why should I risk all my capital by investing it? How do I know what the future will bring?"

"But then your country suffers from poverty and Communism," I observed.

"Yes," he agreed with a sigh, "that is sad; but is it my responsibility? Each person must take care of himself and his family."

"I understand you," I remarked. "Then you must understand the man without a job or without land who cannot take care of himself and his family and who therefore thinks that he can best take care of himself by joining the Communists."

"That is De Gasperi's headache," he declared.

Antiquated business principles and antique minds operating in a country with limited resources and overpopulation gave Communism the strength it had in Italy after the Second World War.

One evening I went with some American friends to a Viennese restaurant in Rome where we ate Viennese food at a long bare-board table and listened to sentimental Austrian melodies. Presently two young men in the black garb of Roman Catholic priests approached and, after asking permission, sat down at the unoccupied end of our table. When I heard them speaking English, I started a conversation. One was from Missouri, the other from Brooklyn, and both were engaged in postgraduate studies which included social work in the slums of Rome. They spoke Italian fluently, they said. I inquired about the political views of the people they met in the slums.

"Most of them are Communists," the Brooklynite asserted.

"Why?"

"Because they are poor and embittered," the Missourian explained.

Communism is opposition. The millions of peasants and working men, many of them illiterate or just barely literate, who vote Communist in Italy, France, India, Indonesia, and elsewhere did not decide to do so after a careful reading of the classics of Communism and of free enterprise and a judicial comparison of the virtues of the two systems. They vote Communist because they are unhappy. The miserable are gullible.

Communism is the most effective vehicle of social protest in Italy against unsatisfactory conditions. If there were a powerful non-Communist opposition party, as in Great Britain, or the United States, or Germany, they might support it. But the small middle parties—the moderate Socialist party led by Giuseppe Saragat, and the Liberal and Republican parties—are weak and collaborate too much with the Christian Democrats to be regarded by the disgruntled poor as effective opposition.

The strength of Communism in Italy, and France, is a measure of the loss of faith in democracy. On the basis of past performance, the unemployed, the insecure, the unhappy do not trust the anti-Communists to help them.

The Italian Communist party serves its adherents by terrorizing "the enemy" and serves itself by terrorizing its adherents. Communist influence in the trade unions and factories may determine whether a worker keeps his job; thousands of owners retain surplus labor on the payroll rather than defy Red shop stewards. This Communist-protected "feather-bedding," is a potent weapon. If a worker leaves the Communist party or speaks against it or is known to have cast his ballot against it the stewards will allow him to be discharged the next time the employer demands the dismissal of unneeded hands. Once unemployed and blacklisted, the unfortunate may remain idle for years. The Communists also attempt to terrorize petty urban merchants by threatening the withdrawal of custom. In the country, Communist pressure and violence often get results. A Red-instigated riot in Calabria might induce the government to parcel out a few estates among impecunious peasants. In Tuscany, landowners fearing Communist reprisals in the shape of beatings or worse have acquiesced in raising the tenant farmer's share of the crop. The peasants who benefit vote Communist either out of gratitude or out of fear of losing their benefits if the Communists should grow weak. That is why a peasant who is better off as a result of reform is just as likely to support the Communists as one whose life has not improved. What counts, what attracts is the Communist role as effective opposition, as a spur and a check on the government. In private industry too the working man may feel that he has something to gain from an organization which has the strength to defy and challenge his employer—even when the employer is generous and progressive. The workers cannot relish complete dependence on the will of the industrialist, even of the good industrialist. They want some power of their own and too often they find it only in the Communist party or Communist-controlled trade unions. The Communists, moreover, constitute a majority in hundreds of municipalities and localities where they consequently control the administration and have many jobs to distribute. Italians can be very practical. Some liberals joined the Fascists. Observant Catholics join the Communist party. One's philosophy of life or religion is separate from politics. Service in governments or memberships in parties, all ephemeral, should feed purse, convenience, or vanity. Men who hold power in contempt are likely to submit to it.

Cynicism and terror are excellent organizational props. During my 1951 visit to Italy, Socialist and anti-Communist circles generally were agog with the resignation of two Communist members of Parliament, Cucchi and Magnani, from the party. A serious split in the Communist movement was predicted. But the breach was quickly healed by energetic measures. Cucchi and Magnani, traveling in a northern city with a friend one evening, were gravely assaulted by Red toughs. This served as a warning to potential defectors. Intimidation by Communist *squadristas* à la Mussolini using harder means than castor oil is not to be underestimated as an instrument of "Marxist education." Money helps too, and the Italian Communist party always seems to have plenty of it.

Energetic police action and government suppression of illegal deeds have some effect in such a situation. But force alone cannot weaken Communism in Italy—or in France. Both movements are a response to a stagnant national economy whose effect reaches into every area of human endeavor including art and culture. One morning I visited St. Clement Chapel, a Roman church maintained by Irish fathers, and saw the fading fourteenth- and fifteenth-century frescoes by Masolino and his pupil Masaccio. At lunch the same day Professor Lionello Venturi, one of the foremost Italian art critics, said Masaccio was probably as great as Michelangelo and the father of the Renaissance. Then Venturi, a fervent anti-Communist, shook his gleaming bald head sadly and said European culture was dying because Europe was deteriorating economically. It takes wealth to support art, artists, and the buildings where art is stored. The decline of culture is not a development that would endear the existing social structure to intellectuals. It might incline some to sympathize with critics of that structure. Communism takes further sustenance from an anticlerical tradition which, in Italy as in France, is sturdy and widespread.

A handful of Communists in a country may be subversive, millions of Communists reveal a national need and reflect official neglect. The state nevertheless continues to bolster the *status quo* with its own and foreign moneys. Italy and France are saddled with government-subsidized or legally protected private monopolies and with methods which hamper production and raise prices. (In France, as a result, the purchasing power of wages fell 5 per cent between 1948 and 1951, despite the influx of colossal Marshall Plan funds.) These arrangements persist because those who benefit by them possess the political power to perpetuate them. In Italy, the feudal landlords and feudally minded businessmen wield enough influence in the Christian Democratic, Monarchist, and Neo-Fascist parties to block measures aimed against them. In France, unproductive middle-class and upper-class groups control enough votes in Parliament to survive. The courage of a strong Prime Minister, backed by U.S. determination, might have dynamited this log jam. But neither virtue existed.

This is one of the major failures of the Marshall Plan. In France and Italy, it poured new gold into leaky economic systems. It did not make capitalist competition, moderate profits, and mass production the condition of its dollar transfusions. It was too modest in insisting on the introduction of American methods. Instead, it yielded to the European inertia which was protecting the obsolete.

Yet it would be wrong to overlook the adamantine will of the old to live. One fine afternoon, walking through the streets of Paris, with a Frenchman, I pointed to the numerous quaint little shops whose turnover could only be infinitesimal. They made the process of distribution complicated and expensive; they tormented the manufacturers with tiny orders for an endless variety of goods, thus obstructing standardization and efficiency. "Yes," he said, "but they are the backbone of French liberty and they live happy lives." Progress, my French companion suggested, might clash with happiness.

Europeans often stress this dilemma of democracy. On the one hand, the elimination and proletarianization of the small artisan and petty tradesman facilitate the capitalist tendency toward bigness and concentration of power which—time will tell—may not lead to the freedom or flowering of the individual. On the other hand, the retention of a large uncreative element in the national economy drags it down, conflicts with modern industrial requirements, and generates the discontent which is wind in Communist banners.

An Italian lawyer I met in Rome in 1951 thought the dilemma produced a strange paradox; Italy, weighed down by her feudal elements and with over nine million Communist and near-Communist votes, and France, handicapped by ancient industrial techniques and many unproductive groups and counting approximately five million Communist votes, nevertheless enjoy more personal freedom, he said, and more relaxation than rich, purely capitalistic United States where the Red vote is negligible.

"We are sometimes as worried about America's future," a French editor declared, "as you are about ours." The statement seemed to contribute enormously to his pleasure.

CHAPTER EIGHTEEN

The Rearmament of Germany

TWO DAYS after I arrived in Germany in January, 1951, my wife Markoosha and I went to see a German film in a Munich cinema. The entrance was like the mouth of a cave surrounded on both sides and above by a hill of bomb debris blackened by fire and time. Cookies and chocolates were being sold in the foyer. The auditorium was roomy and comfortable enough—but cold, and the people kept their coats and gloves on. The picture, entitled *Es Kommt Ein Tag* (*A Day Is Coming*), so impressed us that we sought out the author several days later. The scene was laid in the Franco-Prussian War of 1870 during which a German officer kills a French officer in battle. The Germans advance into France and soon the German officer is billeted with a fine French family that is mourning the death of a son in the war, the very French officer he had shot dead. The German now falls in love with the beautiful sister of his victim, and she with him. From things she says it is established that his family and hers are related, as many West German and French families were. The German officer and the girl are, in fact, cousins. He had killed his cousin, his close kin.

The film was a thoroughly pacifist commentary on the fatuity of war and a plea for friendship with France. The author, Ernst Penzoldt, a gentle person, fifty-nine years old, lived in an isolated house outside the town. Tiny glass figures and toys, mementos of a lifetime of living and travel, filled the glass-door cupboards and shelves. He had stayed in this home throughout the war. It was so far from an air raid shelter that at the sound of the sirens he and his family simply went down into the cellar. "We were never hit," he said, "but when the bombs fell near by, as they often did, we found on returning to the rooms that everything had moved just a little, every glass object, toy, chair, table, had shifted just a little from its previous position. It was so with the human beings too. Every air raid moved the mind a millimeter."

I naturally looked for deep changes in Germany after the war. Deep changes in the behavior of a nation take time. But time does not consist merely of hours, days, and weeks; it has another dimension which is intensity. One may grow older, wiser, sadder in a split second depending on what happened in it. A death, a loss, a success, gives one a sudden insight into real truth and may do more to alter outlook and understanding than years of routine existence or placid living. Every air raid and every lost battle, and, finally, the crushing defeat of Germany and the invasion and occupation of her soil should, I believed, have moved the German mind and made a difference in German psychology. I searched for the changes.

My search and what I discovered were influenced by my own mentality. I do not believe in permanent national characteristics. Traveling from one country to another as I have done for many years and as I was doing in 1951—from France to Germany and back again, from France to Italy and back again, and then to England—one is susceptible to the temptation of making generalizations about nations: "The French like money." And who doesn't? Sitting in a café is no more a French and German national trait than standing in a bar or rushing into and out of a drugstore is an American characteristic. These performances do not reside in the blood or genes. They result from economic and social circumstances which may change and disappear just as the saloon of the American Wild West has survived only in moving pictures. Little remains in Italy, for instance, of that martial prowess which gave the Roman legions and galleys their renown. The French were once eager conquerors whose grand armies vanquished enemies in three continents. The whir of the carrousel of history mocks any notion of permanence in the pattern of national existence. America the isolationist becomes the world-wide interventionist. China, whose armies were a joke, becomes a serious military power. Russia of the backward mujik makes jets and atom and hydrogen bombs. These changes occurred in very few years. They already affect national policy and national behavior.

A look out of any window or door of any house in most German cities included bombing ruins, jagged walls, twisted steel girders, crumbled masonry. Germans went to church and theater amid ruins, bought food and clothing amid ruins, worked amid ruins, and slept amid ruins. Germany as a world power lay in ruins, dependent, as long as the imagination could envisage, on America or Russia. These were the new facts of life for all Germans. The cumulative shakings and shocks of the bombings and war had moved minds.

A German driver of a U.S. State Department auto in Frankfurt said to me, "I had four years in Russia on all fronts, in the mud, ice, and lice. I will never again touch a weapon, not even to fire at a flower in a shooting gallery. I would rather go to jail than kill people. Maybe the youth that has not been in the army will allow itself to be conscripted. I would rather sit in a jail." I repeated this conversation to a junior State Department official in Frankfurt who hates Germans. "They'll bloody well have to join the army if we tell them," he asserted.

My German publisher's reader, a professor in the University of Munich, gave me his class one evening for a "free discussion," as they called it—bull session, in American parlance. There were twenty-four students, men and women in their early twenties. First I made an introductory speech in German about the world situation, then I asked them to express their own views, argue with me and with one another, say anything they liked. We talked for three and a half hours. In the beginning the women were silent, but I encouraged them to express themselves, and soon they were competing vigorously for the floor. It was a spirited affair. I asked them to be personal, to talk about their beliefs, hopes, disappointments.

Since the Nazis had come to power in 1933 and this was eighteen years later, all these young people had, automatically, joined the Hitler Youth. They had believed in Hitler. Hitlerism had a public monopoly. One girl said her father counteracted the Hitler influence to which she was exposed in school and in the Hitler Jugend, but still the movement carried her away by its glamour and dynamics. Then, with the defeat and death of the Fuehrer, everything collapsed around their ears, and now they were afraid to believe in anything. They might be hurt and disillusioned again. The churches were dull and did not attract anybody in search of a faith. Several students said the only idea that thrilled them was a united Europe based on friendship between Germany and France.

"What about Communism?" I tested.

"We had our Communism from Hitler," a young man replied. This was greeted with laughter and assent. "Russia is a backward, barbarous country," another man added. "Our soldiers who returned don't have a good word to say about it."

I directed the discussion to German rearmament. Many heads indicated a negative response. Several of the men had been in the army, but none had fought—too young. If conscripted, the men said, they would serve, reluctantly.

"Raise hands please," I asked, "those who want to see a German national army recreated."

Not a single hand went up.

"Raise hands, please," I said, "those who would welcome a European army with German participation."

Sixteen hands. The remaining eight were opposed to any military service by Germans.

"What about defense against Russia?" I queried.

"We leave that to the Western powers and the atom bomb," an earnest young lady volunteered.

After the session, I inquired of one of the girls how she had voted in the last elections. "Well," she answered, "I don't like a religious party, so I didn't vote Christian Democrat. I don't like Socialism, sounds too dogmatic. So I voted for the Free Democratic party. It sounded liberal. But since then I have learned that the big capitalists finance it. Now I don't know what to do."

From Munich I drove to Frankfurt and then went by a speedy three-car Diesel train to Bonn, once a small university town, now the federal capital. I talked with officials, most of them members of the Christian Democratic party, who admitted that there were former Nazis in high and low government jobs but added that neither Nazism nor Communism menaced Germany from the inside, and that every new public opinion poll heaped up further evidence of the German people's reluctance to rearm.

One evening I took a taxi in Bonn and went up the Venusberg (Venus Hill) to interview Social Democratic leader Dr. Kurt Schumacher, whom I had met in Berlin in 1946 and in New York in 1947. He had grown fatter and was more affable but still bellicose. He lost his right arm in the First World War and a leg in a Nazi concentration camp. It seemed to me that he was blind in one eye but both were blue and bloodshot and when he made a point he stopped and stared and bit his upper lip with his six sawed-down lower teeth, so that the whole was a picture of passion. He was talking about things that would shape the future of Germany and they stirred him deeply. In public speeches his feelings sometimes got the better of him and he occasionally made wild statements. But one forgave him a lot; he had spent eleven years in a concentration camp. In fact, he mentioned this early in our talk. My first question dealt with a recent address by Ivone Kirkpatrick, the British High Commissioner in Germany. I had an appointment with Kirkpatrick the next day and I was curious about Schumacher's reaction to what Kirkpatrick had said. "Why does Kirkpatrick ask Germany whether we have thrown in our lot with the West?" Schumacher exclaimed. "Why do they insult us and then ask us to rearm? When I was in the Nazi concentration camp an SS man insulted me and I gave him a verbal drubbing that made him shiver. Nobody will say I'm a coward. I will say to you what I would say to Kirkpatrick: he asks whether we are with the East or West and yet they want us to have an army. The British dismantle the Dortmund steel mill and transport it to England, they use the German island of Helgoland for bombing practice, and ask us to be their allies against Russia. I was born in West Prussia, near Danzig, forty miles from the Russian frontier, and when mothers wanted to scare their children they didn't say the black man is coming, they said the Cossacks are coming. Later in life, Communism was added to make me a fervent adversary of Soviet Russia. We belong with the West. But we cannot rearm unless we enjoy equality."

He was talking excitedly, stopping only to puff on his cigar so it wouldn't go out. "We will agree to the Western Allies having control over a German army if they let us participate in the control of their armies," he continued. "How is it possible for a nation to have an army yet no sovereignty? Would you Americans stand for that?" He drew on his cigar again, and seemed to rest. I said nothing.

"Some time ago," he resumed, "I asked a wise American why the U.S. army trains its recruits in Arizona or Pennsylvania. Why not bring them over and train them in Germany?"

"'What!' the American exclaimed. 'Bring them here so that a Russian army could come across the line and capture them?' 'And you want us,' I said to him, 'to start training a German army of raw recruits so the Russians can step across and seize them?' Until there is an umbrella of three hundred to four hundred thousand Anglo-

American troops to shield us against the Soviets, I told the American, Germany cannot rearm." He pointedly omitted French troops; Schumacher was very anti-French. Throughout the hour and a half interview he reverted often to the umbrella, the "*Schirm*," as he called it in German.

Soon he was blasting Kirkpatrick again. "Kirkpatrick once told me," Schumacher declared, "that a diplomat should speak in private but not go around making speeches. Now he is making speeches in public, but he hasn't talked to me in months."

"Since when exactly?" I asked.

He took out his thick appointment book and turned the pages. "Since late in November," he reported, "almost two months." Then after a pause, "Do you know when General Eisenhower is arriving here?"

I said he was due the coming Saturday, and there would be a party for him at John McCloy's place in Bad Homburg. (McCloy was the U.S. High Commissioner.) Schumacher expected an invitation to see Eisenhower.

"Actually," I remarked, "I'm sure you know that the Western Allies are always talking to you even when their representatives don't see you."

He looked blank, but I was sure he knew what I meant. In any case, since he kept silent, I explained. "The U.S. and England," I said, "know they have Chancellor Adenauer's support for German rearmament. They want to win yours because German rearmament is impossible if the Socialist party, which might in any election become the government of Germany or of several states in Germany, opposes rearmament."

"We are not pacifists," Schumacher asserted, "but we insist on the *Schirm* first. And there must be a national election on the issue of rearmament." He anticipated a victory; then he would be Chancellor in Adenauer's place. He hoped the German people would trust him to rearm without resurrecting German militarism. The West, he felt, did not realize how dangerous rearmament was to German democracy. America, he said, had no statesmen. Suddenly he again attacked Kirkpatrick.

"You realize," I said, "that when you criticize Kirkpatrick you are criticizing the British Labor government whose official he is. You are criticizing your British Socialist comrades."

"The British Labor party costs us a million votes," he affirmed.

"If the Conservatives were in power in England Adenauer would lose a million votes because the Germans would blame the British Conservatives for the sins of the occupation and vote Socialist. Now they blame the British Socialists and vote Conservative."

For the rest of my 1951 stay in Germany, rearmament remained the chief topic of discussion. Washington and London were pressing it despite the obvious reluctance of Germans and Frenchmen. Tacitly, U.S. High Commissioner McCloy admitted the justice of Dr. Schumacher's position when he said the Germans disliked being wedged in between the East and West. "When we are strong they will ask to be rearmed," he declared. He was saying, in effect, that once the *Schirm* was there the Germans would agree to rearm.

Germany meanwhile gave General Eisenhower a cold reception. He smiled warmly, shook hands all around, and emphasized his own close relationship to Germans. While posing for photographs with McCloy and Adenauer, the Chancellor said to the General, in German, "Do you speak German?"

Eisenhower replied, "The only German word I know is Eisenhower." There are many Eisenhauers, or iron-beaters, smiths, in Germany.

Nevertheless, the Germans eluded his courtship. The Northwest German Radio, the largest broadcasting station in the country, condemned his mission which it saw as an effort to convert Germans to rearmament. Germany had no taste for more militarism. In a month of questioning I had not encountered one German who wanted a German national army.

Germany nevertheless troubled millions througout the world. Her aggressions since 1870 were not easily forgotten. Her cruelties, especially in the Second World War, remained a painful memory. Apart from morality, they were not even practically necessary; they could not have contributed to victory. Many individuals therefore feared the rise of a strong, rearmed Germany.

Often, however, attitudes toward German rearmament were shaped by none of these considerations, but rather by considerations of power politics and party politics. Belgium, which suffered under two German invasions, and knows the Germans well, advocated German rearmament; likewise Holland, occupied and trampled by the Nazis. These small countries are not in competition with Germany as world powers. France is.

In Poland and Russia too, anti-German sentiment undeniably

exists, but whether it determines policy is a question. The Poles are impaled on the horns of a permanent dilemma implicit in their geographic position: if the German menace is minimized and Russo-German friendship grows as a result, there might be another Russo-German deal to partition Poland. If on the other hand the German menace is emphasized, Russia can pose as Poland's protector and keep her dominion over the Poles. Emphasis on the German peril similarly serves to reinforce Russia's colonial hold on Czechoslovakia and other satellites. Is it these imperialistic motives that explain Soviet opposition to German rearmament or is it fear of German soldiers? East German soldiers have no terror for Moscow; it arms them. What bothers the Kremlin is obviously not a German army but West Germany's alignment with the West.

Party politics are another factor. In certain countries, opposition to the creation of German armed forces was good election strategy; it brought votes. This was true inside Germany too. Whereas most German Socialists argued against a German army, most French, British, and Belgian Socialists agreed to it.

Some Europeans simply felt it was being too good to Germany to relieve her of the burden of rearmament and then have to defend her in case of war. Not a few Europeans and Americans had conflicting emotions about Germany; while regretting Germany's failure to manifest a greater sense of guilt about World War II atrocities, they had their own sense of guilt about Germany; they felt that more friendship toward pre-Hitler Weimar Germany and less appeasement of Hitler Germany might have obviated many horrors. This time, therefore, they preferred to reward a little virtue rather than expect complete regeneration. In France, too, a strong current of opinion favored some radical cure of the dread disease that poisons German-French relations. General Pierre Billote, a Gaullist whom I met several times in Paris, wanted France to overcome her "aversions, her disquietude, and her complexes" toward Germany.

As for the Germans, their disinclination to rearm stemmed from wartime bombing experiences, battle casualties, and the defeat, but also, and perhaps more, from the postwar situation: with America and Russia competing for hegemony in Europe, Germany could be a pawn or a castle, but not a great power king or queen. If a third world war came, she would be the battlefield and could not win no matter which side won and survived. These facts set a limit to Germany's international ambitions.

Those who refused, for well-understood psychological reasons, to base their policy on German psychology, quickly discovered, on reaching Germany, that conditions after the Second World War were concretely different from post-1918 conditions. When the First World War ended, the German General Staff was intact. Undefeated German armies stood on Belgian, French, Russian, and Polish soil. They marched back to the homeland with colors flying. Hindenburg, Ludendorff, and other generals were national heroes. The armistice was signed by civilians, thus giving rise to the infamous "Stab in the Back" legend: the politicians, Socialists, and Jews had stabbed the soldiers in the back and ruined Germany. This was one of the chief propaganda weapons in the arsenal of the militarists, monarchists, and Nazis. Early in 1919, the German government, threatened by rebellious soldiers' and workers' councils, called on the army to suppress them, and as a result the General Staff became a second government, the real government. The Versailles Peace permitted Germany an army of one hundred thousand. This highly trained force was the cadre of Hitler's Wehrmacht. Allied attempts to collect hidden arms were sabotaged.

None of these conditions existed after the Second World War. The German army was beaten in the field and all of its units were dispersed, captured or annihilated. The German military machine was in rubble. Most of the generals were in prison, in hiding, or dead, and none, except a few of the handful who had tried to kill Hitler in July, 1944, wore a halo. Every square mile of Germany was under foreign occupation. West Germans welcomed the occupation for the security it gave against Russia, chaos, and starvation. It nourished little resentment. There was no resistance.

After the First World War there was scarcely a break in the political power of the army. After the Second World War, no trace of such power survived. Nor could one ignore the fact that East Prussia and some of Prussia were no longer part of West Germany. East Prussia had been the incubator, and Prussia the drill ground, of German militarism. An entire generation of German generals—Hindenburg and Ludendorff are the best-known examples—were sons of impoverished East Prussian landowners and wilted petty aristocrats whose army careers provided steady employment at good wages and restored their social status. Poor in urban cosmopolitanism and contacts with the West, they imposed on Germany their narrow provincialism and narrower caste system as well as the rigid discipline, brittle manners, humorless sense of duty, and defensive arrogance of the insecure in secure positions. But in 1951, the Junkers were gone from German life. Part of West Germany's antimilitarism was actually due to a resurgence of anti-Prussian feeling in Bavaria, the Rhineland, and other parts.

West Germany, nevertheless, had not got rid of all its Prussianism nor all of its past. Many Germans voiced skepticism about their country's democratic convictions and the depth of its hostility to rearmament. Foreign doubts were therefore justified.

But when a plant is tender it does not help to say that it looks scrawny and ugly. It must be well tended. Here the outside world has a paramount responsibility. Given the present international position of West Germany, the fate of German democracy depends in considerable measure on the virility of freedom in Western Europe and the Americas and on the quality of their friendship for Germany. Hate, suspicion, coldness could freeze the plant. A warm relationship might stimulate healthy development.

CHAPTER NINETEEN

The Exiles

WHILE I was in Munich trying to understand Germany, Markoosha, a native of Czarist Russia, introduced me to Mr. R., a Soviet DP (Displaced Person) who had written a book about his life in and escape from the Soviets. I asked R. why he had abandoned the Soviet Union. "In 1938," he began, "when the Stalin purge was at its zenith, I was living in the town of Voronezh. One day I learned that two of my cousins had been arrested. I considered it my duty, as a Soviet citizen, to inform the authorities that I had occasionally seen those cousins at weddings, birthdays, and similar family gatherings but had never talked politics with them there or anywhere. Nevertheless I was suspended from my government job."

Nothing else happened, R. was not arrested, but it is interesting that his defection and disloyalty to the Soviet government were born in this injustice. It made a scratch that never healed.

Shortly after his suspension, the war commenced, and R. was mobilized. He fought in many battles and at the end of hostilities wound up in Berlin where, now in his late thirties, he had himself demobilized and took a civilian job teaching Russian grammar to Red army soldiers stationed in Germany.

Before long he met a young German widow and a courtship started. Presently the Soviet army major under whom he worked summoned him and inquired about his relationship with the German lady. "Are your intentions serious?" the major asked.

R. said they were.

"Then you must not see her anymore," the major ordered.

If it had been a mere affair the officer would not have objected. But since it was serious, with marriage as the contemplated goal, it would not do. Soviet citizens were not allowed to marry foreigners.

"Two weeks later, I escaped with my friend and her four-year-old daughter from East Berlin to the West," the story ended.

"How is it," I wondered, "that the secret police weren't watching you? They should have known you might try to escape."

"Ah," he exclaimed, "they assumed I would be too paralyzed by fright, as the rabbit is paralyzed by the snake, to run away. That is one of the purposes of the Bolshevik terror."

Mr. R. was one of some thirteen to fourteen thousand Soviet citizens—chiefly officers and soldiers of the Red army of occupation in Germany and Austria—who fled to the non-Communist world in the first four years after the war. More would have come, and their defection might have intensified the demoralization inside the Iron Curtain. But the Western powers did little to encourage this movement and much to discourage it.

It takes a great deal of resolution to break with your native land, family, and army, and steal away into a strange world whose language and manners you do not know, and where you will have no friends or even contacts and may starve because you are unskilled.

Most of the postwar defectors were military people without a civilian profession. The British authorities in Germany opened a technical school to teach them trades. This became known in the Soviet areas and stimulated a few escapes. For the most part, however, the newcomers were picked up by the American, British, or French military police in Germany and brought to special interrogation centers where they were sharply questioned for military information, paid for it, and handed over to one or the other penniless anti-Soviet Russian organizations in Western Germany.

A whole new Russian world had sprouted in the non-Russian West. It consisted of the postwar defectors and the far larger community of "nonreturners" who left Russia during the war. Half an hour's ride from the city of Munich, 4,100 of these DP's lived in a place called Schleissheim Camp. I had gone there to have a general look at conditions—it was one of many similar barbed-wire enclosures maintained by the International Refugee Organization—and to find a Russian poet. Before leaving New York an American woman, who emigrated from the Soviet Union in 1925, told me she had been reading the exquisite verses of a Russian DP now living in a refugee camp near Munich. My wife, then working for an American organization which helped DP's emigrate from Germany to the countries that would take them, said she had heard of him, his name was Ivan Yelagin. I could find him at Schleissheim. There I was directed to Barracks No. 102.

A long, dark corridor divided the wooden structure in two. Doors at frequent intervals indicated small rooms. I knocked at a door to get information and, by chance, this was the Yelagin home: a room with four iron bedsteads covered with horse blankets, an iron stove for cooking and heating, a clothesline hung with wash, a pile of kindling wood, a table, a bookshelf, and several boxes in lieu of chairs. All the occupants were present: Yelagin; his wife who was translating Dickens' *Cricket on the Hearth* into Russian; their daughter Lilya, a beautiful child with huge brown eyes, black hair that fell in bangs over her forehead, and a mischievous smile; and the girl's grandmother who had admitted me.

As I entered, Yelagin rose from his bed. He had had two teeth extracted the day before and was still in pain. He stood about five feet four; was twenty-nine years old; had a thin body, somber face, light olive skin, soft silken hair, and dark, glowing eyes. When he felt well, he cut timber all day in the near-by woods to earn money for food to supplement the meager rations supplied by the International Refugee Organization.

Yelagin showed me two books of his poems published in Russian in Germany. Back home, in Kiev, he had never had any of his verse published. What he wrote after his flight from the Soviet Union was fiercely anti-Soviet and reflected the human tragedy of Russian life. The Bolsheviks had arrested and shot or banished most of his paternal relatives. His mother was Jewish and the Nazis exterminated her family. A terrible choice faced Yelagin as the Red army approached Kiev and the Germans prepared to abandon the city. To stay meant to court Soviet wrath, for the returning Communists would suspect everybody of having collaborated with the Nazis. To go meant to go with the hated Nazis. The Germans solved the problem by forcibly transporting large numbers of Kiev residents, including Yelagin, his wife, and mother-in-law, to Germany.

Some time after I met them, Yelagin, his wife, and child—the mother-in-law had died—sailed for the United States. New York thrilled him. "For the first time in my life I walk around without identification papers," he marveled. "The roadways full, the pavements empty," was his description of Park Avenue. In due course, Yelagin found a job cleaning up in a restaurant after closing hour and putting the slop out on the pavement at midnight for collection. One day I phoned him to say he was to apply at a certain watch factory for a position. He replied that he had been employed only recently, was satisfied with the work, and did not think it right to leave. I told him that in America nobody objected when a person tried to improve his condition. "Yes," he argued, "but if I leave, the management will say all Russian DP's are untrustworthy and won't employ any." He failed to get the job in the watch factory, but did find something better than being a slop man. Later, he studied English, attended college, and now he is employed by a university research project.

Ivan Yelagin was one of several million human granules ground between the Soviet and Nazi millstones during the Second World War. Approximately five million Soviet citizens were taken by the Germans from the Soviet Union during the hostilities and brought to German-held territory either as prisoners of war or slave laborers. Many of these prisoners had surrendered willingly in order to get out of Stalin's Russia. At least 500,000 of them served in the Nazi armies though far fewer saw actual combat. A certain percentage hoped to be used to overthrow the Muscovite rule they hated.[1]

[1] George Fischer, *Soviet Opposition to Stalin; a Case Study in World War II*, Cambridge: Harvard University Press, 1952, is a comprehensive survey of this situation.

In the last part of the war, as the conquering Russian army debouched into Poland and Eastern Germany, it captured camps filled with hundreds of thousands of Hitler's Russian prisoners of war and slave laborers. Some prisoners, however, intent on avoiding the Red frying pan, took advantage of the end-of-the-war chaos in Germany and fled westward into the arms of the Americans, British, and French.

Now occurred one of the least publicized and worst crimes in recent history. It flowed from a brief and innocent-looking resolution accepted at the Yalta Conference in February, 1945, by Russia, America, and Britain, which stipulated that each would return to its two allies any of their citizens it held at the end of the war. The United States, the United Kingdom and France, accordingly, were required to hand over to Stalin all Soviet citizens under their control. Armed with this blanket death sentence and concentration-camp warrant, agents of the Russian secret police fanned out into Germany and Austria to take possession of the Soviet citizens who had rushed westward to get out of the reach of the advancing Red army and also of those who, when hostilities ceased, were living in prisoner of war and slave labor camps in Western Germany. Many submitted. Many resisted.

An ambitious manhunt now commenced in Europe. Squads of the Soviet secret police, co-operating with Communists in the French police, hunted elusive Russians in France. They searched for them in towns and villages. They kidnaped them from Paris apartments, and in some recorded instances when resistance was offered, they shot on the spot. The NKVD's biggest field of endeavor, of course, was Germany. There, bewildered, hungry Russians, fleeing the long arm of the Kremlin, roamed the countryside singly or in bands, plundering to live and killing to be free. But the bulk of the former prisoners of war and slave laborers were concentrated in American, British, and French camps in Western Germany, and it was there that the Soviet police reaped its biggest crop. By arrangement with the administration of these centers, the Soviet agents would appear to receive their victims. Sometimes their ghoulish visits provoked bloody incidents.

According to figures given me by the U.S. authorities in Germany, 1,061,000 Soviet citizens were repatriated up to the end of September, 1945, from the American zone in Germany, and 970,000 more from the British and French zones. Some had to be forced.

The reasons for resistance were many and complicated. Two stand out. First, even wartime Nazi Germany seemed an improvement on the Soviet Union both as regards liberties and groceries, and when the Western occupational armies arrived there was more freedom and more food. But the second reason alone would have been decisive: it was known that the Soviet government suspected all prisoners of war and slave laborers. Had they surrendered or were they captured? Besides, they had lived abroad and might have been infected with anti-Sovietism. Returned prisoners, therefore, were sent directly to Siberia for brain-washing in "correction camps," and many DP's believed this might mean prolonged banishment or death. They preferred to remain exiles abroad.

The violent repatriation of Soviet DP's in Germany became widely known in the Soviet armed forces inside the Iron Curtain and acted as a frighening deterrent to any potential defectors, for how could they know that the Western powers would not enter into another arrangement of the Yalta type for their compulsory return?

For this and many other reasons, the Western nations grew to resent the coercion which the Yalta agreement imposed on them. Soon, they refused to use force and prevented the Soviet agents from using force. Gradually, the number of repatriations tapered off and by 1950 it had shrunk to zero.

An estimated quarter of a million Soviet DP's remained in Germany after repatriation ceased completely. Their condition was unenviable. The majority were cooped up in camps and crowded into temporary wooden barracks. The German economy was still too weak to employ them; nor did the Germans show much sympathy for them. Above all, the DP's feared seizure by the Soviet secret police. Most of them had taken false names, forged false papers, and in every way attempted to conceal their identity.

The fondest dream of most DP's was to go as far away as possible —to Australia, Venezuela, to Thailand in case of the Kalmucks who were Buddhists, preferably to Canada or the United States—acquire new citizenship, and start a new life beyond the shadow of Russia.

But a small percentage, the hard core, of the postwar Soviet exiles hoped to overthrow or at least hurt their former masters in Moscow, and organized various committees for that purpose. Their fondest ambition, shared by similar groups of refugees from Poland, Czechoslovakia, and the other Russian satellite states, was to return home when the dictator fell. Conscious, however, of the formidable might of Soviet totalitarianism, they could scarcely envisage the attainment of their goal except after Russia's defeat by America. In public, they might deny that war was their wish. But an incautious remark sometimes revealed it as their deepest desire.

Once, at a New York dinner party, I fell to arguing with Dr. Hu Shih, the well known Chinese philosopher and proponent of Chiang Kai-shek. Chiang was on Formosa, and Dr. Hu Shih believed he should be helped to recapture the mainland. This, of course, involved active U.S. military support and the possibility of a world war. "Some of my best friends are warmongers," I told the Chinese scholar. "In 1938, the Spanish Loyalists, sensing doom, saw salvation only in the extension of their peninsular struggle into a Europewide or world-wide conflict between the Western democracies and Russia, on the one hand, and the Fascist powers on the other. This is the war that actually occurred—but too late to save the Loyalists." Doctor Hu Shih would not admit being motivated by a similar wish, but he was too honest and wise not to recognize that Chiang Kai-shek's forces alone could not reconquer China. "Likewise my Russian émigré friends, idealists and humanitarians though they are," I continued, "think of their eagerly desired return to Russia only in relation to a third world war."

The dream of the political exile to go home and play a role in the leadership of his native land becomes a febrile obsession, and anything which suggests that the dream may never come true is seriously disturbing. In this connection I always recall a personal experience in New York on January 1, 1948. I had celebrated the New Year until the morning hours, so I stayed in my apartment all day without dressing. At 9:40 P.M., Fira Beneson, the famous dress designer, Countess Ilinski in private life, telephoned. "What are you doing?" she asked.

I told her I was about to go to bed.

"Come over," she said.

"I haven't dressed today," I replied. "I'm not shaved. I can't come." We are close friends and I knew she would understand.

"You must come," she insisted. "I need you."

I shaved, dressed, took a taxi uptown, and arrived thirty minutes after Fira's call. Her husband, Colonel Janusz Ilinski, former aide-de camp of General Wladislaw Sikorski, Poland's wartime Prime Minister, greeted me at the door and introduced me to his comrade, Prince Paul Sapieha. In the parlor, on a couch, sat Stanlinslaw Mikolajczyk, Polish Minister of Agriculture who had just fled from his country to escape arrest at the hands of the Communists. On the same couch, with only empty cushion space between, sat Alexander Kerensky, ex-Prime Minister of Russia, whose government, after overthrowing the Czar, was overthrown by Lenin and Trotsky on November 7, 1917, when Bolshevik troops stormed the Winter Palace in Petrograd. Kerensky escaped from the palace and hid in the city. Later, eluding Communist agents, he escaped to Western Europe. Now he is a permanent resident of the United States, and over the years I frequently saw him in Fira's apartment. Fira is Russian-born, and her father, until the Soviet Revolution, was the president of the Lena Goldfields corporation in Siberia. Kerensky had frequented the Beneson family home in Petrograd.

There they now sat in the same New York parlor, Kerensky, the earliest victim of Communism, an exile these thirty-one years, and Mikolajczyk, one of the latest political refugees, only three months out of Communist-controlled Poland.

I had no sooner entered than I began questioning Mikolajczyk about the manner of his escape, the reasons for it, conditions in Poland, and so forth. He answered gladly and seemed to be eager to talk. Knowing my curiosity, this is exactly what Fira and Janusz had expected and why they had summoned me. The evening had been electric with the tension between the two exiles. I was to be the insulation, diverting the current. Both gentlemen on the couch were urbane, cultured, and self-controlled, but hostess and host had sensed the antagonism.

How explain those long streaks of flame that had crackled across the empty cushion space? Kerensky, the veteran of more than three decades of separation from his native Russia which he loves above all else, saw in the younger man a portent. Mikolajczyk's presence indicated to Kerensky that his chances ever to see Russia were almost nil, for the Pole's flight from Poland was proof of growing Soviet power and exposed as illusion any thought of Moscow's imminent collapse. This embittered Kerensky, and the bitterness affected this first contact with his Polish fellow exile and brother-in-pain.

Hundreds of former Cabinet ministers, members of Parliament, high officials, writers, artists, journalists, and others active in politics have fled from Communist, and Fascist, countries to the Western democracies. Some make the adjustment. But even when they are not poor they are in pain. A plain immigrant goes into the melting pot and becomes part of the mass in a new country. An exiled politician always spins fantasies on how he will redeem his nation, and seeks to conceal, even from himself, the reality of his political impotence. Displaced leaders abroad are happy to be alive but their lives are not happy. They toil on quarreling committees and little magazines trying to keep alive a fighting nucleus which might be transplanted to their country of origin in a moment of crisis. But the moment is postponed month after month, and year after year, and the hair grows grayer, the ranks thinner, the prospects darker. Undaunted, the political exiles remain, nevertheless, miracles of man's will to survive. By some mysterious spiritual chemistry they retain their faith, for without it they would leave the arena and die, and they hate to give their enemies that pleasure. Yet always there is the suspicion that even if a political revolution did take place, the exiled leader, who had lived so long abroad, might not be wanted by the population.

Would Mikolajczyk, I wondered that evening in Fira's apartment, look back someday, as Kerensky now did, on thirty-one years of exile? Kerensky must have had the same saddening thought. How long-lived are dictatorships in peacetime? How rapid can be their evolution, if any, toward democracy? Is internally generated, gradual change a conceivable alternative to the sudden violent overthrow contemplated by the exile?

The world of Russia's political exiles, which now consists of dots in Germany, France, the United States, and a few other places, is a little world full of personal feuds, miniscule civil wars between parties and ethnic groups, long memories, and short tempers. It is an unreal world resembling a superheated hothouse in which minor matters attain unreal proportions. But it is linked to the big, real world which keeps it as a possible subversive reserve in case of war and for subversive peacetime propaganda. It is a brave little world, which hopes despite despair, and has a well-defined place in the present era of mutually subversive peaceful coexistence when neither side wants war but each favors revolution—in the other's territory.

CHAPTER TWENTY

America's Mission

W E HAVE many Europeans here this summer," an English-woman remarked in London in June, 1951.

"I thought there were forty-eight million of them," I suggested.

"No," she corrected, "we are British."

"If we were part of a united Europe," Richard Crossman, Labor M.P., said to me, "all the unemployed Italians would come here."

The fact that Italians and French "don't pay their taxes but we do," was one of a number of arguments against European union which I heard from several Englishmen.

"We and the Scandinavians would have to meet the bills of a federated Europe which included us," is the way a London publicist put it.

On June 16, 1940, Prime Minister Winston Churchill had proposed that "France and Great Britain shall no longer be two, but one Franco-British Union." He wanted "every citizen of France" to "enjoy immediately citizenship of Great Britain" and "every British subject" to "become a citizen of France." This remarkable offer to pool sovereignties, to merge two great powers, came at the moment when France was about to topple into Hitler's repulsive embrace. It therefore represented an effort to save a nation through international-ism. Churchill recognized that self-preservation is best served when separate sovereignty is not preserved. He apparently expected that the comfort of union would stir the French to save themselves.

The proposal, unfortunately, could not be tested; five days later, the Pétain government signed an armistice with the Nazis. Nor has it been repeated, for nations are often more idealistic in the fire of war than in cool, calculating calm of peace.

Nevertheless, the need for European union asserted itself after the Second World War despite all the shopkeeper objections. Europe was bursting at its national seams. Italy knew she could not prosper in nationalistic separateness. Germany, her eastern third lopped off and too dependent spiritually to build up a new rump nationalism on the omnipresent debris of the old, hankered for membership by the side of France in a receptive Western family. France was split between an emotional urge for the restoration of bygone national glory and a rational realization that it was impossible. With one lobe of her brain she sponsored the Schuman Plan Coal and Steel Community, comprising, in addition, Germany, Italy, and the three Benelux lands, which came into force on July 25, 1952, after two years of negotiations. With that same lobe, she conceived the idea of the EDC (European Defense Community) as an international device to hinder the recrudescence of nationalism in a rearmed Germany. With another lobe, in which eighty-year-old sentiments reside and proliferate, she rejected it. Then she tried to rescue some of the international features of the rejected scheme.

England likewise was of two minds. Long committed to the doctrine of noncommitment, she began after the Second World War to forsake her traditional free-lance role as the balance in the balance of power and acknowledged her membership in Europe. The British have always regarded advance commitments as irksome limitations on the "muddling through" procedures so dear and so helpful on occasions to their diplomacy. But England's noncommital policy had not, to say the least, prevented the First or Second World War, and it might have imperiled the strategy of preventing the third. For given Russian strength, a balance in Europe without the United States *and* Britain could not be achieved or maintained. Hence England's readiness, after much hesitation, to collaborate with the Schuman Plan and to undertake to station troops on the Continent for an extended period. Simultaneously, however, she treasured her insularity and stressed the paramount importance of the Commonwealth as against Europe.

Nations knew they could not live alone yet hesitated to live together. Internationalism seemed ready to be born but nationalism refused to die. Both therefore began to live side by side, which is a natural and perhaps not unhealthy means of making the transition from nation states to federations of states.

Nationalism still inspired individuals and institutions to fruitful effort. England is an example. Nationalism, moreover, is still an asset prized by the demagogue, rabble rouser, and mentally impoverished politician. It gives him a platform when he has no program. He wraps himself in the flag to conceal his intellectual nakedness. Economic interests deeply rooted in labor and capital fear the competition which they foresee after the removal of national barriers. Nationalism retains great practical, political, and emotional strength.

The passing of the ancient city states and their empires and of feudal sovereignties was likewise attended by reluctance, regrets, and procrastination, and by wars designed to delay the end which they hastened.

The wars since the summer of 1914 look like the convulsions of our dying nationalistic world. They have destroyed or weakened all the old empires. Lenin, predicting collapse, contended that imperialism was the last phase of capitalism. Instead, it may be the last phase of nationalism. For imperialism is export nationalism under which the political and economic egotism of developed nations represses that of underdeveloped colonial and semicolonial regions and in doing so digs its own grave. China, for example, might not have gone Communist but for the nineteenth- and twentieth-century attempts of European powers and Japan, quarreling among themselves, to slice her into spheres of influence. In obstructing the rise of Asian nationalism, Western imperialism became the breeding ground of Asian Communism.

The Japanese, German, Italian, Turkish, and Austro-Hungarian empires are gone, and the French and British empires have shrunk. Imperialism is out or on the way out except in some corners of Asia and small enclaves in Latin America, Africa, and the Communist orbit. This is part of the gradual eclipse of Western nationalism.

The groping for new international forms is the most distinguishing constructive characteristic of the postwar period. Europe in particular knows that it cannot afford the waste and conflict of nationalism. The process of integrating Europe has been slow and painful, for the old hesitates to yield and, making up in experience what it has lost in agility and virility, jousts shrewdly with the new. Yet the signs of an emerging future are numerous. Benelux, with a name that looks as though it might mean "good light," was the first, and if some of the developments have been below expectation, progress toward economic amalgamation continues. Among the many other integrating bodies are: the Council of Europe with its seat at

Strasbourg, France, where, periodically, the foreign ministers of the member states (Belgium, Denmark, France, Germany, Greece, Iceland, Eire, Italy, Luxembourg, the Netherlands, Norway, Sweden, Turkey, and the United Kingdom, and the Saar as associate) meet "to achieve a greater unity" in conjunction with its Consultative Assembly which is an international parliament representing the national parliaments of the member states; also, the European Payments Union of seventeen European countries founded in 1950; the Scandinavian Council for consultation among the governments and parliaments of Sweden, Norway, Denmark, and Iceland; GATT (General Agreement on Tariffs and Trade), active since 1947, in Europe, Asia, and the Americas; UNISCAN (United Kingdom and Scandinavia) for the freer flow of capital; the OEEC (Organization for European Economic Co-operation) embracing the seventeen European nations which adhered to the Marshall Plan; the important Coal and Steel Community; a host of nongovernmental bodies; and, most important, NATO which, born for military purposes only, began in 1955 to function as a political policy board of its fifteen nation members.

In the intercontinental field there are, further, the Colombo Plan, launched in May, 1950, whose richer members—Canada, Australia, New Zealand, England, and the United States—grant other members—India, Indonesia, Burma, Cambodia, Ceylon, Laos, Nepal, Vietnam, and Pakistan—finances and technical aid for economic development; and, not least, the numerous specialized agencies of the United Nations: WHO (the World Health Organization); UNESCO (United Nations Education, Scientific, and Cultural Organization); FAO (Food and Agricultural Organization); the International Bank for Reconstruction and Development; the International Monetary Fund; ECE (Economic Council for Europe), with Karl Gunnar Myrdal as General-Secretary; the ECAFE (Economic Commission for Asia and the Far East), under Mr. P. S. Lokanathan, an Indian civil servant; and others.

In most of these organizations the United States has, either from the inside as member or from the outside as financier, supported closer co-operation across national frontiers. A big federation itself, the United States favors bigger international units.

The internationalism in United States foreign policy is new. For long decades, the United States was isolationist. Isolationism may be a species of nationalist exclusiveness due to snobbish ideas of supremacy. In the case of the United States, however, it was due to remoteness and the desire to avoid enmeshment in unpleasant, unnecessary, and alien matters. Throughout the nineteenth century, the country abstained from alliances, permanent associations, pressure blocs, overseas commitments, or attempts to achieve world influence.

Nor did the nationalism which finds expression in imperialism emerge in the United States until late in the nineteenth century. Internal expansion toward the Pacific coast, the problem of slavery before and during the Civil War, and the tasks of reconstruction after it absorbed the nation's energies. The possibilities of economic development and personal enrichment at home were so unbounded as to leave little room for frustration and no need of foreign adventures or conquests.

Just before the dawn of the twentieth century, a phase of imperialism commenced with the Spanish-American War and intervention in Latin America. Isolationism seemed to wane. But it quickly reasserted itself, and public sentiment against entry into the First World War was strong enough to postpone participation in it for nearly three years.

After that war, however, the United States relapsed into isolationism. The disillusioning experience of the wartime alliance left no wish for its continuation in peacetime. Economically and diplomatically, to be sure, the United States played an increasingly important role in world affairs, but it was far from commensurate with the country's expanded power. Neutrality, nonalignment, and non-commitment remained the three pillars of U.S. foreign policy, bringing happiness to Fascist aggressors in Abyssinia, Spain, and everywhere else.

Although the Second World War commenced on September 1, 1939, the United States did not fight until December 8, 1941, the day after the Pearl Harbor attack. America's aid to the anti-Axis coalition before that date, and America's belligerence after it, were necessary to prevent one power, Germany, from dominating Europe, and another power, Germany's ally Japan, from dominating Asia. But although the United States thus expensively contributed to the world balance of power, nothing indicated an American intention of becoming a permanent part of it. On the contrary, judging by

U.S. behavior toward Russia during the war and till about the middle of 1946, there is every reason to assert that isolationism would soon have revived.

But Russia's forward urge in Europe and the inability of non-Russian Europe to check it compelled the United States to enter into alliances and other intimate international arrangements to re-establish a balance of power in Europe and Asia against the Soviet Union.

Now the United States had a long-term rival, and when President Truman announced in September, 1949, that Russia had carried out her first atomic explosion it was clear that the rival would be considered a menace. This marks a turning point, a divide, in American history. The United States had lived alone on an estate surrounded by wide moats. Now it became part of a neighborhood. It, therefore, needed a foreign policy, a foreign policy in general and a policy toward Russia in particular.

The foundation stone of the Truman-Acheson policy of the containment of Russia was international co-operation. It made no sense to try to save the countries of Europe from Soviet imperialism without their participation in the effort. Even viewing the American-Russian antagonism as the traditional type of rivalry between the first power in the world and the second, the United States could only succeed through a partnership with Europe, for any attempt to dominate the old independent nations of Europe and use them as American pawns in the fight with the Soviets would have had to end in clash and failure. American imperialism was and is impossible in Europe. Hence the internationalism of the containment period. The Truman Doctrine was a joint effort with Greece and Turkey. The Marshall Plan fostered economic internationalism; the Act of Congress which approved the Plan stressed "the advantages which the United States has enjoyed through the existence of a large domestic market without trade barriers," and the amended Act of April, 1949, stated concisely that it was "the policy of the people of the United States to encourage the unification of Europe." As a result, a whole school of co-ordinating, consultative, and co-operative commissions and institutions was spawned which outlived the Plan and appear to have become permanent features improving Europe's life and reinforcing its will to live. Whereas imperialism seeks to divide the better to conquer, the United States aimed to unite and strengthen in order to prevent the Soviets from conquering.

In a partnership or alliance, attempts by one member to influence fellow members are unavoidable and legitimate. Much depends on the amount of pressure used. A "take it or leave it" ultimatum will antagonize the partners. Nations do not like to be "pushed around." But in the case of German rearmament, for instance, it was the United States that allowed itself to be pushed around, for in view of the passionate U.S. advocacy of a German army, and in view of Chancellor Adenauer's readiness to rearm, the delays to which America agreed for years after Secretary of State Acheson first proposed German rearmament in September, 1950, certainly do not constitute proof of imperialism, dictation, or impatience. Nevertheless, complaints against America for having proposed it at all became a loud chorus in 1951, and contributed to the deterioration of Atlantic climate. American pressure on England, France, and other NATO members to accelerate their rearmament further worsened U.S. relations with Europe. European economic recovery was so recent and frail that many feared its collapse under the weight of too much expenditure on arms. What is "too much" led to numerous debates between governments and in the press.

In mid-1951, moreover, Europe began to feel optimistic about the prospects of peace with Russia, and critics said Americans were too nervous. Europeans saw the earmarks of imperialism in the implacable enmity of leading Americans toward Communist China, in U.S. exclusive domination of Japan, and in the nurturing of "despotic puppets": Chiang Kai-shek on Formosa and Syngman Rhee in South Korea. They feared an American "Go It Alone" policy in Asia which would result in a third world war, with Europe in the role of reluctant and doomed participant.

That these fears were unjustified, or at least premature by many years, has been demonstrated by the absence of events.

Yet some foreign worries are not difficult to explain. For the United States response to the Russian peril was mixed. On the one hand, the country as a whole reacted rationally, and the postwar Administrations, with considerable support from both parties, carried out a peaceful, internationalist policy of economic aid and collective security. On the other hand, Americans in numbers too large to be summarily condemned succumbed to unreasoning panic or siege psychology and struck out at everything that was different. The unaccustomed situation of being accessible to the military might and secret agents of a hostile rival produced hysteria and jitters.

The resulting intolerance, vindictiveness, bellicosity, low boiling point, high temperature, and unforgiveness recalled and sometimes actually recreated the atmosphere of totalitarian countries. It all went under the name of McCarthyism which is kin to Stalinism in its encouragement of anonymous denunciations, unconcern for facts and figures, and disrespect for persons.

Linked with the legislative vigilantism of McCarthy there emerged the specter of American imperialism in Asia which marched hand in hand with hostility to allies anywhere who were not completely submissive.

McCarthyism and imperialism were not identical and did not always overlap but they helped each other and often drew support from the same sources. Both advocated the application of surgery— political or military—on different ideologies at home and abroad. Both generated and flourished in an atmosphere of tension and hate. Their response to Soviet totalitarianism would have been a little American replica of the same, and their response to Soviet imperialism would have been American imperialism.

This nervous revulsion against others who are different was reincarnated isolationism, isolationism in an era when America had to be interventionist. Since the U.S. could not sit alone at home it would at least function alone abroad, insist on having its own way, dictate to friends, and mow down foes.

Such militaristic imperialism being impossible in Europe, America's new nationalists concentrated on Asia where they thought it was. Instead of concerting U.S. policy with more than a dozen allies as in NATO, America would give orders to two or three almost-satellites in Asia and use force to get results. But this imperialist trend never got far. Even General Douglas MacArthur, whom the nationalists regarded as their leader, refused his support. He shared their impatience but declared, in his birthday address in Los Angles in February, 1955, that "war cannot be the arbiter of our survival." President Eisenhower also showed greater wisdom than some of his Senatorial friends.

At home, however, McCarthyism found plenty of scope and sharply diminished the fund of good will built abroad by postwar American policies and aid programs costing billions. Europeans sincerely considered McCarthyism a menace to them. "We are, so to speak," a French author said to me, "sitting in an automobile with Uncle Sam at the wheel and driving fast. But McCarthy, in the front seat next to the driver, is throwing sand into Uncle's eyes and pushing him and telling him to go this way and that way. We are afraid of an accident. Can we trust the driver when he has to please McCarthy?"

Europeans also charged that McCarthyism hampered the fight against Communism. "How can we convince anyone that our cause is democracy," I heard people in Europe argue, "when the United States, the strongest democratic power, tolerates this suppression of freedom?"

Thus every international problem goes back to internal politics, and most aspects of domestic policy as well as many matters that seem unpolitical—like crime, literature, cinema, and racial intolerance—affect international relations. Indeed, the world has reached a stage where there is no such thing as domestic politics. It all gets mixed up with the world situation especially in the present era when diplomats at international conferences keep one eye and sometimes two on their home electorates, or conduct relations with foreign countries by upbraiding them on television.

Nations are more dependent on one another and therefore grow more involved in the internal affairs of near and overseas neighbors. The outcome of a vote in the French Parliament, the size of the Communist vote in Italy, the mood of America, the decisions of the Kremlin, Japanese neutralism, German militarism, McCarthyism, and a hundred other national situations excite keen interest far beyond national frontiers. The fate of any country, large or small, is determined in many other countries. Nations are interlocked with nations while maintaining intact all the forms and fictions of national separatism. Internationalism, finding the front door and direct approach closed, is coming in through the windows, side doors, ventilators, and chimney.

"Why is it," Europeans asked in 1950 and 1951, "that Europe, though so much nearer the Soviet Union and with so many more Communists inside, is less panicky than strong, remote America?"

Later, during my stay in America from July, 1951, to mid-March, 1952, when I left for a trip around the world, I tried to clarify this matter for myself. What actually explained the difference between the American and European reactions to the postwar situation? I looked for the answer in the differences between the United States and Europe. It seemed, and seems, to me that by reason of the width of the country (which makes foreign nations almost an unreality to many mid-continental states of the union) and the width of the oceans, America is still isolationist at heart but has now been forced to become interventionist in deed, and hates that which makes it so. What makes it so is Soviet imperialism.

Before the Second World War the French and British remained complacent in the face of the Nazi peril, appeased it, and were therefore inadequately armed when Hitler struck. America took that as a warning. Europe has also learned the lesson, but hopes fervently for accommodation and compromise.

Looking at some of the countries of Europe separately, we observe that France and Italy have too many Communists to cope with them by suppression, and England and Western Germany have too few to be worried by them. Proportionately, however, the United States has no more than England or Western Germany; for an Alger Hiss in the State Department England had her Klaus Fuchs in atomic energy yet the British took it in their stride.

One returns, consequently, to the resentment of Russia or Communism as a means of forcing isolationist Americans to be active abroad. To which, I believe, another factor that is absent elsewhere should be added: U.S. domestic politics. American anti-Communism has been directed not only against Communists, and perhaps not primarily against Communists, but against the Roosevelt and Truman Administrations and, in one period in particular, against the State Department under Mr. Dean Acheson whose foreign policy the isolationist-imperialists abhorred. For some, but of course not all, Republicans, anti-Communism had been a stick with which to beat the Democrats.

If the political philosophies of the Republican and Democratic rivals in any given area are not far apart, their boasted anti-Communist records may become the chief subject of campaign oratory, and this exalts Communism to the central focus of politics. In England, for example, the clear ideological distinction between Conservatives and Labor would preclude such a development. Nor would Winston Churchill or Attlee be accused of Communism, pro-Communism, or treason by an Englishman who thought they had made mistakes at Teheran, Yalta, or Potsdam. Where politicians are mature and politics serious, mud thrown at a leader sticks to the undignified thrower. A gentleman does not impugn the basic loyalties of a minister of state or make unproved charges. Certain things are just not done in your host's drawing room or in a boxing ring and certain things are not done in the political arena. Maybe it takes more than seventeen decades to evolve a national code of ethics for public behavior.

Of course a Communist party in a democracy poses the problem of espionage; in view of the party's loyalty to a foreign country, any of its members, if asked, would have to obey orders and turn spy. This is a security matter to be handled legally by official experts, not by free-wheeling volunteers. But the point is not to blow up the house while laying traps for the rats. In the United States this means coping with the false revolutionists called Communists without killing the true revolutionary heart of America.

At San Francisco on October 15, 1950, President Truman, returning from his talks with General Douglas MacArthur on Wake Island, made a statement of transcendent significance for the future of America and of the world. Referring to Russian expansion as "this new colonialism," he said, "The international Communist movement, far from being revolutionary, is the most reactionary movement in the world." America, he added, is built on a revolutionary idea, "this endlessly revolutionary idea of human freedom and political equality." The Soviet Union is indeed a reactionary country. That is the biggest truth about Russia. Her peasants are serfs in collectives where they own no land, no machinery, no work animals, and only a very small part of their produce. The workers are chained to their factories, cannot strike, and cannot move from a job without government permission. Writers, journalists, professional persons, scientists, and officials are chained to the party line. The line changes, the length of the chain changes, but the chain is always there. All citizens except a handful of top oligarchs are politically helpless, disfranchised servants of the state. This is a new feudalism, the natural offspring of the feudalism of Czarist Russia.

Feudalism is an excellent clue to the puzzles of the present world situation. Where you find feudalism there will be Communism. To the extent that Italy, China, India are feudal, Communism flourishes. Capitalism—in America, England, Germany—does not breed Communism, except in a neurotic fringe, but feudalism does, for a feudal country slips easily into the pattern of Russian feudal Communism. In a capitalist country the farmer will resist Communist effort to take his land from him. But if feudal barons own the land the peasant is more receptive to the argument that he would be better off under a feudal state. In a capitalist country where the working man is free and adequately paid he will resist Communism. But when he is, in effect, a poor serf of a rapacious, uncontrolled master, he may welcome a system in which the state is his master.

The feudalism inherent in Communism and the feudalism remaining in non-Communist countries is a challenge to the United States and a call to duty. America stands for revolution: rapid growth through adaptability to change, social mobility instead of the class rigidity of feudalism and feudal Communism, equality of rights, equality of opportunity, freedom, and justice under law. These are the most revolutionary explosives on earth. This is why McCarthyism hurt America so much in Europe, Asia and elsewhere; it looked like the abridgment of liberty, the substitution of fear for freedom, and the ascendancy of arbitrary injustice by unchecked accusations. It seemed like an effort to make America conformist and reactionary, to rob it, in other words, of its diversity, flexibility, and courage. Such an America would have less appeal to that large part of the world waiting for a social revolution to release it from feudal backwardness. McCarthyism meant a betrayal of America and, too, a betrayal of those who needed the strength and example of a progressive America. In the same way, imperialism, discarded by the new England, worthy of feudal Russia, would have meant for the United States a turning back of the clock.

America's foreign policy should be internationalism, and liberation from colonialism and feudalism.

America's mission is to carry the technological, industrial, social, and political revolution to all who need and want it. That would be the real anti-Communism.

The living American revolution, embodied in the government's foreign policy, would be a far more effective measure for peace and freedom than verbal attacks on Communism or propaganda for a capitalism whose wealth seems unbelievable and unattainable to the people of retarded countries. American idealism, in action at home and abroad, would hurt Communism more than anti-Communist hysteria or even sensible anti-Communist argument.

Strength is necessary to block enemies and help allies. But only spiritual qualities, translated into deeds, will win friends. In this area, individuals can be at least as effective as governments.

All the bursting arsenals of reactionary Russia contain no weapon for a counterattack on spiritual values or on the revolution of human freedom and progress.

The keystone of United States foreign policy should be revolution.

Part Five

AROUND THE WORLD
IN 282 DAYS

CHAPTER TWENTY-ONE

Wanted: a Revolution

WALKING in the beautiful flower garden of the pension in Taormina, Sicily, where my wife had been living and writing a novel, we met Mario, the gardener. He kissed her hand and then he bowed and kissed mine. On a visit to the kitchen, Antonio, the cook, also kissed my hand. Kissing a man's hand is a feudal custom, a mark of homage, an acceptance of the social inferiority that stems from birth.

I spent three weeks in Sicily at Taormina-Mazzaro by the sea, where the beach is one's front pavement, and in tours of the island, visiting Randazzo, Troini, Enna, and Catania, and villages between these towns. I tarried half a day in the castle of a British lady and lord who inherited their estate from Admiral Nelson. This was a sort of vacation-with-work prior to setting off on a nine months' trip eastward around the world which took me up the Italian peninsula to Trieste, then to Yugoslavia, Turkey, Israel, Pakistan, India, Burma, Siam, Indo-China, Hong Kong, the Philippines, Japan, Alaska, and New York.

Since feudalism is one of the world's major problems, I thought Sicily was a good place to begin. The Sicilians are like their island— mild, relaxed, and picturesque, yet somber, smoldering, volcanic; poor and underproductive (except in babies), yet potentially rich. The people are Roman overlaid with Norman, Saracen, and Greek. More recently, Germans and Anglo-Americans have added their seed to the barnyard of earlier conquerors. It does not seem to have made anybody very energetic, trustful, or inclined toward community effort.

"Duce, duce, duce," "credere, obbidire, combattere, Mussolini ("Believe, obey, fight"), and similar Fascist propaganda on
walls and houses has been whitewashed over so lightly that it is still
legible. I supposed this was a ruse to conform to the proprieties of the
present while retaining the loyalties of the past, but everybody said,
no, the Sicilians were simply too indifferent to Mussolini to care
whether the signs of his vanished glorification were visible or not.
They never followed his foolish slogans anyway.

In Taormina I sought out a landlord, Commendatore Francesco
Atenasio, age seventy-six, who had been mayor of the town during ten
years of the Fascist regime. "Fascism," he said, "was a cloud that has
passed." Mussolini built many roads, and attempted to improve the
economy of Italy, but in the later years he began to think he was
god, and when he made war on Abyssinia he took a wrong turn.
"Italians fought in Spain to earn money," the ex-mayor declared,
"and that humiliated us." Nevertheless, he added, "Fascism brought
order. Italy is not ready for full democracy. Italians need somebody
to discipline them."

The ex-mayor's office, where he received me, was tiny, not much
bigger than a double bed, but I counted eight vases full of bright,
fresh flowers. "I am a landlord," the Commendatore stated, "yet I
think landlords should be compelled to sell large parts of their estates.
Many landowners have so much land they do not cultivate all of it.
Many live in cities. They do not contribute to progress. Mussolini did
not dispossess the landlords or press them to sell; he wanted their
political support. Now the landlords are selling land because they
are afraid the government will be forced to carry out a land reform.
As soon as a peasant has any money he tries to buy land, even if it
is not fertile. He does it instinctively." Land is security and status.
When a peasant has land he ceases to be a hired hand. He is a landowner. He has risen in the social scale.

On an auto tour around Mount Etna with my wife and an Italian
friend who drove the car and interpreted, we stopped on an open field
to talk to a peasant. I asked him about the Communists. "There are
a few of them," he said, "and they work hard. But they have no
religion. The peasants who are devout try to convert the Communists
to religion. My brother, who was in Russia with the Italian army during the war, tells the Communists that under the Soviets the peasants
and workers are against the Red government and only the commissars
are for it."

He told us he was working a plot of land rented from the government. If he could save some money he would buy it. The landlords were beginning to sell because they thought overlarge estates would be cut down in a land reform. "But I know that most of the landlords are not selling honestly," the peasant remarked. "They are selling to relatives who depend on them, or to fictitious legal persons."

Almost everywhere one goes in eastern Sicily, Etna is there for beauty and direction. I saw it first and best from the train as I approached Taormina from the Straits of Messina. The long, gentle slope rises to the peak and then drops down sharply. The sharp side was covered with snow, the gentle slope with pink smoke. The volcano is always smoking; sometimes it erupts and lava comes down from the crater in black rivers, broader than most rivers of Sicily, that end at the road. The lava is in chunks that look like black earth masses ready to crumble but are actually very hard. Across the green countryside these dark streams of stone are dead earth until, centuries later, they disintegrate into fertile soil. Meanwhile, the lava, hewn into manageable pieces, is used to build terrace walls, roads, homes; in Randazzo a church is constructed entirely of lava rock.

Through this lava belt I drove with my wife to the estate of Lady and Lord Bridport, the Duchess and Duke of Brontë, at Maniace, in the province of Catania. The first Duke of Brontë was Admiral Nelson who received his title and the vast Sicilian estate that went with it from King Ferdinand IV of Naples in gratitude for taking the French off his neck by defeating them in Egypt. In the courtyard of the Brontë castle stands a Celtic cross of lava stone with a long stem and a short transverse arm on the base of which is engraved: "HEROI IMMORTALI NILI" ("To the Immortal Heroes of the Nile"). The area is called Maniace after a Christian general from Byzantium who smote the Saracens on the plain opposite Mount Etna in 1032, and erected the castle. It has since been reconstructed, enlarged, and redecorated.

Lord Nelson had no children and the title and estate therefore went to his brother whose daughter Charlotte, the third Duchess of Brontë, was Lady Bridport. The present Lord Bridport is Peter, in his early forties, Lieutenant Comander in the British navy during the war, tall and bald and married to an intellectually and physically attractive woman. They had a beautiful boy of four with wavy blond hair. We were shown through long halls hung with large ancestral oil portraits and tapestries, and then had drinks in a salon prior to eating lunch in a dining room with a long uncovered black wooden table and high-back chairs faced with red brocade. Waiters in livery and wearing white gloves served the meal. It was all very elegant and the more striking in the setting of Sicilian poverty and primitiveness.

Bridport's estate had consisted of twenty thousand acres of orange groves and grain land. In 1950, he sold some four thousand acres to his peasant sharecroppers who converted their shares of the crop into cash to make the purchases. Shortly thereafter, however, he said, they were hit by floods and came to him for help. "If they had not bought the land they would still have been my tenants and the losses would have been mine," he remarked. The answer to the peasant problem in Sicily, he felt, was landlords with a paternalistic interest in their sharecroppers.

Land reform looks like an economic measure only, but it is also deeply social. The peasant's yearning for land is visceral, but translated into social reality, land spells freedom. Land reform strikes the feudal fetters from the peasant's existence. Nevertheless, Lord Bridport's reference to the helplessness of the peasant faced with catastrophe has much cogency. Land alone is no solution and may become an albatross. In Italy, and especially in Asia, the poor peasant who acquires land has to borrow for seed, implements, and animals, and in certain circumstances this leads to a new enslavement—to the loan shark. A land reform must be part of a larger economic program which includes the establishment of rural credit co-operatives, cottage industries, and small canning, tanning, and other factories.

Lord Bridport said many peasants are illiterate. On the day when crops are divided between owners and sharecroppers Communists often appear, he said, to help in the accounting and prevent cheating. No other party gives this service, he told us, though sometimes Catholic priests do. As he showed us through some of the farm buildings near the castle, peasants bowed and took off their hats and caps and held them in their hands till we passed.

The boat and train from Sicily, passing Scylla near Charybdis, took me to Rome. Americans say, "Keep smiling." Romans smile without slogans. Even the poor districts are full of smiles. Every day in Rome seems like a holiday. Even the little Vespa motor scooters are expressions of the Italian personality rather than mere mechanical devices for locomotion. Dashing down or up an avenue, the young man at the wheel races the tiny four-horsepower motor of this metallic bronco to call attention to himself and, sometimes, to the lady passenger riding sidesaddle on the pillion seat behind him. This showing off is sensuous, not social as it might be elsewhere; the driver is displaying himself, not his wealth.

The Vespa, a simple efficient vehicle with two rubber-tired wheels about fourteen inches in diameter and capable of considerable speed and much noise, is, like its four sister brands, an important innovation. It can carry a small trailer attachment for commercial deliveries or a sidecar which will transport all or part of the family. For Italy with its narrower, crookeder streets, milder climate, and lesser wealth, it could become what the automobile has been to America. It has already found a large market at home and is sold in considerable volume abroad. What Italy needs is "Vespa" shoes, "Vespa" clothing, "Vespa" kitchen utensils, farm implements, beds, houses—that is, mass-produced commodities scaled down in price and quality to fit national conditions and the thinner national purse.

Mass production is not an end in itself. It is the road to mass consumption and satisfaction. It means jobs. By raising living standards it brings the poorer classes more level with the upper classes and thereby substitutes balance for the present perilous instability. At the top level in Italy, which encompasses few people, there is far too much elegance, luxury, and spending, while in the broad strata below there are slums, filth, stink, illiteracy, inadequate schooling, unemployment, and despair. With prices high and income low, there are undoubtedly millions of people who have never used a toothbrush, a bed sheet, electric light, a radio, or bought a newspaper.

Offhand one would be warranted in assuming that Switzerland is less likely to succumb to dictatorship than poor Yugoslavia, Denmark has a better chance of remaining democratic than Greece, England than Indonesia, Norway than Venezuela. Prosperity is a key to democracy.

Poverty can be met with mass prosperity or with "discipline," and "discipline" means barring the discontented from political power. Political power is therefore concentrated in the small class that has economic power or in its military or police allies. This explains why Latin-American, Asian, and other countries with sharp social and economic contrasts tend to succumb to dictators who rule by force and assassination until they are assassinated. All their "discipline" still fails to create stability.

Mussolini made the trains run on time, gave Italy parades, pageants, circuses, and wars, and used castor oil to cure indiscipline. But he could not right the disequilibrium between poor and rich, between powerless and powerful. Therefore the reality of Fascism was succeeded by the threat of Communism.

Italy's postwar democracy is infinitely better than prewar Fascism, but under it the social and economic inequality between the small upper class and the rest of the nation continues to be buttressed by the political inequality between rulers and ruled. This feeds Communism.

The Italian disease is imbedded in the feudal elements of Italian capitalism which make it stubbornly static. The brake on change comes from a fear that the changes might gather momentum and sweep away the specially protected positions of those who today possess power, wealth, and status.

Revolutionary America, with a high velocity of adaptation to modern requirements, is not troubled by disruptive revolutionaries. The sluggish society of Italy is.

When I was a student at the Southern High School in Philadelphia, Dr. Charles Hyle, the principal, addressed the morning assembly several times—or was it once?—on his visit to the Uffizi Palace. I never remembered what he reported, I only remembered the name, and that it was in Italy, and I remember the impression that as far as I was concerned it might just as well be on Mars because I would never get there. Now, after a fortnight in Rome, I was in Florence and I went to the Uffizi, perhaps the greatest art gallery in the world, and spent the better part of two vivid, exciting days viewing its treasures of canvas and stone.

Florence is a jewel box of medieval art and architecture set in a modern city that is soft, enlightened, beautiful, tolerant, and conscious of its decline. Politically it tends to swing from Communist to Catholic and back again. The May Day Communist meeting had more of the atmosphere of a picnic than a proletarian protest. Tiring of endless speeches, I went into the church facing the piazza where the demonstration was taking place. A gentle priest showed me the precious Giottos and other paintings on the walls. I asked him about the Communists outside. "Ah," he said softly, "they will repent some day."

In Venice, I floated on the canals in gondolas, walked the streets, and swam in the Adriatic. Then by train to Trieste.

Trieste, far up at the top of the map of the Adriatic, just opposite

Venice, was one of the tumors of Europe, but it could not become malignant because American and British troops occupied the city. The several thousand Americans wore a shoulder patch with the word "TRUST," Trieste U.S. Troops. They, with the British Tommies, were holding Trieste in trust pending a settlement acceptable to Italy and Yugoslavia.

Originally the two zones, one occupied and administered by the Anglo-Americans (Zone A), the other placed under Tito's rule (Zone B), and together known as the Free Territory of Trieste, were to have been united and placed under a United Nations governor, but Russia refused to accept the candidates nominated by the Western powers and they rejected all Russian candidates, so the plan remained in abeyance for years while tempers in Italy and Yugoslavia rose to fever pitch. Both countries claimed the city of Trieste.

Within an hour of my arrival in Trieste—it was the evening of May 7, 1952—I went to a Neo-Fascist rally in the vast Piazza Unita where the leader of MIS (Italian Social Movement), Augusto de Marsanich, leather-lunged, white-haired veteran Black Shirt and colleague of Mussolini, harangued a multitude of approximately thirty thousand persons, or one-tenth the population of the Zone A. Hands on his hips and chin stuck out like his hero the Duce, he asserted that if MIS had power he would march soldiers into Zone B and drive the Yugoslavs out. He would, he added, also take the Dalmatian coast of the Adriatic from Tito and, that done, resume Italy's expansion in "the Mediterranean and Africa."

The next evening I attended an open-air Communist meeting (smaller than the Neo-Fascists' of yesterday), where "Comrade Vittorio Vidali," the Communist leader of Zone A, an Italian, aping the nationalist tone of De Marsanich—without, however, going as far afield as Africa—rained verbal fire and brimstone on the head of Marshal Tito. While Tito was loyal to Moscow the Italian Communist party publicly advocated a settlement that would give Trieste to Yugoslavia. After his break with the Kremlin, Trieste became a fighting word to many Italians and it was easy for politicians to use it to arouse nationalist passions and rally high school boys and others for demonstrations which developed into riots. "Give us Trieste," they shouted, and broke windows in government buildings. During the early postwar years, it became a political issue with the Neo-Fascists and extreme right-wing nationalists. After 1948, they and the Communists built fires under the De Gasperi government to get

Trieste by negotiation or war. In the circumstances, Trieste became a major issue at the polls. Instead of winning more popular support by social and economic reforms between elections, the Italian government tried to ride into office again and again on waves of nationalist frenzy whipped up around Trieste. To support De Gasperi in elections, therefore, the United States government, backed usually by England and France, made concessions to Italy on the Trieste matter during every election campaign. The Italian government could always say to America, "Unless you support us Italy will go Communist." That shut off argument. Support took the form of dollar hypodermics and Triestean mustard plasters.

During my stay in Rome, I had driven out one day to Fregene where, among the pines by the sea, ECA, the Marshall Plan organization, maintained a school to teach factory managers and technical experts American methods of raising output, profits, and wages. This, and the injection of over a billion dollars of ECA money, undoubtedly had a salutary effect on production. But, viewed in the perspective of history, America's role in Italy was to help introduce the basic social and economic reforms which would give more people a stake in the democratic system. But the Trieste issue enabled the powers that be in Italy to divert the United States from this urgent task.

The Italian people did not benefit, relations between Italy and Yugoslavia deteriorated, and across the border Tito was using Trieste for the same purpose: winning popular backing through nationalism where he could not get it by satisfying material needs. Throughout the world there are a number of Triestes—territorial splinters which serve governments and oppositions as political assets when they have nothing healthier to offer.

Italy is living through a conflict between the forces of economic progress and the social rigidities which hamper it. The privileged groups of Italy seek to retain their position even at the expense of the country's welfare. They nevertheless call themselves nationalists.

In a democratic society, a mathematical relationship exists between the velocity of economic progress and social mobility. Widespread prosperity enables more and more individuals to break down social barriers and enlarge what were formerly exclusive groups. As income rises, people of the lower economic strata invade the middle stratum and people from the middle stratum knock for admission to the upper class. The higher levels may try to barricade themselves behind clubs, interlocking families, salons, and so forth. Usually the aggressors press forward and upward on some salients at least. Or they can form their own new social group. In any case, the wealth of the old aristocracy—in the form of a big car or big house or big jewels—ceases to be a distinction when new wealth is being created on all sides. And with the rise of new centers of wealth, power too changes hands.

In Italy, however, those who have power and wealth guard them against loss or diffusion. They do this by obstructing the social mobility which comes in a democracy from material progress. To achieve their purpose, they encourage ignorance, obscurantism, conformity, and poverty. In emergencies they can try to resort to the "discipline" of dictators. At all times they misuse the people's patriotism.

Some enlightened capitalists dislike this situation and many Italians join the Communist movement in protest against it.

The social outlook in Italy in 1952 was somber. The Communists were a negative force, they could not make a revolution yet they blocked reform. The rightists opposed reform. In such circumstances, a far-reaching land or financial or social reform was out of the question. Even minor concessions to the peasantry, for example, might be irritating enough to antagonize the government's conservative friends but too small to weaken its Communist enemies. The result is a political inflexibility which reinforces social immobility and economc rigidity.

The only soluton for Italy at present is a revolt of the progressive capitalists against their feudal brethren. Keeping the mass of the people socially inferior and poor is bad for business and bad for the nation's stability. Italian capitalism cannot prosper with a poor home market; landless peasants, idle or badly paid workers, and a middle class on the verge of starvation make a poor market.

Since Communism cannot make the Italian revolution, capitalism should.

The settlement of the Trieste question in 1954 deprived the Italian government of an emotional-nationalistic asset and forced it to pay more attention to social reform. Reformist capitalists, like President Giovanni Gronchi, therefore flirted tentatively with reformist left Socialists, like Pietro Nenni. Capitalism either regenerates itself, as U.S. capitalism did in President Franklin D. Roosevelt's early administrations, or Socialists enter the field to save capitalism from complete degeneration.

CHAPTER TWENTY-TWO

The New Yugoslav Revolution : 1952

AT THE ITALIAN border, the electric railway system ends, and the wheezy Yugoslav steam locomotive takes over. The young Yugoslav customs official asked me to open one of my four pieces of luggage and gave it a perfunctory dig with one hand. This contrasted with the meticulous examination at a Soviet point of entry.

Yugoslavia, Italy's neighbor to the east and northeast, is about as big as the state of Oregon or the United Kingdom of Great Britain and Northern Ireland, and has a population of seventeen million.

Seen from the car window, and in fact, Yugoslavia is much poorer than Italy. Actually, a closer comparison would be between Yugoslavia and Russia. The scene from the Trieste-Belgrade train took my mind back to numerous trips through the Soviet Ukraine: the same long, single, muddy streets bisecting villages, the same lowly huts and poorly dressed people.

At Belgrade, I got into a taxi, an Opel age thirty-two. As the cabbie tried to start his ancient car it balked, and he motioned to two passers-by who quite simply, with nothing more than an indication from him, put their shoulders to the back of the auto and pushed it for several yards until he got a spark. He chugged along slowly in streets with almost no traffic—"Sunday," I thought—while I tried to sit as lightly as possible to avoid bouncing on the hard springs under the thin, dead upholstery. At the Hotel Moskva (Moscow) the chauffeur could not open the door, it had got stuck. He therefore lifted my bags from the seat by his side and piled them on the steering wheel, and then I crawled out.

Yugoslavia is largely mountainous and 75 per cent agricultural. Farming methods are primitive. An official American expert estimated that an Iowa farmer is ten times more productive than a Yugoslav farmer. Industry too is backward. Not all Yugoslav industries are as out-of-date as Belgrade taxis, but they do need renewal and expansion. The sum of these circumstances is national and individual poverty.

The war made matters worse. Between 1939 and 1945, Yugoslavia was invaded by German, Italian, Bulgarian, and Hungarian troops while Yugoslavs vigorously butchered one another. In the widespread fighting, 21.4 per cent of all arable land was devastated. Out of 75,000,000 fruit trees, 18,000,000 were killed; out of 220,000 hectares of vineyards, 84,500 were destroyed. The number of horses fell from 1,273,000 to 475,000; cattle from 4,225,000 to 1,825,000; sheep from 10,154,000 to 3,830,000; pigs from 3,504,000 to 1,381,000. This is the black arithmetic of war. Small wonder that when peace arrived UNRRA had to save the country from starvation with commodities worth $415,642,000.[1]

On the other hand, Tito began his peacetime rule with the enormous political advantage of having no organized opposition, for the world war coincided with a Yugoslav civil war, and the adherents of the monarchy, the old army, and the bourgeoisie who were not destroyed by the one succumbed in the other.

By contrast, Tito had a lot of trouble with his own Great Red Father, Joseph Stalin. Whereas the Polish, Rumanian, Hungarian, and other East European Communists were lifted into government office on the bayonets of the Russian army and have had to sit on them ever since, Tito fought the Germans and his domestic enemies from 1941 to 1945, and while doing so built up his own army, guerrilla units, state administration, and local party organization. True, the Russian army entered Yugoslavia in October, 1944, and helped liberate Belgrade, the Banat, and near-by districts from the Nazis, but difficulties sprouted when Moscow assumed that this conferred the right to dominate Yugoslavia as it did the other six satellites.

In June, 1952, in Belgrade, I asked Mosha Piyade, member of the Yugoslav Communist Politburo, elder statesman, painter, and journalist, why it had taken them so long to recognize the imperialism of

[1] UNRRA, *Op. cit.*, Vol. III, p. 428.

Moscow. "We had faith," he replied. "There had been a Socialist revolution in Russia and we believed in it. For this reason, we accepted much we did not like." They collaborated against their better judgment; the religion of Communism submerged common sense.

Gradually, faith ebbed and friction mounted. Belgrade resented selling its copper to Russia at $470 a ton when the world market price was $700. It got tired of taking orders from the Kremlin and seeing all its offices honeycombed with Russian agents. The more Tito murmured the more Stalin bullied. At the time of the final rupture in June, 1948, Stalin probably calculated, or miscalculated, that Tito would feel cold in the open and plead for readmission into prison.

Some faith did in fact persist. As late as March 18, 1950, for instance, Milovan Djilas, age forty-one, member of the Politburo and then rated Number Four man in Yugoslavia, spoke of the Soviet Union as a "Socialist" country. In the first of three interviews I had in May-June, 1952, with Djilas, a tall, dark, brilliant, temperamental Montenegrin publicist and novelist, I quoted this statement and suggested that it could only stem from a misunderstanding of Soviet conditions. "Oh," he agreed, "we no longer think that. We are inclined now to regard Russia as Fascist and reactionary rather than revolutionary."

For about two years after the June, 1948, break, the notoriously hardy habits and clichés of a revolutionary lifetime had clouded the thinking and controlled the conduct of the Titoists. In the beginning of that period, in fact, they seemed to be trying to prove that they were better Stalinists than Stalin. The clearest evidence of Tito's lingering Stalinism was the drive to collectivize agriculture. Until 1948, only a few thousand individual peasant households had been pressed into collectives—which meant that they lost the right to cultivate their land and, instead, worked as sharecroppers in a state-controlled co-operative. But in 1949 and 1950, collectivization was powerfully accelerated to the point where 27.2 per cent of Yugoslav farmland was being tilled collectively.

The peasants did not like it. In 1951, their attitude grew menacing. Some collectives petitioned for the right to disband, but the government crushed these efforts.

Toward the end of 1950, or perhaps it was in 1951—such things cannot be clocked exactly—the Yugoslav Communists realized that if they did not mend their methods they would merely be anti-Stalin Stalinists, Stalinists who had fallen out with Stalin because they resembled him so much. So they began to sing a new refrain: "We are different from the Muscovites." I heard it first from the chief of the secret police.

Three days after my arrival in Belgrade, I met George V. Allen, the U.S. Ambassador to Yugoslavia, at dinner in the home of an American Embassy official. Mr. Allen, a friendly and astute career diplomat, asked me to accompany him the next afternoon to the annual wreath-laying on the tomb of the Unknown Soldier at Avala, some miles outside the city. In the car, the Ambassador said he had seen Tito that morning and opened the conversation with a question about Yugoslavia's political problems. "There are no political problems," Tito replied with a broad smile. "It has rained." Until four days before, a prolonged drought threatened another famine like that of 1950, when, but for a fifty-million-dollar appropriation by the U.S. Congress on December 29, 1950, Yugoslavia would have suffered grave privation. Now the country had had heavy rains followed by cool, dark days in which the moisture penetrated deeply. A good harvest was in prospect and Tito felt relieved.

At Avala, the Ambassador introduced me to several members of the Yugoslav government, including Alexander Rankovich, the Minister of Interior, head of UDBA, the secret police, and highest official present. After the wreath-laying ceremony, I stepped up to Rankovich and asked whether I could come see him. He murmured, "Yes," and left me to bid good-bye to the Papal Legate and other departing diplomats. When he returned I said, "Monday?"

"Tuesday at ten in the morning," he replied. I suggested he have an interpreter and he nodded assent. Back in the car, Ambassador Allen remarked that I would be the first foreign journalist to interview Rankovich. But remembering my experience in Russia, where one often got interviews "in principle" but not in fact, I felt doubtful, after the offhand manner in which the interview had been arranged, whether it would ever eventuate.

Four minutes before the appointed hour, I appeared at the entrance of the secret police headquarters, showed my U.S. passport, and was immediately escorted up to the office of Rankovich where he was waiting for me with Franz Kos, a Foreign Office employee, who spoke English well.

I did not beat around the bush. "When people think of a Communist dictatorship," I began, "they usually recall purges, mass executions, concentration camps, and perpetual terror. Do these conditions exist in Yugoslavia?"

"We are completely different from the Soviet Union," Mr. Rankovich asserted. "We have no concentration camps in Yugoslavia and no person has been shot or otherwise executed by our government in the past five years."

He spoke in soft tones, just above a whisper. His face is big, broad, and bony, and the flesh is firm. The eyes are small and the wrinkles around them record many smiles. His is the head of a Slav, surmounted by flaxen hair, the head of a leader in the prime of life who knows how to shoulder responsibility. His manner is gentle, and nothing but his quiet calm, which reflects firmness, would suggest he is the strong man of the Tito regime, a member of the Politburo of Yugoslavia and next only to Edvard Kardelj as Tito's foremost lieutenant.

"The impression that all countries ruled by Communists are alike," he continued, "arose during the period when we were on friendly terms with the Soviet Union. But we differed from Soviet Russia even before our break with Moscow and its Cominform in June, 1948. This is exactly what did not suit the Russian leaders. One of the reasons for the Cominform's rupture with us was just this refusal to adopt Soviet methods of terror. Communist Yugoslavia has witnessed no mass trials, no mass killings, no wholesale deportations, and no annihilation of whole classes as in the Soviet Union."

"Do you have the right to execute anybody?" I asked.

"No," he replied.

"Have you executed anybody since the war?" I persisted.

"In 1946, after a public trial," the Minister declared, "we executed Drazha Mihailovich." Mihailovich led the anti-Communist Chetniks in numerous pitched battles against Tito's Red Partisans during the Second World War. "In 1947," the Minister continued, "we had a trial of Fascist Ustashi, over a hundred of whom, in the pay of a foreign government, entered Yugoslavia to commit acts of terror. They were sentenced to be shot. But since 1947, no one person has been executed by our government."

This was later confirmed by critical foreigners, some of them diplomats, long resident in Communist Yugoslavia.

"Last year," the secret police chief proceeded, "we uncovered a large spy organization planted in the Ministry of Railways by the

Soviet NKVD; it had been serving Russia since 1945. Two of the ringleaders were sentenced to death, but on Marshal Tito's intervention the sentences were commuted to life imprisonment. Here too there was an open trial."

"Nevertheless," I ventured, sipping the black Turkish coffee which was served at every interview I had in Yugoslavia, "you will not deny that an atmosphere for fear exists in the country."

He did deny it.

I pressed the point. "Haven't you forced peasants into collectives?" I demanded.

"It is true," he admitted, "that in the beginning we followed the Soviet pattern on occasions. Nevertheless it would be wrong to speak of compulsory collectivization in the crude sense in which it manifested itself in the Soviet Union. But now such excesses are a thing of the past.

"The Soviet system," Rankovich summarized, "seeks physical control over everybody and everything. Stalin wants to put brains in chains. That won't work. It might succeed in a primitive country like Russia for a time but not forever. The chains in the Soviet Union must be broken and some day they will be. We are happy that we broke them here in time."

That made a happy ending for an interview which had lasted an hour and a half. I took my leave.

Mr. Kos accompanied me to the exit of the secret police building. "Did you," he asked, "in your fourteen years in the Soviet Union, ever interview or meet the head of the Ministry of Interior?"

I admitted that I had not.

Something I had meanwhile learned about the Avala wreath-laying brought out the difference between Russia and Yugoslavia much more. At that ceremony the military guard of honor was reviewed by General Peko Dapchevich, Assistant Chief of Staff. His older brother, Colonel Vladimir Dapchevich, had been arrested for loyalty to Moscow, tried publicly, and sentenced to ten years' imprisonment. In the Soviet empire, and perhaps in some democratic countries, guilt by association or family relation would have cost the general his job.

The day before I saw Rankovich, I had a stimulating talk with Vladimir Dedijer, editor of *Borba*, the daily newspaper of the Yugoslav Communist party, who was just finishing a biography of Tito. He confirmed what I had gathered from conversations with experts in the U.S. Embassy and with foreign correspondents stationed in Belgrade: the whole political situation in Yugoslavia was in flux. The Titoists were re-examining their most basic ideas and reassessing, in perspective, their experience as Russia's satellite. Dedijer said, "Our revolution was different from the November, 1917, revolution in Russia. Ours was born in the national struggle against the foreign invader and in that struggle we had the support of the people. We therefore don't have to fear the peasants as Stalin does."

"Then why have you collectivized?" I asked.

"We are disbanding some collectives," he said. "Our whole policy is subject to change. Collectivization requires central government control, Communist party pressure, and compulsion. We are opposed to bureaucracy. The great evil in Russia is bureaucracy. All orders come from the top, no initiative from the bottom."

"What, then, is the future of the Communist party?" I asked. "Isn't the party the source of all orders, and the root of all bureaucracy?"

"We are re-examining the role of the party too," Dedijer declared. "In the next room," he said, pointing with his thumb, "a meeting is going on of the new Workers' Council of *Borba*. I was in there until you arrived. That Council, consisting of representatives of all the employees on the paper—the writers, office girls, typographers, bookkeepers, etc.—actually manages *Borba*. Since 1951, we have had the same system of workers' management in all factories, mines, publishing houses, wholesale and retail stores, in every economic unit in Yugoslavia."

"But the Communists will dominate the workers' councils," I suggested.

"We will guard against that," Dedijer asserted. "You must discuss this with Djilas. I will arrange an interview for you with him."

A young American who was studying the Serbo-Croat language in a Belgrade university took me to the home of a woman student he had met there. Her father had been a prosperous businessman before the war. Now he was working for the government's Electrical Trust which had directed all the power stations of the country. But under the new decentralization program the government was taking itself out of business and the Electrical Trust was being abolished. Each power station or regional group of stations would be run by its own workers' council. My host had been offered a job in the provinces, but two of his children were studying in Belgrade where he occupied a fine apartment, and he hesitated to leave. I asked him what he would do. "I'll wait a while," he said.

In accordance with recent innovations, each enterprise, operating under a workers' council, was a separate unit free from government interference, except that the state collected taxes, issued currency through a central bank, and performed all the other normal functions of state administration. Each enterprise competed on the open market with other enterprises, and it was the market which determined prices and profits. Profits were distributed among employees after provision had been made for repairs, amortization, and expansion. The first act of the workers' councils when they were introduced was to cut down the size of the labor force; the working men did not want their incomes reduced by unnecessary "feather-bed" employees. In stores, the workers' council system changed the lethargy of the sales force overnight to dynamic hustle. The business, now, was not the government's but their own. They could not sell it, private capitalism was not restored, but if the store earned more they earned more.

The Titoists seemed to be groping toward a new economic system which would alter the very nature of their politics. The workers' councils were reminiscent of Guild Socialism on which Bertrand Russell had written a book I read in the 1920's. The Yugoslav Communists called it Democratic Socialism or Social Democracy. The state would do less, the people more.

The day after I saw Dedijer he sent me two quotes which he had typed out. One was by Tito from *Borba* of March 12, 1952. It read: "In Yugoslavia only the Communist Party carried out the revolution and led the war of liberation. But it too will one day disappear. The process of democratization means the withering away of the state. The state is now withering away as regards its functions in the economy, and one day this will take place in the field of politics too." The second quote was from a speech by Foreign Minister Kardelj in Parliament. He had said: "The alternative between the withering away of the state—and with it of the party system—and the Stalinist theory of the strengthening of the state today constitutes the touchstone of true socialism." Kardelj also referred to "the new partyless system in which each individual citizen will even more directly, without the mediation of parties, take a conscious part in the functions of social management."

Something quietly spectacular was happening in Yugoslavia. Having been divorced by Moscow, Yugoslav Communisim was trying to transform itself. Tito appeared to be scrapping the do-all Communist state and trying to establish a do-as-little-as-possible government. After abolishing private capitalism in industry and trade when their regime was founded they had now abolished state capitalism too. "Marx's commune," a Yugoslav leader called it. This would not only differentiate the Yugoslav system from the Russian but reverse a world trend toward statism noticeable in most capitalist countries and of course throughout the Soviet empire.

I therefore looked forward eagerly to my first interview with Djilas, the leading theoretician of Yugoslav Communism. I met him in the headquarters of the Central Committee of the party, a massive, rock-faced building—it had housed a bank before the war—with two heavy entrance doors that could have served a fortress, a magnificent marble foyer, marble balustrade, and long corridors with marble floors. In the foyer stood a black metal sculpture of Lenin leaning forward from the waist and making a speech.

Djilas is handsome in a tired way with short black hair that comes down in a V at the center of the forehead. His head is a larger V, broad at the temples and narrow at the chin. We sat in his private office in soft, deep leather chairs at a small round table on which, within a few moments, a tray with two cups of hot Turkish coffee and two glasses of cold water was placed by an attendant. He began by saying, "I hear you have seen Rankovich. What do you think of him?" I told him and then brought up the question that interested me most. "I gather," I said, "that you are reconsidering many basic Communist propositions formerly regarded as sacrosanct. Is it conceivable to you," I asked, that" the Communist party, born to power, its every tradition linked with power and loyal to the philosophy of Lenin whose statue I saw downstairs, will ever relinquish power?"

"Yes," Djilas replied firmly. "It will remain to educate and elevate."

"In other words," I interpreted, "it will become a cultural organization."

"A cultural organization of a special type," he amended.

"A cultural-ideological organization," I volunteered.

"Yes," Djilas said.

"With no power?" I asked again.

"With no power," he confirmed.

"Who then will exercise power?" I inquired.

"In the cities, the workers' and producers' councils, in the villages, the peasants," Djilas explained. "We are writing a new constitution for Yugoslavia."

We had been talking animatedly in Russian. His phone rang and while he answered it I walked over to his bookcase and examined a Russian set of Lenin in a blue binding. He put his hand over the mouthpiece and said, "It's the fourth edition, expurgated by Stalin but the best I could get."

When he returned to the table I got into an argument with him about the entire new development in Yugoslavia during which he kept interrupting me and I kept saying, "Wait, let me finish my sentence." My contention, according to a detailed diary entry I made after leaving him, was: The Yugoslav Communists attack the Soviet Union as a state-capitalistic bureaucracy which permits no personal freedom, and I agree with that analysis. But so far, the only cure I have heard proposed here is decentralization. Yet a single factory or a territorial district or one of the six national republics comprising the Yugoslav federation (Serbia, Croatia, Bosnia-Herzegovina, Slovenia, Macedonia, and Montenegro) could be just as bureaucratic as a federal ministry, in fact worse, because it might be less enlightened, less idealistic, and more power-hungry. I did not see, therefore, how decentralization could solve anything unless the power relinquished by the Communist party was exercised by the people. "That is," I stressed, "as long as being a Communist means more than being a citizen you will have bureaucratic rule from above and not democratic rule from below."

"I agree completely," Djilas said. "There must be a diffusion of power and authority. The new constitution will give power to the people. We have taken the first steps. We have launched the workers' councils. In them power resides with those who create the accrued surplus value [he used the German, Marxist word "*Mehrwert*"]. That is the beginning of democracy. Of course," he added, "democracy is a matter of tradition and education too."

I then launched into a discussion of farm collectives. I said that Stalin wanted the satellites to collectivize so that they would be weakened by peasant opposition—"and," he finished the sentence for me, "have to lean more on Moscow for support."

"Collectivization," I said, "is feudalism."

"It is state capitalism with feudal characteristics," Djilas declared.

"No," I objected, "there is some state capitalism in America and

England but they are not feudal. The determining factor is the relationship between the individual and the state, and in Russia that relationship is a feudal one, the peasant is tied to his collective, the worker to his factory, and all good comes from Baron Stalin."

Djilas laughed and told me that Boris Kidrich, a member of the Yugoslav Politbureau, agreed with me. "Let's have an evening with Kidrich," Djilas suggested, and went to the phone, dialed, and made the appointment.

CHAPTER TWENTY-THREE

Dinner at the Villa Toda

DJILAS' secretary fetched me at the hotel in a Packard at 6:45 P.M. and drove me out to the suburbs of Belgrade. A guard shouldering a Tommy gun with perforated barrel stood inside the grille gates of Boris Kidrich's home. On the front wall, in large letters, were the words "VILLA TODA." Toda is a girl's name. This two-story house with a sloping lawn in front and garden space on both sides might have belonged to a well-to-do merchant before the war or to the owner of a small factory, now statified.

Kidrich, the economic brain of the Yugoslav Politburo, Number Five man in Yugoslavia, met me in the hallway. He wore a brown suit somewhat too small for him. With an affable greeting in German he ushered me into a large library and study where crowded bookshelves rose to the ceiling. A desk was piled high and helter-skelter with reports, letters, and litter. Decorations in the room included a relief map of Yugoslavia, a portrait of Tito, and a metal bust of Lenin on a marble base inscribed "To Boris Kidrich."

Kidrich offered me a rakiya, a deadly—I am told—Yugoslav drink, and when I turned it down he poured one for himself, leaned back, folded his hands, and invited questions with one word, "Please."

Since Yugoslavia is an agricultural country and collectivization had upset the peasants I started with that. I said Stalin had collectivized all farms and liquidated the "kulaks" who objected. I could understand such a policy. But how did the Yugoslav party expect some peasants to remain in collectives if they saw private, uncollectivized farmers all around them—"unless the government keeps them in by force?" The necessity of using force against the peasantry would rule out democracy.

Kidrich replied, "We cannot be a Socialist state, we cannot prosper with backward farming. As an economist," he continued, "and even though I am a Socialist, I would accept private-capitalistic farming if I thought it would result in modernized farming. But in Yugoslavia that is impossible"—presumably because the peasant had no machinery and little money with which to buy it.

About 6 per cent of all arable land in Yugoslavia, Kidrich said, was tilled by state farms which were owned and operated by the government just like factories, and 14 per cent more was tilled by co-operatives which, he explained, were not like Soviet collectives. In Yugoslavia, the peasants kept their land but pooled it with that of other peasants; they also pooled their labor and shared the crops which each sold individually. In answer to a question, Kidrich stated that the government had no intention of creating more farm co-operatives.

At this point, Djilas arrived looking sick, tired, and haggard, and coughing occasionally. Because his German was inadequate, we switched to Russian for the rest of the evening.

Kidrich said half the peasants in the co-operatives were satisfied and would not leave, but the other half were under pressure to stay.

"There is too much pressure," Djilas interjected.

Kidrich was a production man, he wanted more food for Yugoslavia and believed in farm co-ops as a means of getting it, but when I asked what he would do if more and more peasants wanted to leave the collectives, he said, "In that case it would be all the more foolish to use compulsion. We are not like Stalin." But any new system would have to wait a year or two.

I next brought up the subject of industrialization. "We never expect to compete with or duplicate the great industrial nations," Kidrich announced. Nor did he expect big credits from capitalist countries for building large industries. They would be content with small industries that served agriculture and consumers' needs; they also intended to develop their mineral resources and from the proceeds pay for imports.

"Have you ever been to the United States?" I asked Kidrich.

"No," he replied, "I know the Continent but not England or America."

"I've been there," Djilas reported. He had represented Yugoslavia at the United Nations. "It's fantastic. Nothing in Europe is like it. Such wealth and technological perfection. We are just small-town provincials, but we wouldn't want to live that way. You Americans live as if you were in a submarine surrounded by machines and mechanical gadgets."

A maid served Turkish coffee. I looked at my watch. It was eight o'clock. I wondered whether I had misunderstood the appointment. I had expected dinner.

"Now permit me to talk politics," I requested.

They nodded agreement.

I said I sensed that this was a period of transition for them, they were trying to escape from Stalinism inside as they had escaped from foreign Stalinism. And my question was, "Must not a one-party system evolve by a fatal compulsion toward Stalinism?"

"No, no, no," they both exclaimed.

I asked them to let me go on. I wanted to make a plea for a two-party system. "Marxists," I said, "claim that parties represent classes, and if you have two or more parties you have class war, which Yugoslavia wishes to avoid. But parties can represent divergent interests in the same class, like the Democrats and Republicans in the U.S.A. For an intellectual like me," I declared, "the value of a two-party system is that it provides an alternative and therefore a threat to the party in office and acts as a curb on power-lustful politicians. But what alternative is there to Tito? All right, Tito is an idealist."

"A devoted revolutionary," Djilas offered.

"But what guarantee have you that Comrade X who will succeed Tito will be the same kind of person?" I demanded.

"With this posing of the question I agree in principle," Kidrich said. "But if we had another party it would bring back into politics all the filth of prewar days, the monarchists—"

"The reactionaries, the Pan-Serbians," Djilas interjected. "Different countries are at different stages of development and must work out their fate in different ways. The two-party system is not for us."

"America is a progressive country under capitalism," Kidrich conceded. "England and France may advance toward Socialism under the multiparty system, although the many parties in France are certainly a hindrance to good government. But for us, two or three parties would mean a setback."

"But if we assume that," I persisted, "where is the control over the party in power?"

Here Djilas went into an elaborate disquisition on the new constitution soon to be published which would give power to Parliament, to the workers' councils, to village councils. No government officials, furthermore, would be members of Parliament. Parliamentarians would not be paid wages; they would have to work elsewhere for their living.

"We know the disastrous development in Soviet Russia," Kidrich interposed. "It is a warning to us of what to avoid."

"There are traditions of democracy in Yugoslavia," said Djilas. "Yugoslavs have never tolerated despots. We Communists know that."

Somebody behind me opened a door, Kidrich shook his head in the affirmative, and invited us into the dining room. The three of us sat down, Kidrich poured red wine, and a ruddy, bashful maid silently served the meal which consisted of hors d'oeuvres (sardines, salami, ham, hard eggs, and vegetables), pork chops with little new potatoes, a salad of lettuce covered with balls of rice, rich, cream-covered cake, and black coffee. Djilas ate no hors d'oeuvres, asked whether the chops were pork and then partook copiously, and had no dessert. Kidrich consumed two pieces of cake. I guessed he was about forty years old—and overweight.

There was no small talk at the table. As soon as the first course was served, Djilas said to me, "Our chief divergence is on collectivization."

"I am afraid of a repetition of the Soviet development," I replied. "I regard the Russian collectives as feudalism, a modern feudalism with tractors and electronics."

"I think the form is really state capitalism," Djilas objected.

"I agree that it is feudalism," Kidrich asserted. "There are also elements of ancient slavery in it.

"On essentials I accept that," Djilas acquiesced. "But we have no feudalism here." He explained that Yugoslavia had had a land reform after the First World War, the estates had been divided, and most peasants owned their land.

(Farmland has always been private property in Tito Yugoslavia, and this is one of the basic reasons why its history has differed from that of the Soviet Union. If the Soviet peasants, who did not own their farms, had to be coerced into entering collectives, the Yugoslav peasants, who had land to lose, would certainly resist the abolition of private farming.)

I took advantage of a shift of plates to change the subject. "I see you have a bust of Lenin," I said to Kidrich. "You reject Stalin and accept Lenin. But isn't Stalin the legitimate political son of Lenin?"

"Lenin was a cultured person, he had a great mind," Kidrich asserted. "Stalin is semieducated and crude, and has no respect for the human being."

"Lenin was a European," Djilas exclaimed with warmth.

"But he venerated the state," I recalled, "and he wanted the Communist party to remain all-powerful."

"He believed in the withering away of the state," Djilas commented.

"Yes," I said, "that was the theory. But how do we know that the same kind of Stalinist dictatorship would not have developed under Lenin when Russia came around to collectivization and the Five Year Plans? Lenin, like Marx, thought that nationalization was the key to all virtues."

"Not Marx," Kidrich demurred.

"Marx at one time," I replied. "All Marxist now, in any case."

"But we know that nationalization is not the key," Djilas declared. "It leads to bureaucratic state control. That is why Stalin is the kind of dictator he is."

"Stalin is an empiricist," Kidrich volunteered. "He has no theories or convictions. He is a reactionary imperialist, no different from the Czarist imperialists."

This led into a lengthy examination of the 1948 break and why Stalin did not follow it up with an invasion of Yugoslavia. They held that Stalin was afraid of war and thought he could destroy them without it. The discussion yielded a piquant tidbit. Djilas and Kidrich, who knew the inside story of Tito Yugoslavia's relations with Moscow, told me that during the war Stalin had urged the Yugoslav Communists to collaborate with King Peter and even with Draza Mihailovich whom they had been fighting and whom they later executed. I recalled that Stalin also urged Mao Tse-tung to collaborate with Chiang Kai-shek. Stalin, they said, feared that their opposition to Mihailovich would antagonize America and England and drive them into cutting off military aid from Russia. I suggested that Roosevelt and Churchill would certainly have refrained from such a drastic step; they did not want Stalin to sign a separate pact with Hitler. "After 1943, Stalin would never have done that," Djilas affirmed.

"In other words," I summarized, "while America and England were worried lest Stalin quit their side, Stalin was worried that they might stop supporting him. Pity they didn't know it."

Djilas admitted to many illusions about Soviet Russia till very late. "We believed the Moscow trials," he said. "Now we know better."

"What do you think of Trotsky?" I asked.

Kidrich screwed up his face in a grimace of disapproval and said, "He was too dogmatic, too doctrinaire."

In my eagerness to know more about their views I put a series of questions on unrelated matters. Djilas said he favored a rearmed Germany.

"You're not afraid of that?" I inquired.

"No," he assured me. "It's even a pity the West allowed Russia to occupy any part of Germany. A strong Germany would weaken Russia's position in Poland and Czechoslovakia and help liberate them."

Djilas declared he would like to see the Soviet puppet regime in Albania overthrown by Albanians of democratic persuasions.

"There was a time," I recalled, "when your regime wanted no change in Albania for fear the Russians would march through Yugoslavia in order to save Albania."

"That was in 1950," Djilas explained. "Now we are not afraid."

About Red China, Djilas said Mao Tse-tung was not a puppet of Moscow; he acts independently; he may have gone into the Korean War without consulting Moscow. "We acted independently in the Greek civil war," Djilas stated, "and for six months didn't tell the Soviet government about it."

By this time, the maid had cleared the table and set a large bowl of cold cherries before us, and we were leisurely munching cherries and chatting. "In 1945, or 1946," Djilas reminisced, "Markos, the Greek Communist leader, came to Belgrade and told us he could win the Greek civil war and make Greece Communist if we helped him. We did."

"And Bulgaria and Russia?" I wondered.

"Bulgaria and Hungary sent sanitary supplies," Djilas asserted. "Russia sent nothing. Much that was said in the United Nations debates about our intervention in the Greek civil war had no basis in fact, but some of it was true. Yugoslavia sent most of the military supplies."

"What happened to Markos?" I asked.

"He was accused of Trotskyism by the Cominform, carried to Bulgaria or Hungary by his Greek comrades and, as far as we know, executed there."

Markos' crime was that he had failed.

We also talked about the unsolved and then seemingly insoluble Trieste puzzle. They suspected England of egging on the Italians. "Don't you think some Italians might precipitate a war with us over Trieste?" Djilas asked.

I said I thought the idea fantastic, Italy was not strong enough, and England and America would never allow her to attack Yugoslavia.

It was now ten-forty. I arose to go. We stood around talking for a few moments. Then Djilas, shaking my hand warmly, said, "Well, we've gotten acquainted. Interesting." He moved to go with me, but Kidrich asked him to stay and so Djilas yelled to the guard to tell the driver to take me to the Hotel Moskva. The streets were getting their nightly bath from a big hose manipulated by two men in high rubber boots.

It had been a rich experience. I left for the morrow the manual labor of typing out an almost verbatim record of what was said during the evening.

CHAPTER TWENTY-FOUR

Power or Freedom?

O N THIS Yugoslav visit I spent some time at the Stalingrad Textile Factory on the outskirts of Belgrade near the Danube. It was built in 1904 and its newest machinery was installed, Director Milovan Bojoc said, in 1916. It looked it. Shortage of cotton, imported from America, had reduced production to 50 per cent of capacity. The management, Bojoc declared, took orders from the workers' council whose fifty-nine members, representing the eleven hundred employees, were likely to know every part of the plant and its needs better than he did.

I spent two and a half hours at the factory's workers' council. It had been elected just three months earlier, in March, 1952, for a two-year term. The trade union nominated a list of sixty-seven. Six additional candidates were nominated from the floor. Almost the entire factory force had attended the election meeting. They were more interested in workers' council elections, I was told, than in elections for Parliament. Thirty-four members of the council were Communists, twenty-five were not.

I counted the women members: twenty-six. Some of the older ones looked like cleaning women, some of the younger ones like secretaries and machine hands. One of the older women took the floor to say that the factory wasted water. A man reported that the water used in production contained sand. Several women were upset by the bad showing the plant's textiles had made at the recent Zagreb fair. "The trouble is," a young engineer asserted, "that we are making coarse products with an old pattern but the people now want something finer."

"What can you do with old machines?" a working man exclaimed.

The meeting listened to several management reports. Before that there was an argument on whether each report should be criticized separately. They decided to discuss them all together.

I had no way of knowing the value of this meeting or of the councils in general. I was sure of one thing: if the members of the workers' council found that the Communists dominated them from the inside or outside, this whole system of economic democracy would die and become part of a new centralized bureaucracy just as the soviets, the organs of local political democracy in Russia, died except in name, and for the same reason.

Dr. Sherwood Berg, the agricultural attaché of the U.S. Embassy, had been telling me about farming conditions in Yugoslavia one afternoon when I said to him, "Couldn't we go out to see a collective?"

"Would you like to go tomorrow?" he asked.

We agreed to leave at eight in the morning, and Dr. Berg and his Serbo-Croat speaking interpreter, an Embassy employee, picked me up at the agreed hour. He had not informed anybody about our trip and received no permission from any Yugoslav authority. We just went—as in a free country.

The village was out in the Voivodina, a flat region fertile when wet. We reached it by jeep in an hour. The central street was rudely paved with cobblestones, the houses were of wood and well built. We went first to the office of the collective and talked to its chairman. The whole village, all three hundred families, had been collectivized. I had noticed quite a number of men standing about outside and asked the chairman why they were not working. He said, "It rained during the night."

In the street I addressed a peasant in Russian and inquired why so many were standing about. He must have understood because I can understand about 30 or 40 per cent of spoken Serbo-Croat. "It's a religious holiday," he replied. In the course of our meanderings through the village in the next three hours a peasant sidled up to me and said the village priest had been sent away for the duration of the two-day holiday to prevent him from conducting services.

We joined a group of men dressed in their Sunday best—which was good by any Central European rural standard—and I put some questions to them. A farmer in his fifties with a merry twinkle in his eye made himself the spokesman for his neighbors. Yes, he replied, they were happy in the collective; yes, they ate adequately; yes, meat too, twice a week; yes, conditions were improving.

While wandering up and down the central street between visits to the village co-operative store and the collective's stables and machine sheds, this same peasant with the twinkle motioned to us to come into his courtyard. When we were in he asked us to enter his house and there he led us into an inside room. "It is all untrue," he declared. "None of the peasants like the collective. We want to get out. We want to work for ourselves."

Back in the courtyard, a crowd gathered. Two peasants had arrived on bicycles from the edge of the village where they tilled strips given them after they had left the collective. "We are not richer," they said, "but we are happier."

"They are not letting any more out of the collective," one elderly Serb stated. "If they did there would be no collective."

A tall peasant joined the crowd. "He's a Communist," the man with the twinkle whispered. The group slowly melted away.

We talked to the tall Communist. "These fellows are content to live as their fathers and grandfathers did," he said. "Yugoslavia must be remade."

Whenever possible in my travels, I make it a practice to visit a school. Our party of three entered the village school, knocked at a door and were beckoned in by the teacher. After listening for a while to the history lesson, I asked permission to put some questions to the class of boys and girls between twelve and fourteen years of age. The teacher gestured to me gracefully to take his place.

I told them I was an American journalist and was asking questions not to examine them but to get better acquainted with Yugoslavia. They nodded as though they understood and were pleased.

"Who is Tito?" I began.

"Marshal Tito is the leader of Yugoslavia," a boy answered. I pointed to a girl. "Marshal Tito is the chief of the Yugoslav government."

"Who elected him?"

"The people," the pupils chorused.

"Who is Stalin?"

"Stalin is the dictator of Russia." "Stalin is the enemy of Yugoslavia." "Stalin is the Soviet chief in Moscow."

"Who is Churchill?"

"Prime Minister of Great Britain."

"Who is Truman?"

"President of the United States of America."

"What kind of country is the United States of America?"

"A capitalist country," came the quick answer from many throats.

"What kind of country is Yugoslavia?"

"A Socialist country." "A Communist country."

"Has the United States-helped Yugoslavia?"

A boy jumped to his feet. "Yes, with food," he exclaimed. "And machinery," another boy added. "We get cotton for textiles from the U.S.A.," a girl volunteered. "American engineers help us in our factories," an older boy asserted.

"How is it," I asked, "that the United States, which is a capitalist country, helps Yugoslavia which is a Communist country?"

Silence. More silence. Then some girls giggled, and a few boys opened their eyes wide and shrugged their shoulders.

I said good-by, shook hands with the teacher, and bowed myself out. The class clapped their hands as we left.

On the street we met the tall Communist. "How is it," I asked, "that capitalist America gives economic and military help to Communist Yugoslavia?"

He eyed me, thought a moment, and said, "I am a simple man. You had better ask Djilas."

Three days later, in Belgrade, I asked Djilas. "National interest takes precedence over ideology," he proclaimed.

Without mentioning the name of the village, I reported to him on the attitude of the peasants toward collectivization. "I just came back from Montenegro and found the peasants quite satisfied," he said.

"Maybe they told you what they thought you wanted to hear," I suggested.

He looked sad and said nothing. "Silly local Communists," he exclaimed angrily when I recounted that the village priest had been sent away for Whitsuntide. "Maybe the peasants don't yet know that they need not be afraid," he added.

"We are evolving a new peasant policy," Djilas informed me. "But the workers' councils have come to stay. There can be no return to state capitalism. I've just been reading Aneurin Bevan's *In Place of Fear*. He is close to us and we regard him as a friend, but he makes a mistake in thinking that nationalization is the cure."

"Don't most Socialists?" I queried.

"We don't," he stated.

Total nationalization in Yugoslavia had given birth to a top-heavy, clumsy, expensive, inefficient, centralized bureaucracy which threatened to run the ship of state aground on a shoal of red tape, papers, decrees, deficits, and thefts. "It militated against personal freedom," Djilas declared. It had been abandoned.

Djilas was a politician and an intellectual. His training as a theoretician made him impatient; he wanted to translate theory into practice quickly. The more practical politicians preferred to wait cautiously. As a key figure in the Yugoslav dictatorship his business was power. As an author and thinker his requirement was freedom.

Djilas, the writer, frequently found himself at the epicenter of literary storms. The most recent concerned Negosh, Bishop Petar Petrovich-Negosh, the ruling prince of Montenegro from 1813 to 1851, who fought Turkish oppression and is revered by most Yugoslavs as the greatest writer of the Yugoslav lands. In 1951, the centenary of Negosh's death was commemorated throughout the country by performances of his epic *Mountain Wreath* and with generous eulogies. Notable among the tributes was a book by Isadora Sekulich, a well-known writer in her sixties, full of ecstatic praise of the bishop's mystic, idealistic, and patriotic qualities. Djilas reviewed the book in *Borba*. He rated Negosh very highly as an artist, he wrote, but it was unbecoming to laud him as a superman. *Nin,* a literary weekly, fiercely denounced Djilas' attack. So did other critics. Addressing an editorial conference of the fortnightly literary review *Svedochanstva (Evidence)*, Djilas said, "After all, maybe I too have a right to say what I think." And he a member of the all-powerful Politburo! In self-defense, Djilas wrote a book taking issue with Miss Sekulich. His book and hers were on sale side by side at bookstores. The April 5, 1952, number of *Svedochanstva* printed an article by Isadora Sekulich on page one and an answer by Djilas on page three.

Literary jousts with editors on paper chargers often rumble through Yugoslavia's cultural life. Eli Finshi, editor of *Svedochanstva*, said to me, "We are in a state of permanent civil war with the fortnightly *Literary Journal*," which he accused of being "conservative and superrealistic." It contends, he explained, that "literature must reflect social life, while we argue that art can be subjective, pessimistic, or optimistic, or whatever the author wishes to make it." Finshi is a Communist.

"But," I asked Djilas during our discussion on freedom of expression, "would a Yugoslav publisher bring out a book attacking Marxist theory?"

He replied in the negative.

"Yet if you learned that a Marxist book had been prohibited in the United States or France or England," I pressed, "you would say that country was not free, wouldn't you?"

Djilas accepted the implied criticism of Yugoslavia but added that they had come a long way since their 1948 break with Moscow. "Give us time," he pleaded.

I left Djilas toward the end of the long lunch hour. On the broad pavement of the Central Committee headquarters three or four persons were walking in one direction and three or four in the opposite direction. At the curb stood a bright new American car, the only one in the block. (Traffic is very sparse in Belgrade at all times.) Nobody was in the car. About a yard from the car I saw a well-dressed man in a felt hat. I looked: it was Rankovich, chief of the secret police whom I had interviewed early in my stay. I walked over to him, shook his hand, exchanged a few words, and walked away. He was waiting for his driver. There was nobody anywhere near him, nobody was guarding him. I might have been an assassin. Apparently, Rankovich felt secure. This could not have happened in the Soviet Union or in the satellites. The head of the Russian NKVD would never expose himself on a street with or without protection. He would enter his auto in a closed courtyard and the car would be preceded and followed by another full of armed agents.

Yugoslavia in May-June, 1952, was a one-party dictatorship, but there are dictatorships and dictatorships. The Yugoslav people were not free but Tito did allow some freedoms and the trend seemed to be in the direction of more.

CHAPTER TWENTY-FIVE

Cross-Examining a Dictator

A WOODEN panel, about a foot square, was pulled back like a window and a man's face appeared. I gave my name. The two halves of the wooden gate swung open. Inside, two officers without visible weapons stood at attention as I passed. This was Marshal Tito's residence at 15 Uzhitska, a public thoroughfare in a suburb of rich villas which once belonged to the Belgrade bourgeoisie.

The low, Moorish-style house was surrounded by a lush garden crowded with old evergreens, a red-leafed tree, hedges, flower beds, and grass plots. To the right of the paved walk stood a breast-high stone pedestal surmounted by a sculpture of the dog that saved Tito's life on a wartime battlefield. Near by a ferocious-looking, square-headed wolfhound crouched and growled suspiciously as I passed. He was excluded from his master's presence for the duration of my interview.

A secretary met me at the step of the terrace, led me to an antechamber, entered Tito's office, and soon came back to invite me in. At the far end of the vast room the Marshal was just getting up from his desk. We met halfway. I greeted him in Russian and asked whether he preferred to speak Russian or German. He said it was all the same to him, and asked how good my Russian was. We continued in Russian.

A photographer who had followed me into the room took some pictures of us in the rose garden. When we returned to the office, Tito introduced me to a man and said, "He's not sure he can take down everything in Russian so I have a tape recording machine here if you don't mind." I said I didn't mind.

Tito was wearing a light gray suit, with a blue pin stripe, a shining blue poplin shirt, a dark blue tie with white dots, and shoes of soft, plaited leather. His authorized biography says he always liked to dress well.

As the three of us sat down at the low table, Tito took out a silver cigarette holder which resembled a miniature pipe. He offered me a cigarette from a white carton and pushed over a metal matchbox decorated with a five-pointed red star made of what looked like rhinestones. A moment later a waiter in short white jacket appeared bearing a silver tray with three little cups of Turkish coffee, three large glasses containing a colored beverage and three smaller glasses containing a colorless liquid. Tito stood up to serve us. I told him I didn't take strong drink. "This is vermouth," he said indicating the bigger glasses, "it isn't strong. And this," he continued, distributing the smaller glasses, "is vodka." It was 10 A.M.

"Vodka?" I exclaimed. "During fourteen years in Soviet Russia I never touched it."

"That's remarkable," Tito commented, "I can't understand how you managed to avoid it."

It was a perfect opening, for in thinking about the interview in advance I had hoped we would start with a discussion of Russia. I quickly asked Tito his opinion of Stalin.

"I visited him several times," he replied, "but then our relations were still friendly. I have the definite impression that he is a man who does not consider individual human beings or the lives of individuals." This, Tito suggested, might be a national trait intensified by Stalin's work in the illegal Bolshevik underground. "Besides," he added, "unlimited power, so to speak, makes some people heartless, rude. They develop a sense of being very strong."

At his first meeting with Stalin in the fall of 1944, Tito recalled, the Kremlin dictator sharply criticized the Yugoslav Communists for certain wartime acts in defiance of Moscow's orders. Tito defended his party, which "somewhat irritated" Stalin. "He gave me to understand," Tito declared, "that he disliked my attitude. . . . He would have wanted me to behave as an inferior whereas I was behaving more like an equal."

"You know," Tito went on, "it is very dangerous when individuals feel that they cannot say what they wish to say."

"Would you apply that to a whole nation as well?" I inquired.

"To a nation as well," Tito agreed. "We speak openly to the country on all matters. I don't know whether you have attended one of our meetings. At meetings I and other comrades speak freely not only of our achievements but also of the failures of government officials from the bottom to the very top. . . . Take the peasants, for instance. Our peasant tells you the truth to your face. He is not afraid; it's his nature. It's a national custom."

Yugoslav farmers have undoubtedly acquired subtle skills in communicating their desires and dissents to the government. They say it with plows and prices; they speak through their work in the fields and their practices at markets. A peasant prefers economic weapons because they win more debates than the most brilliant words.

"Do you enjoy the support of the people?" I inquired.

"Yes."

"How do you know?"

"I see it all around me," Tito asserted. "Many people come to visit me."

"Do they tell you the truth?" I wondered.

He thought they did and could always check whether their complaints were true.

"But does the entire country approve of you?" I asked.

"Of course not the entire nation, but the overwhelming majority," he argued. "Naturally those whose property we expropriated will not smile and be happy. I shall not speak of the past now. But it is foolish to contend, as some foreigners do, that only 10 per cent of the population supports us. If this were true we would have been out of here long ago."

"What could the people do?"

"They could drive us out," Tito said.

"How?"

"Very simply," Tito declared. "Who is the army if not the people?"

This, in effect, was an admission that the people could not do it. On the other hand, the army in a dictatorship is likely to be more democratic, more conservative, and less militaristic than the dictatorial party.

Unlike the Kremlin, whose ideal is a moat between leadership and people, the Yugoslav Communists, whether from weakness or by temperament, seemed to yearn for warmer democratic contacts and approval. In this context, I asked Tito what inspired his work, what made him tick?

"The doctrine of Marxism-Leninism," he replied.

"But I was thinking of something inside you, something personal," I said. "Marxism is a thing you learned."

"Yes," Tito declared, "but it is a view held by workers."

Tito then put his adult biography in capsule form: "I was a worker, went to prison, was captured during the war, which was difficult too, saw the Russian Revolution and participated in it to a slight extent, later returned to Yugoslavia and poverty. In 1921, the persecution of Communists commenced in Yugoslavia, a repetition of the old, only worse. I was often arrested; served six years' hard labor. All this strengthened the man and gave him a definite goal toward which to strive."

I remarked that Stalin's life had run a very similar course. "I believe," Tito agreed, "that Stalin once was a revolutionist and that he fought to destroy the Czarist system. He was in exile in Siberia, I know that. But I do not know what motivated him later or what is now his basic motivation. I don't know, nevertheless I assume it is power. In a vast country, Stalin achieved certain successes, and that, so to speak, turned his head."

Tito warmed to this theme: "Stalin is dizzy with success and underestimates other nations, especially small ones; he puts a low value on individual persons and on small nations. Only big powers exist for him and he recognizes only strength." Therein, Tito emphasized, lay the fundamental cause of the break between Yugoslavia and Soviet Russia in June, 1948. The Soviet, Tito affirmed, failed to understand that the Yugoslav nation, "which suffered much in its history and was struggling to become its own master, had not shed a sea of blood in order to fall into foreign bondage and be a serf."

This led into a discussion of Yugoslavia's break with Russia and the reasons for Stalin's failure to invade Yugoslavia. At all costs, Tito felt, Moscow wanted to avoid war. "I have said many times," Tito declared, "that Stalin will not start a war, that he wants to achieve his end by other means, exploiting the differences among the Western countries."

I referred back to Tito's first statement about Stalin's disregard of persons and said I had found more freedom of expression than I knew existed in Communist Yugoslavia. "On what grounds should we suppress criticism?" Tito asked. "On the grounds that a few people believe they can think for the whole nation and not listen to the voice of the nation? Stalin believes he can think for two hundred million people. But for us here it is very important always to listen to the voice of the people.

"In Yugoslavia, however," Tito continued, "our people have never liked anybody who tries to put himself on a high pedestal. Our people appreciate a man who endeavors to be on the same level with them. In the Soviet Union one still feels the vestiges of Czarist Russia."

I had been taking copious, hurried notes, but my hand tired of its race with Tito's words and I asked him whether he would give me a transcript of the tape recording. He said he would. After that I jotted down an occasional reminding phrase just in case something went wrong with the tape or the promise.

I could now look around. The office in which we were sitting had a tremendous expanse, sixty feet by twenty-five, I judged. A giant rubber plant occupied one corner. Near the windows of the long wall stood a magnificent, highly polished wooden table where fourteen could dine comfortably, and on it were a cut-glass vase with red roses and another with yellow roses. The wall behind Tito's desk at the far end of the room was covered with a painting depicting a battle between rebellious Croat serfs and their masters in 1573. Tito says his slave forefathers fought in that very encounter. He himself looked the sturdy warrior type somewhat gone to fat at sixty. Of medium height, with broad square shoulders, fine big head, shining wavy hair, and friendly yet stern face, he seemed a person whom men would admire and follow and women could love. If Djilas is more intellectual than practical, Tito is more practical than intellectual, yet quick and intelligent with a knack of brushing aside theoretical cobwebs, grasping the hard core of a thought, and formulating it simply.

I expressed the view that "Yugoslavia would not be secure as long as the Soviet Union was ruled by Stalin and as long as Soviet imperialism exists."

"That is true," Tito agreed. He assumed that this uncertainty might continue for ten or twenty years until the West was stronger. "But," he added, "I think that if the West is so strong as to be 100 per cent sure of a victory over the Soviet Union, it would be dangerous if it made use of its power. The West must not use its superiority in war, it can use it for peace by forcing the Soviet Union not to launch a war and to enter into a peaceful and just settlement. The leaders of the Soviet Union recognize only strength. Why did they sign a pact with Hitler? Because they regarded him the strongest power in the world."

I inquired about the nature of the suggested settlement. The basic problem, he said, was Germany.

"Would you want to see a united Germany?" I asked.

"I would want to see a united Germany," he replied directly. "The German people have seen that experiments like the First and Second World Wars brought them only unhappiness. As a country with a democratic system, Germany must enter the international family and permit neither Fascism nor dictatorship."

I asked about German rearmament and he said he favored it but not for militaristic purposes.

"Aren't you afraid of a rearmed Germany?"

"Fear or no fear—logically it is so and it has to be so," Tito declared. "You cannot compel a country to be unprotected for any length of time."

"Would not the restoration of a united Germany result in Russia's loss of her satellites?"

"In the final analysis, yes." Tito said. "In Moscow they are making a mistake: it is better to have a neutral neighbor than an unreliable satellite." The Russians cannot hold the satellites forever, he declared. Czechoslovakia and Poland were advanced countries.

"Is it possible to rise up against a dictatorship?" I asked.

"It depends on conditions," Tito explained. "Now it is impossible because all the armies are mobilized. The Soviet army is prepared."

At this moment the door was opened and a secretary stuck his head and shoulders into the room. Tito looked at his watch and I at mine. The interview had lasted an hour. "We haven't finished," I said quickly. Tito looked at his watch again, said, "I know," rose and took a step toward the secretary. Suspecting that the next caller might be put off for ten or fifteen minutes, and avid for a second long interview, I stood up too and proposed that I come back another time. "Good," Tito exclaimed and gave me an appointment for Sunday afternoon four days hence. He sent me back to the hotel in his Packard, which was a relief after the springless Belgrade taxis.

I took a short walk on Tito Boulevard and then went to the Hotel Majestic where the foreign correspondents had a table at which they habitually lunched. The headwaiter and the waiter had urgent messages for me. Before I sat down there was a telephone call from the Yugoslav Foreign Office. All the messages were alike: The Marshal wanted me back the same day at four; he was planning to go out of town on Sunday to visit Foreign Minister Kardelj, just recovering from a spinal operation.

Same room, same stenographer, same tape recording. I noticed a bust of Lenin in a far corner. When we were seated, a different waiter came in with Turkish coffee, three large glasses of wine, and three small glasses of vodka. "No," Tito said, "after lunch beer is better." The waiter went out and returned with beer. I took one sip for politeness' sake and quickly chased down the taste with a gulp of coffee.

I opened with a question about the domestic political situation. Tito spoke of bureaucracy as "a menace." "People from the outside," he said "don't know—but we inside the country know that it has not been so easy to get rid of bureaucracy. It was even difficult for us at the very top. If we hadn't started this battle against the bureaucrats for another year or two it would have been very difficult to liquidate the bureaucracy without big upheavals."

"Upheavals by whom, by the people?"

"No, on the part of the bureaucrats in the various departments," Tito explained. Now they were sending officials out of Belgrade into the districts. "Let them work there," he said. "That's where they are needed. Foolish things were done: Belgrade used to decide what and where and in what quantity to sow—"

"You have also talked the withering away of the Communist party."

"As the government withers away so—only somewhat later—the party will wither away," Tito declared. "We are doing everything so that the party will wither away, but it is too early to talk about that."

(I made a mental note: Tito is in less of a hurry about this than Djilas.)

Tito declared that their purpose was to introduce "Socialist democracy with a solid economic base." We discussed democracy in various countries. I told him about my talk with Rankovich who had said the government had no right to shoot anybody without a trial. "But," I demanded, "what would prevent the government from doing it?"

"The government," Tito asserted, "must be the first to see to it that people obey the laws. And if it began to break the laws—"

"But what makes you observe the laws?" I interrupted.

"Public opinion," Tito replied.

Would his successor have the same respect for public opinion?

"I don't believe he would behave any differently," Tito said, "unless of course he wanted to lose not only his job but his head."

He was making everything dependent on the person, on the tradition of the revolution, on the leader's regard for the people, I objected. But where was the built-in control over the party and over the government. "If you got a Stalin here—"

"I've already told you," Tito said, "that I don't understand Stalin. Why does he attach such great value to power? I would have a much easier time if I were working somewhere eight hours a day and were a free person. But here I am, I sit here day and night as in a prison. A person in my position has a very big responsibility especially if he has a conscience. . . . Nobody works as hard as our top people. Do you know that our ministers some years ago received only twelve thousand dinars and almost starved?"

"What would you do if you were working only eight hours a day?"

"I would go where I wanted to," Tito smiled. "If I got a two months' vacation, I would go somewhere and have a real rest. Do you think it's a vacation when I leave for Brioni? [Tito's summer place.] I have to think and work there too. Always work and always be informed about all state matters. The only thing is I have fewer telephone calls there."

"And what does your work give you?"

"My reward is success. My entire reward is success, and nothing else."

"And don't you get any satisfaction from power?"

"What do I need power for?" Tito exclaimed. "Do I need it to take revenge on somebody? I don't need it at all. I don't understand people who fight for power. I think you are better off than I am," Tito said pointing to me. "How many nights I don't sleep! I get up at night to look out the window and see whether there will be rain. . . . When we had a drought we got bread from America. Do you think that was easy for us? It was very difficult for us. . . . That's why I say that to be in power is not so easy and I don't understand men who strive for power. One should fight not for power but to help other people live better."

"In what circumstances would you give up power?"

"I don't understand that," said Tito. "We Communists are bound by discipline. I can't say I'm tired, let somebody else take over. That would be desertion. I can't say: I'm sixty years old, I've been working for forty-five years, and I ought to take a rest. Certainly, it would be fine to rest, but I have no right to it."

But suppose he discovered a very talented person? "What will happen when you die? Are you preparing anybody to replace you?"

Tito said there were a number of talented coworkers who could take his place. "But desert, go on vacation—never."

"Aren't you a dictator?" I exclaimed.

Tito leaned back and laughed.

"Why are you laughing?"

"I am laughing because here in Yugoslavia it is dangerous to be a dictator. I want to tell you this: people abroad don't understand that in Yugoslavia a government can adopt stern measures and yet retain popular sympathy." The people had been trained in the hard school of invasions and privations, and if they saw a government which was preserving national independence and striving to make the country prosperous the people would accept many hardships. "But abroad you do not understand that. You think that if a nation tolerates difficulties it means dictatorship."

What about the collectives? Wasn't the government dictating there?

They were no longer forcing peasants into collectives.

"But do the peasants have a right to leave the collectives?" I asked.

"That," he said, "depends on each collective." You couldn't have collectives if peasants started leaving them without the permission of the majority.

I switched the subject to international affairs and put some indiscreet questions about the size of the Yugoslav army and its equipment which he answered frankly, fully, and proudly. He also summarized the nature and extent of American economic and military aid.

"And don't you think that is American imperialism?" I tested.

"I don't think," he replied, "that giving help is imperialism. I believe that it is imperialism when you take something away from somebody, but when you give—that is not imperialism."

I had been with him for an hour and a half and I decided it was time for me to go. Four days after this double-header interview, the Marshal's secretariat sent me a forty-four page Russian transcript of the tape recording of the two talks. All quotations here from those conversations were translated verbatim from that document.

Marshal Joseph Broz Tito, to give him his full official name, was relaxed, urbane, and showed good manners. He obviously withheld many secrets and endeavored to present his regime in the best light during our conversation, but far from attempting to obscure his thought processes he exposed them and seemed to enjoy the intellectual exchange that resulted. I felt I was talking to a European gentleman. Though Yugoslavia tapers off to the East and is geographically Balkan, it is solidly anchored in Western culture, and Croatia, Tito's birthplace, as well as Slovenia, has a definite feel of Western or at least Central Europe. The Yugoslavs have never resented or resisted Europe as Russia has throughout the centuries; on the contrary, they boast of being Europeans. This makes a huge political difference. The Yugoslavs, like some of the other Europeans now caught in the Soviet empire, regard Russia as culturally inferior, the mother, to be sure, of literary and musical titans but on the whole uncouth and backward. Domination is always irksome, but in India, for instance, Britain was never held in contempt; its superiority in many fields was often recognized and its ways copied and assimilated. Even in the days of their friendship with the Soviets, however, the Yugoslavs felt that Moscow was dragging them down—and not alone economically. The humiliation of colonialism was thus accentuated by the unworthiness of its source.

Having spurned Moscow's support in June, 1948, Tito needed more popular support. The government of a Communist satellite antagonizes the people because it is Communist and because it is an apparently willing servant of the alien power. It must therefore lean heavily on Russia and behave despotically toward its hostile citizens. But Tito, minus Russia, had to lean on his people, and this has made a difference in the Yugoslav system.

With all his frankness in talking to me, Tito naturally could not admit the inadequacy of his popular backing. Yet a dictatorship is, by its very nature, a minority government afraid of the people or of some other minority. But whatever the percentage of Tito's popular approval, it rose after June, 1948. Until then, the Yugoslav nationalists believed that Tito had sold their country down the Moscow river. When he asserted Yugoslavia's independence from the Kremlin some patriots took him to their bosom.

The objective need and the subjective wish of the Yugoslav Communists to win acceptance from their people have motivated many of their acts. This should mean more nationalism and less dictatorship. But less dictatorship conflicts with the habits, tastes, ambitions, and pleasures of many local, regional, and central Communists and bureaucrats. Until more Yugoslavs are materially satisfied, the dictatorship cannot wholly dismantle itself. The dilemma of a dictatorship is always this: unless it wins some popular approbation it encounters too much resistance in the performance of its difficult tasks. But if it makes too many concessions to the people they may ask for complete freedom.

The Yugoslav regime in 1952 was walking a political tightrope. It was trying to avoid the evils of a one-party system and the dangers to itself of a multiparty system. It had actually inaugurated an exciting experiment in economic democracy in industry and trade which could be called Socialist Democracy because there was no capitalism in it. But if the peasants were granted economic democracy they would of course scrap collectivization and revert to private capitalism.

In this uncertainty, Tito was holding on to the collectives and to the Communist party, the instrument of political power. The situation was theoretically and intellectually confused because there was a yearning for capitalism in the Communist collectives, an attraction for Stalinism in the anti-Stalinist Communist party, and poverty and inexperience in Socialist industry.

In such a situation dogmatic individuals would be lost and rigid leaders might crack. But the Titoists were flexible and eclectic. Kidrich criticized Trotsky as "too dogmatic." Mosha Piyade said to me, "That is the great service the Stalinists did us, they freed us from dogmatism." Tito was too much of a realist to be brittle, single-tracked, or ruthless.

During my five weeks in Yugoslavia I frequently thought of Asia, particularly of India and Burma. It seemed to me that Titoism, as it slowly evolved, might be a new social-economic form applicable to progressive Asian nations which reject Western capitalism yet do not want to go the way of Soviet Stalinism. And Titoism is just that: not-capitalism plus not-Sovietism.

This is why Yugoslavia stimulated me. It took a new creative approach to urgent world problems. At the same time it reveals that the Soviet Russian system is not the new society of the future but rather the rottenness that forms, like maggots, when an old system decays.

Yugoslavia illustrated for me a mistake in thinking I had made for many years: I had drawn a sharp line between capitalism and Communism, and between capitalism and Socialism. But it was becoming clear that no social system is pure. Each is a mongrel. Most capitalist countries, including the U.S., have been compelled to introduce and tolerate a measure of Socialism. In fact, it may be the measure of Socialism which keeps the capitalism in good health. (Socialism is merely government participation in economic affairs.) Some other capitalist countries retain a considerable measure of feudalism. Italy, for instance, is feudal-Socialist-capitalist. Russia is feudal-state-capitalist. Yugoslavia is Communist-Socialist-capitalist. What ism, then, does one believe in? An ism can be isolated in theory. In practice it combines with other isms, and the nature of the mixture depends on national and international conditions and political forces. Each country is going to evolve its own peculiar social form. The world will long be a coat of many colors, with patches within patches, and time will change the colors. No patch is all white, or all black, or, for that matter, all red.

CHAPTER TWENTY-SIX

Turkey's Immunity to Communism

AT A PARTY in the home of an American Embassy official in Ankara during the summer of 1952 I had dinner at a bridge table with Turkish Foreign Minister Fuad Koprulu and an interpreter who translated our French for Leon Dayton, the head of the Mutual Security Agency (successor of the Marshall Plan's ECA), in Turkey. I repeated some of the things Tito had told me about Stalin.

"Stalin is an Asiatic," Professor Koprulu said scornfully.

"That is a strange statement coming from you," I remarked. "Aren't you an Asiatic?"

"No," he replied, "we are Europeans."

Only the toe of Turkey, comprising the city of Istanbul (the former Constantinople) and a little strip around it, is in Europe. The remaining 97 per cent is in Asia, a rather remote and Asiatic part of Asia, yet the Turks consider themselves Europeans, for Europe to them is an idea, not just a place on the map, and Asia was their past which Ataturk, the founder of the modern Turkey, ordered them to discard.

Mustapha Kemal (Ataturk) was a mixture of Paris and wild Anatolian plateau, of gentlemen and Tamerlane. He was a genius possesed by a demon whose sex-drink-cards orgies, during which he vanished for days—though he was head of state and dictator—were succeeded by monumental outbursts of creative turbulence and a prophet's reforming zeal.

Ataturk was a professional soldier and political doctor. In 1853, Nicholas I called the Turkish Sultan "the sick man of Europe." The imperial ambitions reflected in the Czar's dictum did not diminish its truth. The putrid Turkish empire, the profligacy of the court with its harems and eunuchs, and Islamic obcurantism were indeed a cancer. Turkey, in every way diseased, had commenced to lose its virility and therefore its possessions even before the First World War. Defeat in that war, during which General Mustapha Kemal won plaudits for strategy and stubbornness, reduced Turkey to her hard Anatolian core, and theɪe, in the fresh air and amid the soil, sand, and rock of the wind-swept plateau, Kemal began the cure. He converted the loss of empire into a national asset. Turkey was Turkey again and he made the people proud of it. "Turkey for the Turks" was not the usual chauvinistic slogan of exclusiveness; it meant that the Turks would mind their own business: to build a healthy country.

Ataturk shifted the capital from Asiatic Istanbul, with its twisted streets and devious traders, on the European side of Bosporus, to the European city of Ankara, newly built on the Central Asiatic steppe. He ousted the Sultan and abolished the Caliphate, making Turkey a secular state. He prohibited the veil, the harem, and polygamy. Sunday, instead of the Moslem Friday, became the Sabbath. The complicated, cursive Arab script, so conducive to illiteracy, was abolished in 1928, and replaced by a modified Latin alphabet. The muezzin calling the faithful to mosque had to be in Turkish, not Arabic. Any infraction received condign punishment, for it was treason against the new republic. Ataturk also proscribed the fez and made the Western hat compulsory. Turkish men in towns dressed dapperly and brightly. Women were free and elegant. All clothes are now Western. In Ankara, I saw Turkish military policemen wearing white American army spats and carrying neatly folded kid gloves. The most popular photograph of Ataturk, displayed in many places and engraved on the national currency, shows him in white tie and tails. This is the furthest removed from the traditional caricature of Turkey as a man in oriental fez, baggy trousers, and moccasins with curled-up toes.

The volcanic, intemperate Ataturk rode his horse into the hearts of his people who were close enough to the primitive to admire his rough daring, masculine stamina, and unconventionality after the effete Sultanate. Personally and politically he was a rebel. He broke precedents and heads with equal abandon. Cast in a hero's mold, he gave the nation a feeling of living an epic.

Turks regard Ataturk as the agent of a national metamorphosis. History offered him an opportunity and he bent it to his will. The war, the subsequent economic collapse, the slipping away of empire, and the emergence of a new shrunken Turkey 80 per cent agrarian destroyed the old ruling class of imperial officials, big-power bureaucrats, established-church dignitaries, and merchants. Into the vacuum Ataturk lifted young men, usually ex-soldiers of village origin, unspoiled and enthusiastic. This was the new ruling class and its rise to office constituted a social revolution.

But private capital was extinct, wiped out by the war and its aftermath. Ataturk therefore introduced Turkey to a regime of "etatism," statism, under which the government supplied funds for new industrial enterprises. The government created state monopolies for the manufacture and sale of matches, alcoholic beverages, salt, cigarettes, and other products. The government built a cotton textile mill at Kayseri. There was no theory behind this. Turkey has few thinkers, philosophers, theologians, or theoreticians: the cultural stage belongs to poetry, painting, folklore, and drama. Etatism was a simple, practical expedient in a situation where individuals had no money to go into business. But it also served, for years, to discourage them from doing so.

The Turkey I saw in the summer of 1952 was still Ataturk's Turkey. He died in 1938. But his spirit survived and has sufficed to make Turkey immune to Communism. The Turkish experience, accordingly, holds an important lesson for countries like Italy and India: a strongly rooted, home-grown revolution is the best guarantee of safety against foreign-inspired revolutionists. Or, to put it another way, a healthy nation will not import quack medicines.

Turkey has a long common frontier with Soviet Asia and is contiguous with Sovietized Bulgaria. Yet Soviet influence on Turkey from the outside and Communist support inside are negligible. I asked a number of Turks, "What is the effect of Soviet industrial progress on Turkish border areas?"

Usually they stared and replied, "Effect? None." A wide zone on each side of the frontier is closed, and there are no contacts and visits. "All we hear about," one Turkish journalist said, "is the Russification of Moslem minorities in Central Asia and the Caucasus."

Ataturk prohibited the Communist party and all Communist activity from the very beginning of his harsh regime, but proscription alone has not eliminated Communism in Brazil, for instance, or anywhere. The movement just never has acquired a serious following or given the authorities serious trouble in Turkey.

When I asked why, I was told that the Turks had a profound hostility toward Russia, having fought thirteen wars with the Czar's empire in the 240 years between 1677 and 1917. At Bolu, a small town on the rugged Anatolian plateau, I started a conversation in a sidewalk café with a group of men whose heads resembled the stone sculptures of their Hittite ancestors in the Ankara museum. One happy Turk sat smoking his narghile or water-bottle pipe. His right eye had been knocked out, exposing the pink fleshy socket. A gnarled scar ran from eye to ear. "A Cossack did this to me with one saber slash," he said, smiling. Such walking wounds and many sleeping but unforgotten dead, I repeatedly heard, remind the Turks of recurring conflicts with Russia and turn them against Communism.

I found this explanation unconvincing. For despite the casualties and memories of the thirteen wars between expansionist Czarist Russia and expansionist Sultan Turkey, the relations between Soviet Russia and Ataturk Turkey were most cordial from 1919 to 1939. The Lenin regime denounced Russia's old dream of acquiring the

Dardenelles, and Kemal had no designs on anybody. On this new basis, an effective friendship ripened. In the 1921-22 war with Greece, Kemal's army received military supplies and technical assistance from Russia, and at subsequent international conferences on the Turkish question, Kemal could always rely on Foreign Commissar Chicherin's skillful diplomatic assistance. In the later period of economic reconstruction, Turkey obtained long-term loans from the Kremlin. The ties between the Soviet and Turkish governments in the 1920's and 30's can only be described as reciprocally fraternal.

However, the Stalin-Hitler Pact of August 23, 1939, launched Soviet Russia on her modern career of imperialism and within a few weeks Moscow made demands on Turkey which mounted crescendo till, in 1945, the Soviet government asked for Turkish territory and a Russian fortress in the Turkish Straits. Since 1939, consequently, Turkey's suspicion of and hostility to Russia have been renewed.

The advantage of this look at the historic record is that it reveals cause and effect: Russian imperialism makes Turkey anti-Russian; a cessation of Russian imperialism makes Turkey pro-Russian. But whether Ataturk Turkey has been pro-Russian or anti-Russian it has always been anti-Communist and unaffected by Communism. The reason for this immunity to Communism must, therefore, be independent of what Moscow does or does not do. The reason lies in what Turkey is.

Turkey is twenty-two million people in an underpopulated country as large as Western Germany plus Italy plus Ireland with much unexploited natural wealth.

Turkey is seventeen and a half million peasants who are poor but not discontented. Driving through villages, the children shout, "Gazetta, gazetta," at you and then run after the car in the hope that you will throw out an old newspaper which the family may want for reading or other purposes. In one village where I spent a day, some of the men wore Western clothes which, however, were patched, and the patches were patched and the patches within patches were beginning to shred. Nevertheless, 99 per cent of Turkey's peasants own their own farms. This includes recent refugee arrivals. There is plenty of land. The number of sharecroppers is infinitesimal. No Turkish peasant can look up to the hill crest or horizon and say, "I am poor because of that landlord in his villa." There is widespread poverty on the countryside but no sharp contrast in wealth, and it is the contrast rather than the poverty that generates bitter protest. The government is helping peasants with loans. There were 3,000 tractors in Turkey in 1948, 36,000 in 1952. The peasantry has been especially benefited by an enormous road-building program, part of national defense, which connects village marketers with towns. Crop failures are frequent and stimulate inflation, but in general, agricultural output has risen due to greater productivity per acre and millions of acres of virgin soil brought under cultivation. Growth banishes despair.

Turkey is the small urban middle class—consisting of a few intellectuals not given to isms and not unemployed or unhappy, plus the officials, plus the merchants—which has benefited from the expansion of the national economy.

Turkey is a small, growing working class, new to the city, living better than it did in the village, and not under the influence of a disaffected intelligentsia.

Altogether, Turkey is a proud new nation conscious of its virility and vibrant with faith in its potential progress.

Ataturk gave the Turks a revolutionary push. Defense of the national revolution shuts out the foreign revolution. The statue of Mustapha Kemal Ataturk blotted out the face of Stalin.

But in 1952 a strange change occurred: unseen hands were defacing or breaking statues of Ataturk. Occasionally, reports of such political vandalism even appeared in the press. Generally, they circulated by word of mouth. It was said the faithful objected to graven images. But in that case they would have had the same objection long ago. Now they had found the courage or encouragement to act. From minarets looking like sharpened lead pencils wearing electric-light necklaces the muezzin was once again being called in Arabic instead of Turkish. The government had also sanctioned religious instruction in public schools. A theological seminary was opened in the state university. The repair of old mosques and the building of new ones, formerly frowned upon by the authorities, was now permitted.

A foreigner who might discern in these developments an increase in tolerance was faced with this rebuttal: the government of Prime Minister Adnan Menderes had initiated legal steps designed to deprive the opposition Republican party, fathered by Ataturk, of its daily newspaper *Ulus*, and of its funds and properties. Menderes and other leaders of his Democratic party resented newspaper criticism, placed critical journalists and opposition leaders under arrest, maintained strict partisan control over the national radio network, and hampered the very mild activity of the trade unions, first made lawful in Turkey in 1947.

Thus the apparent tolerance of religion was counterbalanced by intolerance of political dissent, and in combination they seemed not like a trend toward liberalism but the reverse: a reaction against democracy and a retreat into the past. Religious reactionaries were being used to speed the retreat.

The bitterness of the Menderes Democrats toward the Republican party, and to other smaller opposition parties, was the more remarkable since all parties agreed on Turkey's simple foreign policy: Russia, the imperialist neighbor, is again a menace; join the West and be strong. They likewise agreed that, since economic improvement had created fresh capital in private hands, the government should gradually withdraw from Ataturk's state-capitalist etatism. After the May, 1950, elections, moreover, the Democrats enjoyed a seven-to-one majority in Parliament over the Republicans led by former President Ismet Pasha Inonu and Dr. Kasim Gulek, and need not, therefore, have persecuted the minority, especially in view of the fact that it was Inonu who, as dictator, had allowed the Menderes Democrats to launch their party in 1945. While countenancing the formal existence of rival parties, the government had started moving back to an actual one-party monopoly, and as a means to that end, was favoring religious fanaticism and frowning on dissent.

In their rough handling of the opposition, the Democrats, to be sure, were giving a mild imitation of the harshness meted out by Ataturk and Inonu to opponents in their time. But the times are different. The fight for freedom from Communism is not furthered by the suppression of freedom.

Of course, long-ingrained political habits die hard. In Turkey, democracy is young, frail and easily bent to the lust of power lovers. Similar relapses followed by partial recoveries, more relapses, and recoveries fill the history of some of the best Western democracies. Provided the state remains secular Turkey may describe a similar cycle. The roots of Turkey are healthy; the homogeneity of the population and the nation's ties with the West should conduce to further advances toward freedom. The Turks are sensitive to what other countries, particularly France and the United States, think of them. They resent dictation but appreciate applause; they will get it when they earn it by loyalty to liberty. In our age, it is the best weapon against Communism.

CHAPTER TWENTY-SEVEN

Storm Center

ISRAEL is Europe in Asia and that is probably the basic reason why the Arab countries resent it.

Originally, no conflict was anticipated between Jewish nationalism and the Arab world. On the contrary, they expected to co-operate to mutual advantage. "Zionist success," Colonel T. E. Lawrence declared, "would enormously reinforce the material development of Arab Syria and Iraq."[1] Emir Faisal, leader of the Arab revolt and of the Arab army during the First World War and later King of Syria and King of Iraq, wrote a letter on March 3, 1919, to Professor (subsequently Justice) Felix Frankfurter stressing the kinship between Zionism and Arab nationalism. "We are working together," Faisal stated, "for a reformed and revived Near East, and our two Movements complete one another. The Jewish Movement is national and not imperialist. Our Movement is national and not imperialist, and there is room in Syria for us both. Indeed, I think that neither can be a real success without the other."[2] This thought, which he repeated elsewhere, has proved prophetic. For other Arab rulers did not want a reformed and revived Near East. They therefore fought Zionism. As a result, neither Zionism nor Arab nationalism has been a real success.

All the Arab states were the children of the First World War. The

[1] Letter to his friend, Robert Graves, published in Robert Graves, *Lawrence and the Arabs*, London: Jonathan Cape, 1927, p. 398.

[2] *Palestine; a Study of Jewish, Arab, and British Policies*, published for the ESCO Foundation for Palestine, Inc., New Haven: Yale University Press, 1947, Vol. 1, p. 143.

state of Israel came to life on May 14, 1948. In the intervening thirty years the Arabs did so little to consolidate themselves as nations that the 650,000 Jews of Palestine were able, in the war of 1948, to defeat Iraq with 5,000,000 inhabitants, plus Jordan with 1,200,000, plus Syria with 3,100,000, plus Lebanon with 1,100,000, plus Egypt with 20,000,000, not to mention the hostility of Saudi Arabia's 6,000,000 and Yemen's 4,500,000. The Arab world, paradoxically, would have been better equipped to crush the Zionists in 1948 had it collaborated with Zionists during the preceding three decades.

The primary purpose of Zionism, to be sure, was not to help Arabs but to make the Holy Land flow again with milk and honey and build thereon a national Jewish homeland or state. Most of its leaders realized, however, that their small, technologically advanced, European-minded settlement could not long endure as an oasis amidst the blowing sands of a backward Arab desert. They therefore shared King Faisal's dream of Arab-Jewish collaboration designed to raise living standards in the entire Near East (now known as the Middle East) and making it, too, flower. Apart from seeing a potential market for their industrial products in a prosperous Arab continent, the Zionists hoped by uplifting it to forestall the inevitable jealousy between archaic paupers and thriving moderns.

In Palestine itself, and on a limited scale, the sight of blooming Jewish orchards and farms, comfortable housing, rapid transportation, and new factories did spur some Arabs to enrich themselves by discarding Biblical methods and introducing the latest techniques. But two circumstances have militated against Arab-Jewish co-operation. The first was the imposed Jewish trait of self-defensive segregation. Having been rejected by most Western Christian countries and forced into ghettos, walled and unwalled, squalid and gilded, the Jews voluntarily built their own ghetto in Palestine, a well-ventilated, sun-drenched ghetto, to be sure, where manual labor was the ideal, but a world, nevertheless, which isolated itself from the surrounding gentiles. The justifications were legion: the lower cultural level of the Arabs, the absence of a common language and the understandable reluctance of the Jews to learn Arabic when they were intent on restoring Hebrew as a living tongue, and the different geographic origins and social outlooks of the two peoples, but above all the avowed, implacable Zionist design to acquire more land and employ Jews rather than Arabs so as to open additional opportunities for new immigrants from Europe. Dr. Judah L. Magnes, a saintly,

Gandhian person, Chancellor of the Hebrew University, and former New York rabbi, whom I met in Jerusalem in 1934, and again in 1942, was scorned and spurned by the Zionists because he urged Arab-Jewish unity. Many Arabs were equally uncompromising and hostile. Friendship was frustrated and the gulf grew wider.

Alone the tragedy of Arab-Jewish segregation in Palestine and of the subsequent grave Arab refugee problem would not account for the unbending Arab antagonism to Israel. A second circumstance was decisive: the Arab governments aimed to destroy Israel at birth because they correctly saw in it a threat to their outmoded, inefficient regimes. Israel cannot conquer Egypt, Iraq, and the Arabian peninsula. That is not what the Arabs fear. They fear coexistence with an energetic, dynamic, electronic neighbor whose progress would expose their lag and thereby foster popular discontent in the Arab world. In attacking Israel the day after a United Nations resolution made it a state, the Arab rulers aimed to preserve their own obsolete social systems.

But the Egyptian soldier arrayed against Israel had little incentive to fight for corrupt, dissolute King Farouk or the pasha-landlords or the bribable bureaucrats who had given the people such a bad deal. Why should the poor, illiterate peasants die for their rich rulers? The social and economic gulf was too wide for patriotism to bridge. The same is true of the other Arab belligerents. The zealous young Israeli nationalists therefore defeated them.

Having failed to kill Israel, the hatred of Israel is kept alive in the hope that it will sooner or later induce the Arab masses to rally gratefully around their rulers. Anti-Zionism is thus a bid for the popular support which the Arab master classes, having done so little for their people, neither enjoy nor deserve. Israel is a godsend. Instead of improving conditions by social reform, the reactionary, anti-reform upper classes offer a sentimental substitute: sustained hostility to the new Jewish state. It is their counterrevolutionary alternative to that "reformed and revived Near East" of which Faisal wrote to Frankfurter in 1919.

But large social trends are not easily controlled. They have a way of turning into their opposites. In Egypt, for instance, the attempted counterrevolution sired a revolution. It was naturally the army that made the revolution, and not merely because it had the power to compel Farouk's abdication; it was indignant over the faulty civilian leadership which sent it out to invade Palestine with defective munitions. The resulting casualties and setbacks might be hidden from the public. But the officers knew. They knew too the profound social causes of their soldiers' bad fighting morale. Led by General Naguib and Colonel Nasser they avenged their shame and chagrin.

I was in Israel in July, 1952, when Farouk fell and Naguib rose. Jerusalem officials were encouraged by Naguib's symbolic abolition of the title of pasha as a prelude to the land reform soon to follow; they hoped the Egyptian military would henceforth concentrate on domestic reform instead of Israel.

A revolution, however, is never immediately or wholly successful and often finds it convenient to lay the blame for delays and failures on a foreign enemy. The military who took over from the foul monarchy faced the historic task of making Egypt a nation by bringing the classes closer together so that some connecting tissue could form between them. This difficult growth is best fed by material welfare and interclass mobility. But impatient cooks sometimes throw in the hatred of a neighbor as an artificial stimulant. Hostility to Israel would serve the further purpose of silencing opposition at home and guaranteeing that the army, which alone could cope with a foreign foe, remained in the ascendant politically. It also reinforced Egypt's claim, as the biggest Arab state, to leadership of the other anti-Zionist Arab countries.

Ringed by a hostile hinterland, Israel remains an armed camp. Military affairs are the government's chief preoccupation and the constant concern of all citizens, for the Arab neighbors, who shout their hatreds from every housetop and podium, are too near ever to be forgotten. "Passengers on the only railway in the country, which connects Jerusalem, Tel-Aviv-Jaffa, Hadera, and Haifa, for much of the way look straight from their compartment windows into Jordan, and come so close to the Jordan towns of Qalqilya and Tulkaram that they can throw a cherry stone through the window into the streets below."[3] There is hardly any spot of Israeli territory that could not be shelled from Arab territory by a cannon with a fifteen-mile range, and most of Israel is no more than five or ten miles from Arab soil. Much of the country is within rifle shot of the enemy. Jerusalem, one of the most beautiful cities in the world, has been cut in two—one part is Jewish, the other Arab—and the cut is an ugly gash, like

[3] "From Our Jerusalem Correspondent," London *Times*, November 16, 1953.

a wound across a pretty face, with stitches and skinless flesh in the form of coils of barbed wire, stone barriers, trenches, and ruined buildings. Snipers in one segment of the town can fire into many streets of the other section. The Israeli Parliament meets in a Jerusalem building only a few hundred yards from Arab sentinels.

Since "the whole of Israel is a frontier,"[4] and such an insane, indefensible, undefined frontier, frontier incidents are inevitable. The oft-proclaimed refusal of the Arab governments to recognize the existence of Israel would not reinforce any feeling of respect for the new state's boundaries. The Bedouin nomads, moreover, who abound in the region, have no understanding of a frontier, even for a sanctified, meticulously demarcated one; map lines have never confined them; and there is some Bedouin in every Arab. If a sheep strays across the international border he will certainly try to recover it. Smuggling, robbery, and spying also create incidents. Many Arabs had homes and farms in Israel and may infiltrate for various reasons—to damage a crop on their former land or to kill a present owner. When an Arab infiltrator is himself killed the matter grows into a family feud with an unlimited potential for expansion.

Several days after I arrived in Jerusalem five Jews were killed by Arabs on Jewish soil in circumstances which, as always, remained unclarified. The Israelis were expected to retaliate. I discussed the subject of reprisals with Israeli Foreign Minister Moshe Sharett over a quiet lunch for two. "Isn't it possible," I argued, "to break this mad spiral of Arab attack, Israeli retaliation, Arab retaliation for the Israeli retaliation, and so on?" Could not the Israelis forbear this time and refrain from avenging the five Jewish deaths? Or, at least, wait a while?

I thought, or perhaps the wish was father to the thought, that in high Israeli councils Sharett, whom I had known for many years and who told me, when I arrived for lunch, that reading my Gandhi biography had made him want to be a better person, would side with the advocates of restraint. Yet if the Israelis failed to retaliate the Arabs would interpret it as a sign of weakness or cowardice and perpetrate more raids costing more victims. On a lawless frontier, the only deterrent is the power and will to punish crime. Usually, however, the Arab criminals were unknown and an Israeli retaliatory attack therefore meant punishing the helpless innocent for the guilty.

[4] Statement by Israeli Ambassador Abba Eban before the Security Council of the United Nations on November 12, 1953.

But what responsible Israeli could resist the cold logic of the realists: that where there is no law, the choice is between self-defense and anarchy? On the other hand, recurrent recourse to illegal force is itself a virulent form of anarchy. Sharett preferred to negotiate an effective frontier truce and then a basic peace. But the Arab states have always declined to negotiate. King Hussein I of Jordan said on November 1, 1954, "My Government's policy on Palestine remains the same as that of other Arab countries—no peace, no negotiations with the Jews."[5] As a result, haphazard, individual forays turned into planned military raids which amounted to large-scale murder of blameless people. One group, the Herut (Freedom) party, peacetime heir of the pre-Independence terrorists, would solve the problem surgically by achieving what it bluntly calls "the territorial integrity of the Land of Israel within its historic boundaries on both sides of the Jordan,"[6]—in other words, by annexing most of the Hashemite Kingdom of Jordan, whose 330 miles of frontier with Israel constitute the larger segment of Israel's total land frontier of 591 miles. Many outside the party would undoubtedly welcome the expected benefits of such imperialistic expansion but shrink from its international repercussions.

Tension with the Arabs is a constant strain on the manpower reserves, nerves, and finances of Israel. The miracle of the country's transformation into a land flowing with electricity and human energy is all the more remarkable. Water has poured from the rock; roads have been thrust through sizzling wastes; deserts grow rich crops; woods cover the naked limestone of Judea's hills; factories, ports, scientific institutions, housing settlements, hotels, banks, and schools rise in once empty spaces. The United States government and American Jews supply much of the money, but the brains, brawn and blood are Israeli.

Unusual economic growth has brought enormous social and political changes. When I was first in Palestine as a Zionist and volunteer in the British army from the end of 1918 to the beginning of 1920, the new Jewish settlement (as distinguished from the old Jewish residents who came to pray, study Jewish lore, and die in Zion) was in the main agricultural. The pioneers, mostly from Russia and Poland, were more than Jewish nationalists; they were inspired ideal-

---

[5] *New York Times*, November 2, 1954.

[6] Quoted in *State of Israel, Facts and Figures*, 1954, p. 15. This is an official publication of the Israeli government.

ists whose goal was a cultural renaissance, a new type of Jewish life rooted in physical work on farms in the ancient homeland. Some became owners of orchards, vineyards, and wheat fields. But others formed village communes where work and income were shared alike and the emphasis was on egalitarian community living rather than personal needs. They renounced for the common good; it was a religious way of life shaped by persons who were not religious. They owned nothing except a few pieces of clothing, books, and photographs. Constant vigilance against Arab attacks entailed further sacrifices gladly endured for the sake of a better Jewish future in Palestine.

At that time, these colonies, many of which I visited, were to me the most attractive aspect of Jewish Palestine, the signs of growing Arab-Zionist cleavage the most disturbing, and nationalism the least inviting. In subsequent years, when I met Indian Gandhians, some of whom had gone to Palestine and admired the communes, I wondered why they had never felt sufficiently inspired by the Mahatma's love of the simple life and attachment to the village to participate, through their own membership and manual labor, in a similar exciting venture in India.[7] The Jews transmuted their revolutionary zeal for a better world into creative physical work stretching over years, indeed, for some, over a lifetime, and attained considerable practical success.

Since 1920, however, Jewish Palestine has become overwhelmingly urban in its buoyant development. In 1954, the urban population of Israel numbered 1,182,000, the rural, 487,000.[8] Of the new 1948-to-1953 immigrants, the bulk flocked to the towns. The government hoped to draw newcomers to the villages by providing them with housing and jobs. But though these efforts met with some success, the city apparently holds the same attraction for Jews it always had. And in the cities of Israel the cultural rebirth is likely to be limited to language, theater, and so forth rather than grow into a way of life very different, as life in the numerous communes still is, from the old pattern in the countries of the Jewish immigrants' birth.

A further dilution of the Zionism ideal followed its long-desired

[7] "I believe that the life lived in the Kibbutz [commune] can be lived in Burma according to the principles of Buddhism," Prime Minister U Nu of Burma said on his visit to Israel in 1955. (*New York Times*, June 2, 1955.)

[8] *State of Israel, Facts and Figures, 1954.*

translation into reality. The Jewish homeland in Palestine was conceived not as a perfect society and not merely as a cultural Arcadia but as a haven from intolerance and persecution. "The state of Israel will be open to the immigration of Jews from all countries of their dispersion," said the Declaration of Independence of May 15, 1948. Yet bitter opposition to British efforts to close the Palestine door to victims of Nazi persecution in Europe caused the Israeli immigration policy to become an end in itself. Zionists actually discouraged homeless Jews from trying to settle outside Israel and adopted an attitude of hostility or at least nonco-operation toward Jewish leaders who sought alternative immigration outlets. The fitness of new arrivals seemed to matter not at all. "The vast majority of the new immigrants has no trade or calling and is fitted only for unskilled work. . . . Few know Hebrew. Many are without an elementary education," an official publication declared.[9] Many congregated in the cities where they showed greater eagerness to make quick money than to acquire technical training or do productive work.

Of the 717,997 immigrants who entered Israel between May 15, 1948, and December 31, 1953, 17.1 per cent came from Iraq, 4.3 per cent from Iran, and 12.3 per cent from North Africa. Earlier settlers were alarmed by this wave and referred to it as "inferior human material" not easily assimilable with European Jews. In fact, Israelis talked about their "color problem." But ardent supporters of Prime Minister David Ben Gurion's policy of full-throttle immigration said, "A Jew is a Jew; we need people." Now that the river of immigrants has dried up, and with the exodus sometimes exceeding the influx, some Israelis are frightened, for their country does indeed need people to man the walls as well as build them.

The military aspect of immigration was actually the supreme consideration. Israeli law provides for compulsory two-and-a-half-year conscription of men between the ages of eighteen and twenty-six, two-year conscription for men between the ages of twenty-seven and twenty-nine, and two-year conscription for unmarried women between the ages of eighteen and twenty-six unless "they have religious objections." If newcomers know no Hebrew they will learn it in the army, I heard repeatedly; military service will give them a sense of identity with the country and then they will want to learn a trade.

This may be so and in some cases undoubtedly has been so. Never-

[9] *Ibid.*, p. 11.

theless, the introduction, during a brief, five-and-a-half-year period, of 350,000 Asian and African Jews into a nation which, including these, had a total population on January 1, 1955, of 1,716,000, aggravates other grave problems. Israelis say they are not disturbed. They obviously are, else they would not be so irritated over the failure to attract more than a handful of Jewish settlers from America, England, Scandinavia, and Switzerland who, presumably, would excel in technical and managerial skills, and, no less important, if they came in large numbers, disprove the thesis, demonstrated by the immigration to date, that only the homeless, the menaced, the maladjusted, and penurious go to Israel. The others contribute money and gasps of admiration. But Zionism was intended as the "in-gathering" of the dispersed, and when Western Jews refuse to be in-gathered Israel begins to look like refugee relief rather than Zion. In a way, therefore, American Jews build up Israel physically and tear it down spiritually. I suspect some of Ben Gurion's quarrels with U.S. Zionists stem from this dilemma.

The Asian-African influx is not the only discordant element. Indeed, for a nation born in a battle in which "men and women from more than forty countries formed a homogeneous and victorious force," a nation presumably the child of necessity and an idea, Israel, I found, had astonishingly little cohesion. The question of loyalty to the state is not in question here. But in this small country centrifugal factors seemed extraordinarily strong.

Religion is one of these divisive factors, a circumstance which should certainly intrigue those who insist that Jews are a religious community and nothing else. Flying to Israel, my plane from Istanbul stopped at Cyprus where it took on a Jewish passenger who removed his hat and replaced it with a black skull cap. We were late, and reached Lydda Airport, between Jerusalem and Tel Aviv, after sundown, Friday. The Jewish passenger with the skull cap accordingly settled down on a bench in the airport waiting room for a twenty-four-hour stay; being an observant Jew he would not travel till Saturday evening when the Sabbath ended. I planned to go to Jerusalem, about an hour's distance by car through the hills. My boyhood friend, Gershon Agron (born Agronsky), editor of the daily *Jerusalem Post*, had sent his automobile to meet me, but the driver, knowing he must not travel on the Sabbath, had returned when he learned the plane would be late. Since I would now have to pay for transportation, I walked over to the airport exchange bureau to get some Israeli pounds. Closed—Sabbath. I inquired about the airlines limousine or a bus. Neither was available—Sabbath. Taxis? No taxis—Sabbath. Then how could I get to Jerusalem? I couldn't on the Sabbath. After a vehement protest, I finally rented a government car at an enormous price to take me to the renovated King David Hotel in Jerusalem. The front desk was closed—Sabbath. A watchman let me have a room.

Saturday, no buses were running and no taxis could be summoned by phone although one might occasionally be picked up on the street. No telegram was delivered unless it dealt with an emergency. Religious Jews sometimes terrorized people who did not observe the Sabbath, and a government official would not dare infringe it although he might be completely agnostic or atheistic. After working hard in a hot factory for six days, a working man would not find a public conveyance to take him and his family to the beach on Saturday, and he could hardly have a car of his own.

Israel has no civil weddings or civil burials. A marriage is not valid unless performed by a rabbi under the traditional canopy. A corpse cannot be interred except by a religious society known at the Hevra Kadisha. Because the Socialist party of Ben Gurion, Sharett, and President Itzhak Ben Tsvi, the largest party in the country, refused to give this situation permanent legal validity in a constitution, and since the religious Jews would accept no constitution that did not, Israel still was without a constitution.

The Mizrachi political party and the Agudat Israel party are based on the Torah, or Jewish Bible, and its commentaries. Thus religion invades Israeli politics. In turn, religion and politics shape education. In 1952, when I was in Palestine, all schools were party schools. The Mizrachi, the Agudat Israel, the Mapai or moderate Socialist party of Ben Gurion and Sharett, and the Mapam or pro-Soviet Socialist party each had its own parochial school system. In August, 1953, a "unified State-controlled elementary school system with provision for special religious schools was established."[10]

The political struggle between the religious and Socialist parties, between the Socialist and capitalist parties, and especially between the moderate and pro-Soviet Socialist parties is ferocious. The story is told, and it is revealing even if apocryphal, that one day Prime Minister Ben Gurion received a telephone call from his son in London. "Papa," said the boy, "I'm getting married."

Papa Prime Minister, who had a lot on his mind, extended hasty congratulations.

"But Papa," the son went on, "my bride is not one of us."

[10] *Ibid.*, p. 41.

"What!" shouted the father. "From Mapam?"

"No, no," the boy explained, "she's a Christian."

"Oh," said Ben Gurion with relief, "that's all right."

That a pro-Soviet party should have any lure in Israel seemed remarkable, for here was an independent modern nation carrying out a progressive, dynamic policy, experiencing tremendous growth, and full of buoyant self-assurance. In Russia and her empire, the object of Mapam's infatuation, on the other hand, Zionist or Jewish nationalist activity was proscribed and Jewish culture discouraged, and Jews and Zionists were often persecuted. Why should Israeli Socialists, of all people, be attracted by the Soviet Union? The problem intrigued me, but I was handicapped in studying it directly, for I was known as anti-Soviet. Despite the difficulty, I asked Moshe Pearlman, the Director General of the Israeli information office, to put me in touch with Dr. Sneh, the leader of Mapam. He telephoned Dr. Sneh in my presence.

"I shall have to consult my comrades," Dr. Sneh replied.

Several hours later Pearlman called back for the verdict. "If Fischer is in the Knesset [the Israeli Parliament] next week we might meet."

The next week I was in the restaurant of the Knesset and asked an editor of the *Jerusalem Post* to tell Dr. Sneh I would like to talk with him. But during the week I had been interviewed at a press tea where I gave the Hebrew journalists some impressions of other countries, including Yugoslavia which, having liberated itself from Soviet domination, was now free, I said, to conduct an interesting experiment, worthy of attention, in new social forms.

"Tell Fischer to go to Yugoslavia," Dr. Sneh told the *Post* editor.

On that same occasion a more moderate Mapam leader, Mr. Mordecai Bentov, consented to have a glass of tea with me in the Knesset dining room. I had talked with him in Palestine in 1942, and our conversation this time was urbane. Prodded by my questions, he explained the Mapam party line: a third world war would certainly break out soon. The Soviet forces would cut through intervening territory and occupy Israel. Moscow would not be so crude as to allow the anti-Zionist Israeli Communists to form a government. It would give the assignment to a friendly party, like Mapam, which, since it was Zionist, could expect support from the Jewish population.

My argument that a third world war was not inevitable made no impression, or rather it made a ludicrous impression.

Furthermore, said Mr. Bentov, humanity faced the alternative of Soviet Socialism or American capitalism, and Mapam's choice was obvious.

My counterargument (that Soviet feudalism drowned out Soviet Socialism and created sharp inequalities in Russia, whereas America's capitalism, with Socialism added, made for equality of opportunity and fewer class differences) fell on unhearing ears. The idea that capitalism could mix with Socialism was too unorthodox for an orthodox Socialist. I had no more success contending that Israel might avoid choosing between America and Russia by evolving its own social forms; it had already given birth to the rural commune.

In those communes, the Mapamniks, as Mapam members were called, performed the remarkable feat of choosing both America and Russia. Most of them lived on American bounty and enjoyed the farm machines and fine kitchen and dining room equipment which came to them free from the United States. But at meals they sang the praises of Moscow which had ordered the arrest of their fellow members. They wanted to have their cake and eat it and beat up the baker.

The resulting friction with Ben Gurion's Mapai had become so acrimonious in 1952 that almost all the communes which included members of both parties were breaking in two. This was a regretted setback for the ideal of egalitarian living which they shared, which indeed was the very essence of their lives; yet it could not unite that which divergent attitudes toward Russia and Communism sundered.

Zionist politics remain volcanic. Though the hostile neighbors have their ears to the wall, no Israeli thinks he ought to make less noise. Outbursts in Parliament, the press, and public meetings—against official corruption, the dominant role of private capitalists, the low salaries of engineers and members of the professions, the high wages of working men, the mistreatment of Arabs as second-class citizens, the government's leniency toward religious bigots, its religious intolerance, and so forth—are evidence of divisions, but also of democracy. Everybody has a stake in politics and his word to say about it. A problem tackled means a controversy opened. The Jews had not waited almost two thousand years for a state to be indifferent about it. Nor were the Arabs. Inside and out, therefore, the weather prediction was "Stormy."

The best shelter from the storm would be a cover of unbroken negotiations and more negotiations. The best way to calm the storm would be the co-operative coexistence Emir Faisal desired. Common use of water resources would be an important step toward such coexistence. Water in that whole area is the staff of life.

Arab-Israeli coexistence is the best nationalism. Conflict defeats national growth. The Arab middle class is interested in growth; it is truly nationalistic. But the Arab nationalist's desire to destroy Israel is self-destructive. It not only obstructs progress by giving guns precedence over bread and water. It could lead to a dangerous mood within the Arab world and a dangerous alliance between it and Soviet imperialism.

CHAPTER TWENTY-EIGHT

Religion and Status in Pakistan

THE FURTHER east the hotter it gets, the greater the need of cleanliness, and the less cleanliness. There are exceptions, but Karachi, the capital of Pakistan, is not one of them. In the best hotel, flies compete with you for your food and never take no for an answer. An ambassador's wife complained that the herd of water buffaloes in the back yard of her neighbor, a nawab, attracted huge flies which swarmed around her house; that merchants skillfully opened a tiny hole in the rind of watermelons, which sell by weight, and injected quantities of water to make them heavier; finally, that grocers mixed sand with their flour and sugar.

Pakistan is poor; business standards are low; the country is backward. With the usual sensitivity, the Pakistanis object to being called backward, they prefer the more objective "underdeveloped." But the underdevelopment is due to backwardness. Why, I have often wondered, are Asian countries so retarded? Why did the West and not the East invent the steam engine, electricity, and modern machinery? The Chinese invented gunpowder for firecrackers, they made paper, and they knew how to pour bronze before Europe did. India invented the "Arabic" numerals, the concepts of the zero and infinity, and chess. Asia's supply of brains has always been plentiful, witness its great mathematicians, philosophers, writers, architects, and artists in bygone centuries. But good minds usually applied themselves to esoteric subjects for the enjoyment and edification of the select few rather than to practical activity from which the millions might draw tangible benefits. India made beautiful textiles on hand looms but could not compete with European machine-made goods. And when the economy lagged the arts and sciences also lagged. The result was a basic weakness which antedated imperialism and probably invited it.

In the present era too, the independent nations of Asia—and all of this applies to Latin America as well—might import foreign capital or advanced technical know-how or both and yet continue backward and undemocratic because they lack a modern attitude toward social equality, manual labor, and the welfare of the mass of the people. It is not technology that brings progress; it is the other way around: the desire for progress is the mother of inventions.

Perhaps the biggest block to the economic development of backward nations, and one against which Mahatma Gandhi was in constant combat, is social status. In Karachi, at dinner in the home of a Pakastani official, I met the owner of a textile mill. He said the plant was new and equipped with American machinery 30 per cent of which usually stands idle and in need of repair as a result of mishandling by unqualified working men. I asked him how much he paid his workers. "Two rupees a day," he replied—about fifty-five cents.

"Why not ten rupees?" I asked.

"You couldn't get workers worth that much," he asserted.

"Why not attract some of the intelligent young fellows one sees around town and in government offices?" I wondered.

"They wouldn't do it," he explained. "They would rather earn less in an office than more in a factory, because work with the hands lowers your social rank. The white sahib, the Englishman, didn't dirty his hands."

Moslems, like the Hindus, use untouchables for menial work. I asked the guests at dinner whether this aversion to manual labor might not explain the poverty of the entire Indian subcontinent. Somebody suggested that perhaps the Moslem did not work hard in this world because he expects the really good life in the next, to which another guest remarked that Christians held the same belief but probably did not take it as seriously as the followers of Islam. The conversation then drifted to the topic of the democracy of Islam. Everybody is equal in the mosque. "But what equality can there be in Egypt," I protested, "between pasha and peasant, or between feudal master and starving beggar in Pakistan?"

Here the manufacturer interposed that he paid as high wages as anybody else in Karachi. "Why not pay more?" I asked.

"Good God," he exclaimed, "you don't think I would pay more than I have to."

I hinted that this was feudal psychology; a capitalist devoted to his class and country would pay his workers as much as he could afford, not as little as he could get away with.

"I have enough to do taking care of myself," the manufacturer contended.

"But you cannot expect persons living in the physical conditions and intellectual climate of their medieval ancestors," I argued, "to handle your expensive American machines efficiently. Besides, the fact that factory work is socially degrading must impede a nation's industrialization and general progress."

U.S. Ambassador Avra Warren and Mrs. Warren contributed interesting data on social stratification. Their servants, they said, give a guest a social rating and treat him accordingly. Thus former Ambassador William C. Bullitt, and American Socialist Norman Thomas who stayed with the Warrens for three days, were rated as sahibs because of their distinguished bearing and given the red-carpet treatment, while others might find the service slower and less eager. A person's standing in his community goes up or down not only in accordance with the work he does but with the social status of those he works for. The number of servants is a measure of the employer's social status and so is the elegance of their uniforms. There is a hierarchy among servants, and the larger the staff, therefore, the better the servants appreciate their master.

In 1942, when I was the house guest of Sir Claude Gidney, the British Resident of Hyderabad, and Lady Gidney, they told me how much care had to be exercised in inviting Indians. An invitation to lunch gave a person a certain position in the community; an invitation to dinner gave him a higher position; an invitation to a dinner attended by important British officials made it still higher. With the social position went financial credit and even political power. If Sir Claude and Lady Gidney, by an oversight, neglected for some time to invite a person who had previously frequented their palace he might be ruined.

"I have never received a maharaja but that he asked me to increase the number of guns he was entitled to" as an honorary salute, Lord Linlithgow, the British Viceroy, said to me in 1942.

It would not be wise to underestimate the effect of these matters on India's and Asia's development; it might even profit to ascertain how much of the same psychology remains. Certainly the competition for British titles and favors and the education, under British rule, for government office and the law instead of, for instance, engineering, helped to shape India's political and economic fortunes. Indeed, rivalry for government jobs, which were the biggest industry in the country, was not the least and perhaps the most important cause of the Hindu-Moslem disunity which ended in the unhappy partition of India. The Moslems wanted a state of their own because they felt they would be at a disadvantage in competing with the Hindus for office and in business.

In small matters and big, the rivalry between Pakistan and India continues. "You and India," I said to Begum Liaquat Ali Kahn, the widow of the Pakistan Prime Minister, in 1952, "behave like divorced husband and wife."

"Who is the husband?" she demanded.

I said I did not know but that each was painfully jealous and interested in each other's affairs. They were divorced yet not divorced, and the troubles born of partition would last decades.

"We want to be independent of the Hindus," the Begum exclaimed. "Why does the United States take Nehru's side on the Kashmir question?" she said, changing the subject. "U.S. aid to Pakistan has been cut, but India is getting more than her share."

I had heard the exact opposite from my Indian friends. "No doubt," the Begum declared, "but you know the Hindus cannot be trusted." I reminded her that Indians often make the same comment about Pakistanis.

"I suppose," the Begum said with a smile, "India is at an advantage because she has a Communist problem. Maybe if we had more Communists we would get more money."

In another mood, she talked with bitterness about the murder of her husband. Nawabzada Liaquat Ali Khan, Jinnah's successor as Prime Minister, was assassinated on October 16, 1951. Suspicion reached into the highest governing circles. The murderer was killed on the spot by the police though he did not try to escape and might have supplied evidence of a conspiracy. Since then the search for clues had been reported unavailing, and the Begum was only one of many Pakistanis who wondered what powerful circles were obstructing the investigation. The Prime Minister's unsolved murder remained the biggest scandal in the history of Pakistan.

Assassination, a word said to derive from the Arabic, has been used since the Second World War as a political weapon in many Moslem countries—and elsewhere too. Liaquat was an able administrator with the courage to rebuff the mullahs or Islamic teachers, the ulemas, or Islamic theologians, and the landlords who tried to control the government. An assassination does more than remove an obstacle; it is a warning to survivors to respect the unseen wielders of power.

In many Middle East and Asian countries, more than one vote at Cabinet sessions has been cast with a troubled eye on an imaginary revolver in the hand of a lurking assassin. The thought of a less violent, political death is of course a potent vote-shaper in the councils of not a few advanced Western democracies. But bullets are a more immediate and frightening influence than ballots in a future election. On the question, for example, of the disputed territory of Kashmir, no Pakistan government was free to formulate the best solution and try to reach it in negotiations with Nehru. Any yielding might have brought lethal results. Yet the tensions caused by the military hostilities in Kashmir were forcing both Pakistan and India to devote more than 50 per cent of their federal budgets to defense.

Pakistan's claim to Kashmir had been brilliantly defended at United Nations sessions in New York by Foreign Minister Sir Muhammad Zafrulla Khan. A former member of the Viceroy's Executive Council and judge of the Federal Court under the British, his legal ability, experience, and eloquence lifted him high above any rival for his difficult post, yet he was in danger of losing it for religious reasons. The mullahs wanted Sir Zafrulla removed because, though a devout Moslem, they considered him a kafir, an infidel, for he was an Ahmadiya. The Ahmadiyas are a sect of approximately half a million members, most numerous in the Punjab, who regard Hazrat Mirza Ghulam Ahmad (1835-1908) as the modern messiah, a second Prophet; but this is heresy to the orthodox to whom Mohammed is the one and only possible Prophet of Allah. The issue provoked riots in the Punjab province between Ahmadiyas and orthodox which cost the lives of scores of persons. Violence also broke out in Karachi. Punjab Prime Minister Mian Numtaz Muhammad Khan Daulatana subsequently attributed the disturbances to "destructive political elements who seized an opportunity to exploit religious sentiment."

Khwaja Nazimuddin, the Prime Minister of Pakistan, a small, pudgy man with a dark brown, lopsided head, told me, when I inquired about the fate of Sir Zafrulla, that the mullahs were "very much wrought up" about the affair, and had come to see him. Religion, he declared, was a bar to Communism and had to be kept alive. "Our young people who love to dance and drink," he added, "say this sends us back to the Middle Ages. But I hold that the Koran and Sunna [traditions of the Prophet] are adaptable to modern life." Pakistan's constitution, he explained, would be based on Islamic law.

The nation was five years old, but it still had no constitution because the religious reactionaries insisted on basing the country's legal structure on holy writ, and since this was subject to interpretation and could only be interpreted by Islamic scholars, the judicial system would be controlled by backward-facing mullahs, ulemas, and Maulanas who, as a corollary, could also veto legislation and, in effect, dominate the state. Progressive elements opposed such a retarding development. The result was no action and no constitution.

The Prime Minister said he hoped things would work out with Sir Zafrulla, "but we are not yet out of the woods." Ghulam Muhammad, the Governor-General of Pakistan, however, declared, "Nothing will happen to Zafrulla," and his tone carried conviction. He was in fact defending the Foreign Minister against the Prime Minister, and before long he dismissed Nazimuddin.[1]

The Governor-General, though officially head of state and therefore out of and above politics, had actually become the strong man of Pakistan, and this despite a recent stroke. He dragged his feet, slurred an occasional word, and sometimes, as he held the teacup in his shaking hand, it beat a little tinkle against the saucer. But he

[1] Ultimately Sir Zafrulla was kicked outside to the World Court in The Hague.

spoke eloquently for almost two hours while a giant, barefoot lackey in black beard, bulbous pink turban, and ornate uniform served tea and stood behind Ghulam Muhammad swating flies with loud bangs. The Governor-General spoke of his country's poverty and lack of skilled personnel in all branches of government. He wanted peace with India, and I believed him. If Kashmir went to India by international decision he would accept it, he asserted.

At the end of the interview, Ghulam Muhammad held my elbow and, shuffling his shoes along the brightly polished parquet floors, walked toward the exit. "I dislike this pomp," he said. "I live in one simple room." Presently he left me, walked into his room, and came back with a framed photograph of Nehru autographed "Jawaharlal Nehru December 1948." The Governor-General contemplated it morosely for a moment and said, "I have known Jawaharlal for thirty years. We have been friends. I knew his father. Now we are separated. It's sad."

Ghulam Muhammad and Sir Zafrulla belonged to a generation of Moslems who had had Hindu and Parsi friends and were broadminded and tolerant. The mentality of their juniors was being shaped by the tense rivalry with India. To them the past meant not friendly association with Hindus but the bitter quarrels that attended partition and especially the savage slaughter for which each side blamed the other when neither was blameless.

Ghulam Muhammad might speak affectionately of Nehru and Zafrulla of Mrs. Sarojini Naidu, the Indian poet of Gandhian days, but the structure in which they functioned and the atmosphere in which they moved were bequeathed them by Mr. Jinnah who, "up to 1913, when he was thirty-six years old," his authorized biographer writes,[2] "had never attached himself to any human being, in love or friendship. . . . he liked laying down the law to the young . . . was still a celibate introvert, timid of human relations." His vocabulary was "cold." His relations with Lord Chelmsford, Viceroy from 1916 to 1921, were based on "a personal equation. . . . This dislike influenced his conduct and his speeches." He had a "deep, instinctive dislike of the Mahatma's mind." That dislike influenced his determination to create Pakistan.

It is easy to exaggerate the role of individuals in history, but it is wrong to underestimate it. More than one Pakistani has said, in

[2] Hector Bolitho, *Jinnah, Creator of Pakistan*, London: John Murray, 1954.

private, that there would have been no Pakistan but for Jinnah. For Pakistan was no historic necessity. The Moslems of India, to be sure, had serious grievances against the Hindus who often abused their numerical, economic, and cultural superiority. The Moslems of India had reason to fear living as a permanent minority in an independent, Hindu-majority India. The Hindus and the Indian national Congress party of Gandhi and Nehru did too little to calm these justified apprehensions. Nevertheless, adjustments could have been negotiated. The grant of maximum autonomy to the provinces where the Moslems constituted the majority—this was offered by the British but rejected by Jinnah—might have brought them more material, political, and educational benefits than today's Pakistan which Jinnah accepted though he said it was "quite impracticable" and "moth-eaten." But in 1947, unfortunately, Labor Britain was in a hurry to quit India, the Indian Congress was impatient to achieve national independence, and Jinnah, having proclaimed all his adult life that "the constitutional way is the right way," employed unconstitutional violence to obtain British and Congressional acquiescence in the Caesarean birth of Pakistan.

When surgeon Jinnah died thirteen months later he left a state but little strength. Pakistan consists of two parts, West Pakistan with a population of thirty-three million, and, a thousand miles away, East Pakistan with forty-three million. The thousand miles are Indian territory. This insurmountable obstacle to national unity is aggravated by diversity of language (the East speaks Bengali, the West Urdu, Punjabi, Sindi, and several other tongues) and by sectional, economic, and political rivalries. Before partition, Sikander Hyat Khan, Moslem Prime Minister of the Punjab, now partly included in West Pakistan, told Herbert M. Matthews of the *New York Times*, "that he considered a Bengal Moslem as foreign as a Chinese." The reality of Pakistan has not bridged this gulf; if anything it is wider.

In interviews with Pakistan leaders I made a point of saying that "Pakistan is a country of thirty-three million inhabitants." Their protests were formal. For in regard to defense, world influence, and relations with India, East Pakistan's weight is negligible. Traditionally nonmartial, it could be conquered militarily by India in a week.

In a discussion of Pakistan's foreign affairs with me on August 9, 1952, Sir Zafrulla said Pakistan's (that is, West Pakistan's) soldiers and Turkish soldiers were among the finest in the world and should be linked for defense against Russia. But, he declared, Pakistan could turn its attention to the menace of Soviet imperialism only if it had a United States guarantee against an assault by India. Yet when he had broached this matter to Secretary of State Acheson, Mr. Harriman, and former Ambassador George McGhee, he said, they told him it was out of the question since America was averse to giving such assurances outside the United Nations.

In Karachi, diplomats playing the role of secretly briefed armchair strategists talked about a "pincer movement" by Turkey and Pakistan against a Soviet armed force invading the Middle East via Iran and Iraq. Pakistan's army would approach the area of combat through its remote, barren province of Baluchistan where, I was informed, there was now a good road. A trial maneuver had already been carried out with fifty thousand men, and, given the necessary armor, one heard, the action could be conducted realistically with two hundred thousand.

"Your trouble is," I argued with Pakistanis, "that the Russians could slice through the disunited, internally feeble Arab states without much opposition before the Turkish-Pakistan countermove had time to unfold, and then you would be far out on a sawed-off limb." Ambassador Warren said that the Turks were therefore interested in peace between the Arabs and Israelis and hoped, eventually, to draw both into a Middle East defense pact. Most Pakistanis, however, were fiercely anti-Israel. The newspapers gleefully published adverse news about Israel, always printing Israel in quotation marks, which gave them the dual satisfaction of believing the worst about a state whose existence they denied. Yet even an editor whose paper practised this self-delusion emphasized the desirability of bringing Israel into a Middle East defense pact. Sir Zafrulla would have liked to try his hand at an Arab-Israeli reconciliation facilitated by frontier rectification at the expense of Israel and Israeli financial reparations to Arab refugees. It was pointed out, however, that the domestic opposition to Zafrulla by orthodox Moslems would embarrass him in any such efforts. If, as mediator, he showed the slightest friendliness for Israel his enemies would interpret it as further proof of hostility to Moslems and demand his official scalp.

Religion is the blood of Pakistan politics. "We cannot relinquish our claim to Kashmir, 80 per cent of whose inhabitants are Moslems, without undermining the principle on which our country is based," a member of the government said to me. The principle is that all predominantly Moslem areas of India should adhere to Pakistan. Jinnah, himself neither devout nor observant, made religion the criterion of nationhood because there was no other. Without religion there could have been no Pakistan. Therefore the government must yield to the embrace of religion and the theologians. Progressive forces may fight this condition. They will weaken the nation if they succeed—unless they find some new basis of nationhood, as Turkey did, as Western countries have. For the present, religion is the only possible foundation under the cleft house of Pakistan.

The effect of basing the constitution on the Koran and the Shar' or Sharia [Moslem law] was illustrated by an event during my 1954 visit to Pakistan. Jumma, the son of Gulsher, according to the prosecution's story in a Session Court trial, as reported by *Dawn*, "had an evil eye" on Musammat Sara, the wife of Khamiso. Though Jumma was a near relative, Khamiso ordered him to keep away from the house. Several months later, however, when Khamiso was off milking his cows, Jumma entered the house with a hatchet, injured Musammat Sara, her seventy-year-old mother Musammat Memi, and a man named Ismail. The mother died.

Jumma was sentenced to death and the Chief Court of Sind confirmed the sentence. The day of the hanging was fixed. But at the last moment the condemned man's attorney obtained a stay from the Chief Commissioner of Karachi on the ground of a mercy petition by the descendants of the murdered woman in which they stated that they had forgiven Jumma and demanded that he be pardoned and released. This was in accordance with "the rights vested in them by the Holy Koran and the Sunna." The "*fatwas*" or rulings of the ulemas supported the contention that if the family of a victim pardons a murderer he must go free.

"Crime is bad enough as it is," a hotel employee said to me, "without murderers roaming the city by the grace of Islamic law."

Nine days later, however, the Chief Commissioner of Karachi, having consulted the federal government, ruled that Jumma must hang because the Koranic law "is not yet applicable in the land."

But when Pakistan adopts its Islamic Constitution, any murderer could presumably buy himself a pardon from his victim's family. Under the Constitution, moreover, education is likely to be controlled by the theologians with emphasis on conservatism and fatalism —influences inclined to confirm social backwardness and economic poverty. In a clerical Islamic state, above all, women would remain underpriviliged and segregated before the law and in life, and this is one of the major factors, if not the major factor, conducing to the stagnation of the Moslem world. Where one sex, approximately half the population, is regarded, and treated, as inferior the whole country is dragged down and the idea of inequality and discrimination becomes deeply ingrained. No doubt, modern industrial trends militate against the inferior status of women. The theologians can therefore be expected to range themselves against social and economic progress.

The role of religion is thus the key to Pakistan's future, and the dynamic, idealistic, forward-looking Pakistanis one meets will have to gird their loins for a bitter struggle to separate church from state.

CHAPTER TWENTY-NINE

India Is Different

ONE AFTERNOON, when I arrived at the editorial office of Devadas Gandhi, the managing editor of the New Delhi *Hindustan Times,* he said to me, "Don't linger here, I have a sadhu upstairs and kept him waiting for you. He speaks English." This was a most unusual opportunity. A sadhu is a Hindu holy man, and I had never met one who spoke English. I asked Devadas why the sadhu had come and Devadas replied, "He wants me to arrange a demonstration in which he will show that he can be buried in the earth for twenty-four hours and remain alive." I rushed upstairs to the Gandhi living room.

The swami was seated on a chair—not on the floor. He wore a white homespun cotton shirt and loincloth and no shoes. The features of his pleasant, pale-brown face were small and fine. He had a tremendous head of thick, black-gray hair which fell in curls or strands several inches below his shoulders. He was fifty-six. I noticed his very long, squared-off fingernails and asked about them. He said, "One who does not cut his hair also does not cut his nails." But I remarked that the nails of his right hand were short. They had broken off from work, he explained.

"You think you could be buried in the earth and live?" I said.

"Yes, I have done it for forty days," he asserted. "I haven't tried it for a longer period."

"Why do you do it?"

"To achieve self-control. If I attain perfect self-control," he said, "I can bring about world peace."

This is no crazier, I thought, than some other methods of bringing about world peace. His reasoning was that once he acquired absolute self-control his influence would radiate out to millions of others and from them to others still and in that way the whole universe would come under the spell.

The swami, whose name was Narayan, had come to Delhi to visit his wife and child, but usually he lived in the Himalayas at an altitude of ten thousand feet. He had climbed as high as sixteen thousand feet. "What do you wear?" I inquired.

"Just what I am wearing now."

"No shoes?"

"I never wear shoes," the sadhu declared. He walked over snow and ice with bare feet and dressed only in thin cotton clothing. He said he never felt cold; it was a matter of training in detachment from the body. That is Yoga. "Sometimes," the swami elaborated, "I live in a Himalayan cave for three months. The first month I take a little food in the shape of nuts and fruit found in the mountains. The second month I live on water only. The third month on air. Sometimes I go on walks," Narayan said, "but most of the time I am unconscious or semiconscious. Serpents creep over me, rodents run over me, but do no harm." Wild animals abound in the mountains but they never touched him, he affirmed.

"What animals?"

"Tigers and cheetahs," he enumerated.

I asked what he did all those months alone in the mountains. "I think of God and contemplate," he declared. "In this way I reinforce my control over body and mind and prepare to save the peace of the world."

I said that since he could be buried alive for days at a time, couldn't he now hold his breath for three or four minutes? He agreed, though it would be better, he explained, if he had no food in his body. At this point, however, Mrs. Gandhi, who had come into the room and heard the last part of the conversation, began to gather up her sari and prepare to flee. Little Gopu, age seven, Mahatma Gandhi's favorite grandchild, made grimaces of distaste. I said if the swami could live for forty days under the earth, three minutes without breathing would not hurt him. But Lakshmi declared she would not be able to look at such deliberate torture of self, and Gopu continued to twist his face in disgust. Just then Devadas came in dressed in his sleeveles undershirt and a much-wrapped dhoti which dangled between his legs. He liked my proposal. "Yes, why not?" he said. But Lakshmi put her bare foot down and the project was abandoned. When the sadhu stood up to go I saw that he was not over five feet tall.

Six and a half months later the Indian press reported that Swami Narayan, after a fast, entered a wooden box measuring six cubic feet which had been sunk into the ground near Rajghat, where Mahatma Gandhi lies buried. Then the box was closed and four feet of earth were packed down over it to shut out the air.

On February 7, 1953, a bearded disciple of Swami Narayan dug the dirt away, opened the box, and acting on previous instructions, rubbed ghee or clarified butter into the curly hair of his master. Thereupon, according to a statement of the disciple as telegraphed by Robert Trumbull to the *New York Times* of February 8, the sadhu "awakened and held up two fingers" which meant that he intended to emerge from his voluntary grave in two hours. The sadhu also recited a verse from the Gita, the Hindu holy book. Then, suddenly, he died.

The crowd accepted the bearded man's report and pressed closer for a view of the departed saint. A municipal physician, summoned by the police, found that the sadhu must have died between twelve to twenty-four hours before the box was opened. On this assumption, Swami Narayan had survived for eight days in his airless grave.

From New Delhi I drove twenty miles one day to Faridabad, where, with government assistance and under the supervision of Sudhir Ghosh, a follower of Mahatma Gandhi, wasteland had been converted into an industrial-agricultural settlement for thirty thousand refugees from Pakistan. On the return trip, I saw a small eagle sitting on a tree stump, a peacock strutting into a wood, and many monkeys. Monkeys sat on trees and chattered, and some played or quarreled on the much-traveled highway. Newspapers report that monkeys enter private apartments in Delhi in search of food and bite young children. But there is a religious prejudice against killing monkeys, for the monkey may be a reincarnation of your dead mother or sister, or brother, so they infest the countryside and many towns. Often they travel from north to south and back with the weather and cut swaths of destruction across standing crops. About two years ago, the government of one of the Indian states offered a money reward for each monkey tail produced. The resulting uproar among the people was tremendous and the government almost fell. But when the storm subsided the authorities resumed their antimonkey crusade. In some states, hunters are employed to shoot them and get so much per tail. An official told me that he had gone hunting once and shot a monkey with his rifle. A peasant came running, asked for the body, and put it on a pole as a scarecrow. "But the same peasant," the official said, "would have been too religious or superstitious to kill the monkey himself."

When I arrived in New Delhi, in 1952, I could find no hotel accommodations; I had to take an apartment in Maidans Hotel in Old Delhi. Most of my appointments, however, were in New Delhi six miles away. To travel the distance to and fro several times a day was inconvenient but educational, for New Delhi, with its palaces, embassies, office buildings, broad avenues, vast lawns and parks, is old England. But Old Delhi is India, a sizzling, seething, messy, massy, densely packed city. Pedestrians overflow from the crowded pavements into the streets, and the streets are a jungle of men, women, children, automobiles, cycles, rickshas, horse carriages, buses, oxcarts, donkey carts, bicycle caravans, men carrying enormous burdens, boys wheeling giant boards that advertise moving picture shows and, in the midst of all this twisted, clanging traffic, sacred cows and bulls who have the right of way over everything else. They stand or walk in the middle of the busiest thoroughfare or, for their afternoon siesta, lie down on the asphalt so that vehicles and persons must detour around them.

Sometimes, coming home late at night, I would see cows and bulls sleeping in the streets or browsing on the pavements where thousands of families sleep all night on rope beds to escape the heat of the houses. The bulls, very mild-looking bulls incidentally, belong to nobody. A number of them are branded with a mark for a deceased person and that gives them a special sacred status. The taxi drivers said the cows need the bulls. And why should cows live in the middle of a big city? Because they belong to city people who want to have their own clean milk undiluted with water. Isn't it cruel to keep a cow in a city, would it not give better milk on a farm instead of grubbing around in urban slop piles? The cattle bring flies, dirt, and disease; frequently they are quartered inside courtyards and even kitchens. Is this the way to demonstrate love of the cow? "Don't you keep dogs and cats in your homes?" Mrs. Devadas Gandhi argued.

To a Hindu the cow is the symbol of the entire animal kingdom. It provides man with food and works for him. It is the incorporation of humility, the symbol of universal motherhood. Even the poorest peasant will not slaughter a cow.

It was so hot in the south Indian city of Madras during the second week of September that I never walked during the day and got little exercise. The evening sea breezes brought some relief, but even then I had to force myself to go into the streets while they were exhaling the heat absorbed during the many sunny hours. As I stepped beyond the hotel grounds one evening a ricksha puller accosted me. I had thought of going to the beach for a stroll in the salt air but I felt it was wrong to use a two-legged instead of a four-wheeled taxi. On the other hand, if I did not hire him he would remain idle and hungry. I said, "Marina"; he said, "Two rupees." I knew this was excessive and walked on. He followed and came down to one rupee. By this time I decided that the city was interesting, the heat at the end of the day tolerable, and walking desirable. Soon, two little boys caught up with me, one could not have been more than four and he kept silent throughout; the older one, about six, his hair neatly parted in the middle, a narrow strip of cotton cloth about his loins and otherwise naked, started to chant in English, using the broad "a": "No father, no mother, no brother, no sister, one anna, please master." (Sixteen annas in a rupee; a rupee is about twenty cents.) As he spoke he smiled, revealing gleaming-white, perfect teeth. In the beginning I thought he was having fun, playing a game, but he and his little friend pursued me for blocks with the elder repeating at regular intervals, "No father, no mother, no brother, no sister, one anna, please, master." Occasionally he would add "no uncle," or forget himself and ask for two annas. They were competing, along the same street, with a score of beggars of all ages and sizes and in every stage of decrepitude and disease.

The boys remained at a respectful distance when I approached a diminutive shrine in the center of a broad pavement. The small stone building consisted of a short vestibule and a main cubicle which was almost filled by a tomb, as big as a coffin, covered with flowers. Now and then a barefooted worshiper bowed, leaned his forehead against the tomb, then placed a mite in the brass collection urn. Now and then the priest lifted a broom of long peacock feathers and sprinkled holy water on the devout. I watched a man of apparent education make his obeisance and addressed him when he began putting his feet into the sandals he had left on the threshold. This was the tomb of a saint, he told me, who had been buried some ten yards away. Came a day, the British decided to cut a street here and asked the religious community to move the tomb. They refused, whereupon the British engineer brought working men to disinter the holy man. The first worker demurred, the second too. The third lifted his pick but began to bleed profusely and desisted. Then the Englishman exclaimed, "If the saint is so powerful why can't he remove himself so the people have their street?" Straightaway, the tomb rose into the air, sailed over to its present resting place and imbedded itself in the ground. The shrine was built above it.

My informant, who spoke a good English and worked in the post office, said the saint heals the sick. He began at my request to write out the name of the saint but needed the priest's assistance to finish it. The name is Syed Moosa Sha Khadari, a Moslem. Yet all this smacked of Hinduism and, of course, Mohammedans in India have absorbed some features of the Hindu way of life.

"Who are these people?" I asked the postman, indicating a long queue of mendicants.

"These sisters and brothers," he replied, "are fed by the saint." They live on the alms of visitors to the saint's shrine.

"No father, no mother, no brother, no sister, no uncle, two annas, please, master." The child beggars were back again. I gave them half a rupee. Their white teeth gleamed like electric lights.

In the summer of 1952, Jayaprakash Narayan, the leader of the Socialist party of India, aged fifty, went on a twenty-one-day fast, and when he came out of it he wrote an article saying, "For many years I have worshipped at the shrine of the goddess—Dialectical Materialism" but "it has become patent to me that materialism of any sort robs man of the means to become truly human." Jayaprakash or J.P., as many friends call him, therefore "had chosen goodness." He preferred humanism to materialism.

I spent two days with Jayaprakash in Dr. Dinshah Mehta's Nature Cure Clinic in Poona, a medium-sized city, 108 miles from Bombay, where he had lived during the fast and where he was now recuperating from it. I had stayed in the same clinic with Mahatma Gandhi in the summer of 1946. J. P. was in fine fettle, tall and handsome as ever with a relaxed look on his attractive brown face. Throughout the twenty-one-day fast, he had taken no food and lived on water with a pinch of salt to prevent nausea. He lost eighteen pounds in the three weeks. Now, under Dr. Mehta's postfast regime, which included breakfast but no lunch and a heavy dinner plus frequent tall glasses of milk, J.P. was gaining half a pound every twenty-four hours and felt stronger every day.

I asked J.P. why he had undertaken the fast. He said it was in fulfillment of a vow. In 1946 the postmen of India had gone on strike. J.P. was the president of their trade union and he tried to negotiate a settlement with Mr. Rafi Ahmed Kidwai, the Minister for Communications. At one meeting, J.P. understood Kidwai to have promised that if the postmen returned to work they would be paid compensation for the period of the strike. J.P. thereupon ordered the strikers back to work. Subsequently, however, Kidwai denied having made the promise, and the government refused the postmen their back pay. Negotiations on this issue continued for several years until J.P. took a pledge to fast.

"This fast is not against anybody, nor for anything outside of myself," J.P. declared in a public statement to his friends dated June 22, 1952, the day before he plunged into his three weeks' ordeal. The fast, he explained, was for "self-correction" because, in the meeting with Mr. Kidwai, "I found I was guilty of carelessness and negligence," and he now wished to "atone for the mistake which had affected so many working men." The fast, he added, was "an entirely personal affair" and he begged all to refrain from sympathetic public manifestation and publicity.

The fast, nevertheless, was first-page news throughout India. It was discussed in the press and debated in Parliament. In that debate,

Prime Minister Nehru displayed a little irritation with Jayaprakash for fasting, and Mr. Kidwai defended himself against the implication that he had pledged compensation to the striking postmen and then reneged.

Many postmen and railwaymen—Jayaprakash had also been president of the Railwaymen's Union—fasted during the last twenty-four hours of his three weeks' ordeal. The Socialist Party Conference in the Punjab state passed a resolution emphasizing the need for more morality in politics. Letters and telegrams of good wishes reached Jayaprakash from all corners of India. The President of India wrote to him, and so also did the Prime Minister Jawaharlal Nehru, despite his irritation and although their friendship of earlier years had apparently grown somewhat sour because of political differences. Nehru expressed the hope that he would survive the test with health unimpaired. Jayaprakash's life, Nehru assured him, was precious "for all of us and for India."

A fast touches India as nothing else. Soon the government of India announced that it would pay the postmen a total of approximately ten million rupees, about two million dollars.

The first three days of the fast were the most difficult for Jayaprakash. He felt hungry. But after that the desire to eat disappeared. Dr. Mehta told me that this is normal in all fasts.

Prabhavati, Jayaprakash's wife, cared for him throughout the fast. It was not a new experience, for she was, for many years, a disciple and nurse of Mahatma Gandhi. She is a soft, gentle, self-effacing woman eager to serve and anxious to be overlooked. As I talked with Jayaprakash she lay on her bed at the opposite end of the long room, sometimes listening, often dozing, for she too had to recuperate from her husband's fast, in which she did more than nurse him; she was a source of spiritual comfort. Once, when Jayaprakash left the room, I asked her whether there was any difference between Jayaprakash's fast and the two long fasts of Gandhi which she had witnessed. She laughed, whether with embarrassment or amusement I did not know, and walked out into the next room and then came back, still smiling, with Jayaprakash. She had repeated my question to him, and he was now urging her to answer. Her face straightened as she said, "With Jayaprakash the fast was a triumph of will power; with Gandhi a triumph of God." Jayaprakash had taken a decision to fast and had seen himself through the ordeal by virtue of his inner strength, whereas Gandhi, she declared, never decided to fast, the call came to him and the fast was effortless, a spiritual exercise rather than a physical trial.

But, sitting up in bed, Jayaprakash said things which showed that the fast had brought spiritual benefits. It cleansed and enlightened him, he declared. As the fast progressed he thought less of politics and more about philosophical problems. He found inner peace. At certain hours, he read the ancient Hindu Upanishads, or listened to friends recite passages from the Bhagavad-Gita, the Hindu holy book.

"You are becoming religious," I said.

"No," he replied, "but I am attempting to get beyond the material." He spoke of a certain Indian Socialist as a "Commissar."

"And you are the Yogi," I suggested.

"I am trying to be."

As a result of the fast, Jayaprakash said, he realized—he had sensed it before—that the social changes and new institutions through which Socialism expects to improve the world are not enough. "The individual man, the root of society," he subsequently wrote in an article, "must also be cured. That is why we have latterly been laying more and more emphasis on values and the right means." Success could be achieved by reaching for "noble ideals" and not by "the conquest and maintenance of power, as in Stalinist Communism." Conceivably, he declared, the right kind of Socialist institutions might shape man and society, "but who will shape those who undertake to shape these institutions?"

J.P. was obviously moving toward the Gandhian goal of a better man as the means to a better world. Having become a Communist during his student days in America, and then, on his return to India, a Democratic Socialist employing Marxist tactics and violence as his political instruments, he was now transforming himself into a Gandhian social revolutionist whose purpose was not the triumph of an ism or the glorification of a state but the ennobling of the individual.

Jayaprakash was the rare politician who reacted to the best in India.

CHAPTER THIRTY

Sketch of an Indian Leader

I N NO COUNTRY or province in the world has a Communist party ever been elected to take over the government. Communists have seized power by violence but never won it by votes. In 1951, however, Communists made a bid to break all precedents and take office by democratic means. It happened in the south Indian state of Madras which, with fifty-seven million inhabitants, was numerically larger than a majority of the earth's nations. In a democratic election, the Communists had won 16.5 per cent of the seats in the state legislature. Their ally, the left-wing KMP party, controlled 9.3 per cent of the seats. This Communist-led quarter of the legislature, moreover, exercised a tremendous attraction on the Independents who constituted another quarter of the state Parliament. If the Communists were going to form a government the Independents intended to be in it.

Against this potential Communist-dominated coalition, the Nehru Congress party held only 40 per cent of the seats.

The Communists' position was improved by the strength of their party in two other south Indian states. In neighboring Hyderabad, it had won 20.8 per cent of the votes, and in next-door Travancore-Cochin 15.5 per cent. These three southern states were the stronghold of Indian Communism. Together they gave the Indian Communist party 4,030,000 of the 5,370,000 votes it received in the elections to the federal Parliament. Madras city was the headquarters of the national Communist party, and when people spoke in those days of the rising Red tide in India they were thinking of Madras, Hyderabad, and Travancore-Cochin.

Presently Chakravarti Rajagopalachari, or C.R. (or Rajaji), appeared on the Madras scene. He had been the first Governor-General of India, and Minister of the Interior of India. His administrative experience was considerable, his talent as attorney great. He had been Gandhi's close friend.

At seventy-two, Rajaji retired from politics. To inquirers he would have given fatigue and physical frailty as the reasons. Disgruntlement with the central leadership of India might have been the fuller explanation.

In the spring of 1952, the Congress party called on Rajaji to come out of retreat and save Madras from Communism. Apparently the challenge of leading a minority into battle against a potential majority was too enticing to be resisted, and Rajagopalachari accepted the office of Chief Minister of Madras state.

His strategy was direct and simple. It began with a declaration of war. "I am your Enemy Number One," he announced to the Communist lawmakers in May, 1952, and "may I say," he added, "you are my Enemy Number One. That is my policy from A to Z." Using words independent India had not heard, he told the legislature that "I am here to save my country from the traps and dangers of the Communist party."

Great political general that he was, Rajaji next aimed to divide his enemy's forces. He was not concerned, he announced, with the "hotch-potch opposition" in front of him. This served as a shrewd hint to the allies of the Communists to withdraw from their "hotch-potch" coalition with the Reds, to quit the front and get out of the line of fire. Knowing how hot C.R.'s fire could be, a number of wavering oppositionists sought cover behind him or in neutrality.

Having scattered the timid fellow travelers by indicating that no easy Communist victory impended, Rajaji turned to his own demoralized forces. Under the guidance of Gandhi, Nehru, Patel, Azad, Rajaji, and others, the Congress party had won national independence for India. Now it expected humble gratitude from the people. The pleasure of playing with new power and the smell of the fleshpots of patronge intoxicated a number of Congress party leaders who forgot their duties and promises. The country had been led to believe that when the British went Paradise would descend to earth. But too many local and provincial politicians regarded the exit of England as a signal to begin scrambling for jobs, and sometimes the chief qualification of candidates was not ability but imprisonment during the struggle for national freedom. Little men sought their personal reward instead of concentrating on the people's welfare. The opposition fed on these deficiencies.

The original revolutionary impetus of the Congress party was national, not social. Gandhi's was social and national; indeed his social ideals were paramount, he wanted a free India in order to free the Indians. The Congress party, however, had followed Gandhi without accepting either his nonviolence or his program of reform. It rode in his train to Independence Station; some, in fact, got off earlier, as soon as the lights of the fractured independence of the Indian-Pakistan solution appeared on the horizon. The Congress party, accordingly, tended to rest on the achievement of independence rather than press forward to the social revolution. Hence the appeal of the Communists. By implication, they offered to fulfill the Congress party's broken pledges.

Rajaji saw this. As a first step he instructed the district officials to rule and instructed the Congress party to keep hands off. No more nepotism, political favors, or wire-pulling. Contracts were to be let and officials appointed on merit. Quickly, as a result, orderly government was restored and public respect for authority re-established.

Politics in Madras, however, was primarily food. Scarcity had induced an earlier Congress party ministry to ration food and control its distribution. Results: black-marketeering, hoarding, high prices, bribing of officials, and greater distress.

Rajaji decontrolled. Hoards came out of hiding, prices dropped, the people were pleased. Overnight, the political climate of Madras changed from storm to calm. C.R. now had a respite for planning further innovations.

"Do not lay traps for poor people, that is my appeal to the Communist party," Rajaji said in the state legislature. "Do not tell stories, do not exaggerate, do not work up discontent." But trapping the poor is their business and discontent is the wind in their sails. Rajaji, therefore, did not limit himself to appeals; nor did he resort to suppression. He introduced a land reform in the fertile district of Tanjore with a population of three million. Elsewhere he guaranteed peasants against eviction from their farms. Aware that on the countryside teachers are key persons who write letters and petitions for illiterates and guide the perplexed, C.R., whose budget did not permit raising teachers' salaries, granted their children free education through high school.

Everywhere in India, capital is scarce and expensive while labor is abundant, cheap, and underemployed. In villages, unemployment and underemployment are especially high; they may affect 200,000,000 individuals. A 1950-51 survey by India's Ministry of Labor showed that 17,600,000 rural families, or 89,760,000 persons, belonged to the class of agricultural laborers who owned no or little land. Of these, 5,100,000 families, comprising 26,000,000 souls, lived in Madras state. They were Rajaji's problem. Most Indian farmers are too poor to employ others. The Ministry's survey found that 20.2 per cent of the rural population did not engage in farming, 27.2 per cent were themselves tenants with inadequate acreages, and only the landlords (22.2 per cent) intermittently employed farm laborers who, consequently, remained idle 147 days each year, and in India it is almost literally true that if you do not work you do not eat—unless you are rich.

When I talked with Rajaji in Madras in September, 1952, he did not disapprove of the several giant multipurpose projects, such as the Damodar River Valley irrigation, hydroelectric, and water-transportation authority, and the Bhakra-Nangal dam, which the federal government of India had inaugurated, but he observed that they put a strain on the nation's limited resources of money and engineering personnel and tapped only a minor fraction of "India's biggest capital reserve"—labor. Throughout his own state, Rajaji launched a large number of small irrigation and water-conservation schemes which employed masses of men and a minimum of money and machines.

In India the eye explains why Gandhi, and Gandhians like Rajaji, frowned on too much mechanization. The men whose white turbans and white loincloths—that is all they wear—and perspiring chocolate-colored skin gleamed in the tropical sun as they pushed and pulled rubber-wheeled two-ton wagons laden with goods through Madras city streets would have resented being displaced by draft animals, not to speak of trucks. A well-known Indian writer argues that eight million human beings have as much horsepower as the Damodar Valley Project, so why not use them instead of condemning them to starvation? The view would be widely held in India and elsewhere in Asia. Chakravarti Rajagopalachari, in any case, urged that India "must stand erect on the foundation of agriculture. Work on the land and the raising of food must be our principal concern." He felt that the first Five Year Plan for the federal government started at the top instead of in the soil. "Our next main concern," Rajaji continued, was cottage weaving. He wished to revive the hand looms of the villages so that the underemployed and the unemployed could clothe themselves and, also, sell to others. To achieve this, "I declared war," he said, on mill-made dhotis or loincloths for men and saris for women, and appealed to the entire country to buy village textiles. He also demanded that the government prohibit factories from manufacturing dhotis and saris which compete with peasant output. This "is not politics or economics," he explained, "but human fellowship and compassion for the man and the woman and the suckling baby. The weavers know their craft and work hard and produce the best cloth in the world for you to wear. India consists of peasants and weavers. What is left of patriotism or politics if you do not feel for them? Do not turn the weaver away and go and buy factory-made cloth." He met with scant success in the cities. But the peasantry was with him.

Some Westernized Indian minds called Rajaji old-fashioned and said he wanted to turn back the clock. He twitted them and asked, progress at what cost, and for whom? "I belong to an older generation," he admitted in a speech before the All-India Home Science Conference, and now things were becoming different, now people slept in beds, ate at tables, and sat in chairs. In his day, life was lived on the floor, or on the ground. But "let us not imagine," he suggested, "that we have raised the whole of India four feet high. We have raised only a few families, and all our instructions and courses are suited only for a few."

Critics might charge that he was obstructing progress; but by drawing strength from the ancient roots of India, he continued to stress the welfare of the tens of millions, not of the Westernized thousands. The monsoon had passed by Madras six times, giving the state six lean years of drought. "The rains won't come," Rajaji declared shortly after he became Chief Minister, "because we are sinners. . . . I am advanced in years. I have had experience in life, and I am convinced about the efficacy of prayers to bring rain." The people prayed and, luckily, it rained—not much, and not enough to save the crop, but the monsoon next year brought copious rains, and the people's faith in Rajaji must have been reinforced.

He was a devout Hindu and often drove home a political program by tying it to holy scripture. Arguing against the abandonment of the study of English in India, for example, he said it was one of the languages "given us by our Goddess Saraswati." In this instance he was the Westerner tilting at superpatriots with a Hindu lance. Though a high Brahman, moreover, he taught the dignity of manual labor. He told an audience that he had once been a barber and knew the job of laundryman. For a year he even tried to learn shoemaking (though it is forbidden to orthodox Hindus to work leather) but gave it up as too difficult. From religious scruples, Rajaji never touched meat, fish or eggs. Yet as Chief Minister he fostered the fishing industry and poultry farming. Heresy of heresies for a Hindu, he even deprecated the consumption of fodder by the millions of India's overage cows and would, he wrote me, have taken drastic measures to eliminate the tragic waste. By implication, this meant the killing of cattle to promote the welfare of India and her poor.

Although Rajaji was operating in Madras state he remained a national figure. In 1952, throughout India, every political conversation led in five minutes to a discussion of Prime Minister Nehru and within five more minutes to the question of who would succeed him. Usually the first successor mentioned would be Rajagopalachari. In almost the same breath the name of Rajendra Prasad, the President of India, was added as a possibility. Rajagopalachari was seventy-three, Rajendra Prasad sixty-eight, Nehru sixty-three. Occasionally, Jayaprakash Narayan, the Socialist, a younger man in his fifties, appeared in the speculative list of candidates.

India boasts many efficient administrators in the federal and state governments. Several Cabinet members in New Delhi and ambassadors abroad are of high caliber. But even more than having ability and wisdom, India's top political leader must be a national figure, known to the entire country, sanctified by association with the Mahatma, and, above all, judged capable of holding India together. Having become an independent country before she was a nation—which is why she became two nations—India fears dissolution. Indians are aware of their deeply fissiparous, divisive tendencies; they have several emotional loyalties: to a province, a regional language, a caste, a religion. The crowning loyalty to the nation is a new, delicate plant, and it is one of Jawaharlal Nehru's historic achievements that he has been nurturing it successfully. Much as individual Indians might condemn this or that policy or quality of Nehru's they would defend him as the agent and symbol of national unity. Rajaji could have served the same purpose. His appeal to the youth was less than Nehru's, his appeal to the peasants and traditional Hindus greater.

He was superior to Nehru as an organizer. Rajaji could not rival Nehru as an actor, nor could Nehru compete with Rajaji as a political analyst.

"If Gandhi had been sixty when India was liberated!" Indians lamented. "If Rajaji were twenty years younger!" It was mournful to observe Rajaji's big, undimmed Brahman brain in a wasting body. To be sure, when he said, a second time, "I am frail, I was frail as a boy," I argued that since he was frail as a boy and had survived to seventy-three, he could be frail and keep going for many years. But there was obviously a vanishing truth in such logic.

India inclines to worship a hero and follow a leader, and men therefore play a more decisive role in politics there than in most other countries. The weakness of Indian Communism, it is said, is the absence of a popular leader. But neither does hero worship help to inculcate democratic habits.

CHAPTER THIRTY-ONE

Burma, Land of Laughter

BURMA is a blessed land. It is a land of gold and laughter, the solid gold of its pagodas, the rice or "white gold" which is its chief wealth, and the laughter of the people whose round Asian faces are almost always lit up with joy.

After seven weeks in India I flew, in less than three hours, from Calcutta to Rangoon, the capital of Burma. At the airport I realized that during those seven weeks I had lived in a world of tension and frustration. I realized it because suddenly they were gone, replaced by gaiety without reason. In fact, there was reason for gloom. Burma had been fighting a civil war with Communists and others since 1948. Two days before my arrival insurgents blew a hole in the water main at a place thirty-six miles from Rangoon and thereby cut off the city's central supply of water. This dynamiting—the fifth in four months—occurred just four hours after the damage from a similar attack five days earlier had been repaired. It left Burma with no more pipes for replacement. Rangoon, a tropical town of 700,000, was now dependent on its fire hydrants for water. As I drove in from the airport, crowds had assembled at the hydrants and were filling petrol tins and pails to carry home, or were squatting, the men in loincloths and the beautiful women in strapless slips, lathering and then pouring water over themselves with bowls or cups. Brown children splashed in the cooling puddles, and women slapped their soaped laundry on the pavement stones—the Eastern substitute for scrubbing. Though the city was in crisis the people seemed to be at a picnic, and the relation of adults to children and of the men and women to one another suggested a pleasant lightness and love of life.

Since my stay in Burma in 1952, I have been asking what accounts for the contrast between the jolly temperament of the Burmese and the austere mood of India. Some say it is Buddhism. Burma is Buddhist, and Buddhism, one is told, conduces to carefree living. But Buddha was a Hindu, and Buddhism first developed in India about the fifth century B.C. as a reform movement of Hinduism. Today, however, India has no Buddhist community. Hinduism, an absorptive creed, undoubtedly took on some aspects of Buddhism, but not its simplicity. Buddhism is certain where Hinduism is speculative. The Buddhist is extrovert, the Hindu self-tortured and involuted. Buddhism has no caste system with its segregation, jealousies, and hatreds. Burma has none of the Hindu food taboos which aggravate the problem of nutrition in India and deepen religious cleavages. Women in Burma are treated as equals; they do not hide, shyly, in the back room or behind a curtain when nonfamily menfolk appear. Relations between the sexes are free from the restraints of Eastern tradition and Western puritanism. Buddhism teaches equality and moderation. These departures from Hinduism were needed in India and therefore evolved there, but instead of keeping them, Hinduism exported them eastward to Burma, Siam, Indo-China, Indonesia, China, Mongolia, and Japan. En route, of course, they underwent regional modifications.

It may be that Buddhism suits the Oriental. Burma is the beginning of the Orient. India is the product of Aryan, Arab, Persian, and Turco-Afghan (Mogul) migrations superimposed on the original natives. The Mongoloid Burmese, on the other hand, came down in successive waves thousands of years ago from Tibet and China. Burmese culture is Tibetan overlaid with some Hinduism and much Buddhism. In Burmese pagodas, the temples of Buddhism, one finds strange-shaped, unnatural animal figures of a primitive animism guarding shrines of the Buddha who, perhaps more than any person, achieved detachment from man's animal characteristics and rose to the highest pinnacle of spirituality.

Oriental Burma, like non-Oriental Ceylon, is Buddhist and happy. Burma has no ulcers. Are the Burmese happy because they are Buddhist or did they adopt Buddhism because they were happy? Who knows? Economics is a factor. Cares are few. The climate reduces clothing requirements to a minimum. Food is plentiful. (In India it was scarce for centuries.) Bananas seem to grow in every back yard, and rice is available in excess. The size of Texas, Burma has only 19,000,000 inhabitants, or 70 persons to the square mile compared with 250 in India and 500 in Japan. Land is no problem. Anybody can acquire a farm by going out into the near-by jungle and clearing it. These fortunate material conditions, reinforcing the message of Buddhism, make for happiness.

Despite the pacifism which is the core of Buddha's teaching, the Burmese temper can flare wildly, and Burma has had more than her share of murders and fighting. The British, coming from India, were forced to wage three wars, at intervals from 1824 to 1885, before they could defeat the Burmese kings and annex the entire country.

Foreign rule, as always, bred opposition, and under the impact of Western nationalism a demand for independence emerged. The British, in 1937, made a concession to it without satisfying it by severing Burma from India and making it a separate colony.

Resenting British domination, many Burmese welcomed Japan's victories over England in the Second World War and received the Japanese as liberators when they seized Rangoon on March 9, 1942. Partly this was due to illusions skillfully induced by Tokyo's "Asia for the Asiatics" propaganda, and partly, perhaps chiefly, to the irrepressible desire of a colonial people to oust the foreign ruler no matter what may follow and even if what follows is another foreign ruler. The urge for liberation from imperialism is both rational and irrational; it keeps no records of profits and loss.

When the British Labor government granted freedom to India in 1947, it did the same for Burma, and on January 4, 1948, Burma became independent, but, unlike India, Pakistan, and Ceylon, she chose not to join the British Commonwealth. Astrologers consulted by the government fixed 4:20 A.M. as the most auspicious moment for the birth of the new republic. Since then the annual celebrations of the event begin at that unearthly ordained hour.

Seven weeks later the Communists decided to overthrow the new government. The decision was arrived at in a conference held in Calcutta from February 24 to 27, 1948.

The Conference was outwardly sponsored by the World Federation of Democratic Youth and the International Union of Students, but actually it was an important conclave of policy-makers, including men from Russia. At this conference it was laid down that the communist parties should initiate and lead violent insurrections and civil wars in the South and South-East Asiatic countries. Accordingly, uprisings followed in Burma in April, in Malaya in June and in Indonesia in September.[1]

Burma has a frontier of almost a thousand miles with China, yet when I asked U Ba Swe, the Defense Minister of Burma, on October 1, 1952, whether Red China had helped the Burmese Communists, he said, "As far as we know, no." U Nu, the Burmese Prime Minister, gave me the same information as did foreign observers who would gladly have burdened Red China with every demonstrable guilt. Perhaps China was not interested in aiding a Russian policy move.

The Communist uprising, abetted by parallel revolts of the Karens, a tribal minority, of the PVO's (People's Volunteer Organization consisting of pro-Communist, wartime, anti-Japanese resisters), and, later, of at least ten thousand Kuomintang troops who escaped into Burma from China after having been defeated by the Chinese Communists, gave the Burmese government considerable trouble. Its army was small and inadequately trained because, since the Burmese had fought the British in the nineteenth century, Britain never recruited them in her colonial armies. The Burmese government received some arms shipments from England and a gift of ten gunboats from the

---

[1] *The Communist Party of India*, a short history by M. R. Masani, with an introduction by Guy Wint. Issued under the auspices of the Inst. of Pacific Relations, New York: The Macmillan Company, 1954, pp. 89-90.

United States, but its forces always suffered from insufficient equipment. In the mountainous, river-valley and jungle terrain of Burma, moreover, the Communist attackers enjoyed many advantages. When I asked two U.S. military observers and the British military attaché in Rangoon why the Burmese authorities could not guard such an important fixture as the water main which supplied the capital, they said it would require all the government's soldiers to protect the thirty-six miles of pipe from the source to the city and even then two daring rebels with sticks of dynamite could blow up a section of the pipe on a dark night. Notwithstanding all these difficulties, and despite the wide geographic dispersal of the insurgent groups, the U Nu government had broken the back of the revolt by the end of 1952. Mopping-up operations continued long after that.

The Communists wanted control, and if they could not get control they would create chaos. They failed in Burma because the government had the sympathy of the people, and that proved decisive. The population opposed the Communists for three reasons:

1. Eighty-five per cent of the country is Buddhist—the remainder is Moslem, Christian, Hindu, or Animist—and the government leaders were Buddhists, some, like U Nu, very devout Buddhists. Buddhism is intimately intertwined with life. Most youths spend several weeks living with the ascetic monks in their abbeys and go back when they are older for brief refresher courses. Monks preside at birthday, wedding, and other family ceremonies, and are frequently invited to meals. At the fabulous Shwedagon Pagoda—the Golden Pagoda of Rangoon—built atop a flattened hill, one ascends 166 steps to a vast marble floor, 900 feet long and 700 feet wide, which forms the base of a giant, gilded, terraced cone ending in a graceful spire and, also, of innumerable dragon-guarded shrines and niches housing sitting and recumbent Buddhas, some encased in thick layers of gold, others made of white clay to which the faithful attach half-inch squares of gold leaf until the entire image is gold-plated. In the larger shrines, families seated on the stone floors eat from pots and pans of home cooked food brought to the temple. Each group enjoys the company of two or three monks with shaven heads and wearing yolk-of-egg yellow robes. After the rich repast, women, men, and monks smoke enormous cheroots, which make the Churchill cigar look like a pup, while Buddhas smile down enigmatically and children frolic unhampered. The monks are unworldly, and three I engaged in conversation had not heard of Russia or America or Communism. But

they are close to the people and wield enormous influence, and since the leaders of free Burma were good Buddhists and adhered to Buddhist ritual in official ceremonies (U Nu was contemplating a world Buddhist congress), they supported the government.

2. Burma was independent, not a colony, and the government was defending national freedom against conspirators who took orders from abroad.

3. The government was revolutionary. The Communist uprising, therefore, was counterrevolution. As in Turkey and Yugoslavia, foreign-inspired Communists representing outside imperialist interference could not win against a regime with an indigenous program of land and other reform. Burma is 85 per cent agricultural. Its main plague before the war was absentee land ownership. If a peasant's crop failed or if he spent more than he earned (for a wedding, perhaps) he would borrow and lose his farm to the moneylender. In 1937, half of the tilled land of the country had been alienated in this fashion, and "in the richest rice-growing districts of the delta it was higher still, absentee landlords owning 70 per cent of the cultivated area. More than half was in the hands of Indian money-lenders."[2] One of the first acts of the new Burmese government was to nationalize land and make it difficult for foreigners to acquire farms. Big landlords were deprived of their acreage and compensated. As long as peasants till their land it is theirs in usufruct and neither the government nor an individual can deprive them of it. This single piece of revolutionary legislation—the land reform—doomed the Communist uprising to collapse.

The heart and head of Burma's social revolution has been U Nu. ("U" is the equivalent of "Mister.") With Ramon Magsaysay, President of the Philippines, he is the most outstanding and talented of the new Asian statesmen who made their reputations since the Second World War. I first saw him in his family sitting room. He was wearing a white-and-black check *longyi* skirt, a collarless shirt with thin jacket over it, and old sandals which he slipped off and on his bare feet. The sitting room was filled with about thirty Burmese journalists, and U Nu had sent word that I was to attend the conference and then interview him privately. It was the most informal press conference imaginable, more like a friendly party than an official meeting between journalists and Prime Minister. They asked questions. His reply would often be argued by the writers among

[2] London *Economist*, July 15, 1950, p. 125.

themselves, and he would argue it too when he succeeded in getting the floor. Sometimes he asked them questions, and those answers would be debated back and forth. (A press attaché was giving me a running account of the exchange.) Laughter frequently punctuated the proceedings, and U Nu smiled most of the time. He was then forty-five years old. I noticed no tension in him but felt certain he had everything under control. He is usually relaxed, resolute, and forgiving. If he bursts into a temper he quickly apologizes. "To err is only human," he insists, "and to err with sincere motives is pardonable. I feel that it is far more desirable to commit mistakes in the sincere discharge of one's duties than by vacillating and fumbling timidity in the face of work." He was speaking to a national frailty.

Left alone with him, I inquired whether the large framed photograph of Gandhi behind his chair was always there or only today, October 2, the Mahatma's birthday. "Always," U Nu replied. Gandhi, like Buddha, was a reformer of Hinduism, but as Gandhi grew older he became less of a Hindu and more of a Buddhist. He would probably have disputed this assessment of himself and pointed to his fervent faith in God as contrasted with the avowed atheism of most Buddhists. He combined Judean-Christian monotheism with Buddhist rejection of castes, inequality, and formalistic religion. Gandhi's wide acceptance in India may be what Sigmund Freud called "the return of the repressed." Buddhism had remained repressed in India, its birthplace, until it returned to live in Gandhism. Obviously, therefore, U Nu found complete harmony between Gandhi and Buddha. He is Gandhian in temperament and Buddhist in faith. Buddhism is an ethical philosophy. The ubiquitous image of Buddha in the pagodas is no idol, it is the representation of the Gautama, Prince of India, who, in his twenty-ninth year, renounced wife, child, palace, pleasures, and power, and thereby subsequently achieved Nirvana, or complete spiritual liberation from the human body.

U Nu has expressed a desire to retire from politics and become a Buddhist monk. He is up daily at an early hour to say his prayers and recite Buddhist verses. With Hindus and Buddhists, U Nu believes in reincarnation, in a constant cycle of death and life. He adds, however, that a person who has "annihilated not only hate, fear, and carnal desires but also all cravings and attachments" attains the highest peak of enlightenment and "is not reborn at all after his death."

Buddhism is an ethical philosophy; in private talks and in public speeches, U Nu mixes morals with politics. His social revolution is aimed, as was Gandhi's, not at the enthronement of an ism or the exaltation of a system of government or economy, but at the purification of man. "Revolution," U Nu declared, "is none other than a sincere effort to uproot all those factors—ideologies, thoughts, organizations, or the machineries of government—which are opposed to human progress and the mental and physical well-being of mankind." He scoffs at the revolutionary pretensions of Communists who would rule through "a ruthless dictatorship." "A dictatorship," he insists, "is a dictatorship whether it is called 'the dictatorship of the proletariat' or by any other term. In such a regime the political power is not derived from the people; it is derived from a small group of sharpers who know how to perpetuate their power." He therefore regards the Communists as "reactionaries of the first magnitude." He fights Communists not merely because they are violent and owe allegiance to a foreign government but because they cannot contribute to "human progress and the mental and physical well-being of mankind."

Nevertheless, and though the Burmese government had for years been combating Communist insurgence in the field, a Communist party was functioning in Burma. I asked U Nu why. "We are a democracy," he explained. Those who use arms would be met with arms. The others could try to persuade. Even in the midst of a civil war he was not afraid of them. He is a man of faith in men. He summoned the Communist guerrillas, in a speech on August 4, 1952, to "come into the open and lay before the people the plans they intend to adopt if they come into power." They continued to wage war. But his democratic approach laid the basis of their defeat.

U Nu's aim is a state built on five pillars: "physical, intellectual, social, economic, and moral." He is not worried, he has said, about the first four. "But I am worried about the pillar of moral strength." Sometimes he sounds more like a prophet than a politician. "Look where I will," he thunders, "in government circles, political circles, or business circles, I see people out for gain, devoid of all scruples, as if they were possessed by the devil of greed." Nothing will destroy freedom more speedily, he asserts, "than the decadence of character." Accordingly, he talks honestly to the country. "For heaven's sake," he said in one speech, "don't ask for quick results like the miracle of sowing a mango seed now and in the twinkling of an eye make it bear fruit. We don't care to delude the masses like a magician."

The practical results U Nu seeks to attain are modest indeed. He begins by pointing out that thirty of every hundred Burmese babies die at birth. "What a sad story!" The average length of life in Burma is thirty years, he said. Our "soil is incredibly fertile" yet the seventeen and a half million acres which are farmed comprise less than 50 per cent of the available land.

Burma's welfare state program provides for a little hospital here, a new bridge there, roads, wells, schools, reservoirs, artificial lakes, and some government buildings. Beyond these primary needs, the state must train men and women for official positions, technical tasks, and factory labor. The country is woefully deficient in persons equipped to run a modern industrial society. There is a scarcity of good mill hands, good engineers, good teachers, and good heads of government departments. This is another way of saying that Burma lacks a middle class and a working class; proof that it is precapitalist and pre-Socialist.

It is only necessary to walk around the streets of Rangoon and drive out into the countryside to be convinced that Burma is in a precapitalist stage of development with capitalism or Socialism still to come. Most of the business of Rangoon is done with miniscule capital or no capital from sidewalk baskets or in tiny, man-sized kiosks, cubicles, and stalls. Most of the "dining out" is done from paper bags sold by peripatetic hawkers or at old wooden tables and broken benches on pavements. Most of the industry operates in store-sized shops which make or repair household appliances. Such enterprises, and some sawmills and rice mills, comprise the bulk of the "private capitalism" of Rangoon and of Burma.

Before independence, trade, transport, mining, oil production, and rice export were in the hands of Indians and Englishmen, and the profits drained out of the country leaving it poor in capital and backward in development. Today, Burma's policy is to keep business in the hands of Burmese. This economic nationalism, so frequently encountered in newborn states, is the major ingredient of what her spokesmen naïvely call "Socialism."

When U Nu and U Ba Swe, both sons of merchants, and many of their fellow university students came into politics in the mid-1930's, not to be a Socialist meant being a reactionary. The Burmese Socialists and Marxists did not know Marx or Engels. To them Marxism was synonymous with national independence, industrial progress, and certain vague ideas that added up to the welfare state.

Defense Minister Ba Swe received me in his home at nine in the morning. He wore a green silk wraparound *longyi* skirt, a white jacket, and under it a collarless shirt buttoned tight at the neck with gold or gilt heart-shaped studs down the front and gold or gilt cufflinks. On his finger was a gold ring with a pearl.

I began by saying that I had read a speech he delivered in December, 1951, to a trade union meeting in which he called himself a Marxist. "What do you mean when you say you are a Marxist?" I asked.

"I don't understand your question," he said.

"I mean what is Marxism to you?"

"I find it difficult to explain," he commented.

"Well, please tell me," I begged, "just what you think of when you say you are a Marxist."

"I believe in it," he affirmed. "In my student days it was the fashion, but I believe in it. It is a social philosophy and acts as guidance in the class war." He then spoke with feeling and deep understanding of the relationship between Buddhism and welfare state Socialism.

Obviously, however, no class war was possible in the absence of a working class, middle class, and capitalist class. Burma's class war, therefore, was really a national revolt against foreign capital, a struggle for political and economic independence. U Ba Swe saw this. "We cannot be a Socialist state," he admitted, "without a proletariat, and to have a proletariat we must industrialize." Since private capital was not available, the state would serve as the new capitalist. Burmese "state capitalism" in 1952, consisted in government ownership of the country's airlines, railroads, and shipping, and of the one factory, a textile mill with newly imported machinery and employing six hundred persons, which would answer to the description of modern industry.

The biggest and most remunerative state business is the purchase of rice in the country and its sale abroad. Rice is the chief food of the Orient, and Burma is one of the world's chief exporters. The government pays the peasant at least half of what it receives from the exported rice,[3] and the surplus, a considerable sum for Burma—

[3] Frank N. Trager and Helen G. Trager, *Burma: Land of Golden Pagodas.* New York: Foreign Policy Association, Headline Books, March-April, 1954, p. 29. Mr. Trager was Director of the U.S. Technical Co-operation Administration (Point Four) in Burma from 1951 to 1953.

she had 1,600,000 tons available for export in 1953, when the fluctuating world market price was perhaps $130 a ton—goes to expand the country's economy. The government's foreign sales of teak and other woods, and of copper, cobalt, lead, silver, nickel, antimony, tin, and tungsten also yield a profit which becomes national capital for economic development.

Burma is a one-crop country. Industrialization will give it economic balance and presumably raise living standards. A high standard of living creates a middle class—tradesmen, teachers, professional people, officials, and all others who serve without being direct agricultural or industrial producers. The middle class, when employed, lends stability to a society both by reason of its central position and because its welfare depends on national growth and internal peace.

The strength of the new youthful Burma is that its government "with a cabinet averaging under forty years of age,"[4] is the answer to national necessities. Under its present guidance it will become a capitalist-Socialist state.

Small and sensibly led, Burma has no international ambitions. The government chiefs declare that since Burma is within striking distance of powerful Communist China and accessible to mighty Western nations "our foreign policy is a neutral one." Occasionally, to be sure, the government is tempted to play the role of intermediary between the two blocs, but more often it resists the tug of personal or national vanity and minds its own business. By and large, sympathies are with the West. U Ba Swe, who had visited satellized Poland, said what he saw there was "crude imperialism." Kyaw Nyein, Minister of Industry, and the intellectual leader of Burmese Socialism, has vigorously denounced Soviet imperialism as ruthless and dangerous. U Nu is soberly aware of the potential menace of a new Chinese imperialism pouring over Southeast Asia, and he accordingly fears any act of Western appeasement or Eastern naïveté which might encourage aggression.

But nobody can free himself from his own experiences, and U Nu believes that if a country is independent and governed by democratically elected persons devoted to the people and capable of executing plans for their welfare no harm will come to it. Other countries, however, have had different experiences. U Nu's description fitted Finland, but in 1939, the Soviets invaded Finland and, though

[4] *Ibid.*, p. 4.

a united nation fought back, it was crushed under Russia's weight. Norway and Denmark were prosperous democracies with progressive governments, but that did not prevent Hitler from conquering them in 1940 without the aid of fifth columnists. If, in the future, aggression is not easy it will undoubtedly be due to the inner strength of threatened countries but also, and perhaps mainly, to the deterrent of collective military power even though, for adequate reason, the endangered nations do not participate in the international defense system which protects them from foreign attack.

CHAPTER THIRTY-TWO

Peaceful Thailand

THAILAND, the size of Spain, is a nation-wide Venice. Except in the high, dry northeast, the people live on, in, or at the water. A considerable portion of the 1,200,000 inhabitants of the capital city of Bangkok make their homes on flat-bottom boats moored in the wide Chow-Phya River or in its numerous arms and tributaries or in the endless network of tidal canals which lace through town. Peasants from up-country row down to Bangkok with their hand-made pottery, charcoal, fruits, vegetables, and bright birds in cages and live on the canals for days, even weeks, till they sell their wares. The quays are Bangkok's marketplace. Countless thousands of Thais occupy permanent wooden shacks built on piles sunk in the mud of streams and canals.

Children learn to swim as soon as they can crawl. Games are played amid the rushes and lotus plants which grow lush everywhere. Boys and girls up to the ages of six and seven go about naked except for a luck cord around their middles. Housewives step down from their living rooms into the slow-moving brooks to fetch water for cooking, wash their dishes, do their laundry, and bathe. The canals serve as sewage drains, water closets, and mosquito incubators. As the water passes each home its filth content mounts. No doubt the Thais, or Siamese, acquire some immunity to unhygienic living by living unhygienically. But malaria, intestinal diseases, and tuberculosis are big killers. With only two thousand physicians for eighteen million inhabitants, nature takes its course.

So does almost everything else in easygoing, Buddhist Siam. The farmers, who constitute 85 per cent of the population, float lightly on the tide of time; their methods have not changed in millennia. Fruit orchards just grow; the trees do not stand in military formation at the corners of immaculate squares as in Europe and America. They shoot up helter-skelter, undirected by the baton of man: the thin high coconut palm is neighbor to the squat fat banana, the betel nut rises by the side of the pineapple—and in the shade of these flourish sugar cane, mangoes, papayas, and even tobacco. This jumbled jungle condition, the experts say, conduces to balanced bird and bug life. Insects attack and liquidate one another instead of the vegetation. Since this is the spirit of Thailand, the political pests behave the same way, eating or tolerating one another in accordance with mood and season but rarely involving the people who do not know or do not care and could not change things if they did. Thailand, therefore, is not a dictatorship; it is several dictatorships existing side by side with rival accumulations of power. Together they have total power, but none has a monopoly of power. That is the extent of the democracy.

It all began when several young men with European experience, notably Pridi Phanomyong, who had picked up Socialist thoughts in Paris, and Pibul Songgram, who studied at St. Cyr, the French military academy, conceived the bright idea of fencing the absolute King around with a modern constitution. Their method was the coup d'état.

The first theatrical coup took place on June 24, 1932, when Pridi and Pibul, leading a column of no more than a hundred fellows, marched on the royal palace and demanded a constitution. A few shots were fired. Casualties numbered zero. The King complied.

True to Siamese character, this was only a half-coup. The King still had considerable authority. In April, 1933, therefore, Pibul, who was now Assistant Minister of Defense, paraded two or three thousand troops through Bangkok streets and told the monarchist government to step down. It did.

Six months later, the monarchists tried their hand at a *coup d'état*. A royal prince gathered several battalions of soldiers in the provinces, took some towns against no opposition, and advanced on Bangkok. Before attacking, however, he parleyed with the government. Meanwhile Pibul, masterminded by Pridi, mobilized his assault guards. In the interval, desultory fighting occurred and a handful of men were killed.

With both camps poised for battle and neither venturing to precipitate it, a government colonel jumped on a railway locomotive and drove it toward a train of freight cars that contained the rebels' entire supply of ammunition. As the engine sped forward bullets played a staccato tune on its iron sides but failed to stop it before it crashed into the arsenal on wheels and effectively blocked its progress. This melodramatic performance of the gallant colonel ended the royalist countercoup and sealed the fate of the absolute monarchy. In 1935, the King lost interest in his eclipsed crown, handed it to his young nephew Ananda, and voluntarily went into exile in Europe where he died in 1940.

Pibul's star rose; in 1938 he became Prime Minister. Pridi, on the other hand, played at Utopia. He advocated a Southeast Asian federation, government industries, and co-operative marketing.

When the Pacific war broke out in December, 1941, Japan sent an ultimatum to the Thai government demanding the right of transit through the country to Burma and the right to quarter troops. Pridi counseled active resistance. Pibul acted in character: he neither rejected nor accepted. He failed to reply. Thereupon the Japanese invaded the land. Pibul put up a token fight for twenty-four hours, then capitulated and co-operated where he had to. At the same time, however, he flagrantly connived at Pridi's open support of the Western Allies. Pridi, who had been named regent, organized the Free Thai movement which, throughout the war, maintained contact with the American Office of Strategic Services (OSS) and its British equivalent. In the beginning the Americans and British landed in Siam by boat, but later, as the liaison was perfected, they came and departed in their own planes. Pibul's director of police collaborated with the Free Thais and facilitated the work of the Western undercover agents. Japan was mistress of Thailand, but kept no strong force in the country and her Anglo-American enemies enjoyed free access and egress and did not lose a man in all their hazardous operations through four years of war. Despite the Japanese, leading Siamese traveled to Washington and back.

Pibul's bifurcated wartime policy was a classic balancing act. No matter how intricate the somersault, this indestructible political acrobat, by combining luck with skill, always landed on his feet and stayed in office. He survived coups in 1948 and 1949. His most hair-raising adventure and hairbreadth escape occurred one Friday afternoon in June, 1951. At four-thirty, Prime Minister Pibul went aboard a dredger anchored in the Chow-Phya River to accept it as a gift from the United States. At a signal, a squad of Thai Marines on the vessel drew their revolvers, surrounded Pibul, and carried him to a landing boat and then to the Thai navy's flagship upriver. Simultaneously, the navy dispatched armed sailors into Bangkok to seize the city. The army and police prepared to resist. A battle seemed to impend. At 7 P.M. the naval radio announced that the Prime Minister, the post office, and the official broadcasting station were in its hands. The police radio immediately issued a denial. At 8 P.M., the navy thrust a microphone in front of Pibul and got him to broadcast an appeal against bloodshed.

Negotiations during the night between the two sides proved vain. At dawn the Thai air force appeared over the river and proceeded to dive-bomb the navy flagship on which the Prime Minister was imprisoned. Nobody knew whether this was a friendly or unfriendly act. Miraculously, the flagship was hit, caught fire, and began to sink. Pibul, age fifty-six, jumped overboard and began swimming toward Bangkok to reach his friends. But bullets began popping all around him, so he ducked, turned around, and swam back into the arms of his naval abductors.

The navy coup leaders now took fright at these serious developments and telephoned the government forces in Bangkok to come and fetch their Prime Minister.

The coup had lasted from Friday afternoon to Sunday and nobody was killed. Pibul was wroth with the navy for stealing him, the air force for bombing him, and his friends for firing at him while he was breasting the river waves. Several airmen and admirals were arrested and tried.

While I was in Bangkok in October, 1952, foreigners and Thais hourly expected a coup. There had been none for a long time and astrologers said the time was propitious. Rivalries between the contending forces in the country were boiling tempestuously. The annual police parade had been scheduled and the King would review it in the palace square. This offered an opportunity to Chief of Police Pao Sriyanonda to gather his forces and use them for political aggrandizement. His armed strength, one heard, numbered forty thousand men equipped with tanks and cannon. Surely they were not needed to regulate traffic or maintain order among the peaceful Buddhist Thais. But Police General Pao had a rival in General Sarit, the commander of the First Army in garrison in Bangkok. In this rivalry, Pao enjoyed the support of his father-in-law, General Pin, Commander-in-Chief of the entire army, and Deputy Prime Minister. Sarit resented this mighty alliance.

Over the week end—coups in Siam seem to have a predilection for week ends—the kettle was expected to blow its lid. The capital buzzed with excitement and expectation. At dinner, lunch, and cocktails, and in serious interviews, the coup was the central subject of conversation and gossip. The army called all officers and men back from leave. Sunday night I saw police armed with carbines at the four corners of all street intersections—which was most unusual.

The police parade took place on a blazing hot Monday afternoon. Pao, a big, jolly man, staged a great show. For ordinary people—foreign journalists, Thai military and civilians—elaborate marquees with seats were erected on one side of the vast square in the center of which stood an equestrian statue. For the King, the diplomatic corps, and other VIP's, a gold-and-red wooden structure had been built. Since His Majesty King Phumiphol Aduldej would be present the diplomats were required to wear "white tie" outfits including woolen suits, stiff shirts, and vests. Even ordinary mortals like myself had to have on a jacket and tie. Much perspiration ran down backs and brows and in the marquees much free ice-cold Coca-Cola ran down parched throats—the higher-ups were too dignified to get any— before the King's giant, lemon-yellow Daimler rolled out of the palace and into the square. Everybody stood to attention until he was seated on a temporary throne. "He is certainly wearing his armored vest this afternoon," a foreign friend whispered into my ear. "I hope it keeps him cool."

The parade commenced with a collective oath of allegiance by the police to the King. Then Phumiphol, dressed in a white, lightweight uniform, read a proclamation, and the march past began. Policemen in summer khaki, shouldering rifles or light machine guns and wearing short boots reaching six inches above their ankles, goose-stepped across the square. Just after they had saluted their sovereign a Buddhist monk standing in the shade of an umbrella at the top of a movable ramp of steps, like that used by debarking airplane passengers, sprinkled holy water on the steaming faces and uniforms of the marching men nearest to him. As each line of policemen approached he dipped his bamboo broom into a bucket and shook the broom at the marchers. When his arm grew tired a beaming colleague relieved him. The tanks stayed outside the broom's orbit. General Pao had displayed his power.

Perhaps that was his only purpose. Perhaps he was biding his time. Perhaps the army alert had frustrated his coup. A coup would be a gamble; he might lose. If he merely showed his strength without using it he remained a force to be reckoned with in Thailand's politics.

This problem, why no one person or group has assumed supreme dictatorial power, intrigued me during my stay in Siam and I asked many questions about it. I have thought of it often since. The answer may throw some light on the nature of a dictatorship. The dictatorships of the Bolsheviks and Nazis, of Mussolini and Franco, supplanted multiparty democratic systems. But Siam never had a democratic system. Therefore no dictatorship was needed to suppress democracy. A dictator, moreover, endeavors to fill his people with terror and propaganda. He never leaves them alone; if he did they might begin to think and doubt. The dictator craves approval, applause, and 99.6 per cent electoral triumphs. This is a kind of perverse, reverse democracy; the people are active, as in a democracy, but their activity is compulsory and merely demonstrates their impotence and the despot's might.

In Siam, on the other hand, the possessors of power operate in a circle eccentric from the population. Politics is divorced from life. In a backward country it is the middle class which first becomes political and demands democracy or preaches totalitarian revolution. But the Thai coup-masters are spared both these embarrassments, for the country has no native middle class. Deliberately to draw the peasants into the circle of politics is wasteful and unnecessary; they are not interested in politics and not interfering with the politicians. Propaganda would fall flat because the leaders have no ideas or dogmas. The leaders I talked with, Prime Minister Pibul and his acting Foreign Minister, were deft parriers rather than deep thinkers. They had neither a doctrine to implant nor a program to implement. The politicians, accordingly, leave the people in peace and the people leave the politicians in peace so they can play at personal changes of the guard instead of subjecting everybody to a harness-and-muzzle dictatorship.

Moreover, a violent coup by one power man to eliminate all others would entail risks; the victor in the first phase of lethal liquidation might succumb in the next, or the next. To survive, as a wise ambassador put it to me, each tiger would rather share the bullock's carcass than try to destroy his rivals in the hope of devouring it alone.

The tigers are moved by another consideration; they are business associates. Pibul, General Pao, General Sarit, and most other top government officials are active executives of industrial companies and export and import firms. No doubt, occasions arise when one member of a board of directors would like nothing better than to kill a fellow member, but not in tolerant Thailand. Politics in Siam is a kind of exclusive club where the game is played according to rules which prevent anybody from getting hurt and help everybody to amass a fortune. A ministerial portfolio is often the royal road to riches.

Like the Burmese Socialist government, the conservative Siamese government operates a system of state capitalism. In Siam, the government owns sugar mills, cement factories, the railways, airlines, shipping, bus lines, tanneries, canneries, a jute bag plant, the tobacco and cigarette monopoly, the port of Bangkok, a whisky distillery, a national lottery, a paper mill, cotton spinning mills, and so forth. But unlike the Burmese leaders, the Siamese top politicians personally own private shares in these government enterprises. And, in addition, these same men sometimes own private estates and share in private companies, and represent foreign firms. The economy of Thailand is obviously quite mixed.

Needless to say, all this, as usual, is "in the national interest." Thailand is underdeveloped. The Thais are just beginning to show a desire for business activity. If a high government official has money, why not invest it? And if he can assign himself a participation in a government trust and thereby earn a profit with which to promote a private firm, why not? It all fosters national economic growth and squeezes out the Chinese.

To be underdeveloped means to be underindustrialized and poor, but more than anything else it means to have a small middle class. In Thailand, for a long time, the Chinese, numbering at least three million out of a total population of eighteen million, were the middle class. Many of the Chinese first entered Siam decades ago as contract labor to build railroads and roads and remained and applied their industry and commercial acumen to advancing themselves economically. They work hard, trade skillfully, and make good mechanics, whereas the Thais were inclined to be unurban, indolent, and averse to business.

In 1952, chiefly at Police General Pao's instigation, a series of measures was undertaken against the Chinese minority. The annual registration fee for each Chinese man, woman, and child was increased twentyfold, from twenty to four hundred bahts. For poor, large Chinese families this yearly head tax equals three to five months' income. Nor is there any escape for them in Thai citizenship. Naturalization is beset with mountain-high impediments. At the same time, police edicts prohibited Chinese from working as barbers, hairdressers, dressmakers and ricksha men. Cynics said Pao would not enforce these ordinances but allow his henchmen to be paid for nonenforcement. In any case, friction between the well-entrenched Chinese middle class and those leaders who wish to nurture an indigenous Thai middle class is sure to increase and cause embarrassment in domestic as well as international politics, for whatever their ideologies and sympathies, the Chinese will inevitably look to Peking for solace if their situation in Thailand becomes desperate.

To be underdeveloped also means to lack fluid investment capital. The principal source of capital and of foreign currency for the import of machinery is rice, rubber, and timber. As in Burma, the peasant who grows Siam's huge rice surplus for export receives from one-third to one-half of the selling price and the government takes the balance for developing the rich resources of the country.

Anyone who inquires why the peasant is not paid more so as to give him the incentive to produce more, improve his living conditions, and buy city goods hears a cold-blooded answer: "No use. The farmer's needs are primitive; if his income went up he would merely hoard more." Hoarding is a major Asian problem. It sometimes takes the form of burying treasure but more frequently of decking the womenfolk in ornaments. A United Nations economist gave me his private estimate that, in 1952, the Burmese peasant women, despite war and civil war, owned precious stones and gold and silver jewelry worth $240,000,000. Between 1931 and 1938, it is said, India exported $100,000,000 in gold annually because the hungry peasant had to sell his gold. Gold in Asia is an insurance policy and the only kind the people understand. They could no more be persuaded to divest their womenfolk of jewelry than Western women would think of dispensing with their dresses and finery. In Thailand, where the same conditions prevail, government loans have been a failure and money is so scarce and expensive that the legal interest varies from 8 to 15 per cent and the private rate from 24 to 36 per cent.

Hardly anything is more important in Asia than devising means of mobilizing domestic capital for domestic economic development. Actually the peasant is cheating himself, for since he will not buy beds and books, or medical care and radios, or government bonds, the state underpays him for his crops and taxes him and the middlemen who trade with him. The proceeds flow into the federal treasury.

Left to themselves the Siamese would be inactive politically and primitive economically. Political inactivity conduces to the Thai form of co-operative dictatorship, while primitive economics, in a nation which is rich and has a surplus and is therefore ready for capitalism but has no capitalist class, forces the government to invent a new, unique species of mixed state-private capitalism. It is not surprising that the key figures in this peculiar system become persons of great wealth and great power. Power equals arms. Most ministers in the Cabinet are military men. Civilians are of minor importance.

With so little pressure on it from the people, the wonder is how much the government does to develop the country. The King writes songs and the power-men contemplate comic-opera coups, but, considering the circumstances, serious work is being done. In the arid northeast which borders on turbulent Indo-China and is certainly infiltrated by foreign Communists, the Department of Irrigation, assisted by American technicians, has dug innumerable miniature lakes to catch water for use during the rainless season. Strangely enough, the government encourages the organization of local farmer co-operatives to care for these reservoirs and plant them with fish. The Ministry of Co-operatives, raised to that status in 1952 from a mere department in the Ministry of Agriculture, and the Bank for Co-operatives are financing peasants who propose to sow cotton, sugar, and other crops, apart from rice, which will diversify Thai agriculture and protect it from the perils of monoculture.

It is estimated that two-thirds of Thailand are under forests. The possibilities for the extension of agriculture and for logging are obviously vast. In the forests stand teak trees which can be sold abroad; in the ground minerals wait for exploitation. Rivers need to be dredged and opened to navigation. All these tasks have now been attacked and it is unlikely that the world unrest and global drive for better living as a means of defeating totalitarianism will ever let Thailand fall asleep again.

The biggest sleep inducer is climate and the fertility of the land. Nobody freezes or starves in Thailand. Drop a seed in the ground and something grows, drop a line with a hook into the river or sea and the fish rise to bite. Then how stimulate the peasant's initiative or the citizen's incentive? The press, which enjoys substantial freedom, occasionally hints that a land reform might help. Although there is plenty of land for the clearing, much of the used land is owned by absentee landlords who earn enough without bothering about it. The tenant, on the other hand, does not improve his parcel because he could be deprived of it at any time. In a farming area I visited, most of the cultivators were sharecroppers and those I questioned said they had a sense of impermanence.

Not even these folk, despite the primitiveness of their huts and the absence of furniture and comforts, were candidates for Communism. Like all politics, Communism seems very remote. Nevertheless, Communists have been infiltrating into the poor northeast from neighboring Laos and into the Moslem-Malayan south from British Malaya. Pridi, Prime Minister Pibul's student-days friend, seems to have gone to Red China and assumed the leadership there of the "Free Thai" movement—obviously with Peking's blessings. His agents are operating in Thailand. Such "indirect aggression," or aggression by subversion, is difficult to cope with, especially when the gun runners come as advocates of "peace." The Thai government is worried. The greater fear, however, is an actual invasion by Communist China. In such an event, they would look to the United States. The Thais rarely take a clear-cut attitude on anything, but they are thoroughly serious about their alliance with America.

CHAPTER THIRTY-THREE

Why the Communists Won in Indo-China

THAILAND was at peace and indifferent and Indo-China, my next stop on this trip around the world, was at war and indifferent. The war between the French-controlled Vietnam and Communist-dominated Vietminh did not seem to interest the people. In Saigon, the capital of Indo-China, a big, modern city, there was no sign of war though the war had been going on since 1946, no placard calling on the inhabitants to do or not do this or that, no flag except the few French flags over official French buildings. This was a demonstration of the most complete eccentricity of people and politics: people in one circle, politics in another, and never the twain shall meet even in war. Observers called it a civil war because two parts of the country were involved, but it was a civil war with the participation of few civilians.

An American friend in Saigon gathered nine young men, all Vietnamese intellectuals—journalists, artists, teachers—to meet me at a dinner party in his home. They heaped coals of fire on Emperor Bao Dai, the playboy head of the Vietnamese state who usually luxuriated at the French Riviera, on the Vietnamese government, and on France, the imperialist oppressor. Then I asked each one where he came from. Without exception they had come in the last two, three, or four years from the north, from Communist territory. Why had they left to live under French rule? Because they could not bear living under Communist rule, they declared.

The people of Vietnam were between the hammer and sickle and the French anvil, and the difficulty of the choice made them even more indifferent than they would normally have been. Perhaps indifferent is an insufficient word. The Vietnamese—men as well as women—are small, smiling people and have a kind of soft, silken quality. Working in the flooded rice fields within sight of the stone tombs of their ancestors or squatting in city streets or at the Saigon waterfront they seem too tender and gentle for the tough problems of a complicated world; they look as though they would be happier in the seventeenth century than in the agitated twentieth, as though just living is hard enough and still joyful enough to fill their lives and nothing else ought to be in it, nothing like government, politics, and wars. I simply could not imagine, watching them, that most of them had any sense that this was their war or, to many, that this was their country.

At 10:30 A.M., Saturday, October 18, 1952, I was admitted into the presence of the Prime Minister of Vietnam, His Excellency Nguyen Van Tam, or President Tam, as he was known, who had occupied his high office since June 25, 1952. The announcement of the appointment had come to me from Monsieur Claude Cheysson, Tam's French political adviser and later Chef de Cabinet of Premier Mendes-France. Shortly after the interview commenced I said, "Mr. President, I understand you are a French citizen."

"That is correct," he replied in French.

"How is it," I pressed, "that you, the Prime Minister of Vietnam, are not even a citizen of Vietnam but a citizen of a foreign country?"

He explained that he was from Cochin China in the south, and the Cochin Chinese could easily become French citizens before the war and so he was a French citizen.

"But why," I wondered, "now that you are the head of the Vietnam government and seeking independence for Vietnam have you not relinquished French citizenship?"

"Ah," he exclaimed, "the French might feel insulted."

"So the fact remains," I persisted, "that you are the Prime Minister of a country of which you are not even a citizen."

"There are circumstances," he declared mournfully.

An hour after the interview I had lunch with M. Cheysson in the Hotel Majestic and repeated this conversation to him. The matter had never occurred to him, he confessed. He would look into it. The next evening I went to dinner at the home of U.S. Ambassador

Donald R. Heath whom I had known in 1946 in Berlin where he worked for the State Department. Present also were President Tam, M. Cheysson, and Mr. John M. Allison, Assistant Secretary of State in whose honor the function had been arranged. Before we sat down to table, Cheysson called me aside and whispered, "Everything has been settled. The next time President Tam travels abroad he will use a Vietnam passport."

Fine. But I learned subsequently that seven members of President Tam's Cabinet were likewise French citizens. How could he rally the people to fight for their country when it looked as if he and his associates belonged to France and not to the people?

President Tam said his side, with French help, would win the war in two years if the Chinese Communists did not send troops. The war had lasted so long, he explained, because the Communists up north were exploiting nationalism, but the population was beginning to understand that they were Communists and not nationalists.

"We are totally independent," he declared.

"On paper," I commented.

"We have this fight with Ho Chi Minh," he replied, "and we must have French aid. But after victory the French army will withdraw and France will remain only for cultural and commercial purposes."

I asked whether he was convinced that France would give them national freedom. He answered in the affirmative. They had said so. "Why don't they say it in Paris?" I inquired.

"I do not know," he replied, "but for us it is enough that they say it here."

I wondered whether he would consent to a truce with Ho Chi Minh. "No," he affirmed. "He is unreliable. We must defeat him."

It is conceivable that Tam really believed they could defeat the Communists. He mentioned the superior technical equipment of the French army in support of his optimism. He was fifty-seven years old and had worked in the French government service in Indo-China for forty of those years. Gloom on his part would have been discourteous to the French and disruptive of his own position: his present and future were tied to France's role in Indo-China.

But the French themselves were not optimistic. "Ten years from now we may be sitting in the Hotel Majestic in the same situation as today, still fighting," a Paris newspaperman said to me. Events proved this to be a rosy prediction. The French were in a tragic position. Though the policy of France in Indo-China repelled me, I could not help being very sorry for those appointed to carry it out. Their hearts ached for France. And, I must say, so did mine. Frenchwomen in Paris had told me of the terrible gaps made in their families by the Indo-Chinese fighting. France could ill afford to lose her young men in the jungles, swamps, and mountains of Vietnam, Cambodia, and Laos. And the French officials I met in Saigon could not conceal the gnawing feeling that it would all be in vain. Precious blood was being shed in a lost cause. The slaughter had to go on though no one desired it and no one would benefit from it. The fighting, moreover, was growing more intense and costly as time went on. Thirty per cent of the officers and 40 per cent of the noncommissioned officers of the entire French army were now in Indo-China. The usual tour of duty lasted twenty-seven months. Every officer of the French army had served one tour of duty in Indo-China, and some had served two. French military personnel in Indo-China in October, 1952, numbered 140,000 (these included Frenchmen, Africans, and Foreign Legion of whom half, according to statute, had to be French—most of the remainder were German volunteers) plus 110,000 Vietnamese.

Supplying this mammoth force during the Korean War strained the resources of France and the United States. The two hundredth cargo of American military aid arrived in the port of Saigon while I was there. The United States Information Service issued a mimeographed bulletin stating that up to August, 1952, American military assistance had amounted to 90,000,000 rounds of ammunition, 11,000 transport vehicles and trailers, 750 combat vehicles—mostly tanks, 225 military aircraft, 225 ships, 4,500 radio sets, and 80,000 small arms and automatic weapons. Yet as compared to the French forces Ho Chi Minh was stronger than ever.

What was the secret of Ho Chi Minh's power? How could a rebel challenge France and hold a large French army at bay despite enormous American munitions shipments? I listened to a number of French military briefings which yielded facts, figures, and confusion. But they enabled me to ask questions and press for clarification. Finally, a civilized young officer, the finest type of Frenchman, speaking out of great pain and intimate knowledge, told me the truth. It was the truth as he saw it, of course, but the details corresponded to what I had often heard before and the connecting tissue of interpretation transformed them into a living reality. Lieutenant Jean P. Dannaud, Information Chief of Jean Letourneau, the French High Commissioner, had access to all the data and on the occasion of a visit to my hotel he proved ready to impart them. After Ho Chi Minh broke with the French on December 19, 1946, Dannaud said, the French tried to avoid war and arrive at a truce with him. Neither side fought very much in 1947. In 1948, Ho, using guerrilla, American Indian methods, began moving into the rich, rice-growing delta of the Red River in North Vietnam. But by 1949, most of the towns and roads were back again in French hands. In 1950, the advantage seemed to rest with France, and Ho launched few attacks. He was training his guerrillas for regular battle and siege warfare. In the autumn of 1950, he moved thirty thousand men against the five thousand French soldiers guarding Cao Bang, the key to the frontier between Communist China and Vietnam. This region, known locally as the "Land of a Hundred Thousand Mountains," is one of the most rugged in the world. The French lost 3,500 in killed and wounded. After holding on grimly during October and November, 1950, the French had to evacuate the remnants of their forces, retaining only Mon Cay, the one point on the Chinese frontier which could be defended from the sea. Thereafter till the end, Ho Chi Minh was amply supplied with rifles and machine guns and ammunition and with some, though not much, artillery.

Ho now had five well-equipped divisions and ventured to employ them in open, pitched battles against the French. This compelled Marshal de Lattre de Tassigny, the French commander, to withdraw the garrisons from isolated posts and organize them into task forces or mobile groups to meet the Communist assaults. Thus confronted with first-rate troops in conventional combat, Ho's men met defeat time after time. Quickly realizing his error, Ho reverted to guerrilla fighting.

Now commenced the worst phase of the war for the French, the phase they called "total popular warfare." Since Marshal de Lattre de Tassigny had concentrated a large part of his soldiers at fixed points, Ho found it easier to infiltrate into the crucial Red River Delta, and once this process of infiltration started the French found no effective means of coping with it. "If we enter a village with a battalion," Lieutenant Dannaud declared, "nothing happens. If we enter with only a company it will be destroyed." The Communists, he explained, have achieved "an amazing engineering feat"; many villages have a whole network of tunnels under the ground. The fighting men stay in them during the day and come out during the night to pick off a French infantryman here or there and to punish any peasant who has collaborated with the French. Therefore the peasants keep aloof from the French. They know they are being watched by hidden Communist spies and will be reported and punished. And since everything in this kind of war depends on information about the whereabouts and strength and plans of the enemy, the French are "blind," they cannot get the necessary information from the civilian population. As a result, extensive areas nominally under French control were not; nor were they controlled by the Communists. This was twilight politics; tricolor by day, Red by night.

The French officer then discussed various battles and their outcomes. "The trouble is that Ho's regulars never fight when attacked," he said. "They retreat. They are used only for offensive strategy, not for the defensive." Out of this grew another difficulty: the Communists chose to fight major engagements in places where French air superiority, tank superiority, and even artillery superiority did not count. Tanks could not reach into rugged country nor could heavy guns be dragged up mountainsides. In the mountains, French planes could drop paratroopers to aid a beleaguered garrison but could not land to evacuate them in case of necessity. Even air bombing achieved minor results in mountainous terrain. This explains the French defeat in the final and decisive battle of Dien Bien Phu. "The solution," Lieutenant Dannaud thought, "is to hold the plains—if China doesn't intervene. The Vietnamese are people of the plains. Ho needs the plains to get food and recruits. We must force him to come down into the plains."

But in the plains, Ho refused to wage conventional warfare. He contented himself with infiltration and tunneling. In Cambodia the population was not behind Ho because they were anti-Vietnamese and Ho was from North Vietnam. Likewise in Laos. But Vietnam was the bulk of Indo-China—26,000,000 people—and there the French had been unable to invent a mode of warfare which would enable them to face, much less destroy the Communist armed forces.

Those whom this situation baffled wishfully found comfort in a new development: after long hesitation, the French had organized an army of Vietnamese. When they took the field things would be different. The Communists could no longer pose as nationalists in arms against French imperialism, they would be facing their own kin. Vietnamese, moreover, would establish better relations with villagers, obtain more information, and therefore succumb to fewer ambushes. But Nguyen Van Tri, the Defense Minister in President Tam's Cabinet, did not share this optimism. "Nobody in the world," he said, "has found a way of coping with Communism. America failed in China and Korea, so you cannot expect more of us." The Vietnamese army was born in December, 1950, four years too late, he declared, and it took time to create an officers corps. Vietnamese administrators were inexperienced, they had not even known that the delta was infiltrated by Ho's men. Then the Defense Minister blurted out the essence. "We are caught in a vicious circle," he said. "If the French withdrew their army we would be overwhelmed, and as long as they stay our morale is bad."

Pham Van Giao, the Minister for Information and Propaganda, and Vice-President under President Tam, proposed to break out of this vicious circle by asking the French to go home. "I am Minister of Propaganda," he exclaimed after having served sweet coconut water, "but I have nothing to say. There is no Vietnam army; it is a French army made up of Vietnamese. I know, I'm one of its three-star officers. The French conduct this war. What right have they to kill my countrymen on the other side? Why does America help the French? The United States should not aid the French."

The Minister, a pharmacist by profession, age fifty-one, had by now worked himself up to a high pitch of excitement in which he was sometimes incoherent but always revealing. "I'm in this government as the representative of Emperor Bao Dai, but I do not agree with its policy and it does not approve of mine." Here he showed me the minutes of the Cabinet meeting of October 11, 1952, at which he had offered a resolution urging France to "relieve" her army in Indo-China. There was only one vote for the motion, his own. "Let the French withdraw to certain limited areas in Vietnam," he now suggested, "and allow me to fight Ho Chi Minh. I will win. Let the French help us when they're asked."

This was somewhat contradictory, but then that was the dilemma. Though he wanted the French army out he knew he would need it in a crisis. The Minister insisted, however, that American munitions plus the patriotism aroused by French retirement would give them victory. "If we cannot win with American and French aid we should commit suicide."

The Minister, too, seemed imprisoned in the vicious circle. "If the French win," he contended, "they will stay here for a hundred years and we will be unable to lift our heads." He was pessimistic about the French chances of winning and pessimistic about the outlook if they won.

The Vietnamese were confused and naïve, the French were confused and tormented. Nothing was clear-cut. It was that kind of war. Brigadier General Nguyen Van Hinh, the thirty-seven-year-old chief of the Vietnamese General Staff and son of President Tam, had fought in Ho's army for two years, from 1946 to 1948, because he thought Ho wanted Vietnam independence. Then he fled to Siam, stayed there two years, and returned to join the French in Indo-China. Others had moved in the opposite direction, from the French side to Ho, and from similar disappointment. But Ho, of whom the French and Vietnamese spoke with respect, presented an unclear picture too. All his adult life he had worked with the Moscow Third International. Now he received supplies from Communist China, and the Vietnamese feared and hated China which had conquered them in the past. So President Tam and the French branded Ho a Moscow-Peking puppet and Ho excoriated Tam as a Paris puppet.

The Communists enjoyed several decisive advantages, however. Ho, by the testimony of persons engaged in fighting him was a gifted leader, whereas Bao Dai was not and did not even see fit to stay with his people in the midst of a crucifying war; he preferred his palace and women by the quiet, blue, faraway sea. Ho had driven out the landlords, while Tam had only begun to put land reform into effect. Above all, the French were visibly, palpably the masters of Indo-China whereas few Chinese appeared in Ho's territory. Since Indo-China has been a French colony and Ho was fighting the French, the average citizen did not have to be a professor of politics to conclude that if the French defeated Ho they would remain as imperial rulers. Who could prevent it? Then why help them?

To be sure, President Vincent Auriol of France and His Majesty Bao Dai had signed an agreement on March 8, 1949, granting Vietnam formal independence inside the French Union. But I could find nobody who considered that the equivalent of independence. French officials in Saigon never gave an unequivocal answer to the question whether they would get out after the war. They usually answered: "Yes. How could we? Would you? Maybe; it's not so simple." The topmost French official in Indo-China, High Commissioner Jean

Letourneau, said, "I've been in charge here for three years. We have not won because this is a struggle against the entire Communist world. The French people want to get out of Indo-China, they are resigned and do not argue the matter any longer, but we cannot leave before a substitute power has been created. The Administration here is still weak."

"Can any government be strong if you put it in office?" I asked.

"We placed Bao Dai in power," the High Commissioner replied, "but he appointed the government. These people do not realize they are independent. We say to them, 'You have power, you decide,' but when we tell them to govern and guard a province they tell us they are not ready. I have said to Bao Dai, 'What restricts your independence? Tell me and I'll get rid of it,' but he never specifies. I have never believed that nationalism alone will stop Ho Chi Minh. This regime is incapable of assuring its internal and external security. The people have no instinctive desire to support their country or government."

"You are the stronger force," I said. "What does Ho have which prevents you from defeating him?"

"He has nationalism," the High Commissioner replied. "He has terror. Even when we hold a village the peasants are with him out of fear. He has an honest administration; that is the same kind of advantage that Mao had over Chiang Kai-shek. These people do nothing for refugees. Under us, hospitals function perfectly; when we hand one over to the Vietnamese the doctors won't work week ends, the gatekeeper has to be bribed, et cetera, et cetera."

"Then how can you win?" I wondered.

"Voilà," he exclaimed, lifting his arms wide. Then after a pause, "I don't see how it will end. But one must be an optimist."

"Is there any way in which you could make the people feel that this is their country and their struggle?" I asked.

"The French Union is not a prison," he began. "When Ho Chi Minh is defeated we are not going to fight Bao Dai. We will not use force against him. But we cannot tell the French public that after all its sacrifices of blood and money we will get out of here."

"That is the basis on which the United States is fighting in Korea," I remarked.

"It's not the same thing," he asserted, raising his voice somewhat. "We have been here for a hundred years. We have done good cultural work and don't want to see it wasted. We have national pride. '

We do not wish political power. I agree with you that it might have been better to do as the British did in India and Burma in 1947, but England is England and France is France. We are here to defend these good people. If we had left there would have been war anyway. Cambodia is weak, the people are soft, inert children; three million inhabitants in the shadow of Red China. Laos is still smaller, a million and a half. We are the only nation that can save these three associated states from Communism. And if Indo-China goes, Thailand is next. I know Nehru well. He thinks he can mediate between the two worlds. He has illusions about the Communists. We have none."

He finished as he began: "This is part of the world struggle against Communism and we need American aid."

Mr. Letourneau's statements did not warrant the conclusion that France would give up Indo-China. "And do you want us to leave?" Frenchmen challenged. "Do you want Indo-China, with its rice and minerals and key strategic position, to go Communist? Or will the United States send in a hundred thousand American soldiers to take our place? No? Then what are we talking about?"

Some problems are simply insoluble at the time and in the circumstances in which the solution is attempted. That is why statesmanship consists in the prevention of incurable political diseases. President Franklin D. Roosevelt offered a preventive scheme years before the insoluble difficulty in Indo-China arose. In 1943, Mr. Roosevelt began saying privately that the French should not be allowed to return to Indo-China after Japan was driven out of that territory. When Lord Halifax, the British Ambassador in Washington, heard this he asked Secretary of State Cordell Hull whether it was true. Hull reported the inquiry to Roosevelt. Roosevelt invited Halifax to the White House and sent Hull a memorandum on the conversation which ensued. "I saw Halifax ten days ago," Roosevelt wrote to Hull on January 24, 1944,[1]

and told him quite frankly that it was perfectly true that I had, for over a year, expressed the opinion that Indo-China should not go back to France but that it should be administered by an international trusteeship.

France has had the country—30,000,000 inhabitants—for nearly 100 years, and the people are worse off than they were at the beginning. As a matter of fact I am wholeheartedly supported in this view by Gen-

[1] *The Memoirs of Cordell Hull*, New York: The Macmillan Company, 1948, Vol. 2, pp. 1596-97.

eralissimo Chiang Kai-shek and Marshal Stalin. I see no reason to play in with the British Foreign Office in this matter. The only reason they seem to oppose it is that they fear the effect it would have on their own possessions and those of the Dutch. They have never liked the idea of trusteeship because it is in some instances aimed at future independence. This is true in the case of Indo-China.

Each case must of course stand on its own feet, but the case of Indo-China is perfectly clear. France has milked it for 100 years. The people of Indo-China are entitled to something better than that.

When Japan was ejected from Indo-China at the end of the war all eyes and brains were glued to twenty other key and quaking areas, and Indo-China failed to receive the merited attention. As a temporary expedient, troops of Chiang Kai-shek occupied Northern Vietnam down to the sixteenth parallel and British troops occupied the Southern past below that line. Ho Chi Minh's rise to prominence and power dates from this time. His Vietminh party had been operating in the north under his leadership during the Japanese occupation in an atmosphere of suspicion but not of open hostility. At Ho's invitation, Emperor Bao Dai became his "adviser." In the chaos that followed the Japanese evacuation and the entry of the Chinese, Ho took over the administration of large sections of the north and proclaimed a "Democratic Republic of Vietnam," with himself as President. Shortly after this, Bao Dai parted with Ho in circumstances not quite clear, probably a conflict of personalities or prerogatives.

Ho Chi Minh, anxious now to get rid of the Chinese, who have never been liked in Vietnam, invited the French armed forces back into the country, and in March, 1946, an initial agreement was concluded between France and Ho which recognized the "Republic of Vietnam" as "a free state, having its government, its parliament, its army and its finance, belonging to the Indo-Chinese Federation and to the French Union."[2] Several months later, Ho arrived in Paris and was officially received there with the honors usually accorded a chief of state. In September, 1946, he signed a further agreement with the French government confirming previous arrangements. The Communists and the imperialists were getting along very nicely together.

On December 19, 1946, however, hostilities suddenly broke out

[2] Jacques Soustelle, "Indo-China and Korea: One Front," *Foreign Affairs* Quarterly, New York: October, 1950.

between the armed forces of France and Ho in Hanoi, the capital of the north. This startling change from friendship to antagonism sprang from local friction, but it is best understood by reference to the world situation. Ho collaborated with France while the French Communists were in the French government. Maurice Thorez, the leader of the French Communist party, was Deputy Premier, his party comrade François Billoux was Minister of National Defense, and three other Communists were in the French Cabinet. The cold war between Russia and the West had not yet commenced. The French Communists believed they could remain, as a minority, in the French government; they even seemed to believe that France might go Communist by peaceful, parliamentary means. In January, 1947, the French Communist party actually issued a manifesto declaring "it possible to envisage other avenues for the advance of socialism than those chosen by the Russian Communists. In any case, the road is necessarily different for each country." Throughout 1946, Moscow must have viewed with alarm these "opportunistic" and "nationalistic" attempts of French Communism to take a line independent of the Kremlin. The Russians probably suspected that the fruits of office tasted sweet to their French comrades and that the postwar peace had encouraged dreams of peaceful political developments in France and in Europe generally.

There was one easy and simple way to put an end to such backsliding: if France was at war with Ho Chi Minh, the French Communists obviously could not be in the French government. Communists could not be leading the fight against a Communist rebel. The first shot was fired in December, 1946. But in the early months of 1947, Paris made efforts to patch up its quarrel with Ho. When these failed, and since the East-West cold war had grown in intensity with the enunciation of the Truman Doctrine in March, 1947, the French Communists resigned from the French government on May 4, 1947. Thereafter, the Indo-China War flared.

Indo-China was thus a victim of the struggle among the great powers, and the problem, therefore, should have received international attention much sooner than it did. France could not hold Indo-China singlehanded nor was it desirable for her to relinquish it to the Communists. The loss of all of Indo-China would have opened the sluice gates to a Communist flood that might inundate Malaya, Thailand, Burma, and Indonesia and splash against the walls of India. Indo-China, consequently, concerned Southeast Asia first of all. Yet as long as a rebel proclaiming himself a nationalist engaged in an armed struggle against a Western imperialist power, the threatened governments and peoples of Southeast Asia would inevitably side with him even though he was a Communist and their enemy. Not only did the France-versus-Ho alignment spell ultimate defeat in Indo-China, it widened the breach between Asia and the West and created sympathy for Communism and, as a corollary, for Red China. Western diplomacy showed complete intellectual impotence in the face of this dark prospect. Neither did any Asian democratic leader have the imagination or vigor to lift himself out of the rut of barren recrimination and do something, wrest the initiative from the West, and offer a creative idea that would end the bloodshed and bring national freedom to Indo-China yet halt the spread of totalitarianism in Asia. The poverty of statesmanship in all quarters was astonishing; it left the fate of the hapless Indo-China people to the arbitrament of force.

Having lacked the wisdom, or maybe it was the time, to prevent the Indo-China conflict in 1945, the democracies might nevertheless have internationalized it in 1947 or 1948 or 1949 or 1950. They missed that opportunity too; they were seeing the struggle only in terms of soldiers and materials. But those are inadequate weapons in any war and certainly in a war between Communism and colonialism. Then the crisis descended and all solutions became impossible.

With North Vietnam lost to the Communists by the Geneva agreements of 1954, the situation grew more difficult but less confused: the South Vietnam government found that to establish its authority and resist Ho Chi Minh it had to combat feudal armies and French imperialism simultaneously; this had always been the only way of checking the Communists.

CHAPTER THIRTY-FOUR

Looking at Red China

HONG KONG, a pimple on the big body of Red China, is a minor miracle. Twenty-seven miles from China—twenty miles as the airplane flies, the Communists could seize it any month. That apparently does not worry the Chinese who inhabit it, the English who rule it, the Americans who tour it.

Before the Second World War, the Crown Colony of Hong Kong had a population of 700,000. Today—2,500,000. The additional residents are refugees from China. They voted for British imperialism.

About a century ago, the British saw a barren rock seven miles off the coast and decided to make it a city, their gateway to China. Hong Kong now consists of that rock—the island of Victoria—and, opposite it on the mainland, a little peninsula called Kowloon. I lived in a Kowloon Chinese-owned, Chinese-operated hotel named, of all names, Shamrock. It was immaculate, efficient, orderly, and interesting. In the barbershop across the street the barber wore a gauze mask over his mouth and nose, like those worn by doctors and nurses, to keep his breath off the customer (and vice versa).

The Western world often thinks of the Chinese as a laundryman or a comic figure of the vaudeville stage shuffling along in carpet slippers with his hands in his broad sleeves and a long black pigtail down his back. But in the mass in Hong Kong the Chinese are most impressive: intelligent, industrious, cheerful, quick, clean, good businessmen, good craftsmen, good working men. Hong Kong sets one thinking about the future of China. These are talented people.

Nights, the skylines of Victoria and Kowloon are crazy mazes of red, blue, green, and orange neon lights in Chinese curlicues. The face of Hong Kong is Chinese: the white rectangular pillars of shops painted with large black and red Chinese characters; the poor mother with her baby in a pouch on her back and the baby's head dangling as it sleeps; the high-pitched songs and cries of peddlers; the rickshaw coolies with their mighty leg muscles; the persistent beggars; the young men who rush to your taxi as it stops and expect a tip for turning the door handle; the handsome hatless women in body-clinging neck-to-ankle gowns with slits down the sides from the knee to the ground to facilitate walking; the special, onion-with-fat smell of outdoor cooking; the junks with their purple sails in the bay between Kowloon and Victoria—everything is Chinese. White faces are few. The Chinese police the city. The British hand is unseen.

Hong Kong is the New York of Asia, overcrowded, dynamic, in a hurry, always building more offices, factories, and apartment houses. Yet in the United States, the British Vice-Chancellor of the University of Hong Kong, most of whose students are Chinese, collected only blank stares when he appealed for funds to expand the school's facilities. Why build on a volcano? Why build what Red China may soon take? But why build in Berlin? What is the difference nowadays between twenty-seven miles and two hundred or five hundred miles? Why build in London or Lyons? or Milan? Yet man always builds where the lava stream ends. British officials in Hong Kong say a Communist attack on the city would mean that China is ready for a world war and then Liverpool and Seattle might be as unsafe as Kowloon.

"When will the Chinese seize Hong Kong?" I asked the top British Foreign Office representative there.

"Oh," he replied, "maybe in five years, maybe in twenty, or perhaps never. It's an advantage to them, you know, for us to hold it."

Hong Kong is Red China's contact point with Western business. But seizure by China, even if the seizure did not provoke a war, would reduce trade with the West and make the Chinese still more dependent on Moscow-controlled commerce than they already are— and that, they know, is not in their national interest. So long, therefore, as economic considerations, which are also partly political, prevail, Hong Kong is likely to remain British.

At Hong Kong it is difficult to resist the temptation of taking a peep at Red China. One would not see much, but little is better than nothing.

The twenty-seven-mile highway winds through good country which, however, is too limited in area to feed Hong Kong. The sea comes almost to the road at a number of places where an aggressor in boats could make a landing and advance on the British colony. Hong Kong would be difficult to defend.

There is no iron or bamboo curtain at the Chinese border, only a chin-high twenty-mile-long, British-built fence of crisscrossing metal wire ending in unprotected spikes to keep out unwanted escapees and smugglers. The barrier opens at two places, one to admit food from China which enables Hong Kong to live, the other, at Lowu, where pedestrians and animals come and go. Here, in the center of a short wooden bridge, stand several wooden frames covered with barbed wire which are moved aside for authorized passengers who alight from a daily train a few hundred yards back and walk across the bridge to a waiting train on the other side, and for peasants with their water buffaloes as well as for coolies, in black cotton pants and smocks, carrying heavy burdens. I saw them carrying crates of Made-in-Germany chemicals into China.

In the middle of the bridge stand four young Hong Kong Chinese policemen in stiff caps, short-sleeve khaki shirts, khaki shorts, long woolen stockings, black, shining shoes, and revolvers in holsters on their left hips. Not a yard away, are four other young Chinese, in tan trousers that fall like cylinders to their shoetops, military tunics, and soft caps with red-star insignia, cradling burp guns in their arms. The two quartets of Chinese remain there for hours and never exchange a single word: that is the real Iron Curtain.

Immediately behind the Communist sentries, facing the Hong Kong side, is a wooden board with white lettering: on the top line, in Chinese: "TEN THOUSAND YEARS OF PEACE"; on the second line, in smaller, Russian letters: "LONG LIVE PEACE IN THE WHOLE WORLD"; third line, in English: "LONG LIVE PEACE"; finally: "VIVE LA PAIX." On a second board near by—a crude drawing of a dove.

After I had taken in the scene, I started photographing it. A Red officer appeared and began to photograph me. I smiled, but he did not.

Behind that officer and his guardsmen lay Communist China with its boasted six hundred million inhabitants, and behind China lay the Soviet Union with two hundred million, and then the Soviet satellites with a hundred million—a third of humanity that are a puzzle or a worry to the other two-thirds. Nine hundred million persons ruled by dictators, not free to work, live, or speak as they please, and not free to change something if they do not like it.

Having peered into Red China, I returned to Hong Kong wondering what was happening there. I put the question to John Keswick, head of Jardine, Matheson, and Company, a British firm famous throughout the Far East. He, like his ancestors before him, had spent most of his life in China. When Mao came John Keswick stayed, convinced that business was still possible. Later he left—disappointed.

"What is happening in China?" Mr. Keswick repeated. "Here, have a look at this," and he rose, walked over to his desk, and picked up a thin book which he handed to me. On the blue, hard-back cover was the imprint, in gilt letters, *What I Know About China, by John Keswick.* I turned the cover. The title page was blank. I turned another page; another blank. And the page opposite was blank, and the next page too, and so on, fifty blank pages and then the back cover. That is what John Keswick, the old China hand, the China trade tycoon, knew about China.

"Everything I ever learned about China is invalid," he asserted. If this was excessive self-deprecation, the reason he gave had great validity: he intimated that Communist China was unrecognizable because it was imitating Soviet Russia.

The Mao regime undoubtedly did pattern itself after the Moscow model. Indeed, in respect to terror and psychological warfare against the individual it overtook the Bolsheviks in the first few years. For Lenin and many of his colleagues, except Stalin, had taken a few sips at the fountain of European enlightenment and the French Revolution ("Liberty, Equality, Fraternity"), whereas the Chinese Communists began imitating Russia at a time when the Kremlin had already crushed every vestige of party opposition, political freedom, and personal initiative.

In Hong Kong, and later in Tokyo, I read reams of English translations of the Chinese Communist press and had a strange feeling, a feeling that "I've read this before, in Russian." The same breast-beating confessions of accused intellectuals and distrusted officials which the world had come to associate with "the Russian soul" and Dostoyevsky! The same deunciations of "cosmopolitans," "lackeys of American imperialism," and "international spies." The same unrestrained, immodest, and incredible tales of economic progress.

The old Chinese professor of English, Wu Mi, for instance, crying, "I sinned," confessed,

I failed to employ the class viewpoint and the history of social evolution to explain individual historic facts in the History of English Literature and the History of World Literature. . . . And, since I felt that the students were on a higher ideological and political plane than myself [he added with his tongue, perhaps, in his cheek], I relied upon them to make criticisms by themselves. This is a wrong attitude. From now on I must be able to criticize everything, and I must look for Russian reference books on world literature so as not to make mistakes. (In my recent teaching of Shakespeare I have done so.) I must . . . keep a firm stand in the matters of resist-America, and aid-Korea, of germ-warfare, etc.[1]

Chinese education toed the Kremlin line. The Soviet Union was China's teacher and guide. "To Learn from Our Soviet Elder Brother," said the Communist propaganda bureau, "has become a common motto among Peking citizens." The Soviet-China Friendship Association, with almost 39,000,000 members, NCNA asserted on November 5, 1952, is "China's largest mass organization." Wu Yu-chang, vice-president of the Association, in an article in *China's Youth* called on the new Chinese generation to learn from the Soviet people "not only their advanced knowledge and construction experience but their good political character."

Premier Chou En-lai told a celebration of the Soviet Revolution's thirty-fifth anniversary on November 7, 1952, that "in the past three years the Government of the Soviet Union has given us great help both in material and in technique. Many Soviet experts have eagerly assisted us in China's national construction. The generous, selfless aid of the Soviet government has enabled us to strengthen our national defenses, overcome the economic blockade by the imperialist countries, and bring about speedy successes in the restoration of our national economy."

Chou En-lai then quoted Chairman Mao Tse-tung as saying that the unity of Soviet Russia with Communist China was "eternal, unbreakable, and impregnable."

But throughout history eternal, unbreakable, impregnable unities between nations have been shattered when disunity appeared more profitable. And not only stupid capitalists are fooled by assurances of eternal love. When Nazi Foreign Minister Joachim von Ribbentrop congratulated Joseph Stalin on his sixtieth birthday, December 21,

[1] *Hsin Hua Jih Pao* (*New China Daily*), Chungking: July 8, 1952.

1939, Stalin wired back, "The friendship of the peoples of Germany and the Soviet Union, cemented in blood, has every reason to be lasting and firm." It was "lasting" for eighteen months, till June 22, 1941, the day Germany invaded Russia.

In the case of China and Russia, too, one would do well to look for the cake under the icing, for the reality under the sweet sentiment. In 1952, China was deep in the Korean War and needed Soviet munitions; she has needed them to this day. She also wants Soviet machines and experts to accelerate industrialization, and gladly pays with avowals of eternal unity. But help from Moscow does not preclude Chinese acts against Moscow. In fact, China is in a position to exact a better price for not-so-good relations with Russia than for abject good relations.

A Soviet satellite exacts no price, it pays the price of its weakness. China is too big and strong to be a satellite. Russia actually courts China, and with courtship go gifts. China also courts Russia—it is that kind of complicated courtship—but Mao's gifts are verbal bouquets.

The relationship between the Soviet Union and Communist China is shot through with contradictions, because a powerful, united China is both a boon and an obstacle to Russia. In present circumstances, Red China can keep Japan off the Asiatic mainland and impede American power in the Far East. China thus becomes Russia's buffer against the West and Japan. China helps to protect the vast, exposed Soviet territories in Asia. Moreover, the antagonism between America and China deflects considerable U.S. strength and attention away from Russia. These are services for which Moscow is ready to pay.

Indeed, logically, Moscow should try to aggravate the hostility between China and America. Yet this is a delicate matter, for if the Chinese thought Russia was deliberately involving them with America they might resent it. The Kremlin must also be careful not to allow the Sino-American antagonism to deteriorate into military hostilities, because in that event Russia would have to deplete her own stockpiles to supply China with munitions. China, moreover, might, after all, succumb to defeat, in which case Western power would be dangerously entrenched on the Soviet Union's long Asiatic flank.

But short of war, Moscow can only benefit from the strains in Chinese-American relations. To play this role, however, China must be strong, and Russia is therefore willing to reinforce the military and economic power of the Chinese Communists especially since

Moscow would be afraid to refuse Peking the aid it asks. Moscow is perceptibly nervous about its relations with China. China is Moscow's biggest foreign headache. For though China is still the weaker country, Russia has been under uncomfortable Chinese pressure.

This is Russia's dilemma. A strong China blocks Japan and America. But a strong China also stops Soviet expansion in the Far East and has already compelled Russia to retreat.

For decades, China had been under Czarist and Soviet pressure to relinquish territory. Now China has undertaken to halt this process and, what is more, to retrieve Chinese areas previously lost. Communist China has expanded at Communist Russia's expense.

In this remarkable territorial tug-of-wag between two co-operating Communist states, the first prize was North Korea. When the Korean conflict erupted, North Korea was a Muscovite satellite and invaded South Korea at the Kremlin's instigation. But most observers agree that in the course of the Korean fighting North Korea became a Chinese satellite. An outsider cannot know whether Mao Tse-tung had this result in mind when China first intervened in the Korean War late in 1950, but it is not impossible, for the Chinese Communists must have surmised that one of Stalin's motives in launching the North Korean forces into South Korea was to strengthen Russia's strategic position against Red China. Be that as it may, once China had sent hundreds of thousands of her "volunteers," together with "volunteer" tanks, artillery, and trucks into North Korea, her power there was inevitably enhanced. Moreover, masses of Chinese and of Koreans long resident in China were brought into North Korea to replace the huge number of civilian casualties and refugees. With this military and nonmilitary leverage, a pro-China group in the North Korean Communist party gained control of it and purged the pro-Russians. More recently, the Soviet government has contributed toward North Korean economic rehabilitation and will not hesitate to seek political benefits therefrom, but, as the Chinese radio has emphasized, imports and technical assistance are coming to North Korea not only from Russia but from China, Outer Mongolia, Eastern Germany, Czechoslovakia, and other parts of Eastern Europe.[2] Furthermore, foreign aid is sometimes an irritant and never as effective as physical control, and that, in North Korea, is exercised by Red China.

The Korean War likewise reinforced China's and weakened Russia's

[2] *New York Times,* April 11, 1954.

position in Manchuria. The biggest industrial center of China, with thirty-five to forty million inhabitants, Manchuria is economically and strategically the most crucial area of the country. Russia has coveted it since the end of the nineteenth century. In 1896, the Czar's Prime Minister, Count Witte, an exponent of Russian expansion into Asia and father of the Trans-Siberian Railway, induced the Chinese government to permit the extension of the Trans-Siberian through Manchurian territory to Russia's Pacific Ocean city of Vladivostok. This shortened the route by 342 miles and gave Russia special rights which enabled her to compete with Japan for control of Manchuria.

The Russian railway through Manchuria, named the Chinese Eastern Railway, which included a southern spur down to the port of Dairen, was ready in 1903. Whether or not this projection of Russian power served to hasten the Russo-Japanese War of 1904-5, the Czar's government was forced, after its defeat in that conflict, to cede the southern spur to Japan and to retire to a Russian sphere of influence in Northern Manchuria. Japan took over South Manchuria.

The Bolshevik Revolution shattered Russia's position in the Far East and enabled Japan to seize the entire Chinese Eastern Railway. But in 1924, after protracted negotiations with China and with Marshal Chang Tso-lin, the Manchurian war lord, the Soviets took it back.

On July 10, 1929, Chang Tso-lin's son, Marshal Chang Hsueh-liang, confiscated the Chinese Eastern. In November, the Kremlin sent troops into Manchuria and forced the young Marshal to return it. This is an indication of the importance Russia has always attached to Manchuria.

In September, 1931, however, Japan entered Manchuria with troops. Japan continued to jockey with Russia in Manchuria until 1935, when Moscow, rocked by internal difficulties, and fearing a simultaneous Japanese-German invasion, sold the Chinese Eastern Railway to the Japanese puppet regime of Manchuria.

Just as Russia had attempted to penetrate into Manchuria, so she endeavored to make herself at home in Outer Mongolia, Manchuria's vast, underdeveloped, thinly populated Buddhist neighbor to the west. The effort began in 1911, with the overthrow of the Manchu rulers of China. The Czar, certainly no champion of freedom or anti-imperialism, insisted that the new Chinese Republic founded by Dr. Sun Yat-sen grant Mongolia maximum autonomy, and under persistent pressure, China agreed. This was Russia's opening wedge into Outer Mongolia.

The Soviet regime continued the Czar's policy of absorbing Outer Mongolia, and by 1924, the territory had become a Soviet satellite.

During the Second World War, Stalin several times expressed to American and British officials his eagerness to fight Japan. U.S. Secretary of State Cordell Hull records in his memoirs that as he was sitting with Stalin at a dinner in the Kremlin on October 30, 1943, the dictator turned to him and declared that "when the Allies succeeded in defeating Germany, the Soviet Union would then join in defeating Japan." Stalin, Hull states, "brought up this subject entirely on his own, and authorized the Secretary to inform President Roosevelt on this in the strictest confidence." At the very first session of the Teheran Conference with Roosevelt and Churchill in December, 1943, Stalin again asserted that after Germany had been beaten "we shall be able by our common front to beat Japan." By the time the Yalta Conference was held (February, 1945) Germany's collapse was visibly imminent, and Stalin accordingly made arrangements to collect advance payment for his participation in the war against Japan. Roosevelt and Churchill promised Stalin in writing at Yalta on February 11, 1945, that "the status quo in Outer Mongolia (the Mongolian People's Republic) shall be preserved," and that after the defeat of Japan, Russia would receive southern Sakhalin Island, the Kurile Islands off Japan, the Manchurian harbor city of Dairen and the near-by naval base of Port Arthur, which Russia had held until 1905, and the Chinese Eastern Railway and the South Manchurian Railroad which were to be operated by a joint Soviet-Chinese company.[3]

Under the coercion of American and Soviet diplomacy, Chiang Kai-shek acquiesced in these arrangements as far as they concerned China. Moscow's representatives immediately commenced to transport great loads of booty from Manchuria to the Soviet Union. Not only did the Russians take machinery; they blew up permanent installations like dams. They wished to impede China's rise as an industrial power.

But no sooner had Mao Tse-tung established himself in Peiping on October 1, 1949, than the Chinese counterpush began. On February 14, 1950, Moscow consented to return Port Arthur and the Manchurian railways, but not Dairen, to Red China "not later than the end of 1952." On September 15, 1952, China's Foreign Minister Chou En-lai "requests" the Soviet government to stay in Port Arthur, and Moscow, in a published reply, obligingly "expresses its agree-

[3] *Ibid.*, March 17, 1955, page T31.

ment." This was apparently a concession to Russia for supporting China's military effort in the Korean War. But on February 23, 1955, China announced that the Soviets were leaving Dairen and Port Arthur. Mao had the natural desire to be master of Manchuria. Russia was forced to yield.

Nobody expected, however, that Communist China could make a bid for influence in Outer Mongolia after all the decades of Russian monopoly control. Yet this is happening.[4]

The same process of reassertion is manifest in Sinkiang, a northwestern Chinese province five times the size of Poland, where, thanks to its proximity to and good rail, air, and road contacts with the Soviet Union, and its distance from the heart of China, Moscow had done more business and exercised more political power than Chiang Kai-shek. Mao quickly busied himself redressing the balance in favor of China.

The rivalry between Russia and China is likewise reflected in their competitive striving for domination over several Asian Communist parties; their struggle for control of the Japanese Communist party has been particularly fierce because of Japan's importance to both of them. In this contest, China enjoys tangible advantages. She is Asian. Europeans and Americans sometimes think of the Soviet Union as semi-Asiatic, which it is; but to yellow and brown Asians Russia is European, white, and remote. With the passing of Stalin, moreover, Mao certainly, and even Chou En-lai, outranked or outshone all the Communist leaders of the Soviet Union. Presumably the Japanese, Indonesian, or Indian Communists could be asked to pay homage and own allegiance to the two great Communist powers, but it is more human to want to choose one, especially when Moscow and Peiping play favorites and do not always see eye to eye on policy and theory.

Thus China is Russia's indispensable ally and boisterous rival. Watching the new China with her half-billion or more[5] inhabitants, the Soviet leaders cannot help being as troubled about future pros-

[4] Robert A. Rupen, "Notes on Outer Mongolia Since 1945," *Pacific Affairs*, New York: March, 1955.

[5] Premier Chou En-lai, while visiting India in 1954, spoke publicly of China's six hundred million inhabitants. But the official *A Guide to New China*, 1953, published by the Foreign Language Press of Peking, which I bought in East Berlin in 1954, puts China's population at "about five hundred million" (page 1). Red Chinese figures cannot be too exact or reliable.

pects as they are about current problems. Russia is probably no less perturbed by China than many Westerners are by Russia.

This situation evokes the best efforts of Moscow's and Peiping's wiliest strategists, shrewdest intriguers, and sweetest phrasemongers. The Chinese are probably the most subtle people in the world, and their phrases, to this day, have been sweeter than those of the Russians. But there is an old saying that China's love is a greater threat than her hatred. The Chinese are past masters at the art of "open obedience, hidden rebellion," and the Soviet Russians are artists in subversion. Each side is constantly trying to outfox and outbox its beloved partner. In fact, there are not only sides, there are sides within the sides, and, given the circumstances of Moscow's head start as dictator to the world Communist movement, one is not surprised to hear that a pro-Russian faction existed within the Chinese Communist party. Its leader was Kao Kang (also spelled Kaokang). Franz Borkenau, an authority on the world Communist movement, writes,

Meanwhile the Russians sought to exert pressure on Mao by installing Li Li-san as boss in Red Manchuria. Li Li-san was not only a left extremist, but Mao's bitterest personal enemy inside the Chinese Communist movement. Mao was strong enough in the end to get him removed, but his successor, Kaokang, likewise followed an extremist line, apparently on orders from Moscow.[6]

In 1952, Kao Kang was listed as one of the six Vice-Chairmen of Red China under Chairman Mao. In the spring of that year he openly demanded a more radical policy with "complete expropriation of the industrial bourgeoisie and the total collectivization of the land as an *immediate* aim."[6] In November, 1952, he organized China's State Planning Commission and became its chairman.[7] Moscow's man was riding high in China. But by the beginning of 1954, his political career seems to have ended, and in April, 1955, the Chinese authorities in Peking announced that Kao Kang had committed suicide following a "warning" issued to him over a year earlier by the Central Committee of the party.[8] Mao had got his Moscow man.

[6] Franz Borkenau, "The Peking-Moscow Axis and the Western Alliance," *Commentary*, New York: December, 1954. Mr. Borkenau is the author of *European Communism*, New York: Harper & Brothers, 1953.

[7] *A Guide to New China*, p. 38.

[8] *New York Times*, April 5 and 6, 1955.

Kao Kang succumbed in the first important purge of the Red China regime. The Made-in-Moscow extremism for which he paid with his life represented consistent Soviet policy throughout the new Russian empire. In 1952 and again in 1953 when I visited Belgrade, members of the Yugoslav Politburo told me that the Kremlin sponsored farm collectives and other unpopular radical measures in all the satellites so as to create friction between people and government. Thus weakened, the satellite government would be more dependent on Moscow. This, too, was the Kremlin–Kao Kang strategy in China. But Mao refused to be undermined for the greater glory of the Soviet Union.

From the very birth of Red China a mysterious hand appears to have been busy embarrassing its relations with all countries except Russia. On October 24, 1949, Chinese police, probably under orders from Li Li-san, Kao Kang's predecessor, arrested Angus Ward, the U.S. Consul General in Mukden, Manchuria, and four employees of the Consulate. January 5, 1950, Great Britain broke off diplomatic relations with Chiang Kai-shek's Formosa government and recognized Red China. But Peiping did not reply for a long time, and when it did and agreed to admit a British diplomatic representative he was denied full status. China also rejected Yugoslavia's proposal to establish diplomatic relations. On January 30, 1950, Secretary of State Acheson delivered a conciliatory speech in which he recalled Russia's aggressions in northern China and wisely urged that "we must not undertake to deflect from the Russians to ourselves the righteous anger, and the wrath, and the hatred of the Chinese people, which must develop. It would be folly to deflect it to ourselves. . . . That, I suggest to you, is the first and greatest rule in regard to the formulation of American policy toward Asia." The Chinese missed Acheson's point or chose to ignore it. But the Russians apparently read his speech. Forty-eight hours later police raided the U.S. Consulate General in Peiping.

Nevertheless, the door to the United Nations remained open for Red China. Yet the Chinese Communist government deliberately closed it. The facts were given to me subsequently by Ambassador Jean Chauvel, Permanent Representative of France to the UN. In January, 1950, he said, France decided to vote for Red China's admission to the UN. Egypt, then a member of the UN Security Council, had taken a similar decision. This would have given China seven votes—the Soviet Union, United Kingdom, France, India,

Norway, Egypt, and Yugoslavia—enough for admission. Secretary of State Acheson had stated publicly that the United States would not veto Red China's admission, and, presumably, in that case, pressure could have been applied to prevent Nationalist China from using its veto. Yet just when the chances of admission to the UN seemed so good, Moscow and Peiping on January 29, 1950, granted diplomatic recognition to Ho Chi Minh who was fighting France in Indo-China. This move, Ambassador Chauvel explained, made it impossible for France to support China's admission.

Other events too suggest the existence of some influence, either an extreme wing within the Chinese Communist party, or Moscow, that interfered with Peiping's contacts with the non-Soviet world. It was an obvious advantage to the Kremlin to be Red China's spokesman abroad; it put Peiping under an obligation and gave the Soviet government a means of steering China's foreign policy.

If Russia could make trouble for Mao inside and handle his troubles outside, he could make less trouble for Russia.

China naturally preferred to use other intermediaries or to handle her foreign affairs directly.

But despite all the friction and suspicion, the Russo-Chinese alliance will endure as long as fear of or antagonism toward Japan and America holds it together. That alliance tips the international balance of power dangerously against the West. There are two ways of breaking it: one is to go to war with China or Russia.

A war with Russia would be a war to the death since neither side would consent to die without using all its resources. It would therefore be an atomic-hydrogen war. A war with China means direct United States action. Professor Hu Shih, Chiang Kai-shek's former Ambassador in Washington, said in San Francisco in 1954, that the Nationalists could not invade the China mainland "without logistic and perhaps military support of China's allies."[9] Japan was in a better position geographically and militarily to fight such a war, and fought it against a China weaker than the present one, but though the battle raged from 1931 to 1941, and involved millions of Japanese soldiers, Japan had not won it when the Second World War commenced in the Pacific. An American war against China would be fought without allies and would involve greater losses than any war in American history.

The second way of loosening the Russo-Chinese alliance is much
[9] San Francisco *News*, April 8, 1954.

cheaper: try to improve relations with China or Russia or both. In international politics nothing is impossible, no alignment permanent, no policy unalterable, no combination inconceivable. I imagine myself addressing an audience, say, in San Francisco, on May 1, 1945. The newspapers and radio that day had reported Japanese sinkings of American battleships, American bombings of Japanese cities, Japanese atrocities against American soldiers, and so forth. The hatred of Japan is unbridled, implacable. In my lecture I state that of course Japan must be defeated, but after the war the United States should give Japan hundreds of millions of dollars to rebuild her economy and insist that Japan restore her military power, should in fact finance the new Japanese army, navy, and air force. My listeners, I am sure, would have said to themselves, or even aloud, "This man is mad." Yet what did the United States, with no objection from its citizens, actually do after Japan's defeat? On May 1, 1955, exactly a decade after my imagined lecture, the Kyodo News Service of Japan announced that in the past year alone the United States had supplied Japan with $277,800,000 in armaments.[10] And this process of rearming Japan had commenced much earlier. The enemy, with whom peace seeemed ruled out forever, was now a friend. The same change had occurred in the relation of the Western powers to Germany.

It might be argued that the differences with Communist China and Soviet Russia are deeper because they stem from clashing philosophies and rival social systems. They are not deeper. The United States gave eleven billion dollars in lend-lease to the Communist dictatorship of Russia during the war and has supported Communist Yugoslavia since the war. Nations behave like nations, and if it suited the Chinese Communists they could be anti-Russia and pro-America, and America could be pro-China or pro-Russia, and Russia could be anti-China and pro-America. Peace with China or Russia is just as possible as peace with Japan and Germany despite the many differences.

[10] *New York Times*, May 2, 1955.

CHAPTER THIRTY-FIVE

From Garage Mechanic to President

OFFICIAL United States missions in non-Communist countries are far better informed than they were before the Second World War because America is more intimately involved in economic affairs everywhere. I had a deep and broad briefing about the Philippines from the Embassy staff in Manila, and collected an armful of publications, and then one attaché suggested I see the Ambassador, Admiral Raymond A. Spruance. "Navy brass plus State Department striped pants," I thought to myself. "It will be formal and dull and a waste of time."

His office certainly suited an admiral hero of the Pacific war. Outside the window lay Manila Bay. In the distance one saw Bataan, with Corregidor not far away. The foreground was a naval graveyard: here the cannon mouths of a submerged Japanese cruiser sunk by the U.S. air force, there, there, and everywhere tips of masts, decks awash, and the iron skeletons of dozens of freighters lying on their sides or standing upright where they were bombed. The Filipinos are waiting till the Japanese pay them to salvage this scrap treasure.

Greetings and preliminary small talk behind us, the Ambassador said, "Did you ever read a book called *Progress and Poverty* by an American named Henry George?"

"Yes," I replied, in astonishment, "I read it as a young man and, like Prince Kropotkin's *Memoirs of a Revolutionist*, it influenced my thinking."

"I read it as a young ensign," he exclaimed, "and after marriage my wife and I read it aloud together." He added that he would like to have an abbreviated version published in Manila. The book is a plea for Single Tax and for a radical new system of land tenure.

This was the surprising first gambit of an interesting, enlightening conversation. The Philippines needed a drastic land reform, and the United States favored it. In fact, the official Bell Mission recommended to President Truman that financial assistance to the Philippines "be strictly conditioned on steps taken by the Philippine Government" to carry out tax and land reforms.[1]

But why had the United States failed to introduce a land reform during all the forty-seven years from January, 1899, when President William McKinley ordered a civilian government established in the Philippines, to July 4, 1946, when President Truman proclaimed its independence? Americans have just cause for celebrating the voluntary renunciation of a colony, and there is likewise much to laud in America's rule of the Philippines.

With all its progressive policies, power, and money, the United States, however, did not bequeath the Philippines a stable social system. Indeed, independence, by withdrawing the restraining foreign hand, actually made political corruption and feudal servitude worse. The Huk uprising was the result. It wore the new Red dress which became stylish in Asia after 1945.

American officials, Filipino Defense Minister Ramon Magsaysay, spokesmen of the Roman Catholic Church, and others agreed that the Huk revolt was not Moscow-made or Peking-paid; it grew in Filipino soil. The Hardie Report, prepared by Robert S. Hardie for the Mutual Security Agency (the successor of the ECA Marshall Plan administration) stated the problem in stark terms:

Chronic economic instability and political unrest among farm tenants has culminated in open and violent rebellion. The rebellion derives directly from the pernicious land tenure system. . . . There is no reason to believe, unless the cause be remedied, that rebellion will not spread. Neither is there any reason to believe that the rebellious spirit, nurtured by years of poverty and strife, will be broken by force of arms.[2]

This report so stirred the anger of President Elpidio Quirino that he

[1] *Report to the President of the United States, by the Economic Survey Mission to the Philippines*, Washington, D.C.: Department of State, Publication 4010, October 9, 1950.

[2] *Philippine Land Tenure Reform, Analysis and Recommendations, Special Technical and Economic Mission, Mutual Security Agency, United States of America*, Manila: 1952, p. 7.

told Ambassador Spruance he did not want it circulated in the Philippines.

Public opinion, the Hardie Report stated, "seems overwhelmingly favorable to a land reform," but "a small minority which owes its position to the wealth and prestige derived from land ownership in a feudalistic culture" said no, and "the political strength of this minority group has in the past proved dominant." How then could the people believe in democracy? The feudal barons had economic strength, social prestige, and political power, and were loath to relinquish any one element for fear of losing the other two. "The Philippine farmer," the Bell Mission found, "is between two grindstones. On top is the landlord, who often exacts an unjust share of the crop. Beneath is the deplorably low productivity of the land he works. The farmer cannot see any avenue of escape." He escapes into the jungle to join the Huks and avenge himself on his tormentors.

A map of sharecropping tenancy makes the whole situation almost incredibly simple. In the Philippines 33.5 per cent of the land is tilled by sharecroppers. But in the district of Tarlac it is 51.2 per cent; in neighboring Nueva Ecija 64.9; in Pampanga 67.9; and in Bulacan 60.5. These four districts, grouped together in the center of Luzon Island, were the home of the Huk rebellion.

My first day in Manila I heard a reminiscent sound under my hotel room window, a sound I had not heard in all the months of my absence from the United States, the steady, brushing swish of heavy automobile traffic. I raised the Venetian blinds and looked out on Dewey Boulevard (named for the Admiral). An endless traffic column passed, bright new cars, Packards, Lincolns, Chryslers and Cadillacs and smaller makes, and great station wagons. This was excessive, conspicuous consumption in a small, poor country. The upper class spends while the rest of the population suffers. I asked Filipinos why the government did not put a heavy tax on imported automobiles.

"It does," came the reply. "New cars are heavily taxed. Our rich accordingly buy 'used cars,' that is, cars which they or their agents have driven a hundred miles or so in America. That way they avoid the tax."

"Why aren't such practices stopped?" I demanded.

"Because the people who could stop them are the people who benefit from them."

Karl Marx and Friedrich Engels, convinced that capitalism would always make the rich richer and the poor poorer, prophesied the collapse of the capitalist system. Had their analysis been correct their prediction would today be a reality. But in the century since Marx the poor in advanced industrialized countries have grown richer. However, where, as in mixed capitalist-feudal nations like the Philippines, the rich do grow richer and the poor poorer, Communism indeed becomes a menace.

Feudalism in the Philippines—and it takes similar forms in other countries—is poverty plus aspects of slavery. The sharecropper or tenant is required to vote for the landlord's political candidates, buy in the landlord's retail store, render free extra services to the landlord like helping to build his house, mend his fences, and plant his fruit trees, use the landlord's transportation facilities at exorbitant fees, and allow the landlord to keep the sharecropping accounts—a right which the landlord can easily abuse. If the tenant objects to being a serf he is beaten by the overseers or ejected from his land without appeal. The landlord is not merely lord of the land; he is lord of the men who till the land, he is a princeling independent of the state. This modern feudalism is an elusive system rooted in custom and in the peasantry's defenselessness, and the landlord can usually reckon on the tolerance or even connivance of the authorities. It is more than economic exploitation; it is an insult to human dignity, and it not surprisingly breeds rebels.

In 1950, the armed, Communist-led Huks[3] threatened to capture Manila and overthrow the government. Alarmed, President Quirino, on September 1, 1950, appointed Ramon Magsaysay his Secretary for National Defense. Magsaysay had made a reputation for bravery and energy leading a group of anti-Japanese guerillas in the Second World War. Then he found a job as a garage mechanic with a private transportation company and rose to the post of general manager. As Defense Minister, he developed enormous activity in combating the Huks. Soon his name was the biggest in the Philippines, and not merely because he went with his troops into the field against the Huks. Rather because he understood the rebels. A son of the poor people, he knew what motivated the Huks and therefore knew how to cope with them.

Magsaysay's home was seven miles outside Manila in a military

[3] Huk originally stood for Hukbalahap, a shortening of *"Hukbong Laban Sa Hapon"* ("Army Fighting Japan"). After the war it was changed to *"Hukbong Mapagpalayang Bayan"* ("Army Liberating the People").

cantonment named Camp Murphy for the late U.S. Supreme Court Justice and former Governor of Michigan and of the Philippines. I went there for lunch on November 5, 1952. Magsaysay was wearing white slacks, leather sandals, and an over-the-trousers, deep purple, wooden-buttoned blouse printed over with a confusion of light blue open-fan petals, sharp bright yellow petals and darting arrows. Taller than most Filipinos and massively built, Magsaysay is an impressive person with a big head and rich crop of black hair. As he spoke his nervous eyes flashed, his heavy facial muscles moved, and his brown arms, naked to the elbows, described wide arcs. He seemed to be packed full of power, eagerness, seriousness, will, and fascination. He was forty-three.

He asked me about my work. "You write books," he said with naïve awe and admitted that he had too little education and had read too few books. He wanted especially to hear about Gandhi.

I asked him about his work.

The Huks, he stated, are highly organized and intelligently directed. In one mountain area alone they had five hundred good dwellings, basketball courts, schools, and leveled training grounds. "For five years," he asserted, "our army had been fighting the Huks with little success. It had never gone into the jungle to grapple with them. It simply reported, 'Huk detachment annihilated.' I bought thirty-eight hundred cameras and gave one to each commander in the field. If he brought back the photo of dead Huks he was promoted. A general must go into the forests with his men. Otherwise the men stop to catch fish and the Huks vanish."

He unclenched his fists and gulped some coffee. "A few hours ago," he continued, "three Huks surrendered to me right here. Formerly this would have been news and got into the press. Now we are accustomed to it." He shouted, "Garcia." Captain Garcia, who had been tending the telephones around the corner from the dining room alcove where we sat, came in and stood to attention. "How many Huks have surrendered since I became Secretary of Defense?" Magsaysay asked.

Several moments later the young captain, in summer khaki with a revolver hanging by a strap from his shoulder, brought the answer: "9,970." That was for the period from September 1, 1950, to October 31, 1952. The total number of armed Huks was estimated at twenty to thirty thousand.

"Before I came in," Magsaysay asserted, "the country hated the army and the constabulary because they divided their time between fighting the Huks and looting, seizing crops, and extorting bribes. In this struggle everything depends on information, and if the population refuses to co-operate you fail."

Magsaysay ordered the soldiers to punish the Huks instead of persecuting the peasants. Secondly, he saw to it that the civil war ceased to be a series of occasional forays and became a single, uninterrupted harassing campaign. That insured persons who gave information to the military against reprisals by returning Huks.

But the men with most information were Huks who capitulated —provided they felt safe from Huk kidnapers and triggermen. Magsaysay made them his special wards. More than that, he began settling them on farms. So far, he told me, he had given land, equipment, electricity, and financial credit at low rates to three hundred families—eighteen hundred individuals. He was launching his own land reform.

Magsaysay called for his collection of photographs. He gave me one of José Avilla, a former tailor, subsequently a Huk commander, recently captured, who had lectured on dialectical materialism at the underground Stalin University. The picture shows him fitting Magsaysay for a pair of trousers. Another snapshot depicted a Huk officer who had surrendered and been helped to set up a retail village shop where he sold bananas and Coca-Cola.

On January 3, 1951, the chief of the Moro rebels, Datu Tawan-Tawan, a fanatic Moslem, surrendered to Magsaysay at Lanca, on the island of Mindanao. "I sent him on a pilgrimage to Mecca," Magsaysay said. "That earned me the sympathy of Filipino Mohammedans."

He left the room and came back carrying a straw-covered scabbard in one hand and in the other a sword with a handle and hilt of delicately carved wood and a blade two feet long whose two cutting edges tapered to a point in a series of quarter-moon curves. "Take it," he said. "It's Tawan-Tawan's sword. He gave it to me when I captured him." (I shipped it home.)

Magsaysay's understanding of psychology taught him that the Huk problem had to be met with force, humanity, and basic reforms. He knew that even if the hard core of the Huks laid down their arms and melted into the peasantry it would only be to wait sullenly for another opportunity to rise. Every unhappy tenant, he said, was a potenial Huk looking for a chance to stab the society that treated him so unfairly. Hence Magsaysay's burning faith in a land reform, "the best anti-Huk weapon."

But a land reform had to be passed by the Congress of the Philippines, and both parties, the Liberals who controlled the Quirino Ministry and the Nationalists who controlled the Senate, opposed the land reform for a simple reason—they were financed by landowners, real estate speculators, and other moneyed men who profited from the feudal structure of the system. "I do not wish to make a *coup d'état*," Magsaysay said to me. He was too democratic to undermine democracy by violence. Obviously, however, he craved the political power to carry out his program. How could he get it?

I told Magsaysay of my lunch with Laurel two days earlier. José P. Laurel, a graduate of the Yale Law School and former member of the Philippines' Supreme Court, had been President of the Philippines under Japan's occupation and was therefore widely regarded a Nippon puppet. But the best American authority informed me that General Douglas MacArthur and President Quezon of the Philippines had, before leaving Corregidor in the face of the Japanese advance, instructed Laurel to stay behind and do what he could for the people. When I asked Admiral Spruance about Laurel he said the Senator was a patriot, never feathered his nest, and lived modestly.

In 1949, Laurel ran against Quirino for President and lost after a very bitter fight which left permanent scars. Now all political talk again centered on the Presidential elections in November, 1953. "I will not be a candidate," Laurel said to me.

"Adlai Stevenson," I remarked, "was also reluctant to run." (We were lunching the day before the U.S. elections.)

"A few weeks ago," he declared, "I publicly offered to withdraw from politics if Quirino did."

"Quirino won't agree," I said.

"Then we must defeat him," he affirmed. "But I am tired."

"Don't you think that the only other man who can defeat Quirino is Magsaysay?" I asked.

"I do," Laurel replied.

A little later, Laurel said he favored the expropriation of big estates. I mentioned Magsaysay's known support of a land reform. "I would back Magsaysay for President if he joined our party," Laurel asserted. (Laurel was a Nationalist, Magsaysay a Liberal, but party-switching is not an unusual procedure.)

I gave Magsaysay a detailed account of this lunch with Laurel. He was visibly excited and ordered more cold drinks. "Now everything depends on Recto," he exclaimed. Senator Claro M. Recto was, with Laurel, the leader of the Nationalists.

"I am having lunch with Recto tomorrow," I said.

"Everything depends on Recto," he exclaimed. "If you could convince Recto to support me it would be wonderful. If you get Recto, oh boy!" he said, and snapped his fingers. "Then I will get the nomination, and if I am nominated I will be elected President. You will come back to the Philippines to visit me."

I grimaced to indicate reluctance. "We will arrest you in New York and bring you here," he said with a laugh.

"All I need is the nomination," he repeated. "After that I will go into every village. Walk from street to street in the cities. Visit every island. I'm not worried about the elections."

"Won't they steal the election?" I probed.

"Quirino will try to get me out of the Defense Ministry so that he can run the army and prevent it from supervising honest elections," Magsaysay said. "But the officers and men are loyal to me," he added. "All I need is to be nominated. You must talk to Recto."

I promised. "Get him to put it in writing to you," Magsaysay advised.

"But I am leaving for Tokyo tomorrow," I said.

"Ask him to write you to Tokyo," he said, "and draft the text with him." Obviously, Magsaysay would bolt his party and join the Nationalists.

Before parting, we made an appointment for five the next day so that he could hear what had happened at the lunch with Recto.

I arrived at the New Europe restaurant at twelve-twenty-five for my twelve-thirty appointment and found Senator Recto waiting. He was a great legal authority, age sixty-three, and much respected. He ordered a Coke and I asked for a tomato juice, and then he waved the waiter away. "Later," he said. This meant we would have a long talk. I began by intimating that I thought Philippine society corrupt. Politics in many countries was corrupt, and no social system was ethical, but in the Philippines the corruption of politics permeated all of life. "I am told that everything depends on bribes, even down to the lowest village level where the peasant must bribe the landowner's overseer, sometimes with his daughter."

He agreed and gave me several examples of malfeasance in the highest circles.

After we ordered the meal, I raised the question of the 1953 Presidential elections. "Don't you need somebody who will sweep out the corruption?" I queried.

"Laurel," he replied, "is tired and does not wish to run. I am tired too."

"Where will your party find a strong candidate to defeat Quirino?" I asked.

He shrugged his shoulders.

"What about Magsaysay?" I said.

"He is not a member of our party," Recto stated.

"I believe he would join it," I asserted.

"Do you know?" he pressed.

"Yes."

"Then I will support him," Recto declared.

"Would you put that in writing to me?" I asked, and when he shook his head affirmatively I took from my pocket a page of a United Press bulletin which I had been receiving from Gene Symonds, its correspondent in Manila,[4] and began writing as Recto watched: "I don't want to be a candidate. I would support Magsaysay if he bolted his party and joined ours." Here he put his finger on the paper and said, "and ran against Quirino." The hatred of Quirino was great, and Recto, like Laurel, wanted a candidate who could defeat him. I wrote, "and ran against Quirino."

Then I asked whether other Nationalist leaders would join him in backing Magsaysay. "I will see to it that they take the same position," he said. I recorded his words.

"We would require of Magsaysay," he dictated, "that he appoint a majority of his Cabinet from our party—of course, decent men, and that in selecting candidates for the Senate and House he agree with us."

"What about social changes?" I asked.

He pointed to the paper and I wrote as he spoke: "That we should agree to a minimum program of constitutional reform and a social program . . ."

He paused. "I am sure," I said, "that Magsaysay would insist on land reform."

Recto nodded, and continuing where he paused I wrote "including." He said, "Better say particularly. Particularly land reform."

At the end of the long lunch I asked whether he wanted the paper.

[4] Mr. Symonds, unfortunately, was killed while observing a riot in Singapore on May 13, 1955.

"No, I will remember," he promised. I gave him my Tokyo address. He drove me to my hotel in his Cadillac.

That afternoon at five, Magsaysay phoned and said he was downstairs. I invited him up. He was wearing white trousers and a white, transparent shirt with embroidered front made of pineapple fiber. He asked what had happened at lunch. I showed him the paper which Recto had dictated. "It's wonderful," he exclaimed. "You were sent by God. It's a miracle. I was in touch with Laurel and Senator Tanada today and they said they agreed to my candidacy, but final approval depended on Recto, and it was too early to approach him, they confessed, because if he wanted it himself they would support him. Now you have won Recto. It is lucky you came here just at this moment." He shook both my hands.

We discussed his immediate strategy. Recto had told me, I reported, that Magsaysay must resign immediately from the government. But I argued with Recto that this would be unfortunate; Quirino would immediately begin purging the army and appointing officers who could not be trusted to guard the elections against fraud and force. Therefore, I had said to Recto, the whole matter should be kept secret till the Nationalist party's nominating convention in May, 1953, and Magsaysay ought to try to remain Defense Minister as long as possible. Recto had concurred. I had asked him how many secrets were kept in the Philippines. He smiled and hoped this one would be.

Magsaysay thought well of the secrecy idea. He said he would be "correct" in his relations with President Quirino and give no hint that he was planning to run against him. He studied the Recto luncheon paper again and declared, "A photostat of this will make an interesting page in your next book." After more conversation about the crucial matter of guaranteeing an honest poll he inquired when I was leaving. "My plane leaves at ten this evening," I informed him. He invited me to dinner at eight; he would call for me. I escorted him downstairs. The hotel was agog and the lobby full of guards, Magsaysay's and, no doubt, Quirino's, observing. I went upstairs, put the Recto document and my diary notes about the lunch into my bosom pocket and went off to keep my last appointment before dinner.

At eight Magsaysay took me and my luggage aboard and we drove to the U.S. Officers Club for a steak dinner. Again the talk centered on future procedures. He said, "Next week I am going into the field to fight the Huks. I'll stay there as long as possible so Quirino cannot dismiss me."

I suggested discreet land-reform agitation in the army, and also propaganda against corruption. I said Recto told me that he, Magsaysay, had tape recordings of Quirino telephone calls. "I have more than that," he confirmed. "bought a special German camera to make photostats of some income tax returns."

After dinner he insisted on taking me to the airport. Captain Garcia joined us at the door of the club and a jeepful of Magsaysay's bodyguards followed the car as soon as we moved away.

The routine checks and examinations at the airport were speedy and perfunctory. Then I urged him to go home, but he said he would stay and so, while spectators gaped, we sat on a bench in the big central waiting room and talked. At one point, Magsaysay beckoned to Garcia, who had remained, ever-vigilant, at a respectful distance, and told him to send in so-and-so. "That's the driver of the bodyguards' jeep," Magsaysay explained. "A former Huk."

"You certainly trust people," I commented.

"He is very loyal to me," Magsaysay assured.

The ex-Huk, a young man about twenty-one in summer khaki shirt and trousers, approached, saluted, and stood at attention. He had a tight, thin body, copper-colored skin like an American Indian, a long bony face, and bushy, wavy hair that ended in a crescent curl at the sideburns. His only weapon was a knife in a long sheath on his left hip. Magsaysay addressed him in English and he answered in the same language. I asked him about himself and his family. Would he ever go back to the jungle? No, he wanted to serve the Minister.

All that night I slept soundly in a berth until a sudden silence and lack of motion woke me. "What's this?" I called to the steward.

"Okinawa," he replied.

I fell asleep again and he had to wake me half an hour out of Tokyo.

Immersed in Japanese affairs, I had nevertheless commenced to wonder about Recto's promised letter when, on November 25, I received a three-line telegram from Magsaysay indicating that he was in contact with the Senator and expected good results. Several weeks later, after he had undergone an appendectomy, he wrote me again. In due course, he was nominated for President by the Nationalists with Recto's concurrence. American officials scarcely concealed their delight and expressed a hope in clean elections. I wrote Magsaysay from New York in September, 1953, that American friends trusted he "would have a fair chance in honest balloting. The rest depends on the will of the voters and I imagine that if you convince them that you will introduce the reforms which could destroy feudalism and make the Philippines a more progressive nation they will vote for you." He replied on the eve of the November, 1953, elections, "I would like to confirm your belief," he said, "that the victory of my political party could only be assured if there would be no irregularities at the polls. As for the Filipino electorate, my own personal observations have convinced me that throughout the Archipelago the prevailing sentiment is favorable towards the success of my political crusade." He was right. He received 70 per cent of the four million votes cast. No irregularities.

The experience of the Philippines demonstrates that national independence is an incomplete solution of Asia's problems. With the exception of a few spots and dots, Asia, from the Arab world to the China Sea, has achieved national liberation. But the Communists still have an appeal because colonialism was only one form of inherited inferiority; other more personal forms of that same abomination, such as feudal peonage and limited opportunity, remain, and because they are more personal, and since nationalism is new and not deeply ingrained, these intimate manifestations of inferiority dominate and motivate while national independence seems a disappointing shell. Without national freedom there would be revolt in Asia, but even with it unrest continues because feudal injustice persists.

President Magsaysay's task is to translate constitutional democracy into individual reality, into the day-to-day economic life of men, women, and children. This is a revolution which the Filipinos themselves have to make. With all America's influence in the Philippines and favorable attitudes toward the land reform, nothing can happen unless the Filipinos do it. Outsiders cannot introduce basic social changes. This ought to curb some of the conceit which assumes that foreign nations can be won or lost by what the United States does. American policy and action are certainly important, but the fate of a nation lies in the hands of that nation.

Inevitably, of course, President Magsaysay's efforts at land reform met the stubborn resistance of rural proprietors and their political agents. Magsaysay, therefore, undertook the tedious, time-consuming process of expanding his popular support, building his own political machine, and restraining the rebels while preparing to pass laws which would restrain the landlords. Finally, in August, 1955, the Filipino Congress, at a special session called by Magsaysay for the purpose, passed a land reform bill giving the President the power to break up large landed estates for distribution among tenant farmers.[5] It made Magsaysay happy. And it spelled defeat for the Communist Huks.

CHAPTER THIRTY-SIX

The Future of Japan

THE POROUS limestone of the Imperial's outer walls and the flower ponds in front of it give the hotel the appearance of a mellowed medieval Japanese temple. In the lobby stands a single chrysanthemum plant, "The Golden Moon," with eighty big yellow blooms; a scarcely visible wire frame holds up the heavy branches. Near by in the large ground-floor dining room guests at any table can look through the windows and glass panels in the side walls and see the sky. The only objection I had to the hotel was that in an otherwise commodious room and bathroom the top of the sink was just three inches above my knees.

Frank Lloyd Wright, the American, designed this Japanese hotel.

[5] *New York Times*, August 11, 1955.

All around it in the center of Tokyo, are harsh, American-type sky-scrapers designed by Japanese. Often as I walked in the area, with its straight wide streets and Western buildings, and suddenly caught a glimpse of men playing baseball in a vacant lot it seemed strange, for a moment, that the people everywhere were Japanese.

The Japanese have played baseball for many years; a professional game sometimes attracts seventy thousand spectators. In Hibiya Park, across the street from the Imperial, I watched two amateur teams. With the exception of one barefooted fellow in shorts all the players wore American-type baseball outfits and shoes and used American terms: "batter up," "strike," "ball," "home run," "nice one," etc. When a player struck out or made an error he laughed and the spectators laughed. Laughter plays a special role in Japanese life; it hides discomfiture, saves face, relieves tension, and indicates that though the matter is serious the person involved can "take it." I noticed that the muscular response of the players was quick and perfectly co-ordinated, but where judgment was needed they lagged. They caught and hit the ball and ran the bases with expert precision; if, however, there was a man on first and another on third base and the outfielder caught the batted ball he took an extra second to decide what to do. I asked some Japanese and several foreigners about this and they said, out of their experience, that the Japanese requires a pattern, a system which he can follow. He has dexterity without resourcefulness. Faced with the necessity of making something new he remakes the old.

One hears all kinds of generalizations about Japan in Japan. A sensitive young American, daughter of a diplomat, who had lived in Germany and Japan, thought the Japanese were the Germans of Asia: hard-working, romantic, literate, easily regimented, inclined to hero worship. I found the Japanese mind very oriental and far more inscrutable than the Indian or Russian. In search of clues I dipped into their poetry.

A Japanese author gave me a 1952 book of Japanese poems in English translation. The volume has a hand-sewn binding of black paper that feels like silk. The lettering on it is in gold: "*Lacquer Box,* by Shoson Yasuda." Mr. Yasuda wrote the introduction, the verses are by poets ancient and modern. Educated Japanese, I learned on inquiry, can recite from memory many of these five-line sonnets, or tankas, and regard them as an accurate reflection of Japanese mentality. The tanka, says Mr. Yasuda, "is the very act and rhythm of living." One tanka reads:

If but my life be spent
just as now within this world
very merrily,
In the next life I'll be content
whether bird or bug I be.

The devout Hindu endeavors, by penance and sometimes by good deed, to improve his status in the next incarnation, but the Japanese, who likewise believes in reincarnation, is reconciled to an insect's existence in the hereafter if only he can be gay in the here-and-now. Merriment, however, is neither riotous nor raucous. The Japanese are a small, quiet, minor-key people. Their warmed saké is a gentle wine, and drunkenness is rare. Drink is regarded not as an end in itself, but as a means, together with music, good food, mellow surroundings, and friendly companions, of creating that harmonious pleasure which is the goal of life.

The poet Motoori, who died in 1801, wrote:

Should ever someone
inquire what the spirit is
of Japan, declare:
In the radiant morning sun
mountain cherries bloom so fair.

That, I was assured, remains the spirit of Japan: love of color and love of nature, cherry blossoms on a mountain in the bright morning—almost a definition, a trade-mark picture of Japan.

Japanese poems resemble a wisp of cloud, a smell, that melts away quickly, nothing profound, no philosophy, only a sentiment that evokes a mood. A tanka by the present Emperor reads:

On the wild plateau
The mountain rhododendrons
Are blowing
In lovely gathered clusters
Where birds are fluttering[1]

Ochikochi, a ninth-century bard, sang of the unity and harmony of nature:

When the autumn breeze
blows on Suminoe strand
whistling through pine-trees,
Snowy waves far out at sea
join their voices rhythmically.

Harmony seems to be the major goal of Japanese living, and

[1] Translated by Kenneth Yasuda and published in *Perspective of Japan*, an *Atlantic Monthly Supplement*, 1954.

harmony is art. Even cheerfulness, though so highly desired, must not be a discord. Japanese plays and films often end with a suicide or a heart-rending, permanent separation or a series of deaths, yet such tragic conclusions may felicitously resolve the conflict presented in the preceding acts and are therefore satisfying, whereas a happy ending, dragged in for optimism's sake, is mournfully incongruous. Hamlet with a happy ending would be shocking, the climactic deaths rhyme with the character of the drama and make the art immortal. Japan has produced no one remotely resembling Shakespeare in dimension or depth, but her creative spirits know they must not, by omitting violence, do violence to the national love of harmony. Equally, harmony, which is harmony with life, and therefore truth, may require that a play or novel end indeterminately, without solution, as life often does.

In Tokyo I asked why the Communist party, which had had twenty-two seats in the Japanese Diet, won none in the last election. Because, came the unanimous answer, in their May Day parade, in 1952, the Communists had thrown Molotov cocktails at bystanders, overturned automobiles, and injured innocent spectators, and the Japanese do not like violence; therefore, they did not vote Communist.

As politely as possible I suggested that I seem to remember a great love of violence in the late war. "Oh, yes," they agreed, "in war we are violent, but in peacetime one must be peaceful."

"Japan's motto is: Everything in its place," Ruth Benedict wrote in her book, *The Chrysanthemum and the Sword*.[2] The title itself contains an important clue to Japanese culture, sensitivity to beauty blends with killing.

One day I drove out to the town of Kamakura with my friend Herbert Passin, an American scholar who had spent seven years in Japan and speaks excellent Japanese. We went to see the Enkakuji Temple of the Zen Buddhist sect. After viewing the enormous Buddha statue with the red mark on its forehead we looked for the Abbot, the chief of Japan's Zen Buddhists who number many millions. A young monk in saffron robe and shaven head sank to his knees as we approached his hut to ask for information, directed us to the High Priest, and then touched his brow to the floor as we thanked him. We walked through a vast grove whose floor had been swept clean, and presently, among the trees, women in exquisite silk

[2] Ruth Benedict, *The Chrysanthemum and the Sword; Patterns of Japanese Culture*, Boston: Houghton Mifflin Company, 1946, p. 87.

kimonos appeared. Soon we reached a wooden structure which was nothing more than a floor six steps above the ground and a roof. The steps, which ran the length of the house, were covered with pairs of little wooden shoes left by the ladies who were sitting upright with their lower legs under them listening to a lecture by the High Priest who stood, dressed in silk robes and scarf, at a rostrum. He was talking on the Tea Ceremony.

When he had finished he invited Passin and me to his room on the second story of a wooden building in the grove. We sat on blue cushions on the floor. The Abbot's head was closely shaven, he wore glasses, and fingered a long rosary which consisted of 108 beads. There was a radio on the floor, an electric fan, books and newspapers on a shelf, and, in the corner, the alcove or Tokonoma one finds in every Japanese house; his showed a little skull of Buddha, a long decorated scroll, and fresh flowers.

Immediately we were settled and the High Priest began preparing tea on an electric plate, I asked him how come he, the head of Japan's Buddhists, was lecturing on tea pouring. He laughed . . . and explained. It was not just a matter of serving cups of tea. The Tea Ceremony nurtured poise, composure, and harmony. The tearoom had to be appropriately decorated, a scroll in the Tokonoma to suit the occasion, and specially selected flowers. The hostess must know how to face people. She has to be sure about the kimono she picks for the event. Every detail is important. The Tea Ceremony is disciplined relaxation, a symphony, it is art, and of course it is related to religion because the purpose of Buddhism is peace and happiness, and peace and happiness are found through inner harmony and the Tea Ceremony is an exercise in that harmony.

While he was pouring tea I asked him his name. He wrote "Sogen Asahina" on his Japanese visiting card; all the urban Japanese I met had cards and when two Japanese meet or when a Japanese meets a foreigner they bow to one another several times and exchange cards. He said he was sixty-two; he looked fifty.

I quoted to Mr. Sogen Asahina the statement of a student at the big Waseda University in Tokyo. I had taken a class and talked to it about conditions in the United States and the world in general. At question period, the student asked, "How can I know what is right and wrong if the government makes mistakes?"

The High Priest agreed that his country's defeat in the Second World War had created a deep psychological crisis. A mistake, he said, is humiliating, and defeat in war is of course the crowning mistake. Japan, which had never been invaded or defeated, was forced to surrender in 1945, and as a result everybody lost authority; the Emperor dedeified himself, announced that he was not a god. But the Japanese, the Zen Buddhist leader declared, incline to dependence on authority. Japan had been a country led by men who were considered gods. That is Shintoism. "I opposed all that," Sogen Asahina stated, "and suffered for it. Buddhism has no gods and no prayers."

"Do you believe in God?" I asked.

"No, I do not believe in God," he affirmed. "I believe in the common brotherhood of all men, I co-operate with Kagawa, the Christian leader. Self and universe are one. We must be at one with the universe."

"What happens after death?" I wondered with a laugh.

"I don't know," he replied. "I haven't had the experience of being dead. But since we are one with the universe the essence lives after physical death and we do not recognize death. If a person I love dies, I am sad, but there is really no reason for mourning. In death you unite with Buddha, just as in life you unite with Buddha."

"Then why would killing be wrong?" I inquired.

"Because every person has value and beauty," he said, "and should not be destroyed."

"Regardless of faith, social status, occupation, or geographical location," writes Professor Iichi Oguchi, a Japanese authority on religion, "the sense of close relationship between the living and the dead is the outstanding characteristic of Japanese religious consciousness."[3] This fosters ancestor worship; it also diminishes fear of death. Death is not a frightening phenomenon. "To encourage a boy who is worrying about his final examinations from middle school, a man will say, 'Take them as one already dead and you will pass them easily.' To encourage someone who is undertaking an important business deal, a friend will say, 'Be as one already dead.' . . . During the war Japanese soldiers said, 'I resolve to live as one already dead.' "[4] Being "dead" while alive banishes fear. It might also banish all consideration for others.

Every society is held together by one or more cements like fear, authority, common experiences, common interests, common origin, and so forth. Japan, where most structures are of wood, is a country of earthquakes, typhoons, tidal waves, and great fires which, by destroying the present, threaten to wipe out the past of future genera-

[3] *Perspective of Japan,* An *Atlantic Monthly Supplement,* 1954.
[4] Ruth Benedict, *Op. cit.,* pp. 249-50.

tions. Ancient survivals are therefore particularly treasured, and tradition is strong.

Tradition plus a ready submission to authority produce a conservative society, and Japan was conservative, the more so since it had become powerful and successful while conservative. But in the war Japan failed and authority failed. My impression is that Japan nevertheless remains conservative. Yet the conservatism lacks its old self-confidence. Youth seeks a new pole of faith, the intellectuals are critical of everybody in office, and the working class craves new gods. A nation shattered by defeat begins a quest for stability and clings to sources of strength. General MacArthur was such a source; he had conquered the Japanese, and since they had thought highly of their own military prowess they thought highly of the foreign general who had crushed it and who, in addition, was now the Emperor's emperor. What could be more impressive? It gave him an unprecedented opportunity to transform Japan, and he did not hesitate to use it.

Remote as Douglas MacArthur may seem in social philosophy and personal characteristics from Franklin D. Roosevelt, he was Japan's F.D.R., he gave the Japanese a new deal. Japan lay inert in MacArthur's hands. Japanese tell me the people expected to be ground into dust. But with unequaled generosity of spirit and purse, MacArthur, acting in obedience to his superiors in Washington but contributing his immense ability and understanding, proceeded to make Japan's problems his own. This was so very American; the Americans would have been unhappy merely to occupy and govern, and were certainly incapable of oppressing, or exacting reparations from, the defeated nation. They had to reform, rebuild, improve. They had to make things work.

MacArthur gave the women of Japan the vote and equal rights. "Women," said Chief Justice Kotaro Tanaka of the Supreme Court of Japan, "are no longer inferior. The legal relationship between husband and wife has been radically changed." The new constitution allows a wife to obtain a divorce and dispose of her property without the husband's approval. Parents can no longer marry off a daughter without her knowledge and consent. More women marry for love. More girls are working in offices and attending coeducational colleges. President Tadao Yanaihara of Tokyo University told me that they already had four hundred women students—out of a total enrollment of eleven thousand—and the women are as good students as the men. Nor has their presence created any special behavior problems.

Like President Roosevelt, General MacArthur breathed new life into the trade union movement. Before the Second World War, trade unions were illegal in Japan. In 1952, they had approximately seven million members.

MacArthur released the Communist leaders from jail, and they came and stood in the street in front of his headquarters in the resplendent Dai Ichi building in the center of Tokyo, bowed stiffly from the waist many times, and greeted him with loud and repeated "Banzais."

He sanctioned and some say he drafted Article 9 of Japan's new Constitution whereby "the Japanese people forever renounce war as a sovereign right of the nation and the threat or use of force as means of settling international disputes."

He introduced a land reform which eliminated absentee landowners and transformed tenants into owners and thereby conferred very great benefits on the peasantry and the nation.

He disbanded the Zaibatsu, the giant industrial and banking trusts or cartels which controlled a large share of Japan's economy.

Before the war, the courts were agencies of the Ministry of Justice and obeyed the executive branch of the government. Now, the Chief Justice told me, they are "self-administered." The prewar federal police was dissolved, Parliament assigned greater powers, the Emperor shorn of authority.

MacArthur's office-made revolution should perhaps be viewed as the second installment of another American revolution in Japan, the one that began almost a century earlier when Commodore Matthew C. Perry on the flagship S.S. *Susquehanna* appeared, with three other U.S. men-of-war, in the Bay of Yedo (now Tokyo) in 1853; he returned with more ships in 1854, and thrust open the closed door which had shut out the West. Prior to that, for two centuries, the Japanese allowed no foreigners, except a handful of Dutchmen, to live in or enter their country. Perry gave the Japanese their first view of the steamboat and of big cannon. It stirred the nation's jealousy, imitativeness, and fear of weakness. Thousands of Japanese went to study in European and American universities. Western techniques were naturalized in Japan. With their brilliant adaptability, the Japanese, in fact, sometimes improved on them. Japan became the foremost power of Asia with the strength to defeat Russia and encroach on China.

This startling and rapid metamorphosis could not help influencing the manners and thought patterns of the people. Yet many have wondered how great the influence was. Perry unlocked the gate to Japan; did he push aside the sliding door that opens the Japanese home? When the Japanese businessman, or factory or office worker rejoined his family he put away his Western clothes and put on his kimono. This was symbolic. The Japanese house was hardly touched by modernization; its materials may have been factory-made, but the samurai would have had no difficulty recognizing its design, cooking facilities, and plumbing and heating fixtures or the absence thereof. Perry ended Japan's isolation but could not invade the fortress which is the Japanese family. Did MacArthur?

The moment it went into effect MacArthur's revolution underwent Japanization; it was refracted, modified, diluted not by ill will or sabotage but by passing through the personality of the Japanese people. As in China, the dominant social unit of Japan is the family. The Communist revolution of China, being totalitarian, seeks to transfer the individual's primary loyalty from the family to the state. MacArthur's democratic revolution as written into the new Constitution undertook to make the individual supreme. Its purpose was not to break up the family but to break the dictatorial power of the head of the family over all aspects of the lives of all its members as long as they lived. "The new Constitution," Chief Justice Tanaka said, "abolished family power and makes the individual uppermost."

A constitution, however, is merely a step toward reality; it does not automatically become reality. Most Japanese agree that the new, the democratic, is gripped in a ferocious grapple with the old, the feudal. The old has charm and beauty and the Japanese like it. But some of it has gone and more of it will go. Women, for instance, are unlikely to lose their franchise or their right to hold public office. "Men now know that they cannot do as they please," Mrs. Hanako Muraoka, writer, critic, and social worker said to me in her home; there are more divorces on women's initiative; the government is helping in the dissemination of birth control information; girls are somewhat freer and therefore happier. On the other hand, wives, daughters, and daughters-in-law are undoubtedly still treated as inferiors in many families.

After I had been in Japan several weeks serious Japanese and foreigners began inquiring whether I had been to a geisha house. I said, no, I was too busy collecting information. "You are making a mistake," was the frequent rejoinder. "You can't understand Japan without seeing the geishas." So I went. The visit threw light on the Japanese family.

Some geishas are prostitutes, but they are not typical. Some geishas are concubines, or permanent lady friends of city husbands, but they are not brought into the family as in China. Most geishas are nothing more than educated entertainers, and men go to a geisha house for something they usually do not get at home. I once took the owner of a newspaper chain in India to a New York dinner party. He said it was his first social experience in the company of women who were not members of his family. Men in a number of Asian countries are similarly deprived. The Japanese male, however, has had the inventiveness to provide himself with a beautiful outside substitute. He sits with a number of men friends on the floor in a delightfully furnished room sipping harmless saké and listening to one or two or three geishas strumming their long samisens and singing. Then the geishas may dance together or with the men or play innocent little tricks like the one that involved me: I was standing after a dance when a geisha in front of me pushed me and I rolled over the back of a geisha who was hunched on all fours behind me. There is conversation and laughter and holding of hands, and the geishas tell stories or recite tankas, and the atmosphere is light, gay, and relaxed, and then the Japanese husband goes home to his wife and children. The geisha supplements the home and relieves family life of some tedium. The wife may get the bill in the mail and understandingly pay it.

Miss Shiho Sakanishi, literary critic, translator of Japanese poetry into English, Chief of the Japan Section of the Library of Congress in Washington, D.C. for twelve years, with whom Herbert Passin and I spent many delightful, fruitful hours in her home, in the Imperial, and in her office in the House of Peers where she lectured members of the Upper House of Parliament on world events, gave us some interesting interpretations of the role of the family in Japan. "The predominant mentality," she said, "is 'One man rules, the other man bakes cakes,' each to his place, and the cakes must excel for the sake of the family, not for the sake of the customer." There are no horizontal ties in society, she explained. "The head of the family must care for his family, but if a neighbor starves it is not his concern. If you're impolite to a stranger it is not impoliteness. Every family for itself, is no basis for democracy. Social consciousness is weak. But it is developing," she added. "Subordinates are no longer subservient. Children talk back to parents. With the emergence of individualism has come a new sense of nationhood. Japan was never nationalistic. We loved the Emperor and obeyed him but the average Japanese had no feeling of nation. The wars with China and Russia made us realize we were a nation and then the defeat made everybody conscious of a common fate and that feeds nationalism. But friendships are rare. Most Japanese have no trust in others and no confidence in themselves. The individual prefers to share responsibility with a group rather than shoulder it himself. The family is his refuge from the world."

The family is of course more tightly knit in the village than the city. But the provision in MacArthur's Constitution abolishing primogeniture was aimed at the absolute power of the head of the family in rural areas. The eldest son is no longer the sole heir; property is divided among all children. Now come the modifications made by life. Since division of the land causes fragmentation of farms, orphaned sons may agree to work their parcels in common or, as Chief Justice Tanaka explained, younger sons and daughters renounce their inheritance in favor of the eldest son. Thus custom defeats the law. But such renunciation assumes openings for the younger sons either in the armed services or in the cities. If these avenues are blocked by too little rearmament or by urban economic stagnation, social explosives will begin to accumulate. The Japanese village is already overcrowded. Breaking up a father's farm into three farms for his three sons and nine farms for their sons would ruin agriculture. As an alternative, the city must provide employment for surplus villagers. In that case, Japan needs bigger foreign markets. Intensive birth control and emigration might be tried as contributory solutions. MacArthur's land reform was a huge success, and in villages I visited the farmers were happy about it, but his reforms have raised new rural problems.

The American occupation authorities quickly became aware of the power of the head of the family, or perhaps one should say, in more psychological terms, the power of the father figure, in the cities too. Some aspects were visible, like the devotion of the people to the Emperor. But one phenomenon eluded investigators for several years. They sensed some kind of hidden power, a patriarchal system which established a loyalty tie between superiors and inferiors in various fields, especially in labor. The Japanese, it was learned, called this attachment "*Oyabun-Kobun*" or "Parent-Child" or "Father-Son." The *oyabun* might have several *kobun* who in turn were *oyabun* to several lower *kobun*; it was, in other words, a hierarchy. In industry, for instance, an *oyabun* is, in effect, a labor boss who recruits working men for an employer, and receives the workers' wage and shares it with them. But the *oyabun* has duties too. He and his *kobun* are members of a gang or clique and make pledges of mutual loyalty and service at a solemn ceremony. The *oyabun* will finance a wedding in his *kobun's* family, or pay sickness and unemployment benefits. One *kobun*, involved in a serious automobile accident, did not ask to see his wife and children, he asked for his *oyabun* and on his deathbed pledged the *oyabun* to support the family. Japanese regard such obligations as binding.

The *oyabun-kobun* relationship, undoubtedly a holdover from the feudal lord-and-vassal relationship, was in fact kept alive by the suppression of the trade union movement in prewar years as well as by the absence of an inclusive social security system. It remains so elusive and traditional that no effective way has been found of combating it. It persists just as the Zaibatsu families, like Mitsui, Mitsubishi, and Sumitomo, which controlled so much of Japan's big business under the militaristic regime, have survived all efforts to stamp them out. The old in Japan is resilient, the new forces are still weak. The old is a web, a pervading, interlocking network hallowed by custom. The new is unorganized sentiment.

MacArthur's Constitution, aiming to end the Emperor's absolute power as the nation's father, decreed that "he shall not have powers related to government." He is merely the symbol of the State and of the unity of the people, deriving his position from the will of the people with whom resides sovereign power." The people are sovereign, not the Mikado. This is new and revolutionary.

By all available evidence, the royal family remains immensely popular. Crowds always stand around the palace in the center of Tokyo and bow to its high stone walls. I was in Tokyo when Akihito, the eighteen-year-old eldest son of the Emperor, was officially installed as Crown Prince. The nation treated it as a momentous event. At birth he had been hailed as the 125th direct descendant of the Sun Goddess. But by his father's announcement of dedeification, the young man is now a human being, rides a horse, goes to school, and behaves more democratically than his ancestors did at his age. The public seems to like it and want more of it. "To be a symbol does not mean that you have to be a doll," a high school student wrote in a letter printed in a Tokyo newspaper during the events attending the Prince's formal investiture as Heir Apparent. "I want you to be human-like and share joy and sorrow with us." I doubt whether such a letter would have been printed before the war. The Empress goes to concerts and sits in the front row and then meets the performers and shakes hands. The Emperor consorts more with commoners.

Nevertheless, *Yomiuri* was not the only daily which warned that the Crown Prince must not become a "new god." The danger is not great, but it exists, probably because in times of uncertainty and weak governments a nation yearns for a pole of authority. Human beings often go very far afield to find a father-god. Some Japanese chose Stalin, others chose Mao. Some needed an idol, others were reacting against a master, the United States.

The American military occupation was rather mild and the Japanese reaction to it remarkably co-operative. Nevertheless, no nation enjoys the presence of the armed forces of a foreign conqueror, particularly of a conqueror whose manners are so different from those of the conquered. An American or Englishman need merely imagine how he would feel if his country were occupied by Japanese.

Japan accepted the occupation with considerable docility and adaptability. I think the trouble began brewing after April 28, 1952. On that date, the occupation officially came to an end and Japan was again a free, sovereign nation. Yet on December 6, 1952, during a street parade of left-wing trade unions, United States Military Police displaced Japanese civilian policemen at a number of intersections and directed traffic with their whistles. I saw and heard them. The parade had been preceded by a mass meeting in Hibiya Park. After the speeches the audience formed a column and began the march through the city. Just where they emerged from the park stood an American jeep with two U.S. army lieutenants making notes on board pads which rested on their knees. Anybody with brains would have left these tasks to the Japanese. Why give critical and hostile persons free proof that America was still dominant in Japanese affairs? Why feed the cry of "American imperialism"? In 1955, U.S. armed forces stationed in Japan engaged in artillery practice on the slopes of beautiful Mount Fuji which the Japanese consider sacred. This is not the way to make friends.

During my five weeks in Japan the press reported a statement by Republican Congressman Joseph W. Martin, of Massachusetts, urging the use of Japanese soldiers in the Korean War. This may have made sense in the United States or in Mr. Martin's home state where parents naturally wanted fewer of their sons to go to war in far-off territories, but in South Korea President Syngman Rhee said that if Japanese were brought into Korea he would turn his army around to fight them (there is an ancient feud between Japanese and Koreans), and in Japan opponents of rearmanent said this was an additional argument against it, the Americans were merely looking for Japanese cannon fodder. Americans sometimes forget that their words may sound differently in foreign ears.

The Japanese reluctance to rearm was very widespread, indeed overwhelming. It did not take much wisdom to grasp the change which had taken place in world affairs: Russia was strong and China was strong and no territory could be torn from them by an aggressive Japan. Neither would the United States, Great Britain, and France permit Japan to engage in profitable imperialist adventures in Southeast Asia or anywhere in the Pacific. "What about defense?" I argued.

"Russia is on our doorstep in the Kurile Islands," some Japanese replied. "We can easily be invaded. Later you might liberate us, but we would lose in both operations." Japan's experience in offensive warfare in 1941 and 1942 has undermined faith in defensive operations. Unspoken yet present is the conviction that in an emergency the United States would have to defend them, so why ruin one's own economy and again expose the nation to the dangers of militarism and dictatorship? Some Japanese also probably had a lurking suspicion, especially after the Korean War, that the United States might not win.

In the village of Nawa, sixty miles from Tokyo, an astonishingly prosperous village (4,000 bicycles to 8,600 inhabitants), I met the headman and his committee at the village hall. I polled them on Japanese rearmament: The Mayor was opposed, the doctor was opposed, the left Socialist was opposed, all eight were opposed though they belonged to the whole rainbow of parties from rightest Tory to pinkest pro-Communist.

American diplomacy nevertheless persistently insisted that Japan rearm. It did not make the United States more popular or create an impression of American sincerity, for Washington was asking the Japanese to violate MacArthur's Constitution. The new ground forces were first named National Police Reserve, then National Safety Force, then Defense Forces, and their equipment included tanks and artillery, but this was not called rearmament. Japan leased frigates from the United States, but frigates, Prime Minister Shigeru Yoshida told Parliament, are not warships. (The newspapers printed photos of the Director-General of the National Safety Corps inspecting a leased Japanese frigate carrying heavy guns.) Though the Constitution declares that "land, sea and air forces, as well as other war potential, will never be maintained," soldiers and sailors in uniform walked the streets, lived in barracks, and maneuvered with military equipment, yet the Japanese government, by a verbal legerdemain which fooled none, said this did not constitute rearmament, it was merely self-defense. Nevertheless, the Prime Minister promises disarmament if the world disarms. Such tactics would hardly increase the people's faith in their government or Constitution or in democracy.

Many Japanese are pessimistic about the future of Japanese democracy and economy. Japan is a highly developed nation of almost ninety million inhabitants with a very high living standard (higher, it seemed to me, than in large parts of Italy and even France) but narrowly limited resources.[5] It has water power, and practically every house enjoys electric light; and it has the sea, and, unlike the Indians, the Japanese have no food taboos, they eat everything, and a fish store is like a museum of strange creatures and weeds from the deep. Every square foot of soil, the road embankment, the ditch, the farmyard, is cultivated, by hand where necessary, and the yields per acre are enormous. One sees few working animals in a Japanese village, there is so much manpower, and one sees few cows; it is sometimes more economical to grow food for them than to let them graze, so the cattle remain in their stalls and are massaged to make up for lack of movement, and the result is that Tokyo restaurants supply the best steaks in the world, massaged, marbled beef.

Labor is plentiful but not land and not minerals. The country therefore must import food and raw materials, and either pay for its imports or take subsidies in one form or another (financing of rearmament is a subsidy) from the United States. The population is eating better and multiplying rapidly, despite birth control, and that means more food imports; wages have risen since the war and the renewal of industrial machinery has lagged since the 1930's, and that means bigger difficulties in finding foreign markets. For a number of years, nevertheless, American pressure prevented Japan from trading with China. One is not sure how much business the Japanese could find in Red China, probably less than they expect—Russia is trying to corner that market—but it would be healthier to let them find out than to dream of remote nonexistent fleshpots from which the United States bars them. Meanwhile the forced separation strengthens the yearning for better ties with China. Moreover, America is under a moral and practical obligation to cover any deficits which result from

[5] "As has often been pointed out, the total area of Japan today is slightly less than that of the state of California, and only 16% is arable. If California were as densely populated as Japan, her population would be 93,500,000, or 60% of the present population of the United States." John D. Rockefeller, 3rd, "Japan Tackles Her Problem," *Foreign Affairs*, New York, July, 1954.

the restrictions on Japan's trade with the Chinese Communists.

When I came home from India in 1948, my interest in that country led me to make a public proposal of a triangle, consisting of India, Japan, and the United States, for the rapid economic development of India. The scheme might have been expanded to include all of Southeast Asia. I am not sure how well it would work. Asians are suspicious of Japan because of her militaristic, aggressive past. A formidable combination of American dollars and Japanese genius might frighten them as a design for conquest. Besides, the pride and economic nationalism of Asian countries inspire them to want to do things with a minimum of foreign aid and personnel. On the other hand, India has reaped a rich advantage by borrowing Japanese methods of rice culture. If fears and prejudices could be banished, all countries would benefit from co-operation.

What is no longer open to question is that the modern age has confronted Japan, and Germany, and Great Britain, and to a lesser extent France and Italy, with this serious problem: the exploitation of backward, agrarian colonial regions by advanced industrial nations is at an end or rapidly coming to an end. Most of the newly independent Asian countries are eager to industrialize. Retarded European countries both sides of the Iron Curtain are industrializing. The Soviet Union is the second greatest industrial power of the world and China is following the same path. There are no new fields to conquer by military force, and old markets have shrunk because each country is bent on maximum self-supply. If the world is entering a period of national autarchy or self-sufficiency the industrialized peoples will have to reduce their living standards and the industrializing countries will pay an exorbitant price for their progress.

Nobody in the world would be unemployed if humanity were humane and civilized enough to undertake the simple task of making available a school for every child, a hut or house for every family, an adequate number of calories for every human being, a doctor for every village in all the continents, clothing to suit the climate, and some rudimentary provision for transportation, entertainment, higher education, and so forth. At present more than a billion persons out of the two and a half billion on this earth live on the level of animals. I suspect that few American farmers would keep their cattle in the accommodations which most Asians and Africans call home all their lives. No wonder there are no markets for Japan and other countries. We need some international economic planning. The business of diplomacy should be the welfare of peoples.

Part Six
THE NEW ERA

CHAPTER THIRTY-SEVEN

The Revolt That Failed

SOMEDAY the Soviet empire will inevitably go the way of all empires. In the fourth century B.C., King Philip and his son, Alexander the Great of Macedonia, conquered Danubian lands, Greece, Persia, Palestine, and penetrated as far as India and what is now the Soviet Union. Today Macedonia is a tiny, scarcely known area part Bulgarian, part Greek, and part Yugoslav. The Grand Duchy of Lithuania was once a powerful empire with which Europe had to reckon; under Algirdas, who reigned from 1345 to 1377, it extended from the Baltic to the Black Sea. But after the First World War, independent Lithuania was a miniscule country with just over a million inhabitants, and in the second it was absorbed by Moscow and ceased to exist. In the seventeenth century, the Duchy of Courland, a part of Latvia, possessed colonies in Africa and America. In modern times, Turkey embraced the Crimea, large parts of the Ukraine, a large segment of the Balkans, and most of the Arab world. Now Turkey has shrunk to the Anatolian plateau and a toehold in Europe. The withdrawal of Britain from India and of Holland from Indonesia is fresh in memory.

Why, then, should it be assumed that Russia will forever rule Poland or Czechoslovakia or Hungary or Albania? The power of states waxes, stagnates, and wanes. Fractions of one country become independent or adhere to another. Parts of the Soviet Union have much more in common with China than with Russia. Tajikistan in Soviet Central Asia is kin to India rather than to Muscovy. Azerbaijan, Turkestan, and Uzbekistan have deep ties with Turkey and probably deep resentment of their present Kremlin rulers. The fascination of maps is that looking at them the imagination wanders to combinations very different from existing ones. Coming centuries will operate surgically on many of today's sovereignties and, very likely, on the concept of sovereignty itself.

When the Soviet empire dies somebody will write its "decline and fall." The germ of ultimate destruction has been present from the start, for the empire was born in the cynical Hitler-Stalin Pact of August, 1939, which precipitated the Second World War and achieved its expansion by means of invading Russian armies operating without popular consent. The actual decline began with the defection of Yugoslavia which showed that Russia held her colonies not by the comradely bonds of Communism or any other common interest but by force alone. Exactly five years later, Soviet imperialism experienced a worse moral defeat. For whereas in the case of Yugoslavia a government slipped out of the Kremlin's steel embrace, in East Berlin and East Germany, in June, 1953, it was the people, and especially the working class, who rebelled against their Communist masters. Since then the fact of Soviet oppression in Europe has been undeniable.

Because the insurrection in East Germany failed is no reason to conclude that it was wasted effort. The Edward Gibbon of the Soviet empire will know that anti-imperialist energy is stored and never lost. Rome was not wrecked in a day. The mere fact that the East German revolt took place at all makes it a remarkable historic event. For eight years, the eighteen million inhabitants of the Russian zone of Germany had borne their Red star, working hard, living badly. Muscovite despotism, transplanted to East Germany, Hungary, Rumania, Poland, Bulgaria, Czechoslovakia, and Albania, was so harsh, ubiquitous, and frightening that the people did not dare complain, much less oppose. Indeed, the silent suffering had continued long enough for the social scientists to assume that a population without weapons and penetrated by spies could never rise against a dictatorship in peacetime. Wrapping themselves smugly in this comforting thought, the Communists asserted that they enjoyed "the unanimous support of the masses." It never occurred to them that this fiction could be shattered. Then came the revolt.

It began at dawn on June 16, 1953, when eighty construction workers on the Stalinallee in East Berlin protested against Russian speed-up methods and wage cuts. By evening this small strike had burgeoned into a city-wide general strike and the next day it ballooned into a zone-wide national uprising in which over a million persons, marching through the streets of more than two hundred towns and cities in the Soviet zone, burned Communist banners and pictures of Stalin and other Red gods, unlocked Communist prisons and liberated the inmates, raided government offices, and shouted, "We want free elections," "We don't want to be slaves." The German police was swept away, the German Communist government's authority crumpled.

Thereupon the entire Russian army of occupation was called out, twenty thousand troops in East Berlin alone, more than two hundred thousand in the entire Soviet zone, with hundreds of tanks, armored cars, antitank guns, and machine gunners on motorcycles. Defiant Davids hurled stones at the giant tanks, pushed logs between their wheels, stuffed bricks, brief cases, and refuse into their cannon mouths, and even clambered up their steel sides and broke their radio antennae.

But when the machine guns began to chatter, the unarmed multitudes crept back into their homes and scores of young rebel leaders escaped to freedom in West Berlin. Nevertheless, the martial law imposed by Major General Dubrova, the Soviet commander, at 1 P.M. on June 17, remained in force throughout Eastern Germany until zero hour, Sunday, July 12, twenty-four days later. It obviously took the Communists a long time to calm the zone and compose their nerves.

The Communists were too shocked, confused, and dishonest to offer a logical or convincing account, much less an explanation, of what had occurred. *Pravda*, echoed by the carbon-copy newspapers of East Germany and the East European satellites, referred to the revolt as "the adventure undertaken by foreign hirelings in Berlin on June 17." This short sentence contained three big lies contradicted by photographs, scores of eyewitness reports, and statements in the Communist press itself. The first lie was the implication that nothing happened in East Berlin on June 16; the second, that nothing happened outside East Berlin on June 17; the third, and most damaging to Moscow, that the people of the Russian zone had responded to foreign adventurers.

The morning of June 18, after reading the New York newspaper reports about the events in East Germany, I said to myself, "This is too important to miss."

Six days later I left for Berlin. I stayed four weeks.

I spent the first evening at the home of Melvin J. Lasky, editor of the U.S. State Department's *Der Monat* magazine, where friends filled me with stories about the new crop of German heroes, not generals or warriors, but young working men, engineers, and students who had defied Communist power on June 16 and 17. Some, they said, had fled to West Berlin and I could find them through Dr. Rainer Hildebrandt who had helped plan the attempt on Hitler's life in July, 1944,[1] and fostered East German opposition to Moscow ever since the end of the war.

The next afternoon, more than a dozen of the East German rebel leaders were crowded into Dr. Hildebrandt's living room. Eagerly, they related their experiences. One of them, who seemed in his early thirties, was wearing old, abbreviated shorts, a white shirt that was too tight for him, brief ankle socks, and heavy old shoes. I invited him to visit me the following morning at the Hotel am Zoo on the Kurfuerstendamn.

He came in the same clothes. They were all he had and they were borrowed, for he had escaped from Magdeburg, an East German city sixty miles from Berlin, on the night of the seventeenth, made his way on foot cross-country, and then, clad only in underpants, swam the last three hundred yards across a lake to West Berlin. I asked him to tell me his story in the greatest detail and took almost verbatim notes:

Konzertmeister Hans Herzberg, age thirty-six, had never been active in politics of any kind. With his wife and three children, he had lived the life of a solid, middle-class German burgher, leading his orchestra, and composing music in the Richard Strauss manner. The evening of June 16, dressed in white tie and tails, he conducted *Die Fledermaus* before an appreciative audience that packed the Magdeburg Opera House. At home later, he listened to a late RIAS broadcast about demonstrations in Berlin but paid no special attention to it and went to bed. (RIAS is the State Department's Radio in the American Sector of West Berlin.)

The next morning neighbors told him about some sort of "events" in Magdeburg. At 9 A.M., Hans Herzberg took a walk into town to see for himself. A long column of striking streetcar employees was

---

[1] He recorded the experience in an eloquent, enlightening book, *Wir Sind die Letzten, aus dem Leben des Widerstandskaempfers Albrecht Haushofer und Seiner Freunde*, Neuwied-Berlin: Michael-Verlag.

moving toward the Hasselbachplatz in the center of the city to the accompaniment of bystander applause. Several pedestrians tagged along, and so did he.

By the time the column reached the square in front of the railway station it was already crowded. Seeing a group of about forty to fifty demonstrators enter the near-by seven-story Free German Youth building on Otto von Guericke Strasse he joined them. They met no resistance and went from room to room throwing posters of Stalin, Otto Grotewohl, the head of the East German government, Walter Ulbricht, the head of the East German Communist party, and others, as well as red flags, propaganda leaflets, newspapers, and office files out the windows.

Herzberg remained inside the Youth building for about half an hour, then descended to the railway station plaza and kicked in a wooden propaganda booth. I asked him why he did it. "I did it impulsively, without thinking. I had come to hate their lying words. No, I had no fear of the police; there were no police around." He never gave the Russians a thought.

Now a railroad employee who had seen Herzberg kick in the kiosk told him that a passenger train from Cologne, in West Germany, would soon be pulling in at the station. Herzberg waved his arm and called on the crowd to come to the platform and greet the train as a symbol of national unity between West and East Germany. Before the train stopped a sign reading "INTER-ZONAL INSPECTION OF DOCU-MENTS HERE," was destroyed. "No more zones," the people shouted. Eight Vopos—"Volkspolizei" or "People's Police"—tried to interfere, but the demonstrators disarmed them, locked them in a service room, and hammered their rifles on the stone pavement.

"Didn't you want the weapons?" I asked.

"No," Herzberg replied, "it never occurred to me that we might have to use arms."

As the train came to a halt, some passengers put out their heads and seemed to be wondering whether this was not a Communist attack on them as travelers from West Germany. On being reassured, they distributed chocolates, cigarettes, cake, and fruit among the Magdeburgians and joined in acclaiming the end of the zonal partitioning of Germany.

A few minutes after the Cologne train continued on its journey, one from East Berlin to Halberstadt arrived. Herzberg and three other unarmed men went from compartment to compartment in the train and ordered passengers with Communist part pins and Soviet-

German Friendship buttons in their lapels to remove them. "This is all over," Herzberg told them. "The Magdeburg population has risen against the Communist government." Nobody resisted. Many passengers were jubilant.

Informed that a train from Halberstadt with a prison van attached would soon come in on Platform 5, Herzberg summoned the demonstrators to follow him there. As the train slowed down, a Vopo guard on the prison car drew his pistol, but a working man hit him on the head with a bottle and he dropped his pistol, jumped to the platform, and fled.

"I entered the car with two other men," Herzberg recalled, "and ordered the two Vopos inside to hand over the prisoners' papers. Seeing the crowd on the platform they complied; they also obeyed my instructions to remove their shoulder straps and insignia and disappear. I looked through the documents and found that there were no criminals in the transport, only politicals, twenty-four in all including two women. Each prisoner occupied a tiny individual cell with a little window and bars to the outside and a door to the corridor inside. One by one we opened the doors, gave the prisoner his papers, and advised him to leave at once."

Stimulated by this accomplishment, Herzberg led the platform crowd of about fifteen hundred to two thousand to the police headquarters on the Halberstaedter Strasse in the center of Magdeburg, near his house. He thought of liberating more prisoners. It was now about 1 P.M. and as they marched he heard the grinding sound of tanks. Two T-34 tanks with six wheels inside their caterpillar treads came up from behind and moved toward the marchers. The column opened and let the tanks through. A Russian in uniform stood in the turret of each tank but did nothing and the crowd made no hostile move either. "When we reached the police headquarters," Herzberg continued, "we found that we had been preceded by other insurgents who used rocks, crowbars, and clubs to break open the gates and storm into the courtyard. As my column surged through the entrance, Vopos fired from the roof of the building. I saw three dead and eight wounded. Nevertheless, some townspeople forced their way into the building and demanded the release of political prisoners. An official announced from the balcony that the prisoners would be liberated in half an hour, but the people yelled 'Pfui,' and said they wouldn't wait. Everything was confusion now; I heard that twenty-five prisoners were freed."

Between fifteen and twenty thousand people had assembled around the police headquarters when, at 2 P.M., ten Russian tanks and ten armored cars drove into the multitude and tried to disperse it but failed. After a brief delay, Russian infantry arrived in company strength, 350 men, according to Herzberg's estimate, and began herding the crowd off the square into the side streets. Tanks followed the infantry, and Herzberg testified, "Russian civilians, armed with submachine guns, popped up in the crowd. I was near one of them and heard him give orders in Russian to the demonstrators. They drove the people toward the Russian foot soldiers who seized some Germans and dragged them into the police headquarters."

Here Hans Herzberg went home to see to his family. He drove them in a car to the town of Quedlinburg, thirty-five miles from Magdeburg, where he had once lived and then returned to Magdeburg to see what there was to be done for the insurrection, but on learning that the tanks ruled the city and that his apartment had been searched, he began walking toward West Berlin. His role as insurgent leader had lasted six hours and ended as suddenly as it began leaving him rather lost and wondering whether his future was to play politics in East Germany or music in West Germany.

In ones or twos other leaders of the revolt came to tell me their stories. Meanwhile I read the East Berlin dailies delivered at my hotel by the corner newspaperman together with the Russian papers which he had twenty-four hours after their appearance in Moscow. They still tried to keep up the fiction of "the Berlin adventure of June 17," but: on June 30, the *Taegliche Rundschau* and *Neues Deutschland*, East Berlin Communist dailies, published a detailed report of the revolt in the important city of Leipsig; on June 30, the *Taegliche Rundschau* reported that rioters on June 17 had killed a government store manager in Rathenow and released prisoners in the city of Halle; on July 7, the Weimar daily *Das Volk* published an account of the trial of a clergyman named Sammler, a former town mayor named Wille, a peasant named Thybusch, and a Herr Lux, who, having heard the RIAS broadcast on June 16, addressed a meeting in the marketplace of a little spa called Bad Tennstedt on June 17 under the slogans, "Down with the Communist party" and "This is the end"; on July 8, *Neues Deutschland* said the gate of a big factory in Madgeburg had been smashed in on June 17 and that many factories were on strike that day; on July 9, the *Taegliche Rundschau* referred to peasant insurgents. There were other statements of a similar character. Unable to maintain the pretense any longer, the East German government admitted on July 15 that disturbances had taken place on June 17 in East Berlin "and several other cities of the German Democratic Republic." The "several" included the important towns of Halle, Merseburg, Fürstenwalde, Bitterfeld, Chemnitz, Cottbus, Thale, Jena, where strikers from the Zeiss and Schott factories stormed the government office building and trade union headquarters and strewed the files on the street (photographs of these scenes were later published in the West German press) and released political prisoners from jail; Leipzig, Brandenburg, Rosslau, where the entire work force of the Elbe shipbuilding wharf downed tools, marched to the marketplace for a mass meeting, and liberated 180 political prisoners; Wolfen, Görlitz, Weimar, and Dresden. Each day the newspapers of East Germany were forced by their desire to publish news about the punishment of rebels to reveal additional centers of the revolt. Thus, toward the end of July, for instance, the East German daily *Neue Zeit* reported the trial and conviction of sixteen persons in the small East Saxon town of Niesky for assaulting the buildings of the secret police and of the Communist party and maltreating party officials. One defendant, a photographer, was sentenced to life imprisonment.

By the testimony of eyewitnesses as well as on evidence in Communist newspapers, the revolt reached into every corner of East Germany's totalitarian "Democratic Republic." But the uprising began in East Berlin and it was there that its causes and dramatic course showed most clearly. In fact, it is quite likely that but for the unique situation of Berlin, bisected as it is between the West and Russia, the revolt would not have taken place. The Soviet authorities could administer their part of Berlin but were unable to keep its inhabitants from traveling to West Berlin or to prevent West Berliners from entering East Berlin. East Berliners normally enjoy easy access, by subway and urban railway and on foot, to West Berlin, and vice versa.

One afternoon in July, 1953, I left West Berlin by urban railway and within fifteen minutes I was at Alexanderplatz, a square deep in the heart of East Berlin. During the next two and a half hours I walked slowly, meandering through main thoroughfares and side streets, looking at people's faces and clothes and at automobiles, taxis, trolleys, and other vehicles, and going into shops, restaurants, and bookstores. I had known this part and most other parts of Berlin since I first lived in the city in December, 1921. The Eastern sector had been subjected to universal and heartbreaking bombing, but so had many wards of the Western sector. In the latter, however, some ruins had been torn down and replaced with new buildings and, where this was not the case, they had been reconstructed up to the knee—that is their first and second stories had been rebuilt into new stores, cafés, restaurants, and homes. In the Soviet part, however, literally nothing new or bright or elegant greeted the eye except the huge housing project for government officials and similarly privileged persons in the Stalinallee—the usual Russian idea of demonstrative achievement or display for Communism propaganda boasts.

East Berlin (population 1,200,000) was gray and bedraggled, with the best, halfway usable buildings occupied by government and party offices. Nobody was well dressed and most men, women, and children were poorly dressed. The dyes seemed of such pitiful quality that everything melted into a kind of dull grayish brown. Men's suits and women's frocks were made of shoddy, loosely woven material and instead of keeping their shape assumed the shape of the wearer with bulges at the hips, waist and knees. Shoes were inferior and few persons wore hats. In the once-fashionable Friedrichstrasse, the rue de la Paix of Berlin, a woman sold children's socks on a stand, but the white socks were dirty cream and the pink of the pink socks had run and was spotty, and I had a feeling that a youngster would go through them in three days. I watched a long queue at a state-owned vegetable shed, each customer with a bag or brief case or shopping net, and when, after a long wait, they finally made their purchases, they shuffled off with a bunch of tired carrots or old lettuce. The windows of the HO (Handels Organization) state stores displayed propaganda posters, wine and vodka bottles, and dusty models of goods supposedly on the shelves; inside, many shelves were empty; commodities lacked firm texture; cigarette boxes were misshapen and faded.

In all my wanderings in East Berlin, I saw no moderately inviting restaurant, only government eateries, and not one outside café, although Germans love them. The buses and street cars were of pre-Hitler vintage and seemed to have received their last coat of paint in the 1930's. The few taxis were aged and weary and groaned as they moved. Even Unter den Linden (the Park Avenue of Berlin) had little traffic.

The whole aspect of the Eastern sector of the city made me think back to a second-rate Soviet town, say Kiev, or Minsk, in the 1920's. East Berlin had been Russified, dragged down to the Soviet economic level. The pedestrians reflected the depleting effect of this process; their gait lacked the spring, their faces lacked the glow of vitamin-rich, hopeful persons. The obvious deterioration in East Germany may have been the result of a conscious Muscovite policy; the Kremlin does not want Russia to suffer by comparison with the satellites.

In West Berlin an attempt was being made, despite difficulties arising out of its geographic isolation inside the Iron Curtain world, to beautify life. In Eastern Berlin the opposite was true. The difference invalidated every word of official Communist propaganda pumped into East Berliners and East Germans. Trudging through West Berlin on Sundays or holidays or any day, they learned by visual arithmetic a lesson in the cost of Soviet domination. Each man and woman undoubtedly added up the total he or she paid, and many thereupon decided to substract themselves from the East. In the first five months of 1952, the number of East Germans who emigrated to West Berlin averaged 4,400 per month. Others probably stole across the frontier between Russian and Allied zones without going through West Berlin; some who entered West Berlin might not have registered at refugee headquarters. In June, 1952, the figure rose to 8,219; in July, to 13,182; and from August to the end of the year it averaged 15,000 a month. In January, 1953, the number jumped to 25,340; in February, 39,962; in March, 48,724; in April, 35,182; in May, 41,338; and the first two weeks of June, 1953, 33,183. These were the thermometer readings of East German discontent. On June 16 and 17, the mercury column rose to the top and cracked the glass.

Rebels never make a rebellion; they are pushed into it by their oppressor. The East German revolt was made by Stalin. After the war, food, industrial products, and machines from dismantled factories flowed out of East Germany into Russia as reparations for the cruel German depredations in the Soviet Union during the period of military hostilities. Industry languished, farm output fell, and human suffering grew. Stalin reacted in typical fashion; he tightened the screws. His new program, inaugurated in July, 1952, provided for the seizure of private farms and their conversion into Germany's first collectives, bigger investments in nationalized heavy industry and less money for the production of consumers' goods, the expropriation of additional privately owned factories, the opening of more state retail stores and the closing of more private stores, intensified persecution of the church, and the creation of the East German army under the transparent title of "People's Police in Barracks." The entire program was called "Bolshevization" and achieved an immediate rise in the production of anti-Bolsheviks. Similar policies wrought similar havoc in Russia's other satellites. Everywhere the evil of misconceived plans was aggravated by the ineradicable inefficiency inherent in centralized government bureaucracy.

Overtaken by a short confessional mood after the revolt, the Communists showed that they knew what was wrong. "It is not simply," wrote the prominent Communist author Stefan Heym, in the East Berlin *Berliner Zeitung* of July 15, 1953, "that June 17 came because it was organized from the West and because agents and provocateurs were at work. Without a real, existing discontent in broad strata of the population the provocateurs might have yelled themselves hoarse and nobody would have paid any attention to them." There were two kinds of discontent, Mr. Heym explained. One arose "from the mistaken measures of the government and the bureaucracy." These, he assured his readers lightheartedly, would soon be eliminated. But there is another "which will not die so easily. This dissatisfaction is best expressed in the little word, 'Before.'" The "Before," he says, refers to the Hitler period when, he writes, "many Germans," including sections of the German working class, enjoyed "quite good" conditions.

It is possible that truthful reports about the temper of the people had been sent to Moscow before the revolt. Stalin, however, had never been well equipped to recognize the failure of his policies or, if he did, to amend them, and in his old age blind stubbornness conquered him completely. But his youthful heirs, especially Beria and Malenkov, knew that it would not hurt their prestige to avow and undo Stalin's blunders. In May, 1953, therefore, V. S. Semyonov, Russia's Viceroy in East Germany, was summoned to Moscow and after protracted consultations there he returned to East Berlin on June 5 and handed the Communist government of the "German Democratic Republic" its new instructions. A faithful German translation of these was published in the press on June 11 as the decisions of that government. The East German Politburo, the communiqué declared, had met on June 9, and resolved that the Communist party and government had committed a "series of mistakes" which would now be corrected. Accordingly, "Peasants who . . . had fled to West Berlin or the Western zones would be granted the possibility of returning to their farms," and in the "exceptional instances" where this could not be done they were to receive full compensation for confiscated property. All other East Germans who had fled to the West could return and get back their property at "no disadvantage." Private artisans and merchants and also private industrial, construction, and transport firms could obtain "adequate short-term credits" from the state "with a view to increasing the output of mass-production goods." Toward the same end government stores would employ private retailers as agents. Furthermore, ration cards would be reissued to persons recently deprived of them (for political reasons), trolley car fares would be reduced, price rises for marmalade, synthetic honey and other sweets annulled, travel between East and West Germany facilitated, students expelled from high schools and colleges on account of social origin (for having been born in the wrong families) could re-enroll, and "forceful measures in the collection of delinquent taxes" from private farmers and businessmen were to cease.

These concessions were one of the main causes of the revolt. I heard East Berliners say: "Before the concessions were announced on June 11, anybody who criticized the government or party for its errors was branded a Fascist or traitor. Now the leaders themselves beat their breasts and loudly admit their errors. Why don't they resign?"

Moscow had publicly spanked Grotewohl, Ulbricht, and other East German Communists and compelled them to confess, repent, go into reverse, drop Stalin's Bolshevization and promise benefits to some groups. East Germans sensed confusion at the top. The arm of the driver which had hitherto held the reins so firmly now communicated a quiver of uncertainty, the men who had cracked the whip had themselves been whipped and were not, for the moment at least, fit to wield the whip themselves. By some unerring intuition, the public knew that the East German regime was timid and vacillating and could not hurt anybody, and this, indeed, proved to be true during that fraction of historic time in which the insurrection occurred.

The autopsy of the revolt reveals a second cause: working men's bitterness toward the so-called workers' state. The concessions of June 11 in favor of farmers, merchants, and manufacturers came on the heels of an East German Council of Ministers' announcement, on May 28, which decreed an additional "minimum average" increase of 10 per cent in the production norms of state enterprises. The norm is a special Soviet managerial invention for the sweating of labor under the nation-wide piecework system; it is a unit of production for a unit of the working man's pay, say, ten screws for ten rubles, or ten marks. But once the employees in a given plant achieve that unit of production, some "shock-troop" workers, incited by the management or the party, begin to turn out twelve screws in the time it used to take to do ten, and so twelve becomes the norm, but the pay is not raised, in fact anybody who cannot produce twelve screws suffers a pay cut till he can.

This is the kind of 10 per cent norm increase decreed for all factory workers in East Germany on May 28.

In a postrevolt postmortem, when the Communists, for a moment, publicly ate humble pie, Kurt Meier, a top official of the East German "trade unions," admitted in an article in the *Taegliche Rundschau* of June 30, 1953, that "many government factory directors unjustly and illegally reduced the wages of working men, shortened their vacations, and neglected safety regulations." But before the revolt, the Communist leaders obviously assumed that whereas they had to compensate the farmers, merchants, and industrialists for the co-operation which might otherwise have been withheld, the workers had no choice—they had to work to eat. Events proved that the workers had very powerful weapons at their disposal.

May 31, workers at the Sachsenwerke in Nieder-Seidlitz won a two-hour strike against a 10 per cent norm increase. June 3, strikers forced the management of a factory in Eisleben, near Halle, to drop a 12 per cent norm rise. June 10, two thousand steel workers in Henningsdorf, on the edge of East Berlin, staged a sit-down strike which achieved the cancellation of a norm boost and the liberation of strike leaders. June 13, a similar strike was victorious at the Abus machine plant in Gotha.

June 14 fell on a Sunday. At picnics and in courtyards, conversation centered on the norm increase and how to oppose it. Anna Seghers, the well-known and gifted German Communist novelist, writing in the East Berlin Communist *Taegliche Rundschau* of July 7, recalled a chat she had after the revolt with some laborers on the building site of the new Friedrichshain hospital. That June 14, she wrote, the workers "brought the strike motto home with them from a Sunday excursion on a steamer." Unfortunately, she complained, no Communist was present to explain that "this nation is your nation, this government is your government." She apparently suspected the workers of thinking it was not their nation but Russia, not their government but the Kremlin's own. She knew, in other words, that the strike was a strike but that it was also a protest against Communist colonialism, against an exploiting employer who doubled as alien ruler.

Monday, the workers on the Stalinallee housing construction talked strike. Tuesday, June 16, at seven in the morning, eighty bricklayers and others downed tools and announced they were marching to government headquarters on the Leipzigerstrasse in the center of town. One of them seized a Communist banner and painted, "WE DEMAND REDUCTION OF NORMS" on the reverse side. Behind this device the men circled in and out of the Stalinallee project chanting the rhymed slogan,

> Kollegen, reiht euch ein
> Wir wollen keine Sklaven sein.
> (Colleagues, join our ranks,
> We don't want to be slaves.)

Hundreds joined, and the march into town began. Women shoppers joined, working men joined. Passengers left their trolley cars and joined, then the motormen and conductors joined. The column grew at every block. Six burly hodcarriers in leather aprons walked in the front row. The column made a detour to the State Opera House which was undergoing repair. Five hundred builders joined. At the near-by Humboldt University students left their classrooms and joined. They passed the Soviet Embassy on Unter den Linden in silence and proceeded down the Wilhelmstrasse to the House of the Ministers on the Leipzigerstrasse. By this time, they numbered four to five thousand. (Published photographs of the scene confirm the estimate.)

The guards of the government building withdrew into the courtyard and closed the iron gate. The crowd commenced to shout, "We want Grotewohl," "We want the Goatee." ("The Goatee" was the bald and bearded Communist party chief Walter Ulbricht.) Instead, Fritz Selbmann, Minister of Steel Production, appeared and stood on a table brought out of the building. At first, the crowd did not let him speak and when he did make himself heard the demonstrators heckled him. Finally, Hanne, one of the hodcarriers, naked to the waist, stretched out a muscular arm and pulled Herr Selbmann down from the table. (This too shows on a photograph.) Hanne himself now made a speech atop the table; a girl in a Communist Youth jacket then climbed on the table, ripped off her jacket and threw it to the crowd, and denounced the government. She was followed by a housewife who complained of high prices. Meanwhile the growing multitude cried, "Down with the government," "We demand free elections."

"The Goatee," the meeting learned, was in Leipzig, so, after further speeches and some waiting, the column resumed its serpentine progress through East Berlin. At several places, police tried to stop them but, "we put our fingers into our mouths, whistled, and then, linking arms in the front rows," one of the leaders told me, "we walked straight ahead." The police desisted. Near the Oranienburg Gate the strikers blocked a government loudspeaking van which was urging the marchers to disperse because the May 28 norm increases had already been annulled. Working men climbed on the van and twisted its antennae. Later the demonstrators captured a radio van and broadcast antigovernment slogans to passing pedestrians. Many joined the column. Returned to the Stalinallee, the original strikers parked the van under an overnight guard.

Early in the evening rain descended in torrents, yet until midnight agitated groups stood on street corners, or sat over their beers in bars and commented on the surprising events of the day. Communists returning from a mass meeting who tried to argue with the outdoor groups were beaten. Police cars sent to rescue the Reds were overturned and their uniformed occupants mauled. The streets no longer belonged to the Communists regime. Political weathermen predicted "Storm" for the morrow. The norms by now were a vanishing issue. The strikers had become insurgents pursuing a political aim, they wanted a new government. The events of the day had encouraged them; the tyrants they had feared seemed powerless.

From dawn till dark on June 16 citizens of East Berlin beat a track to the door of RIAS in West Berlin and reported on the strike and the procession. For years RIAS had played an enormous role in the life of East Germany by giving them news about their own affairs. The station, operated by America's State Department from West Berlin, enjoyed the advantage of innumerable volunteer informants, many of them working men, foremen, engineers, and executives in Communist factories, some of them important employees in government offices, who slipped unheralded into the RIAS building to report about conditions and decisions in East Germany. A number of these informants, always taking care not to be detected, came at regular intervals to RIAS; others came irregularly, and at times they brought with them documents which they took from Communist government files at the end of the working day and replaced the next morning after RIAS had photostated or copied them. Years of experience taught the Germans and Americans at the radio station whom to trust and how to check information before broadcasting it. They rarely went wrong. Often the mere fact that RIAS told the East Germans about a secret decision of their government meant that it could not be enforced. Whenever RIAS reported resistance in one factory or area to a certain official measure opposition usually spread to other places. This was the effect of the minute-by-minute broadcasts by RIAS on June 16, 1953. Mr. Gordon A. Ewing, a State Department official and political director of RIAS, realized the significance of June 16 the moment the day dawned, and thereafter throughout the day, without cease, music and entertainment having been dropped, every act and word of the East Berlin strikers was beamed far and wide. News bulletins were repeated again and again because in some parts of the Russian zone of Germany the Communists occasionally succeeded in jamming RIAS.

Without RIAS, East Berlin would have learned about the strike—the news spread like wildfire by word of mouth—but East Germany outside Berlin might not have heard of it for days and the nationwide insurrection might never have taken place. As befits modern times, the June, 1953, revolt was a revolution by radio. The radio of the sedate State Department fomented revolution—in other people's territory. In effect, RIAS was the signal corps of the revolution telling one sector of the front about moves and changes on other sectors. It helped them to know the political slogans that had won approval in various places. It urged the East Germans "to exploit the uncertainty and insecurity of the authorities," but it cautioned them against "exposing yourself to avoidable dangers."

RIAS broadcasts about East Berlin on June 16 would not, however, have caused the insurrection to flare in all of East Germany if the strike news had not fallen on the fertile soil of popular unhappiness. RIAS merely supplied the spark; the fuel, thoroughly soaked in misery, was already there—stockpiled by Communist misdeeds.

Via RIAS, the June 16 East Berlin work stoppages and marches fused the discontent in the Russian zone of Germany into a revolutionary flame on the seventeenth. They naturally produced the same repercussions in East Berlin itself.

East Berlin's many factories were paralyzed by strikes from early morning, June 17. Shortly after daybreak, groups of strikers commenced waylaying cars occupied by Communist officials going to their offices, forced them to step out, removed their party buttons or pins, and then, in some cases, set fire to the autos. The police remained absent or neutral. Many policemen, judging by the number of them who escaped to West Berlin before and after the insurrection, undoubtedly sympathized with the anti-Communists.

Thousands of working men congregated at the gates of their factories, but not to work; they demonstrated. After preliminary meetings at which the government was denounced they usually formed up to march into the center of town. One of the most exciting events of that day was the march of the four thousand men of the Henningsdorf steel plant. On and on they came, a solid phalanx eight abreast in their grimy, oil-sodden overalls and gray-black work caps, the goggles of the furnace tenders hanging from their necks. It was raining, and dirty water dripped from their clothing and down their faces. Some were in bare feet, many wore clogs, and the "clop, clop" of their wooden shoes on the asphalt resounded through the streets bringing heads to every window and endless multitudes to the sidewalks. Twelve miles they marched in formation, from their plant on the border to East Berlin, through a part of East Berlin, then by a diagonal short cut through West Berlin, and back into East Berlin again. In East Berlin the people shouted encouragement to them, girls ran out to kiss them, old women embraced them. In the Western sector, they were acclaimed by spectators massed along the curbs and by thousands waving from windows and rooftops. Restaurants and cafés brought out trays of sandwiches and fruit; pedestrians ran into stores and got all the cigarettes and chocolate the money in their pockets would buy to distribute among the steel men.

Workers in the front ranks of the procession carried crude banners reading, "DOWN WITH THE GOVERNMENT" "WE WANT BUTTER," "WE WANT NO ARMY," "WE DEMAND FREE ELECTIONS."

"Free elections," came the deep-voiced cry from four thousand throats.

"Free elections," the spectators on the sidewalks echoed. This *was* a free election: four thousand pairs of legs were voting anti-Communist, they voted by walking, they voted in the rain.

Not far away, on a parallel thoroughfare—this too was photographed—six thousand striking railwaymen were likewise taking a short cut through West Berlin toward the heart of East Berlin. By 11:45 A.M. fifty thousand East Berliners had assembled in the Lustgarten (now renamed Marx-Engels Platz.) The streetcars, buses, and subway were on strike. Everybody walked. Walked, shouted, demonstrated and thereby voted. They and their brothers and sisters throughout the city and the Russian zone, were marching and voting for liberty. June 17 was election day throughout Communist East Germany, and the Communists elected nobody. The revolt exposed them as political bankrupts.

If anybody doubted this the tanks proved it. At 11 A.M., the tanks came roaring down the main thoroughfares of East Berlin; bumper to bumper they slowly rumbled forward, trying to clear the streets. Photographs show young Germans on the tanks attempting to open the turrets to attack the crews. Youngsters heaved rocks at the armored monsters.

The rebel leaders from East Berlin were unaminous in asserting that the discipline and technique of the Soviet tankist were exemplary. They held their fire except under extreme provocation, usually to defend their equipment. Quite a number of spectators testified that at times the Soviet military waved friendly greetings to the demonstrators. After all, they might have read in their Soviet schoolbooks about just such popular revolts against the Russian Czars, and here it was—a graphic enactment of Bolshevik texts—only this time it was directed against the Bolsheviks and their German Communist puppets.

The Soviet tanks also performed other tasks. They whisked away the family of prominent Communists to country hideouts. The ministers themselves were nowhere to be seen. Moscow's German puppets no longer functioned as a government.

Russian tanks filled this political vacuum and recaptured the streets. They defeated the people and the proletariat. It was good marksmanship but bad Marx. The Soviet Revolution, turned counterrevolutionary, reactionary, and imperialist, used steel and fire, the weapons of all oppressors, to crush the two-day East German revolution.

During the month of the East German revolt, antigovernment strikes and riots also occurred in the Pilsen area of Communist-dominated Czechoslovakia. Writing in the Chicago *Sun-Times* of March 22, 1954, about a tour of Poland, Frederick Kuh, veteran student of European conditions wrote: "There is strong opposition to the regime . . . secret police are hated and feared. . . . The Polish people have been suffering from an acute shortage of merchandise." The same situation maintained throughout the Soviet satellites: forcing of heavy industry, limited quantity and low quality of consumer goods, food in short supply, discontent, terror, political impotence of the people, no immediate threat to Russia's mastery but not a favorable starting place for further imperialist expansion or for a war against the West. Stalemate, immobility.

Equally, the Western powers had not been able to take advantage of the East German insurrection. The Eisenhower Administration quickly learned that running a government was very different from running and winning an election campaign. In the campaign the voters had been promised a "roll-back" of the Soviet empire in Europe. But when the brightest opportunity presented itself in June, 1953, RIAS was ordered to moderate its encouragement to the rebels, and the U.S. military in West Berlin, fearing a Russian invasion—of all things—took precautionary measures of withdrawal. Again stalemate, immobility.

The two contending world forces were in a condition of deadlock. Neither side could advance. This bred the hope of adjustment through negotiation.

CHAPTER THIRTY-EIGHT

The Englishman and His Country

IN THE tug-of-cold-war between the West and Russia, Moscow suffered two major disappointments: it could not acquire additional colonial territories by force or threat; and the unsovietized countries of Europe refused to collapse. In fact, one of the most striking developments in the decade after the Second World War was the resurgence of Britain as a great power despite the loss of empire and the rise of Germany as a great power despite the loss of half her territory to the Communist orbit. Both achievements were the fruit of economic recovery, and that recovery gave new hope to the Western world.

The vogue of Marxism in the 1930's was due to the coincidence of business depressions and Hitler and Franco in the West with the successes of the Soviet Five Year Plans. By the 1950's, however, the vogue had ebbed, for the remarkable recuperation of Europe and the liberation of India, Burma, Ceylon, and Indonesia now contrasted with economic difficulties inside Russia and the sins of Soviet imperialism. In the drab decade of Stanley Baldwin's and Neville Chamberlain's spineless appeasement many intellectuals lost their hearts to Moscow and Spain, but the national heroism of the wartime Churchill era and the Labor government's peaceful postwar revolution repatriated them and restored faith.

Karl Marx himself, had he risen from the dead and returned to his native Rhineland or resumed his studies in the British Museum, would have been astounded by the reversal of roles: his closest avowed followers, the Communists, were unscientific idolators of a remote feudal dictatorship over the proletariat, while the British working class had, by a democratic election, nationalized important industries without provoking violent resistance from the capitalists. Not only had there been no barricades, British class barriers were lower. Chancellor of the Exchequer R. A. Butler revealed on April 26, 1955, that no more than 450 Britons had an income after taxes of over £6,000 ($16,800) in 1954, and only fifty Britons had earned over £10,000 net ($28,000) during that year. Upper-class strata had been depressed to a middle level (luxury spending, which abounded, therefore came out of capital or depended to a great extent on how many Rolls-Royces, dinner parties, trips abroad, and entertainments could be charged to taxes); whereas the proletarian depths had been uplifted by free state medicine, family allowances for newborn children, social insurance, government-favored housing, and, perhaps most surprising to Herr Doktor Marx, the disappearance of unemployment under what he used to call the capitalist system but which had in fact become a capitalist-Socialist welfare state. Indeed, historians may decide that the greatest discovery of the mid-century— and the best guarantee of the non-Soviet world's survival—was not fission but fusion, the capacity of capitalist elements to fuse with Socialist elements to form a nonexplosive whole.

England, the classic capitalist society according to Marx, has probably carried this process of social chemistry further than any other country, and that was not unexpected, for the British, in Isaiah Berlin's terms, are foxes not hedgehogs, they are pluralists and coexisters, they try to blunt dissent by living with it and prefer creative compromise to conflict.

England, however, attained this mature stage of democracy through conflict. The British won their freedom gradually, one class at a time, by fighting for it. From that month of June, 1215, when the barons met King John at Runnymede, near Windsor, and forced him, under the threat of civil war, to grant them certain rights under the Magna Carta, each section of the population had to apply pressure before it won the franchise; the last were the women (1917) and working men. As a result, Britain began, in the second half of the nineteenth century, to resemble its present very democratic self. And after the first five decades of the twentieth century—especially at the dawn of the sixth in 1951—England's democracy, while far from classless, approximated the definition which Aristotle gave in his *Politics*: "The most pure democracy is that which is so called principally from the equality which prevails in it . . . that the poor shall be in no greater subjection than the rich; nor that the supreme power shall be lodged with either of these, but that both shall share it." Exclusive control by or in the name of any one category, whether it be the feudal aristocracy, bourgeoisie, or workers, is obviously not democracy of any kind, and the British have shown that they will have none of it.

One day in London, Sir Robert Boothby, Conservative Member of Parliament and writer, was discussing with me how various classes of Englishmen vote. In the end he said, "Well, I hope enough workers vote Tory to keep us from going too far to the right, and enough middle-class people vote Labor to keep it from going too far left." Neither party can succeed over a long period unless it cleaves as a unit to the middle of the road, unless, in other words, it appeals to more than one social class.

Sir Robert was concerned with the opposition as well as with his own party, for an opposition makes a major, if not the major, contribution to the smooth functioning of a democracy, and the party in office must permit it to do so. Democracy flowers best when the opposition has a reasonable expectation of turning out the government; it then tends to behave with responsibility in the hope of winning over the voters who are uncommitted by party or class allegiance. "The only sound policy for the opposition to follow in deciding its policy," Hugh Gaitskell, former Chancellor of the Exchequer in the Labor government, declared in November, 1953, "is to ask in each case what they would do if they were in power. If they felt they would do the same as the Government was doing, then to attack the Government was not only dishonest and irresponsible, but foolish." This is the fair play and sportsmanship which puts so much decorum into British democracy.

While I was in London late in 1953, a team from Communist Hungary, wearing red shirts, played the unbeaten British football champions before 100,000 spectators at Wembley. I listened to the B.B.C. play-by-play report. "There's a wonderful shot by a Hungarian halfback!" the commentator exclaimed. "Another goal for Hungary," he shouted a moment later and one could hear the British crowd roaring its congratulations. "Our chap was too slow," the broadcaster explained. Hungary won the game, 6 to 3, and British cheers. The next evening I saw the same match at the newsreel theater and here too the audience applauded the visitors' skill. I spoke of this to an Englishwoman who came to lunch. "That's all right," she remarked. "Other nations should have their innings. You can't always win." The Communists, on the other hand, proclaimed that Hungary's victory proved that the bourgeois world was dying. But the British ability to take defeat with equanimity reflected more confidence in the future than the strident tones of their opponents. (On July 4, 1954, the Hungarian team lost the world championship to West Germany, 3 to 2; the United Press reported that "most of the Hungarian players broke into tears at the finish.")

The craving to be always right and always victorious and to destroy the vanquished, mirrors and breeds totalitarianism; the quality of a democracy, on the other hand, depends on the number of its people who are kind and co-operative. Just as dictatorships differ (one might plot an ascending curve of tyranny beginning with Salazar's Portugal and rising to Stalin's Russia or Mao's China), so democracies vary according to the individual behavior of their citizens. Democracy means personal responsibility. But the personal responsibility is not merely and not chiefly a matter of going to the polls and voting for the best candidate and of trying to influence the successful one. The personal responsibility runs much deeper; each person bears the enormous responsibility of shaping the policies of his country by his daily conduct at home, at work, and in the street.

The British man in the street or driver on the road, that is the individual performing the numerous nonpolitical acts which make up most of his life, displays many other characteristics which influence high politics. He is polite and patient; he "queues up" in the most orderly manner and nobody tries to get ahead of the other. He does not expect immediate, 100 per cent solutions or easy victories; his history has no record of any. He is tolerant; the London *Times* recently referred to "our national dislike of arbitrariness, love of hearing all sides, and genius of compromise." He is not too suspicious in personal matters or overly competitive in business. His slogan is "Live and let live." Violence and destruction are prohibitively expensive in a little island tightly packed with fifty million inhabitants. Everybody lives close together and the frontier is a lost memory. Grievances must be adjudicated and wrongs adjusted peacefully.

Sweet reasonableness and a seasoning of doubt sound better in British ears than invective or brashness. When Aneurin Bevan referred to the adversary as "vermin" it hurt him and his party. A fiery oration in the House of Commons would provoke astonishment and smiles; the correct tone is conversational with an occasional hesitation or a pause for thought; even a stammer does no harm and an admission of error or ignorance is good form. Nobody expects perfection of a human being; he is only expected to be human. Strong opposition and tenacious debate between parties are in order, but crude personal hostility boomerangs, and a mud-slinging, character-assassinating, irresponsible rabble-rouser would expose himself to ridicule and empty benches and, soon, to political death. Inkwell-throwing or fisticuffs and brawls after the manner of some Continental parliaments would of course be inconceivably silly in the House of Commons.

Not that the British lack faith in their convictions. But it is faith without fanaticism. The fanatic is too dogmatic and dangerous. Nothing is so repugnant to the British mind as a rigid set of principles or an unbending doctrine. Since he abhors the strait jacket of ideologies and fixed formulas, the Englishman thinks he ought to keep his mind open to the cleansing winds of argument and dissent. In a way, this is part of the national conceit: The British, he is saying, can be trusted to separate the chaff of propaganda from the kernel of truth and do not need an official censor to decide what they are to hear and read. Early in January, 1955, for instance, Mrs. Margaret Knight, a lecturer on psychology at Aberdeen University, Scotland, spoke on the B.B.C. and classed the Bible with other ancient mythologies, like the Greek, et cetera. Immediately, some listeners accused the B.B.C. of "coddling atheists." But the conservative *Daily Mail* said, "We are not among those who think Mrs. Knight . . . should be banned from the air. . . . Christianity is not so weak a faith that its adherents should run screaming from those who attack it." Actually, many of the B.B.C.'s critics limited themselves to urging that Mrs. Knight be faced with an opponent in a debate, and this, in the spirit of fairness, was subsequently done.

The Honorable Michael Astor, of the famous British family, commenting on a visit to America, expressed his dislike for the "loose uniformity of values" and the process of "living up to the neighbor." "I personally," he wrote,[1] "favour a little eccentricity from time to time." Englishmen enjoy controversy and like to think of themselves as nonconformists. To be sure, they delight in formal attire and meticulously observe many ancient rituals. They are not iconoclasts or rebels. But they do not "keep up with the

[1] London *Sunday Times*, November 29, 1953.

Joneses" as much as Americans because each family proudly regards itself as the Joneses. The British are individualists. Women do not look like ready-made products of the same beauty parlor; nor do the men seem to have obtained their clothes from the same factory. Caps, bowlers, hats of all shapes and materials and many uncovered heads add variety to the street scene. No variety in men's umbrellas, however.

Eccentricity would not be so important if it were confined to appearances. But it cannot be. The same deviation from center manifests itself in thought and political action. Britain welcomes orthodoxy but does not condemn, in fact by tolerance encourages departures from it. If the departures are too extreme they are killed slowly with bursts of laughter and barbs of sarcasm. Anybody can stand up in London's Hyde Park and express his views, however singular. Those who do not like them walk away. As long as listening is not compulsory speech can be free.

England has the same approach to Communists. Their right to talk is not abridged, the privilege to air ideas is uninhibited unless they commit overt acts of treason, sabotage, or subversion or otherwise break the law. Some have called this approach too gentle, but British officials say it pays good dividends in civil peace. "Moreover," one Minister of the Crown argued, "the moment you begin whittling away anybody's rights you set a precedent for witch-hunting and arbitrary persecution by the executive branch."

Notwithstanding this open-mouth and open-mind liberty, modern England has in fact rarely been rocked by convulsions of any kind; indeed the country remains even-keeled though ideological and other storms rage destructively elsewhere.

Perhaps the whole picture of the Englishman's character and its effects on British democracy should be set in a frame of climate and nature. The British climate is temperate. Sometimes it gets very cold and often there is sun, but many days of the year are mild and gray. In nature, too, the contrasts are rarely sharp. The country is gently rolling with winding roads good for relaxed walking, and the average height of all dwellings and buildings is probably less than two stories. Somehow, man reflects the soft contours of his surroundings; extremes of black and white do not flourish in England, moderation and a sense of proportion do. It is the general grayness, incidentally, which may generate the inner need for colorful pageantry and royal ceremony.

That this small island, poor in natural wealth—except in coal, which is a dwindling asset—and unable to feed itself, should have become a rich and mighty power is one of the world's wonders. Three centuries ago its inhabitants numbered five million; now they are fifty million who have no doubt about their future. "Britain is going to continue to be a Great Power," Sir Oliver Franks, former British Ambassador in Washington, said firmly in the first of his six Reith Lectures in 1954. "This is something the British people assume and act upon."[2] That is indeed the popular attitude; it shapes foreign policy and economic policy. The British, an old seafaring nation, know how to weather storms on land. They combine the dynamism of the fisherman and navigator who fights his way through the tempest with the mystic confidence of a deeply rooted race inured to losses at sea (and in coal pit tragedies).

Sometimes, indeed, they seem overconfident and inclined to be too complacent. Since "there will always be an England," the British do not hustle when the situation demands change. Their postwar social reforms, for instance, have not been matched by a technological revolution of equal scope. Numerous firms have, often with government help, rebuilt and retooled their plants and are creating new capitalist fortunes, but just as many go on the principle that "the methods which were good for grandfather, or great grandfather, are good enough for me"; then they worry about German and Japanese competition and contend that the financial burdens of socialized medicine and other social benefits are too heavy for the country to bear.

British trust in the inevitability of gradualness at times conduces to too much gradualness and too little progress. Geoffrey Crowther, editor of the brilliant *Economist*, and Graham Hutton, formerly a British official in the American Midwest, have been the intellectual burrs-under-the-saddle, stimulating the interest of industrialists in "the three charmed S's of high productivity . . . Simplification, Standardization, and Specialization."[3] Numerous British teams of managers, engineers, and directors have visited the United States under the auspices of the Anglo-American Council on Productivity to study and, if convinced, adopt or adapt American methods. Since he has no inferiority complex and loves his country the Englishman is not

[2] *The Listener*, London, November 11, 1954.

[3] Graham Hutton, *We Too Can Prosper; the Promise of Productivity*, London: George Allen and Unwin Ltd., 1953, p. 96.

too proud to learn from other countries. Certainly there is no harm or indignity in learning from a country where, according to Mr. Hutton, "eight hours' work buys for an American from two and a half to four times the quantity of goods that eight hours' work buys for a British or West European worker." This is the kind of technological lend-lease that wins ideological battles. A managerial NATO, open to all countries and disposing of peaceful atomic resources, would soon reduce the Communist peril to easily manageable proportions and empty the world-encircling ocean of human misery.

CHAPTER THIRTY-NINE

Man Against the Mass

FROM ENGLAND, in November, 1953, I flew to Switzerland and thence to Yugoslavia and Germany. In wealth per head, Switzerland is the first nation of Europe. In Zurich, the richest city in Switzerland, the secretary of an anti-Communist organization came to see me to discuss how to combat Swiss Communism. "But my dear man," I exclaimed, "why should any Swiss be a Communist?"

He thought a second, and said, "From boredom."

The human mind does interesting things. The moment he uttered the word "boredom" my mind jumped back twenty years. I recalled that in New York, in the 1930's, a considerable number of dentists were Communists, and suddenly I understood why. The dentist stands for eight or ten hours a day executing minute, meticulous motions in other persons' mouths, and what could have been more natural, in the circumstances and atmosphere of the period, than that in the evening and on week ends he should revel in the illusion that he belonged to a vast global movement which, with giant hammer blows, was crushing the old world and preparing to build the new?

Not only discontent, poverty, and inequality breed Communists. Contentment, security, mediocrity, monotony, middle-class smugness and mental obesity also make rebels, and the rebels may become Communists or juvenile delinquents or neurotics or psychopaths or simply unhappy. Modern man is held in the clutches of powerful, constraining social forces which can break his spirit, rob him of his originality, and turn him into a pea in a pod, a digit, a conformist. Some persons submit unconsciously or willingly. Some retreat into a private nook inaccessible, they hope, to outside pressures. Some protest, and of these one may be tempted by Communism, the other by crime or alcohol or hot-rod auto-speeding or frivolity or publicity—just to find excitement, to register opposition to conditions which do not allow him to be a full individual.

In a slow-moving community most adults are either not aware of dullness or do not resent it and find satisfaction in their work or in the process of amassing fortunes and relief in an occasional voyage or adventure. But in a dynamic, highly urbanized and mechanized society, especially one which glorifies individualism yet insists on conformity, youth often sows its wild behavioral oats before submitting to life's heavy shackles. Do not their sedate elders escape from suburban placidity and professional and social exhaustion into the vicarious pleasures of murder stories and other forms of fictional violence? Or go on the longest possible trips away from home—to the moon or Mars in space ships—like the dentist who flew from his last patient's mouth to Moscow?

The four Brooklyn boys who tortured an old man on a park bench and then threw him into the river where he drowned probably had an urge to add spice to life; they killed to be thrilled. Often youthful crime is attributed to the reading of horror comics which might be called "How to Be a Criminal" literature. But why blame the young folks when their seniors are gorging on sex-sadism books and the gory details of sensationalized murder trials, and when the radio and television are full of shootings and beatings?

This is not merely a city problem or a New York problem. J. Edgar Hoover, director of the U.S. Federal Bureau of Investigation (FBI) reported that the over-all estimated crime rate in the first half of 1954 rose 8.5 per cent over the same period in 1953; "rural murders increased 5.8%, burglaries rose 16.7%, larcenies 13.6%, robberies 10.8%, and aggravated assault 1.8%."[1] "This is a city terrorized by crimes of violence and brutality," wrote the St. Louis *Globe-Democrat*, a serious, unsensational newspaper, on May 8, 1955. "Men, women, even children are not safe at their home or on the streets. . . . Armed robberies here showed a 30% increase in 1954 over the previous year. The incidence is still rising."

"What had caused this situation?" asks *Newsweek* magazine. "The most important factor, criminologists believe, is the unrest that has gripped the world since 1939. The two major wars had an unsettling effect on the nation's social structure." But other countries were closer to those wars than the United States. Yet the British national police reported a decline of one-sixth in juvenile offenses in 1953; "Crime as a whole dropped by 7.9 per cent. Preliminary figures indicated the downward trend continued in 1954."[2]

World unrest and H-bomb and A-bomb scares undoubtedly act as disturbing influences, but tensions and pressures within nations seem to be the decisive factor. "Life in Laos, where no one has ever suffered a nervous breakdown, is incompatible with Communism," Crown Prince Savang of that remote and relaxed little Buddhist kingdom recently told Homer Bigart.[3] He was wise to relate the absence of Communism to mental health.

One quiet Sunday afternoon in June, 1955, I addressed two London bobbies who were chatting peacefully on the pavement before my hotel. They were in their late twenties at the oldest and wore the traditional high felt helmet, navy blue uniforms, and pale blue shirts with neckties. The shirt collar of one was frayed. "Do you mind if I ask you a question or two?" I began.

They smiled permissively.

"How is it you go unarmed, without even a club?" I said. "What would you do if you had to deal with an armed criminal?"

"Most of our criminals are unarmed," the taller bobby replied. "Besides, they know that anybody who shoots a policeman will hang."

"That is the record," the other concurred.

---

[1] New York *Herald Tribune*, September 23, 1954.
[2] *New York Times*, February 25, 1955.
[3] New York *Herald Tribune*, January 8, 1955.

"But what would you do?" I persisted.

"Oh," the second declared, "we would wait till he had used up all his ammunition and meanwhile cut off his escape. If he fired at us he would be caught in the end."

"In any case," said the first, "we are a law-abiding people."

It may be that nonviolence begets nonviolence.

The violent juvenile gangs of America, according to persons who have studied them, band together for friendship and power, power of the leader over the members, power to overpower a rival club, and power in relation to the police. Those who successfully elude or defy the police and especially those who beat up a "cop" are lionized. This is in the nature of a revolt against authority, and it may reflect not only the disturbed state of the world but also the general lawlessness and arbitrariness of the government toward the citizen and the feeling that the individual's only revenge against a too forceful society lies in force.

Most youths in the United States are well behaved and law-abiding, but the incidence of juvenile delinquency, which reaches into all social strata, is high, and no single circumstance can explain it. "The causes of delinquency," said Senator Estes Kefauver, chairman of a Senate subcommittee which investigated them, "are as complex as our society." The role of the family, the decline of conversation in the home, the condition of schools, racial rivalries, personal idiosyncrasies, and many other aspects of life affect the situation, but since delinquency does mirror society it would naturally mirror the outstanding, and for youth the most irksome, characteristic of American society—the pressure toward uniformity.

U.S. Chief Justice Earl Warren has said that "if man is free only to be what his neighbor wishes, then he is not truly free," and he added, "American patriotism requires political allegiance, but not uniformity in faith, in culture, or in sentiment." Yet even after the deserved eclipse of virulent McCarthyism the number of groups and persons in America who insist on conformity is legion, and they frequently succeed in creating an atmosphere of safety-first compliance with the demagogue's standards and the government's norms of loyalty. Whereas, for example, American undergraduates of the 1920's, according to Professor Arthur Mizener of Cornell University, "were conducting a running fight for the freedom of Americans to be eccentric and subversive and to do in private what they chose,"[4]

4 *Ibid.*, September 19, 1954.

the student of the mid-century, many find, is timidly orthodox, politically pallid, solemnly uncontroversial, and properly unsubversive.

A letter issued to its eight thousand congregations by the General Council of the Presbyterian Church of America deplored "the almost exclusive concentration of the American mind upon the problem of the threat of Communism."[5] For it may be that Communism is the symptom, and that the disease is the uniformity required by the modern age, by big government, Big Business, Big Labor, and big church. It is not always their concept or motivation which is evil; it is their effect, apparently inevitable, on the individual.

In the United States these matters are freely discussed. In the Soviet Union where more than conformity, where abject and absolute obedience is required of every man, woman, and child, and where the price of deviation is death, the concentration camp, or silence in some other form, the phenomenon of the shrinkage of man under modern pressures is never mentioned. On the contrary, the Kremlin argues that the man-robot it has produced is civilization's highest flower. This creature operates factories, farms, government bureaus, newspapers, laboratories, and schools, and its only deficiency, no doubt temporary, is that it wants love and food. Love actually appears to be a vanishing necessity; sex is an adequate substitute. Food, however, remains a problem. Under this system, the factory and the harvest become ends in themselves, almost animate objects, whereas the human being is a regretted encumbrance.

Thinking Soviet citizens are aware of this situation and it is sometimes cautiously, obliquely reflected in Russian literature, in Ilya Ehrenburg's latest novel *The Thaw*, for instance.[6] But no psychiatric institutions record its effects. A nervous breakdown is put down as "inability to cope with one's duties"; the usual cure is demotion or worse. Individuals—and they remain individuals despite it all—resort to many devices, conscious and unconscious, in an effort to save themselves. A great poet like Boris Pasternak translates Shakespeare and Rustavelli into Russian and writes verse "for the drawer," that is, for his desk, for himself and a few friends. Several of the best Soviet novelists have not produced a book for many years. Cynical artists paint well-paid portraits of factory

[5] *New York Times*, November 3, 1953.

[6] *Ottepel*, Moscow: Sovjetski Pisatel, 1954. *The Thaw*, Chicago: Henry Regnery Company, 1955.

directors and party bureaucrats or, on a higher plane, of Moscow bosses. Toward the end of my stay in the Soviet Union—up to 1938 —many people were seeking comfort and forgetfulness in prerevolutionary literary classics, heavy drinking, old-world sentimental music, "capitalist" jazz, and political indifference while going through all the required political motions of loyalty pledges, obeisance before Communist idols, et cetera. The greatest price the Soviet individual pays is in the currency of self-respect; since so many of his acts are responses to compulsion and the absence of choice he loses his inner dignity and looks upon himself as a hypocrite. He would like to protest but dare not; he would like to rebel but cannot. Or— and this is true of the millions—they become habituated to automatic repetition of official slogans and unthinking acceptance of official policies and heroes.

Russia too has her juvenile delinquents and her eccentrics who seek refuge from the ubiquitous state. Tarzan has a great vogue in the Soviet Union and some young men wear their hair long in jungle fashion and utter Tarzanesque grunts and words. Then there are the "Stylyagi," as Soviet publications call them, or Style-kids, who dress in bizarre colors. A poem in a satiric Moscow magazine mocks the type; the verse reads:

> He lives, like a strange shadow,
> Apart from people.
> Beneath his green jacket,
> His spirit is a vacuum.[7]

The female of the species, according to *Soviet Culture*, "wears dresses that reveal her figure to point of indecency. She wears slit skirts. Her lips are bright with lipstick. In summer she is shod in 'Roman' sandals. Her hair is done in the manner of 'fashionable' foreign film actresses." Obviously a decadent bourgeois apparition who has somehow evaded the Kremlin assembly line.

There, here, and everywhere, the enemy is grayness, sameness, uniformity, and the central problem is, Man versus the Mass.

[7] Moscow *Krokodil*, February 20, 1955. Words by Lev Oshonin, Music by A. Ostrovsky.

CHAPTER FORTY

Tito, Lenin, and Thomas Jefferson

ARE YOU a Communist?" I said teasingly to a fat peasant woman who obviously was not the type.

"When I have money in my pocket I'm a Communist," she replied.

That year she had money for the crop had been good, and the pigs were fat and the litters big. It was December, 1953, in a Yugoslav village. On my first visit, in June, 1952, its three hundred families were inside the collective and hated it. But after the government's March 28, 1953, announcement that peasants were free to leave the collectives, all but twelve families asked for their former holdings and animals. An equally heavy exodus from Socialist agriculture took place throughout Yugoslavia.

During the last two years in the collectives the harvests had been bad owing to weather conditions. But the first year out of the collectives the crops were excellent. "God is on the side of private farming," the peasants said.

I asked one peasant whether he was for Tito. He answered, "Yes." I asked another. "I am for the government," he replied. By letting them be capitalists Tito had made them "Communists."

While I was standing on the main street talking to the chairman of the village and another Communist, a tall, wiry peasant approached them. He was wearing a cone-shaped fur hat and a rawhide coat with the animal hair inside. The weathered skin of his bony face was the color of mustard and deeply furrowed and his luxuriant handle-bar mustache was black streaked with gray—a stalwart Serb. Knowing what exercised the peasants I inquired whether he had received all his animals when the collective was disbanded. "No," he shouted, shaking a mighty fist at the chairman. "I put in two cows, I got back one; I put in two horses, I got back one."

The peasantry, who constitute 65 per cent of Yugoslavia's population, are a tough lot. They have fought invaders and oppressors for centuries. The Russian peasant is meeker; he was a serf until 1861 and landlord-ridden until 1917. Even so, Stalin had to apply armed force and banish millions of recalcitrants to Siberia before the Soviet peasant submitted unco-operatively to the yoke of the collective. Tito had no Siberia, his land is not so big and rich as Russia's, and the peasants are not so ready to starve or comply. The Yugoslav collectives simply proved an economic and political liability. The Communist leaders saw this truth and allowed the village to revert to capitalism.

In urban industry and trade, however, the new Socialist regime of management by workers' councils without government interference remained in force. It had been somewhat modified since birth and still needed improvements. The chief difficulty was the workers' councils' inclination to distribute to the working force all the income from the sale of their products leaving nothing for amortization and expansion. The authorities tried to cope with this by taxing the plant heavily in order to create capital for use by the local commune. In other respects, each factory or store could operate as it pleased. Svetozar Vukmanovich-Tempo, Tito's right-hand man for economic matters now that Boris Kidrich was dead, told me that a factory could, without consulting anybody, withhold goods from the market till prices went up; shift from the production of one commodity to another; compete for raw material with other Yugoslav plants (I knew of a case where two Yugoslav textile mills were competing in the purchase of American cotton); raid other factories for skilled labor; raise prices when demand rose; and put a competitor out of business by lowering prices. This, therefore, was a system of free enterprise without private capitalism; competition under Communism; personal initiative despite Socialism. Something new under the sun, and quite entrancing in itself and by comparison with the Soviet Union.

In Russia, nothing is self-starting or automatic. Billions of tons of energy are expended each year by government bureaucrats and propagandists persuading workers to produce more, and inducing peasants to harvest their crops on time, take better care of collective cows, plant corn instead of wheat, and get rid of weeds. Nothing happens unless Moscow pushes the buttons, sends speed-up agents with punitive powers, broadcasts orders, editorializes and threatens.

Belgrade's whole approach to persons and problems differs from Moscow's. Edvard Kardelj, second to Tito among Yugoslav leaders, told me of a conversation he once had with Soviet Foreign Minister Molotov. Kardelj explained to Molotov that the Yugoslav government was bound by the requirements of national honor and truth. "I don't understand such terms," Molotov commented. "When you effectively control a country you are meeting all the requirements of honor and truth."

The Yugoslav Communists were the Soviet system's most devastating critics. Speaking to a gathering in Oslo in October, 1954, Kardelj condemned Soviet Communism because "it does not begin from the basic socialist principle, that is, from the liberation of labor, from the freeing of creative will-power of the man who works on the social means of production. . . . On the contrary, it transforms every single person and every single working collective into blind executors acting on behalf of mysterious technocratic plans which in most cases are unknown to the masses." Under it, he added, there is indeed an economic incentive in the form of high living standards for the bureaucrats who "control those who work" but not for "those who work." The consequences? "Economically," Kardelj asserted, "they are expressed in the more or less slow-down of productivity. . . . This system, like every monopolism, gives birth to stagnation and rotting of forces of production. Such situations, naturally, require the corresponding political system of control and pressures which is founded on political despotisms and on the atmosphere of general mistrust and fear."[1]

Yugoslavia, Kardelj promised, would not go that way; neither could it, for historic and other reasons, take the path of more advanced Western nations which could reach Socialism via bourgeois democracy. Yugoslavia, he said, was trying to develop a "mechanism of direct democracy, which would in time remove every necessity for political monopolies either in the 'one-party' form or in the

[1] These quotations and others that follow are from the English translation supplied by the Yugoslav Information Center, New York 21, N.Y.

'multi-party' form." This "direct democracy" was the workers' council of each economic enterprise. These combined to form a local commune which in turn combined with other local communes to form a district commune, and so on up to the highest "People's Committee of Communes," the ultimate parliament-plus-government that will replace the withered-away state. Only communes make real Communism. It is Yugoslavia's goal. It is Moscow's nightmare.

The Yugoslav Communists had discovered that Soviet Russia's Achilles' heel was the dead hand of bureaucracy, and they intended to avoid it by farmer freedom and worker's self-management.

These measures increased Tito's popularity. No outsider can know exactly how much support a dictatorship enjoys among its people; the dictator himself would like to know. But the death of the rural collectives and the birth of the workers' councils certainly reinforced the Communist regime.

Nationalism is another source from which Tito draws popular strength. When Yugoslavia was Russia's carbon-paper satellite many people felt that Tito had sold the country to Muscovy. When he broke with Stalin and reasserted his independence the nation was proud and pleased. Tito is the worker-warrior type of natural leader who is very sensitive to mass reactions. In the formulation of policy, he keeps his ear close to the national heart. In a crisis he acts quickly by an instinct which is often unerring. This showed with particular vividness in the 1953 Trieste episode. On October 8, 1953, the United States and Great Britain decided to withdraw their troops from Zone A of the Free Territory of Trieste and hand it over to Italy. The same day Tito was so informed. The same day demonstrations against the decision erupted throughout Yugoslavia. Within hours, Tito ordered military reinforcements into Zone B which borders on Zone A, and Belgrade announced that it would regard Italy's entry into Zone A as "an act of aggression" and an infringement of Yugoslavia's right in Zone A.

Impressed by Tito's ferocious reaction to the October 8 plans, the British and United States governments postponed its implementation indefinitely. A year later, after many official conferences which included Tito, a Trieste settlement was adopted with slight alterations in Yugoslavia's favor. But these changes were less important than the principles which Tito had established: that no decisions affecting Yugoslavia be made in her absence.

It was a victory for Tito, and the nationalists, jealous of Yugoslavia's independence, and prestige, probably rewarded him with an additional slice of their loyalty.

The Trieste episode caused a cooling of the theretofore very warm Yugoslav government feeling for the United States. This phase passed quickly but left a residue of suspicion. Leading Yugoslavs interpreted the October 8 decision giving Trieste's Zone A to Italy as an unfriendly act. "We expect friends to consider our internal problems," Kardelj said to me. In other words, it would have been impossible for Tito, in view of the nationalist sentiment for Trieste, to bow to the October 8 fiat. Kardelj also regarded the United States move in Trieste as the overture to the Eisenhower's get-tough-with-Russia, roll-back policy. "Until 1948, Russia was on the offensive, now it is the United States," he declared. He feared a preventive war launched by America. Subsequent events completely disproved this interpretation, but, as often happens in human affairs, the suspicion persisted and was a factor in the somewhat more neutralist tones one heard in Belgrade at the end of 1953. "Isn't it possible that America will become the slave of its creatures Chiang Kai-shek and Syngman Rhee, and be dragged into war?" a former Yugoslav ambassador who is close to Tito asked. "Isn't it time for a new United States policy of negotiations now that Russia will not go to war?"

The broadening of Tito's popular base which resulted from his blocking the Anglo-American move of October 8, as well as from the ending of compulsory collectivization and the further evolution of the workers' councils and communes produced some remarkable repercussions on Yugoslav domestic politics, notably the "Djilas Affair."

When I talked with Milovan Djilas in Belgrade in the first half of December, 1953, he was Number Four Yugoslav leader, Vice-President of Yugoslavia, President of Parliament, a much-respected member of the Politburo of the Communist party, and prominent writer —age forty-two. A month later, he was tried and purged and stripped of his positions and power. The reason was the publication of a series of articles by Djilas in the daily newspaper *Borba*, organ of the Yugoslav Communist party, between October 11, 1953, and January 7, 1954, and, as a climax, an article in the January issue of *Nova Misao* (*New Thought*), which added up to an undisguised, vigorous attack on the methods, leadership, and philosophy of the Yugoslav Communist party and a plea for its abolition.

Tito and Kardelj had likewise proposed to put an end to the party's power. At the Djilas trial before the January 16 and 17, 1954, Extraordinary Session of the Central Committee of the League of Communists (the new name of the Communist party), Tito said, "I was the first to speak about the withering away of the Party, about the withering away of the League, but I did not say it ought to take place within the next six months, nor within the next year or two; I said it was long-range process."[2]

Merely the difference, however, between the Djilas timetable and the Tito timetable would not have caused all the turbulence. What troubled Tito and his associates was that so many people agreed with Djilas.

"The revolution is finished," Djilas said to me during my interview with him. "The collectives have been disbanded," he explained, "but I do not fear the capitalist village, it will not be completely capitalist, elements of Socialism will exist in it—co-operatives, small voluntary farm collectives, et cetera. Besides, the city and political power are Socialist."

The workers' councils, Djilas argued, had eliminated centralized bureaucratic government control of industry and trade. The liquidation of agrarian collectives had eliminated government management of farming. In city and village everything was now based on economic self-interest, personal initiative, and competition. Then why not eliminate the Communist party which is a bureaucracy with power to interfere and dominate? The existence of the party as an instrument of power divides the country into two parts: Communists who are trusted, and ordinary citizens, the bulk of the population, who are not automatically trusted. Such inequality is the negation of democracy, and such mistrust necessitates the use of a secret police. Inequality and mistrust frustrate freedom.

Commenting on Djilas' analysis, Tito said at the trial, "We have, namely, never believed that there were so many people who thought (and especially that comrade Djilas thought) that we had already liquidated the class enemy in our midst. In his thinking, there are no classes, there is no class enemy, they are all now equal. And it is his case which shows how dangerous the class enemy is in our country.

[2] The proceedings of the trial were broadcast in the official Yugoslav radio and published in full, verbatim text in the Belgrade *Borba* and other Yugoslav newspapers. The English translation cited here and below is from *The Case of Milovan Djilas*, New York: March, 1954, by the Yugoslav Information Bureau, New York, 21, N.Y.

The class enemy exists. . . . He exists also in the League of Communists."

During my first visit to Communist Yugoslavia in May-June, 1952, I had talked with Djilas and other leaders about the role of Lenin. The Titoists had rejected Stalin who stood for Russian imperialist domination of Yugoslavia, and, in addition, for the do-all state managed by a mighty bureaucracy. But they had not rejected Lenin who stood for rule by a paramount party exercising all power over the people in the name, allegedly, of the workers who actually had no say in the matter.

Now, at the end of 1953, Djilas was ready to throw Lenin overboard. Clearly, Stalin was Lenin in a later political incarnation; if the party kept control how could the workers' councils and city communes be democratic? The party would try to run them, and the result would be Stalinist bureaucracy, the very system from which Yugoslavia wished to escape.

Thus the issue in the Djilas affair was really: Thomas Jefferson versus Lenin, Democracy versus One-Party Dictatorship; and also, Guild Socialism or the Voluntary Co-operative Commonwealth versus Soviet Communism.

In dissecting Djilas's deviations, Tito ascribed them, in part, to the West. "Then," Tito said at the January, 1954, trial, "there is the influence of the West, there is the influence of travels abroad." Djilas had spent time in England with British Laborites and represented his country for a long period at the United Nations in New York. Tito admitted in his speech that what finally convinced him to order the trial was the friendly reception Djilas' article had found abroad: "I saw how promptly they have all seized upon the theory of Djilas. . . . They maintained that in this way Yugoslavia had come closer to Western democracy. It is correct that there is a *rapprochement* between Yugoslavia and the Western democracy, but not as regards the question of the internal system, rather as regards the question of co-operation in the matter of foreign policy." At a later stage of the controversy, Mosha Pijade, Djilas's successor as President of Parliament, charged that the "spiritual address" of Djilas was the United States.

West and East were struggling in Yugoslavia's breast. Djilas was West and he would be rejected. But Yugoslavia was obviously not the Soviet East. Many Soviet leaders had been shot in the back of the neck for far less than Djilas had done. But at the trial, which was little more than a hearing, not only Djilas' life, even his feelings were spared. Tito spoke of him as "comrade," sometimes called him by his nickname "Djido," and recommended forgiveness. "We do not have to seek to ruin and annihilate people who make mistakes, even the greatest mistakes," Tito said, "but can afford to make it possible for them to see their errors and to do, from now on, whatever lies in their power to repair, to a certain extent at any rate, what damage they have done."

Facing the Extraordinary Session of the Central Committee which conducted the hearings, Djilas was not very contrite and made only a brief, formal apology. In fact, he defended himself and served notice of storms yet to come. "I have been from my early youth and I hope I shall remain to the end of life," he declared, "a free man and a Communist. I do not see and I cannot at all see that the two things are in conflict with each other."

Despite this unyielding stance of the independence-loving Montenegrin, the Central Committee merely excluded him from its membership, deprived him of his functions in the League of Communists, or Communist party, and gave him "a final warning." The Titoists were not only treating Djilas with a mildness born of personal affection and a basically European tradition; in psychological terms they may have been trying to save him from himself, for at times it seemed that he was trying to commit political suicide.

Djilas was no babe in the Communist woods, he knew his articles in *Borba* were dynamite. As far back as March 23, 1952, he urged in *Borba* that the party should fight with ideas and political weapons only. Otherwise there might be a "return to Stalinism."

On January 4, 1953, in *Borba*, Djilas advocated the elimination of required Communist party "cell" or small-unit meetings which had become "sterile" with "churchlike" insistence on dogma.

Then in October, 1953, *Borba* commenced publishing the fateful series of unorthodox Djilas articles which proved his undoing. Laying the groundwork, and writing as a poet, he said, "Our enchanting country is breathing with the same spirit and beating as one heart." The Peoples of Yugoslavia, the Serbs, Croats, Slovenes, Montenegrins, Macedonians, and others were all equal. "Particularities are not abolished," but there is a "fusion of our peoples. . . . This is in fact the new Yugoslavism . . . this is socialism." Socialist Yugoslavia belonged to "the new Europe in which the spirit of justice and freedom is awakening."[3] He was saying that the Titoists were strong in a united European country.

A week later, commenting on the recent elections, he expressed the hope that "democratic tendencies" may "make it possible for the voters to elect future deputies . . . who are not imposed from above."[4]

Discussing "New Forms," on November 1, 1953, Djilas revealed that there had been dissension in the Communist party. "This is quite natural," he wrote. "As soon as the centralized management of the whole life of society . . . disappeared, differences had to come. . . . Free socialist economy requires a corresponding form, a socialist democracy. . . . Here discussion and differences are inevitable." There was "nothing bad" in this. "Broader and firmer unity through differences, that is the democratic way, that is socialism . . . scolding, haughtiness, imputation, hair-splitting, unnecessary vehemence, personal insult, etc." should be discarded. "We must learn to respect the opinion of others. . . . We must also accustom ourselves to be, with out attitudes, in the minority, even if we are right." From a Communist, such language was new.

In a contribution entitled "Is It For All?" on November 22, the "It" is democracy "which all must enjoy," but, he contended, "the bureaucratic forces are trying to justify their arbitrariness and rule over the people by the danger of counter-revolution although, by their pressure and despotism, they are provoking the resistance and dissatisfaction even of ordinary working people." Yes, democracy even applied to the bourgeoisie. "The true Communist-democrat," therefore, "fights for the equality of all, including the bourgeois, before the law, and at the same time he carries on an ideological struggle against bourgeois conceptions and against capitalism." Then Djilas aired his idealistic views: "For democratic development," he preached, "internal purity, culture, love of truth, discussion and criticism, bringing words into accord with deeds (or respect for the law) are more important than anything else."

"No one," he wrote in December, "should be persecuted because of his ideas. Because only in such an atmosphere can these new ideas . . .

[3] Article entitled "Yugoslavia," in Borba, October 18, 1953. The English translation from Serbo-Croat is from the translation service of the United States Embassy in Belgrade. Likewise below.

[4] "Small Electoral Themes," Borba, October 25, 1953.

come to the surface." Always he pleaded for elasticity, flexibility, no dogma, no attempt at exact theoretical formulations. "Theory is gray," he quoted. "Only the tree of life is eternally green." Life cannot be compressed into a formula.

Djilas' articles obviously represented a distinct departure from Communist practice and thought. Edvard Kardelj, active head of the government (Tito was in Slovenia taking a cure), felt much disturbed and had a talk with Djilas on December 22, in which he expressed his disagreement with the content of the articles. Djilas, according to Kardelj,[5] became "very nervous" and "offended." He told Kardelj that "Comrade Tito is the defender of bureaucratism and that he [Djilas] must sooner or later come into conflict with him." Furthermore, Djilas said—again according to Kardelj's report of the conversation which Djilas did not deny when he heard it at the trial: "Comrade Rankovich [Minister of Interior and chief of the political police] and I [Kardelj] agree with him, with Djilas, but we are opportunists, and therefore do not wish to quarrel with Comrade Tito." In addition, Djilas declared heretically that "one cannot exclude the possibility that in our country two socialist parties will develop."

Kardelj would normally have conveyed this conversation to Tito. In any case, Tito gave orders from Slovenia "that the articles be stopped immediately."

Nevertheless, Djilas now committed the crowning sin, he published a satire of the whole ruling Communist world of Yugoslavia in *Nova Misao*, a serious monthly magazine. Entitled "The Anatomy of Morals," it told the story of General Peko Dapchevich, Chief of Staff of the Yugoslav Army, whose twenty-one-year-old bride, an actress named Milena Vrsajkov, had been boycotted by the wives of the top Communist brass because she was an actress and had not fought in the wartime civil war when she was ten or eleven years old. Describing the mode of life of these wives, and parenthetically of their husbands, Djilas referred to the expensive automobiles, villas, clothing, and food which they permitted themselves. He castigated this "inner circle" as personally immoral and politically corrupt.

"Comrade Djilas," Tito said at the Djilas trial, "knew my negative views before he published his last article in *New Thought*. He published it hurriedly. And what did he want to achieve thereby? . . . His objective actually was to make us, that is to say those of us who

[5] *The Case of Milovan Djilas*, p. 14.

constitute the 'circle' he had attacked in *New Thought*, morally disqualified to argue on an equal footing and with full authority against his theoretical and other assumptions."

Conceivably Tito's guess may not be far from the mark. Yet unless Djilas had lost his political compass completely, he knew he could not win against Tito, Kardelj, and the party. He was bound to lose, and he did, though the punishment—freedom in his own private apartment where he could do translations and work on his novel—was certainly mild by any Communist standard.

Thus he lived, quietly, for almost a year. In December, 1954, however, Vladimir Dedijer, the biographer of Tito, friend of Tito and Djilas, and the only member of the Central Committee who stood by Djilas at the trial, was summoned before the control board of the Central Committee to declare whether he had reformed or still agreed with Djilas. Instead of submitting peacefully to this legitimate inquiry by a party of a recalcitrant member, Dedijer and Djilas made an unusual move, they attacked their country's system in the foreign capitalist press. Dedijer gave an interview to the London *Times* and Djilas to Jack Raymond of the *New York Times*. Djilas knew what he was doing. "I am taking a risk," he told Raymond,[6] "but one cannot go on without some risk. In our present system, we cannot know what will happen. However, I think that nothing bad will happen, and it will mean a lot for our country to have a citizen say what he thinks." He had known, he said, when he wrote his articles that "a discussion would start and that I would lose. But I supposed that the discussion would be democratic as in the West. I did not expect an inquisition.

"In 1950 and 1951," Djilas continued, "we had a new atmosphere of freedom developing. The police were no longer putting people in jail. But it is clear now that we have obtained only certain freedoms, as in art and literature, which can be distinguished from the stupid Soviet 'socialist realism,' but not in basic ideological and political questions. I have felt that the political aspect of our system is in essence close to Stalinism."

Djilas accordingly advocated a second Socialist party for Yugoslavia. "In ten years perhaps," he suggested, "possibilities for political democracy will develop, perhaps sooner. The situation is ripe for it, but the regime is preventing it. Inevitably, however, it will have to

[6] December 25, 1954.

relent." And he was still a young man. He had faith in the future. "The party is depressed," he explained, "and without an ideology. The dogma was taken from it through the democratization trend, and nothing has replaced it. The party apparatus actually rules. If we have peace in ten years, modern technology will make it impossible for this small country to retain a totalitarian apparatus." In ten years Tito would be seventy-three, Djilas, fifty-three.

"I am a democratic Socialist," Djilas announced. "The name Communism is good but it has been compromised. It is a synonym for totalitarianism in this country as well as in Russia."

Then he told Mr. Raymond that he had resigned from the Communist party, another unprecedented act in a Communist country. "I handed in my Communist card for moral and political reasons. Why remain in the party when I cannot say anything? Why pretend?"

The interviews, especially Djilas', provoked a furious storm in official Yugoslavia. However, when tempers cooled, Djilas was still in Belgrade, writing, walking the streets, entertaining friends, and being entertained. This, obviously, would have been impossible if Yugoslavia had been a Stalinist nation.

Milovan Djilas is perhaps the symbol—and victim—of a dilemma which the Titoists created for themselves, the dilemma of fractured freedom, of mixing democracy with dictatorship. For, as Djilas had stated, literature and art were free in Yugoslavia and political persecution had waned. With the dissolution of the collectives the peasants acquired economic freedom, and the workers' councils are an advance toward industrial democracy. Tito did this to escape the pitfalls of Stalinism. But he was afraid to go the whole length and adopt Jeffersonian democracy.

The Communists were accustomed to get things done by drastic measures, pressures, and threats. They were power men and felt reluctant to relinquish their power and the material advantages it brings. Djilas could tilt with his pen against this phenomenon, he was the theoretician. Tito had to reckon with it, he is the practical politician. Djilas might argue that the government would have more popular support if there were no Communist party. Tito could not gamble, he could not destroy the party which is the instrument of Communist rule as long as he was not completely sure of the people.

Djilas is a complicated composite. The spirit of his wild Montenegrin mountains mingles in him with strong strains of Western culture and the influence of his recent experience. His trip to India and Burma early in 1953, for instance, may have had an appreciable effect on him, for he told me he had had some enlightening talks with U Nu, Burma's Buddhist-Socialist Premier, and with Jayaprakash Narayan, Indian Socialist turned Gandhian, and Asoka Mehta, another Indian Socialist leader. Perhaps Djilas is a mixture of West and East, but not the East which is Moscow. Also, he is an intellectual, a writer, and he believes in the power of thought, in the ability of man, by taking thought, to alter his outlook. A human being is not merely object; he is subject too, he is not only the result of material forces acting on his personality, he can generate ideas and change his attitudes.

This seemingly abstract matter stood very close to the center of the controversy between Djilas and the Yugoslav Communist party. At the trial on January 16 and 17, 1954, the main attack on Djilas was delivered by Kardelj who continually stressed that Socialism and democracy would emerge from "mechanisms." "Democracy," he insisted, "is not only discussion, and above all it is not only a discussion between talkative and philosophically minded intellectuals, but in the first place it is a democratic social organizational mechanism which enables masses of citizens to decide directly, personally, in a democratic way on concrete social problems in the light of their general aims." And again: "There is being created there"—in the workers' councils and people's assemblies—"a mechanism which is the only one able to actually insure the development of a Socialist democracy."[7]

On the other hand, the key word in much of Djilas' writing was not "mechanism" but "human consciousness." "If an idea takes root in the masses," he said in one of his *Borba* articles, "it becomes a material force capable of changing the reality."[8] The human consciousness, if it animates an organization, "is a material social force, even a decisive one."

Kardelj, the materialist, trusted in mechanisms, in workers' councils, to bring democracy. Djilas, the idealist, said everything depends on the spirit which moves those who sit in the councils. Spirit alone, ideas alone, without an organizational mechanism, may not conquer. But a mechanism without an idea—like the soviets in the Soviet Union—is dead.

Marxists incline to depend on mechanisms, on institutions, to make man better. Idealists, like Jayaprakash Narayan, for instance, ask,

[7] *The Case of Milovan Djilas*, p. 13.
[8] November 25, 1953.

how can an institution do good when the people who control it are not good? In modern communities, much of life, whether we like or not, is lived through and in mechanisms. Their form is very important. But democratic forms can be and have been abused and distorted by the hates, prejudices, and power of undemocratic men. Freedom is man-made, it is trust in man.

CHAPTER FORTY-ONE

How Democratic Is West Germany?

DURING my 1946, 1948, and 1951 visits I tried to discover why Germany had gone Nazi in 1933. Now, too, in December, 1953, the same phenomenon troubled me. The Germans are virile people, and they are a creative people, witness their music, literature, and other arts, as well as their scientific and industrial achievements. What made the nation of Kant, Liebnitz, Bach, Goethe, Alexander von Humboldt, Lessing, and Beethoven succumb to a corporal named Adolf Hitler? Sometimes, when I put this question, in exactly those words, to Germans, they avoided a reply. But I wanted an answer, and above all I hoped to learn whether they might repeat the folly.

Faced with critical problems, the United States evolved the New Deal, Britain in 1945 elected a Labor government, but Germany went Nazi-totalitarian—and might do it again in an economic crisis, Germans admitted to me both privately and in discussion groups. Aware of their inadequacy as a political unit, they said, they now wanted to be integrated with the West—for education, guidance, social-system safety, and defense. This is still a desire for leadership

—but by England and America, not by a second Hitler. "A child that has burned his fingers fears the fire," a sociologist said at a day-long round-table seminar. "We Germans are more accessible to dictatorship than other peoples, but experience with the Nazi brand at home and the Soviet type on the battlefield has taught us a bitter lesson."

"Nevertheless," a neighbor at his elbow remarked, "Germans are again conscious of their superiority, this time in the economic field. Our people are boasting that while the French flounder, we are performing miracles of reconstruction." They also think the Russians and the East Germans under Russian rule are inefficient.

It was natural that Germany should concentrate on work, there was so much rubble to remove, so much to rebuild, so many homes, house furnishings, clothing articles, books, and so forth to be replaced after the bombings. The emphasis now is on material things. Power has less interest for them.

Power was formerly a primary German preoccupation. But aspirants to hegemony pass from the stage like everything else. In the first seventy years of the nineteenth century, France was feared, France was bidding for the mastery of Europe;[1] in the next seventy-three years, Germany was feared, Germany was bidding for domination. Today, many Germans have swung to the other extreme: some wish to be neutral and powerless, some would pool their power with the powerful. This of course raises the question of a possible future alliance with the Soviet Union. But too many Germans hate Russia and Communism, and, on religious, social, and other grounds have chosen the Western family as their own—provided it admits them as full members, not as unwanted stepchildren.

Both these alternative approaches, neutralism and Western alignment, are an escape from power headaches and, to some extent, from nationalism. The nationalism which aspires to freedom from colonial rule has creative attributes and so has normal pride in one's native land. But frenzied exaltation of country in the spirit of "Deutschland Ueber Alles" is harmful; it promotes arrogance, exclusiveness, and ideas of supremacy at the expense of weaker nations. Thus the creative becomes destructive, and in a strong, mature nation, therefore, internationalism is healthier than nationalism.

[1] A. J. P. Taylor, in his The Struggle for Mastery in Europe, 1848-1918, Oxford University Press, 1954, p. 126, writes of France in 1861 as "the traditionally restless Power."

Hitler abused and debased German nationalism. Aggressive German nationalism also used Hitler and lent itself willingly to his aberrations. It is difficult to know how much of this psychology remains. Some say nationalism in Germany is weaker, some say it is merely dormant. I had the impression in 1953 that German nationalism lacked passion. Germans are wary of causes and skeptical of military and nationalist solutions. They are afraid to think and cannot believe. The twelve heavy Hitler years—representing a lost generation which could not create because it was trained to hate, lie, and fight—still act as a dead weight on art and literature and as a damper on public enthusiasms. Passions are channeled into work and the acquisition of things. Germans ask only to labor and reap the reward in comfort and quiet.

The young man's ambition is not to become an army lieutenant but to own a motorcycle. Working-class families aspire to middle-class living standards: a cozy apartment, the biggest obtainable bed, the heaviest armchair, and—highest ideal—a Volkswagen auto. Sociologists call all this "Americanization." Erich Ollenhauer, Chairman of the Social Democratic (Socialist) party of Germany, said to me in Bonn, "The workers are contented and in a petty bourgeois mood. They join trade unions to protect their financial interests, but it is very difficult to organize them politically."

The reluctance to be politically active is in sharp contrast to the pre-Hitler period with its plethora of political organizations and political meetings. Not only were there far more parties then than now; each party had its junior department which sometimes consisted of hundreds of thousands of militant teen-agers and older youths who rejoiced in marching under political banners. Sundays and holidays saw frequent political picnics, with speeches. If rival groups met on such occasions they often commenced by hurling names at one another and went on to stones or the use of their iron-tipped walking sticks. Special squads of juniors, operating at night, painted their party's slogans on every available and accessible wall space and erased those of its competitors. Senior party members were no less belligerent. Throughout most of the pre-Hitler Weimar Republic's brief history (1918-1933) the German atmosphere was electric with civil war.

This has come to an end. Germans stay at home, or go on excursions in couples, families, or small groups. Political meetings are few. There is no such preoccupation with politics as in the pre-Hitler and Hitler days. When I mentioned this to Chancellor Konrad Adenauer on December 28, 1953, he said, "But 86.2 per cent of the eligible voters went to the polls." That is true, they cast their ballots and thus created a delegated authority which they watched more or less passively though intelligently.

This passivity is, in a way, a guarantee against totalitarianism. For the marching, the shouting, and the violence of many parties in the period before Hitler was the prelude to the marching and shouting and violence of one party, Hitler's. The dictator heats the political atmosphere until mass emotion blots out individual reason and the demagogue rises, like scum, to the top; he panics and excites the public; he keeps the people in motion and commotion; he craves loud acclaim, incessant applause, and repeated approval. Hysteria is his meat. Indifference, apathy, and silence, or laughter would deflate and then defeat him. In West Germany, the temperature is low. No fever, no Fuehrer.

Three manufacturers: the owner of a leather factory in Offenbach-on-the-Main employing one thousand persons, the owner of a metal factory in Frankfurt employing three thousand, and Hans Reuther, General Director of Demag, the giant machine-tool company at Duisburg in the Ruhr, told me that employer-worker relations are excellent. Working men said the same thing; so did Chancellor Adenauer. Dr. Eugen Kogon, editor of the *Frankfurter Hefte*, declared that the class war had been extinguished by prosperity and the widespread revulsion against extremism of all sorts. Socialist Leader Erich Ollenhauer stated that though some of his party members were atheists, atheism is no longer the policy of the party. "Hardly anybody in our party," he added, "now accepts Marxism as a dogma. Our workers enjoy higher living standards than Karl Marx thought possible; and Marx was wrong in supposing that the middle class would be proletarianized. Instead, the proletariat is becoming middle class."

Germans want a better life with more quiet. "We seek safety in the center," a factory worker exclaimed. "We have had enough exciting adventures." Hans Reuther's chauffeur, who drove me to the railway station on my way back to Bonn, spoke of his years in the German army on the Russian front. It was a harrowing experience; he is happy to have survived; he hopes nobody will have to go through it again. "My slogan is, 'Russia for the Russians,'" he said. A huge proportion of his comrades-in-arms who lived through the same horrors have had the same reactions. They yearn for no wars of conquest.

Germany's ambitions are less national and political, more personal and economic. Sociologists have given this phenomenon the clumsy name of "privatization." The private personality of the German is said to predominate; individuals are turning from the clamor of the street and forum to the calm of the family.

Another factor is new in post-Hitler Germany, and that is the impression made by the American GI and the British Tommy. (I did not visit the French zone.) The easygoing manner of the soldiers, the camaraderie within the forces and between them and the Germans, has brought home the fact that authority does not require the constant use of the jack boot or blackjack, or of scowls, howls, repression, and oppression. The foreign occupation left the German pretty much to himself yet with no doubt as to where the ultimate power lay. The occupying armies were merely being true to themselves, but their conduct was an object lesson to Germans in liberty within the framework of authority, and that is democracy.

Nevertheless, German democracy is very weak in a basic component. "The biggest problem," a famous German university professor said, "is the absence of any tradition or deep comprehension of liberty. My classes listen with rapt attention to lectures on the true essence of freedom because it is all so new to them, neither their parents nor teachers could have taught it to them during the twelve years of the Hitler regime"—and even before that, in many academic circles, national power was valued more highly than individual liberty. "Germans can still be organized to follow," the professor added. "But Nazism and Communism have no chance." Moderate conservatism has vanquished extremism. The students, he said, were long on brains and short on ethics; civil rights to them means their own rights, not those of their fellow men.

Dr. Kogon, the Catholic editor, asked whether Germans had changed, replied, "Yes and no." Privatization is a negative thing, he said. "The people cannot stand public life." They are for justice in general but do not react to injustice when they encounter it. A German driver is likely to help another driver having mechanical trouble, but in traffic each one tries to get ahead of everybody else. Refugees from East Germany receive no help from individuals; the state helps. The emphasis is on aid by institutions, not by persons. The gulf between private and public morality, which was the source of Nazism, remains. There is little sense that others must not be hurt, and political idealism is rare. The citizen resents government interference in his life; on the other hand, he does not like to tangle with officials. A Hitler would be resisted. The younger generation is opposed to militarism and some would refuse to be conscripted, he believed, but the majority will co-operate, reluctantly. In all these respects, Protestants and Catholics react in the same way.

I inquired about Chancellor Adenauer, who, like Kogon, is a Catholic. "I see him now and then," Kogon stated, "and have told him to his face that he is a cynic. I tell him that if West Germany and East Germany were reunited the CDU [Adenauer's Christian Democratic Union party] would be weaker. Adenauer denies this, he thinks the East would vote CDU. He is a Latin. East Germany is to him a colony. For Hundhammer [Bavarian Catholic leader] even Frankfurt is uncivilized. Adenauer is for reunification, but coldly. He is cold, calculating, flexible, ignorant of economics, an authoritarian, and compares himself with Bismarck."

I found Adenauer quite remarkable. The physical side of his personality alone is astonishing. In a week from the day I saw him in Bonn he would be seventy-seven. He was a giant, tall and erect. His hands were big and powerful, a farmer's hands, and his face was enormous and flat. I came into his office at 5:45 P.M., at the end of what, for him, must have been an exhausting day. He recalled that we had met before in 1928, when he was Lord Mayor of Cologne. (He held that elected post from 1917 till the Nazis ousted him in 1933.) We sat down, he on a straight-back chair, I on a soft sofa, and then he began interrogating me about how I did my work as a foreign correspondent: how did I collect material? how did I make contacts? when did I write? did I compare countries? did countries change from one visit to another? and so on and so on. This continued for twenty minutes. One never knows how long an interview with a leading statesman will last. "If he has a dinner appointment or a session with a Cabinet minister or if he gets tired he may dismiss me at any moment," I said to myself, "and I have been getting nowhere." But he seemed in no hurry. I asked him whether he was planning to go into journalism and offered my help. He chuckled and inquired about a foreign correspondent's life in Soviet Russia. He had been reading a book about Russia, he said, and wondered about its accuracy. "What is your opinion?" I gave it and wondered why he was reading the book. "Oh," he replied simply, "somebody sent it to me." At last, I was on solid ground. He talked about Russia. He thought Soviet strength had been exaggerated, the Bolsheviks faced grave problems at home, especially in the collective farms and the national minorities. From here it was an easy transition to international affairs and Germany. He answered questions freely and fully; in fact, he seemed to be in a relaxed, conversational mood and scarcely needed the prodding of my queries. Suddenly the big clock in the room chimed seven times. A woman secretary brought in a slip of paper which might have said anything or nothing and given him an excuse to send me home. But he continued talking, and I stayed till 7:15 P.M. He seemed fresh and chipper to the end.

If I had to summarize in a sentence everything Chancellor Adenauer said, I would write, "He made a plea for internationalism." The EDC (European Defense Community) was pending at that time, its fate hung on the vote of the French Chamber of Deputies. The Eisenhower Administration was strongly pro-EDC. Adenauer would consider no alternative. When I asked, "Nevertheless, what would you do if the Chamber defeats EDC?" he would have none of it; EDC had to win. "The Communists here are a negligible quantity," he asserted, "but you know the Germans, they are emotional and romantic, and if the West shuts them out I fear the worst." They might turn to Russia. Neutralism would expose Germany to Soviet power. "The Austrian solution," as it then existed— a united Germany under four-power occupation—was completely unacceptable to the Chancellor. "Only EDC," he kept reiterating. Under EDC there would be German contingents in a European army, but no German army or German General Staff or German armaments industry. He did not want a German national army or navy or a German armaments industry, only European arrangements with United States backing would suit him. Theodor Blank, Adenauer's Director of the Federal Office for Security and Defense, had written an article for the London *Times* of December 21, 1953, in which he declared that the EDC was "the best way of averting the revival of so-called German militarism." This was Adenauer's view, except that he omitted the "so-called." "It has to be remembered," Herr Blank said further, "that the aversion from the rigid Prussian forms of military service is very marked among the German people and especially among the German youth. The spirit of the barracks-square perished in the horrors of total war and defeat." Adenauer was especially conscious of these facts. Hence his insistence on a European army instead of a German army.

Adenauer's mind was magnificently single-track. He was, in fact, a monorail: "Only EDC." He saw his life's purpose as the elimination of the German-French antagonism which had plagued Europe since 1870. EDC would accomplish that.

In opposing EDC in the French Chamber, former Premier Daladier, the man of Munich who had helped sell Czechoslovakia for nothing to Hitler, contended that France could not take the hand of Germany unless Britain took Germany's other hand. He did not want to leave Germany a free hand with which it could swing around and hit France. Adenauer was willing. He advocated a large Western hand-holding ring, the larger the safer.

France defeated the EDC, and instead, Germany was admitted to NATO, which meant the Germans would have a national army. Thus France gave birth to something which, presumably, she least wanted.

The German Social Democrats also opposed the EDC. The party's leader, Erich Ollenhauer, said the EDC discriminated against Germany. "It is not in a spirit of nationalism that I say this," he added self-consciously.

I reminded him of the statement his predecessor, Dr. Kurt Schumacher, had made to me in Berlin in 1946 that if the Western powers would not allow them to be Socialists they would become nationalists. "It is true," he agreed, "that we use nationalistic arguments against the EDC. But it is better that we should be the nationalists, for we are not chauvinists."

The Social Democrats also used nationalistic arguments against German rearmament. They contended that it would prevent the unification of Germany because Russia would not relinquish East Germany unless all Germany were unarmed and neutral. This stand brought them the votes of antimilitarists as well as of prounification nationalists, and I could not help feeling that it was devised at least in part with an eye to just that result.

In a time of prosperity a Socialist opposition has difficulty finding a program that will win elections. The search may lead in strange directions. I do not doubt that the German Social Democrats sincerely desire the unity of West and East Germany; the partition is an abomination. I am certain that many Socialists fear rearmament under CDU auspices. It is equally true that the British Bevanites have deep-seated objections to German rearmament and are honestly critical of the United States. But when workers are satisfied with conditions and since experience has shown that the nationalization of more industries is not a great vote-getter, a Socialist politician may occasionally be tempted to stray from his internationalist convictions and try a bit of nationalistic demagogy. In other words, when ideology does not suffice, spice it with nationalism.

The objective fact is that whereas Konrad Adenauer, a Catholic conservative authoritarian, and many British conservatives were following an internationalist policy, the German Socialists and a few British Laborites had adopted nationalism.

German conditions—prosperity, the desire for peace and order, the class-war truce, the disillusionment with extremism, and the revulsion from marching-shouting politics—favored a democratic development. But certain inherited German mental attitudes did not. In such circumstances, Germany's close association with Western democracies would strengthen freedom, just as her association with the Soviet Union would strengthen unfreedom and love of dictatorship. International relations influence national conditions. Moreover, if a united Germany (and Yugoslavia) became firmly attached to Western civilization, which one identifies with freedom, Russia, where Western and Slavophile tendencies have been in conflict for centuries, would also be drawn toward the West and personal liberty. This is one reason, a chief reason, why Moscow objects to German reunification and tries to draw Yugoslavia eastward.

The day after my evening interview with Chancellor Adenauer I went to Frankfurt; in order to see the scenery along the Rhine I traveled by train. Then I flew down to Zurich and there took another plane which rose almost perpendicularly and flew over the entire solid, snow-covered mass of the Swiss Alps with the angular Matterhorn, gleaming white in the sun, towering above it all. One saw more than even the most intrepid mountain climber ever saw, all the mountains at once and the deep, steep, spaces between them. Suddenly, far below, Lake Como, and Lago Maggiore appeared, blue framed in green. A few minutes later we landed in Milan and, after an interval, proceeded to Rome.

I spent New Year's Eve at a jolly party given by Robert Neville of *Time* and *Life* to a number of Italian, Indian, British, and American friends, got in a number of interviews in the next few days, and then flew to Karachi, Pakistan, by the British Jet Comet.

"Don't go by the Jet," Bob Neville said, with a worried look. But it was a pleasant trip. Between Rome and the first breakfast stop at Beirut we made 625 miles an hour.

I left the Jet Comet at Karachi, spent three days there, and boarded the next Jet for Bombay. I spent a month in India. It was my first winter visit, and I found it delightful. I could sunbathe on my balcony in the Taj Hotel in Bombay, something one cannot do in the summer. I also went swimming in the Arabian Sea up the coast from Bombay.

While I was in India a Jet Comet crashed with all on board, and a little while later another went down. Rumors of sabotage and other evils circulated, but the experts attributed the horrible accidents to "metal fatigue." Ever since then I have been happy that my Jet Comet was not tired.

From India westward, I stopped again in Karachi, three days in Beirut to view an Arab country, three days in Rome, three days in Paris, and on February 17, I was in icy, freezing Berlin to study the last phase of the Big Four Foreign Ministers Conference on the fate of Germany and Austria.

"Everybody's here," I reported to my family, "sixteen hundred journalists, and probably as many diplomats," though the latter were not quite so visible. Each correspondent received a yellow card which admitted him to the Allied press building in West Berlin and the Soviet press center in East Berlin. Newspapers, magazines and books of all countries were on sale in both; for the duration of the conference the Iron Curtain was pulled aside. In the East I bought two volumes of Mao Tse-tung translated into Russian and in the Western press center the Moscow dailies. The journalists never attended any of the conference sessions; these were strictly for officials. In the evening, however, the press chiefs of the Big Four held "briefings" where they told the newsmen what had happened at the talks. Between briefings, one might, if one was lucky, buttonhole a diplomat and attempt to get the "low-down." Usually the writers took in one another's journalistic wash. I elected to go to the Russian briefings in the East sector; it was an opportunity to see the Communist part of Berlin again, and I had one more touch with the Soviet mind. Whereas, the British, American, and French press chiefs usually gave a running account of what Dulles, Bidault, Eden, and Molotov had said, adding their slant of course, the Russian briefing was straight propaganda and confined itself to the brilliant discourse of Mr. Vyacheslav Molotov.

No electronic brain counted the number of hours the journalists and diplomats, separately and together, devoted to speculating on the solutions and combinations of part-solutions that would settle the Austrian and German problems. They must have totaled several decades. Since war's end, top and below-top representatives of the Four Powers had survived over two hundred conferences on Austria; they finally boiled down to five the points on which the Anglo-French-Americans refused to yield to Moscow. At Berlin, John Foster Dulles, with the consent of Anthony Eden and Georges Bidault, conceded those points to Molotov. Now, Dulles said in effect to the Soviet delegate, will Russia leave Austria and allow her to be independent? Molotov replied in the negative. This was a spectacular diplomatic joust in which Mr. Dulles skillfully unhorsed the stammering Molotov. It clarified the situation: the Kremlin wished to keep its troops and occupied zone in Austria.

No such clarity was achieved on Germany. Nobody put the question bluntly to the Soviet Foreign Minister: Will you permit democratic, internationally supervised elections in your part of Germany as we will in the West? This would have been the prelude to Germany's unification as a free, unoccupied nation. Molotov's answer would have had to be no. For in November, 1953, just three months earlier, as I learned in East and West Berlin, between nine and ten thousand private apartments in the Russian zone of Germany had been seized for the use of the families of Soviet army officers. Theretofore, the officers had been quartered behind barbed wire in military cantonments and at least some of their dependents remained in Russia as hostages. With the mounting political influence of the marshals and generals on the Kremlin, however, these arrangements, imposed by the untrusting secret police, had been canceled. Hence the need of the apartments. It was proof that Moscow had no intention of relinquishing its armed power in Eastern Germany.

Having failed to solve the German and Austrian problems, the Big Four Conference decided to hold a conference on Indo-China at Geneva in April.

What was the connection between Germany and Indo-China? French domestic politics supplied the link. Growing sentiment in France demanded an end of the war in Indo-China. Pierre Mendes-

France had promised to end the war if he became Premier. The Berlin decision to convene the Geneva conference therefore resulted in the selection of Mendes-France as Premier. And he and the neutralists who supported him had no enthusiasm for the EDC. So by calling the Indo-China conference, Molotov defeated the EDC.

Molotov did not want the EDC in 1954 for the same reason that Moscow rejected the Marshall Plan in 1947: it would promote the unification of Europe. Thus the Soviets, the German Social Democrats, and some in Britain and France, though their motives differed, took a position which impeded European internationalism and German democracy.

CHAPTER FORTY-TWO

India's Number One Problem

OF ALL THE new nations of Asia, India is the best administered, has made the greatest progress, and gives the biggest promise. There had been considerable improvement in the national economy between my visits in the summer of 1948 and the summer of 1952, and still more from then till my return in January, 1954. Factories were producing more goods and fertilizer, and most important—for a country where so many have died of hunger for so many centuries—India was now self-sufficient in food and was importing none except, at times, to build up a reserve for an emergency.

Nevertheless, the margin between sufficiency and misery remains paper-thin. The outstanding indication of India's weakness is the enormous number of unemployed. Mr. Chester Bowles, former U.S. Ambassador to India, wrote in the *New York Times* Magazine section of April 3, 1955, that in India "there are eighty million partly or wholly unemployed." This figure seems unbelievably high, but is probably an honest underestimate. In the villages, where 67 per cent of India's population resides, "a very large percentage of the people who derive their livelihood from agriculture remain unemployed," according to an Indian expert on the subject, "for at least five to seven months of the year."[1] The main reason, he declares, is that "while India's population rose from 275,500,000 in 1931 to 361,000,000 in 1951 [the latest census] there has been no corresponding increase in the amount of land brought under cultivation, nor has there been any appreciable change in farming technique."

Part of the surplus village population overflows into the cities, and town population has accordingly mounted from 31 million in 1931 in the present area of the Indian Union, including Kashmir, to 44 million in 1941, to 62 million in 1951. Here again there has been no corresponding increase in work opportunities. Witness the fact that in all of India the average number of persons employed in factories in 1951 was only 2,599,000.[1] "Each year," moreover, Chester Bowles states, "Indian universities graduate 50,000 young men and women, most of whom have liberal arts degrees and a gentlemanly reluctance to tackle the grueling task of raising the nation by its bootstraps," or, in less polite terms, to dirty their hands and do some hard work. Politically significant: between 1921 and 1951, village population rose 38.7 per cent, but the population of the cities, where misery is greater and discontent more easily exploited, rose 119.5 per cent in the same period. Meanwhile, the population of all of India in 1955 was officially stated to be 376,000,000 and mounting at the rate of four million annually. The per capita income per year, however, hovered around fifty dollars—nearly the lowest in the world, and the calorie intake, despite good crops, remained insufficient. I was traveling one day in a train from Poona to Bombay with Dr. Dinshah Mehta, Gandhi's physician, and remarked that the people seen through the window were clean and energetic. "Yes," he said, "but they are undernourished and their growth is stunted."

Science aggravates the population problem. Better sanitation, improved medical service, lower infant mortality, and control of epidemics and malaria—in all of which India has registered appreciable advances—are bringing down the death rate. It is accordingly esti-

[1] Dr. N. Das, *Men Without Work* (*An Essay on Unemployment*), Eastern Economist Pamphlets, Calcutta: 1953.

mated by specialists that even at the present relatively low rate of increase—less than 2 per cent per year; it is higher in many other countries—India's population will reach 730 million in 1986. No amount of economic development can cope with such a situation. Every addition in agricultural and industrial output is quickly canceled by the new mouths to be fed and the new bodies to be clothed and housed.

The gravity of the situation is greater than the demographic figures would indicate. For India, with more than twice the population, is only two-thirds the size of the United States and has meager natural resources. Large areas are deserts and mountains. One of India's chief deficiencies is fuel, and instead of using cow dung for manure, therefore, the peasants burn it for cooking purposes, and this, in turn, creates another difficulty: since the heat from dung, or charcoal, is not intense the Indians have become accustomed to eating rice, which requires a weak fire, rather than wheat, and the result is that in India, and in the Far East generally, the poorest people of the world eat rice, which is the most expensive and least nutritive cereal and in short supply, instead of wheat which is cheaper and abundant.

Even assuming the early use of atomic energy for industrial purposes and sun reflectors for domestic purposes (cooking, heating, and air-conditioning), assuming, too, further progress in the introduction of more efficient agricultural methods, the expansion of the arable acreage through irrigation and drainage, and the extension of soilless hydroponic farming—in water pans covering vast areas—India's overpopulation in relation to available necessities must remain for decades her Number One problem.

This of course raises the question of birth control, or family planning as it has been called for delicate ears. The subject is best discussed against the background of the reality which is India:

One hot summer morning, under the guidance of Sardar Datar Singh, an Assistant Minister of Agriculture, I drove out to a village development project some nineteen miles north of Delhi. We stopped in a field to see a stall used for the artificial insemination of cows and peered into a thermos flask full of phials of sperm ready to use. But before artificial insemination by pedigree bulls could be made to work, all the bulls belonging to the ten villages in the project had to be castrated, else the peasants would have allowed their own bulls to spoil the new, superior cattle strains now being developed.

We also visited a farmyard where Sardar Singh, in black beard with gray fringe and bulbous white turban, showed me the difference between the ordinary village hen and one produced by an imported high-bred cock. Suddenly, spying an emaciated village cockerel, he stamped his foot, shouted angrily, and upbraided the worker who had allowed the cockerel to get into the farmyard. "You are fined ten rupees," the Assistant Minister yelled. He then explained to me that one native cockerel could ruin the results of months of scientific breeding. But I was not sure the peasants knew what it was all about, for even a score of miles from the capital of India they may be ignorant and profoundly conservative. This is not to say that they do not learn. They have, for example, been taught the advantages of co-operative dairying. In this district they now bring their cows for milking to a village shed, wash their hands and disinfect them with permanganate, wash the cow's udder, and then take the milk. The milk is sent to New Delhi where hotels which cater to foreigners pay more because it is pasteurized, clean, and not thinned with water. The higher price is distributed among the peasants who therefore submit to the new system.

But village life is very, very primitive. In one mud house I saw a baby about a year and a half old sitting naked and alone on a rope bed; flies literally covered a round sore, about two inches across, on its left cheek. More flies camped on the child's eyelids. Women veiled their faces completely with the ends of their saris as I approached and then hid. The men were more advanced. I interviewed groups of them in each of the three villages. In one, two brothers had inherited a twenty-five-acre farm from their father. They halved it; each now has twelve and a half acres. Together the brothers have seven sons. Each son, since India has no law of primogeniture, will inherit an equal segment of his father's land. In this way farms are more and more fragmentized and efficient farming is hampered.

I asked the peasants, through Datar Singh who was interpreting, whether they did not see the damage which this system of land inheritance inflicted on their children. "God will look after our children," they replied. One farm of sixty acres had been subdivided among four brothers. "Can't you work it co-operatively?" I asked.

"Our wives quarrel," they replied. Sardar Singh explained that petty quarrels and feuds in villages often impede official efforts to raise living standards; peasants distrust one another but they will follow outside leadership which comes in to organize them for building a road or digging a ditch.

I requested the Assistant Minister to question the peasants on birth control. Would it not be better for them to have fewer children? "Yes," one farmer said, "males should be castrated—like our bulls." This proposal provoked general male laughter. The only notion the peasants had of birth control was through castration—and this within easy reach of the national capital.

Under the able, assiduous leadership of Lady Rama Rao, wife of the former Indian Ambassador to the United States, assisted by many upper-class and middle-class women who, throughout the country, consider volunteer social work a duty, an unofficial family-planning association has been coping with the mammoth, heartbreaking task of carrying the necessary information and equipment to the 500,000 lowly villages of India. In the cities, of course, their work is easier but the obstacles remain numerous and the results meager though encouraging. In 1952, Dr. Sushila S. Gore showed me through the health and welfare unit for lower income groups which she supervised near the Bombay dockyards. It was a lying-in hospital, dispensary, and kindergarten operating on a tiny budget in one inadequate building. When a woman came to give birth to her baby she was offered enlightenment and the paraphernalia to help her determine the interval before the arrival of the next. Usually, according to Dr. Gore, the woman said, "You must speak to my husband," and, startlingly enough, the men were ready to discuss the matter with a female physician and, in most cases, agreed to accept guidance.

In 1954, Dr. Gore took me to her Family Planning Center at the Western Railway Central Station in Bombay. It consisted of three small cubicles, one for waiting, one for an office, and a third where the women were examined and fitted with the desired appliance. I asked Dr. Gore to show me some of the individual records, and as she drew them at random from the steel filing cabinet I could only marvel at the heroism of the devoted people who tackled this tremendous job with such limited means. I took some of the dossiers with me and they lie here on the table as I write. One woman, married in 1940 at the age of fourteen, was the mother of five children in 1954. Another, married at thirteen, had her first child at the age of fourteen and now had twelve children; she had never menstruated.

Here are the summaries of several files:

Husband 50 years old, wife 35—7 children.
Husband 44, wife 39—11 children of whom 7 survive; all live in one room.
Husband 35, wife 27—5 children. The woman was married at 16 and the marriage consummated when she was 17.

Husband 55, wife 35; she married at the age of 14—6 living children, 3 others died of "weakness."

Husband 40, wife 30; she was married at the age of 12—9 children of whom 8 survive.

Husband 33, wife 26; first child born when the wife was 13—4 children.

Husband 30, wife 25—7 children of whom 6 are alive. First child born when the wife was 14. She had had 5 daughters but refused birth control aid because her husband wanted a son. When a son was born they decided to try to prevent further births. The entire family of 8 occupy one room in a tenement.

Dr. Gore stated that the women who came to the clinic for birth-limitation advice were outnumbered by those in search of fertility. Fertility is highly prized in India; newspapers print advertisements on how and wherewith to achieve it. Shrines to the phallus are seen in cities, and some Hindu temples contain its sculptured form.

Child marriages, in contravention of the law, likewise obstruct planned-parenthood activity. A child marriage is of course not consummated immediately, but it does bear fruit much too early for the health of the individuals and the nation. The earlier they begin the more offspring they procreate. In the state of Madhya Pradesh, for instance, according to the 1951 census, 56 mothers had 22 or more children, 53 had 20 or 21 children, and 6,000 had between 15 and 19 children. Altogether, therefore, these 6,109 women had more than 104,000 children.

To reduce the number of children born in India, it seems, it would be necessary to reduce the number of parents who are children and the number of children per parent. The undertaking is a formidable one; old customs die hard. Yet new knowledge, though difficult to obtain, is welcome. There is, fortunately, no religious taboo against birth control and no delicacy about advertising or displaying "hygienic rubber goods for family planning." On the other hand, planned parenthood meets many obstacles. The Moslems in one village believed that the Hindus wished to weaken them numerically by preaching birth control, and an American was suspected of wanting to weaken India. More seriously, Gandhians like Morarji Desai, the Chief Minister of Bombay, told me he favored birth control by self-control but in no other manner and remained unconvinced by the argument that even if a couple were continent for eleven months out of every twelve they could still have a baby each year. How, moreover, can one preach abstinence to the young and passionate?

Another Gandhian, Rajkumari Amrit Kaur, whom I first met in the Mahatma's *ashram* where she served as his English language secretary, is now federal Minister of Health, and she too has certain qualms about birth control.

In general, as Dr. S. Chandrasekhar of Baroda University told the Third International Conference on Planned Parenthood which met in Bombay in 1952, "The Government of India seems to be of two minds" on birth control.[2] Prime Minister Nehru himself, reluctant to abandon the progressive abstraction that, given the proper social and economic auspices, the earth should be able to support all those born onto it—which may be correct in the very long run but not in India for the next few generations at least—is also of two minds. Speaking in London in June, 1953, for instance, he mentioned India's potential of economic expansion and alluded to "large tracts in India which are totally unpopulated still." He accordingly concluded that "while I am for the limitation of population, the problem is not quite so simple as some people imagine it to be."

India's poverty and backwardness are undoubtedly the products of history; they are not solely the result of natural phenomena, and need not endure in the modern age. The future prospect, however, is not yet present fact, and today, in view of the country's capital and commodity shortage and crushing unemployment, overpopulation is a grave menace to the standard of living. The large number of births is the public enemy of every Five Year Plan. Without family planning, economic planning defeats itself and all the heroic efforts of the Indian people and their leaders to raise the nation out of the dismal depths of the past will have been in vain. That would be a pity.

[2] *New York Times*, November 28, 1952.

CHAPTER FORTY-THREE

Nehru

PUPUL, whose small, smiling face is wreathed in black hair parted down the middle, is a short-story writer and poet. When I met her at a dinner party in Bombay I asked about new writing in India. She said that in recent years very little of value had been produced except a novel or two also published in England and the United States. "The reason?" she anticipated. "Because our writers imitate the West. And that makes no sense. For Western literature, in the last fifty years, had been under the sign of Freud, seeking the subconscious through sex. But we in India have been searching for the subconscious these last four thousand years."

A minute later we were discussing Nehru's foreign policy, and the transition was easy and direct. In the West, Pupul .explained, the sexual is individual and Freudian psychoanalysis is personal, whereas India is so old that sexual traits have been transmuted into racial or mass mental habits. Thus the pornographic sculptures seen in Hindu temples have lost their intimate suggestiveness and reflect, instead, the adoration of potency. Indians worship the symbol of their strength. "Politically, that is Prime Minister Jawaharlal Nehru," Pupul stated.

India gained her independence so recently that she is still afraid to lose it by internal division or outside subjugation, but Nehru, an attractive, dramatic figure endowed with eloquence and a high degree of personal courage who temperamentally scolds domestic opponents and big foreign governments, reassures the nonconfident Indians. He stands for their power and must not be weakened. This is a central source of his great influence and popularity.

451

At an election meeting in Travancore-Cochin state on February 4, 1954, Nehru asked his countrymen to love him. "If you and the millions of India give your love and affection to me for the moment," he declared, "and make me your leader, then I am no longer small, because I am your symbol. If I can speak for the whole nation," he added, "I am a proud leader of a proud nation, and I am unwilling to bow to any country in the world."

I cannot remember that Mahatma Gandhi ever asked anybody to love him. He loved and was therefore loved. Persons close enough to Nehru to know him well believe that he has never loved, he loves himself too much. He wishes to be loved and is loved by many, but he does not love. He is proud and often speaks of pride. In a way, pride conflicts with love, for love is a surrender and pride is a refusal to surrender.

Nevertheless, many Indians find pleasure and solace in Nehru's proud sentiments. "The Prime Minister said that he wanted to tell the people of the world, 'If you want peace then you have to accept the path shown by India.' "[1] Such talk is balm to the Indians' inferiority complex.

Nehru makes no secret of his conceit. Long ago, in November, 1937, the Calcutta *Modern Review* printed a peculiarly revealing article about Nehru signed "Chanakya," a pseudonym. Subsequently the article was republished under Jawaharlal Nehru's own name, and a one-page excerpt from this self-portrait appeared in his autobiography.[2]

The article begins with a description of how Nehru, who was then president of the Congress party, behaved in the presence of an adoring crowd. He greeted them with a palm-to-palm salute and smiled. Then the smile passed away and again the face became stern and sad, impassive in the midst of the emotion that it had roused in the multitude. Almost it seemed that the smile and gestures accompanying it had little reality behind them; they were just tricks of the trade to gain the good will of the crowd whose darling he had become. Was it so?

Watch him again. There is a great procession and tens of thousands of persons surround his car and cheer him in an ecstasy of abandonment.

[1] *Indiagram*, issued by Embassy of India in Washington, D.C., October 13, 1953, reporting a speech by Nehru in Bombay on Oct. 9, 1953.
[2] *Toward Freedom; The Autobiography of Jawaharlal Nehru*, Appendix E, "Excerpt from the Article About Himself Written Anonymously By Jawaharlal Nehru in the *Modern Review* of Calcutta." Copyright 1941 by The John Day Company, Inc.

He stands on the seat of the car balancing himself rather well, straight and seemingly tall, like a god, serene and unmoved by the seething multitude. Suddenly there is that smile again, or even a merry laugh, and the tension seems to break and the crowd laughs with him not knowing what it is laughing at. He is godlike no longer but a human being claiming kinship and comradeship with the thousands who surround him, and the crowd feels happy and friendly and takes him to its heart. But the smile is gone and the pale stern face is there again.

Is all this natural or the carefully thought out trickery of the public man? Perhaps it is both and long habit has become second nature now. The most effective pose is one in which there seems to be least of posing, and Jawaharlal has learnt well to act without the paint and powder of the actor. With his seeming carelessness and insouciance, he performs on the public stage with consummate artistry. Whither is this going to lead him and the country? What is he aiming at with all his apparent want of aim? What lies behind that mask of his, what his desires, what will to power, what insatiate longings? . . .

With an energy that is astonishing at his age [Nehru continues] he has rushed about across this vast land of India, and everywhere he has received the most extraordinary of popular welcomes. From far north to Cape Comorin he has gone like some triumphant Caesar passing by, leaving a trail of glory and a legend behind him. Is all this just a passing fancy which amuses him, or some deep design or the play of some force which he himself does not know? Is it his will to power . . . ? One wonders as one hears [his voice] or sees his sensitive face what lies behind them, what passions suppressed and turned to energy, what longings which he dare not acknowledge even to himself. . . . Joy may not be for him, but something greater than joy may be his if fate and fortune are kind—the fulfilment of a life purpose.

What is that purpose? "He," Nehru says of himself,

has all the makings of a dictator in him—vast popularity, a strong will directed to a well-defined purpose, energy, pride, organizational capacity, ability, hardness, and, with all his love of the crowd, an intolerance of others and a certain contempt for the weak and inefficient. . . . In normal times he would just be an efficient and successful executive, but in this revolutionary epoch Caesarism is always at the door, and is it not possible that Jawaharlal might fancy himself a Caesar?

When it became known who wrote this remarkably honest mirror-study, Motilal Nehru, Jawaharlal's father, fiercely berated his son for being so arrogant and vain. Yet today it is clear that that script was merely a pale forecast. Nehru's skill in manipulating crowds is now artistically perfect, his vanity is in full flower; he possesses the power of a dictator, and abroad he has in some respects out-Caesared Caesar, for without marching armies he has carved for himself and for India an empire of influence of indeterminate size.

Some would argue that this empire has no substance since it consists of equal parts of Indian self-delusion and foreign flattery. Nevertheless it is a political reality for, what with the numerous comings and goings of Mr. Nehru and his chief foreign representative, Mr. Krishna Menon, India since independence has played a prominent world role which responds to the Indian people's deep sense of mission, the mission of peace. Mr. Nehru in the toga of the Caesar-of-peace is certainly an attractive figure to Indians; it salves the painful wound of a thousand years of humiliation under invader rule, it appeals to their vanity as well as his, it gives them a feeling of being a nation and an important one on the world stage. "If we align ourselves with one or other bloc we cease to count,"[3] Nehru declared on July 7, 1950, and as a good Indian he wants his country to count. Long ago, Mr. Nehru wrote, "India will count as a Great Power or not at all; no other position attracts me."[3] He has already boasted in public that India is the fourth world power—after the United States, the Soviet Union, and Communist China.

Prime Minister Nehru is too independent and too independence-minded to make India a satellite of the Communist bloc, and while association with the democratic coalition might have enabled him and his government to play a more effective, if also less dramatic, role in promoting world peace, there is no question but that the policy of nonalignment and the opportunities it affords of spectacular attempts at interbloc mediation is best calculated to focus the international spotlight on him oftenest.

A highly placed Indian, friend of Gandhi's and universally respected by his countrymen, after exacting a pledge from me not to reveal his identity (this happened with distressing frequency in 1952 and 1954, for the fear of irritating Nehru had spread throughout the land), said, "Jawaharlal's foreign friends have done India a disservice. They have built him a world stage and now he performs on it." He added that he was "an actor." Nehru is indeed a superb actor. At Kalyani, near Calcutta, in January, 1954, I watched a crowd, estimated at nearly 200,000 strong, which had assembled for one purpose: to see the Prime Minister. Squeezed together in a temporary enclosure, the unruly mass pressed forward toward the platform to get a better

[3] Quoted by Philip Deane, British foreign correspondent, on the B.B.C. *Listener*, December 2, 1954.

view of its hero. The ushers and the speakers at the microphones failed to introduce the slightest semblance of order or discipline, and for some frightening moments it seemed as though hundreds would be trampled to death. But within seconds of Nehru's appearance on the platform he had that huge assemblage under complete control; they sat down on the ground at his command and then they laughed or clapped or listened silently according to his will. The relationship between the people and Nehru was like that between theater audience and star. They came to see a spectacle and saw it and paid with applause, while he blossomed under their approbation.

When Mahatma Gandhi met a crowd it was a spiritual experience. The saint's impact is different from the actor's. The saint gives his love, the actor displays his talent. Nevertheless, Nehru's success on the smaller stage at Kalyani is surely due in part, perhaps in large part, to his successes on the international stage where India, starved of prestige for centuries, has frequently played a stellar role. No politician is above politics, he is in politics; and Nehru's foreign policy, like the foreign policy of every other country, is domestic policy, it is expected to win elections. Nehru's has.

The foreign policy of Prime Minister Nehru also serves as a weapon against the Indian Communists who are his most menacing political opposition. Through ignorance or malice, some foreigners have accused Nehru of being a Communist. They could not be further from the mark. He has perhaps suffered from an arrested ideological development since the 1930's when the Soviet Union and Communists elsewhere were regarded as revolutionary, but in India, as often as the Communists fight him, he fights back passionately. For years he used to say that India's internal dangers were Hindu-Moslem communal tensions and provincial rivalries; he did not mention the Communists. But later they irked him by their tactics, and he attacked them. He has charged that the Indian Communist party "leans on, depends on, and looks to a foreign country," that "their body is in India but their mind is somewhere else," and that they have been "posing as if they were Russians."

Nehru has been overestimated as a person and underestimated as a politician. Shrewdly, he has been using Russia to beat the Indian Communists. Moscow has had reason to be pleased with many of his policies. He condemned West German rearmament when it was a project,[4] but never criticized Soviet rearmament of East Germany although it was already a fact. He condemns the South-East Asian

4 *New York Times*, April 1, 1955.

Treaty Organization (SEATO), but not the Soviet-Chinese military alliance. He has harsh words for NATO but none for the Soviet empire's military bloc in Europe. Like Moscow he repeatedly advocated the immediate, unconditional destruction of atomic and hydrogen bombs which would have put the West at a disadvantage in the face of Russia's overwhelming superiority in army divisions and conventional weapons. He has attacked every form of Western imperialism not only in Southern and Southeastern Asia, where it might be said to concern India directly, but ranging free and far, referred to "Zionist imperialism" in Israel,[5] and excoriated French imperialism in Tunisia and Morocco,[6] and took to his bosom Dr. Cheddi Jagan, of Indian origin, and Mr. L. F. S. Burnham, Prime Minister and Education Minister respectively of the Progressive People's party government of British Guiana which the British government had deposed. Nehru dined these visitors from across the Atlantic and introduced them to meetings of parliamentarians, and on instructions from New Delhi, Mr. S. K. Patil, President of the Bombay State Congress Party Committee, made a public appeal for funds in support of their cause. Prime Minister Sir John Kotelawala, on the other hand, barred them from Ceylon as Communists, and the British Labor party informed its local branches in writing that the "leaders of the Progressive People's party pursued a Communist policy."

Such is Mr. Nehru's political eyesight that though he can discern the minutest imperialist speck on the Western horizon, the towering fact of Soviet imperialism in Eastern Europe eludes him to this day. Reporting the proceedings of the Afro-Asian Conference in Bandung, *Indiagram*, the news service of the Indian Embassy in Washington, said,[7] "Mr. Nehru also referred to Sir John Kotelawala's observations and pointed out that many of the East European countries, mentioned by the Ceylon Prime Minister as colonies of the Soviet Union, were members of the UN. One of them, Poland, was a member of the International Commission in Indo-China. . . . Mr. Nehru said it would be extraordinary in the circumstances to challenge the very basis of their existence." Strange that Mr. Nehru did not recall that Yugoslavia was a member of the UN and recognized by many countries as a technically independent nation before it broke out of the Soviet empire in June, 1948, because it did not wish to be a Russian colony. Did Marshal Tito, in all his hours of private

[5] *Indiagram*, April 25, 1955.
[6] *Ibid.*, May 19, 1954.
[7] April 26, 1955.

conversation with Nehru, never explain this to the Indian Prime Minister? Tito has said it often enough in public. The Soviet Ukraine and Soviet Byelo-Russia are members of the UN, and of international commissions, and would Nehru say that they are independent? Soviet imperialism is simply a very modernistic form of imperialism under which colonies like Poland, Czechoslovakia, Hungary, and the others formally retain national sovereignty; Moscow finds that quite convenient. For a statesman to shut his eyes to this situation is to ignore one of the major world developments since the war, and perhaps the one that has caused most trouble in making the peace of Europe.

When India's Chief of State, President Rajendra Prasad, a consistent and lovable Gandhian, speaking on January 26, 1955, referred to India's foreign policy as "the policy of what I may be permitted to call active and purposeful neutrality," he was expressing an unfulfilled wish. For Nehru regards his policy as one of nonalignment and noninvolvement; he objects to the term neutrality, and on the basis of the evidence it would be difficult to dispute his contention that he has not been neutral. This unneutrality inescapably leads to the defense of principles at variance with the best in India's traditions and philosophy. I choose two instances:

After both belligerents in the Korean War, convinced that neither could win and that further fighting merely meant a waste of life, limb, and wealth, agreed to a truce, Indian diplomacy produced a plan for the repatriation of prisoners of war. On January 17, 1953, Mr. Nehru told the All-India Congress party that this plan "did not recognize voluntary repatriation of prisoners, nor was there any question of prisoners being asked whether they wished to return or decline to do so. . . . The presumption," he added, was that all prisoners "would go back to their country of origin."[8]

In my hearing, in a private home in New York, Mr. Krishna Menon asserted that the end result of his involved scheme concerning the Korean prisoners of war would be to return them to their native countries. This was the Communist aim. In all the negotiations, North Korea, Communist China, and the Soviet Union insisted on compulsory repatriation of prisoners—either because they did not want the world to know that any of their subjects would refuse to return or because they feared that military discipline in future wars would be undermined if the principle were established that a man taken prisoner during hostilities could, when peace was

[8] Official text supplied by the government of India.

restored, decide not to go home. The prospect of such a freedom of choice would naturally encourage desertions, and the Communists therefore objected to it.

The United States, on the other hand, favored prisoners' choice for this very reason. It hoped that the Communist fear of desertions would serve as an additional deterrent to future wars. The American position, furthermore, grew out of the traumatic experience after the Second World War when the United States and other occupation authorities in Germany forced more than a million Soviet citizens to return to Russia against their will in accordance with a Yalta Conference agreement.

With the United States and the Communists at cross-purposes on this fundamental issue, a most delicate situation developed in the neutral zone of Korea where the screening of prisoners took place. The Indian army detachments, whom Prime Minister Nehru, at the request of the UN, assigned to police this zone, performed their difficult duty with great tact, skill, and success, combining firmness with kindness and nonviolence, and thereby preventing many incidents and casualties. In doing so, Lieutenant-General K. S. Thimayya, who proved himself a good diplomat as well as a good organizer, and his officers and soldiers earned the deserved tributes of the entire world. But—an Indian army film of the Korean prisoner exchange, incidentally showing the Communist prisoners at their best and the South Koreans at their worst, closed with a statement by General Thimayya in which he, aware of Nehru's and Krishna Menon's attitude, expressed the hope that "the principle of prisoners not wishing to return to their homes at the end of a war is never encouraged." For, he added, "it may set up a dangerous precedent and it may act as a strain on the loyalty of those who participated in future wars."[9]

How sad that such a militaristic, undemocratic viewpoint should emanate from the country of Mahatma Gandhi!

The second instance concerns the unification of Germany.

The proceedings of the General Assembly of the United Nations always begin with speeches by the chiefs of national delegations about the world situation. At the Ninth Session in New York on October 6, 1954, it was Mr. Krishna Menon's turn as head of India's delegation. He dealt first, as he said, "with general problems and with Asia and with the United Nations," and "I now come," he con-

[9] This text was officially supplied to me after I had seen the film exhibited.

tinued, "to some specific problems. . . . The first of these problems is Germany." He made no apology for India's interest in Germany, he stated, for, "We think that Germany is the center-piece of this peace fabric—or non-peace fabric. What happens in Germany will decide, to a very considerable extent, the question of peace or war." On this he was certainly right.

He then outlined the position as he saw it: "On the one hand, one side, the West, wants, quite rightly from its point of view and, as the plan is presented, quite unexceptionally—universal elections in Germany, presumably controlled by the United Nations, out of which will come some organ which will seek to unite Germany or will express the voice of a united Germany. . . .

"On the other hand," Mr. Menon added, "the Eastern side—that is, the Soviet Union—while wanting a united Germany . . . asks for a different solution. The Eastern side asks that the two Governments, one in Eastern Germany and one in Western Germany . . . should together, and presumably on an equal basis, arrange for these elections as a coalition government; that is to say it is proposed that there should be unity before the holding of elections. On this matter the two sides have been at loggerheads, with the result that Germany remains divided."

Now how did India suggest meeting the problem? "On behalf of the Government of India," Mr. Menon declared, "I would say that we think it is time that there should be direct talks between the two sides, in order to bring about this unity which is of so much concern not only to Europe but to all of us. . . . We do not for a moment want to say—in fact, it is not our place at the present moment to say—what status or contents these talks should have, what form they should take. . . . But, if there are now two independent communities, as has been proclaimed, and if, as I have no doubt, the governments of these communities have the support of their people, it appears to us that it should be possible for Germans to talk to Germans in order to find ways—or at least the beginning of ways—to establish the unity of their own country."

That was Mr. Menon's suggestion, and he said, "My delegation wishes it to be placed on record that these observations represent my Government's view in this matter and its concern."[10]

[10] United Nations General Assembly Ninth Session Official Records, 492nd Plenary Meeting Wednesday, 6 October 1954, at 3 P.M., New York, Agenda Item 9, p. 219-36.

Clearly, Mr. Menon's suggestion about Germany had Mr. Nehru's sanction. Clearly, too, the suggestion coincided with the Soviet proposal: that the two German governments first form a coalition and thereby bring about German unity.

Mr. Menon's treatment of the German question aroused great indignation in many circles. First, there was his assertion that the two German governments, and therefore the East German government, had the support of its people—this after the East German revolt of June, 1953, which conclusively proved the contrary. In view of that uprising which swept away the East German Communist authorities only to have them returned under the guns of Soviet tanks, no West German government could have risked its popular support by sitting down with East German puppets of Russia to discuss German unity. It would discuss this vital subject with the Soviet government which exercised power in East Germany, but not with Moscow's discredited agents. No British or French or German neutralist organization would have made Mr. Menon's suggestion. It was a purely Communist suggestion. In this matter on which, as Krishna Menon said, the fate of Europe and perhaps the world depended, India took Russia's side, the undemocratic side. Moscow was grateful.

On October 5, 1952, Prime Minister Georgi Malenkov, in his report to the Nineteenth Congress of the Communist Party, still listed India among the "colonial and dependent countries." But within a few months Nehru became the recipient of effusive Kremlin praise. This paid dividends in India. A political leader, especially in a country like India where, however great the government's achievements, much poverty, undernourishment, and unemployment remain, must always be mindful of the opposition, in particular of an opposition as unscrupulous, assiduous, and destructive as the Communist party. Jawaharlal Nehru therefore could not refrain from pointing out that "now when these Communists saw that even the world they respected, the Soviet world, had praised India's foreign policy and called it a policy of peace they were in a big quandary."[11]

Soon they were in something deeper than a quandary. Andhra, the new Telegu-speaking state with twenty-two million inhabitants carved out of Madras state in October, 1953, was holding elections in March, 1955, and since the area had been a Communist stronghold, the Communists expected to win control of the state government. This would have been a serious setback for the Congress party over

[11] *Indiagram*, November 30, 1954.

which Mr. Nehru presided, and he personally toured the state, speaking frequently at election rallies, and the Congress sent its best organizers to make sure the province did not fall to the Communists. Suddenly, when the campaign was at its hottest, the Moscow *Pravda* printed an article which lauded Nehru's foreign policy. The Congress party, grateful, no doubt, for this outside interference in Indian domestic politics, made sure that the contents of the article became known throughout Andhra. The Communists suffered a crushing defeat. They contested 159 seats in the state legislature but won only 15. Congress won 119 seats, and its two allied parties 27. The Socialists took 13 seats. It was noted, however, that the Congress coalition polled 4,200,000, the Communists 2,600,000 and the Socialists 482,000.[12] The Communists therefore remained a power to be reckoned with in the future.

Three months later Prime Minister Nehru made a triumphal twelve-day tour of Russia. On his departure he stated he was leaving "part of his heart behind" in the Soviet Union,[13] and in Vienna, a few days later, responding to a journalist's request for his impression of conditions behind the Iron Curtain, he exclaimed, "What Iron Curtain? I never noticed any curtains, iron or otherwise," to which the London *Times* correspondent commented: "This remark caused some surprise among those present who were acquainted with the electrified double-barbed-wire fence and 10-yard-minefield which separates undefended Austria from her Soviet satellite neighbors."[14] The real Iron Curtain, however, is not a fixture which hangs from heaven; Russia hasn't enough metal. It is the totalitarian system, the fettered press, the one-party system, the fear. Even if it were true that the secret-police terror had recently been relaxed, Mr. Nehru could have recognized without difficulty that Russia was not a free country, like India for instance. In London, later, Nehru stated that he had not had an opportunity to visit any of the Soviet agricultural areas, "but it seemed to me they were all very well fed."[15] The same month Mr. Ajoy Kumar Ghosh, general secretary of the Indian Communist party, received an invitation to Moscow for a month's "cure." It is not the first time a foreign Communist party had been sacrificed, at least temporarily, to the Soviet government's foreign-policy re-

[12] *Ibid.*, March 11, 1955.
[13] London *Times*, June 24, 1955.
[14] *Ibid.*, June 28, 1955.
[15] *Ibid.*, July 11, 1955.

quirements. In this case, Moscow especially appreciates Nehru's efforts, for it knows that in present world conditions it cannot acquire new colonies or satellites; its best hope is to weaken the non-Soviet orbit by strengthening neutralism. Nehru cannot make Poland or Hungary or Czechoslovakia neutral, they are bound; but if he can increase the neutralism in Japan or Germany or Yugoslavia or anywhere, Russia benefits.

But the explanation that Moscow was using Nehru to promote its international aims while he was using it to defeat his chief domestic enemies is too simple for such a complicated person as Nehru. He undoubtedly harbors a real enthusiasm for the Communist regimes of Russia and China, and whether that is a survival from the United Front days of the 1930's when I first met him in Geneva, Paris, and London, or whether he thinks of Communism as the wave of the future destined to rid the world of capitalism one would not like to guess. He is probably fascinated, yet repelled, by the brutal methods of the Soviet and Mao governments, and awed by their remarkable power at home and abroad even though it has been achieved at great human expense.

In assessing Nehru it would be wrong to let the picture of himself he gave the world in his autobiography get in the way of a full view of his present personality. For even that picture was frankly egocentric. Today too, to be sure, he is capable of irresistible charm, and the visitor, taken on an exciting mental excursion, is impressed with the grace, versatility, and culture of the man. But he is not only the contemplative Hamlet; he is also a power man, an intellectual with a Caesar complex. His foreign policy, which consists so largely of advice to others, may appear idealistic. At the same time, he is a hard, down-to-earth, practical, political realist.

Thus when Communist China in 1950, militarized Tibet—there was never any question of her right to do so nor yet of the threat the move constituted to India—Mr. Nehru, having twice protested to no avail, ultimately, on April 29, 1954, concluded a Tibetan treaty with China setting forth Five Principles which have since been adopted by many countries as the basis of coexistence: "(1) mutual respect for each other's territorial integrity and sovereignty, (2) mutual non-aggression, (3) mutual non-intervention in each other's internal affairs, (4) equality and mutual benefit, and (5) peaceful co-existence."[16] These high and wholly innocuous principles, so easily

[16] *Indiagram*, December 14, 1954.

disregarded by the Soviet government when it invaded Finland and Poland and annexed the three Baltic countries in contravention of treaties embodying just such provisions, were the idealistic aspect of Nehru's handling of the Tibetan affair.

He also took other steps. A new, Northern Army Command was created to protect India's theretofore unguarded Himalayan frontier, and the three principalities, Nepal, Sikkim, and Bhutan, that lie between India and China up near the roof of the world, were quietly taken under New Delhi's wing. When Mr. M. P. Koirala, Prime Minister of Nepal, described the situation of his country to me in Calcutta in January, 1954, I said, "You have, it seems, become a dependency of India."

"Semi-dependency," he corrected.

In a debate in the Council of States, Nehru announced that "during the recent visit of the King and Ministers of Nepal to Delhi it had been reiterated that Nepal would co-ordinate her foreign policy with that of India."[17] Nepal's economic and military affairs have likewise been co-ordinated with India's. Sikkhim, land of orchids, rhododendrons, and high mountains, and Bhutan, a feudal state under an absolute maharaja, are also Indian protectorates. This was the practical aspect of Nehru's handling of the Tibetan crisis.

In 1954, when it became known that the United States intended to give military aid to Pakistan, Nehru aroused India to near-hysteria and then took advantage of the furor to integrate Kashmir with India although the Kashmir dispute, provoked by Pakistan's military aggression, was still before the United Nations and India had agreed to a plebiscite which would decide whether the state would adhere to India or Pakistan. The theory that Kashmir should go to Moslem Pakistan because the majority of its four million inhabitants are Moslems is a vicious one even if it conforms to the doctrine of racial and religious self-determination which is so open to abuse, and I have no doubt that the Kashmiris, given normal conditions, will fare better under New Delhi than under Karachi. But Nehru had delayed, and has now apparently abandoned, the plebiscite project because he feared it would go against him and he would be robbed of his beloved Kashmir (he is a Kashmiri Brahman), and the way in which the incorporation of this beautiful area into India was executed, beginning with a kind of Moscow-Trial amalgam accusation that Adlai Stevenson, a visitor to Kashmir,

[17] *Ibid.*, May 20, 1954.

had conspired with Nehru's friend, Sheik Abdulla, Prime Minister of Kashmir, to sell out the state to American imperialism, and going on from there to the arrest of Abdullah and detention for years without trial, and then the annexation, is scarcely a suitable stage background for Nehru's idealistic posturings before his world audience. Governments, however, are governments, and none is completely ethical, and if they cannot attain their goals by fair means they often use others. Prime Minister Nehru cannot escape the operations of this unfortunate law of the inherent immorality of national states.

Yet he tries to have the best of all worlds. He lectures other countries on the dangers of accepting foreign aid, but when it is called to his attention that India has accepted foreign aid, he writes, "One of the reasons why we have not said that we shall not accept aid from outside is that our saying so would itself be a gesture of lack of friendship if not of hostility. We do not want to behave in this unfriendly and discourteous way to any country."[18] He lectures against alignments and blocs, but his government is in the British Commonwealth, which carries an implied guarantee of military and financial assistance. And in the Commonwealth there is also South Africa, whose indecent injustices toward colored people Nehru properly wants all civilized nations to condemn, but when, on his return from a London conference of Commonwealth Prime Ministers, he was asked by the press whether the racial problems of South Africa were taken up, he brusquely replied, "We do not discuss such matters at the Prime Ministers' Conference."[19] He lectures other nations about reducing armaments. But when a Gandhian, writing in Harijan,[20] the weekly magazine founded by Mahatma Gandhi and now published by his disciples, challenged Nehru to reduce India's armaments, he met with no positive response. No wonder Vallabhbhai Patel, the strong man of the Congress party during Gandhi's day, called Jawaharlal Nehru a "disjointed idealist."

It is noteworthy, to say the least, that the two sober Indian voices raised against the frenzy into which Nehru whipped the country at the first news of U.S. aid to Pakistan were Gandhian voices. One was this article in Gandhi's Harijan, and it called for consistency: if Nehru wanted the West to believe in Russia's and China's peace-

[18] Ibid., July 8, 1954.

[19] Ibid., Feb. 11, 1955.

[20] Article entitled "Defense vs. Development," by P. Kodanda Rao, Harijan, April 17, 1954.

ful aims why did he not believe Pakistan's peaceful avowals? "Against a possible aggression of Pakistan which spent about seventy crores of rupees[21] on her military might, need India spend 200 crores?" the writer asked.

If India must be prepared for Pakistan aggression in spite of assurances of Pakistan's innocent intentions, Pakistan also feels it necessary to be prepared for defence against possible Indian aggression, and supplement her military might with American aid. Perhaps the best solution seems to be that the military strength and expenditure of both India and Pakistan should be reduced approximately to the same level.

The second voice was that of Acharya (Scholar) Vinoba Bhave, Gandhi's spiritual heir, the Mahatma's closest disciple and spiritual heir, whose walking tours through India to collect land from the rich for the poor had thrilled Indians as nothing else—for there is a spiritual or religious chord in the Indian on which Gandhi could play whole symphonies and from which Vinoba Bhave was now getting rich tones. In the midst of the clamor against the Pakistan-U.S. agreement, the Indian press, under a New Delhi dateline of January 12, 1954, reported that

Acharya Vinoba Bhave said here yesterday that he failed to see how any new threat or danger to India could be created by the reported Pakistan-US military pact. While he did not deny the existence of dangers, he said these dangers came from within the country and arose from the evils of caste, sectarianism, unemployment, landlessness, hunger, disease, and social injustice. . . . He appealed to all citizens to become conscious of this internal danger which was more real and ever-present than any external threat to their security.

In private, other persons also took a quiet view of U.S. aid to Pakistan, but they did not speak out because of the excited national temper, for Nehru had been proclaiming that "American aid to Pakistan will certainly bring world war nearer in the matter of time and also nearer India's frontiers."[22] A member of Nehru's government predicted that "it would certainly destroy the peace of the whole world," and Krishna Menon, speaking in New York, asserted it would "bring armed conflict nearer to India."[23] According to rumors and press reports Pakistan was receiving, or had already received,

[21] A crore of rupees is ten million rupees, approximately $2,000,000.
[22] Bombay *Sunday Chronicle*, January 31, 1954.
[23] New York *Herald Tribune*, March 14, 1954.

THIS IS OUR WORLD

three thousand tanks and squadrons of jet planes from America. It developed, however, that no arms had yet been delivered, that they would begin arriving only in October, 1954, and that their total value, in the first year of the program, would be less than $27 million[24]—with no jets, and probably no tanks, and no military or other bases for the United States.

U.S. aid to Pakistan has not, according to latest available reports, yet caused a world war. Nor is it likely to. But then Nehru's evaluation of international events sometimes tends to be alarmist and is often subjective. In 1946, for instance, neither he nor Krishna Menon believed that the British Labor government would liberate India; it did in 1947. Possibly, however, Nehru was forced into his extreme hostility to the American-Pakistan arrangement by the exigencies of the internal situation: if he had not taken the initiative in denouncing it the anti-Pakistan orthodox Hindus and the anti-American Communists might have taken the propaganda ball away from him and captured public opinion. Instead, Nehru called the aid to Pakistan "a challenge to India's manhood,"[25] and summoned the nation to unite around him in this hour of peril. It undoubtedly did to a considerable extent. In the tense atmosphere, few cared to comment on the fact that just before and during this agitation about aid to Pakistan India received a free grant of 200,000 tons of steel from the United States and $20 million for the purchase of railway locomotives and rolling stock. The steel might have been used directly or indirectly for munitions; the railway equipment was presumably needed, and India would have spent her own money for it; that money was saved by the U.S. gift, and at least some of it went to pay for the jet airplanes India bought in France. In the same period, moreover, India purchased from America thirty Sherman tanks, and twenty-six C-119 Flying Boxcars as well as some helicopters. She likewise acquired, at one time or another, British destroyers, minesweepers, frigates, and a cruiser. In 1954, moreover, India was already capable of manufacturing an internal combustion engine and rubber tires for jet planes and of assembling airplanes. India is indubitably Pakistan's military superior, and only a regrettable lack of confidence would engender a contrary view.

But, whether from fear or hate, Pakistan and Moslems are emotional issues with most Indians, and Nehru, who has been accused of being pro-Moslem—though actually he is the impartial champion

[24] *New York Times*, May 20, 1954, and July 3, 1954.
[25] *Times of India*, February 6, 1954.

of Hindu-Moslem peace—could not have dealt with them solely in terms of logic and fact. In general, governing India is a bed of nails suffused, sometimes, with the incense of adoration. Jawaharlal Nehru, "an eighteenth-century patrician," according to a British lady who, with her husband, has lived in the Prime Minister's house, a nineteenth-century aristocrat, according to others, is not to be envied his difficult task. If at times he wants to lay it down one is not surprised. Nor is he personally happy: "Joy may not be for him." History will probably forgive him a number of his mistaken policies and blunders, as his intimates usually forgive him his tantrums and tempers—but not the halo which he affects, and not the ill-conceived ideas which, through his support, have gained currency in Indian minds and obstruct clear thinking.

Prime Minister Nehru has repeatedly contended, for instance, that "if India did not have any independent policy, then her policy would be dependent on the wishes of others. Thereby she would lose her independence of action."[26] And, "If we become foolish enough to accept military help from outside and stretch out our hands and beg for such aid, we will be only mortgaging our freedom and losing it ultimately."[27] But the evidence proves the contrary. Yugoslavia remained Communist, established friendly relations with nonaligned India, and had a *rapprochement* with Soviet Russia although she received heavy military and economic assistance from capitalist, aligned America. Has Tito lost one jot of his independence? Are England, Norway, Denmark, Belgium, Holland, France, and Italy less independent because of U.S. military aid? In fact, the opposite has been true: without foreign aid, Greece would have lost her independence, and perhaps Turkey and Italy and even France too. During the Second World War, moreover, the Soviet Union, the United Kingdom, and many other states survived with military help from the outside.

The law of life, love, and international affairs is interdependence. No country is independent—not Russia, not America, not England —all are interdependent, dependent on somebody else, and Nehru's constant insistence of India's independent policy suggests not only lack of trust in others but also lack of faith in herself. India's independence is undisputed and safe. What she needs is to cultivate skillful interdependence.

Nor is it correct, as Nehru frequently argues, that an unaligned

[26] At the Kalyani Congress, *The Statesman*, January 22, 1954.
[27] Bombay *Sunday Standard*, January 31, 1954.

area enhances the prospects of peace whereas the multiplication of collective security agreements brings the adversaries right up against one another without a buffer and thus intensifies the war danger. Many European neutralists took this view, saying that if West Germany was included in NATO and rearmed, the chances of negotiations with Russia would be reduced if not completely destroyed. Yet immediately after the ratification of the Paris pacts which provided for German rearmament and membership in NATO, Moscow finally agreed to the long-delayed liberation of Austria, the Kremlin invited West German Chancellor Adenauer to Moscow for diplomatic discussions, and the Geneva Conference "at the summit" in July, 1955, became possible.

Sometimes it is difficult to understand Nehru's present rejection of collective security. The idea was first proposed by Soviet Foreign Commisar Maxim Litvinov and won general acceptance in liberal, Labor, Socialist, and Communist circles of Asia, Europe, and America in the 1930's. The idea simply was for countries to unite against the menace of aggression. "With the growth of the Nazi power," Nehru wrote in 1940, "the Congress [party] condemned Fascism and Naziism and disapproved of their theory and practice. We approved of collective security to check aggression and noticed that British policy, in spite of occasional declarations to the contrary, was deliberately sabotaging this idea, on which the League of Nations had been based, and was often encouraging aggression."[28]

Why was collective security right against Nazi imperialism and wrong against Soviet imperialism?

In and outside India I have heard collaborators of Nehru discreetly refute some of his favorite propositions on international affairs; he often gets more acquiescence than agreement. They also have criticized: his excessive preoccupation with foreign policy at the expense, they say, of domestic developments; his tendency "to want to get in on the act" of every major international event; his encouragement of the formation of a world color bloc—it would be the darkest mark on the epitaph of one who is without conscious color prejudice; his excessive flirtation with Russia and China;[29]

[28] Jawaharlal Nehru, "India's Demand and England's Answer," *Atlantic Monthly*, April, 1940, p. 455.

[29] When Nehru returned from his trip to Europe in the summer of 1955, the Bombay *Times of India*, July 16, 1955, wrote: "Today the air is thick with missions and delegations flying to and fro between Delhi and the Red Meccas of Peking and Moscow. If our foreign policy is independent, let us for our own sakes, if for nobody else's, have a little less of this political commuting."

his too close association with Communist fellow travelers; and his weakness for Krishna Menon whose virulent anti-Americanism, aired in America, has hurt India's role as mediator between America and other countries.

I do not know whether Mr. Menon's influence with Nehru rose as Mrs. Pandit's fell because of her friendliness toward the United States. Certainly, and despite the show of affection they stage by embracing at airports, no respect, much less love, is lost between her and Krishna Menon. The courtship of Jawaharlal Nehru is an international sport, and jealousies abound. His extraordinarily seductive personality alone, to which now has been added his lofty position, invites competition for a station close to his heart or in his shadow. Something like a Mogul court has been built up around him where flattery and figurative throat-slitting are considered legitimate means of advancing toward the powerful prince charming who sits on the throne. Even sisters, and of course many other women, are numbered among the suitors.

Power is a powerful thing, especially with those who have long been deprived, and it affects relations in the palace as well as in the world. When England had power in India, Indians were anti-British. But today India and Britain are equal members of the Commonwealth, they are in the same caste, so to speak, and that conduces to close ties, whereas America represents power, not in India to be sure, but globally, and the hand which habitually twisted the British's lion's tail takes particular delight in twisting the American eagle's feathers or Uncle Sam's coat tails. The defiance of power gives one a sense of power; Americans, alas, are far too insensitive to this aspect of their problems on the international scene. Why India does not have the same defiant attitude toward the powerful Russian and Chinese regimes would be a subject for examination. Perhaps it is because they are new and aspiring rivals of America which is Number One. India, Russia, and China therefore have in common the wish to clip U.S. wings or, at least, to teach America that she is not omnipotent. Secretly, and in some cases openly, other nations applaud the effort.

Whatever the complaints against Nehru's foreign policy by discerning Indians and irrespective of the court intrigues, there is no denying that the policy is popular and has given Nehru the power not only to curb his Communist and other opponents, but also to further reforms which a ruler with less support would have hesitated to sponsor. He has, for example, defeated a bill introduced in Parliament by Hindu extremists which would have banned the killing of any cow. Arguing against the measure, Mr. Nehru, according to an Associated Press report from New Delhi dated April 2, 1955, called the idea "most silly. We are totally opposed to it," he exclaimed. "We stand or fall by it."

"Shame, shame," cried the obscurantist Hindus.

"I don't get excited over any animal," the Prime Minister retorted, "not even the cow."

It takes courage to make such a statement in India, and it is political dynamite. Hindu sentiment and religion are deeply opposed to ending a cow's life even if its existence robs young cows of necessary pasture and fodder.

In May, 1955, Nehru guided through Parliament another precedent-breaking bill which gives Hindu women the right to demand a divorce. Hitherto only men had enjoyed this privilege. When Hindu conservative members of Parliament argued that marriage was sacramental and unchangeable, Nehru cried out, "What is sacramental? Is it sacramental to be tied to each other for life, all the time hating each other, biting each other, beating each other, making life hell for each other?" Divorce can now be obtained by mutual consent. The new law also bans polygamy and marriages of girls under eighteen and men under twenty-one, and permits women to inherit property.

To facilitate the land reform, Nehru also piloted a bill through Parliament empowering the federal and state legislatures to fix the compensation for expropriated private property. Theretofore, estate owners had, in some areas, delayed the division and sale of their lands by protracted litigation in the courts regarding the indemnification they were to receive.

Mr. Nehru, who has always called himself a Socialist but not a Marxist, now advocates "a Socialist pattern" and a "classless and casteless society"[30] for India. These purposes, though no doubt sincerely conceived, still belong to the music of the future and seem intended in the first place as bait for Westernized intellectuals and an attempt to court and confuse Communists or Communist sympathizers. "Socialist pattern," Vinoba Bhave has said, "tends to be vague," and he added that "he did not believe in collective farming which had proved a failure."[31] He preferred voluntary

[30] *Indiagram*, December 29, 1954.
[31] *Amrita Bazar Patrika*, January 22, 1955.

co-operatives with ownership of the land vesting in voluntary village-size co-operatives. But to Nehru Socialism means more state industries and more state-bureaucratic control over private industry. Such concentrated power at the summit can only be at the expense of individual freedom.

The central Indian problem is the village not only because it accounts for more than two-thirds of the national population, but especially because the village is the floor on which India, "vast, poor and industrially backward,"[32] stands, and unless it can be lifted the country will remain at its present indescribably low economic and cultural level. Mr. Nehru has now promised that the second Five Year Plan will concentrate on the village. Gandhians have chided him for not making that the aim of the first. But Nehru's taste, at home as well as in international politics, runs to the spectacular, and the four truly gigantic hydroelectric projects, for power, flood control, irrigation, and navigation, appeal to it. These undertakings, invaluable and ultimately indispensable to an expanding economy, will, before they yield large results, swallow a considerable percentage of the capital of India whose chief problem is capital deficiency. Meanwhile, according to Finance Minister Sir Chintaman Deshmukh, unemployment has been increasing despite the rise in employment under the First Five Year plan.[33] In the village, on the other hand, India's greatest supply of capital—the peasants' labor—lies misused and largely unused. But the village needs technological help and leadership, and though the Community Development Projects, an American idea financed with a little American and much Indian money, have commenced the reformation of the countryside, the great difficulty is that the urban-educated Indian, after four, five, or six years of university study, can find no place in a village and naturally seeks a city job, preferably with the government. As a result, apart from the Community Development Projects and where agriculture extension work has penetrated, the peasantry is scarcely aware of the existence of the government—except during election campaigns—and has not yet tasted the fruits of national independence.

India's independence movement was nationalistic and anti-imperialistic. Mahatma Gandhi tried to turn it to social reform—against caste, untouchability, status, and peasant poverty—but succeeded

[32] Statement by S. Radhakrishnan, Vice-President of India, cited in *Indiagram*, March 21, 1955.

[33] *Indiagram*, December 15, 1954.

only partially. So today in India, as Communications Minister Mr. Jagjivan Ram has said,

Every educated citizen, for example, pays lip service to the fundamental principle of democracy that man is the measure of everything and man's measure is his inherent goodness, not his wealth, power, caste, or birth. And yet, all who say that they believe in this principle continue to think in terms of old values and beliefs.[34]

India needs a moral as well as economic and social revolution.

Jawaharlal Nehru was born November 14, 1889. Though astonishingly agile, ambitious, energetic, well preserved, and handsome for his age in the cruel climate of India, he cannot of course finish the enormous task of lifting his big country out of its lethargy, poverty, debilitating customs, and interprovince, intercaste, interracial, interlinguistic, interreligious, and intravillage feuding. That will take generations.

Within four minutes of the beginning of any political discussion in India it becomes a discussion of Nehru, and three minutes later someone will have asked, "But who will succeed him?" I do not believe in the "great man" theory. Roosevelt was greater than Truman, but Truman proved himself an excellent President. The dimensions of Churchill's personality far exceed Attlee's, but Attlee was a historic godsend. Morarji Desai, Chief Minister of Bombay state, (born February 29, 1896), U. N. Dhebar, President of the Congress party, and Finance Minister Deshmukh have been mentioned as possible successors. Nehru at times seems to be grooming Krishna Menon who, however, is almost as unpopular in certain high circles in India as he is in New York and would certainly arouse endless opposition and chagrin in non-Communist circles. Jayaprakash Narayan, the Socialist turned Gandhian, who accuses Nehru of striking "totalitarian attitudes,"[35] has likewise been named as a possible future Prime Minister. He might not meet the approval of some Congress party leaders but he has what may prove infinitely more effective: the support of Vinoba Bhave, the Mahatma's spiritual heir. Both Jayaprakash and Bhave are anti-Communist, not as Nehru is (because the Communists have a foreign allegiance and believe in violence), but as U Nu, the Burmese Prime Minister, is (because Communists methods and aims are inherently immoral).

For a generation, and no matter who succeeds Nehru, India prom-

[34] *Sunday Statesman*, April 11, 1954.
[35] London *Times*, September 6, 1955.

ises to be a turbulent mixture of Gandhism, more state capitalism, modern private capitalism, decadent obsolete capitalism, infiltrating Communism, crass materialism, high-minded spiritualism, reactionary religious influences, extremely advanced Western intellectualism, parliamentary democracy diluted with personal politics, nepotism and party-bossism, quality journalism mottled by crypto-Communists, impressive progress, crises galore, inflation, an inflated bureaucracy, and all kinds of baffling, irritating, interesting, suffering, and lovable people.

Nehru, like Tito, wishes to have a strong government and foreign influence. These are pleasant for the leadership but do not always contribute to the welfare of the people. Power is a snare. Yet Nehru, though traditionally a democrat, is more interested in power than in freedom at home or freedom abroad.

CHAPTER FORTY-FOUR

Russia Since Stalin

WHEN Moscow was gently wooing Nehru and Tito and Vienna and the world in general in 1955, observers said this meant that Russia had really changed after Stalin's death, a new era had dawned. History does seem to be divisible into periods, sometimes by coincidence, sometimes by content. Thus Franklin D. Roosevelt became President five weeks after Hitler came to power in Germany and died one month before Hitler. 1933 to 1945 might therefore be called the Roosevelt-Hitler era, or the Roosevelt-Hitler-Churchill-Stalin era, an era of social change, preparations for war, and war.

There followed the years of postwar consolidation, containment, and competition: the cold war, which was also the first stage of the Atomic-Hydrogen Age, dominated by the personalities of Truman, Attlee, Stalin, Churchill, Adenauer, Mao Tse-tung, Nehru, Tito, and Pierre Mendes-France, and marked by the inflation of America's world role and the emergence of Communist China and independent India.

Another era commenced in 1953: on January 20, Dwight D. Eisenhower was inaugurated President. Seven weeks later, on March 5, Joseph Stalin died. New faces appeared in place of his: Beria, Malenkov, Khrushchev, Bulganin, Zhukov, Konev, and others. This might be called the Eisenhower–Stalin-succession period.

From March, 1953, to the present, experts, officials, and laymen have argued whether, how, and how much the Soviet Union has changed since Stalin's passing. While this debate raged the world press reported almost daily shifts in policy and personnel inside Russia. Yet doubts remained regarding their profundity, permanence, and significance.

What one has to understand is that the post-Stalin present represents a reaction against the Stalinist past. Joseph Stalin tried for two decades to become "The Father of the Peoples" and only succeeded in being hated by most people, including many of his closest lieutenants who developed a high respect for his talents and a deep contempt for the man. Immediately after his death the orgiastic personal glorification, thickly smeared praise, fawning adulation, and tasteless obeisances ceased abruptly. Some foreign Communists had argued that these reflected real love, some that backward Russia needed a political idol. Apparently they merely reflected his wishes. For no sooner had his mummy been deposited in the Red Square mausoleum than the love evaporated—or was it that the Soviet citizenry suddenly grew mature? In either case, Stalin became the forgotten Soviet man. To be sure, he was mentioned, usually in conjunction with Lenin's name, but never in the breathless, worshipful manner which his sick ego seemed to have required and relished.

This revulsion against Stalin was so strong that certain foreign commentators suspected foul play in connection with his death. They contended that the Moscow announcement, on January 13, 1953, of the arrest of nine prominent Soviet physicians, most of them Jews, for alleged complicity in the death of Andrei Zhdanov, Politburo member, in 1948, and for trying "to put out of action" a number of army marshals portended a new nation-wide purge, like that of 1937-38; Stalin, they claimed, was having another attack of paranoia which usually preceded a purge, and how could anybody know who might be among its victims? Perhaps Beria himself, perhaps Zhukov, or Budenny. Men as high, and higher, in the Soviet hierarchy had been executed before. Accordingly, the argument concludes, some top Soviet leaders with a premonition decided to put Stalin out of action.

There is surely distortion and exaggeration here; possibly the attack of paranoia brought on the cerebral hemorrhage which officially caused Stalin's death. But the "Doctors' Plot" was somebody's political machination against Beria, the leader responsible for the secret police at the time of the "conspiracy." He, by implication, had been negligent, or perhaps had encouraged the doctors to kill Zhdanov and the marshals. But Zhdanov's rival had been Malenkov and suspicion would have fallen on him. Did he wish to shift it to Beria? Malenkov, moreover, no sooner became Prime Minister than he appointed Marshal Zhukov Assistant Minister of Defense and Marshal Voroshilov President of the Soviet Union. Did Malenkov propose to use the army for his coming struggle with Beria? A feud had always existed between the secret police and the army, for the Soviet secret police is not merely an intelligence service, it has fully armed divisions which fought at the front in the Second World War, and it, not the army, guards the frontiers, railways, roads, et cetera. It is a second army which the regular army never liked. Was the "Doctors' Plot" Malenkov's way of fanning the army's hatred of Beria by suggesting that he wanted the doctors to poison the marshals?

Beria, and perhaps others, apparently did connect Malenkov with the "Doctors' Plot." On March 21, 1953, *Pravda* announced that Prime Minister Malenkov had, "at his own request," been relieved of the post of Secretary of the Central Committee of the party, the more crucial of his two offices, and replaced by Nikita S. Khrushchev. Simultaneously, public praise of Malenkov was muted. And on April 4, Lavrenti P. Beria released and exonerated the doctors and charged that their "confessions" had been obtained by methods "impermissible and strictly forbidden by Soviet law"—as though that had ever mattered. Beria also dismissed some top secret police chiefs who presumably had concocted and revealed the "Doctors' Plot" without his sanction.

When Stalin died a triumvirate succeeded him in which Malenkov stood first, Beria second, and Molotov a low third. Now Malenkov had sunk and Beria had risen. In fact, beginning about April 12, by all the signs—appointments made, positions in published photographs, and so forth—Beria was first.

And first to die. On July 10, 1953, *Pravda* announced that the Central Committee of the party, "having heard and discussed a report" by Malenkov on the "criminal anti-party and anti-government activities of L. P. Beria," expelled him from the party "as an enemy of the Communist Party and the Soviet people." He had been arrested, according to reliable data, in the last week of June. He was executed in December.

It is not necessary to believe the stereotype official version that Beria worked "in the interest of foreign capital." He did demonstrably use the power of the secret police to make himself Number One and then began to behave too much like his fellow Georgian, Stalin. Nobody relished the idea of a second autocrat in the Kremlin. Without exception, Stalin's survivors had silently witnessed him liquidate their friends and intimate collaborators at all levels, even the highest, and the fear of being added to the black list of dead and banished must have been ever-present in the mind of each one of them, from Malenkov and Molotov down. All Stalin's heirs had suffered too much at his hands to view with equanimity the possible emergence of another personal despot. That sealed Beria's fate. And that, to a considerable degree, determined the form of Russia's post-Stalin leadership. It was a directorate.

This directorate, in place of Stalin's personal dictatorship, took more definite shape with Prime Minister Malenkov's "resignation" on February 8, 1955. On a motion of Nikita S. Khrushchev, first secretary of the Communist party, the Supreme Soviet elected Nikolai A. Bulganin, until then Minister of Defense, as Malenkov's successor. Marshal Zhukov was promoted from Assistant Minister to Minister of Defense; the army, it seems, had to be compensated for acquiescing in changes in the leadership. But Malenkov was not shot or exiled or purged or reviled; he was appointed Minister of Electric Power, an important post which may—such matters are of course highly secret—include responsibility for atomic energy, and he remained a member of the small central oligarchy which rules the country.

I believe this was the first resignation in Soviet history. Instead of calling for a subordinate's resignation Stalin would call in the executioner who, in the last years, had been Beria. Then the executioner executed Beria. But Stalin's remaining heirs were afraid to perpetuate this custom which, depending on the turn of the wheel, might cost any one of them his life. That saved Malenkov.

Equally important, perhaps more important, a division of power, if not a balance of power, had been achieved at the apex of the Soviet hierarchy. In Stalin's day, which lasted two and a half decades, he ruled absolutely and therefore ruthlessly. Now power was shared. Khrushchev, as party secretary, might, at a given moment, exercise more power than any one of his fellow oligarchs. But he needed the support of Bulganin, a political marshal who had been the head of the political police in the army, and Bulganin, in turn, depended on Zhukov who, however, had a rival in Marshal Ivan Konev. Molotov was wanted for his experience and ability in foreign affairs and he and Khrushchev seemed to be linked in their dislike of Malenkov. In February, 1941, Malenkov had attacked Mrs. Molotov's conduct of the Soviet cosmetics industry—such things count even in the kingdom of dialectic materialism. But Malenkov was not without friends in the army. Moreover, he had been associated with industry and had much in common with the numerous technocrats and managers who play a key role in domestic affairs.

Thus the Stalin monolith had been converted into a mosaic capable of constant rearrangements but held together by a desire to keep the general design intact in the interest of self and the movement. There evolved a kind of limited and conditioned democracy within the directorate whose members, less afraid of one another than they had been of Stalin, seemed to find greater joy in life, showed themselves oftener in public and at diplomatic receptions, and gave the impression that tensions at the top of the political pyramid had waned. Some of this relative relaxation trickled down into lower strata. Rank and membership in the directorate, however, remained exposed to the exigencies of the personal power struggle, for the entire system lacked the sanction of a freely expressed popular will.

Under Stalin there were no politics in Russia, for politics are a struggle for power and Stalin held all power irretrievably. Today, however, politics have returned because power is shared and can be won and lost in quiet competition. The political power of the secret police, for instance, has shrunk, and General Serov, its chief, sits at the far end of the table at official dinners and jumps obediently to the least crook of Khrushchev's or Bulganin's finger, whereas Marshal

Zhukov bulks large at the center of the official picture and the Central Committee of the Communist party has regained some of the influence which Stalin drained out of it. In Stalin's time, moreover, subservience to the Communist Czar was a prerequisite to survival and promotion. Now ability is paramount. Besides, a younger generation of leaders is pressing upward against the old, and the veterans seek to protect themselves by dressing up in the armor of Leninist ideology. The supremely intelligent, modernist Malenkov, however, is less interested in phrases out of Marxist textbooks or in foreign expansion and more interested in production for popular use.

Human rivalry is tightly interlaced with policy differences. On March 12, 1954, when he was still Prime Minister, Malenkov, for instance, stated that with modern weapons a new world war "means the death of world civilization." Foreign Minister Molotov took the first possible opportunity—the session at which Malenkov was deposed—to reply angrily that it would mean only the death of world capitalism,[1] a sentiment subsequently echoed by Voroshilov— as though the H-bomb and A-bomb were class conscious, as though Marxist ideology supplied each Soviet citizen with a two-foot-thick protective shield of lead against radioactivity. Moscow may cry "Peace, peace," but it wants no pacifism in Russia induced by fear of the big bombs.

This little controversy about man's future on the planet would suggest that Malenkov was the "moderate" seeking conciliation with other countries whereas Molotov took a more aggressive stand. There is evidence in support of this distinction. On the other hand, Molotov said on April 1, 1953, twenty-six days after Stalin's death, "This proposal allows . . . for an armistice in Korea," and in the preceding week Prime Minister Kim II Sung of North Korea and China's Premier Chou En-lai had spoken in favor of a Korean truce. Stalin apparently impeded the settlement in Korea because he felt that the longer North Korea, Red China, and America bled, the better off Russia would be. He likewise stood in the way of the normalization of Soviet international relations in other areas. His passing enabled the directorate to remodel Soviet foreign policy.

Stalin, for instance, had made territorial demands on Turkey and tried to force the Turks to agree to a Russian fortress in the Straits. The only result was to drive Turkey into a firm Western embrace. But Stalin was too inflexible to relent even when nothing

[1] *New York Times*, February 9, 1955.

could be gained by continued hostility. On May 30, 1953, however, Mr. Molotov told the Turkish Ambassador in Moscow that the Soviet government had "found it possible to renounce its territorial claims on Turkey" and wished to re-establish "neighborly relations."[2] Similarly, Stalin had antagonized Tito and caused the break between Yugoslavia and Russia. He knew from 1948 to 1953 that Tito could not be brought back into the fold, yet he refused to establish normal diplomatic relations with Belgrade. The *rapprochement*, commenced during Malenkov's administration, was completed by Khrushchev and Bulganin during their personal visit to Yugoslavia in 1955. As far as Yugoslavia and Turkey were concerned, the new Moscow masters were closing dead accounts with the notation: "Not responsible for debts incurred by our predecessor."

In other respects too they behaved like pliant realists. They permitted some Soviet wives of foreigners to leave Russia, released many slave laborers from the concentration camps, admitted more foreigners into the country and allowed them and resident diplomats and foreign journalists to travel more widely in the Soviet Union, opened a gate in the Iron Curtain through which a large number of Soviet scientists, athletes, and others went on visits to all the continents, and themselves attended foreign parties in Moscow where they mixed freely with the guests and contributed to the gaiety and interest of the occasions. Soviet representatives abroad, as though at the pull of a string, smiled more often and dropped some of the artificial reserve which they donned for protection during the Stalin era. All these were inexpensive trivia, but by their contrast with the previous period and by seeming to portend a new deal they improved the international atmosphere—a not negligible factor in world affairs.

The Muscovite rulers appeared to be painfully aware of the two new major facts in Russia's foreign position: the rise of a united China and the active role of the United States in Europe and Asia. Both these circumstances obstruct Soviet expansion. The Soviet Union cannot expand in the Far East without incurring Chinese hostility or elsewhere without encountering American counteraction. Friendship with China, even at high cost, is a first Moscow principle, and so is the avoidance of war, any war, and of course a war in which the United States might participate.

An American general who had years of contact with the highest

[2] Moscow *Pravda*, July 19, 1953.

Soviet military in Berlin once said to me, "The army is the most conservative force in Russia." The Soviet army, to be sure, is not in the saddle in Moscow, but neither can the rider ignore the moods and wishes of its powerful, popular commanders, and generals and marshals do not always thirst for battle; on the contrary, many prefer peace with armaments.

No war, more smiles and contacts, and less tension were the bugle call that opened the negotiating season, which may last years. The first negotiations gave the seven million inhabitants of Austria the independence promised them in 1943, but delayed by Moscow until October 1955. The little country, permanently neutralized, regained its freedom on payment of a huge ransom to Russia for giving back to the Austrians their own properties seized by the Nazi invaders and seized by the Russians from the Nazis. Many signs indicated that Moscow hoped Austrian neutralization would set a pattern for West Germany.

In the absence of war, and since no country was likely to enter the Soviet empire voluntarily, the best and perhaps the only means left to the Moscow directorate of weakening the West and strengthening Russia was the neutralization of others, and this they therefore pursued with characteristic persistence, vigor, and skill. That spelled cold war, the cold war continued with colder methods.

It was peaceful coexistence, of course; coexistence is an empty slogan because it describes a condition which neither side intends to alter by ceasing to exist. But how competitive would the coexistence be? And does coexistence imply that its advocates insist on or accept the permanent colonial status of Russia's East European and Central European satellites? One of the satellites is East Germany. If Moscow relinquishes it, the Soviet empire might rock. If Moscow holds it, Germany cannot be united, European security is jeopardized, and coexistence remains highly competitive.

The heart of Stalin's foreign legacy is the colonies. Depending on the angle of vision these have been regarded as a protective *cordon sanitaire* for Russia or a springboard for coming Soviet aggressions. This military aspect is less real than it seems; in the age of jet planes and guided missiles the geographic width of the Soviet satellite belt is a negligible quantity, and in wartime unrest might make it a minus quantity for Moscow. But the political aspect is of transcendent importance. For the outsider it raises the moral issue. For Russia it raises the whole big question of the future of Soviet society.

Nobody has argued convincingly that Moscow rules the peoples of the empire by consent. Some do assert that the satellites benefit from Soviet rule. To debate the point is fruitless. Even where benefits are tangible and visible, nations want to be free. If that is true in Africa it must certainly be true of European countries with ancient advanced cultures.

Imperialism, sitting on the lid of popular dissatisfaction, can never be a contribution to world peace. We believed this when the imperialism was brown, black, rising sun, Union Jack, and red white and blue. Why abandon the principle because the imperialism is Red? I have heard Asian intellectuals sizzle with opposition to French rule in Morocco and Dutch rule in West Irian and in the next breath condone Russian rule of Czechoslovakia and Poland. Should not anti-imperialism too be indivisible?

Logical propositions, however, will not persuade Moscow to withdraw to its prewar frontier. Stalin created the Soviet empire partly because he could not resist the opportunity when it presented itself, but largely because he hoped thereby to solve pressing domestic problems: since the Soviet regime had failed to give its people material contentment he offered them, as a substitute, nationalism and export-nationalism which is imperialism; sentiment instead of groceries, clothes, and housing. Before Moscow will agree to relinquish the satellites it must either grow very weak, too weak to hold them, or it must introduce reforms which conduce to greater happiness and bring the Soviet government more popular support at home.

The surrender of colonies is always closely related to internal social change. The loss of empire induced or at least helped Ataturk to undertake his social revolution in Anatolia. France's reluctance to abandon her colonies is linked with a hesitation to renovate her domestic social system. England liberated India to liberate herself for a new era of social progress. The same law applies to Soviet Russia.

Soviet leaders never mention basic problems of the social system; they consider its form final—as though anything ever is—and merely discuss surface questions: the volume of heavy industrial output as compared to consumer goods, the productivity of collective farms, and so forth. But these surface issues stem from grave faults of the system. The most fundamental fault is agricultural collectivization.

The Bolsheviks had no Socialist agrarian program when they seized power in November, 1917. Lenin therefore extemporized: the remaining estate owners were expropriated, land was nationalized, and the peasants were permitted to hold the redistributed land in usufruct as private cultivators. After the civil war, this mixed Socialist-capitalist arrangement worked fairly well, and production rose. But the peasant wanted factory goods for his produce and the city was incapable of meeting his demand. Leon Trotsky said: tax the peasantry heavily, make it pay for urban industrialization, and meanwhile promote world revolution so as to rescue industrially-backward Russia from the peasant counterrevolution. This was Trotsky's "Permanent Revolution." Bukharin coined the slogan: "Peasants, enrich yourselves." A village freed from the landlords' yoke and working for itself would be wealthy enough to pay for a moderate flow of imported consumers' goods and also for urban industrialization. Stalin, who shared Trotsky's fear of the peasantry, rejected Trotsky and Bukharin. He did not trust private-capitalist peasants under any circumstances; they would soon overwhelm and dismantle the Communist state. He therefore decided to lock them all up in collective farms where the land, the working animals, and the machinery—the capital—would belong to the state as would a part of the yield.

This was a political solution designed to place the hundred million or more Soviet peasants under government control. But it had its important constructive side, for with characteristic thoroughness Stalin undertook to collectivize and industrialize simultaneously; new industries would produce the tractors, combines, fertilizers, and so forth which would make agriculture more profitable.

Out of the mouths of Stalin's heirs we now know that it has not worked. Even before Nikita S. Khrushchev became First Secretary of the Soviet Communist party, he expressed his dissatisfaction with both the political and production aspects of collectivized agriculture and experimented with remedies. It was perhaps his preoccupation with this most important Soviet problem that made him the most important member of the directorate—that and his drive, energy, and bull-in-the-China-shop manner. As long ago as March 4, 1951, *Pravda* published an address by Khrushchev advocating what has come to be known as the Agrogorod, or Agricultural City: villages would be abolished and the peasants of several villages would be moved into an urban settlement whence they would go forth each morning to till the fields. The very next day *Pravda* made it clear that this was not government or party policy; somebody must have called Stalin's attention to the havoc which such a proposal might cause in the collectives. But Khrushchev never really dropped this startling idea of tenements on the steppes.

At the 1952 Nineteenth Communist Party Congress, Georgi Malenkov, who delivered the chief address—this made it clear that Stalin had trapped him as his Number One successor—reported that 254,000 small collectives had been merged into 97,000 enlarged ones,[3] a development he welcomed; but he also complained that in this process "a few of our leading officials" made mistakes, forced the tempo, allowed cottages to be destroyed, and robbed the peasants of the one-acre or half-acre plots around their homes where they raised chickens, a pig, et cetera for family use or for private sale on the free market.[4]

Thus despite *Pravda's* repudiation of Khrushchev's speech the Khrushchev plan did go into effect, at least partially. The reason is basic to an understanding of Russia. Stalin, fearing the peasants, converted them into collectivized serfs. But the collective, or kolkhoz, was still the old village, mechanized to be sure, modernized in its production methods, but still the same old village with the rude huts, the one long central street, and the high-steepled church. The collective farmer retained his small private plot to which he and his wife and children devoted more care than to the big work on the fields and in the barns of the collective. This left even the collectivized peasant some sense of independence, as did the whole village life where the handful of Communists who ran things could never become too ruthless, for the peasants might beat them up some dark night, or murder them—such deeds were reported in the Soviet press—or refuse to allow their children to intermarry. Khrushchev's Agrogorod, as well as the enlarged kolkhoz, was intended to rob the peasant of his last shred of economic freedom and personal independence, place him under closer secret police surveillance, and transform him into a proletarian on the land. Stalin himself, in his last published work, had referred to the incongruity of having a mercantile economy on the countryside "where the collectives

[3] *Otchotni Doklad 19. Syezdu Partii O Rabote Tsentralnovo Komiteta VKP (B)* (*Report to the Nineteenth Congress of the Party on the Work of the Central Committee of the All-Union Communist Party* [Bolsheviks], October 5, 1952, Government Publishing House of Political Literature, 1952, p. 48.

[4] *Ibid.*, p. 55.

agreed to give up their produce only as goods in return for which they wish to receive the goods they desire," side by side with nationalized industries where the workers are paid in money.[5] This is what troubles Khrushchev and all his comrades; the peasants, even though corralled into collectives, still possess economic power. That is embarrassing for political reasons. In the Soviet Union, nobody but the state should have economic power which is convertible into economic or other pressure.

No less embarrassing, the collectives have been disappointing as producers. One would have thought that Moscow's truly colossal investment of money, machines, skilled personnel, and science in the collective farms would make them enormously successful and raise their output. Yet in animal husbandry alone they have proved a disaster, and the evidence was supplied by Khrushchev. In a speech remarkable for frankness and figures—instead of past percentages—Mr. Khrushchev, on September 3, 1953, painted a gloomy picture indeed of the livestock situation of his country.[6] Comparing the number of animals on the first day of January of several years: 1916, in the midst of the First World War when Czarist Russia had a population of 150,000,000; 1928, before collectivization when farming was still capitalistic; 1941, before the Soviet Union entered the Second World War; and 1953, when the U.S.S.R. had more than 200,000,000 inhabitants, Khrushchev showed that the country had 28,800,000 cows in 1916, 33,200,000 in 1928, 27,800,000 in 1941, and 24,300,000 in 1953. The figures for sheep and goats were 96,300,000 in 1916, 114,600,000 in 1928, 91,600,000 in 1941, and 109,900,000 in 1953. For pigs, which should multiply quickly: 23,000,000 in 1916, 27,700,000 in 1928, 27,500,000 in 1941, and 28,500,000 in 1952. For horses: 38,200,000 in 1916, 36,100,000 in 1928, 21,000,000 in 1941 and 15,300,000 in 1952—but the deficiency in horses was balanced by the introduction of thousands of tractors and combines. Party Secretary Khrushchev added that milk yields per cow were very low, meat production had dropped steeply, and in vast Siberia, with its increased population under the Soviet regime, butter manufacture had declined from 75,000 tons in 1913 to 65,000 tons in 1952. Obviously, therefore, the average Soviet citizen had less meat, leather, eggs, dairy and other animal products than a subject of the Czars.

[5] J. Stalin, *Ekonomicheskie Problemi Sotsialisma V SSSR* (*The Economic Problems of Socialism in the USSR*), Gospolitizdat, 1952, p. 16.

[6] *Pravda*, September 15, 1953.

Cereals, which probably consitute two-thirds of a Soviet person's diet, have also been a severe headache. Georgi M. Malenkov boasted, in his report to the Party Congress on October 5, 1952, that "the grain problem, formerly regarded as the most urgent and serious problem, has been successfully solved, solved finally and irreversibly."[7] The delegates, who included Stalin, rewarded the announcement, according to the official stenogram, with "stormy and prolonged applause," for they knew how vital the matter was. But after Stalin the truth could be told, and a party decree of March 2, 1954, declared that "the present grain production level . . . does not meet the growing needs. . . . The quantity of grain remaining on the collective farms after the fulfillment of their obligations to the state does not cover the needs of the collective farms."

Nikita S. Khrushchev accordingly made himself the spearhead of an enormous drive, a truly historic venture, to increase the area under grain by seventy-four million acres by 1955, an area, according to Soviet Deputy Premier Mixim Z. Saburov, "approximately equal to the entire sown area of France and Italy."[8] It is also equal to the "total harvested acreage of wheat in the United States."[9] But it is all "virgin soil and wastelands in Kazkhstan, Siberia, the Urals, the Volga Valley and Northern Caucasus."[8] This is a laudable undertaking which, however, reflects desperation, for these lands were virgin and unused for a reason, and the reason is that they lie either in cold or in arid and semi-arid regions. One can only wish Khrushchev luck. Acting with customary forcefulness he has mobilized several hundred thousand "volunteers," young men and women from the cities who can drive machines, and sent them out into these uninhabited districts to increase Russia's supply of bread and gruel.

The fundamental question is, Why has it all happened? Grain, the Soviets say, is insufficient because of the growth of the population, especially city population. But in the United States too the national and urban populations have risen steeply yet there is an insane superfluity of cereals and dairy products in government warehouses.

The explanation of the Soviet Union's persistent food problem is the collective farmer's refusal to work as well and as loyally as he can. He sees economic disadvantages to himself in collective

[7] *Op. cit.,* p. 48.

[8] *New York Times,* November 7, 1954.

[9] Chauncy H. Harris, "Growing Food by Decree in Soviet Russia," *Foreign Affairs* Quarterly, New York: January, 1955.

farming and, above all, he is irked by the system itself. It is compulsory, restrictive, and collective, and he prefers to labor for himself instead of being an entry in the collective farm's bookkeeping ledger, a factory working man on the farm. Tito recognized this basic peasant resistance to collectivization and disbanded the Yugoslav collectives. Can Moscow do the same? The private peasant would represent not only a defeat but a danger, for the peasant would then demand consumer goods in return for his crops and Moscow's emphasis is still on heavy industry, not light industry which makes consumer goods. Heavy industry makes products which the Soviet citizen cannot eat or wear—armaments, and machines for the industrialization of China and the satellites and for luring neutrals like Egypt into Russia's orbit.

What we are witnessing in Russia is probably a gigantic, slow-motion sit-down strike of more than a hundred million collectivized peasants in protest against modern, mechanized feudalism. Stalin's heirs think they can break this resistance by offering the cultivator more money, more freedom to work his private half-acre, and nationalism-imperialism. But the directorate is dealing here with something quite visceral, unconscious or subconscious, intuitive, inherited, and, above all, perfectly normal and natural. The peasant wants to be independent. He dislikes Communist or other supervisors bending over his bent back, watching, reporting, ordering, collecting.

The core of the Kremlin's difficulty is the same in city and village. It is bureaucracy. Since Stalin, the directorate has tried to transfer some tasks from the federal government to the governments of the constituent republics of the Soviet Union. It remains bureaucracy. Hardly an issue of any Soviet daily newspaper or magazine is without some illustration of or complaint against bureaucracy. The evil is recognized. But the cure proposed is usually the same as the disease: send more Communists: dismiss the manager; "increase vigilance"; "the party demands rhythmic production" instead of feverish spurts to fulfill the plan. The prescription is always a ukase from above. *Pravda* and *Izvestia* editorials, read mostly by city people and Communists and couched in their language, regularly exhort the peasant to harvest his crop on time, to plant his seed now, to give better care to cows and sows; the timberman is told the Fatherland needs lumber; Moscow pleads with the miner to dig more coal and not to leave the pits. Moscow dispatches thousands of agents all over the country to remove bottlenecks—and how these visitors are resented

on the spot! Thousands of factory managers, planners, and technicians daily arrive in Moscow and republican capitals for instructions.
Speeches by leaders and articles in the press demand that specialists
leave their swivel chairs and go out into the plants and farms. I
used to read such appeals, threats, and summonses in the fourteen
years I lived in the Soviet Union, and now I continue to read them
in Soviet publications.

My family and the Soviet families we knew always complained that
the shops offered summer goods in the winter and winter goods in the
summer. The leading editorial of *Pravda* of October 5, 1954, makes
the same point: "There must be an end," it says, "to such abnormal
conditions when summer goods in many instances appear in the
shops only in the fall and winter goods—in spring." How many
editorials of this kind I collected in Moscow between 1922 and 1938!

Faced with similar and seemingly inescapable defects of a political
system in which the state owns and operates everything—all factories,
mines, lumber camps, railroads, and so forth—Tito resorted to radical
surgery. He withdrew the government from management and transferred each industrial and mercantile unit to a workers' council
elected by the employees. He thus substituted a real Socialist experiment for what the Kremlin Fathers have chosen to call "Communism."

Of course, the Soviet government is strong and can apply heavy
pressure to its citizens, and Russia is richer than Yugoslavia and
can afford more mistakes longer. Besides, the wealth of the Soviet
Union and its industrial progress enable an upper and upper-middle
class to live comparatively well by Czarist standards and by East-
European standards, and these privileged strata numbering, one
estimates roughly, 5 to 10 per cent of the population, or ten to
twenty million persons, are satisfied and uphold the regime, as do the
students who enjoy educational opportunities, and they give the government enough support and technical talent to prolong the life
of the present life-sapping bureaucratic system in town and village.

But as long as it continues, Moscow cannot introduce civil liberties. If the peasant had them he would bolt from the collectives, and
the working man would insist on less state capitalism and some
Socialism or workers' control of industry.

The Soviet people are a wonderful people with endless talent.
The Czarist system held them back, now the Soviet system holds
them down. But the post-Stalin directorate does seem less brittle and

dogmatic than the Great Red Father who preceded it. Khrushchev, for instance, has decided that the Soviet peasant can learn more from the Iowa corn farmers than from Karl Marx and Professor Lysenko. No longer does Moscow insist that Russia has nothing to learn from "the decadent capitalist West." The directorate seeks contacts—in trade, culture, science, and sports.

Quite a number of Westerners, being Westerners, put their trust in education. When the late U.S. Presidential candidate Wendell Willkie interviewed Stalin, he said, "If you continue to educate the Russian people, Mr. Stalin, the first thing you know you'll educate yourself out of a job." Stalin laughed. He was right—he kept his job till he died. But another Westerner, Mr. Allen W. Dulles, Director of the United States Central Intelligence Agency whose chief task is to estimate the power and future of the Soviet system, reporting the Willkie incident, said, "There remains the possibility that newly created wants and expectations, stimulated by education and perhaps by more exposure to the West, will in time compel great and almost unpredictable changes in the Soviet system itself. . . . In introducing mass education the troubled Soviet leaders have loosed forces dangerous to themselves. It will be very difficult for them henceforth to close off their own people from access to the realities of the outside world." And once the Iron Curtain is raised, Mr. Allen Dulles ended, the people "surely will come to realize the inevitability of the great precept, 'And ye shall know the truth and the truth shall make you free.' "[10] Amen. Allen Dulles is no dreamer. He is a tough screener of information and he reflects and helps to formulate official American thinking on Soviet affairs.

Such profound changes take time and peace is the mother of time. The outside world must give the Soviet Union the time and the incentive to change. The incentive would be more and warmer, mutually profitable ties of all kinds. Those who regard this as a gamble should have the courage to gamble. For if the game is won Russia will be saved for freedom and the world for peace and Russia's colonies will win their independence.

[10] Commencement Address at Columbia University, June 1, 1955. Complete text supplied on request by Mr. Dulles' office.

CHAPTER FORTY-FIVE

America Under Eisenhower

A FEW weeks after Dwight D. Eisenhower became President Stalin's death opened the road to the conclusion of a truce in Korea. Thus the dictator, in dying, enabled the democratic leader to fulfill his implied election pledge to end the Korean War.

Stalin tried hard for decades, sometimes working at his job sixteen hours a day, to be accepted as the father of his country, but failed. Eisenhower, on the other hand, has often preferred golf to memoranda even when they are only a page long. Nevertheless, he has become the national father figure, the first, unless I am mistaken, in United States history.

Certain qualities in his personality made Eisenhower Papa to America. This unprecedented phenomenon, however, would not have occurred but for a sense of insecurity in the American people. Stalin's truculent postwar bellicosity, especially after Russia's first atomic explosion in 1949, inaugurated a period of painful puzzlement and uncharacteristic fear in the United States. Fear, a nation's worst counselor, is the demagogue's best friend and he keeps him well fed. So McCarthyism waxed and grew fat and its constant company gave many good Americans the jitters—which is not a comfortable condition when it lasts very long. The alternative was the calm, protective, paternal confidence of President Eisenhower.

Before Mr. Eisenhower could impart confidence, however, he had to acquire it himself and that took time, and meanwhile his Administration was being demoralized. The army, usually the synonym of courage, crawled on its belly to appease the fire-belching demagogue.

(The facts were brought out in the public hearings which helped reduce Senator McCarthy to his natural weight.) The Secretary of State, while seeking to impress allies and adversaries with big words about negotiating from strength, robbed them of much of their impact by giving demonstration after demonstration of weakness in the face of one terrorizing man.

Mr. John Foster Dulles began his tenure in office by volunteering to be investigated; the offer was in tune with the spirit of the times but not with the spirit of democracy, for loyalty should be assumed in a democracy and if disloyalty is assumed then one investigation is not enough, there should be continuing investigations and constant snooping on all, including the snoopers—the open door to an ubiquitous secret police. Nevertheless, Secretary of State Dulles earned America's gratitude for showing that investigations could be heaped on investigations until they became ridiculous. For example, John Carter Vincent, Career Minister in the U.S. Foreign Service —this is its topmost rank—had been investigated time after time. The reason is not far to seek. "From 1936 to 1947, except for a short interruption," Secretary Dulles declared, Mr. Vincent "served in key positions in China and in Washington in relation to Chinese, Japanese, and Far Eastern matters," and "was largely relied upon by his superiors, notably the President, the Secretary of State and George Marshall when he headed a special Presidential mission to China in 1945 and 1946." He had therefore become, as Mr. Dulles stated, "the subject of inquiry and controversy" and repeated hearings. When Mr. Dulles took office he very properly called for the dossiers and studied them with his trained legal brain. He concluded, and asserted in a public statement,[1] that Mr. Vincent was not a security risk and was not disloyal. Despite this he asked for John Carter Vincent's resignation on the ground that "Mr. Vincent's reporting of the facts, evaluation of the facts, and policy advice during the period under review show a failure to meet the standard."

Mr. Vincent's career was thus cruelly ruined. But perhaps he found some comfort—and humor—in the publication, a year and a half later, by the State Department itself of a volume of official U.S. documents including one in which he warned in 1938 that "the Japanese military is psychologically an aggressive force which should not be expected to become satiated. . . . From the long viewpoint our involvement in the Far East may not be avoided unless Japanese

[1] Full text in the *New York Times*, March 5, 1953.

militarism is defeated," and he therefore advised that "the best chance of defeating the Japanese without United States participation in the fighting would be to take early and stern steps to aid Generalissimo Chiang Kai-shek."[2]

I call that good reporting, excellent evaluation of facts, and policy advice of a high standard. Now all of Mr. Vincent's dispatches to the State Department have not been published, and it is plausible to assume that some of his information and prophecy was bad. But so is everybody's. If a top official is to be dismissed ten or fifteen years after the fact because events have proved him wrong then (1) many government offices would be emptied, (2) most men in U.S. embassies and missions abroad will stop sending Washington their honest opinions and write "on the one hand . . . and on the other hand" briefs, and (3) a democracy would begin to resemble a dictatorship where errors are fatal.

But, as Secretary Dulles said, Mr. John Carter Vincent was "the subject of . . . controversy"—possibly because he had foreseen that the Communists might take over China—and he therefore had to be investigated, and if the investigations yielded no incriminating data he had to be discharged anyway. Mr. Dulles accordingly threw Mr. Vincent to the Senatorial wolves. A Secretary of State must get along with the Senate, otherwise he cannot function, and some Senators are carnivores. The trouble is that carnivores have to be fed the same diet at regular intervals, and Secretary Dulles therefore fed them John Paton Davies, Jr., a forty-six-year old official with a service record of twenty-three years in the State Department, who had been investigated nine times, and he fed them several devoted anti-Communists employed by various U.S. offices abroad. The evil consequences on American officialdom were visible to the naked eye when I traveled abroad in 1953, 1954, and 1955. *The Foreign Service Journal*, organ of the Foreign Service Association, wrote at the time that the ouster of John Paton Davies, Jr would have "a serious effect on service efficiency and morale." It urged that American diplomats "must nevertheless continue to call the shots as they see them." Apparently it suspected that some cynics would not; why destroy a life career for the sport of calling a shot which may seem right today and off tomorrow when the wind changes on a hill in Washington, D.C.?

John Carter Vincent, John Paton Davies, Jr., and the others were

[2] *New York Times*, December 19, 1954.

victims of a fierce Republican party vendetta against the Democrats which was after bigger game. One of Mr. Dulles' Cabinet colleagues impugned President Truman's loyalty by charging that he had knowingly kept in the government employ an American who was a Russian spy. Vice-President Richard M. Nixon, according to a dispatch in the New York *Herald Tribune* of October 5, 1954, "blamed the Truman-Acheson foreign policy for getting us 'in the war in Korea.'" New York Governor Thomas E. Dewey said that the blood of Americans who had died and been wounded in Korea was on the hands of the Democratic party. Senator Joseph R. McCarthy of Wisconsin frequently referred to the Roosevelt and Truman Administrations as "twenty years of treason," and the Republican Party National Committee sponsored the same phrase. These attacks were in effect assaults on the basic principle of democracy which is that in a democratic system, especially in a two-party democratic system, a party is entitled to try to weaken the other but not to destroy it, for that would leave only one party, in other words, a dictatorship. And what but destruction, or suppression, would logically follow on the acceptance of the charge that the Democratic party was treasonable and its leaders disloyal?

With the Republicans attempting to pin the label of traitor and subversive on Democrats and Communists, and Democrats joining in the hunt on suspects, investigations multiplied, secret denunciations increased, and all kinds of people were expected to proclaim their non-Communist purity: In Indiana, for instance, the State Athletic Commission required professional boxers and wrestlers to swear that they were not and never had been Communists. In Cincinnati and other cities, street cleaners had to make a similar oath. In New York, the attendant of a municipal lavatory was dismissed because he had been a Communist between 1936 and 1939. The Philadelphia Common Pleas Court Number Six upheld the constitutionality of the Pennsylvania Loyalty Oath act in the case of a hospital nurse who refused to take the oath on the ground that it infringed her individual rights, but in doing this Judge Curtis Bok agreed that the act was so broad that its "rationale ceases when applied to nonsensical positions," and added, "The loyalty or disloyalty of a ditch digger or leaf raker would be so irrevelant to the safety of the state as to render the entire loyalty system not only absurd, but oppressive." Loyalty oaths had become absurd and oppressive, and self-defeating, for the more security-conscious the country became the more insecure it felt until a condition was reached which Paul G. Hoffman, chairman of the board of the Studebaker-Packard Motor Company and friend of President Eisenhower, described as "near-panic."[3] A nation frightened by threats to its existence becomes incapable of normal existence and of coping with the threats.

Solid citizens with authority in the American community and concern for their country were plainly alarmed by the spreading hysteria. Henry R. Luce, Editor-in-Chief of *Time, Life,* and *Fortune* magazines, addressing the annual commencement of Temple University in Philadelphia, on June 18, 1953, said, "the loudest voices that issue from the Senate and Congress of the United States today are not always the voices of liberty. They are too often the voices of hate, of fear, of vulgarity." He complained, moreover, that "in America today, liberty is not loved sufficiently," and, too, that "here in America, we have gone far toward developing a form of brainwashing. Its name is anti-Communism and it has become for millions of Americans a substitute for thinking."[4] Many applauded these precise words; no one could deny them. Catholic Bishop Bernard J. Sheil, speaking in Chicago, denounced Communism but asked, "What kind of anti-Communism is proper in a freedom-loving country like ours?" Unless anti-Communism was moral, he declared, "it is not effective. You cannot effectively fight immorality with immorality," and he cried out against "the phony anti-Communism that mocks our way of life." Expatiating on this point, he said, "As you see, I take a pretty dim view of some noisy anti-Communists— one in particular, the junior Senator from Wisconsin."[5] In a subsequent address, Bishop Sheil flayed the "demagogues," "emotional charlatans," and false prophets who "in their effort to preserve freedom destroy it."[6] Dr. Vannevar Bush, a prominent scientist and President of the Carnegie Institution, deplored the "thought control in our midst" and cautioned that "the stifling of opinion can wreck any effort of free men, but it can wreck science more rapidly and completely."[7] The Association of American University Presses inserted a page advertisement in the *Saturday Review* of June 26, 1954,

[3] Article in the *New York Times* Magazine, November 14, 1954.
[4] Full text published as booklet by Time Incorporated, 1953.
[5] Verbatim text, New York *Post,* April 18, 1954.
[6] *New York Times,* August 19, 1954.
[7] *New York Times* Magazine, June 13, 1954.

stating that "we now seem to live in an age of unreason," and advising the individual "who hears scholars slandered and their loyalty questioned because they believe in freedom of opinion" not to "sit back in indifference or in helpless bewilderment," but "to stand up and declare himself," Mr. H. Rowan Gaither, Jr., President of the Ford Foundation, asserted in his annual report that "there is an unfortunate tendency for donors to select the safe and sure—safe in the sense that few will criticize the gift,"[8] a timidity, one hoped, to which his own, mighty organization had not succumbed. Arthur Hays Sulzberger, publisher of the influential and widely read New York Times, in a speech at a dinner in his honor, decried the "negative and sterile" approach of "our spate of loyalty oaths," and affirmed that risks of freedom must be taken in order to preserve democracy and avoid "a tightly controlled society in which every dissenter, every man who wishes to think for himself, is enchained in a futile effort to insure conformity in the name of security."[9]

President Eisenhower could probably have made any one or all of these statements. By family upbringing—to judge from the religious pacifism of his mother, the way of life of his father, and the known views of his brothers—and by his own temperament, Dwight D. Eisenhower belonged in the broad American liberal tradition. He gave a number of indications that "book burning" in U.S. official libraries abroad and Senatorial hysterics at home were repugnant to him. Yet he seemed reluctant to enter the thick of the fight against fear.

In December, 1953, when I saw Chancellor Adenauer, a shrewd administrator, in Bonn, he expressed the opinion that during his first year in the White House, President Eisenhower was the general who delegated tasks and observed their execution but now he was beginning to realize that the politician must go in and do things himself. One might add that a general does not relish the idea of entering a battle with half his forces while the other half is shelling him from both flanks and the rear. The Republican party was divided, and Eisenhower, lacking experience, did not know his own strength in it.

Gradually, it must have dawned on Mr. Eisenhower that this was a political kidnaping, he was being kidnaped by a band of iron-faced Senators who, having captured the inner fort of the State Depart-

[8] New York Times, September 19, 1954.
[9] Ibid., November 10, 1954.

ment, were moving themselves into the White House and him out of it. The alternative now was McCarthyism or Eisenhower, demogoguery or democracy, government by jitters or by deliberation. The investigators had never intended to stop at investigation. Nor did inquisition satisfy them. Their plan was usurpation of the executive power, and the Administration indeed seemed in a state of dissolution.

The turning point was the Army-McCarthy hearings in mid-1954. Somebody apparently told the army to stop retreating and test the Senator's fire power. The whole circus could be seen on television and heard on the radio, and the entire nation or a large segment of it looked and listened, certainly most of the women did their housework whenever the show was not on. The upshot of it all was that Humpty Dumpty had a great fall and was never the same thereafter. The public's long close-up view of the Senator from Wisconsin did not help him. The reactions varied: contempt, disgust, entertainment, puzzlement, but not awe or fear.

Fortunately for the United States, the Republican party, and for Eisenhower especially, the Democrats won control of both houses of Congress in the November, 1954, elections. The smooth functioning of the government now depended on co-operation between the President and the Democrats who, therefore, could no longer be accused of treason by responsible Republicans. The Democrats were quite happy to collaborate, and Mr. Eisenhower consequently found himself, in effect, leading the Democratic party and at least three-fifths of his own party. This domestic political peace blossomed when the incipient depression of 1954 yielded to the roaring prosperity of 1955.

Eisenhower's foreign policy, in deed, is a continuation, in changed circumstances, of the Truman-Acheson foreign policy, and while he is no New Dealer (his Administration, for instance, prefers private to public electric power production) he certainly is no Herbert Hoover Republican. What with price supports for farmers, subsidies to industry, and the extension of social security benefits to many additional millions, the U.S. government remains a major active factor in the nation's economy. Mr. Eisenhower has, of course, paid lip and other services to private capitalism, but private capitalism is not what it used to be when Henry Ford II, commenting on his company's guaranteed wage agreement with the United Automobile Workers' Union, tells the Detroit *News* of June 20, 1955, that "a lot of people call everything we do 'creeping Socialism.' They called social security that and they called pensions that. I really don't know what creeping Socialism is. . . . We have to keep up with the times. Every time we do something new, people cry that it's either Communism or Socialism." Mr. Ford also asked his critics for a definition of creeping Socialism. I am not one of the critics but I would define it as the slow infiltration of capitalism by Socialism in the interests of the better health of the former. The founding fathers of free enterprise would look with horror on what has happened to their child. However, as Mr. Ford says, "We have to keep up with the times." And the times demand that Mr. Ford be a revolutionary.

Truman and Acheson are very hard for Senators Knowland and McCarthy to swallow and even a watered-down Roosevelt, in a 1955 Ford, is anathema to many Republicans. But the Democrats are pleased and most Republicans acquiesce because they have no substitutes to offer which would work and win votes.

Fortunately, too, for the United States, the world, and especially for President Eisenhower's role as Papa to America, reports about the unimaginable power of the hydrogen bomb began to penetrate into the public's consciousness and with it a realization that in the Hydrogen-Atomic Age, hysteria and intransigence are too combustible to have around the machinery of government. Secretary of State Dulles declared in his press conference on November 9, 1954, that "any idea of a preventive war is wholly out of the question as far as the United States is concerned," and the President lent his authority to statements with the same content on several occasions. In fact, on November 8, 1954, Mr. Eisenhower, addressing a meeting in Boston of the National Council of Catholic Women, made an impassioned appeal—and not his first—for eternal peace. "We must now resolve," he exclaimed, "there must never be another war." Indeed, he went further. "Why must the people of one nation," he asked, "continue to hate or fear the people of another? . . . Above all we need the religious quality of compassion—the ability to feel the emotions of others as though they were our own," and he said we must go even beyond that and arrive at those "fundamental urgings, the bonds which make brothers of all men."

President Eisenhower is a moral man even if some of his associates are not. He is also a military man and, as his press conferences show, when he is dealing with questions about war and armaments he really knows what he is talking about. He knows therefore that the

H-bomb has changed all previous concepts of military superiority and preparedness. Russia does not have to possess more H-bombs than the United States; she just needs three, or maybe one, to make war even more thoroughly unattractive to America than it always has been. The American people fought in the First World War, the Second World War, and the Korean War with great zeal for victory but with less conviction and no thought of gain except that which would accrue to all humanity from the defeat of the enemy. Now the existence of a nuclear weapon one specimen of which might obliterate a city like Seattle, Milwaukee, New York, or Chicago, and contaminate a whole state with prolonged radioactivity, made war, preventive or other, completely unwanted.

President Eisenhower's firm rejection of advice from professional military men that might have led to hostilities in the Far East and his refusal to countenance any step such as the rupture of relations with Moscow, as openly urged by several Senators, or a categorical statement that the United States would leave the United Nations if Communist China entered it, therefore made him increasingly popular. Actually, toward the end of 1954, his popularity no longer depended on any single declaration or anything he did or did not do. Criticism of his perpetual golf playing no longer hurt him. For his moderation, calm strength, and self-confidence gave the nation a feeling of inner quiet which was a tremendous and welcome relief from the extended period of jitters induced by Congressional fire-brands. Now the Eisenhower face with its broad smile eclipsed the dour visage of McCarthy. The Senator was an isolated isolationist-nationalist; the President was the national father.

With this new American look, with Moscow wearing its best manners, and the rest of the world in a mood for friendly talking instead of bellicose shouting, the meeting "at the summit" at Geneva in July, 1955—where Mr. Eisenhower made his celebrated proposal for mutual Russian and American air photography—and the subequent direct negotiations at a high level between Washington and Peiping, inconceivable a few months earlier, came as no surprise. International politics are capable of startling reversals, astonishing combinations, and constant changes of temperature. American foreign policy is no exception to this law.

The "Geneva spirit" generated at the "summit" conference registered the concrete fact that nobody wanted a world war and everybody would try, in self-interest, to avoid it. Hence the subsequent relaxation. Despite the failure of the Four-Power Foreign Ministers' meeting in Geneva in October-November, 1955, which I attended, the relaxation persists. But it is obviously relaxation with rivalry, relaxation with expansion. Russia does not propose to expand by military means and cannot expand through ideology. She therefore will seek to expand through neutralization. Her attempt to gain a foothold in Egypt, whence Soviet influence could fan out into all of Africa and into the entire Arab world, is a striking example of this new type of Soviet expansionism. Simultaneously, perhaps similarly, the West finds new recruits for its collective security system: Iran, for instance. Both sides continue their balance-of-power struggle, both compete for the favor of the neutrals who are ready to accept gifts now from one quarter, now from the other. In this mighty contest, which will shape the face of the future, one's own attitude is determined by personal philosophy rather than by national loyalty. I think that the spread of Soviet influence will mean the spread of bureaucratic state capitalism and the further eclipse of individual liberty, whereas the advance of the West, with all its imperfections and inter-nation frictions, cannot but conduce to a flowering of freedom, for the realization grows in the West that freedom, for man and his country, is the heart of the struggle and best weapon with which to win it.

CHAPTER FORTY-SIX

What to Do?

HAVING seen that the Second World War was preceded by a period of appeasement, military weakness, and division among the democracies, it is only human that people should have preferred nonappeasement, military preparedness, and collective security as the means of preventing another war. History may show that NATO and the hydrogen bomb were the ultimate war deterrents. In any case, let the country that has disarmed throw the first stone of criticism at those nations which hesitate to lower their guard in the presence of dictatorships laden with the guilt of past aggressions and annexations.

Needless to say, disarmament is a noble and desirable goal and some measure of it can probably be attained through patient international negotiations. But man being the animal he is, he will be more likely to discard old weapons than new. The chicken-or-the-egg conundrum applies here: would disarmament eliminate distrust or must trust precede disarmament? Arms limitation by stages might enable governments to grope toward the answer.

Today a major factor, one is tempted to say *the* major factor, in the formulation of the foreign policies of various nations is the dread of war. This is particularly true of Soviet foreign policy. The Second World War was a harrowing experience for the Soviet people: Hitler's legions penetrated farther into Russia than any invader in her history and before he had been defeated fifteen million Soviet citizens paid with their lives and an estimated thirty million were wounded and incapacitated. Immense areas were deliberately devastated or ruined in the course of battle. Talk of another war, this time with worse horrors, frightens the Soviet population. Under Stalin, the Soviet propaganda line to its own people after 1945 therefore was: The imperialist, reactionary capitalists are plotting to make war on the Soviet Union, so rally around your government, work harder, accept privations, the enemy threatens; but do not fear, the progressive forces of capitalist nations, led by the Communist parties, will stay the hand of the militarists. Apparently, however, the more the Kremlin and its minions cried, "Peace, peace" at various international "peace conferences" manipulated by Communists the greater the fear grew inside Russia. In his last published work, a booklet ninety-four pages long in the Russian original, and dated September 28, 1952,[1] Stalin accordingly evolved a new theory: that the capitalist nations would fight among themselves.

"Some comrades assert," he wrote, "that in view of the development of new international conditions after the second world war, war between capitalist states has ceased to be inevitable. . . . These comrades are wrong." America, he declared, was enslaving many

[1] *The Economic Problems of Socialism in the USSR, op. cit.*

capitalist countries and they would not tolerate it forever. "Would it not be more correct to say," he stated, "that capitalist Britain, and after her, capitalist France will ultimately be compelled to tear themselves from the embrace of the United States and go to war with it . . . ?" The defeated nations, Germany and Japan, would likewise come into conflict with America, Stalin added.

"It is said," he continued in the next paragraph, "that the contradictions between capitalism and socialism are greater than the contradictions among capitalist countries. Theoretically that, of course, is true." But it was just as true before the Second World War, he wrote, yet that war commenced as a war between capitalist nations. After further argument, Stalin concluded that "the inevitability of wars among capitalist states remains in force."

The concoction was obviously designed to allay the Soviet population's deep fears that their country would again be attacked, but it could convince nobody, and when Mr. Stalin died, his heirs found it necessary to abandon such nonsensical speculations and substitute peaceful gestures toward foreign governments. There followed a number of friendly conferences, including the one "at the summit" in Geneva, and a spate of "summit" tourism, with Mr. Nehru, U Nu, and others going to Moscow, and Mr. Khrushchev and Prime Minister Bulganin going to India, Burma, London, et cetera. These certainly made the Soviet people happy.

The Eisenhower Administration likewise felt the need of reducing international anxiety. McCarthyism at its zenith had frightened many Asians and Europeans, as well, indeed, as Americans, into thinking that the United States might launch a war, most probably in the Far East. The fear was unjustified, but in view of the tension within the U.S., it was understandable. Washington too, accordingly, became more amenable to serious discussions with Communist powers.

It seems, therefore, that the world has entered a phase in which all governments have a stern mandate from their people to avoid war—and they will avoid war. At the same time, however, nations fear disarmament though they want it, and hesitate to make the sacrifices of position and power that must precede the settlements so eagerly desired. In these conditions, top-level conferences and official visits, even if they do not result in immediate solutions of basic problems, are beneficial, and so are exchanges of cultural, agricultural, scientific, sports, and other delegations—provided they refrain from ideological propaganda. Human contacts do not necessarily guarantee peace;

high British Admiralty officers were on a friendly visit to the German fleet at Kiel marked by warm personal relations with the Kaiser himself a month before Britain and Germany went to war in 1914. Nevertheless, the "summit" and below-summit tourism and negotiations with smiles may prove to be the net which the peace-yearning public is weaving around its statesmen to compel them to keep the peace. This peculiar phase of history is, therefore, an expression of democratic will and thus a step away from war and from dictatorship. And the more clearly science demonstrates the utter folly and ineffectiveness of war as an instrument of national policy the louder will grow the cry for peace and the more attention politicians will have to pay for it.

If trust is a condition precedent to disarmament and peace, the test of trust must be the extent of relaxation within countries, for relaxation between countries can be simulated and artificially stimulated. Yet it is also true that every official avowal of peaceful intent, even when insincere, is a tribute and encouragement to the public's love of peace and a commitment to peace. Moreover, trust, however undeserved, sometimes begets trust.

When the burden of armaments causes grumbling against high taxation in rich America and the fear of war obsesses mighty Russia, how much more so in France, Great Britain, Germany, Japan, and similarly situated countries? In a recent debate on the defense budget in the French National Assembly, former Premier Paul Reynaud was reported as saying that "modern armaments had become too expensive for France and the only solution lay in a union of European military forces based on a political community."[2] M. Pinay, the French Foreign Minister, went beyond European union and gave his official blessing to a conference on world government which met in Paris in August, 1955. At that conference, Lord Russell (Bertrand Russell), the British philosopher and political writer, declared, "You can preserve peace for some time by negotiation, but without world government there will come a time when negotiation breaks down."[3] His proposition is a forceful argument, but negotiations for a world government have not yet commenced and are not envisaged in the foreseeable future.

The arguments for a United States of Europe, Atlantic Union, world government, and other forms of internationalism are as power-

[2] London *Times*, July 25, 1955.
[3] *Manchester Guardian*, August 3, 1955.

ful logically as nationalism is emotionally. Here common sense, necessity, and indeed the preservation of the human race are in conflict with ancient sentiments, and the latter prevail. Progress toward international co-operation has been registered in many fields since the Second World War and is certain to grow, but as Reinhold Niebuhr, the eminent American liberal and theologian has demonstrated,[4] the long step from such co-operation to a world government is beset with numerous impediments, notably the probability that it would be a "world" government of only the non-Communist world and not even of all of it. Certainly, Moscow and Peiping are not going to join a world government with capitalist countries before such friendly and comparatively similar nations as England and the United States or England and France or Italy and France show them the good example of forming a common government.

How, moreover, is national frustration in Germany, Korea and Vietnam to end when the Communists reject unification by means of free internationally supervised elections because that would probably strengthen the non-Communist side, and the non-Communists reject neutralization, because that would certainly strengthen the Communist side?

One is forced to the conclusion, however regrettable, that while relations between the Soviet government, the Chinese Communist government, the United States, and the other Western powers can be expected to improve, the present cleavage will remain, and the cold war will continue though at a lower temperature and less explosively and with little likelihood of becoming a hot war. The nationalist-Communist regimes of Russia and Red China may want peace, but like all national states they also want power, and they will do their best to attain it by augmenting the number of neutral states in the non-Communist orbit (as America would in the Communist orbit if she could) and by weakening or dissolving the Yugoslav-Greek-Turkish entente, the Turkish-Pakistan-Iraq-Iran defense interest, NATO, SEATO, and similar combinations.

In this new period of colder war and warmer relations, therefore, one of the primary concerns of the democracies should be to combat neutralism, which thins their ranks. Neutralism has a special attraction for weak countries which can think of the next war only in terms of annihilation if they join it, but would like to believe that survival by nonparticipation is possible in an age when colossi like

[4] *The New Leader*, New York, August 2, 1954.

Russia and America might fight with intercontinental, transoceanic guided missiles and world-circling bombers flying over the heads of neutrals. The slightest rumor of war brings further popular support to the policy of "sitting this one out," and the great democratic powers must therefore avoid any appearance or act of belligerence or intransigence, as well as "arm-twisting" in the United Nations or elsewhere. On the other hand, it is equally true that as the danger of war recedes nations will feel more independent of foreign military aid and less inclined to submit to defensive combinations like NATO, etc. Moscow and Peiping will try to lull as many countries as possible into the illusion that America's presence in Europe and Asia is no longer indispensable to their safety.

President Eisenhower has emphasized that the United States wants to be the partner of her allies and friends, not the leader. This is good policy; a partnership of nations has a better chance of holding together under stress provided no partner tries to dictate. For the United States, for example, to insist that Formosa is China and a great power entitled to a veto in the United Nations is an insult to the world's common sense, and to force this on the UN when everybody knows that, but for America's wish, Red China would be admitted to the UN, is an example of dictation in international affairs which clashes with avowals of democracy and partnership, and, moreover, drives other nations to the thought, however unfounded, that America is still thinking of a war against Communist China.

Moderation within a partnership and the readiness to give sympathetic consideration to the views of others will win friends and keep the non-Communist world intact despite the assaults of neutralism.

The urge of recently liberated countries to offer constant evidence of their national independence and of colonial areas to achieve independence is a factor which the major democracies can ignore only at their peril. Individuals may regard the arrogance of new nations as a regrettable sign of immaturity, but governments must take account of it without, however, nurturing it, an admittedly delicate task on which amicable relations between Asia and the West depend.

The small remaining colonial spots and dots in Asia and the large dependent areas of Africa present the Western powers with a painful problem. "We are in a hurry for independence," Tengku Abdul Rahman, the new leader of Malaya, said recently.[5] Some colonies are in a hurry to be free even before they are ripe for freedom. This

---

[5] London *Times*, August 6, 1955.

argument was used against India's freedom and there it has been proved a thousand times incorrect. But an Asian ambassador stationed in New Delhi once startled me by making the point himself: certain countries, he said, must be given their independence simply because they insist on it so vehemently that orderly administration by the imperial power becomes impossible. Britain anticipated this and withdrew from India. Nevertheless, the ambassador added, some of these newly independent nations lack the cohesiveness and talent to manage their own affairs, and in the early stages, accordingly, they need outside help. He had thought out no solution for the problem, and it is, indeed, a most baffling one. United Nations trusteeship is designed for very backward colonial peoples and would be offensive to an independent nation. Guidance by one big power, as in the case of Libya by Britain, is too reminiscent of old-style imperialism. Perhaps the United Nations needs a new department for this complicated mission. Or small, politically disinterested yet highly developed nations such as Sweden, Switzerland, or Austria might find stimulus to idealism and the legitimate spirit of adventure in taking new, retarded nations by the hand and assisting them toward administrative, financial, and economic stability. With Africa coming to a boil it would be far wiser to plan for the future instead of waiting for an explosion. In fact, time may be the essential element. What might recommend itself is a calendar of liberation, internationally approved and subject to acceleration, designating the date on which each colonial possession can expect statehood. The effect could be miraculous, eliminating the riots, bloodshed, hate, and poisoned relations which often attend proindependence movements and inaugurating, instead, a period of sincere co-operation between the mother country and the colonial people which might continue after national freedom had been attained. Apart from self-interest, it was probably the British offer of independence outside the Commonwealth which kept India in the Commonwealth, and it seems beyond dispute that India free is a greater economic and political asset to England than Indo-China, Morocco, Algeria, and Tunisia have been to France since 1945.

Except in the Communist orbit, all colonial peoples are "colored." I dislike the word. When I think of a sheet of white paper, or a white cloud, or a whitewashed cottage, no human being is white, and I know "colored" persons who are much lighter than "white" persons especially after the "white" man or woman has succeeded in acquiring a good healthy tan in a sunny summer. However, I use the terms because they are understood.

If I were asked what worried me most in world affairs I would say the color problem, for it embraces the twin troubles of colonialism and the technological backwardness which spells poverty plus inequality, and it therefore enables the Communists and other irresponsibles to fish in the muddied waters of racial animosities that exist from one end of the world to the other including even the dark interiors of Latin America whose tensions between people of (red) Indian and non-Indian stock have been studied by Moscow for any explosive potential they may contain. In the period that is now dawning, ideology will play a diminishing role in politics, and the appeals will therefore be to emotions that reside in the viscera or in the nervous tissue, appeals to nationalism, blood, race, and color. To nurture color passions is the greatest imaginable crime against mankind, not so much because it could result in a world war, but because it would create more divisions and hatreds and thereby obstruct the advance toward a civilized life. One thinks with horror of a cold war between white and colored blocs.

What to do about the color problem is not an easy question to answer. Of course, nations should refrain from discrimination against colored citizens and visitors and perhaps remember an act of the late Czechoslovak Foreign Minister Jan Masaryk: filling out a questionnaire before entering a certain country he wrote "human" in response to item "race." To be sure, J. Saunders Redding, an American teacher, and Carl T. Rowan, a columnist in the Minneapolis *Tribune*, both excellent writers and Negroes, touring India recently and telling about the marked improvement in the status, condition, and treatment of Negroes in the United States in past decades, were accorded impolite incredulity by audiences whose only criterion was the assumption that the white man simply could not be fair to a Negro. Nevertheless, the truth will ultimately penetrate and produce a good effect. The decision of the U.S. Supreme Court against racial segregation in schools has favorably impressed the whole colored world. Racial superiority is un-Christian and evil, and when practiced by white settlers in Africa it sows the whirlwind which they or their sons will reap when the Negroes imitate them. On the other hand, a handful here and there of technological missionaries serving the retarded people of Asia and Africa in love and unselfish devotion with a view to improving their health, education, and material welfare build solid interracial bridges. Some true Christians like the Rev. Michael Scott make similar contributions.

Human contacts are the most convincing, but financial help from rich countries to poorer areas is naturally of tremendous significance. This kind of giving, however, has pitfalls and needs to be studied much more closely than it has been. The United States, for instance, has made gifts of more than fifty billion dollars to foreign nations since the Second World War. That is a sum whose size still awaits the invention of an adequate adjective, yet, critics, sceptics, and cynics to the contrary notwithstanding, it has neither enslaved nor humiliated the recipients and resulted in no kidnapings or tortures. It has saved some countries from enslavement and raised production in all. But with the exception of the small though very effective fraction of this sum which came from private persons and institutions, the great bulk has consisted of aid from the United States government to foreign governments, and if those foreign governments are oppressive and unpopular and allow only a minimum to trickle down to the neediest levels, America becomes unpopular too. This by-product might be transitory and tolerable if it did not reflect a misuse of funds. To bloster rickety governments which do little for their people furthers neither international good will nor democracy. Usually, it accentuates distinctions between rich and poor; sometimes it reinforces antisocial, historically obsolete dictatorships. Yet to instruct foreign governments on how to spend American money would be resented as the hated "strings", and to withhold the money altogether might provoke grave crises. I have discussed this dilemma over the years and heard various suggestions: Send us agricultural implements which the government will have to distribute among the peasants; send prefabricated huts, mobile hospital units, small village power plants, pedigree breeders suitable for use in our country, and so on. Or, allocate funds for special projects as the International Bank does—wells, roads, and schools, for instance; do not make grants to the federal government. Or, make loans to cities, provinces, and progressive corporations.

Idealism and practical politics will keep aid flowing to retarded countries for decades until the imbalance between nations is at least partially corrected. The aid should accordingly be applied to creative purposes and not used to perpetuate the misery it is designed to eradicate. If national governments cannot cope with this primary problem in world affairs they should retire from the field in favor of an international agency. Citizens of the United States, and of Canada, England, and other members of the British Commonwealth who have given foreign assistance do not do so, or should not do so, to keep morally corrupt and politically bankrupt regimes in office, but to help underprivileged persons live a better, freer life.

As the danger of war ceases to obsess the world mind it is proper to hope that the motivation of giving foreign aid will change from military expediency to humanity, from hastily building a wall against Communist imperialism to erecting a decent home for democracy. The elimination of war and with it the gradual reduction of spending on armaments could open up enormous new possibilities of international trade, travel, and cultural cross-fertilization of varying civilizations. (The West has much to learn from the East and vice versa.)

The peaceful uses of atomic energy, moreover, are a multiple challenge. We literally reach for the moon and permit slums on earth even in wealthy America. Material advancement in many lands, rich and poor, can now be telescoped and accelerated. Then modern man will have to prove that he is capable of more than speed, science, and engineering feats.

In fact, this is the whole point. We desire freedom from war, freedom from want, and freedom from the fear of governments, police systems, and tyrannical majorities, minorities, and dogmas in order that human beings may be free, free to grow and soar. Man flies in planes and may soon fly in space ships, yet he himself remains pinned to the earth by anxieties if he is short of money and anxieties if he has plenty of money, by a wish for more leisure and insufficient knowledge of what to do with it, by imprisonment under mass media which stunt his individuality, by an inability to convert faith in God, where it exists, into faith in the goodness of people, and by a limited capacity for love and friendship within nations and between nations. We want to abolish the Iron Curtain while erecting little iron curtains between groups all around us. Why should we wonder at the cruelty of countries to countries and governments to citizens when we are so cruel to one another? It is probably this last cruelty that is the parent of the others. Mahatma Gandhi could combine truth with kindness and opposition with affection.

The age of atomic peace may now force man to deal with these subtler and bigger problems of worldly existence.

MY THANKS TO

The hundreds of persons in many countries of the world who helped me gather the information and impressions out of which this book grew.

Simon Michael Bessie, Cass Canfield, Marguerite Hoyle, John Fischer, and Jean Carter at Harper & Brothers, and to my relatives, friends, and acquaintances: Markoosha, my son George, Nina Raditsa, Frank Trager, Kasim Gulek, Dean Acheson, Peggy Korn, Moshe Pearlman, Pearl and Joseph Willen, Thomas Finletter, Joseph Freeman, Pupul Jayakar, Philip Jessup, Maurice Hexter, Harry Sigmond, Dorothy Norman, George F. Kennan, Herbert Passin, Molly Castle, and others who have read the entire manuscript of this book or one or more chapters and given me their helpful criticisms without, of course, accepting the slightest responsibility for the contents.

Mrs. Hannah D. Rabinowitz who typed the manuscript.

Louis Fischer

Index

Abdulla, Sheik, 464
Abyssinia, 83
Acheson, Alice, 154
Acheson, Dean, 80, 81-82, 85, 91, 151,
    154-55, 158-59, 160, 161, 162,
    217, 220, 294, 356, 357, 496
Adenauer, Konrad, 4, 68, 198, 199,
    217, 436, 438-40, 441, 468, 474,
    494
Aduldej, King Phumiphol, 326
Agron, Gershon, 282, 284
Agudat Israel, 283
Ahmad, Hazrat Mirza Ghulam, 291
Ahmadiyas, 290-91
Ahmedabad, 138-39
Airlift, Berlin, 110-16, 147, 167
Akihito, Crown Prince, 382-83
Albania, 94, 97, 248
Alexander, Albert V., 15, 16
Alexander the Great, 388
Alexandria, 9, 11
Algeria, 152
Ali Kahn, Begum Liaquat, 289-90
Ali Kahn, Nawabzada Liaquat, 290
Allen, George V., 236
Allison, John M., 334
American Office of Strategic Services
    (OSS), 324
Ankara, 83, 268, 269
Anti-Zionism, 276
Antonius, George, 24
Antonius, Kathy, 24
Antwerp, 40
Appeasement, diagnosis, 72-78
Arab states, 274-75
Aristotle, 408
Arnold, Mayor, 65
Asahina, Sogen, 375-76
Astor, Michael, 411
Ataturk, Mustapha Kemal Pasha, 51,
    179, 268-71, 272, 273
Atenasio, Commendatore Francesco,
    225
Athens, 83
Atomic-hydrogen war, 169, 497, 499

Attlee, Clement R., 7, 11, 26, 31,
    33-34, 220, 472
Auriol, Vincent, 339
Avala, 236, 238
Avilla, José, 364
Azad, Maulana Abul Kalam, 16-17, 19,
    134-35
Azzam Pasha, 11

Bakarich, Stjepan, 105
Baldwin, Stanley, 407
Banat, 234
Bangkok, 322
Bao Dai, Emperor, 332, 338, 339, 340,
    342
Barker, Lieutenant General Evelyn, 23
Bath, 27
Baudouin I, King, 39
Bebel, 108
Bedouins, 278
Beethoven, Ludwig von, 68
Beirut, 442
Belgium, 35-36, 109, 199
Belgrade, 103, 106, 233, 234-67, 356,
    422, 424
Bell Mission, 360, 361
Benedict, Ruth, 374
Benelux, 213
Beneš, Dr. Eduard, 97, 98-99, 100
Beneson, Fira, 208, 209
Ben Gurion, David, 281, 282, 283-84,
    285
Bentov, Mordecai, 284-85
Berg, Dr. Sherwood, 251
Beria, Laventh P., 43, 398, 474, 475,
    476, 477
Berlin, 4, 52-64, 65, 67, 70, 107-8,
    110-16, 389-406, 442
Berlin blockade, 107-8, 111-16, 149,
    167
Berliner Zeitung, 398
Bevan, Aneurin, 30, 253, 410
Bevin, Ernest, 11, 24, 33, 34, 43, 45
Bhave, Vinoba, 465, 470, 472
Bhutan, 463

513